COMPLETE HOME REPAIR MANUAL

COMPLETE HOME REPAIR MANUAL

PRENTICE HALL PRESS
NEW YORK

Time-Life Books Complete Home Repair Manual
was produced by
ST. REMY PRESS

MANAGING EDITOR	Kenneth Winchester
MANAGING ART DIRECTOR	Pierre Léveillé
Editor	Dianne Thomas
Art Director	Philippe Arnoldi
Designer	Marie-Claire Amiot
Editorial Assistant	Michael Mouland
Contributing Writers	Gérard Sénécal, Donna Lee Smith
Contributing Illustrators	Gérard Mariscalchi, Jacques Proulx
Technical Illustrator	Robert Paquet
Index	Christine M. Jacobs
Administrator	Denise Rainville
Coordinator	Michelle Turbide
Systems Manager	Shirley Grynspan
Systems Analyst	Simon Lapierre
Typesetter	Rodolfo Narvaez
Proofreader	Billy Wisse

Time-Life Books Complete Home Repair Manual was adapted from
the Home Repair and Improvement series, produced by
TIME-LIFE BOOKS INC.

EDITOR	George Constable
Executive Editor	Ellen Phillips
Director of Design	Louis Klein
Director of Editorial Resources	Phyllis K. Wise
Editorial Board	Russell B. Adams Jr., Dale Brown, Bobbie Conlan, Thomas H. Flaherty, Lee Hassig, Donia Ann Steele, Rosalind Stubenberg, Kit van Tulleken, Henry Woodhead
Director of Photography and Research	John Conrad Weiser
PRESIDENT	Christopher T. Linen
Chief Operating Officer	John M. Fahey Jr.
Senior Vice President	James L. Mercer
Vice Presidents	Stephen L. Bair, Ralph J. Cuomo, Neal Goff, Stephen L. Goldstein, Juanita T. James, Hallett Johnson III, Carol Kaplan, Susan J. Maruyama, Robert H. Smith, Paul R. Stewart, Joseph J. Ward
Director of Production Services	Robert J. Passantino

THE CONSULTANTS

Richard Day, a do-it-yourself writer for nearly a quarter century, is a founder of the National Association of Home and Workshop Writers and the author of several home repair books. He has built two houses from the ground up, and now lives in southern California.

Mark M. Steele, a professional home inspector in the Washington, D.C. area, is an editor of home improvement articles and books.

Maurice Gagnon, special consultant for Canada, is a professional woodworker. He specializes in custom woodwork in Montreal.

Copyright © 1987 by Time-Life Books Inc.

All right reserved,
including the right of reproduction
in whole or in part in any form.

Published by Prentice Hall Press
A Division of Simon & Schuster, Inc.
Gulf+Western Building
One Gulf+Western Plaza
New York, NY 10023

PRENTICE HALL PRESS is a trademark of
Simon & Schuster, Inc

Library of Congress Cataloging-in-Publication Data

Time-Life Books Complete Home Repair Manual.

Includes index.
1. Dwellings-Maintenance and repair—
Amateurs' manuals. I. Time-Life Books.
TH4817.3.T56 1987   643.7   87-16252
ISBN 0-13-921636-7

Manufactured in the United States of America

10 9 8 7 6 5 4 3 2 1

First Edition

CONTENTS:

The Ins and Outs of Home Repairs

This book has been created in response to a growing trend—do-it-yourself repair. Compiled from the best-selling Time-Life Books Home Repair and Improvement series, the material included in these pages provides the specific step-by-step advice that has built the Time-Life Books reputation as how-to experts. Whether you are an experienced do-it-yourselfer or a novice to the world of home repair, this guide is designed to show you how. The repairs—organized from inside the house out—are those commonly encountered by homeowners; many of the repairs are listed at right. The subjects range from major jobs requiring specialized tools, such as jacking a porch roof and replacing a support, to fixing minor annoyances, including leaking faucets and sticking doors.

In addition to the repairs themselves, there is advice on how to use important techniques—working with electrical wiring and spray-painting your house, for example. Where needed, the book guides you in tool and material selection—how to choose the right paintbrush for the job, which wall-covering material to buy and the types of weather stripping available.

The result is a comprehensive guide designed to demystify the techniques and tools needed for successful home repair —a reference book that can be used time and time again to save time, money and aggravation and build do-it-yourself confidence and skills.

Browse through the pages in each section, and start making a list of repairs to be done around your house. Inspect each room for interior repairs that would improve the appearance—and convenience—of your home; notice where a new paint or wallpaper job is needed. Think about your home's heating and cooling systems, and whether their efficiency could be improved. On a daily basis, watch out for faults in your home's electrical and plumbing systems. Outside your home, inspect for damage, peeling paint and other problems requiring exterior repairs. Remember, this book is designed to help you make hundreds of repairs in—and outside—your home, with the satisfaction that you did it yourself.

1 INTERIOR REPAIRS

• Plaster • Wallboard • Ceramic tile and accessories • Ceiling tiles • Squeaks • Floorboards • Sagging floors • Molding and baseboard • Refinishing • Sealing • Hard surfaced and resilient floors • Carpets • Squeaky treads • Balustrades • Doors and windows • Sticking windows and doors • Sashes • Cords and balances • Swinging windows • Cranking windows • Doorjambs • Hollow-core doors • Door and window trim • Locks • Sliding doors • Screens, blinds, shutters and shades • Working with glass • Cleaning glass • Furniture joints • Dowels • Platform chairs • Frame chairs • Tables • Cabinets • Drawers • Casters • Beds • Damaged wood • Pegs, splints and braces • Damaged finishes

2 PAINT AND WALLPAPER

• Painting the interior and exterior • Planning • Choosing the paint • Tools • Preparing and repairing the surface • Using a roller • Sequence for painting • Cleanup and storage • Choosing an exterior coating • Tools • Diagnosing problems • Estimating time and paint • Techniques for brushwork and spraying • Choosing a wall covering •Wallpapering tools • Removing paper • Estimating wallpaper and materials • Where to start and end • Professional wallpapering techniques • Matching patterns • Dealing with obstacles • Repairing damaged paper • Maintaining wallpaper

3 HEATING, COOLING AND WEATHERPROOFING

• Increasing heating efficiency • Forced-air systems • Liquid-heat systems • Thermostats • Gas and oil burners • Cleaning a furnace •Hot-water heat • Convectors and radiators • Heat pumps • Troubleshooting air conditioners • Weather-stripping windows and doors • Sealing cracks and crannies • Storm windows and doors • Where to insulate • Choosing insulation • How much is enough • Insulating attics and basements • Unheated and warm spaces • Calculating heating and cooling needs

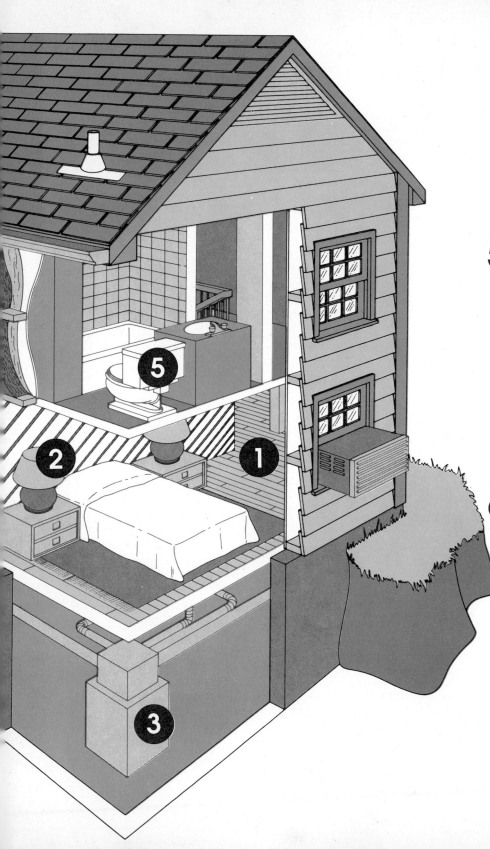

4 ELECTRICITY

- The basics of electricity • How electricity works • Turning the power off • Reading an electric meter • An electrical safety checkup • Common electrical terms • Safeguards that shield against dangers • Circuit breakers and fuses • Grounding • Polarization • GFCI protection • Working safely with electricity • Protecting yourself • GFCI extensions • Safe ways to test for voltage • Electrical emergencies • Techniques and repairs • Checking your work • Safety tips • Working with wire • Electrical repairs • Replacing plugs and cords • How to rewire a lamp • Lighting fixtures • Switches • Receptacles • Doorbells and chimes • Outdoor lighting

5 PLUMBING

- A guide to the home plumber • Shutting down the system • Minimizing water damage • Your home's system • Tools • Unclogging drains • Lavatory and sink drains • Drains below floors • Bathtubs • Toilets • Main drains • Access from the cleanout and house trap • Repairs for seven types of faucets • Other kitchen and bathroom repairs • Spouts and stoppers • Tubs and showers • Traps and tailpieces • Sink strainers • Lavatory pop-ups • Pipe repairs • Emergency repairs • Working with copper, CPVC and polybutylene pipe • Frozen pipes

6 EXTERIOR REPAIRS

- Roof repairs and materials • Ladders and scaffolds • Hoisting heavy loads • Roof leaks • Asphalt shingles • Slate and wood shingles • Flat roofs • Flashing • Gutters • Cornices • Siding materials • Wood shingles • Metal and plastic • Clapboard • Porch posts and floors • Columns • Deck supports • Masonry • Mixing and using mortar • Brick • Restoring and maintaining concrete • Broken steps • Wet basements • The battle against moisture • Walkways • Driveways

How to Use this Book

The *Time-Life Books Complete Home Repair Manual* is divided into seven main sections. Organized and color-coded for easy reference, the first six sections provide step-by-step instructions for specific repairs that you are likely to encounter in your home. Before deciding whether you should attempt a repair, read all the instructions carefully. Then be guided by your own confidence and experience, and the tools available to you. For repairs which may seem too complex or time-consuming for your level of expertise, you may wish to call for professional service. You may still save time and money by diagnosing the problem yourself, and you will be better equipped to find the right professional for the job and to discuss the repair in an informed manner.

The first six sections also offer information on basic how-to techniques, from preparing a room for wallpapering to working safely with electricity. In many cases, charts aid you in diagnosing a problem or selecting the proper materials for the job. Exterior paint problems, for example, are easy to diagnose using the photographs of typical symptoms in Section 2. Extensive charts in the same section advise you on which paints are best suited for covering different surfaces.

The final section presents the basic tools that you are likely to need for most of the repairs in the *Time-Life Books Complete Home Repair Manual*. If you are a novice when it comes to home repair, read this section before undertaking a major job. A detailed discussion of tools and their proper uses provides insights into how to choose quality tools that will serve you for many years.

Doing your own home repair is easy and safe if you work logically, follow instructions and safety precautions, and use safety equipment whenever necessary. Before beginning any electrical repair, for example, turn off power to the circuit, then confirm that the power is off, as instructed. Likewise, many plumbing repairs require closing the main shutoff valve and draining supply lines. Ask local authorities about electrical, plumbing, building or sanitation codes that might apply to your repair.

Name of repair or technique

Introductory text
Describes key techniques, maintenance tips and other information about the repair, based on the experience and advice of professionals.

Close-up illustrations
Highlight specific points mentioned in the text.

Boxed features
Give details on the selection, use and care of tools, or special techniques that will speed the repair.

Exploded and cutaway diagrams
Locate and describe the various parts of the fixture or system.

Cross-references
Direct you to important information elsewhere in the book, including disassembly and access steps.

Variations
Show you different types of damage commonly encountered in the home.

Fine Points of Applying Paint

The basic rule for easy, efficient interior painting is simple: Use a roller whenever and wherever you can. In recent years even professional painters have been abandoning their cherished brushes for ceiling and wall work, and with good reason. A roller covers these areas more than twice as fast as a paintbrush and requires less skill and effort. Guidelines for picking a good roller and for matching a roller to a specific surface appear on the opposite page.

A roller alone, however, will probably not suffice for the whole job. Most interior painting calls for a combination of roller and brush; a single brush, as a matter of fact, may not be enough for the most efficient work. You need a brush for surfaces that a roller is not designed to cover—a delicate, ridged molding, for example, or the narrow divider between windowpanes. You also need a brush—not necessarily the same brush—to use in corners that a roller cannot reach. And you may turn to a brush to paint certain flat areas, such as the wall above a built-in cupboard, where working with a roller can be awkward.

Choose a brush of the right size and shape for the kind of work you are doing. Use as wide a brush as possible, to make the painting go faster, but not wider than the surface you are covering. A 1- or 1½-inch trim brush is good for window dividers, a 2- or 2½-inch sash brush for baseboards and window frames and

sills. For large, flat areas use a 3-inch or, at most, 4-inch brush. (Professional painters regularly use 4-inch or even 5-inch brushes, but it takes long practice and a powerful wrist and forearm to handle them with ease.)

Choose a brush shape that is tailored to the job, using the pictures on page 155 as a guide. The familiar flat brush with squared-off ends is a general-purpose brush; for precise edges and lines, pick a flat trim brush with a beveled, chisel-shaped working end. An angular sash brush, especially designed for certain hard-to-reach surfaces, cannot normally be used on flat surfaces but is ideal for the insides of window- and door frames or the louvers of a shutter. Round or oval brushes have the largest paint-carrying capacity and splay out when applied to a surface; they work best on thin, curved surfaces, such as pipes.

Finally, match your painting tools to the type of paint you are using. Latex paint, which is likely to be used for at least part of every job, calls for a brush or roller with synthetic bristles or nap. Natural bristles and fibers absorb water from latex paint and lose their resiliency. For oil or alkyd paints, which give a smooth gloss to trim, professionals have long preferred a finely tapered hog-bristle brush. However, a good synthetic-bristle brush will also do a fine job and can double as a cutting-in brush if you are using latex on the rest of the room.

Designed for flow. This cutaway shows the desirable elements to be found in a typical flat brush. The bristles, whether natural or synthetic, are "flagged"—that is, split or frayed—at the working end to provide greater area for holding paint. At the other end, the bristles are embedded in hard plastic. One or more "plugs," or spacers, made of metal, wood or hard rubber separate the bristles where they are embedded (you can see a plug by separating the bristles with your hand). The bristles along the sides of a plug "toe in" and meet at the tip in a firm, trim edge from which paint flows evenly. A metal band called a ferrule holds the bristle base to the heel of the handle.

FLAGGED BRISTLE TIP
BRISTLES
PLUG
FERRULE
HEEL
HANDLE

What Makes a Good Brush Good?

When you are shopping for a paintbrush, carefully check the points that are listed below. These guidelines apply to both synthetic and natural-bristle brushes of any size and shape, and can help you to make a knowledgeable on-the-spot appraisal of quality.
□ Grip the handle of the brush as you would for painting (page 164). The shape and the weight should feel comfortable in your grasp. The metal ferrule should be attached solidly to the handle, preferably with nails. If the handle is made of wood, it should have a glossy or rub-

berized coating, which resists moisture and is easy to keep clean.
□ Press the bristles against the palm of your hand. They should not separate into clumps but should fan out slightly in an even spread. When you lift the brush away from your hand, the bristles should readily spring back to their original position.
□ Examine the bristles with care. They should be smooth and straight and the tips should be flagged, as shown in the drawing above. If you are comparing brushes that are the same width, select

the one with the longest, thickest bristles; it will hold the most paint.
□ Part the bristles and examine the way they are set into the base. The plug or plugs should be no more than half the thickness of the setting.
□ Slap the brush against the palm of your hand to shake out any loose bristles—any brand-new brush may have a few. Then tug on the bristles once or twice. No additional bristles should come out. If any do, be wary; badly anchored bristles will seriously hinder the efficiency of the brush.

160

Repairing Wood Molding

Molding is vulnerable to daily abuse; it can also suffer from aging. Outside joints may be hit once too often by the vacuum cleaner, or a baseboard could be gashed or badly scratched when you move a piece of furniture. As an older house settles, the moldings may start to gap at the corner joints, or dry out and split.

If your moldings are painted, many repairs can be quickly and simply done with fillers such as wood putty and vinyl spackling. Natural wood moldings require more careful work and a filler—such as wood putty—that will absorb stain or varnish. Badly cracked moldings—whether painted or finished—are best repaired with yellow glue (page 108).

The two most common types of molding often used together—are shoe molding and baseboard (right, above). If either type is gouged, split, cracked or nicked, you may be able to repair the damage with one of the quick, simple techniques shown at right, below. However, for more extensive damage, you may have to replace an entire section of molding.

When repairing damaged shoe molding or base cap, remove only the section to be repaired; to replace a section of baseboard, you must first remove the shoe molding and base cap, if any, then the baseboard itself. If your molding is natural wood finish, there may come a time when it needs refinishing; for the most professional-looking results, remove it first and number the sections for easy replacement.

The toughest part of molding repair may be finding a matching replacement. If your home is relatively new, chances are the local lumberyard has an identical replacement in stock. However, for older-style, more ornate moldings, you may have to visit second-hand building supply yards or have the piece custom made—an expensive option.

Types of molding joints. Moldings consist of the baseboard, shoe molding and—in older homes—the base cap. Sections of molding may be joined in a number of ways: At an outside corner, a miter cut is common (page 39). An inside corner joint may be mitered, or coped (pages 37-38) for a better fit in a corner that is not perfectly square. Along the wall, 90°-cut sections may be joined at a butt joint or 45°-cut sections at a scarf joint. Joints are secured by nails, angled at corners (inset).

INSIDE COPED JOINT
OUTSIDE MITER JOINT
SCARF JOINT
BASE CAP
BUTT JOINT
SHOE MOLDING
BASEBOARD

Two Common Molding Repairs

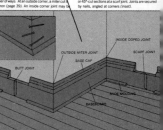

Common repairs for damaged molding. The most vulnerable part of your wall, molding is often damaged when furniture and children's play equipment are knocked and scraped against it. With time, an older house settles, causing gaps where molding intersects at corners. An outside corner is most often marred by daily household activity; it also most obviously reveals a house's structural settling.

Often, the quickest and easiest way to repair the damage is by using a wood filler. Use a putty knife to force the filler into a gouge or open joint (above, left) or damaged length of molding (above, right). Overfill the depression slightly to compensate for shrinkage when the putty has dried. Then use fine-grit sandpaper and a sanding block (page 157) to sand the putty flush with the surface; paint or finish the molding.

36

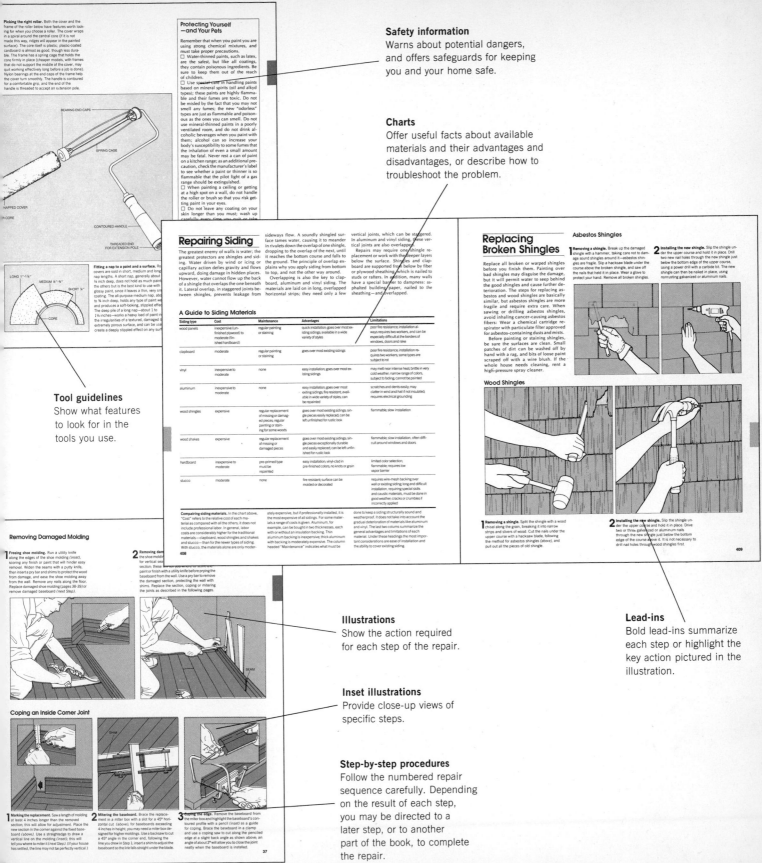

Safety information
Warns about potential dangers, and offers safeguards for keeping you and your home safe.

Charts
Offer useful facts about available materials and their advantages and disadvantages, or describe how to troubleshoot the problem.

Tool guidelines
Show what features to look for in the tools you use.

Illustrations
Show the action required for each step of the repair.

Inset illustrations
Provide close-up views of specific steps.

Step-by-step procedures
Follow the numbered repair sequence carefully. Depending on the result of each step, you may be directed to a later step, or to another part of the book, to complete the repair.

Lead-ins
Bold lead-ins summarize each step or highlight the key action pictured in the illustration.

Protecting Yourself —and Your Pets

Repairing Siding

A Guide to Siding Materials

Siding type	Cost	Maintenance	Advantages	Limitations
wood panels	inexpensive (unfinished plywood) to moderate (finished hardboard)	regular painting	quick installation, goes over most existing sidings; available in a wide variety of styles	poor fire-resistance; installation always requires two workers, and can be especially difficult at the borders of windows, doors and rake
clapboard	moderate	regular painting or staining	goes over most existing sidings	poor fire-resistance; installation requires two workers; some types are subject to rot
vinyl	inexpensive to moderate	none	easy installation; goes over most existing sidings	may melt near intense heat; brittle in very cold weather; narrow range of colors; subject to fading; cannot be painted
aluminum	inexpensive to moderate	none	easy installation; goes over most existing sidings; fire resistant; available in wide variety of styles; can be repainted	scratches and dents easily; may clatter in wind and hail if not insulated; requires electrical grounding
wood shingles	expensive	regular replacement of missing or damaged pieces; regular painting or staining for some woods	goes over most existing sidings; single pieces easily replaced; can be left unfinished for rustic look	flammable; slow installation
wood shakes	expensive	regular replacement of missing or damaged pieces	goes over most existing sidings; single pieces exceptionally durable and easily replaced; can be left unfinished for rustic look	flammable; slow installation; often difficult around windows and doors
hardboard	inexpensive to moderate	pre-primed type must be repainted	easy installation; vinyl-clad in pre-finished colors, no knots or grain	limited color selection; flammable; requires low vapor barrier
stucco	moderate	none	fire resistant; surface can be molded or decorated	requires wire-mesh backing over wall or existing siding; long and difficult installation; requiring special skills and caustic materials; must be done in good weather; cracks or crumbles if incorrectly applied

408

Replacing Broken Shingles

Asbestos Shingles

1 Removing a shingle. Break up the damaged shingle with a hammer, taking care not to damage sound shingles around it—asbestos shingles are fragile. Slip a hacksaw blade under the good shingles and saw off the nails that held it in place. Wear a glove to protect your hand. Remove all broken shingles.

2 Installing the new shingle. Slip the shingle under the upper course and hold it in place. Drill two new nail holes through the new shingle just below the bottom edge of the upper course, using a power drill with a carbide bit. The new shingle can then be nailed in place, using nonrusting galvanized or aluminum nails.

Wood Shingles

1 Removing a shingle. Split the shingle along the grain, breaking it into narrow strips and slivers of wood. Cut the nails under the upper course with a hacksaw blade, following the method for asbestos shingles (above), and pull out all the pieces of old shingle.

2 Installing the new shingle. Slip the shingle under the upper course and hold it in place. Drive two or three galvanized or aluminum nails through the new shingle just below the bottom edge of the course above it. It is not necessary to drill nail holes through wood shingles first.

409

Removing Damaged Molding

1 Freeing shoe molding. Run a utility knife along the edges of the shoe molding (inset), scoring any finish or paint that will hinder easy removal. Widen the seams with a putty knife, then insert a pry bar and shims to protect the wood from damage, and ease the shoe molding away from the wall. Remove any nails along the floor. Replace damaged shoe molding (pages 38-39) or remove damaged baseboard (next Step).

2 Removing damaged baseboard.

Coping an Inside Corner Joint

1 Marking the replacement.

2 Mitering the baseboard.

3 Coping the edge.

37

9

1 INTERIOR REPAIRS

Repairs Inside Your Home

At first glance, any well-maintained home may hide a multitude of needed repairs. A closer look, however, usually reveals a variety of problems ranging from major structural damage to minor breakdowns which, if not repaired, could lead to serious, costly or even potentially dangerous future problems.

The walls and ceilings of a typical house are its single most extensive feature, presenting a surface measured in thousands of square feet and occupying roughly four times times that of the floor. Yet, when they are doing their job well, walls and ceilings go almost unnoticed—until the plaster cracks, the wallboard or baseboard is gashed or brown spots appear on a ceiling panel. The repair may be as simple as replacing one ceiling tile, or more involved, and require locating a concealed stud (below) when patching a wallboard panel. Often, with a few tools and some professional techniques, these repairs are quick and easy to do.

Floors—also intimately linked to the structure of a house—are stressed by natural shifts in the house structure, as well as moisture, abuse and age. Whatever the cause of the damage, repairs are usually possible. Some are major projects—replacing the supports beneath a sagging floor, for example (pages 34-35)—but most require only the right materials and a few professional tricks. You can replace or tighten worn or loose flooring (pages 28-33) or sand yellowed or stained wood, then refinish the floor with permanently transparent polyurethane (pages 40-43). Similarly, new adhesives ease the repair of resilient flooring (pages 46-49), and new bonding agents simplify the resurfacing of concrete floors.

As for stairways, some faults—such as squeaky treads (pages 58-59)— may be annoying, but they can also be dangerous; in actual fact, more accidents happen on stairways than in bathtubs. Accordingly, any sign of faulty stairway parts (pages 56-61) should be investigated immediately. Among the leading causes of stairway accidents are defects in treads and handrails. Each step should have exactly the same rise; uneven heights may be a factor in three fourths of all stairway accidents. Missing railings can also cause accidents, and the railings in place must be safe. A balustrade (pages 60-61) should be strong enough to take the weight of a falling adult.

The only moving parts in the structure of a house are windows and doors, intricate little machines that are designed to open and close thousands of times a year. Most common repairs—such as freeing a stuck window (pages 63-66)—are relatively simple, and require only a few basic tools. Some trim repairs, however, call for some knowledge of carpentry techniques. The parts of a door or a window, and the joints and cuts that fit the parts together, are identified by a very specific language, described on page 62.

Although not a fixed part of a house's structure, furniture is an important part of every home that often needs repair. Whatever else is involved, restoring furniture to usefulness commonly begins with repairs to the joints and frame, which generally means regluing and replacing the parts of a joint. Often the challenge of such a repair is indentifying the type of joint (pages 110, 119), disassembling the parts without causing further damage and choosing the right glue (page 108) for the job.

In most areas of your home, proper cleaning and maintenance will not only prolong the finish on most household surfaces; over a period of time, it can also help avoid the need for many repairs. Resilient floors, for example, should not be scrubbed too often (page 49); stained carpets should be treated immediately with solution appropriate to the stain (page 53) and laundered at least once a year (pages 54-55). Windows and chandeliers—though both made of glass—should be cleaned using different methods (pages 100-107). Even when your home's interior is well cared for, age and use eventually take their toll. A well-done refinishing job—on a wood floor (pages 42-43), for example—can add extra protection and add years to the life of much of the woodwork in your home.

Locating Concealed Studs and Joists

For most work on walls and ceilings, it is necessary to determine the positions of concealed studs and joists, and there are several techniques for doing so. You can tap lightly along the wall or ceiling until you hear a solid sound, which usually indicates a stud or joist, then move over 16 inches—the most common distance between framing members—and tap again. It is also possible to locate structural supports by driving finishing nails into the wall or ceiling at several points until they meet resistance.

To confirm the spacing indicated by either technique, drill a small hole in an inconspicuous spot and probe behind the surface with a stiff wire; when the wire hits a joint or stud, place a finger on the wire where it enters the hole, to record the distance to the stud.

If the repair work makes it necessary for you to remove a baseboard, it is usually easy to check behind the baseboard for visible seams or nails where the wallboard panels cross a stud. You can also examine a ceiling close up, standing on a chair or ladder, for traces of tape seams or nailing patterns along the joists; this is best done at night with an overhead light on.

Many hardware stores sell a simple device, called a stud finder, containing a magnet that reacts to the nails driven into studs or joists. Many such magnets are weak, however, so the device is most useful if the nails are fairly large and near the surface of the wall.

Once you have located one stud or joist you can mark its path simply by measuring out an equivalent distance elsewhere on the surface. Then snap a chalk line between the two points.

Simple Patches for Plaster

If you live in a home built before World War II, walls and ceilings are likely to be plaster, applied in two or more layers over a lath backing of wood, metal or gypsum. Small cracks, holes and irregularities are simple to fix; major repairs to larger areas, however, require considerable skill, and in some cases, the services of a professional.

Cracks and holes need some enlargement for a neat repair. And the best approach to a large and unsightly bulge is to first take a hammer and knock out the humped plaster. Then patch the hole by making a wallboard patch *(pages 18-19)* and screwing it to the laths (remove any broken laths and attach other braces if necessary). Smaller holes and cracks are easy to fill using the instructions on this page. For both large and small holes, a shallow depression is built up with several thin layers of vinyl spackling compound or wallboard joint cement. When the spackling compound or cement is dry, sand it smooth *(page 157)*, blending its edges into the surrounding plaster until the area that was damaged is flush with the surface of the wall.

If the old plaster was deliberately stippled or left rough, use a stiff brush, sponge or comb to duplicate the texture on the patching material while it is still damp. Apply a latex primer to the patch before painting *(page 153)*.

Repairing a Crack

1 Cleaning. With the tip of a beverage can opener, scrape away crumbling or loose plaster along the edges of the crack. The drawing shows a hairline crack being widened a fraction of an inch to make a large surface for patching material to adhere to. A wider crack would require undercutting as described in Step 2 on page 14. Lengthen any crack slightly by removing a bit of the firm plaster at each end. This helps the patching material grip the sound surface, and keeps the crack from extending farther in the future. Vacuum the cleaned crack or, with your eyes shut, blow out the plaster dust.

2 Sealing. Using a clean paintbrush, wet the inside of the crack and a little of the surrounding area with clear water. With a flexible-blade putty knife, spread wallboard joint cement or vinyl spackling compound along the length of the crack in a long, smooth ribbon, pressing the material in firmly. Be sure that the patch overlaps some of the solid plaster surfaces along the edges and at both ends of the crack. Let the patching material dry for a day or so; if it shrinks add another layer. When the material is completely dry, smooth it with fine-grit sandpaper, wrapped around a sanding block *(page 157)*.

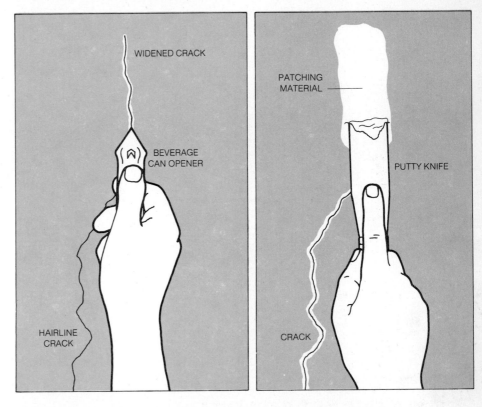

Repairing a Hole

1 Preparation. With a putty knife, chip any loose or crumbling plaster from the edges of the hole until only solid plaster remains. (Caution: If you find seriously damaged lath underneath, the lath must be repaired before replastering; repair generally calls for the skills of a professional.)

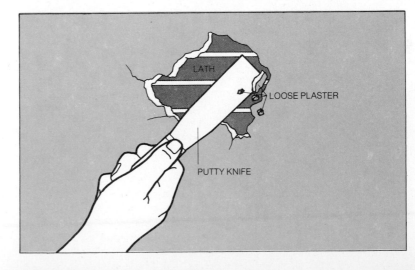

13

2 **Undercutting.** All holes in plaster (and all cracks wider than ⅛ inch or so) must be undercut, a procedure in which some of the old—but intact—plaster is removed along the inner side of the hole (or crack) so that the patching material that is used as a filler will bond securely to the solid plaster around the opening. To undercut, use the tip of a beverage can opener and scrape away a bit of the plaster under the rim of the hole. Then bevel the scraped area to make a V-shaped hollow under the surface. Vacuum or blow out the plaster dust from the undercut area.

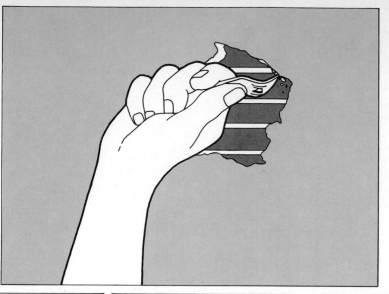

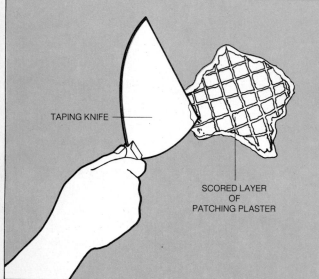

TAPING KNIFE

SCORED LAYER
OF
PATCHING PLASTER

SECOND LAYER OF PLASTER

3 **Applying the first layer.** Mix enough patching plaster to fill the hole almost completely. Moisten the back and edges of the hole with a sponge. Beginning at the undercut surfaces at the edges of the hole, apply the patching plaster with a taping knife. Continue to fill the hole until the patching plaster is about ¼ inch below the surface of the undamaged plaster around the hole. While the patching plaster is still wet, score its surface with the tip of the taping knife (drawing, above). This scored surface will provide a firm grip for a second layer of patching plaster. Let the first layer set for about a half hour.

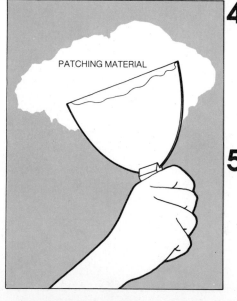

PATCHING MATERIAL

4 **Applying the second layer.** Mix a fresh batch of patching plaster. Dampen the scored layer of patching plaster and 2 or 3 inches of the undamaged surface around the hole. Using a taping knife, preferably wider than the hole, fill the hole with plaster to the level of the undamaged area, spreading the plaster onto the surrounding surface for an inch or so. Smooth this layer by drawing the knife blade evenly over the patched area. Let the plaster set.

5 **Completing the patch.** Cover the filled hole with a smooth layer of wallboard joint cement or vinyl spackling compound, using a taping knife (drawing, left). Continue spreading the cement or spackling to an inch or so beyond the edges of the patching plaster. Let the patched area dry for several days. When completely dry it will feel hard and will have lost the clammy feel of wet plaster. Sand the dry area smooth with a sanding block and feather the edges of the compound (page 157) into the surrounding surface.

Repairing Wallboard

The material commonly used today for constructing and repairing walls and ceilings is wallboard, also called gypsumboard, drywall or plasterboard. Wallboard is cheaper than plaster, can be put up faster and is less likely to develop cracks or holes. It is also easy for the average homeowner to install or repair. Special water-resistant wallboard is used behind tiles in bathrooms, providing a barrier against moisture that can lead to deterioration of the wall. But wallboard has its disadvantages too. It is easily punctured and, because of expansion and contraction as weather conditions change or a house settles, the taped joints between the panels may open up and nails may pull out or pop away from the wallboard surface.

Joints between sheets of wallboard are generally concealed and reinforced by perforated paper tape or, less commonly, adhesive fiberglass mesh tape. The tape is embedded in at least three increasingly wide layers of joint compound. The first and third layers of compound are usually thinner in consistency than the second layer. The edges of panels are slightly tapered, allowing space for the tape and compound; this ensures flat and even joints *(page 16, top)*.

The tools for working on wallboard include three wallboard knives—resembling putty knives but with broader blades—in 5-, 8-, and 12-inch widths; a hammer with a slightly rounded poll; a Phillips screwdriver; a roll of perforated wallboard joint tape; a bucket of pre-mixed joint compound and 120 grit sandpaper. For securing wallboard screws, a wallboard-screw countersink can be attached to a variable-speed electric drill. You can apply the joint compound neatly and easily by following a few simple techniques. Dip the knife sideways into the bucket, loading only half the width of the blade. To avoid leaving scratches in the wet compound as you draw the knife over it, keep the blade clean, especially of dried bits of compound. Clean the blade by drawing it over a scrap of wood, not over the edge of the bucket where the debris will accumulate. Use the knife to feather the outer edges of the wider second and third layers until they become smooth, as shown on page 21.

Apply the first layer of joint compound directly to joints *(pages 20-21),* then cover immediately with a strip of tape. (To make taping easier, bend a wire coat hanger into a V shape that will hold the roll of tape, and hook the coat hanger on your belt.) Be sure a layer of compound covers the nail heads and any metal bead along the outside corners. Before applying a subsequent layer of compound, allow the compound to dry at least 24 hours, longer in humid weather. Keep sanding to a minimum; sand between layers only where there is too much compound buildup. Use a sanding block to carefully smooth the final layer; remember that scuff marks on the paper surface will show through the paint.

After your repair is complete, smooth the surface of the leftover compound and reseal the container. If the compound will not be used again for several days or weeks, pour 1/2 inch of water onto its surface; pour off the water when you reopen the container again.

Before painting, wallboard must be smooth and clean. Use a latex-base primer-sealer paint *(pages 148-149)* to prime all repaired and patched areas. Store sheets of wallboard flat on a dry floor. This will prevent the sheets from warping and the slightly tapered edges from being damaged. When working overhead on wallboard, wear goggles to prevent fragments of wallboard and repair materials from getting in your eyes; wear a hard hat to install full sheets of wallboard on a ceiling.

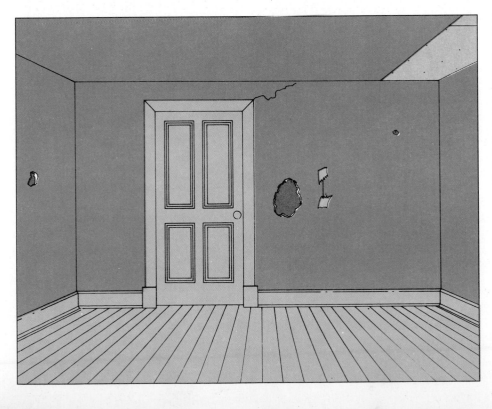

Potential wallboard problems. Wallboard can take the brunt of structural settling and accidental wear and tear. Water from a leaking or overflowing upstairs fixture can seriously warp a ceiling, making a patch necessary. Holes and dents, big and small, result when large appliances are carelessly moved, or the thrust of a hammer head misses a nail. A house's structural settling will cause sections of wallboard to loosen and warp; joint tape will blister and peel leaving an unsightly seam on a living room wall. Failed joints should be resealed and retaped with joint compound and wallboard tape.

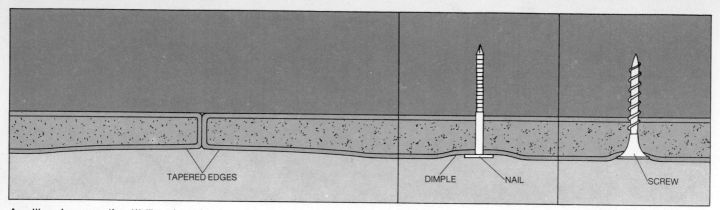

TAPERED EDGES   DIMPLE   NAIL   SCREW

A wallboard cross section. Wallboard consists of a gypsum core covered front and back with heavy paper. The long edges of the panel are slightly tapered *(above, left)* starting 2 inches from the edge, so that when two boards are butted together, they form a shallow trough, simplifying the job of covering the joint.

Special drywall nails, which are made with ringed shafts for extra grip *(above, middle),* can be used to fasten the wallboards to wooden framing members or to furring strips. The nails are driven until their heads are slightly below the surrounding paper surface, leaving a hammer-made dimple that is later filled with joint com-

pound. Neither the nail head nor the dimple should break the paper surface.

Screws *(above, right)* can be used with either metal or wood framing structures. The screws should be sunk to just below the wallboard surface, leaving the paper intact.

Securing Popped Nails

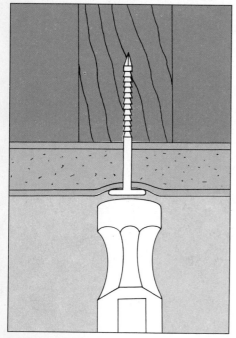

Countersinking a nail. Popped nails may occur wherever a panel is attached to a wall stud or a ceiling joist; the nail head may be covered or partly covered by tape and joint cement. The remedy is the same in all cases. Using a nail set, countersink the nail at least $\frac{1}{16}$ inch below the surface. If the popped nail is in a stud *(above),* install one drywall screw 2 inches above, and one 2 inches below the nail using a Phillips screwdriver. If the popped nail is in a joist, install the screws in the joist 2 inches to each side of the nail. Make sure that the fasteners are countersunk properly by running a taping knife over them; if you hit metal, drive the fastener deeper.

Hiding Fasteners and Joints

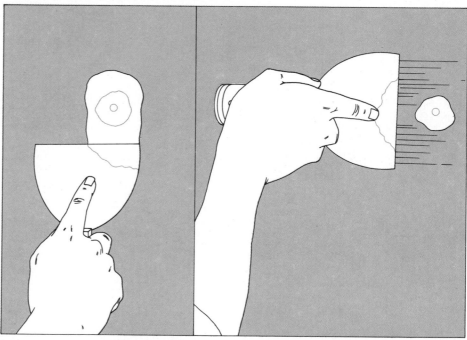

Covering the heads of fasteners. Load half the width of a 5-inch knife blade with joint compound and, holding the blade almost flush with the wallboard, draw the compound across a fastener head and the depression surrounding it *(above, left).* Then raise the knife blade to a more upright position and scrape off the excess with a stroke at right angles to the first stroke *(above, right).* Repeat for other fastener heads. Let the compound dry completely; its color will change from dark to light beige. Apply a second and third coat in the same fashion. Allow each to dry and sand any rough edges *(page 157)* so any depressions are no longer visible.

Filling Holes

1 **Small and large jobs.** Fill a tiny wallboard hole with ready-mixed vinyl spackling compound, let it dry and sand smooth. A hole up to 1 inch wide should first be stuffed with a wad of newspaper; cover the paper with patching plaster and let the plaster set. Add a layer of spackling compound or wallboard joint cement; when dry, sand the surface smooth. The procedure on this page is designed for still larger holes, from 1 inch to about 6 inches wide. (For a bigger hole, see pages 18-19.) First, remove the loose or torn wallboard from the opening. Cut a piece of wire screen that is slightly larger than the hole, thread a length of string through the screen and set it aside. Moisten the edges of the hole with water and apply patching plaster to the moist edges with a putty knife; make sure that plenty of plaster projects behind the wallboard. Now curl the screen's edges and insert it all the way into the hole *(right)*. Pulling the ends of the string gently, draw the screen flat against the inside of the hole and embed it in fresh plaster.

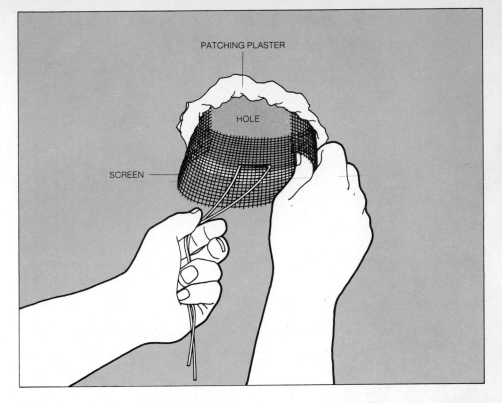

2 **Initial filling.** Secure the screen to the back of the hole by placing a dowel across the opening and tying the string ends firmly around it *(above)*. Fill the screened hole with plaster to a level almost—but not quite—flush with the wallboard surface, then turn the dowel slightly to increase tension on the screen. Let the plaster set for about a half hour, then remove the dowel by cutting the string as close to the plaster as possible. A spot of bare screen will be exposed where the dowel was tied; wet the dried plaster around the spot with water and fill the spot with fresh plaster. Cover the patch with a second layer of plaster to bring it flush with the surface.

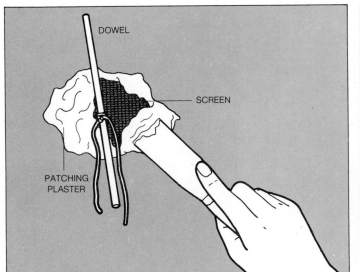

3 **Final sealing.** When the plaster has set, cover the patched hole with wallboard joint cement or ready-mixed vinyl spackling compound (both are easier to sand than patching plaster), using a wide-blade taping knife. Extend the layer of patching material slightly beyond the edges of the patch, so that it covers a little of the surrounding wallboard *(above)*. Spread the material evenly and smoothly with slow, steady sweeps of the knife, and remove any excess. Let the patching material dry for about 24 hours. Finally, sand the patch with fine-grit sandpaper wrapped around a sanding block *(page 157)*; be careful not to roughen the surface too much.

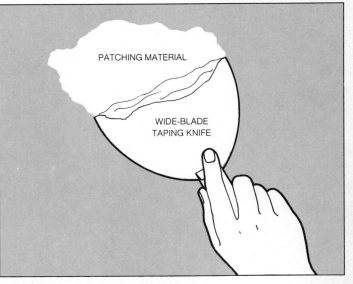

Repairing a Large Hole

1 **Assessing the damage.** If the damaged area is
larger than 6 inches, repair it with a new piece of
wallboard. First, remove any torn or dangling
pieces of wallboard. With a carpenter's square
and pencil (ballpoint ink can bleed through
paint) draw a rectangle or square around
the damaged area. Make the corners as square as
possible, so the new piece will fit neatly.

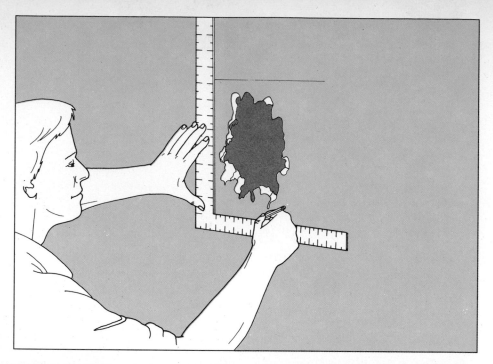

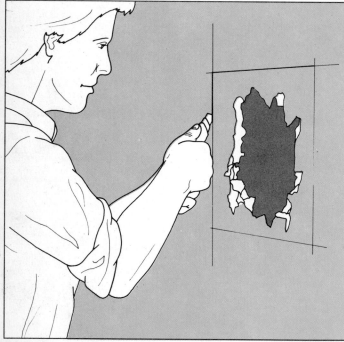

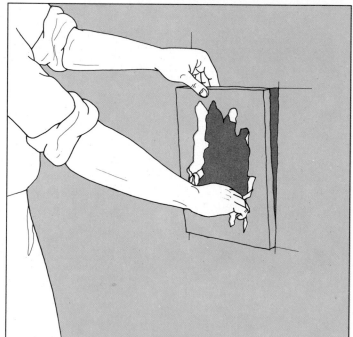

2 **Scoring the damaged area.** Using a utility
knife, lightly score the pencil line of the square
or rectangle drawn in Step 1; hold the knife
with both hands for good control. Then repeatedly
score the lines, cutting a little deeper on each
pass until the knife cuts completely through
the wallboard and paper backing.

3 **Pulling away the damage.** When the edges around
the damaged wallboard section have been
completely scored with the utility knife, clear away
any gypsum or paper backing in the middle of the
hole and pull the damaged section out. If the
section comes away unevenly, or if any paper
backing remains, cut it away. Trim any rough
spots around the perimeter of the hole that could
prevent a patch from fitting snugly in place. If the
insulation lies behind an outside wall surface, take
care not to damage the vapor barrier (page 271).
If the vapor barrier is damaged, reseal it using
the methods described on page 272.

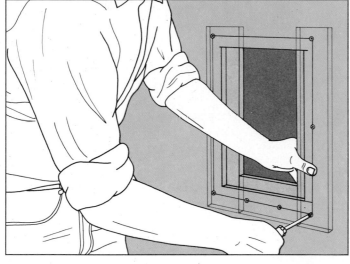

4 Cutting the patch. Transfer the measurement of the cut-out square or rectangle to a piece of wallboard of the same thickness; the replacement piece should fit into the cut-out area with no more than a ⅛- to ¼-inch gap. Using the straight-edge as a guide, score the wallboard until the utility knife cuts through the top layer of paper and into the gypsum core *(far left)*. Then align the cut along the edge of the sawhorse or table and, with one hand holding the board in place and the other holding the end, give a quick firm push down on the end. Turn the wallboard over, bend it and score the crease with the utility knife *(near left)*. Snap off the patch.

5 Bracing the patch. Cut four braces from pieces of 1-by-4-inch lumber. First cut two vertical braces about 5 inches longer than the height of the opening in the wall; then cut two horizontal braces to fit between the vertical ones. Insert each brace behind the wall as shown; this will provide anchorage for the wallboard screws when the patch is put in place. One at a time, insert the braces behind the wall and, using wallboard screws, screw through the wall into the brace about 1 inch from the edge of the opening. Drive the screws at 8-inch intervals around the opening as shown.

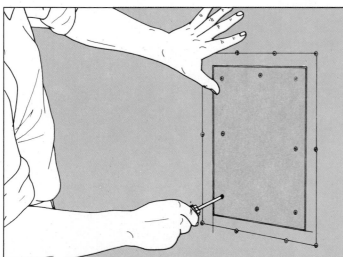

6 Installing the patch. Place the new piece of wallboard in the opening and fasten it to braces with wallboard screws—in the four corners and approximately every 5 inches along the sides and 1 inch from the edge *(above)*. Then plaster the joint, filling the gaps with a fast-setting filler or patch plaster. Try not to add too much filler or plaster; otherwise the joints will show.

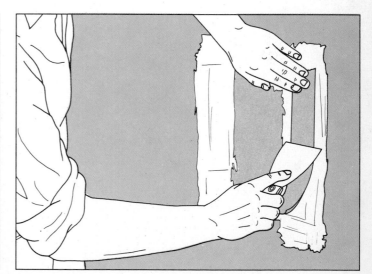

7 Taping the joint. After the filler or patch plaster has set, sand any high spots using a fine-grade sandpaper. Then tape the two vertical edges of the repair, and the top and bottom joints, using the methods described on page 20.

Taping to Make a Joint Stronger

 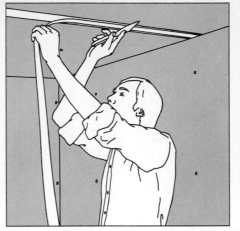 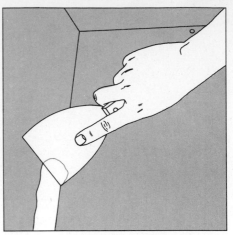

1 Applying joint compound. Scoop a 5-inch knife sideways into the compound so as to load only half the width of the blade. Center the blade over the joint, cocking the blade at a slight angle so the loaded side of the blade is the leading edge. Hold the knife almost perpendicular to the wallboard at the start of the stroke, but gradually angle it closer to the board as you draw it along the seam, forcing the compound into the depression created by the tapered edges of the board. Leave a smooth surface that more than fills the depression. Reload the knife as necessary to fill the longest seam length you can conveniently tape at one time. For an end-to-end joint, where the boards do not have tapered edges, apply compound over the joint in a layer about 1/8 inch thick.

2 Embedding the tape. Center one end of the tape over one end of the joint and press it into the wet compound. Guiding the tape with one hand, run the blade of a 5-inch knife along the joint to force the tape against the compound. At the far end of the joint, press the knife into the tape and wallboard and use it as a straight-edge to tear off excess tape. Run the knife over the joint a second time, pressing firmly to push the tape into the compound and to scrape off excess compound. Go over the joint a third time, leaving a thin film of compound through which the tape can be clearly seen. After 5 minutes check that the tape has no air bubbles under it. At an end-to-end joint, where the paper tape rides on the surface, do not scrape out the excess compound completely. Leave a combined tape-and-compound thickness of about 1/8 inch.

3 Applying compound to an inside corner. Load half the width of a 5-inch knife with joint compound and run the knife along one side of the corner joint, angling the loaded edge of the knife into the corner to create a slightly thicker layer of compound right at the joint. Similarly apply compound to the other side of the joint; do not be concerned if, in applying compound to the second side, you scrape off some of the compound on the first side.

4 Embedding tape into a corner joint. Fold the tape along its lengthwise crease line and press it lightly into the joint compound, using your finger tips to force the crease into the corner. Begin the tape at one end of the joint and use additional lengths to reach the other end. Run the 5-inch knife blade lightly over the surface of the tape, first along one side of the crease, then along the other, just enough to make the tape stick to the compound. Then repeat, using more force to squeeze out excess compound. Finally, coat the tape lightly with some of the excess, and run the knife over it one last time, leaving a thin film of compound on the tape.

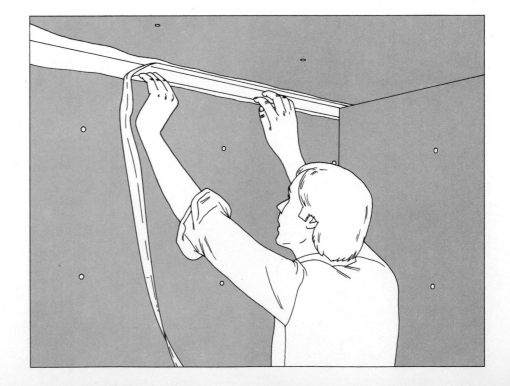

Feathering for a Smooth Finish

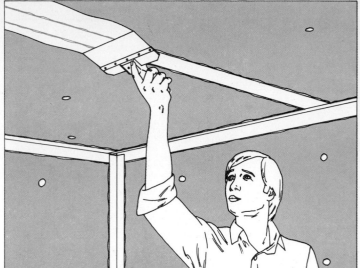

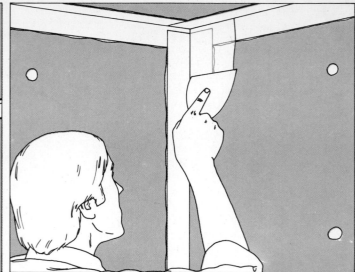

Feathering a taped joint. Load the width of an 8-inch knife with joint compound and lay a second layer of compound over the first *(page 20)*. Then, holding the knife slightly off center so that it laps the joint unevenly, draw the knife down the joint again. This time bear down on the knife edge that is farthest from the joint, to feather the compound on that side, and lift the other edge of the blade about ⅛ inch from the wallboard surface. On a third pass, feather the other side and create a slight ridge, roughly ¹⁄₁₆ inch in height, along the actual joint line.

Apply a third layer of compound with a 12-inch knife, making two passes—one to feather each side of the ridge.

Feathering a taped inside corner. Load the full width of a 5-inch knife and apply the second layer of joint compound to one side of the corner. Scrape off any compound that laps onto the second side, then draw the knife down the first side again, this time bearing down on the outside edge of the knife to feather the compound. Remove any excess from the first side, leaving a smooth surface, and scrape off any compound left on the wall beyond the feathered edge. After the first side of the corner has dried, apply a second layer of compound to the second side. Then repeat this procedure with a wider, 8-inch knife for the third layer of compound.

Working with Corner Bead

Attaching a corner bead. To protect an outside corner, fasten a metal corner-bead strip over the wallboard joint by driving nails or screws through holes in the bead into the stud. The easiest way to trim a corner bead to the correct length is to cut through the flanges with tin snips.

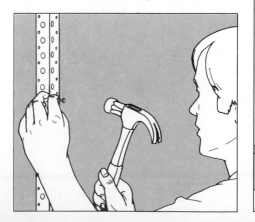

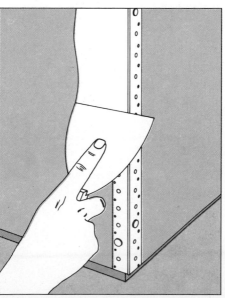

Covering a corner bead. Load about two thirds of the width of a 5-inch knife with joint compound and, lapping the knife blade about 2 inches over the corner, apply the compound by drawing the knife along one face of the bead. Repeat on the other face, then scrape off the excess compound and smooth the joint by alternately running the knife down the two faces.

Apply a second layer of joint compound, filling the knife blade two thirds full, as above, but using the full width of the knife, so as to feather the second layer out about ½ inch beyond the edge of the first. For the third coat, use an 8-inch knife, and feather the compound out an additional 2 inches on each side.

A New Look for Flawed Ceramic

The decorative parts of the bathroom—ceramic tile, soap dishes and towel bars, and the porcelainized surfaces of the fixtures—often need repairs as much as the pipes. Gleaming chrome dulls with layers of mineral deposits; ceramic or porcelain enamel is discolored by rust stains—usually because of a dripping faucet that should have been repaired—or by chemicals in water. A hair dryer slips from the hand—and you have a chipped fixture. Ceramic tiles may even loosen and fall from the wall because of poor installation or the cumulative effects of time and humidity. And one of the most common bathroom repairs—sealing cracks in the joint between the bathtub and the wall—is a repetitive chore because of changes in the weight of the tub as it is filled and emptied time and time again.

The chart and instructions on the following pages provide solutions for these problems. In some situations you may have to combine two techniques to get a job done. On page 25, for example, you will find instructions for replacing a broken grab bar or towel rack. If it turns out that the mounting plate for the new bar does not cover the scar left by the old one, modify the instructions: replace the entire tile by the technique shown opposite, then mount the towel bar on the new tile by the technique on page 25, Steps 2 and 3.

Whatever job you tackle, take precautions. Wear eye protection when you shatter a tile; when you work with powerful cleansers, wet grout or acid, wear neoprene or natural rubber gloves and chemical-splash proof goggles. And when surrounded by the brittle surfaces of a bathroom, handle heavy tools carefully—a single slip can mean a new repair.

Cleaning Tiles and Fixtures

Problem	Solution
Tile adhesive on the surface of the tile	Wash it off quickly with a damp cloth. If it has set, scrape it off carefully with a razor blade or window scraper—without scratching the tile—and then wash the tile with paint thinner.
Dirty seams between tiles Cloudy, filmy tiles	Wash with a toothbrush and detergent. Remove light film with detergent. Heavily soiled tiles need to be washed with trisodium phosphate, available in many paint stores (if phosphates are banned in your community, use a heavy-duty household detergent). Dilute 1 teaspoon of the trisodium phosphate in water. For discolored tiles, sprinkle the phosphate on a moist cloth and wipe, then rinse and dry with a clean, soft cloth.
Rough, grainy surface on tiles or enameled bathtub from the lime deposits in hard water	Dissolve lime deposits by soaking with vinegar.
Discolored bathtub	To improve the appearance of an enameled tub, use a mixture of cream of tartar and peroxide. Stir in enough peroxide to make a paste and scrub vigorously with a small stiff brush.
Soiled or discolored toilet bowl	Flush to wet the sides of the bowl, then sprinkle toilet cleaner or chlorine bleach on the wet surfaces. Let stand a few minutes (longer if badly stained), then brush with a long-handled toilet brush and flush. Never try to strengthen the cleanser with chlorine bleach or add ammonia to either: the mixture will cause a chemical action that liberates toxic gases.
Dirty or sticky chrome	Wash with a mild soap or detergent and polish with a dry, clean cloth. Use vinegar to remove mineral deposits. Do not use metal polishes and cleaning powders: they will damage the plating.
Iron rust stains on sinks or bathtubs	If the fixture is lightly stained, rub with the cut end of a lemon. If seriously stained, use a 5 per cent solution of oxalic acid or 10 per cent hydrochloric acid. Apply with a cloth, leave on only a second and wash off thoroughly. Repeat if necessary. Caution: if your skin or eyes come in contact with acid, flush the area immediately in a sink or shower.
Green copper stains on sinks or bathtubs	Wash with strong solution of soapsuds and ammonia. If the stain persists, try a 5 per cent solution of oxalic acid.

Replacing a Ceramic Tile

1 Removing the tile. Using a hammer and cold chisel and wearing goggles, smash the center of the tile, then pry off the pieces. If a tile falls out in one piece and can be reused, scrape away the old cement on its back. Remove all loose or uneven cement from the tile bed.

2 Resetting the tile. Apply tile adhesive to the back of the tile and, holding it by its edges, set it into place. If the tile does not have little spacer lugs on two sides, place toothpicks in the joint to space it. Secure the tile with masking tape, and let the adhesive dry overnight.

3 Applying the grout. Use already-mixed tile grout to fill and seal the joint spaces around the new tile. First force the grout into the joints with the tip of your finger, then use a moist cloth or window squeegee to remove surplus grout from the tiles on either side.

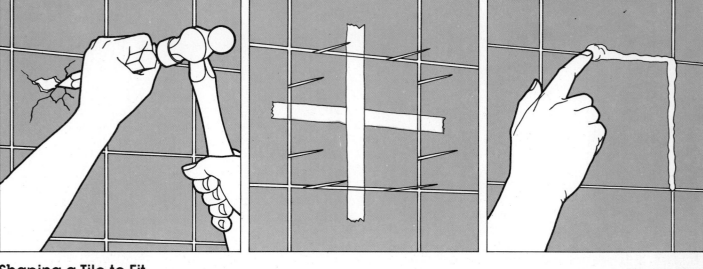

Shaping a Tile to Fit

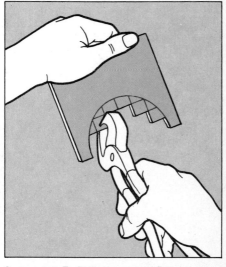

A straight cut. If a tile must be cut to fit into a narrow rectangular space alongside a fixture, outline the part to be removed with a grease pencil. Score the line with a glass or tile cutter: press firmly on the cutter and pull it along the pencil line with a smooth motion *(left)*. To break the scored tile in two, place a pencil on a flat surface and position the tile on the pencil so that the scored line is directly over it. Press down equally on both sides of the line until the tile snaps *(center)*.

A curve cut. To fit tile to a curved fixture, outline the excess part of the tile in grease pencil, and with a glass cutter score a grid over the area to be removed. Using pliers or tile nippers, chip away the grid area. File the edges smooth.

Sealing the Joint between Wall and Tub

Caulking the joint. The simplest way to fill the joint between wall and bathtub is with flexible bathtub caulking. Slowly squeeze the compound out of its tube, using as steady and continuous a motion as possible. Wait at least 24 hours before using the bathtub.

Edging tiles. If caulking will not stay in the wall-bathtub joint, apply quarter-round ceramic edging tiles, which are available in kits. These tiles are easily attached around the entire rim of the tub with a caulking compound.

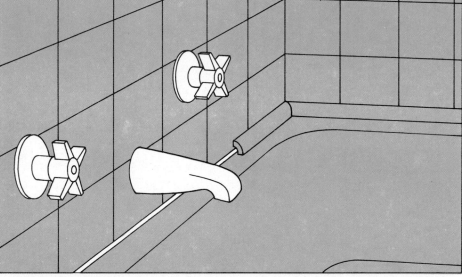

Repairing chipped enamel. Chips on a bathtub or sink can be covered by building up thin coats of epoxy paint, available in touch-up kits in many colors. Clean the surface of the chipped area with alcohol. Then mix a small amount of the paint and hardener in a small container such as a baby-food jar. Apply the paint in several coats with a tiny brush, blending it in toward the edges of the chip. Allow the paint to dry for one hour after each coat. Leftover mixed paint can be kept in a refrigerator for as long as 72 hours.

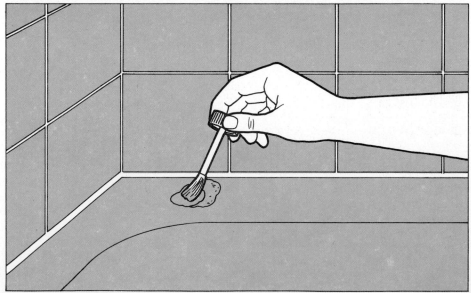

Ceramic Accessories

Broken soap dishes, towel racks and grab bars are replaceable—but as a rule should not be duplicated. In most cases, it is easy to use a replacement accessory that is attached differently.

Most accessories are originally set into tile walls with mortar which is messy to handle. It is therefore best to replace a grab bar or towel rack with a type that can be screwed to the wall. A light soap dish can be simply applied with tile adhesive; be sure to select one without a grab handle, so that you will not be tempted to pull yourself up on it, which could yank it out of the wall.

Replacing a Soap Dish

1 **Removing the dish from the wall.** With a utility knife, score the grout around the soap dish. Protect the adjacent tiles by covering their edges with masking tape. Then, wearing goggles, lightly hammer the broken parts of the dish to loosen them. Set a cold chisel in the groove made by the knife and tap it to force out the dish. Remove the old grout and tile adhesive.

2 **Replacing the dish.** Select a replacement dish that will take up exactly the same number of tile spaces as the old one. Attach the replacement by applying a coat of tile adhesive to the back of the soap dish, then hold it in place with masking tape until the adhesive sets. Wait at least 24 hours for the cement to dry thoroughly, then seal the joints with grout.

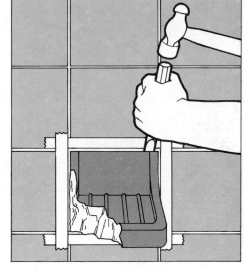

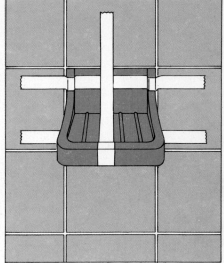

Replacing a Grab Bar or Towel Rack

ANCHOR

1 **Removing the old accessory.** If a grab bar or towel rack breaks, do not gouge out the cement or remaining ceramic piece, but try to get it as flush as possible with surrounding tiles. Protect the tile with masking tape and, wearing goggles, use a hammer and cold chisel, then the sanding attachment on an electric drill to remove as much protrusion as possible. At the inner edges of the tape, sand the surface by hand.

2 **Drilling through tile.** Position the plate for your new rack or bar so that it conceals the old cement bed. Use a metal punch and hammer to knock small chips off the surface of the tile so that the drill bit will not skid, then drill holes for the plate with a masonry bit.

3 **Fastening the mounting plate.** Most contemporary bathroom accessories have "hidden" plates; that is, plates that are attached to the wall with screws and are concealed by the final assembly. If the tile is set in mortar, insert plastic or lead anchors for the mounting-plate screws (above); if you are fastening the unit to a dry wall, use toggle bolts or hollow-wall anchors. Complete the assembly of the unit according to the manufacturer's directions

New Tiles for Damaged Ceilings

Ceiling tiles and panels are often used to cover an unsightly ceiling or reduce noise. Made of wood or mineral fibers, ceiling tiles are permanently attached to the ceiling with nails, staples or adhesive, or to wooden furring strips through tongue-and-groove edges. Suspended ceiling panels are much larger, and rest in a metal grid hung by wires from the ceiling; they may be removed with ease for cleaning or painting.

If your suspended ceiling panels warp because of humidity, try improving ventilation in the room; however, if you live in an extremely humid area, you may get longer-lasting results by replacing the old panels with fiberglass ones. Another common problem is rusting metal grid, which can be caused by humidity or pipes that leak or sweat. Before replacing any tiles or panels, be sure to correct any ceiling problems which may be affecting them. When replacing any portion of your ceiling, wear safety goggles to protect you from flaking or crumbling tiles or panels. In adddition, some tile and panel materials contain asbestos or fiberglass; in that case, wear a respirator and protective gloves. Use a sturdy stepladder when taking down and replacing ceiling tiles, and have a helper on hand for handling large panels.

With regular cleaning, you can keep ceiling tiles in good condition for many years. Dust them periodically with a broom covered with a rag, or a soft-bristled vacuum attachment. When non-washable tiles or panels get dirty, clean them with wallpaper dough (page 221) or sponge lightly with a solution of bleach and water. When washable tiles and panels need cleaning, wash with a detergent-and-water solution and rinse well. Try camouflaging small water spots and stains on light-colored tiles with liquid shoe whitener or talcum powder with a cotton ball. If a discolored or damaged ceiling will not come clean, a new coat of latex paint will often renew it; to avoid clogging the holes of the acoustical tiles, thin the paint first and spray it on rather than brushing it.

Replacing a Suspended Ceiling Panel

Removing and replacing a panel. Wearing safety goggles and standing on a stepladder, gently push up the panel with both hands to free it from the grid. Hold the panel's long edges, turn it sideways (below) and tip it, sliding it out of the grid short edge first. Handle the panel carefully; its edges are very easily nicked. Then replace the panel, sliding it through the grid, short edge first. Align it with the grid and lower it in place, making sure it is properly seated.

PANEL GRID

Replacing a Ceiling Tile

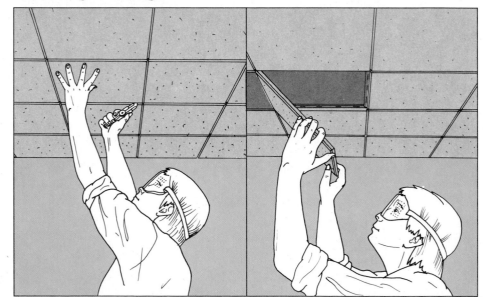

1 **Removing a tongue-in-groove tile.** Wearing safety goggles and standing on a stepladder, insert the blade of a utility knife in the tile's joints; cut through the flanges of the tile on all four sides (above, left). Then pry out the tile (above, right); use a putty knife if necessary. Using a screwdriver, remove flanges left stapled to the ceiling. Remove and replace other tiles if necessary (Steps 2 and 3); or replace the one tile you have removed (Step 4).

2 Removing adjacent tiles. Use a utility knife to cut a cross through the center of the next tile, then slide out any loose pieces; you may have to cut through some of the joints and break off pieces of tile to remove the rest *(below)*. Continue in the same way, removing all the damaged tiles. Then pry off any remaining staples and scraps of flange left in the ceiling *(Step 1)*.

3 Placing new tiles. Slide a tile into one corner of the space; after making sure that the flanges fit together properly, staple the exposed flanges to the ceiling with a staple gun. Insert and staple adjacent tiles, as shown below, in the order in which they best fit. Cut off protruding flanges only where absolutely necessary *(Step 4)*. Install all but the last tile.

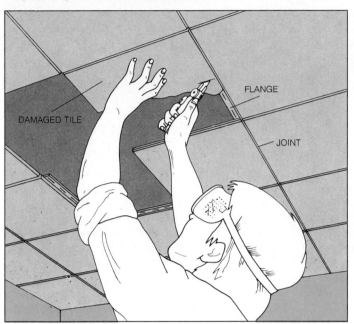

DAMAGED TILE

FLANGE

JOINT

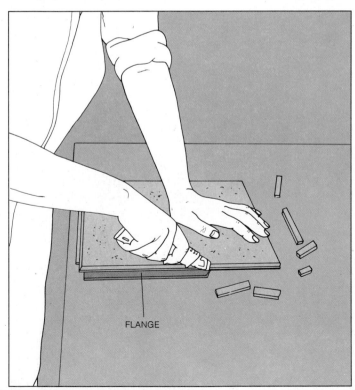

FLANGE

LAST TILE

4 Preparing the last tile. Holding the last replacement tile in place on a flat surface, use a utility knife to cut off all protruding flanges as shown above.

5 Securing the last tile. Insert the tile in the ceiling space, then drive a finishing nail through it at each corner. Use a nail set to recess the nail heads just below the tile surface.

27

Quick Cures for a Wood Floor's Ailments

Although wood, the most common flooring material, is one of the most durable, it does crack, stain, burn and loosen, causing it to squeak or bounce. Fortunately the remedies are simple.

Cracks can be filled, stains and burns sanded away and loose boards retightened in a number of ways. For serious damage, you can replace boards without leaving any scars. Most squeaks arise from subflooring that is no longer firmly attached to the joist below. When the ceiling underneath the floor is unfinished, have someone walk on the floor while you stand below searching for movement in the subfloor over the joist. Then eliminate the squeak by filling the gap with wedges (opposite, top). If the subfloor is inaccessible, refasten the subfloor to the joist by driving nails through the finish floor above.

Squeaks can also result from rubbing between loose finish floorboards. Ask someone to walk over the noisy area while you watch for play in the floor and feel for vibrations. Where the subfloor is accessible, the squeaky boards can be secured from below (opposite, bottom). Where it is not, first try remedies that do not mar the finished surface. Force powdered graphite, talcum powder, wood glue or triangular glazier's points into the joints between boards. Should these solutions fail, nail through from above; be sure to drill pilot holes first, since hardwood flooring is difficult to nail.

Squeaks and vibrations may also mean that the bridging is poorly installed, rotted or inadequate. It should provide reinforcement for all joist spans of 8 feet or more. If it does not, install prefabricated steel bridging, which comes in sizes to fit between joists spaced at 12, 16 and 24 inches. Install solid blocking in place of bridging wherever the joists are unevenly spaced. Cut the blocks to fit tightly between joists, using 2-inch lumber of the same width as the joists. Line them up with the bridging and drive 16-penny nails through the joists into the ends of the blocks; in cramped quarters, drive eightpenny nails at an angle through the blocks into the joists.

Even more common than squeaks are cracks arising from humidity and temperature changes, which cause boards to shrink unevenly. Cracks can be plugged with a mixture of sawdust and penetrating sealer. Use sawdust from the floor itself, gathering the dust by sanding boards in a corner of a closet. Work four parts sawdust and one part sealer into a thick paste and trowel it into the crack.

Surface defects, such as stains and burns, can be erased by sanding if they do not go too deep. To determine the extent of the damage, go over the blemished area with a wood scraper. If the defect starts to lift out, the board can be saved by refinishing. Otherwise, the damaged boards must be pried out of the floor and replaced (page 31). When replacing rotted floorboards be sure to inspect for decay in the surrounding subfloor. With an ice pick or awl, pry up some wood. If it feels spongy or cracks across the grain, rot has set in. Treat lightly decayed subfloors with a good indoor wood preservative, but if the rot has penetrated through the wood the board must be replaced.

Anatomy of a wood floor. A typical wood floor is constructed in layers. Parallel 2-by-8-inch joists, laid on girders and braced by diagonal bridging, provide structural support for the subfloor. In older homes the subfloor is often made of wide planks or tongue-and-groove boards, which are sometimes laid diagonally for extra stability. Today sheets of ¾-inch plywood are preferred, and they are usually glued as well as nailed to the joists. A moistureproof and sound-deadening underlayment of heavy felt or building paper is laid atop the subfloor.

The final layer is the finish flooring, most commonly strips of oak, ¾ inch thick and 2¼ inches wide, that have tongues and grooves on sides and ends so they interlock when installed. They are attached by driving and setting eightpenny nails at an angle above the tongues, where they will be concealed by the upper lips of the adjoining grooves (inset).

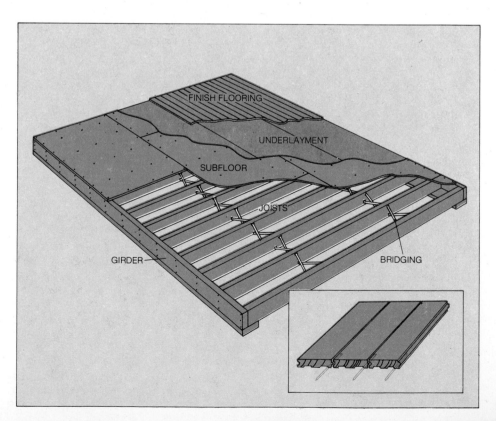

Eliminating Squeaks

Shimming the subfloor from below. Wearing safety goggles, wedge a wood shingle between the joist and a loose subfloor to prevent movement. Do not force the subfloor boards upward or you may cause boards in the finish floor to separate.

Securing inaccessible subfloors. Through pilot holes drilled in the finish floor, drive pairs of eightpenny finishing nails into the subfloor and joist below *(right)*. Angle the nails toward each other. Use a nail set to countersink the nails and cover them with wood putty.

Anchoring finish floorboards from below. Insert screws fitted with large washers into pilot holes drilled through the subfloor and drive them into the finish floor. Use screws that will reach to no more than ¼ inch below the surface of the finish floor. To make the holes in the subfloor, use a drill bit with a diameter at least as large as that of the screw shanks, so that the screws will turn freely in the subfloor. Avoid penetrating the finish floor by marking the thickness of the subfloor on the bit with a ring of tape.

Next drill pilot holes into the finish floor with a bit slightly narrower than the screws. As you turn the screws, their threads will bite into the finish floorboards and pull them tight to the subfloor.

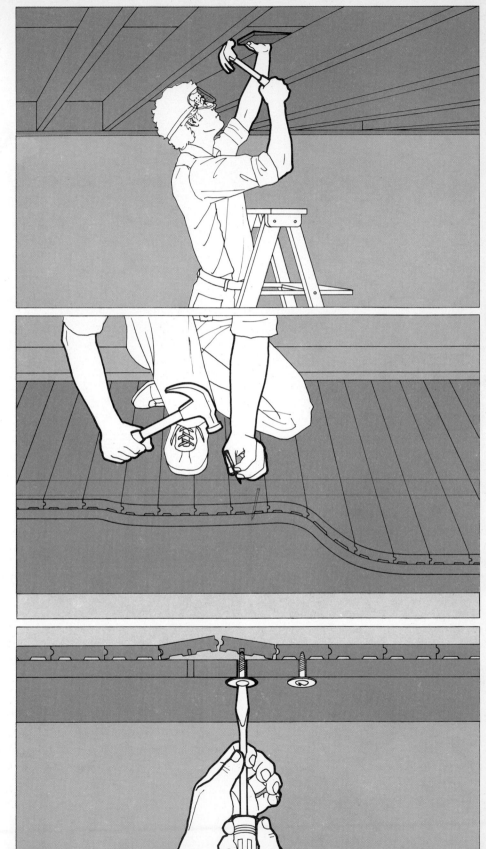

Silencing finish flooring from above. To stop finish floorboards from rubbing together, force glazier's points—the triangular metal pieces that secure glass into frames—into the joints between the boards. Coat the points with powdered graphite and set them below the surface with a putty knife. If the pressure of the knife is insufficient to push the points down, use a hammer and small piece of scrap metal to tap them into place. Insert one point every 6 inches until the squeak is eliminated.

Installing steel bridging. Wearing safety goggles, hammer the straight-pronged end of the bridging into one joist near the top. Then pound the L-shaped claw end into the adjacent joist near the bottom. Alternate the crisscross bridging pattern from joist to joist.

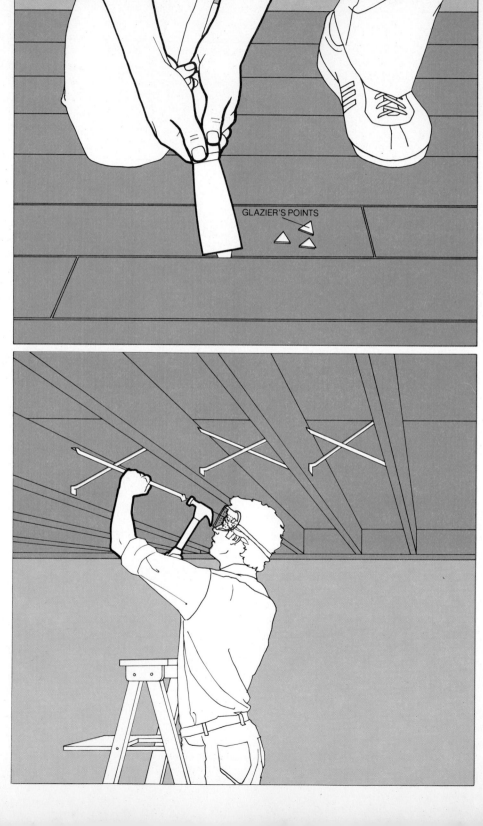

GLAZIER'S POINTS

Custom-Made Patches for Injured Boards

Replacing damaged boards is a job to put off until winter, when dry furnace heat will shrink the wood and make the gaps between pieces larger, permitting maximum play for sliding in replacement boards. Old floors, having acquired wider gaps over the years, are often easier to work on than new ones.

Cut out damaged boards in a staggered pattern with end joints no closer than 6 inches. Then take a sample to a lumberyard to get matching replacements. To install the new ones, follow the sequence illustrated; you will be able to wiggle most of the boards into position, sliding them forward or sideways and blind-nailing them so the repair is invisible. If a board proves obstinate, or is too wide for the space to be filled, plane it on the groove side until it fits. Only one or two should have to be dropped into place from above and face-nailed.

1 **Starting to remove a board.** Make vertical cuts across damaged boards with a 1-inch wood chisel, keeping its bevel side toward the portion of the board to be removed. Then, working back toward the vertical cut, angle the blade and drive the chisel at about 30° *(inset)*, along the board. Repeat this sequence until you have cut all the way through the board.

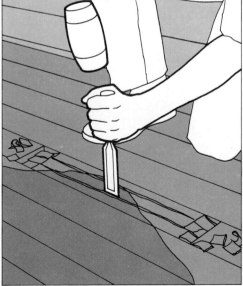

2 **Splitting the board.** Make two rows of incisions with a chisel along the face of a floorboard that has been channeled *(above)*. Pry the board up just enough to split the wood. Proceed until the boards to be removed are split *(right)*.

3 **Prying the board out.** Insert a pry bar into a lengthwise crack in a damaged board. Pry the middle strip out, then the groove side and finally the tongue side. Work from the center of the damaged area, and be careful not to damage good boards. Remove or drive down—with a nail set—exposed nails.

4 Inserting a new board sideways. Using a scrap of flooring—one with a clear groove along its edge to fit the tongue of the replacement piece—as a hammering block, wedge a cut-to-size replacement into place, grooved side over the tongue of the preceding course.

5 Blind-nailing a board. Drive and set eightpenny finishing nails at a 45° angle through the corner of the tongue of the replacement. Pilot holes are not essential but may be helpful. If existing boards around the repair have separated slightly, try to match their spacing by inserting thin shims such as metal washers between the new board and the old one while driving the nails.

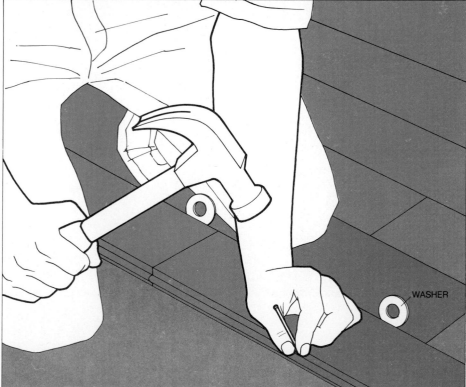

WASHER

6 **Inserting a new board lengthwise.** To slide a replacement between two boards, lay it flat on the subfloor and work the tips of its tongue and groove into those of the existing pieces. Using a scrap hammering block, tap it all the way in.

7 **Inserting a new board from above.** With the last few pieces, which cannot be slid into place, chisel off the lower lips of their grooves as indicated by the colored line above. Then gently tap the board into place from above.

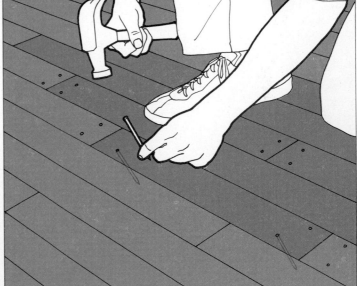

8 **Face-nailing.** To fasten the last replacement boards, which offer no access for blind-nailing, you must drive eightpenny finishing nails every 12 inches into predrilled pilot holes. Drill the holes about ½ inch from the edges of the face. Then set all face nails and cover them with putty that has been tinted to match the color of the boards.

Supports that Bolster a Sagging Floor

A dip in a floor is irritating, but not necessarily dangerous. If you have such a dip, measure it by the method shown on the opposite page. A small dip, less than 3/4 inch deep and 30 inches long, can be repaired in the same way as a squeak, with hardwood wedges driven between a joist and the subfloor (page 29). A larger sag, or a sag that grows worse over time, may be a symptom of trouble. If it occurs in conjuction with such seemingly unrelated problems as a sticky door, cracked plaster or leaky plumbing, it may eventually be followed by structural damage in the supporting framework girders, posts and joists. The solution is to raise the floor and also reinforce or replace the faulty supports.

Sags usually occur in older houses, built with wood posts and girders rather than steel columns and beams. They are most common on the first floor, which is generally accessible from underneath if you have to make repairs. If you have a second-story sag, an entire floor or ceiling may have to be torn out to get at the trouble, but the repair techniques are the same as those used downstairs.

To repair a sag, your first task is diagnosis. Inspect the framework underneath the floor for faulty construction (below). Test for rot and insect damage by stabbing an awl into joists, girders and posts. If you find rotten wood—that is, wood that feels spongy and does not splinter—paint it heavily with penetrating preservative. A honeycomb of long, channeled voids is a sign of termites; call an exterminator.

To straighten a floor before making permanent repairs, jack up the joists or girder under the sag. Always use a screw jack, which is stronger and more reliable than the hydraulic type, and be sure to grease the threads before you begin. If you are working in a basement, rent a house jack—essentially a telescopic metal post fitted with plates at the base and top (opposite, center). If there is only crawl space, use a contractor's jack—a squat, bell-shaped jack with a screw that extends about a foot (opposite, bottom).

Once a sagging joist has been jacked up, it can be permanently straightened by doubling—that is, by nailing a new joist to the weak one. The technique works even on a badly rotted joist, so

long as the ends that rest on the girder and foundation wall are sound and the wood in between will hold nails. A joist that has rotted through must be replaced. Before starting either job inspect to make sure that pipes, electrical wires and ventilating ducts will not prevent you from slipping the new joists into place. You will have to move any obstruction or have a professional do it; in some cases it may even be easier to leave a jack in place as a permanent support and not try to repair or replace failed joists.

Jacking is also the first defense against a sag in a girder, but the final remedy is more complex. If a girder sags over a post, a jack on either side of the post will raise it. But the jacks must be left in place and set on concrete footings; it is often easier to replace the post with a steel column. Similarly, a sag in the middle of a girder can be jacked up if the girder is in good condition and made of softwood; hardwood beams are too stiff to be straightened. A better solution is replacing the wood girder with a steel beam. Replacing a post or a girder can be strenuous work and requires a building permit.

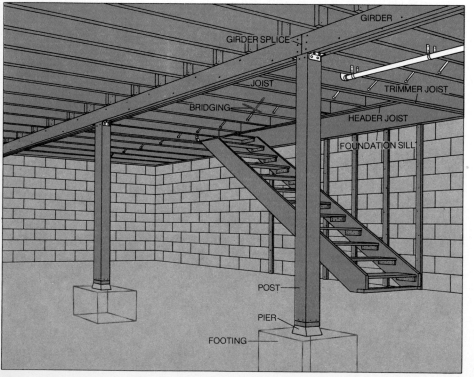

Why floors sag. This drawing shows the horizontal and vertical supports that carry the weight of the ground floor (page 28) in a typical house. Beneath the subfloor are joists, laid in parallel rows, outer ends resting on the foundation sills. Bridging (page 30) strengthens the joists and keeps them in alignment. In the center of the basement the joists rest on a wood girder. The ends of the girder rest in pockets in the foundation wall; the center is supported by wood posts on concrete piers, anchored in footings.

Shifts in the positions of these parts can cause sags in the floor above. Any of the wood members could be damaged by rot or termites. Posts that are not set on piers will absorb moisture from the basement floor, and posts that have piers but no footings are likely to sink. The built-up girder shown, made of overlapping lengths of lumber, would sag if it were spliced in the middle of a span rather than over a post. The header and trimmer joists that frame the stairwell carry extra weight and must be doubled to keep them from sagging. Finally, joists that have notches or holes for electrical and plumbing lines should be reinforced. For that reason it is best when installing such lines to leave the joists intact if possible, as shown.

Jacking Up a Floor

Measuring a sag. Lay an 8-foot straightedge—a 2-by-4, an iron pipe or best of all a rigid strip sawed from the uncut edge of a sheet of plywood—across the sagging area, measure the gap between the straightedge and the floor and mark the floor where the sag is deepest.

Measure from the mark on the floor to two different reference points—walls or stairways, for example—that lie at right angles to each other and that also appear in the basement. In the basement, take measurements from the reference points to position the jack.

Jacking from the basement. If you are straightening a floor—and do not plan to reinforce it—lock the tubes of a telescopic house jack with its steel pins, set the bottom plate on a 4-by-8 pad, and while a helper steadies a 4-by-6 beam at least 4 feet long between the joists and the top plate, screw the jack until the beam presses against the joists. Use a level to be sure the jack is plumb, then nail its plates to pad and beam.

Once a day raise the jack 1/16 inch until the floor is level. If necessary, slip an 18-inch pipe over the jack handle for leverage. Caution: a faster rate of jacking can cause structural damage.

If you plan to double or replace joists, remove their bridging and, when you set up the jack, insert 2-by-6 blocks on the beam between joists. Jack the floor 1/4 inch higher than level.

Jacking from a crawl space. Set a contractor's jack between a pad and a beam, following the instructions above for using a telescopic house jack. Turn the screw of the jack until the beam presses against the joists. In most crawl spaces, the jack will not rise from the floor to the joists even when fully extended. To raise the base of a jack, set its pad on a pyramidal framework called cribbing, made of rough hardwood 6-by-6s, available from dealers in structural timber. Stack the beams in parallel pairs, with each pair at right angles to the one beneath it; the top beams should be about 18 inches apart.

Raise the jack a maximum of 1/16 inch a day until the sag disappears.

STEEL PINS

PAD

JACK HANDLE

Repairing Wood Molding

Molding is vulnerable to daily abuse; it can also suffer from aging. Outside joints may be hit once too often by the vacuum cleaner, or a baseboard could be gashed or badly scratched when you move a piece of furniture. As an older house settles, the moldings may start to gap at the corner joints, or dry out and split.

If your moldings are painted, many repairs can be quickly and simply done with fillers such as wood putty and vinyl spackling. Natural wood moldings require more careful work and a filler—such as wood putty—that will absorb stain or varnish. Badly cracked moldings—whether painted or finished—are best repaired with yellow glue (page 108).

The two most common types of molding often used together—are shoe molding and baseboard (right, above). If either type is gouged, split, cracked or nicked, you may be able to repair the damage with one of the quick, simple techniques shown at right, below. However, for more extensive damage, you may have to replace an entire section of molding.

When repairing damaged shoe molding or base cap, remove only the section to be repaired; to replace a section of baseboard, you must first remove the shoe molding and base cap, if any, then the baseboard itself. If your molding is natural wood finish, there may come a time when it needs refinishing; for the most professional-looking results, remove it first and number the sections for easy replacement.

The toughest part of molding repair may be finding a matching replacement. If your home is relatively new, chances are the local lumberyard has an identical replacement in stock. However, for older-style, more ornate moldings, you may have to visit second-hand building supply yards or have the piece custom made—an expensive option.

Types of molding joints. Moldings consist of the baseboard, shoe molding and—in older homes—the base cap. Sections of molding may be joined in a number of ways: At an outside corner, a miter cut is common (page 39). An inside corner joint may be mitered, or coped (pages 37-38) for a better fit in a corner that is not perfectly square. Along the wall, 90°-cut sections may be joined at a butt joint or 45°-cut sections at a scarf joint. Joints are secured by nails, angled at corners (inset).

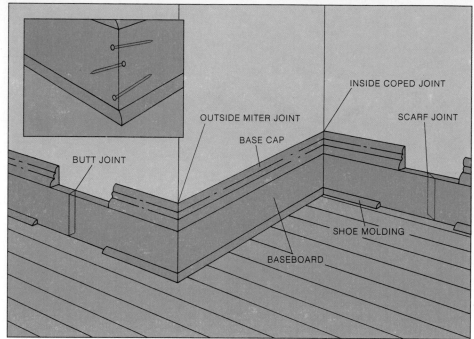

INSIDE COPED JOINT

OUTSIDE MITER JOINT

SCARF JOINT

BASE CAP

BUTT JOINT

SHOE MOLDING

BASEBOARD

Two Common Molding Repairs

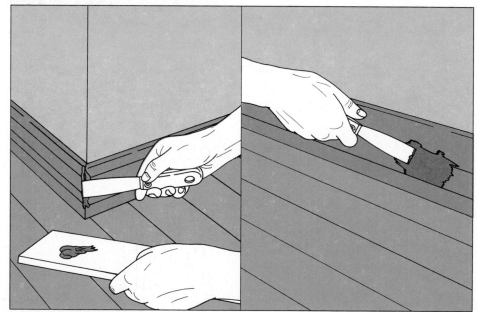

Common repairs for damaged molding. The most vulnerable part of your wall, molding is often damaged when furniture and children's play equipment are knocked and scraped against it. With time, an older house settles, causing gaps where molding intersects at corners. An outside corner is most often marred by daily household activity; it also most obviously reveals a house's structural settling.

Often, the quickest and easiest way to repair the damage is by using a wood filler. Use a putty knife to force the filler into a gouge or open joint (above, left) or damaged length of molding (above, right). Overfill the depression slightly to compensate for shrinkage when the putty has dried. Then use fine-grit sandpaper and a sanding block (page 157) to sand the putty flush with the surface; paint or finish the molding.

Removing Damaged Molding

1 Freeing shoe molding. Run a utility knife along the edges of the shoe molding *(inset)*, scoring any finish or paint that will hinder easy removal. Widen the seams with a putty knife, then insert a pry bar and shims to protect the wood from damage, and ease the shoe molding away from the wall. Remove any nails along the floor. Replace damaged shoe molding *(pages 38-39)* or remove damaged baseboard *(next Step)*.

2 Removing damaged baseboard. After freeing the shoe molding *(left)* and base cap, if any, look for vertical seams on each side of the damaged section; these will tell you where to score the paint or finish with a utility knife before prying the baseboard from the wall. Use a pry bar to remove the damaged section, protecting the wall with shims. Replace the section, coping or mitering the joints as described in the following pages.

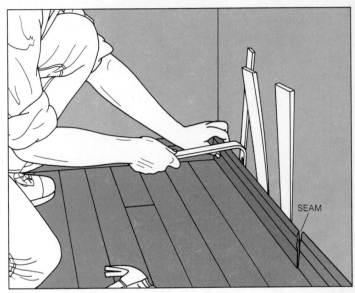

SEAM

Coping an Inside Corner Joint

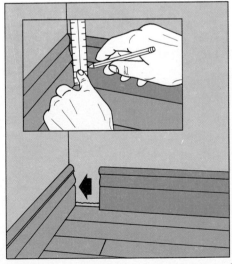

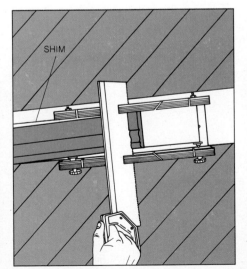

SHIM

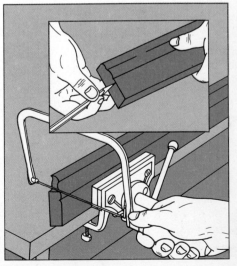

1 Marking the replacement. Saw a length of molding at least 4 inches longer than the removed section; this will allow for adjustment. Place the new section in the corner against the fixed baseboard *(above)*. Use a straightedge to draw a vertical line on the molding *(inset)*; this will tell you where to miter it *(next Step)*. (If your house has settled, the line may not be perfectly vertical.)

2 Mitering the baseboard. Brace the replacement in a miter box with a slot for a 45° horizontal cut *(above)*; for baseboards exceeding 4 inches in height, you may need a miter box designed for higher moldings. Use a backsaw to cut a 45° angle in the corner end, following the line you drew in Step 1; insert a shim to adjust the baseboard so the line falls straight under the blade.

3 Coping the edge. Remove the baseboard from the miter box and highlight the baseboard's contoured profile with a pencil *(inset)* as a guide for coping. Brace the baseboard in a clamp and use a coping saw to cut along the penciled edge at a slight back angle as shown above; an angle of about 2° will allow you to close the joint neatly when the baseboard is installed.

4 **Placing the new molding.** Push the new section into place in the corner. Then run a pencil along the gap between the existing section of molding and the new section; this will mark any high points that prevent a good fit.

In most cases, the baseboard edge that you coped in Step 3 *(page 37)* should fit properly; if the fit is not snug, file any remaining high points with sandpaper, a chisel or the coping saw blade. Check the fit again.

5 **Marking the scarf or butt joint.** After the coped inside corner joint has been fitted, use a pencil to mark the opposite end of the replacement baseboard where it should fit into place along the wall *(below)*. If the joint is a scarf joint as shown, use a miter box and backsaw to make a 45° cut; cut the diagonal in the direction that will accommodate the piece into which it fits. For a butt joint, make a simple 90° cut in the miter box. The more precise your cut, the more neatly the sections will fit together.

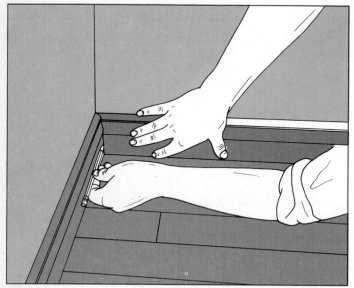

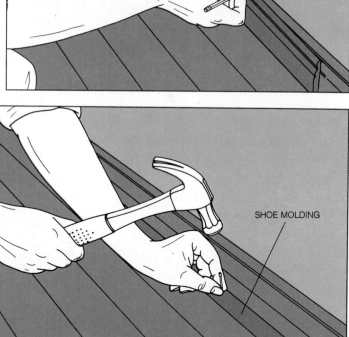

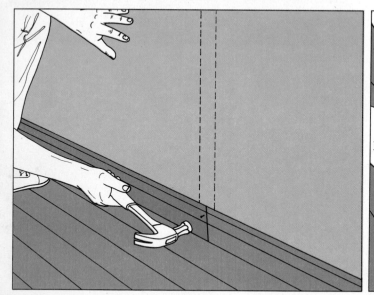

SHOE MOLDING

6 **Securing the baseboard and shoe molding.** Examine the wall behind the new baseboard section and mark with a pencil, slightly above the top of the baseboard, the position of the old nail holes. In most cases, sections are joined over a stud *(dotted lines above, left),* providing firm anchorage for nails. Depending on the combined thickness of your molding and wall, use 2½- to 3½-inch finishing nails to nail the baseboard in place *(page 36, top)*. Next, replace the shoe molding if damaged *(opposite, top)* or nail the

old shoe molding back into place using any existing nail holes as a guide. Countersink the nails with a nail set *(opposite, bottom right)*.

For a clean and professional looking job, fill the nail holes and any gaps in the joints with wood putty; let the filler dry according to the label instructions and use a fine-grit sandpaper *(feathering technique, page 157)* to smooth the filler into the wood. Finally, either paint or finish the molding. If necessary, touch up a stained or varnished finish with a wax pencil *(page 143)*.

Coping Shoe Molding

1 Preparing the replacement. Remove the damaged molding *(page 37, top)*, then miter the corner end of the replacement piece as shown at the bottom of page 37. Highlight the contour of the shoe molding with a pencil *(inset page 37, Step 3)*. Extend the molding over the edge of a work table and cope following the penciled outline as shown below.

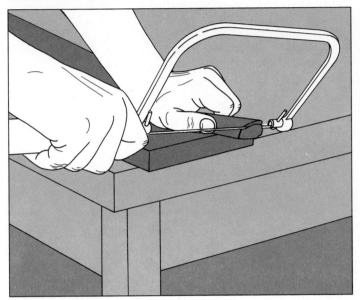

2 Placing and fitting the shoe molding. Slide the coped shoe molding into place and make any necessary adjustments to the fit with sandpaper, a chisel or the coping saw blade. Then use the miter box to make a 45° cut for a scarf joint or a 90° cut for a butt joint on the opposite end of the molding. Secure the molding to the floor using finishing nails *(page 38, Step 6)*.

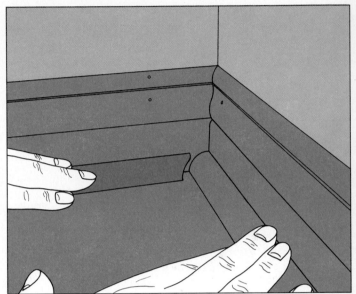

Making an Outside Miter Joint

1 Mitering an outside corner. Remove the damaged section of molding *(page 37, top)* and saw a replacement length of molding at least 4 inches longer than the original piece. Place the molding in a miter box and make a 45° cut at the corner end. On the other end, use the miter box again to make a 45° cut for a scarf joint or a 90° cut for a butt joint *(page 36)*.

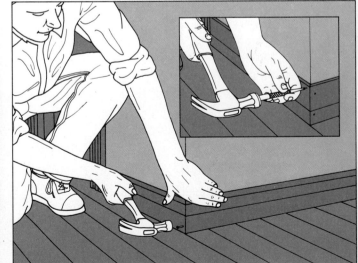

2 Securing the molding. Put the new section in place, and nail the baseboard at the scarf or butt joint: Joints usually occur over studs in the wall, providing firm anchorage for the nails. Next, cross nail the corner joint as shown at the top of page 36 and nail the shoe molding back in place. Use a nail set to countersink the nails *(inset)*. Refinish or repaint the new section, as needed.

Putting a New Face on an Old Wood Floor

Your vanished wood floors may be so worn and scuffed that no amount of waxing and polishing will restore their gloss. Or perhaps you have decided to expose the natural texture and grain of a painted floor. In either case, you must refinish your floors. It is a four-stage job: sanding off the old finish, bleaching out stains, treating the wood with a sealer that gives the floor the tone or coloring of your choice and applying a new, durable, polyurethane-base finish.

A refinishing job calls for professional equipment, available from most tool-rental agencies. You will need a drum sander, in which sandpaper is fitted over a large revolving cylinder; make sure the machine you rent has a tilt-up lever that lifts the spinning drum from the floor (not all have this feature). Also rent an edging machine with a rotating disk for hard-to-get areas that the drum sander cannot reach. In addition, you will need a respirator to block the dust raised by sanding, and ear muffs to deaden the sound of the sander—a brutally noisy machine. Finally, to smooth the floor after applying each coat of sealer or new finish, rent a professional polishing machine; it polishes with a round pad of steel wool.

To help determine the cost of these rentals, estimate in advance the time the job will take—normally, you can sand and seal 200 to 250 square feet of flooring in a day. You can economize by completing the work with the drum sander and edger before you rent the polisher, and use two workers simultaneously, if possible—one to operate the drum while the other operates the edger.

You need to use sandpaper of three grades—coarse, medium and fine. The coarse paper for the first sanding may have any of a variety of grit ratings, depending on the existing surface of the floor. To remove paint or to sand rough floorboards, start with a very coarse, 20-grit paper (the lower the grit rating, the coarser the paper). To take varnish or shellac off a strip or plank floor, use a 36-grit paper; for parquet or herringbone floors, use a 50-grit paper. For the second sanding, use a medium, 80-grit paper, and for the final sanding, a fine, 100-grit paper will do a good job.

Have the dealer supply you with plenty of sandpaper—at least 10 sheets and 10 disks of each grade for an average room. You will pay only for the paper you actually use. Be prepared during the job for a sudden, accidental wastage; a protruding nailhead can tear a sheet of sandpaper to shreds in a split second. Before leaving the shop, check that the machines are working, that their dust bags are clean and that you get any special wrenches you may need to load the drum sander (have the dealer show you the loading method). Because the sanders need grounding, they must have three-pronged plugs; make sure the room you are working in has a three-slot receptacle.

To prepare a room for sanding, remove all the furniture. If you prefer not to take the drapes down, fold them over a coat hanger hung on the drapery rod; then slip a large plastic bag over them and seal it with tape. Remove the floor registers and cover the vents with plastic. Tighten any loose boards and replace badly cracked or splintered boards (pages 31-33). Using a nail set, drive protruding nailheads one eighth of an inch below the surface of the floor, and to make sanding the edges of the floor easier, remove the shoe moldings from the baseboards (below). Sanding produces highly flammable dust: turn off lights and electrical appliances. Seal the doorways with plastic and open the windows for ventilation.

Sanding Down to the Bare Boards

BAGGED DRAPES

CHISELS

SHOE MOLDING   WEDGES

REGISTER GRILL

1 **Removing shoe molding.** Beginning at a doorway, use a utility knife to score any paint seams between the shoe molding and baseboard or wall. Using two sharp chisels a few inches apart, gently pry the molding away from the baseboard and up from the floor. You may have to tap the chisels lightly with a hammer to insert them. When you have loosened about 1 foot of the molding, slip small wood wedges behind and under it to prevent it from snapping back into place. Advance along the length of a section of molding, repeatedly prying out the molding and moving the wedges. As you remove each section, number it so you will know where to replace it after the job. When all the sections have been removed, pull out any finishing nails that remain in the floor or baseboard.

2 **Loading the drum sander.** With the sander unplugged, thread a sheet of sandpaper into the loading slot, turn the drum one full revolution and slip the other end of the sheet into the slot; then tighten the paper by turning the nuts at both ends of the drum with the wrenches provided by the dealer. (On the widely used model shown here, the paper is tightened when you turn the left-hand wrench away from you and the right-hand wrench toward you.) When using fine paper, insert a folded paper wedge of the same grade between the two ends to keep them from slipping out of the slot (inset).

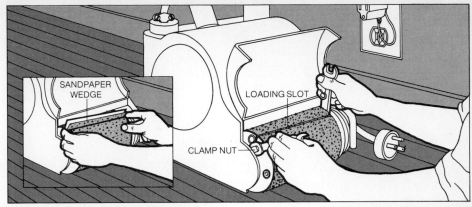

SANDPAPER WEDGE

LOADING SLOT

CLAMP NUT

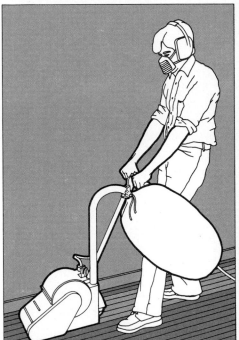

SECOND SANDING   FIRST SANDING

FINAL SANDING

3 **The first sanding.** Lift the drum from the floor with the tilt-up lever, start the sander, and when the motor reaches full speed lower the drum to the floor and let the sander pull you forward at a slow, steady pace. Sand a strip or plank floor along the grain of the wood; on parquet or herringbone patterns, which have grains running two ways, do the first sanding in a diagonal direction. When you reach the far wall, raise the drum from the floor, move the cord behind you to one side, then lower the drum and pull the sander backward over the area you have just sanded. Caution: keep the sander in constant motion to prevent it from denting or rippling the wood.

Then lift the drum and move the machine to the left or right to overlap the first pass by 2 or 3 inches. Continue forward and backward passes, turning off the sander occasionally to empty the dust bag. When you have sanded the whole width of the room, turn the machine around and sand the strip of floor against the wall.

4 **Second and third sandings.** Load the edger with coarse paper and sand the areas missed by the drum sander. Now repeat both the drum and edge sandings, first with medium paper, then with fine. On strip or plank floors, the second and third drum sandings, like the first, should be made with the grain. On parquet or herringbone floors (inset), do the second sanding on the opposite diagonal to the first, and the final sanding along the length of the room.

5 **Scraping the tight spots.** In areas that neither the drum nor the edging sander can reach, use a paint scraper to remove the finish. At a radiator, remove collars from around the pipes for a thorough job. Always pull the scraper toward you, applying a firm, downward pressure on the tool with both hands, and scrape with the grain wherever possible. Sharpen the scraper blade frequently with a file. To complete this stage of the job, sand the scraped areas by hand.

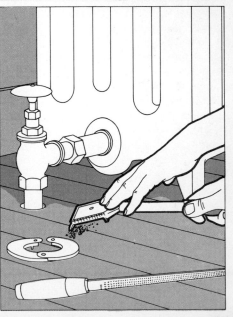

Two Protective Coats that Seal and Beautify

A new floor finish will last a long time—and so will any blemishes that are visible beneath it. Before you seal a floor, check it for stains that were not removed by sanding. If you cannot remove them by hand-sanding, use undiluted household bleach. Wearing gloves and goggles, apply a small amount of bleach to the center of the stain. Wait a few minutes to see how much the bleach lightens the spot, and then apply enough to blend the stained area with the rest of the floor. When you get the right tone, wash the bleached area with warm water and let it dry. Then vacuum the floor and go over it with a tack cloth, a rag moistened with turpentine and varnish, to pick up all dust before applying the sealer.

To emphasize and protect the grain of the wood, use an oil-based penetrating sealer. Such sealers come in both natural wood hues and a clear, colorless form, and unlike conventional wood stains, they sink deep below the surface and cannot be scuffed or walked off.

Some, known as pickling stains, are tinted with pigments that give a floor an arbitrary color—blue or green, for instance—but accentuate the grain so that the floor retains the look of wood.

When a penetrating sealer has sunk into the wood, any excess remaining on the surface must be wiped off promptly before it dries. One person can apply the sealer and mop it up, but two workers make the job faster and easier (right, top). For a pickling stain, two workers are essential to prevent discolorations from the uneven drying of excess sealer.

For a final—but optional—protective glaze over the sealer, select a finish made with polyurethane, a synthetic resin that becomes exceptionally tough as it cures or hardens. Older finishes—varnish, shellac, lacquer and wax—yellow with age, wear easily and must be completely removed when a floor needs refinishing; a polyurethane finish is non-yellowing and far more durable. And, if it is never waxed, it can be renewed by running a polisher loaded with steel wool over the floor and adding a coat of finish.

1 Applying penetrating sealer. Wearing rubber gloves, lay on the sealer with a rag in long, sweeping strokes along the grain of the wood while a co-worker wipes up the excess. Start next to a wall and away from the door (so that you will not have to walk over wet sealer to get out of the room) and apply the liquid liberally over a strip of floor 3 feet wide. Between eight and 20 minutes after it is applied, the sealer will have penetrated the wood, leaving shallow puddles of excess liquid on the surface. At this point your helper, using rags in both hands, should begin mopping up. Start applying a second strip of sealer as your co-worker begins, and try to work at a pace that keeps both of you moving together with your knees on dry floor until the job is almost finished. On the last strip, the helper must do his part while backing across wet sealer to the door. Let the sealer dry for about eight hours.

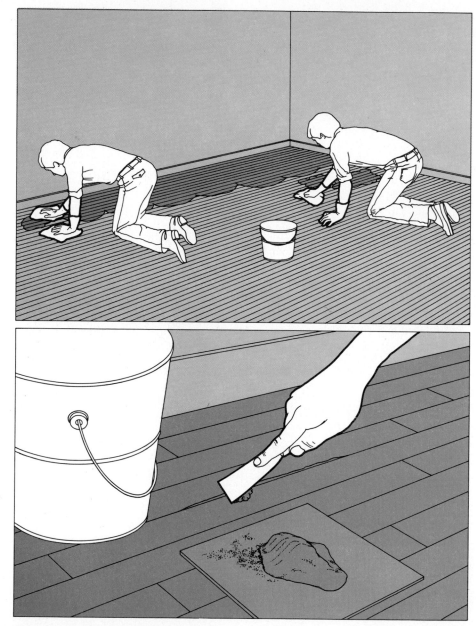

2 Filling cracks and holes. When the sealer has dried, force wood putty into cracks and nail holes with a putty knife. To match the color of the sealed floor, buy a tinted commercial putty or mix your own by using dust from the final sanding and enough clear varnish to make a thick paste. When the surface of the putty has dried, hand-sand it with 100-grit paper.

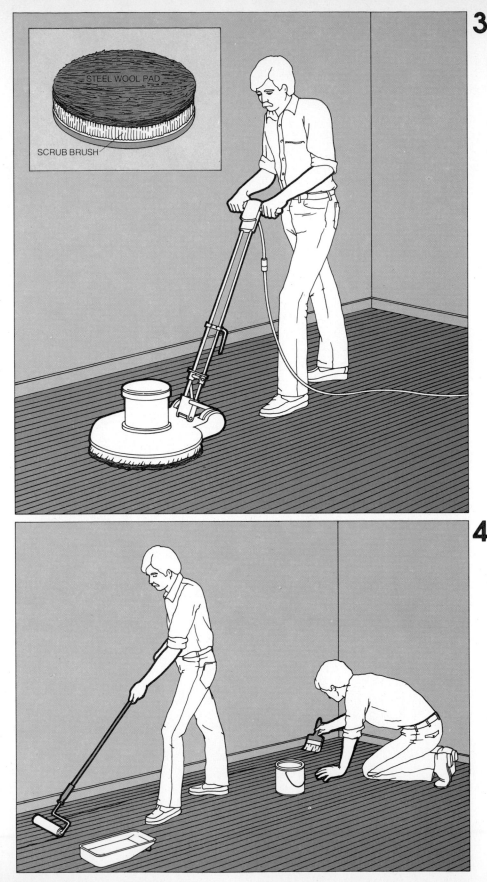

3 Smoothing the sealed wood. Run a polishing machine loaded with fine steel wool over the floor to cut down irregularities in the surface caused by tiny bubbles in the sealer coating. To load the polisher, use a precut pad of steel wool obtained from the rental agent; fit the polisher with a heavy-duty scrub brush and press the pad into its bristles (*inset*). Scour the edges and corners of the floor by hand with small pads of steel wool, then vacuum the entire floor and go over it thoroughly with a tack cloth.

4 Finishing the floor. Apply polyurethane finish to the main part of the floor with a long-handled mohair roller, and to edges and corners with a small brush; if you are working alone, do the edges and corners first. When using the roller, work along the grain and apply the finish slowly and evenly. Wait at least eight hours, then smooth the surface with fine steel wool (*above, Step 3*). When you have gone over the floor with a vacuum and tack cloth, apply a second coat of finish across the grain. Wait another 24 hours for the floor to dry before replacing the shoe moldings, floor registers and radiator-pipe collars.

Some Easy Repairs for Hard-Surfaced Floors

The hard flooring materials—concrete and marble, slate or ceramic tiles—are the most durable. They are also the most inflexible and brittle. All of them can be cracked by the fall of a heavy weight from above. If they are inadequately supported from below, they can be pulled apart by normal settling of a house. Under this invisible but constant stress, tiles will loosen and break; concrete will crumble and crack. A tile floor that is cracked throughout a room is usually a sign of trouble in the structure beneath it. You may have to replace the entire floor by clearing out the old tile, tightening the subfloor (pages 28-30) and laying new tile.

Ceramic tiles are generally laid in an organic or thin-set adhesive if the subfloor is wood. Slate and marble, as well as ceramic over concrete, are generally laid in mortar. When only a few tiles are cracked your job is easier—replace the tiles, one by one, using a flexible adhesive to simplify the job. Use organic adhesives for replacements laid directly on a wood subfloor or smooth, dry concrete. To replace tiles on damp, damaged or irregular mortar beds, use epoxy adhesives consisting of resins and hardeners that require mixing before application.

A new tile must be regrouted. One choice is silicone grout, which comes premixed in squeeze tubes, cures quickly and adheres to both old and new tile. Silicone grouts come in a variety of colors, but if you cannot match the existing grout you can custom tint standard premixed grout. It comes as a powder that you activate with water or latex grout additive. The techniques shown on these pages illustrate a professional's way of replacing an irregular tile at the base of a fixture or pipe. Replacing marble or slate tile involves only slight variations in this procedure.

Like the flexible adhesives that simplify repairs to tile floors, recently developed materials make it easy to patch concrete. Cracks less than an inch wide can be filled with a premixed vinyl or latex patching compound. Larger cracks can be repaired by using premixed concrete and special bonding agents. At one time, the most skilled craftsman could not guarantee a large concrete patch. The dry concrete around the patch absorbed water from the new concrete so the new material could not form a bond with the old. The patch cracked because it could not cure without water. But an epoxy bonding agent applied to the old concrete just before the patch is made (page 425) prevents water loss. And the patch itself, reinforced with wire mesh, can be given flexibility with premixed patching concretes. Even if a concrete slab settles slightly, the patch will not crack.

After patching concrete, you can restore the appearance of a floor or give it a completely new look with paint (page 427). New paints, especially formulated for concrete and available in a variety of colors and textures, resist blistering and peeling. Allow concrete repairs to dry completely before painting or disturbing them; drying times vary, depending on the depth of the patch and how heavily the patching material is applied.

A Tight Fit around a Fixture

1 **Removing the grout.** Wearing protective glasses, use a small cold chisel and hammer to chip out the grout at the edges of a damaged ceramic tile. Make a hole in each line of grout by striking a small cold chisel straight down, then angle the chisel to 45° and chip outward from the hole. Caution: tap the chisel lightly; heavy blows can cause cracks in the surrounding tiles. Use a wire brush to clean out any excess grout.

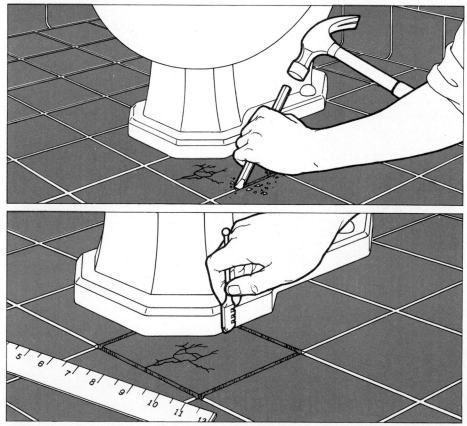

2 **Taking out the tile.** Score an X in ceramic tile from corner to corner, then along the base of the fixture, using a straightedge and glass cutter. Drill a hole through the center of the X with a ¼-inch masonry bit. Hammer a cold chisel into the hole and, working toward the edges, break the tile into small pieces. Clean out the fragments of tile and scrape the old adhesive beneath them with a putty knife. On a marble or slate tile, mark an X with a grease pencil and drill ¾-inch holes ½ inch apart along the X and into the tile along the base of the fixture, using a masonry bit. Then break out the tile with a hammer and cold chisel.

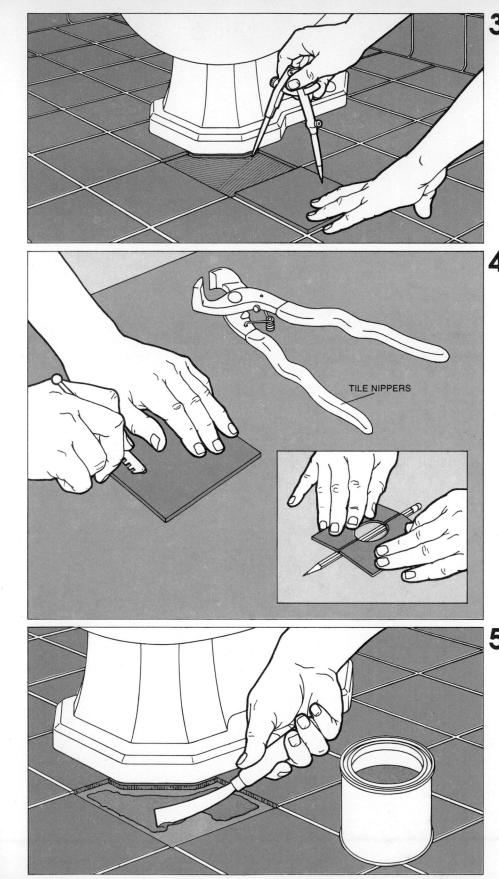

3 Marking the new tile. Set a new tile over the tile adjacent to the space you have cleared. Replace the pencil in a school compass with a grease pencil and open it to span the width of a single tile, then set the pencil at the edge of the new tile and the point of the scribe at the corresponding point on the base of the fixture. Steady the tile with one hand and move the scribe slowly along the base of the fixture with the other until the pencil has marked the shape of the base on the new tile.

4 Cutting the tile. Using a glass cutter, score the line you have marked on ceramic tile, then score a crisscross pattern over the area to be cut away, as shown at left. Snip ⅛-inch pieces of tile away from the scored area with the tile nippers. Angle the nippers so that you use only the corners of its blades; otherwise, the tile may break. Check the fit of the tile and smooth the edges with an emery cloth. To cut a marble or slate tile, use a saber saw fitted with a tungsten-carbide blade or a hacksaw fitted with a tungsten-carbide rod saw.

A replacement for a tile around a pipe is easier to make. Measure the diameter of the pipe and drill a slightly larger hole in the tile using a carbide-tipped hole saw. On marble or slate, mark the hole for the pipe on the tile, drill a starter hole at the center, and, using a saber saw fitted with a tungsten-carbide blade, cut out the pipe hole. Score the tile from the pipe hole to the edges, using a glass cutter for ceramic or a circular saw and masonry blade for marble or slate. Set the tile over a pencil on a flat surface and press down on both sides until it breaks *(inset)*. Smooth the edges with an emery cloth.

5 Setting the tile in place. Using a putty knife, spread adhesive over the exposed subfloor or mortar bed; use organic adhesive on a dry, smooth surface, epoxy adhesive on one that is moist or uneven. If the new tile has tabs on its back, spread the adhesive over the bottom of the tile, covering the tabs completely, and leave the border uncovered so that the same adhesive does not ooze out when you press the tile in place. In either case, apply enough adhesive to raise the tile slightly higher than the ones around it. Use toothpicks or coins set on edge as spacers to keep the joints between ceramic tiles open and even; marble and slate tiles normally butt tightly against each other. Then, lay a 2-by-4 across the tile and tap it down with a hammer. Let the adhesive set for 24 hours, remove the spacers and fill the joints with grout.

TILE NIPPERS

The Care and Repair of Resilient Floors

Resilience is the ability to bounce back, and most types of resilient tiles or sheet flooring—cork, asphalt, linoleum, rubber, vinyl and vinyl-asbestos—do that in several senses. They are more or less bouncy underfoot. But also their tough surfaces bounce back from wear and stains, helping to retain their like-new appearance for many years. Common-sense precautions help. A resilient floor should be kept as dry as possible, even when being cleaned (page 49), so that water does not get underneath it and destroy the bond of the adhesive that holds it in place. Resting furniture feet on plastic or rubber coasters will help protect the floor from punctures and gouges. When furniture or appliances too heavy to lift must be moved across the floor, slide them over pieces of hardboard.

If, in spite of careful maintenance, your resilient floor is accidentally damaged, you usually can repair the injuries yourself—or at least reduce the visibility of the scars. Loosened tiles can be glued down (opposite, bottom right), but first determine whether water from leaking plumbing caused them to come adrift; if so, repair the leak before fixing the floor. Shallow scratches in asphalt and vinyl-asbestos floors can be sanded down with a very fine-grade sandpaper, then waxed. If the floor is vinyl or rubber, gently rub

the scratch lengthwise with the rim of an old coin. This will press the edges of the scratch together so only a thin line remains in the flooring.

Small holes in vinyl, linoleum or cork floors can be filled with homemade putty (Steps 1 and 2). Holes in asphalt, rubber and vinyl asbestos cannot be filled, and neither can large holes or tears in any resilient flooring. The best remedy for a tile that is badly damaged is a replacement (opposite, bottom left); the best remedy for badly damaged sheet flooring is a patch (page 48).

If you do not have spare matching tiles or sheet flooring and cannot buy any, look for replacements in inconspicuous areas of your floor—under a refrigerator or at the back of a closet. Remove the desired tile or section from the hidden area and replace it with a nonmatching material of equal thickness, using the techniques for replacing a damaged tile or patching damaged sheet flooring (page 48); take special care not to break the piece you are removing. (It is almost impossible to remove cork without destroying it, but cork tiles usually can be matched from a dealer's stock).

Two basic types of adhesive are used when repairing resilient floors: water-based latex adhesive and solvent-based adhesive. Because latex can be applied

in thin coats with a paintbrush and clings firmly to other adhesives, it is the best for recementing loose tiles and for gluing down blisters in sheet flooring (page 49). Solvent-based and some water-based organic adhesives are thicker, can be applied with a notched trowel and should be used when replacing whole tiles or sections of sheet flooring. Caution: solvent-based adhesives are highly flammable and give off noxious fumes; use them only in rooms that are well ventilated, turn off pilot lights before starting and keep adhesive containers tightly closed when they are not in use.

Which type of thickened adhesive you should use will depend on the resilient flooring material and the surface on which it is laid—wood, concrete, ceramic tiles, hardboard, felt or an older resilient floor. Give your flooring dealer detailed information so he can prescribe the correct adhesive.

If your resilient floor is glued to an asphalt-felt underlayment, you may tear the felt while removing damaged flooring. If so, glue the felt together with latex adhesive and allow it to dry before continuing the job. If the felt is too badly torn to stick together, glue down enough layers of replacement felt to maintain the same floor level. Use 15-pound asphalt felt and thin latex adhesive.

Filling Small Holes

1 **Mixing the putty.** To make a paste filler for vinyl sheets or tiles, fold a spare piece of the flooring with the top surface on the outside and scrape along the fold with a utility knife, catching the powdery flakes in a bowl. Refold the material as you wear down the surface and continue scraping until the bowl contains what appears to be more than enough powder to fill the hole. Then add a few drops of clear nail polish, stirring with a small stick until the mixture is the consistency of putty.

To make putty of cork flooring, scrape a bottle cork and mix the shavings with clear shellac.

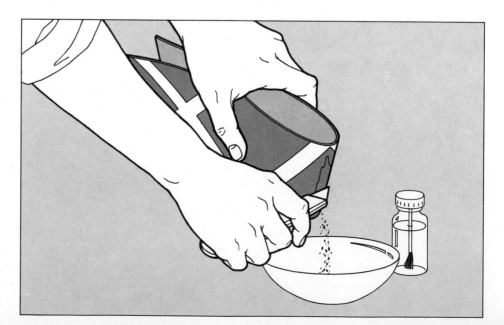

2 Filling the hole. To protect the undamaged floor, surround the hole with a border of masking tape at least an inch wide and then force the filler firmly into the hole with a putty knife. Scrape off the excess and smooth the surface of the patch with the knife. Let the paste set for 30 minutes; then remove the masking tape and buff the patch with 00-grade steel wool. If the repaired area is duller than the surrounding floor, brush a thin coat of clear nail polish on it.

Replacing a Damaged Tile

Removing a tile. For vinyl-asbestos or asphalt flooring, lay a towel on the tile and warm it with an iron set at medium heat until the adhesive softens and you can lift one corner with a putty knife. Pull up the corner while you slice at the adhesive underneath with the putty knife, reheating the tile with the iron if necessary, until you can remove the entire tile. Wait for the adhesive remaining on the subfloor to harden—allow about an hour—then scrape it up.

To remove a damaged vinyl or rubber tile, chip it out with a hammer and chisel, starting at the center. If you are removing a good vinyl or rubber tile you plan to reuse, pry up one edge with a chisel and gently chip through adhesive beneath the tile. Scrape up old adhesive.

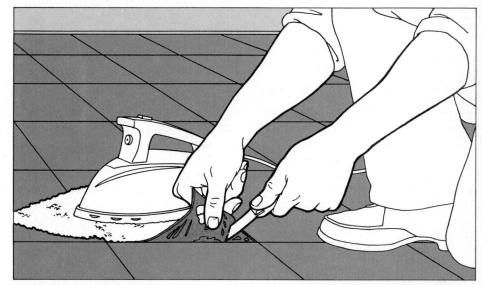

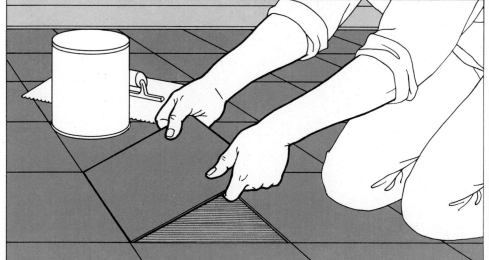

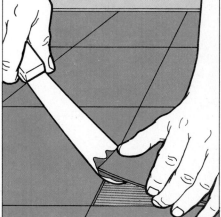

Installing a replacement. Spread a thin layer of adhesive—not more than half the thickness of your tile—on the subfloor with a notched trowel, then butt one edge of the new tile against the edge of an adjoining tile, carefully aligning the pattern. Ease the tile into place. Make sure it is level with the surrounding tiles; if it is too high, press it down and quickly wipe up any excess adhesive before it dries; if the tile is too low, pull it up and add more adhesive beneath it. Then put a 20-pound weight on it for the time specified by the tile adhesive manfacturer.

Securing a loose tile. Lift the loose portion of the tile and spread a thin coat of adhesive on the underside with a narrow, flexible spatula. If only a corner of the tile is unstuck, loosen more of it until you can turn the tile back far enough to spread the adhesive. Press the tile into place, making it level with the rest of the surrounding tiles, and hold it down to set with a 20-pound weight.

Patching Sheet Flooring

1 **Cutting the patch.** Tape a piece of flooring over the damaged area, aligning its design with that on the floor. With a metal straightedge and a utility knife, score the patching material in the shape of the patch you want, following lines in the design wherever possible. Using the scored line as a guide, cut through the replacement material and the floor covering underneath. Keep slicing along the same lines until you have cut through both sheets. Clear away the floor and loosen the adhesive, if any, under the section you are replacing *(page 47)*.

2 **Installing the patch.** Remove the damaged section and examine it to determine what type of flooring material it is. If the color runs through to the backing it is inlaid vinyl; a printed design just under the surface of the flooring will indicate a rotogravure. In either case, the vinyl flooring will be adhered in one of two ways: adhesive will be spread evenly over the entire surface area of the floor to hold it in place or it will be used only around the perimeter. Look at the floor where the patch has been removed; if there are signs of dried adhesive, remove it with a paint scraper before applying new adhesive and setting the patch into place. If there is no adhesive on the floor or on the back of the damaged section, apply a band of adhesive—sold for this type of floor covering—around the perimeter of the patch. Then set the patch into place, matching it to the pattern. If you are replacing inlaid vinyl floor covering, you can make the floor more pliable by using an iron with aluminum foil sandwiched between the iron and the floor covering; be extra careful not to melt the patch when using this technique. If you have rotogravure floor covering, check to see if a commercially available vinyl floor seam sealer can be used to finish the job.

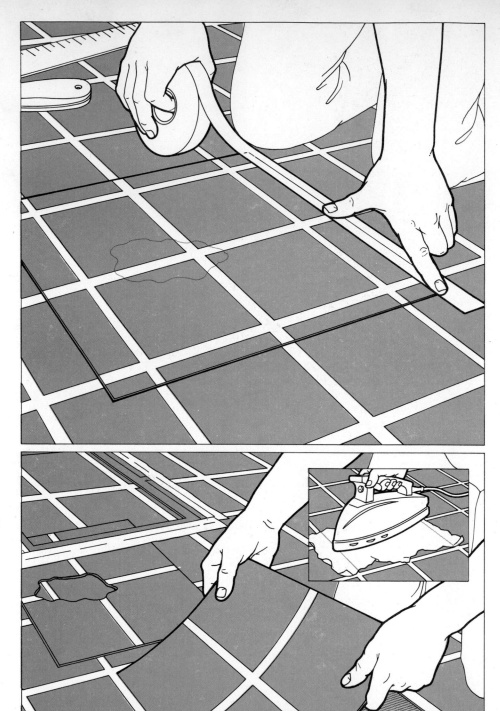

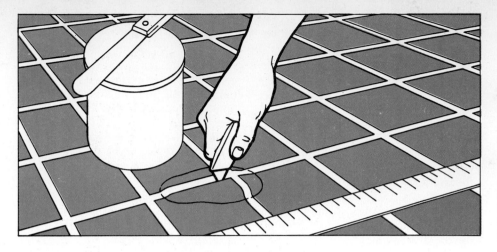

Flattening Bulges in Sheet Flooring

Deflating a blister. Score, then slice, along the length of a blister with a utility knife, extending the cut ½ inch beyond the blister at both ends. Try to cut along a line in the pattern to make the repair less conspicuous. With a spatula, spread a thin layer of latex adhesive through the slit onto the underside of the flooring. Press the sheet down; if one edge overlaps because the flooring has stretched, use it as a guide to trim the edge beneath. Remove any trimmed-off scrap, then press the edges together and put a 20-pound weight on the repaired area for at least an hour.

Keeping That Resilient Beauty

The basic maxim for keeping a resilient floor clean and shiny is: less is better. Although many people think a resilient floor needs a weekly scrubbing, and then a coat of glossy polish, with modern materials, polishing is rarely necessary. Most contemporary resilient flooring has a permanent finish that not only is as hard, smooth and shiny as wax but also functions as wax is supposed to: it has a tough film which guards against stains and dirt.

How often your floor should be cleaned depends on the material it is made of—some are more resistant to dirt than others—and the traffic it bears. But the general rule of less is better is always applicable: do not polish when wet-mopping is sufficient; do not wet-mop when damp-mopping will do; do not damp-mop when a good sweeping is enough. Remember, too much washing can loosen the adhesive.

Restraint with the scrub brush is particularly important when you are caring for a newly installed or recently repaired floor. Do not wash it for at least four days after the job is done, to give the adhesive time to form a solid bond. Then remove dirt with a damp mop or cloth and carefully scrape up spots of adhesive with a putty knife.

For regular cleaning, a good daily sweeping plus an occasional damp-mopping is normally sufficient to remove dust and dirt. If you think your floor really needs washing with detergent and water, avoid doing it more often than every three to six weeks.

However, even so-called permanent finishes can dull with age and wear. If you insist on a high-gloss finish, restore one to old flooring with water-based floor polish in thin coats. To prevent discoloration, take off the polish once or twice a year with commercial wax remover and steel wool.

The tough finishes that normally eliminate the need for polish also protect new resilient floors against a wide range of stains. Even so, you should quickly soak up any spillage and wash the area. If stains remain, they can generally be removed by a cleaner suited to the stain substance. Caution: some of the chemicals used give off noxious fumes and can irritate skin, so work in a well-ventilated room and wear rubber gloves to protect your hands. The following treatments are recommended for common stains:

☐ Alcoholic beverages: rub the spot with a cloth that has been dampened with rubbing alcohol.

☐ Blood: sponge with cold water; if that does not work, sponge with a solution made from 1 part ammonia and 9 parts water.

☐ Candle wax, chewing gum and tar: cover with a plastic bag filled with ice cubes. When the material becomes brittle, scrape it off with a spatula.

☐ Candy: rub with liquid detergent and grade 00 steel wool unless the floor is a "waxless" vinyl; in that case use a plastic scouring pad, warm water and powdered detergent.

☐ Cigarette burns: rub with scouring powder and grade 00 steel wool.

☐ Coffee and canned or frozen juice: cover for several hours with a cloth that is saturated in a solution of 1 part glycerine (available at drugstores) to 3 parts water. If the stain remains, rub it gently with scouring powder on a damp cloth.

☐ Fresh fruit: wearing rubber gloves, vigorously rub with a cloth that is dampened with a solution of 1 tablespoon oxalic acid, a very powerful—and toxic—solvent available at hardware stores, and 1 pint water.

☐ Grease or oil: remove as much as possible with paper towels, then wash the stain with a cloth dampened in liquid detergent and warm water.

☐ Mustard or urine: cover for several hours with a cloth soaked in 3 to 5 percent hydrogen peroxide (available in drugstores) and cover that cloth with another soaked in ammonia.

☐ Paint or varnish: rub with grade 00 steel wool dipped in warm water and liquid dishwashing detergent.

☐ Leather and rubber scuff marks: scrub with a cloth soaked in a solution of 1 part ammonia to 9 parts water.

☐ Shoe or nail polish: rub with grade 00 steel wool that has soaked in warm water and scouring powder.

Unseen Repairs for Unsightly Stains and Tears

The most carefully tended carpets can suffer accidental damage. The flick of a cigarette or a fragment popped from the log of a fireplace can cause small but noticeable burns. The sharp edge of a child's broken toy cuts a swath through the pile of a carpet or rips the backing underneath. And stains from some spilled liquids stubbornly resist detergents and spot removers. But with a few scraps of matching carpet and some inexpensive tools and materials, you can make durable, almost invisible repairs.

Set scraps aside when the carpet is laid or ask for some from the seller when you buy a carpeted house. If no scraps have been saved, take them from unseen areas such as within closets.

Many jobs call for a tuft-setter, which is a special tool for fixing tufts of pile in place. If you cannot find a tuft-setter at a hardware store or carpet supply dealer, you can easily make your own *(below)*. Depending on the task, you may also need latex seam adhesive in a plastic squeeze bottle.

Before you begin to repair a damaged carpet, familiarize yourself with its special characteristics. Loop pile, for example, requires techniques different from those used on cut pile, and carpeting that is installed over padding is handled differently from carpeting that is bonded to a foam backing.

Although most carpeting repairs are not difficult, they do demand patience.

When you replace tufts, for example, do not hurry the work; the best results will come from building up the pile over the damaged area carefully, one tuft at a time. Apply latex adhesive sparingly, making sure that no excess oozes onto the surface of the carpet. Before you cut a patch, check to see that it will match the pattern and the tilt of the pile in the area that is damaged.

You should always use the smallest piece of scrap carpet first, so that if you make an error, there will be larger scraps available to correct it. And when you embark upon a job that is new to you, take the time to practice on unneeded scraps of carpet before tackling the real thing.

A Tool for Setting Carpet Tufts

A device for implanting new pile, called a tuft-setter, can be purchased, but you can make one yourself from a large needle—the type used for sewing squares of knitting together—and a ⅜-inch wood dowel. Cut a 4-inch length from the dowel and drill a ¹⁄₁₆-inch hole about 1 inch deep into its end. Insert the needle point into the

hole and tap the other end of the needle with a hammer, driving the point into the wood. Using wire cutters or the cutting section of a pair of long-nose pliers, clip most of the eye from the needle, leaving a shallow V-shaped end *(inset)*. To complete the tuft-setter, round and smooth this end with a small file or sharpening stone.

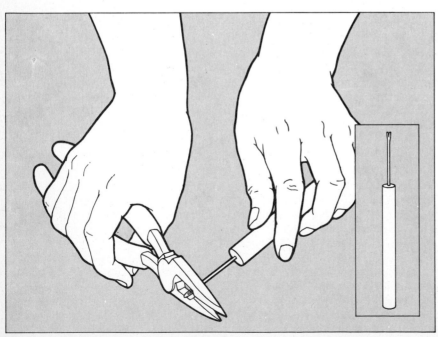

Restoring a Small Area

1 **Removing the pile.** Using scissors with short, curved blades—a pair of ordinary cuticle scissors will do—cut the damaged pile down to the carpet backing, then pick out the stubs of the tufts or loops with tweezers. For replacement pile, pick tufts or unravel lengths of looped yarn from the edge of a carpet scrap.

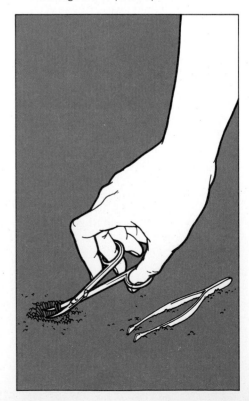

2 **Applying adhesive.** Squeeze a little white wood glue onto a carpet scrap, dip a cotton-tipped swab into the glue and lay a spot of the adhesive at the point where you will begin setting new tufts of loops. The glue dries rapidly—apply it to one small area at a time.

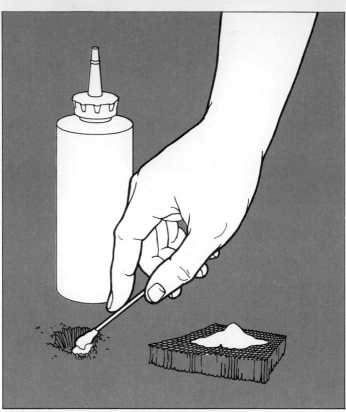

3 **Replacing the pile.** For a cut-pile carpet, fold a tuft into a V over the tip of the tuft-setter and punch it into the glue-swabbed carpet backing with one or two light taps of a hammer. Repeat the process, setting the tufts close together and spreading more adhesive as it is needed. Do not drive the tufts so deep that the replacement pile is lower than that of the surrounding carpet; to get the best results, set the new pile high and trim it even.

For a carpet with loop pile *(inset)*, punch one end of a long piece of yarn into the backing with a tuft-setter, then form successive loops from the same piece and set the bottom of each loop. Check each loop to be sure that it is the same height as the existing pile. Pull a short loop up from the backing with tweezers; punch a long one farther into the backing with the tuft-setter.

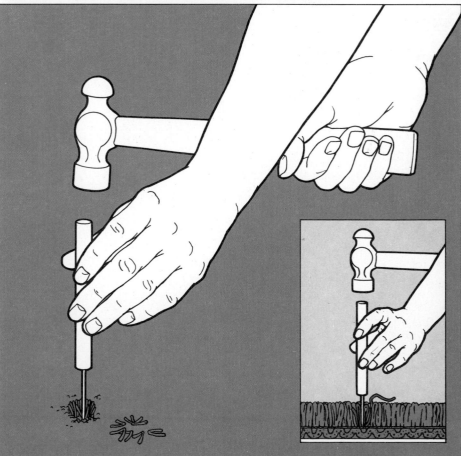

Mending a Surface Rip

1 **Cementing the area.** If the backing is un-damaged, lift the torn section of carpet face away from it, clean out any loose pile or dried cement and apply white wood glue to the backing. Smear the glue into a light film over all of the exposed backing.

2 **Closing the rip.** Push the edges of the rip together and hold them in place with one hand while you rub the carpet surface with a smooth object, such as the bottom of a soft-drink bottle. Rub firmly from the rip toward the sound carpet to work the glue well into the fibers of the backing without forcing it out of the rip. If any glue does ooze up to the surface, clean it off immediately with water and detergent. After four or five hours, when the glue has dried, replace any missing pile (pages 50-51).

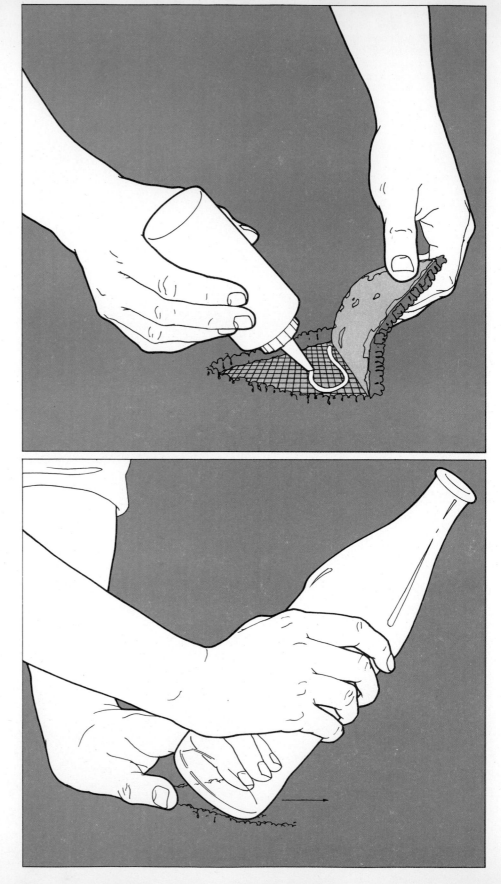

Keeping Carpets Spotless

Routine carpet care requires common-sense procedures. Using a vacuum cleaner once a week, with a touch-up in between on paths of heavily trafficked areas, diminishes the danger that abrasive, tracked-in grit will cut the fibers. The occasional rearrangement of the furniture reduces wear on specific areas. To avoid sun bleaching, draw the blinds. Once a year or so, shampoo or steam clean the carpet *(pages 54-55)*.

But routine means will not do when you confront that perennial household emergency, the spilling of substances that can leave stains. Clean up promptly; even if the spill does not seem sticky, walking on it will probably darken the stain. After picking up solids with a spatula or dull knife, consult the chart at the right for the correct cleaning agents and techniques for more than three dozen common staining substances.

Finding the right treatment. In the alphabetized column at the left of this chart, find the material that has stained your carpet and treat it by the method given in the right-hand column. You may have to apply several cleaning solutions in succession. One is a standard nonflamable dry-cleaning fluid; do not use carbon tetrachloride, gasoline or lighter fluid. Mix the following three solutions yourself, according to these recipes:
☐ Shampoo: one teaspoon of carpet shampoo in one cup of water.
☐ Vinegar: one-third cup of white vinegar and two-thirds cup of water.
☐ Ammonia: one tablespoon of clear household ammonia in one-half cup of water.

Wet a pad in the solution, test the carpet for colorfastness in an inconspicuous place and then blot the stain. Work the pad from the center of the stain to the edge in a circular motion. Follow shampoos by sponging with water. Finally, cover the spot with a pad of paper towels weighted by a book and leave for five or six hours.

Removing nail polish, furniture stain, household cement, dried paint or large quantities of oil, paint or ink is very difficult. For these stains and for unknown materials that you cannot clean up with shampoo followed by a dry cleaner, call a professional cleaner.

Treatments for Every Stain

Cause of stain	Treatment
Alcoholic beverages	Apply shampoo and vinegar. If traces remain, apply dry cleaner.
Bleach	Apply shampoo and vinegar.
Blood	Sponge with cool water. Apply shampoo, ammonia and vinegar.
Butter, margarine	Apply dry cleaner. If traces remain, apply shampoo.
Candle wax	Apply dry cleaner.
Candy, chocolate	Apply shampoo and vinegar. If traces remain, apply dry cleaner.
Catsup	Apply shampoo.
Chewing gum	Chill with ice cube until gum is brittle. Scrape off with dull knife. Apply dry cleaner.
Coffee, tea	Apply shampoo and vinegar. If traces remain, apply dry cleaner.
Cough syrup	Apply shampoo.
Crayons	Apply dry cleaner and shampoo.
Egg	Apply shampoo, ammonia, vinegar and if traces remain, dry cleaner.
Excrement	Sponge with cool water. Apply shampoo, ammonia and vinegar.
Fruit, fruit juices	Apply shampoo, ammonia, vinegar and if traces remain, dry cleaner.
Furniture polish	Apply dry cleaner and shampoo.
Gravy	Apply shampoo, ammonia, vinegar and if traces remain, dry cleaner.
Grease	Apply dry cleaner.
Ink, washable	Apply shampoo.
Lipstick	Apply dry cleaner, shampoo, ammonia and vinegar.
Milk, ice cream	Apply shampoo, ammonia and vinegar.
Motor oil	Apply dry cleaner, shampoo, ammonia and vinegar.
Mud	Let dry, brush gently, vacuum, then apply shampoo.
Mustard	Apply shampoo and vinegar. If traces remain, apply dry cleaner.
Paint, wet oil-based	Apply dry cleaner.
Paint, wet water-based	Apply shampoo.
Perfume	Apply dry cleaner and shampoo.
Salad dressing	Apply dry cleaner. If traces remain, apply shampoo and vinegar.
Shoe polish	Apply dry cleaner, shampoo, ammonia and vinegar.
Soft drinks	Apply shampoo, ammonia, vinegar and if traces remain, dry cleaner.
Syrup	Apply shampoo and vinegar. If traces remain, apply dry cleaner.
Tar	Apply dry cleaner.
Urine	Apply vinegar and then shampoo, ammonia and more vinegar.
Vegetable oil	Apply dry cleaner. If traces remain, apply shampoo.
Vomit	Sponge with cool water. Apply shampoo, ammonia and vinegar.

Two Ways to Launder a Carpet by Machine

About once a year—or more often if they need it—you should clean your carpets with water and detergent. There are two kinds of machines you can use: foam-action shampooers like the one shown in the picture at right and the more thorough water-extraction cleaners like the one at the top of the opposite page. Both kinds can be rented, sometimes from grocery stores or drugstores.

Shampooers come with wheels, for shag carpets, and without, for low-pile carpets. In either form, a motorized rotary brush scrubs the carpet with a foam that comes from detergent and water mixed in a tank on the wand, usually in proportions of 1 to 12 (but check the container label). The foam loosens particles of dirt and dries around them; you then vacuum up both foam and dirt. Use only detergent intended for use on carpets; other household detergents, which are chemically different, require rinsing and may leave a sticky film that gathers soil, quickly making the carpet dirtier than it was before cleaning.

Shampooing is easier and less expensive than water extraction, but repeated shampooing leaves a buildup of detergent residue. Some professionals do not recommend shampooers at all; if you do use one, switch to a water-extraction machine at least every third cleaning, to remove detergent residue.

When renting a water-extraction cleaner, you will probably have to ask for a "steam" machine—the manufacturers use the word, in quotation marks, to imply high heat, although the machines actually dispense hot water. These cleaners spray a nonfoaming detergent solution onto the carpet under pressure and immediately suck up at least 75 per cent of the solution—and the dirt—from the carpet. To accomplish this, an extraction machine has two electric pumps as well as dispensing and receiving tanks. The machine is prepared by filling the dispensing tank to within 3 inches of the top with tap water (hot for synthetics, cold for wool). The detergent is added as directed on the container label—usually 2 ounces per gallon of water. Cover the bottom of the receiving tank with cold water plus 8 ounces of defoamer to neutralize sucked-up detergent residue.

Before starting, prepare the room by removing light furniture and protecting the rest with plastic sheeting under and around the legs. Vacuum the carpet and spot clean *(page 53)*.

When either shampooing or cleaning by water extraction, be careful not to overwet the carpet and go easy on the solution-dispensing trigger. Excess water can cause the carpet's jute backing to shrink and pull the carpet from its fastenings. It can also dissolve the colors in the backing and pad, which then rise to the carpet surface and leave a stain.

For both methods, drying takes two or three hours—more on very humid days. You can speed drying, and restore pile depth, by brushing low-pile carpets with a clean broom and by sweeping shag carpets with a plastic shag rake. Put plastic sheeting under the legs of furniture as you move it back into the room, to prevent dampness from rusting the metal glides and staining the carpet.

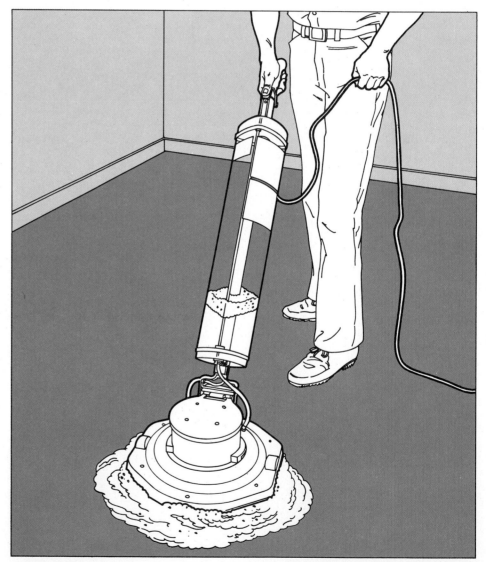

Shampooing. With the brush rotating, push the shampooer over an area about 3 feet square while pressing the thumb trigger to release detergent solution. Then go over the area again without releasing detergent, scrubbing the foam into the carpet. Move on to the next area and repeat. Caution: do not dispense solution onto the same section of carpet twice, or you will overwet it. When the carpet dries, vacuum it and move the furniture back into the room.

Water-extraction cleaning. Turn on the machine's two pumps and, starting near a corner with the vacuum-head opening flat on the carpet, push the head away from you while squeezing the spray-release trigger. Move slowly; cover a swath 3 to 4 feet long in about 10 seconds. Stop spraying, and pull the vacuum head back over the sprayed area. Run the head over the area two or three times without spraying. Then clean another strip that overlaps the first. If a strip does not look clean, spray and vacuum again, but avoid overwetting; do not spray an area more than three times without letting it dry.

When the supply tank runs empty, turn off the switches, drain the receiving tank into a pail and wipe the tank clean of dirt and fibers before resuming the operation.

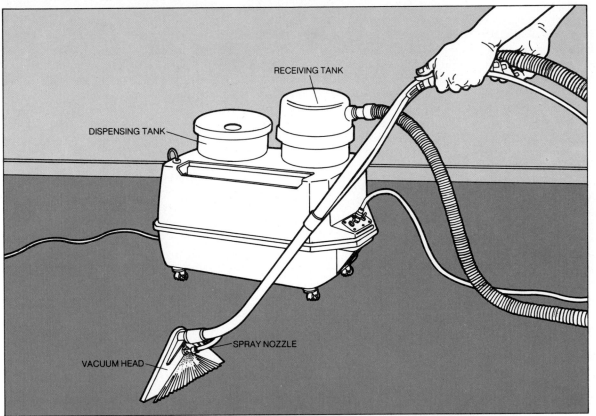

RECEIVING TANK

DISPENSING TANK

SPRAY NOZZLE

VACUUM HEAD

Cleaning stair carpet. If you are renting a water-extraction machine, you may also be able to rent hand tools for stair cleaning. Otherwise, make foam by squeezing a sponge repeatedly in carpet-shampoo solution, scoop up some of it with a clean scrub brush and work the foam into the carpet. Wring out the sponge in the shampoo solution and wipe up the excess foam. Brush or rake the pile erect. When the carpet has dried, go over it again with a stiff brush to loosen dried foam and dirt. Finally, vacuum.

Intricate Structures, Simple to Repair

The structure of a stairway goes beyond that of hammer-and-saw carpentry to the stronger and more elegant techniques of cabinetwork, with its generous use of finish hardwood and ingenious joinery. For this reason a properly built stairway is not likely to present major problems. If it sags or bounces or seems unsafe, the cause is probably settling of the floor under the newel post or at the landing, which throws the stairway out of plumb and level and skews its right-angle joints. Jacking up the floor (page 35) may restore the stairway's health, but if the damage is extensive (or if you judge that the original craftsmanship was poor), it may be wise to install a new prefabricated stairway.

But the most common problems are relatively manageable ones such as squeaks, broken parts, a wobbly newel post or worn treads. The following pages offer an assortment of solutions. For many of these repairs you need to know how your stairway was built. Rough stairways, such as outside stairs or basement stairs, are sometimes made by simpler methods, and metal spiral stairs are a special case, but among finished interior stairways made of wood there are only two basic types, defined by the way the treads are supported.

In most old stairways (right), and sometimes in new ones built for special cases, thick sawtooth-notched boards called carriages support the treads and provide surfaces for nailing the risers, the vertical boards between treads. On a closed side, a baseboard called a skirt-stringer, carefully sawed to fit against the treads and risers, covers and hides their ends. In the modern prefabricated stairway (opposite, top), the functions of the carriage and the skirt-stringer are combined in one board, the house stringer, grooved 1/2 inch deep to receive the ends of the treads and risers.

To discover which type of stairway you have, inspect the underside. In case the underside is enclosed behind walls, push a thin knife under the stringer at a tread end; if the knife is stopped by wood at a depth of 1/2 inch, the stairway has a housed stringer. If this test seems inconclusive, you will have to break a peephole through the enclosing wall.

Either kind of stairway may be open to the stair hall on one side or both. In such cases the visible rim is usually an open stringer cut to fit under the protruding tread ends and against the riser ends. In carriage stairways, it hides the rough wood of the carriage. In prefabricated stairways, the open stringer is cosmetic and structural: The treads rest on it and the risers are nailed to it.

Except for runs of four steps or fewer, open-sided stairways require a post-and-railing fence—an angled balustrade—as a handhold. The pickets, or balusters, are joined into the railing and,

usually, also into the end of the treads.

Two precautions are in order when repairing finished-wood stairways. Treads, risers, balusters, newel posts, railings and moldings are all made of hardwood—usually oak, birch, poplar or beech—and will split unless pilot holes are bored for all nails and screws. Secondly, glue will not bond to dried glue; old joints must be scraped before they can be reassembled. Glue can also mar the finish of any wood it drips onto. Use it sparingly; if it runs, wipe it away immediately with a damp cloth, let the area dry and sand it.

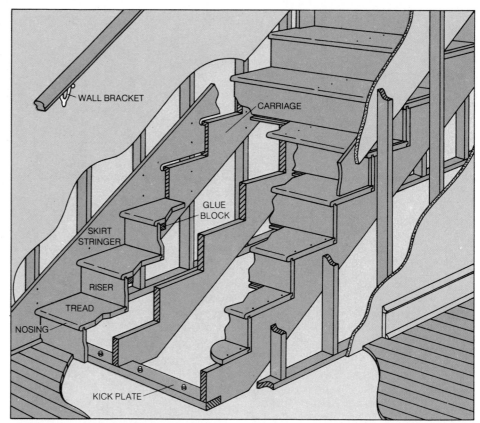

A carriage-supported stairway. In this stairway, which is constructed on the job at the same time that the house goes up, three 2-by-12 carriages with cutouts for each step run between floors, the two at the sides being spiked to the wall studs. At the bottom the carriages fit over a kick plate, a 2-by-4 nailed to the floor to keep them from sliding. After the 3/4-inch risers are nailed to the carriages, the 1 1/16-inch treads are pushed into place so that their back-edge tongues fit into the risers' grooves. At the same time a groove under the front edge of the tread drops over a tongue on the riser below. The tread is then nailed to the carriages. Each tread projects beyond the riser beneath it—usually by 1 1/4 inches—and ends in a rounded edge called a nosing. Glue blocks are used to reinforce the joints between the treads and risers at the front, and nails through the back riser into the tread strengthen that joint. The skirt-stringer that covers the tread and riser ends (and also hides nailheads there) is a 3/4-inch piece of finish softwood, scribed and cut to fit perfectly. Wall brackets support handrails on each side.

A prefabricated stairway. Cut and assembled—minus the balustrade—in a mill, the stairway now used by most builders employs glue wedges to clamp the ends of the treads and risers in V-shaped notches, which are routed into the side of the housed stringer. The treads and risers usually meet in rabbet joints and are glue-blocked and nailed. A walled stairway would use housed stringers on both sides, but an open-sided stairway like this supports the outer ends of the treads on an open stringer cut like a carriage. Since it is too light to serve as a true carriage, the studding of the wall beneath it must be used to provide extra support.

The vertical cuts on the open stringer are mitered to match a miter at the end of the riser, thus concealing the end grain. The end of each tread has a return nosing nailed on, also hiding end grain. A return molding at the end and a scotia molding at the front complete the tread trim.

The parts of the balustrade. Structural support for the railing comes from strong newel posts at the bottom and the landing. At its base the starting newel has slots called mortises to receive the ends of the first riser and the open stringer, and the newel sometimes extends through the floor to be bolted to a joist. Landing newels, similarly mortised, are bolted to the header joists behind them. The railing is joined to the newels with rail bolts *(inset).* The lag-bolt end is screwed into the newel post, and the machine screw end runs into a shank in the end of the railing. A washer and a nut are attached to the machine screw through an access hole bored from underneath the rail. The nut is tightened by driving a nail set against the notches of the nut. Then the access hole is plugged.

The railing rises to the upper newel in a curved piece called a gooseneck. Vertical balusters are installed between treads and the railing, usually with dowels but sometimes at the bottom with dovetail joints *(page 61, Step 2).* Often the top dowels are press-fitted into their holes to stop glue from dripping down the balusters.

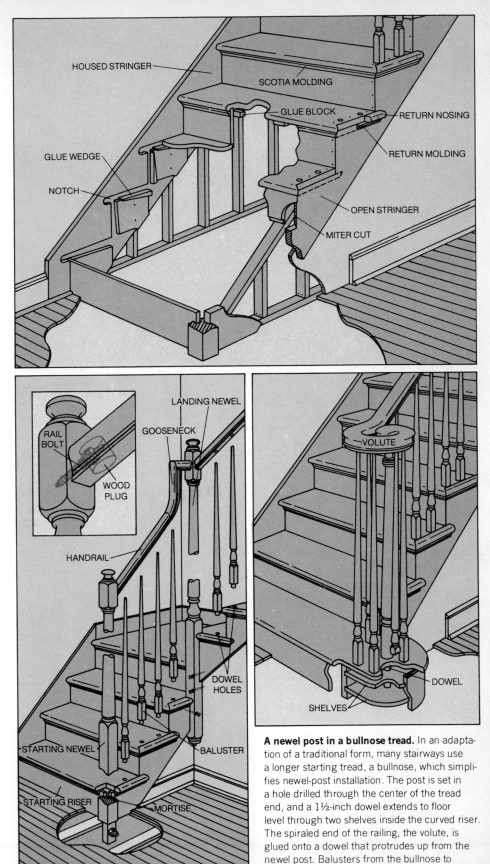

A newel post in a bullnose tread. In an adaptation of a traditional form, many stairways use a longer starting tread, a bullnose, which simplifies newel-post installation. The post is set in a hole drilled through the center of the tread end, and a 1½-inch dowel extends to floor level through two shelves inside the curved riser. The spiraled end of the railing, the volute, is glued onto a dowel that protrudes up from the newel post. Balusters from the bullnose to the volute further support the rail.

Silencing a Squeaky Tread

Squeaks, a common problem in older, carriage-supported stairways (*page 56*), are caused by treads that rub against other stair parts when stepped on. The rubbing movement indicates that some portion of the tread has separated slightly from the carriage or the riser, because of warping or shrinking in these parts; the separated portion is pushed down by a footfall and then springs back up. You can stop tread spring by making the separated portion stay down, or by inserting a thin wedge as a shim underneath it.

First, locate the movement. Use a level to find warps, twists or bows. While a helper climbs the stairs, listen, watch for rise and fall and—resting your hand on the tread—feel for vibration.

After you find the spring, you can repair it if it is minimal with pairs of angled nails. If the tread movement is substantial, use wedges.

Such repairs from the top are usually sufficient. But if you can get to the stairway from underneath you can make a sound and simple fix, preferable because it is invisible, by adding glue blocks (*opposite, top*) to the joint between the tread and the riser under its front edge, the most common source of squeaks. If the tread is badly warped or humped in the center, rejoin it with a screw through the carriage (*opposite, center*).

Squeaks in modern housed-stringer stairways (*page 57, top*) are uncommon. If the squeak comes from between a tread and a riser, try nailing or wedging. If it comes from the end of the tread, the glue wedge that supports it has probably worked loose from shrinkage or the hammering of footfalls. If accessible, replace the wedge (*opposite, bottom*) with a new one from the lumberyard or a home-made one cut from 1-inch hardwood.

Working from Above

Nailing the tread down. Drive two eightpenny finishing nails into ³⁄₃₂-inch pilot holes drilled at opposing angles through the tread and into the riser at the point of movement. Have a helper stand on the tread during both drilling and nailing. If the squeak comes from the ends of the tread, angle the holes into the carriage. Sink the nails with a nail set and wood-putty the holes.

If the tread spring is too great for nails to close, fasten the tread with a No. 8 wood screw 2½ inches long driven through an ¹¹⁄₆₄-inch shank hole in the tread and into a ³⁄₃₂-inch pilot hole in the riser (*inset*). Apply paraffin wax to the threads to make the screw turn easily in oak. Glue a piece of dowel into the countersink hole and sand it off level with the tread.

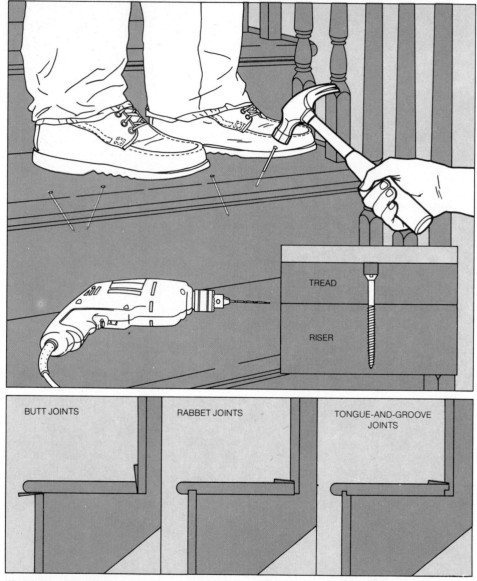

TREAD

RISER

BUTT JOINTS

RABBET JOINTS

TONGUE-AND-GROOVE JOINTS

Wedging treads tight. Remove the scotia molding under the tread nose and insert a knife into the tread joints to discover the kind of joints used. If they are butt joints, the knife will slip vertically into the joint behind the tread and horizontally under the tread; if the knife-entry directions are reversed, the joints are either rabbet or tongue-in-groove (*above, center and right*). Drive sharply tapered wedges coated with glue into the cracks in the indicated directions.

Most wedges tighten a shrunken joint or force the tread down to the carriage, and should be driven hard. The wedge under the tread in a butt joint should prevent a bowed tread from moving by shimming it up; drive it just enough to stop the squeak without increasing the bow.

Cut wedges off with a utility knife and replace the scotia molding. The joints at the back of treads can be covered with shoe molding.

Working from Below

Installing glue blocks. Coat glue on two sides of a block of wood 1½ inches square and about 3 inches long, press it into the joint between the tread and the riser, and fasten the block with a nail in each direction. Add two or three more blocks. If the joint has old blocks that have come partly unstuck, either install new blocks between them, or pry them off, scrape the dried glue on the stair parts down to bare wood and use the new blocks as replacements.

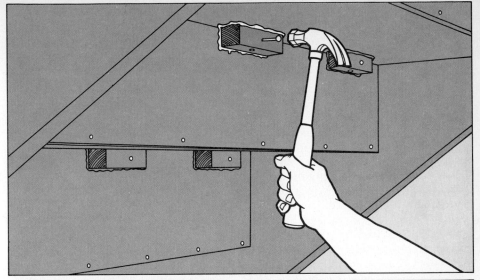

Installing a screw through the carriage. About 2 inches below the tread, chisel a shallow notch into the carriage and with a helper standing on the tread drill a ⅛-inch pilot hole angled at about 30° through the corner of the carriage and ¾ inch into the tread. Enlarge the hole through the carriage with a ¼-inch drill. Spread a bead of construction adhesive along both sides of the joint between the tread and the carriage, and, with the helper off the tread, work the adhesive into the joint, using a putty knife. Have the helper stand on the tread again and install a No. 12 wood screw 3 inches long.

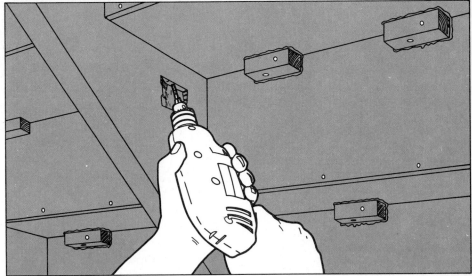

Wedges for a Prefab Stair

Replacing loose wedges. Split out the old wedge with a chisel, and pare dried glue and splinters from the notch. Plane a new wedge to fit within an inch of the riser. Coat the notch, the bottom of the tread and the top and bottom of the wedge with glue. Hammer the wedge snugly into the notch, tap it along the side to force it against the notch face, then hit the end a few more times to jam the wedge tightly under the tread.

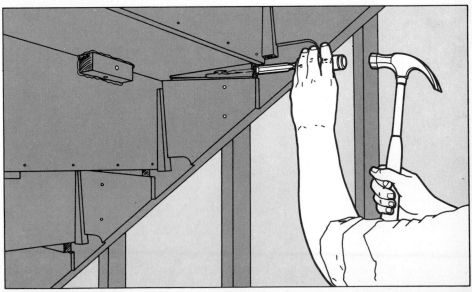

Repairing a Balustrade

With its graceful molded railing and its row of slender balusters, the stairway balustrade, essential for safety, is also the set piece of the cabinetmaker's art in most homes. Thus a broken baluster or a shaky railing affects not only the safety but also the appearance.

A baluster that is merely loose can be tightened with glue, nails or small wedges, but if it is cracked or badly scraped or dented, it should be replaced. Begin by determining how your balusters are fastened. Square-topped balusters usually join the railing by fitting into a shallow groove just as wide as the baluster is thick. Blocks of wood called fillets are nailed into the grooves between balusters. In some staircases such balusters may also end at the bottom in the groove of a lower rail, called a buttress cap, that lies on top of a stringer of uniform width nailed to the ends of the treads and risers (opposite page, Steps 1 and 2).

Turned balusters rounded clear to the top go into holes in the railing. At the bottom, if they do not overlap the return nosing (the piece that hides the endgrain of the tread), they are also doweled, even though they may have square ends. But square-ended balusters that land on the tread slightly overlapping the return nosing are probably joined to the tread by a dovetail joint, and you will have to remove the return nosing not only to be sure but also to make the replacement. Save the broken baluster and use it as a pattern for a new one. If you cannot find a match at a lumberyard, you will have to locate a cabinetmaker who will turn one. You can buy a square-bottomed replacement for a dovetailed baluster and cut the dovetail yourself, or you can simply pin a doweled baluster into the dovetailed tread with a nail.

The cause of a weak and wobbly railing is usually a bottom newel with poor fastenings or loosely cut mortises for the riser and stringer. In carriage stairways the cure is to reinforce the post with a lag bolt driven into structural boards behind it. For posts on bullnose treads, you can run a bolt up through the floor into the floor of the post.

Replacing a Doweled Baluster

1 Removing the damaged baluster. Saw the baluster in two and sharply twist the bottom piece with a pipe wrench to break the glue joint at the base. Remove the top piece; if it is stuck or glued, use the wrench. If the joints do not break, saw the baluster flush, using cardboard on the tread to guard it from the saw. Drill out the dowel ends with spade bits the size of those on the new baluster.

With a folding rule held against the high edge of the dowel hole in the railing (inset), measure to the tread. Cutting from the top, shorten the new baluster to this length plus ½ inch. Saw the bottom dowel to a ³⁄₁₆-inch stub.

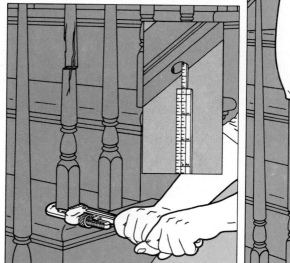

2 Installing the new baluster. Smear glue in the tread hole, angle the top dowel into the railing hole and pull the bottom of the baluster across the tread, lifting the railing about ¼ inch. Seat the bottom dowel in the tread hole. If the railing will not lift, bevel the top dowel where it binds against the side of the hole.

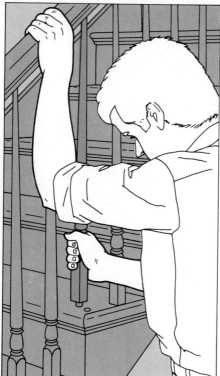

A Dovetailed Baluster

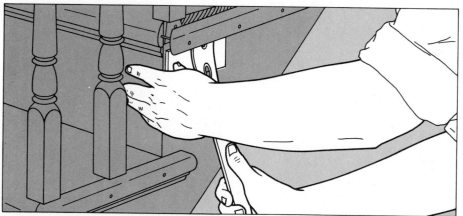

1 Removing the return nosing. Use a chisel to crack the joints, then insert a utility bar and pry off the return molding and return nosing. Protect the stringer with a pry block. Saw through the old baluster and hammer it out of the dovetail.

2 Nailing in the new baluster. Insert the top of a cut-to-length doweled baluster into the railing hole and set its base in the tread dovetail where the old baluster was, shimming behind the dowel if necessary. Drill a pilot hole through the dowel into the tread, and drive a nail through the hole. Replace the return nosing and return molding, driving finishing nails through the old holes, and putty over the nailheads.

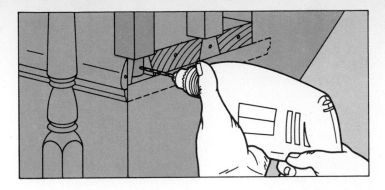

A Filleted Baluster

1 Taking out the old baluster. With a chisel, split the fillets below the butt of the old baluster and above the top into several pieces and pry them out. Drive each end of the baluster toward the chiseled-out grooves, breaking the nailing, and remove the baluster. Scrape old glue from the grooves. Obtain the angle for the new baluster ends and fillets using a T bevel between an adjacent baluster and fillet. Mark the angle on the new baluster and saw it to length.

Tightening a Shaky Newel

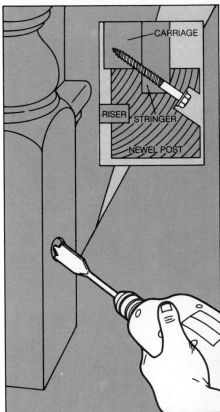

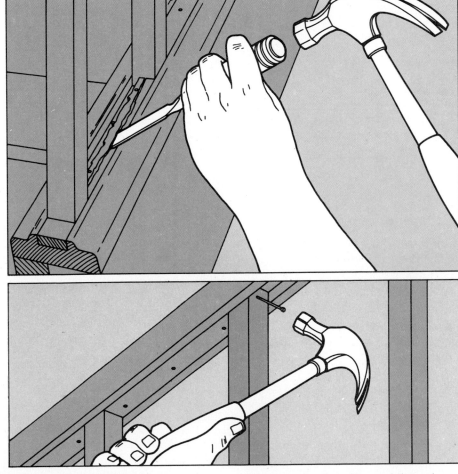

2 Fastening the new baluster. Set the baluster against the existing fillets and toenail two finishing nails through each end—into the railing and buttress cap. Start the nails where the new fillets will hide them, and set the heads. Measure the length of each new fillet, mark the angle cuts with the T bevel and cut with a miter box. Coat the backs and sides with glue and attach them in the railing and buttress-cap grooves with fourpenny finishing nails.

Installing a lag bolt. With a ¾-inch spade bit aimed at the carriage, drill a countersink hole ¾ inch deep in the newel post 4 inches up and centered. Extend it into the carriage with a ⁷⁄₃₂-inch bit and ream it out to ⁵⁄₁₆ inch through the newel. With a socket wrench, screw in a ⁵⁄₁₆-inch bolt 4 inches long fitted with a washer (inset). Plug the hole with a dowel.

To steady a newel set in a bullnose tread, start by driving two nails through the flooring short distances from the newel. From beneath, measure from the nail points to locate the bottom of the newel dowel. Drill shank and pilot holes and install a ⁵⁄₁₆-inch lag bolt 3 inches long. Pull the nails and wood-putty the holes.

The Common Ailments of Doors and Windows

Doors and windows are the Achilles' heel of a house. These covered holes in the house walls must seal out wind, rain, snow and ice, but they must also break the seal at the touch of a hand.

Every door and window is a compromise between these conflicting demands. Like most compromises it eventually breaks down—and doors and windows do in fact require frequent maintenance. The most common repairs are straightforward, once you know how to get at the problem. Broken sash cords and crank mechanisms, for example, can be replaced (pages 67, 68, 73); the cords of a balky Venetian blind can be rethreaded (page 97); a new pane of glass can be cut and set (pages 100-105). You can cure more serious ailments with tricks handed down through generations of carpenters. If need be, you can replace a rotted finish sill and stool (pages 82-85). Somewhat more simply, you can adjust the parts of a window frame to free a tight or frozen sash (pages 65-66), straighten a doorjamb without removing it from its place (pages 74-76), or cut a curved pane of glass for an exotic window (page 103).

In addition to letting in the weather, doors and windows can also let in burglars. If you are concerned about security, you might want to increase protection by replacing the cylinders in your locks (pages 86-87) or by adding better locks as shown on pages 88-91.

If you decide to replace a door or window these days, you may be in for some surprises. Over the last few decades, door and window makers have revolutionized their products with new materials, designs and methods of manufacture. An exterior door, for instance, is as likely to be made of metal as of wood. Metal resists damage better than wood, lasts longer, and is fabricated more efficiently. In fact some metal doors—those with cores of rigid plastic insulation—are even better insulators than their wooden counterparts.

The greatest revolution has taken place in the form in which doors and windows are generally made and delivered for installation. Traditionally, replacing a unit called for precise fitting to close tolerances; most of the parts were fashioned by hand and required a professional to install them. Today, that work is done at the factory. A prefabricated, or prehung, door or window is shipped as a whole unit, with the frame already assembled, the door or window hinged and mounted, and any lock holes cut. The entire unit, leveled and plumbed, is simply nailed into a wall opening—a job that takes, at most, a couple of hours, and one that a beginner can do almost as easily as a professional.

The Language of Doors and Windows

APRON: The inside trim that lies flat against the wall beneath the interior window sill, more properly called the stool (below). It hangs like an apron over the joint between the stool and the wall and covers the gap.

BRICKMOLD: Trim around the outside of the door or window.

CASING: The trim around the top and sides of a window or door visible from inside the house.

DADO: A rectangular groove across the width of a board, designed to accept the end of a second piece.

FINISH FRAME: The stationary pieces immediately adjacent to the movable parts of a window or door. Those at the side and top are called jambs. The bottom piece on a window is the sill; on a door it is the threshold.

JACK STUD: A vertical support that holds up the beam laid across the top of the opening for a window or door.

JAMB: A piece at the side or top of the frame around a window or door, adjoining the moving parts. The top piece is called the head jamb; the term jamb used alone refers to the side pieces.

KERF: The cut made by a saw blade.

MITER: An angle cut into an edge to make it fit a matching angle in another piece; many trim ends are cut at 45° angles to form a right-angle joint.

MORTISE: A recess cut in one piece to hold another. A shallow mortise is usually fitted with hardware, such as a hinge; a deep one holds a tenon, forming a mortise-and-tenon joint.

MUNTIN: A narrow vertical or horizontal strip separating the panes of glass in a window.

PARTING STRIP: A narrow piece of molding along the inner top and sides of the frame of a double-hung window, separating the upper and lower sashes.

RAIL: The horizontal top or bottom piece of a door or a window sash.

ROUGH FRAME: The framework, usually made of heavy boards, surrounding a door or window opening and covered by trim.

SASH: The movable part of any window, or the frame that holds the glass.

SHIM: A thin, usually wedge-shaped piece inserted under or between other pieces to adjust their position.

SILL: The horizontal piece at the bottom of a window frame, generally slanted down toward the outside of the house to shed water. The inside, shelf-like piece commonly mislabeled the sill is properly called the stool.

STILE: A vertical side piece of a door or a window sash.

STOOL: The horizontal piece of inside trim at the base of a window, resting on the sill and projecting into the room.

STOP: A narrow strip of trim along the face of a door or window jamb, which prevents a door or a casement window from swinging too far and serves to create channels for double-hung window sashes.

THRESHOLD: A strip fastened to the floor beneath a door; a doorsill.

Why Windows Stick—and How to Free Them

Like the walls of a house, windows must withstand rain, snow, wind and sun. But walls are solid, permanent barriers, protected from the weather by layers of siding, building paper, sheathing and insulation; a movable window is a relatively fragile machine, fitted with gears, springs, counterweights or rollers to make it open and close. Like all machines, windows at times move reluctantly and occasionally freeze outright.

The basic parts of a window are almost always the same. It has glazed sashes that slide or swing open, a frame, and narrow strips at the sides and top of the frame to hold the sash in place. But each type of window has a different mechanism and a few special parts, and in each type the parts fit together in a different fashion and serve slightly different functions.

Wooden windows like the ones shown on these pages are the easiest to repair because the parts are assembled with carpentry techniques. Metal windows, less common because only costly ones insulate as well as wood, generally combine the functions of the several parts of a wooden window frame in one-piece metal channels.

The most common cause of balky sashes—and the easiest to cure—is a layer of old paint and dirt that narrows the channel between the stops until the sash binds. This layer can be removed with a wood chisel and sandpaper *(page 65),* though in some stubborn cases you may have to remove the sash *(page 67)* to do a thorough job.

If the channel is clean but the sash jams partway open or will not stay open at all, the mechanism is probably at fault. You can repair an older double-hung window, whose weight is counterbalanced by a pulley and a metal or masonry bob, by simply replacing a cord *(pages 67-68).* In newer double-hung windows, the counterbalance is one of several types of spring devices that generally cannot be repaired and must be replaced if faulty *(pages 69-71).* Casement and awning windows can be fixed by replacing the crank assembly *(pages 72-73).*

If the sash sticks in a window with clean channels and a sound mechanism, check the jamb with a straightedge, to see whether it is bowed, and slip a piece of paper along the joints between the stops and the sash, to see whether the sash is binding there. Once you find the point of friction, you may be able to free the sash by driving the jamb or stop away from it slightly with a block of wood and a hammer *(page 65, bottom).*

A sash that will not budge may be literally nailed—by long-forgotten nails. In order to remove finishing nails, drive them completely through the sash with a nail set; pull any large-headed nails with carpenter's nippers *(page 77);* then try to free the sash by the techniques described on page 66.

If none of these standard remedies works, you will have to dismantle the window. A sash that binds against a stop can be freed by removing the stop *(page 77),* moving it back slightly and renailing it to the jamb—but be sure to move the stop only a fraction of an inch, or the sash will rattle in the wind. When a jamb is badly bowed, something behind it—wallboard, plaster, shims or insulation—is probably forcing it out of line. In this case, remove the casing, the apron and the stool *(pages 77 and 82),* pull out the shims in the vicinity of the trouble, and then square, level and plumb the window frame as you would when installing a new window. Do not try to use the easy trick of removing the sash and planing down its sides—no matter how little wood you shave away, you will almost certainly end up with a rattling sash.

The Four Basic Window Types

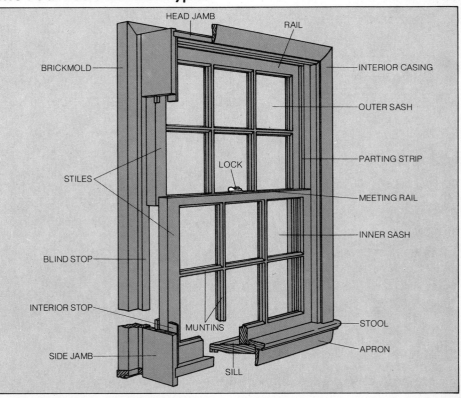

A double-hung window. The frame consists of two side jambs; a head, or top, jamb; and a two-piece bottom of sill and stool. Sliding inside the jambs are an inner and an outer sash. (In a single-hung window only the lower, or inner, sash moves.) The sashes are held by three thin pieces: a blind stop on the outside, a parting strip between the sashes, and an interior stop. Each sash has two horizontal rails and two vertical stiles. Many sashes are divided by muntins, which secure panes of glass. Inside, a horizontal stool fills the bottom of the frame and an apron fits underneath it; outside, the bottom of the frame is filled by a finish sill. The joints between the jambs and the wall indoors are covered by three pieces of interior casing; the joints between the jambs and the exterior siding are covered by exterior casing, called brickmold.

A casement window. These sashes, hung singly or in pairs, have hinges mounted to top and bottom rails; because the sashes swing outward there are no exterior stops. In most modern casement windows the sash is moved by a mechanism called an operator, which consists of a geared crank and an extension arm that slides in a track on the lower rail; in many older windows, the sash is simply pushed or pulled by hand or by a hand-held rod. The latch and lock are mounted on the stile and side jamb opposite the hinges. Casement windows often have no stool or apron; instead, a bottom stop and a fourth piece of interior casing complete the frame.

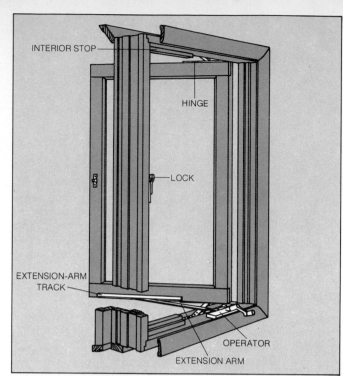

An awning window. The sash, hinged near the top of each stile, swings out at the bottom, ventilating a room while blocking rain. In this widely used design, the sash is moved by an operator with two scissor arms that fold against the sill when the window is closed. Like a casement window, the awning window often has interior casing on all four sides.

The construction of a hopper window, which swings out at the top, is virtually identical to that of an awning window.

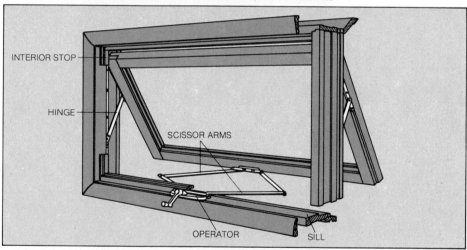

A sliding window. Sashes slide horizontally, generally on plastic rollers along the channels of metal or vinyl jamb liners at the top and bottom of the window frame. A latch and lock are mounted on the meeting stiles. In most models, the sashes can be removed without dismantling the window frame—you simply lift them up and tilt the bottom rail out of its channel.

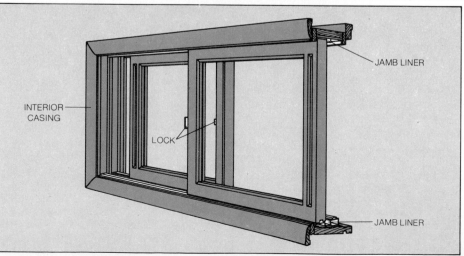

Easing a Tight Sash

Cleaning the channels. On wooden or metal channels, run a chisel, flat side out, along the surfaces touched by the sash. Clean the jambs first, then the sides of the stops and the parting strips, if any. Apply steady pressure to pare away dirt and paint. Sand cleaned wooden channels. Plastic channels and weather stripping of any sort should be cleaned with steel wool, since a chisel might damage the surfaces.

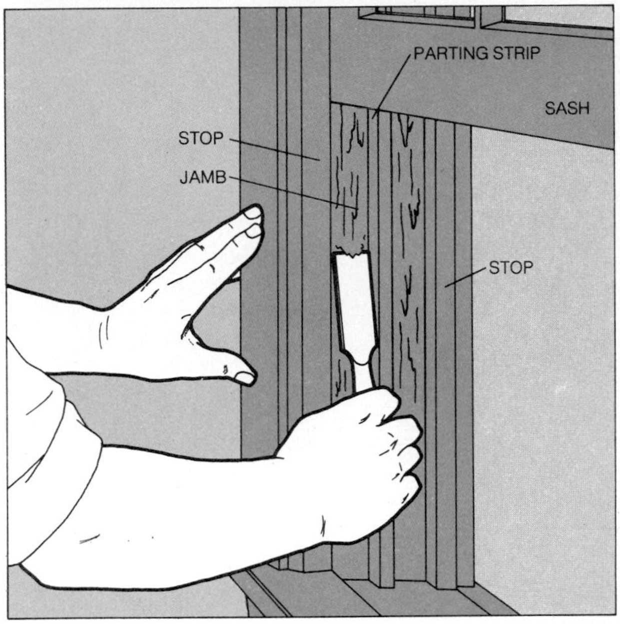

Lubricating the channels. A block of household paraffin run up and down the channels three or four times will apply a light coat of wax to wooden jambs, stops and parting strips. But if you intend to paint the window, be sure to do that job first, before you wax the channels. Silicone spray lubricant can also be applied to wooden parts, and it is better than wax as a lubricant for metal or plastic window parts.

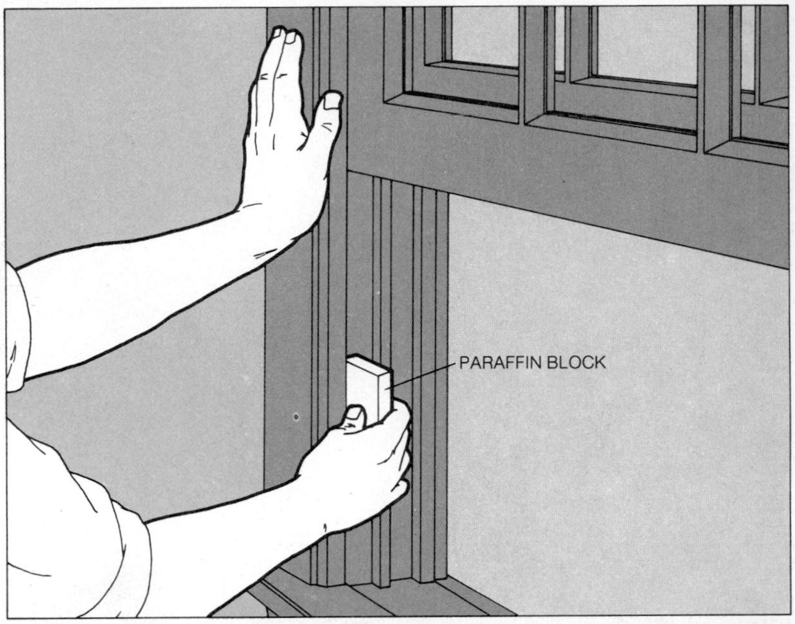

PARTING STRIP

SASH

STOP

JAMB

STOP

PARAFFIN BLOCK

Straightening bowed jambs and stops. Set a block approximately 6 inches long against the back of the channel at the point where the sash sticks, and strike the block five or six times—but no more—with a hammer (*near right*). If this treatment makes the sash slide more easily, drive screws approximately 3 inches apart through the jamb and into the jack stud behind it to secure the jamb permanently. If hammering the jamb does not make the sash slide more easily, do not repeat the procedure—continued pounding could damage the window frame.

If a sash binds against a stop, set the block against the side of the stop and tap it with a hammer several times (*far right*), but use less force than you would on a jamb and do not drive screws into the stop.

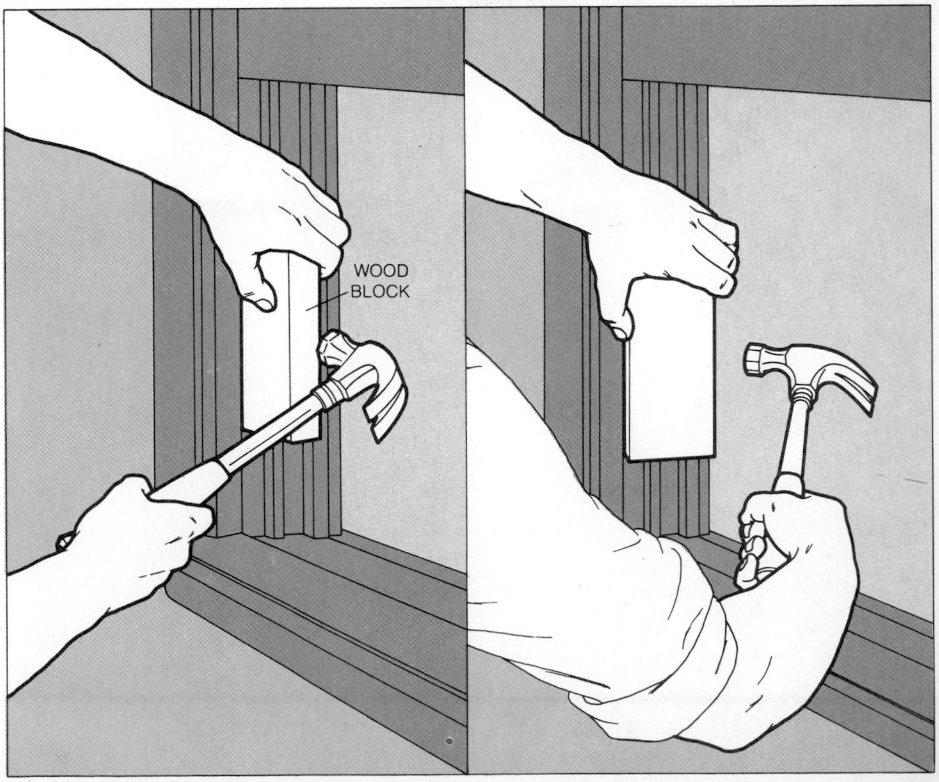

WOOD BLOCK

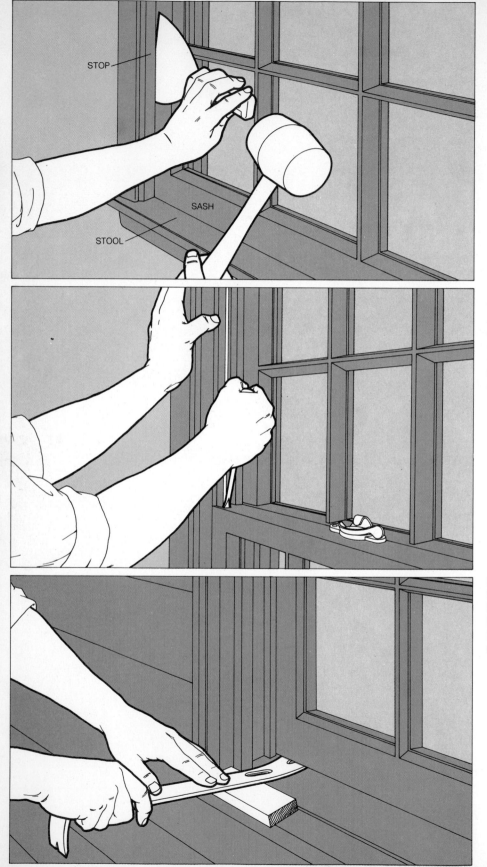

Freeing a Frozen Sash

Breaking a paint seal. Force a wide-blade putty knife into the joint between the sash and the stop. Work the knife around both sides of the sash, then force it into the joint between the sash and the stool. If the sash still will not move, go outside the house and check the joint between the sash and the parting strip; repeat the procedure there if necessary.

Prying open a double-hung window. Force the blade of a heavy screwdriver between the sash and the jamb; if the sash has a groove for a sash cord, use it as the point of entry for the blade. Pry the sash away from the jamb, then repeat the procedure at the other side of the sash. Continue to work the sash to the right and left until you can slide it open.

Prying the sash up from outside. If all else fails, go outside the house and wedge a utility bar between the finish sill and the sash. Set a block of wood on the sill under the utility bar for leverage and pry the sash up, working first under the corners of the sash.

Replacing a Broken Sash Cord

Without some kind of support, the sashes of a double-hung window would slide to the bottom of the window frame every time you raised them. The traditional support method, standard from the 1600s up to about 1950, uses a system of counterweights much like those of an elevator or a dumb-waiter. Two pulleys, one for each sash, are built into the top of each vertical window jamb; from the sides of the sashes, cords run over the pulleys to metal or masonry weights hidden within the jamb. This simple, reliable system has only one drawback: eventually a cord breaks and the sash jams in its channel or falls to the bottom of the window frame.

To replace the cords of the lower sash, generally the first to break, you must remove both the sash and a wooden access plate that covers the sash weight inside the jamb, then thread a new cord over the pulley and tie it to the sash and weight. (While you have the sash out, check the unbroken cord for wear; you may avoid trouble later by replacing it as well.) To get at the upper sash cords, first take out the lower sash and the parting strip between the sashes.

You can replace the broken cord with a length of new sash cord—do not use ordinary rope, which wears too quickly—or solve the problem permanently with sash chain, available at hardware stores. To use chain, however, you must have a metal pulley with a wide groove at the center: a pulley with a narrow groove is likely to jam the chain; a wooden pulley will splinter.

Sash weights are occasionally involved in seemingly unrelated window problems. Long nails driven through the casing or jamb can interfere with the weights, jamming the sash or leaving it unsupported; pull such nails with carpenter's nippers *(page 77)*. And if sash cords stretch, so that the weights lie on the bottom of the window frame, a sash will not stay fully open. You need not replace a stretched cord; simply remove the sash and the access plate in the side jamb, then cut a few inches from the end of the cord and retie it to the weight.

1 **Removing the lower sash.** Pry off the stop *(page 77)* on the side of the window where the cord is broken. Then raise the sash slightly, angle it toward you and pull it sideways until the other side is free of its stop. Pull the knot at the sash end of the broken cord down with a pair of long-nose pliers, untie it and set the piece of cord aside. Pull out the knot at the end of the other cord from the other side of the sash in the same way but untie the knot, slip the cord out of the sash, tie a large knot in the end and guide this knot up until it rests against the pulley. Remove any weather stripping from the lower part of the jamb. If your window has interlocking weather stripping, which fits into a groove in the sash, remove the stop and have a helper raise the sash and hold it at the top of the window frame. Using carpenter's nippers, remove the nails that fasten the metal weather-stripping track; then carefully angle both the weather stripping and the sash out of the window frame.

2 **Taking out the access plate.** Remove the wood screws at the top and bottom of the access plate and pry the plate out of the jamb with a wood chisel. Reach into the access hole revealed by the plate, take out the sash weight and untie the broken cord. Add 1 foot to the total length of the broken cord and cut a new cord or a chain to this length.

If the parting strip covers one edge of the access plate, remove the strip *(page 68, bottom)* before prying out the plate. If the access plate is completely concealed by paint, rap on the lower part of the sash channel with a hammer. When the outline of the plate appears, cut around it with a utility knife, then remove the screws and pry out the plate. If your window does not have an access plate, you will have to remove the casing *(page 77)* to get at the sash weight.

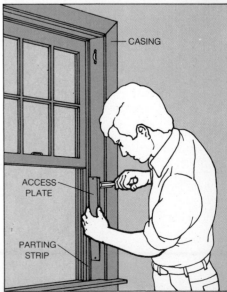

3 **Putting in the new cord.** Tie a bent eight-penny nail to a piece of string, tie the other end of the string to one end of the new sash cord, and feed the string over the pulley until the nail appears at the access hole; then pull the cord over the pulley and down to the access hole. Untie the string and tie the cord to the sash weight, leaving about 3 inches of surplus cord. Rest the sash on the sill and refasten the undamaged cord on the opposite side.

If you are using a sash chain, put a nail through a link at one end to keep the chain from slipping through the pulley and feed the other end over the pulley until it appears at the access hole. Put the end of the chain through the eye of the weight and fasten the loop with thin wire or with clips provided by the manufacturer.

4 **Attaching the new cord to the sash.** With the sash still resting on the sill, pull down on the new cord until the sash weight touches the pulley, then lower the weight about 2 inches and thread the cord into its groove in the sash. Tie a knot in the cord at the level of the hole in the side of the sash, cut off any extra cord and insert the knot in the hole. Hold the sash in its track and slide it all the way up; the bottom of the weight should be visible in the access hole, about

2 inches above the bottom of the window frame. If necessary, adjust the cord by retying it at the sash weight. Replace the access plate, the weather stripping (if any) and the stop; use short nails that will not touch the sash weight and do not drive any nails into the access plate.

To attach a sash chain, thread the chain into the groove in the sash and run wood screws through two of its links into the sash (*inset*).

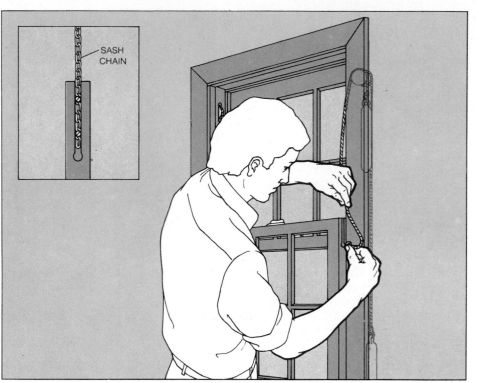

Removing the Upper Sash

Pulling the parting strip. After removing a side stop and the lower sash (*page 67, Step 1*), lower the upper sash. Drill a pilot hole in the parting strip about 3 inches from the top and thread a short wood screw into it. Caution: do not run the screw clear through the strip into the jamb. Pull steadily on the screw with a pair of pliers until you can slip a wood chisel behind the end of the parting strip. From this point, pry the strip out a little at a time with the wood chisel, moving the chisel downward as the gap widens between the jamb and the parting strip. When the top half of the strip is free, slide the sash to the top of the window frame, then continue to pry out the lower half of the parting strip.

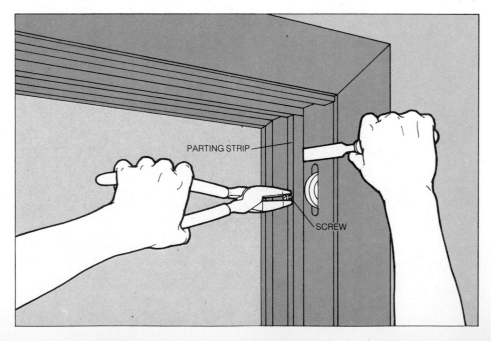

Replacing Spring-Loaded Sash Balances

During the years after World War II, manufacturers of double-hung windows discarded the sash-weight balancing system described on page 67. In its place, they began to install several varieties of less expensive spring-loaded balances. The signs of a broken balance and of a broken sash-weight cord are the same—the sash either jams in its track or falls to the bottom of the window frame—but the remedies are different. A broken balance cannot be repaired. You must remove it and get an exact replacement at a hardware store or a window-repair shop.

The techniques for removing an old balance and installing a new one depend on the type of balance mechanism you already have. These mechanisms come in four general categories:

□ Channel balances, which combine the functions of balances and weather stripping, have sheet-metal tracks nailed to the side jambs of the window frame. Tabs protruding from the tracks hold the sashes up; the tabs, in turn, are supported by tension springs hidden behind the tracks. In a channel repair job, always replace both the left and right balances; the act of removing the sashes usually bends both channels beyond repair.

□ Tube balances are metal or plastic cylinders that fit into grooves in the sides of the sashes and are screwed to the tops of the jambs. Inside each cylinder, a spring-loaded spiral rod fastened to the bottom of the sash holds the sash up by a spring. The tension on the spring can be adjusted by turning the rod (page 70, Step 2), and this alone may free a sticky sash.

□ Tape balances are spring-loaded drums fitted into pockets at the tops of the side jambs or the corners of the head jamb. Thin, flexible metal tapes, hooked to the sides of the sashes, unreel from the drums as the sashes are lowered.

□ Cord balances—a spring-loaded variation of the old sash cord—fit into pockets in each corner of the head jamb, behind a vinyl jamb liner. Each balance contains one reel for the upper sash and one for the lower; a nylon cord runs from each reel to the side of a sash.

Channel Balances

1 Removing the channels. With carpenter's nippers, pull the nails or staples that fasten the channels to the side jambs; then remove the interior stops, if any, from the side and head jambs *(page 77)* and slide both sashes to the middle of the window. Working at one channel while a helper works at the other, tilt the tops of both channels inward, let the bottoms slide partway outdoors from the window, and remove both the channels and the sashes as a single unit. Set the bottoms of the channels on the floor and, while your helper holds them upright against the sashes, slide the sashes up and out of the channels.

CHANNEL BALANCES

2 Installing new channels. While your helper holds the new channels upright on the floor, with the angles cut by the manufacturer at their bottoms matching the slant of the window's finish sill, slide the inner—that is, the bottom—sash into the channel tracks, then the outer sash. Working with the helper, lift the entire unit into the window frame, using the technique described in Step 1 *(above)*. Position the channels against the blind stops of the window frame and fasten them to the side jambs with fourpenny galvanized nails inserted at the top and bottom of each track. Replace the interior stops.

Tube Balances

1 Removing the balance. On the side of the window with the broken balance, remove both the stop *(page 77)* and the screw that fastens the top of the tube to the side jamb; then raise the sash about 8 inches, angle the side of the sash out of the window frame and support the sash on wooden blocks. If the spiral rod is fastened to the mounting bracket on the bottom edge of the sash with a detachable hook, unhook it; otherwise unscrew the bracket.

If your tube balances are built into channels like those shown on page 69, remove the channels and sashes together *(page 69, Step 1)*.

2 Installing a new balance. Set the new tube into its groove and screw the top of the tube to the side jamb. Pull the spiral rod down until it is fully extended, then tighten the spring inside the tube by turning the rod about four complete revolutions. Let the rod retract into the tube until you can screw the mounting bracket to the bottom of the sash.

Slide the sash up and down in its frame. If it creeps up when you release it, loosen the balance spring by turning the rod; if it creeps down, turn the rod to tighten the spring. When the balance is correct, replace the stop.

TUBE

MOUNTING BRACKET

SPIRAL ROD

Tape Balances

Replacing the drum. On the side of the window with the broken balance, remove the stop *(page 77)* and angle the sash out of the frame; then unhook the end of the tape from the sash and feed it back into the tape drum. Remove the screws that secure the drum and pull it out of its pocket in the side or head jamb.

Slip the new tape balance into the jamb and fasten it with wood screws. Pull the end of the tape from the drum with long-nose pliers and hook it to the sash. Angle the sash back into the window frame and replace the stop.

Caution: Because a tape end escaping your grip could injure an eye, consider wearing safety goggles for this repair.

TAPE BALANCE

Cord Balances

1 Removing the jamb liners. With both sashes at the bottom of the window frame, remove the two screws that fasten the vinyl liner to the head jamb and pull out the liner *(below, top)*.

Raise both of the sashes and unscrew the lower of the two pieces of vinyl that make up the left jamb liner; always remove the left jamb liner, regardless of whether the left or the right balance is broken. Then gently bend the bottom of the liner toward the center of the window and pull the liner down and out *(below, bottom)*.

2 Replacing the balance. Lower the inner sash and angle the left side of the sash out of the window frame; unhook the balance cord and guide it up to its balance. Unhook the right-hand cord, guide it up to its balance and set the sash aside. Lower the outer sash, unfasten its cords similarly and set it aside.

Remove the two screws that secure the faulty balance in its pocket in the head jamb. Install a new balance, hook its cords to the sashes and replace the sashes and jamb liners.

HEAD JAMB LINER

SIDE JAMB LINER

CORD BALANCE

Working on Windows that Swing

A window sash designed to swing rather than slide can stick fast in paint or at its edges, but it can then be freed by the remedies on pages 65-66. More often, it is the mechanism that moves the sash, not the sash itself, that binds. You may solve the problem by cleaning and lubricating the hinges and the accessible moving parts (right). Otherwise you will have to remove and repair or replace the sash-moving mechanism, which is technically called the operator.

In both casement and awning windows, the operator is essentially the same. It consists of a metal housing, a shaft with a crank handle at one end and a worm gear at the other, and an extension arm (or, in an awning window, two scissor-like arms) pivoting in the housing at one end and linked to the bottom of the sash at the other. When the crank is turned, teeth at the pivot end of the arm or arms mesh with the worm gear, swinging the arm—and the sash—in or out.

If the grease inside the operator is thick with dirt, clogging the works, you can clean and relubricate the gears. But if the gears have become so worn that they do not mesh, then you will have to replace the entire operator with a new one. The replacement must match the old operator exactly and, on a casement window, it must move the sash in the same direction as the old one—to the right or to the left as viewed from inside the house. Although most hardware stores stock some replacement operators, you may have to send the window to the manufacturer or to a specialty shop for the particular operator you need.

Repairing the crank handle or latch of a swinging window generally involves simply unscrewing the old part and installing a new one; the most difficult part of the job may be finding a matching part. The crank handle, which is secured by a setscrew, slides off its shaft; the latch is fastened to the jamb by screws. If the latch fails to pull the sash tight to the weather stripping, you can shim the latch, by slipping a piece of either cardboard or sheet metal behind it.

Lubricating the window. On a casement window (top), apply a few drops of household oil—or, for a better and longer-lasting job, an aerosol spray of silicone lubricant—to the hinges, the pivot of the latch and the joint between the crank handle and the operator. Open and close the window several times to work the lubricant into the joints. On an awning window (bottom), lubricate the hinges, the joints between the scissor arms and the sash, the pivot joint in the middle of each scissor arm and the joint between the crank handle and the operator.

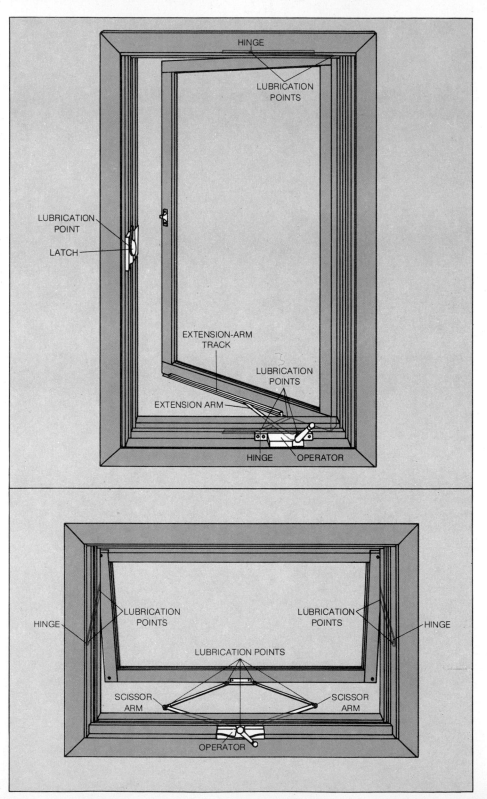

Cleaning an extension-arm track. Open the window fully and scrape hardened grease, paint and accumulated dirt from the track with a wire brush. Scrape away any remaining debris with an old screwdriver, taking special care to remove obstructions inside the lip of the track. Coat the inside of the track with a thin layer of silicone spray or petroleum jelly.

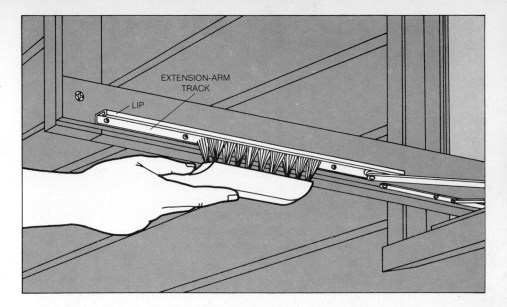

Fixing a Faulty Operator

1 Unfastening the operator. Open the window and remove the screws that fasten the operator to the jamb; if the screws are not visible, pry off the stop above the operator (*inset*) by the method on page 77 to gain access to them. On a casement window like the one pictured here, remove any screws or spring clips that hold the arm in the track at the bottom of the sash.

2 Removing the operator. On a casement window, pull the crank mechanism inward, sliding the extension arm along its track until the end of the arm slips out of the track. Pull the arm completely through its slot in the window frame. On an awning window, unhook the scissor arms from the bracket at the bottom of the sash and pull the operator indoors.

Inspect the gear on the extension arm or arms. If the teeth are rounded or broken, install a new operator. If they have sharp, distinct edges, wash the housing out with kerosene to remove the old grease and let the operator dry completely. Coat metal gears lightly with petroleum jelly or graphite powder and turn the crank handle several times to spread the lubricant. Caution: do not lubricate nylon gears; if they do not work smoothly, replace the operator.

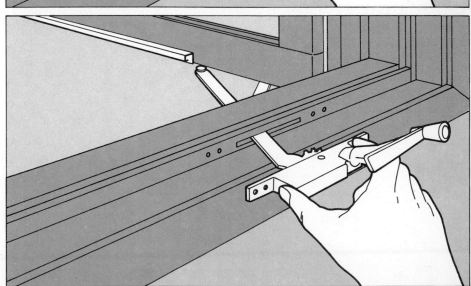

Getting a Door to Fit

Few working parts of a house cause more frustration than a door that rattles, sticks or refuses to lock, or even close at all. Each problem has a number of possible causes. Repairs are much the same for wooden doors, like the ones shown on these pages, as they are for metal doors and usually require no special tools or skills—except in the case of sticky doors which may require planing. Two types of planes are used—one for long edges; the other for short edges and for pieces that cannot

be clamped in place *(pages 460-461)*.

An easy repair for a rattling door uses weather stripping. For a sagging or sticking door check the hinges: the screw holes in the jambs may have become enlarged, preventing the screws from being tightened. Fill the holes with wooden plugs and replace the screws.

When a door sticks even though the hinge screws are fastened securely, the hinge leaves may not have been recessed, or mortised, to equal depths—preferably flush with the surrounding wood.

Remove excess paint preventing a door from moving freely; use a wood chisel and sandpaper as you would for a window *(page 65)*. Paradoxically, lack of

paint can also cause sticking; prevent expansion in hot and humid weather by sealing a door's six sides with paint or varnish.

For a warped interior door with two hinges, move the stop molding or strike plate to accommodate the warp and install a third hinge. Warped exterior doors usually need replacement.

A jamb that bows in the opposite direction must be pried away from the jack stud and straightened, as shown below, with shim shingles (available in lumberyards) driven between the jamb and stud. A jamb bowed more than ½ inch should be replaced rather than straightened. As an alternative, try planing the door to fit the space.

Trimming the edges. If a door sticks at the top, wedge it halfway open and use a block plane to trim the top. Plane from the sides of the door toward the center until there is ⅛ inch of clearance at the head jamb.

If a door sticks all along a long edge, take the door off its hinges—drive the pins up and out, bottom hinge first, then the middle, and finally the top hinge. Remove the hinges and support the door with a door jack or have a helper hold it on edge; trim the hinge-side edge with a jack plane; deepen the hinge mortises if necessary before replacing the hinges.

Straightening a Jamb

1 Marking the bow. Wedge the door open, set a long, straight scrap of plywood against the jamb and mark the high point of the bow. For an exterior door, remove only the casing that is inside the house *(page 77)*. For an interior door, remove the casing on both sides of the partition.

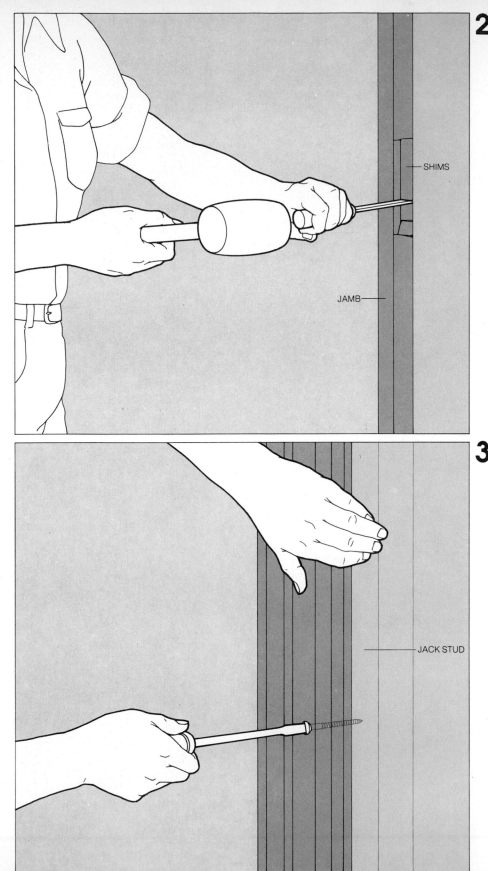

2 **Removing the shims.** Pry the entire length of the bowed jamb away from the jack stud and, using a mallet and a ¼-inch wood chisel, split the shims that are nailed between the jamb and the jack stud and pull out the fragments. If the shims do not split easily, cut the nails with a hacksaw *(page 83, Step 3)*.

— SHIMS

JAMB —

3 **Eliminating the bow.** Using a nail set or pin punch, drive the cut nails through the jamb into the jack stud; putty the holes left in the jamb. Then, at the high point of the bow, use a counterbore bit to drill a hole through the jamb for a 2½-inch No. 12 flathead wood screw. Drive the screw through the high point of the jamb and into the jack stud as shown, tightening the screw until the jamb is vertical.

— JACK STUD

4 **Reshimming the jamb.** On an exterior door, insert the butt end of a shim between the jamb and the jack stud just below the screw used to straighten the jamb. Cut 3 inches from the thin end of a second shim and tap this end into the opening alongside the first shim. Drive two 16-penny finishing nails through the jamb and shims into the jack stud. Install a pair of shims at the level of each of the shims on the other side of the door, and add two more pairs in the unshimmed spaces.

On an interior door, insert full-sized shims, thin end first, from opposite sides of the jamb, nail them, then score and break off their ends.

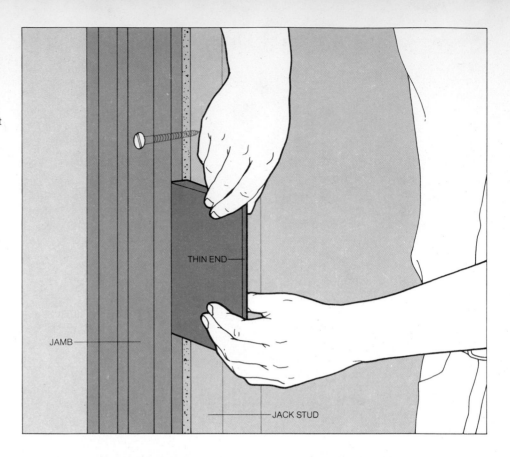

THIN END

JAMB

JACK STUD

Patching a Hollow-Core Door

Filling the hole. Loop a cord through a piece of wire screening slightly larger than the hole, moisten the area around the hole, then insert the screening in the hole and pull it flush to the inside of the door. Holding the cord taut, spread spackling compound around the edges of the hole, working gradually toward the center. To hold the screening while the compound dries, tie the cord to a dowel or pencil long enough to bridge the patch, and turn the dowel until it fits snugly against the face of the door (inset).

When the patch dries, remove the dowel, cut the cord flush to the surface of the patch, and lightly sand the first layer. Apply a second coat of compound, allow this layer to dry, then sand the patch to a smooth finish.

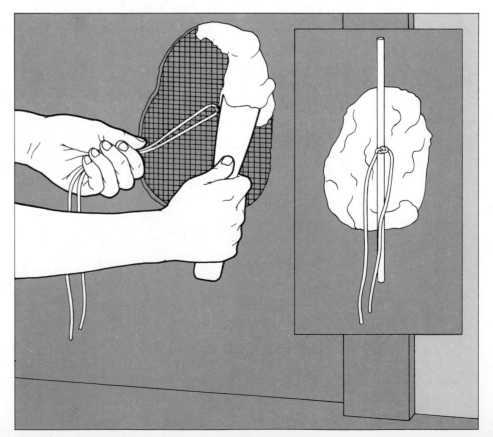

Remedies of Last Resort: Working on the Trim

Trim for a door or window is more than decoration. The stops—the strips of trim inside the top and sides of the opening—keep a door or the sash of a casement window from swinging too far and help to seal the gaps between the door or window and the jambs. On a window with sliding sashes the stops define the channels in which the sashes move.

The interior sill of a window, the stool, acts as a kind of bottom stop; the exterior sill, the finish sill, is angled to carry water away from the window, and forms the window frame base. The molded interior casing strengthens the framework of jambs and conceals the shims that level the door or the window.

The following pages explain how to remove old trim and install new; though the illustrations show the trim work on a door, the instructions apply to both doors and windows. On prehung units, the stop and jamb are one piece of wood. To remove the trim, first chisel off the stop,

then any splintered parts of the jamb. Use a wider material such as 2³/₈-inch casing to cover damage, or putty the damage and work it smooth with a taping knife. Install the new stop.

Lumberyards carry trim pieces in a variety of shapes, thicknesses and widths, but to match the trim of an old house, you will have to check secondhand building-supply yards. Otherwise you can have the piece cut specially—and usually quite expensively—at a mill.

The casing is one of the most carefully fitted elements of door and window trim. Its position depends on the type of unit it surrounds. On doors and casement windows, the casing is conventionally set back ¹/₈ inch from the inside edge of the jamb. On double-hung windows, the casing is generally set flush with the inside edge of the jamb, forming a three-part joint with the interior stop.

Where pieces of casing meet, the joints are generally mitered. The top piece has

two 45° miter cuts, fitting similar cuts at the tops of the side pieces to form right angles. Some windows are cased like picture frames, with four casing strips miter-cut to 45° angles.

Stops may also be mitered. On molded stops, however, the professional technique is to cope the side stops to fit the contour of the head stop *(page 81, Step 2),* making a joint that will not separate as easily as a mitered one.

Both casing and stops should be nailed with special care. Drive each nail until the nailhead alone projects above the wood surface, then complete the job with a nail set. Be sure never to drive the nail in at a sharp slant—by doing so you could pull the jamb out of alignment. On a double-hung window with sash pulleys and weight pockets *(page 67),* be careful not to drive the nails into the pocket. And when nailing door casing, do not drive a nail at the location of a strike plate *(page 91).*

Removing Casing and Stops

Pulling out the stops. Score the joints between the stop and the jamb with a utility knife, then, starting at the bottom of a side stop, set a ¾-inch chisel between stop and jamb, with the bevel of the chisel against the jamb. Tapping the chisel with a mallet, work up the stop to pry it away from the jamb. Repeat the procedure on the other side stop, then on the head stop.

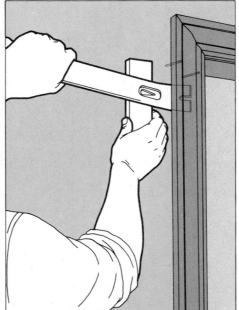

Prying off the casing. Take the casing partway off with a chisel, as for a stop, then insert the flat end of a pry bar behind the outer edge of the casing. Place a thin scrap of wood behind the bar to avoid marring the wall. Slowly pry the casing completely free, working up from the bottom of the side casing. Remove the other side casing and the head casing in the same way.

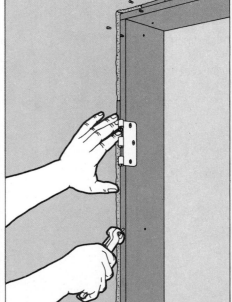

Extracting nails. If a finishing nail does not come out with the casing but remains embedded in the jamb or wall, grip the head with carpenter's nippers and roll the nipper head against the wall to twist the nail free. If the nail is in a stop or casing that you plan to reuse, grip the shank of the nail protruding at the back and pull the head end completely through the piece.

Cutting New Casing

1 **Measuring the head casing.** For doors and casement windows, use a combination square to mark at several points the conventional setback of the casing, ⅛ inch outside the inner edge of the jambs; the marks for the top and side pieces of casing should intersect at a precise corner point. On most double-hung windows, you need not make these marks, because the casing is positioned flush with the inside of the jambs.

Measure the distance between the side jambs at the top; for doors and casement windows, add ¼ inch to allow for the setbacks at the sides. Mark this distance on the edge of a piece of casing that is long enough to leave room for the miter cuts, which will fan outward from the marks.

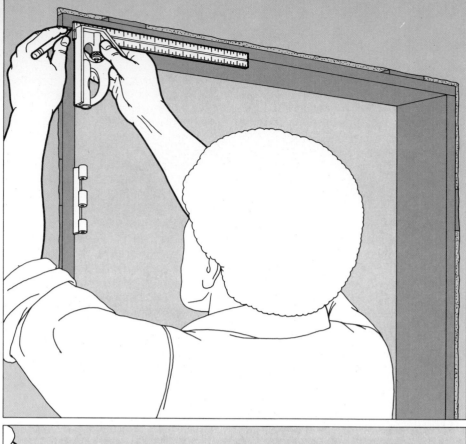

2 **Cutting the miters.** In a miter box bolted to a workbench, place the casing flat side down, set the saw for a 45° cut outward from the mark and, using long, even strokes, saw the strip just outside one of the marks you have made. Reverse the 45° angle and cut the second miter just outside the mark at the other end.

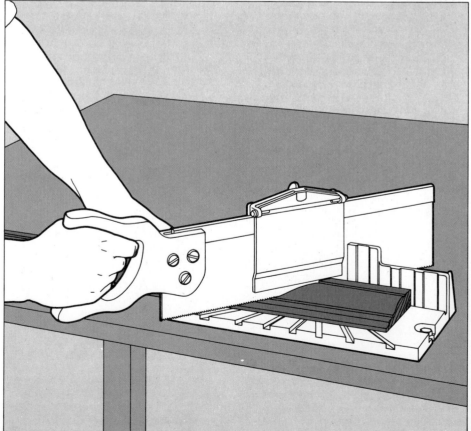

3 **Coping the backs of the miters.** To make the joints fit smoothly, use a coping saw to cope *(pages 38-39)* a crescent-shaped piece from the back of each mitered end of the top casing strip. Leave an uncoped ½-inch margin at the top and bottom edges of the strip.

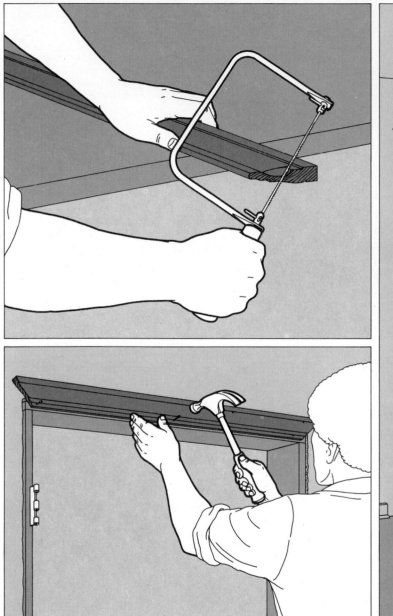

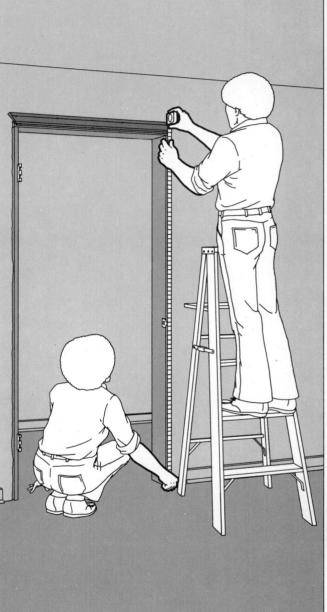

4 **Nailing the top casing.** Set the narrow edge of the casing at the corners of the jambs of double-hung windows or at the marks on the jambs of doors and casement windows, then tack the ends of the casing to the head of the jamb. Starting from one end, drive fourpenny finishing nails through the bottom of the casing into the jamb and sixpenny finishing nails along the outer edge of the casing into the header — the supporting beam at the top of the frame inside the wall; space the nails at least 12 inches apart. Set the nails and spackle the holes.

5 **Measuring the side pieces.** For a door, measure the distance from the bottom of a miter in the top casing to the floor; for a window, measure to the stool. Add 1/16 inch to this and mark the total length on the narrow edge of a casing strip that is long enough to allow for an outward miter at one end. Square off the strip at one mark and make a 45° outward cut from the other *(page 78, Step 2)*. Stand the side casing in place to check the fit of the miter; pare the side miter with a utility knife if necessary. Similarly mark, cut and fit the other side casing.

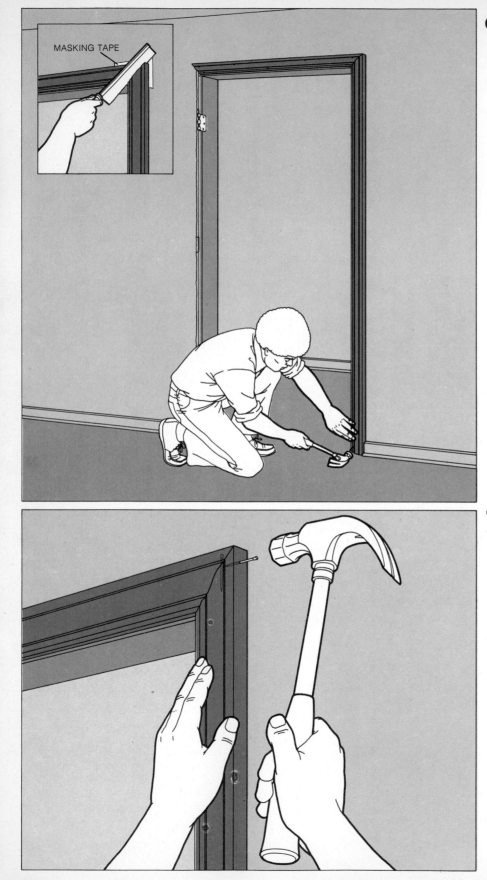

MASKING TAPE

6 **Attaching the side pieces.** With the mitered joint aligned, tack the side casing in position—⅛ inch from the inner edge of the side jamb on a door or a casement window, flush with the jamb edge on a double-hung window. Starting at the top, nail the casing to the jamb and the studs, using fourpenny finishing nails at the jamb, sixpenny at the studs. If there is an uneven gap in a miter joint after the casing is nailed in place, you can improve the fit by cutting through the joint with a dovetail saw *(inset)*. To avoid damaging your paint or wallpaper with the dovetail saw, cover the adjoining wall area with masking tape then, working slowly, angle the saw slightly towards you; be sure to stop sawing as soon as the saw blade touches the masking tape. The casing pieces are so flexible that lock-nailing *(below, Step 7)* will close the cut left by the saw.

7 **Lock-nailing the joints.** An inch from the outside corner of the casing, drive one fourpenny finishing nail vertically down through the top edge of the top casing into the side casing, and another horizontally through the edge of the side casing and into the top casing. The joint should now be even and tight.

Adding New Stops

1 **Positioning the head stop.** Cut stop molding to fit between the tops of the side jambs and nail it in place temporarily. Its position depends on the fixture you are trimming. For a door or a casement window, set the square edge of the stop against the closed door or sash. If the door or window has been removed or has not yet been hung, as in the drawing at right, note the direction in which it will swing and, starting from that side of the opening, mark the thickness of the door or sash on the head and side jambs and set the square edge of the stop at the marks.

For a double-hung window, the head stop fits against the closed sash and generally fills the space between the sash channel and the inside edge of the head jamb *(inset)*. On double-hung windows that slide in tracks *(page 69),* set the stops against the raised edges of the tracks.

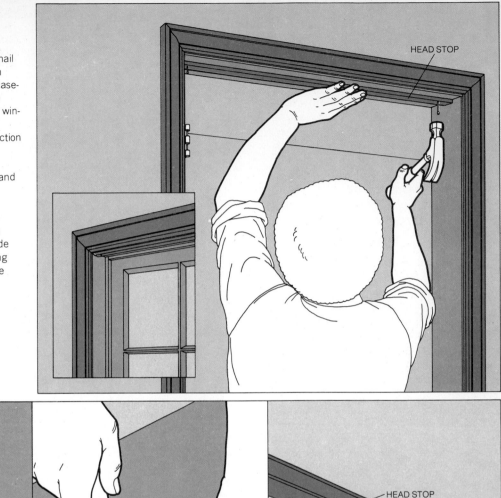

2 **Coping the side stops.** For a door, cut two lengths of stop stock an inch longer than the distance from the head jamb to the floor; for a window, measure to the stool. Flat stops can be butted together; for mitered stops, cut a 45° miter across the molded face at the top end of each piece, angling from the molded face to

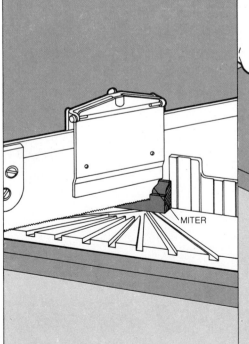

the flat face that fits against the jamb *(left)*. The cuts will leave a scalloped profile on each molded face. Trace the profiles with a pencil and, following the marks, make a 90° cut through each piece with a coping saw *(center)*. The ends of the coped pieces will fit snugly against the head stop *(right)*. Measure the lengths of the side

stops, trim them at the bottom and nail them in place temporarily as you did the head stop.

If a door or a casement window binds or rattles against the tacked stops, move the stops for a better fit. Then secure each stop with fourpenny finishing nails 16 inches apart.

The Base of a Window: Sill, Stool and Apron

The parts of a window that are most vulnerable to damage and decay are the trim pieces at the base, which are frequently bumped, banged and rained on. Each has a special name *(right)* that can be confusing because the terminology is often mixed up in common usage. The finish sill, for example, is exposed outdoors only; the indoor window "sill" is properly called a stool.

The finish sill is usually the first piece to show signs of wear. If it is merely cracked or pitted, try to restore rather than replace it. Remove all the paint, splinters and wood chips, using paint remover, putty knife and wire brush, then coat the sill with wood preservative. Let it dry for a day and give it two coats of linseed oil, allowing a day for drying after each application. Fill cracks and holes with putty, let the putty dry for a couple of days, then prime and repaint the sill.

A rotted finish sill is best replaced promptly to prevent the spread of rot. You should be able to match your sill at a local lumberyard. Otherwise, you can make a new sill *(page 83);* use caulking to seal any gaps. When buying a new sill, choose one with a drip groove under the outside edge to prevent water from creeping up the bottom of the sill, and with an angle cut along the inside edge to make this edge vertical when the sill is in place.

On some older windows you may find an intricate pattern of sill-to-jamb joinery almost impossible for an amateur to duplicate. You can have a professional replace the sill, replace the entire window or make the replacement piece yourself and fill any gaps with caulking.

Sometimes replacing a stool calls for a new piece that will fit your sill and walls—and these may vary from the modern standard. If your window needs a stool wider than the standard available stock, either adapt the new stock by gluing and tacking a strip of wood to the edge that fits against the window sash, or use the next larger stock size and cut it to fit.

The trim at the base of a window. In a double-hung window, a finish sill fits into side jambs seated in dadoes *(inset)* that slope down outward 15° for drainage. Outside, the sill rests on a horizontal 2-by-4—the rough sill. Extensions of the finish sill, sill horns, fit against the outside edges of the jambs, providing a base for the exterior casing, or brickmold *(not shown)*. These horns vary in length, but need extend no farther than the outer edges of the brickmold. Inside the house, a stool fits over the finish sill, with stool horns generally extending ¾ inch beyond the edges of the interior casing. The bottom of the stool has a beveled rabbet that is angled to set it firmly on the sloping sill. An apron under the stool conceals the gap between the finish sill and the rough sill beneath it, and adds support to the stool.

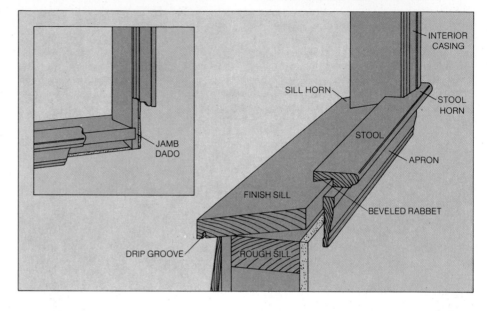

Getting at the Sill

1 **Removing the stool.** Take off the interior side casings and stops *(page 77)*, pry off the apron with a chisel and pry bar, and raise the bottom sash. If you plan to replace the stool, simply hit the stool from underneath with a hammer, but if you wish to reuse the stool, you must pry it off from outside *(above)* after several preliminary steps. First check to see if the stool has been nailed to the studs through the horns; if so, drive the nails completely through the stool with a blunted nail. Then lean out the window, ease a pry bar between the stool and the sill, set a scrap of wood under the bar and gently pry the stool off.

2 Removing the finish sill. Measure and make a notation of the exact distance between the side jambs, then make two cuts approximately a foot apart through the middle of the sill with a crosscut saw. Pry off the cut section and pull the end pieces out of their dadoes (*inset*); if you cannot free the end pieces easily, pry the bottom of the brickmold on each side slightly away from the wall. Caution: work slowly and carefully in order to avoid racking or splitting the jambs.

If the jambs have moved inward, use a hammer and a block of wood to tap them back to their original position. If there are no shims behind the jambs at dado level, install shims to prevent the jambs from moving too far apart.

3 Removing the nails. Working inside the house with a hacksaw blade, cut off the exposed parts of the nails that secured the sill inside the dadoes. The blade can be held in a gloved hand, but the job will go faster with an inexpensive blade holder like the one pictured. Next, either install a purchased replacement (*Step 5*) or make one (*Step 4*).

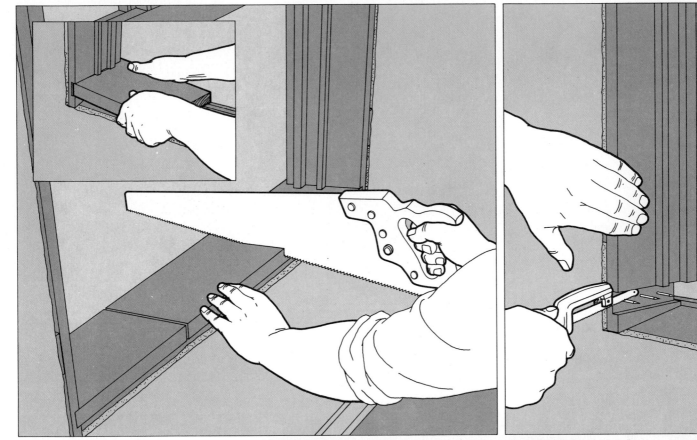

4 Making a new finish sill. Using sill stock such as pressure-treated wood which will not rot, cut the replacement piece as long as the distance between the outer edges of the brickmolds. Working inside the house, have a helper center the piece—right side up with the inside edge toward him—against the jambs, at the level of the dadoes, while you set a combination square across the piece and into a dado. Note the position of the dadoes; they should be angled slightly so that the finish sill will slant downward toward the outside. Mark a line across the new sill for an exact fit inside the dado; repeat for the other side.

On the lines you have drawn, mark off the length of the dado, measuring from the inside edge of the sill. Draw perpendicular lines from these marks to the ends of the sill (*inset*). Cut out the inside corners to fit the dadoes and leave sill horns; saw on the waste side of the lines. Finally, add a grip groove by running a circular saw along the bottom edge of the sill.

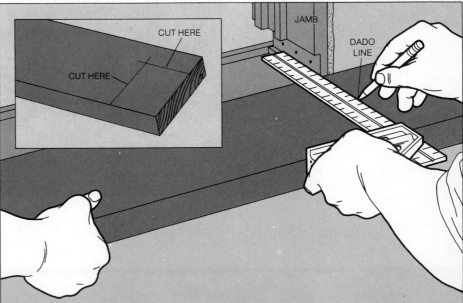

5 **Installing the sill.** Push the inside corners of the sill 1 or 2 inches into the dadoes in the jambs, then set a piece of scrap wood against the outside edge of the sill and tap lightly with a hammer until the inside edge of the sill is flush with the inside edges of the jambs. If the sill is a little too thick to slide into the dadoes, sand the bottom of it; if the sill is too thin, shim and wedge it tight from underneath.

Inside the house, drill pilot holes angling through the inside edge of the sill into the side jambs and toenail the sill in place nailing eightpenny nails at an angle *(inset)*. Outside the house, drill pilot holes straight through from the front edge of the sill horns into the studs of the rough frame; secure with nails. Caulk all exterior joints.

Fitting a Stool and Apron

1 **Marking the stool.** Measure the distance between the outer edges of the interior casings (their positions will be visible on the wall even after you have removed the casings) and add 1½ inches; measure the depth of the window from the inside edge of the jamb to the far edge of the interior stop and add the thickness of the interior casing plus ¾ inch. Cut stool stock to this total length and width. With a helper centering the stool piece—right side up, inner, molded edge toward him—against the jambs, level with the finish sill, set the blade of a combination square across the piece and against the inner face of each side jamb; draw lines from the jamb faces across the stool. Extend these lines down across the squared, outside edge of the stool.

Starting at points directly above the inner corners of the rabbet on the stool's underside, draw lines from each end of the stool to intersect the jamb lines at a right angle *(inset)*. Cut out corners for the stool horns on the waste sides of the lines. Slip the stool into position, with its rabbet fitted to the top corner of the sill, and close the window sash. There should be a ¹/₁₆-inch gap between the sash and the stool; if you find too little clearance, plane the stool down and sand the planed area smooth. Finish the ends of the horns as shown at the bottom of page 85.

2 Attaching the stool. At points in the corners of the stool that will be covered by the side stops, and at two additional points to the left and right of the center, drill pilot holes and drive eight-penny finishing nails down through the top of the stool into the sill. Then replace the casings and the stops *(pages 78-81).*

3 Installing the apron. Cut a piece of apron stock 1½ inches shorter than the stool, finish the ends *(bottom of page)* and set it in place, centered under the stool. Fasten the apron with three sixpenny nails along the top—one at the center and one at each end—and three fourpenny nails similarly spaced along the bottom.

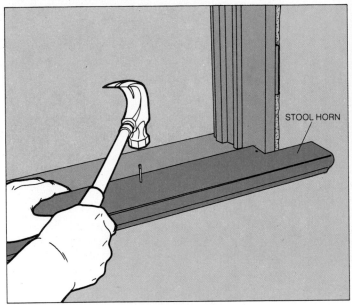

STOOL HORN

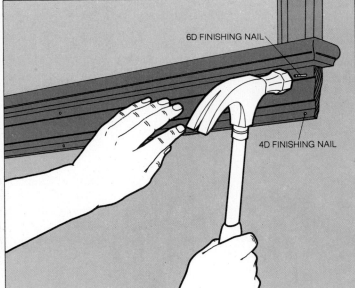

6D FINISHING NAIL

4D FINISHING NAIL

Three Ways of Shaping the Ends

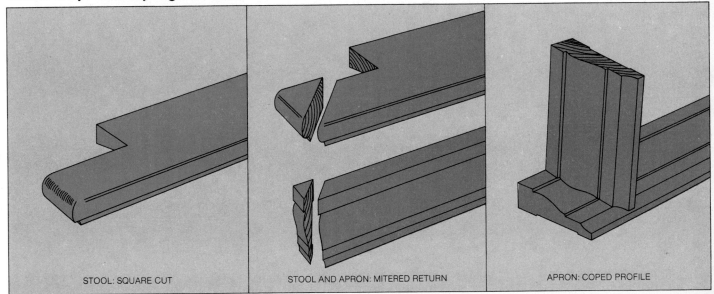

STOOL: SQUARE CUT

STOOL AND APRON: MITERED RETURN

APRON: COPED PROFILE

Rounded, mitered and coped. You can, of course, simply square the ends of a stool or apron with a backsaw and miter box, smooth the cuts with sandpaper, then nail the piece in place. Most professionals, however, prefer to use techniques that give the window a more finished appearance. For a stool, they may cut the ends square, then round them with a rasp and sand them smooth *(above, left)*. For both a stool and an apron, a more elaborate technique is the mitered return *(above, center)*. Cut the stool or apron to length and miter the ends inward at 45°. Cut two scrap pieces of trim into triangular wedges, with a miter cut at one end to fit the mitered end of the apron and a square cut at the other end to fit against the wall, then glue and nail the wedges in place. A third finishing method, which is used for an apron with a molded pattern on its face, is to cope the ends to the same profile as the face. Cut the apron about an inch too long at each end and mark the correct end positions on the face. Set a scrap piece of apron stock on end at the marks *(above, right)* and trace the profile of the piece; then cut the apron along the traced line with a coping saw, keeping the saw straight, and smooth the cut ends of the apron with sandpaper.

Putting On a Better Lock

Often, a good lock on a door leading outside will persuade a would-be burglar to try his luck elsewhere. If you are concerned about the safety of your home, determine the types of locks installed on your doors, and decide if your home is as secure as it could be.

With a key-in-knob, or spring latch, lock, a burglar can pop the latch out of the strike. The dead-bolt lock offers better protection because its bolt does not work automatically, but must be opened and closed by a thumb turn or a key. Such a lock is generally installed in addition to one of the spring-latch type.

The simplest dead-bolt is a rim lock, in which the lock and a set of strike rings are fully exposed on the inside faces of door and frame. Far stronger than any rim lock is a dead-bolt that is mounted inside the door and locks into a strike box inside the door jamb. A mortise lock combines a dead bolt and spring latch in a single handsome, expensive unit.

Some improvements to existing locks can be very simple, involving nothing but a change of keys. Others require the addition of new locks or, if you want to use a mortise lock, a brand-new door. For all lock installations except the simplest, careful and precise carpentry is essential, but it is greatly simplified by the use of a special drilling guide *(page 91)*. Installing a mortise lock demands a very high degree of skill, and may be best done by a professional locksmith.

If keys to existing locks have been lost, you can have the cylinders re-keyed, a job that can be done in minutes in a locksmith's shop. If the existing cylinders are not of the comparatively tamperproof type offered by a rim, dead-bolt or mortise lock, they ought to be replaced. Either re-keying or replacing a cylinder will require disassembling the lock. In dead-bolt locks, you can free the cylinder entirely; in many key-in-knob locks you will have to stop when you free the outside knob from the lock body and then take the knob, with the cylinder still inside, to a locksmith.

The work involved in installing new locks depends on the lock. A rim lock or a dead-bolt can generally be added to a door without making any changes to the locks already in place. If you replace an existing built-in lock, get a model that will fit into the old knob and bolt holes; otherwise you may have to replace the entire door. Before you buy a built-in lock, make sure the door will accommodate it; the door must be thick enough for the bolt mechanism.

If you plan to use a key-in-knob lock, a mortise lock or some models of rim locks, study the way your door swings open; the lock salesperson will need to know the "hand" of the door. If, like most exterior doors, your door opens inward, stand outside the house and look at the hinges. A door with hinges on the right side is a right-hand door; one that has its hinges on the left side is a left-hand door. If your door opens outward, be sure to tell the salesperson.

Replacing Cylinders

A spring-latch lock. If screws secure the interior rose, remove them; if none are visible, use the tip of a screwdriver to depress the small metal tab projecting through a slot behind the knob. Pull the knob from the knob stem, push in the spring clip that protrudes from the rose and insert a screwdriver into the notch at the rim of the rose to pry away the rose. Remove the two screws in the mounting plate under the rose and, from the exterior side of the door, pull the outside knob, which contains the lock cylinder.

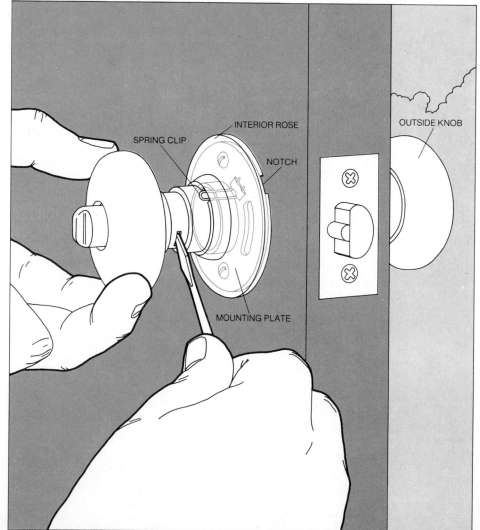

A rim lock. With the door unlocked, remove the screws or nuts that secure the lock case (*below, left*). Wiggle the case off the door and the cylinder drive bar; then remove the screws of the reinforcing plate (*below, right*) and, from outside the door, pull out the cylinder.

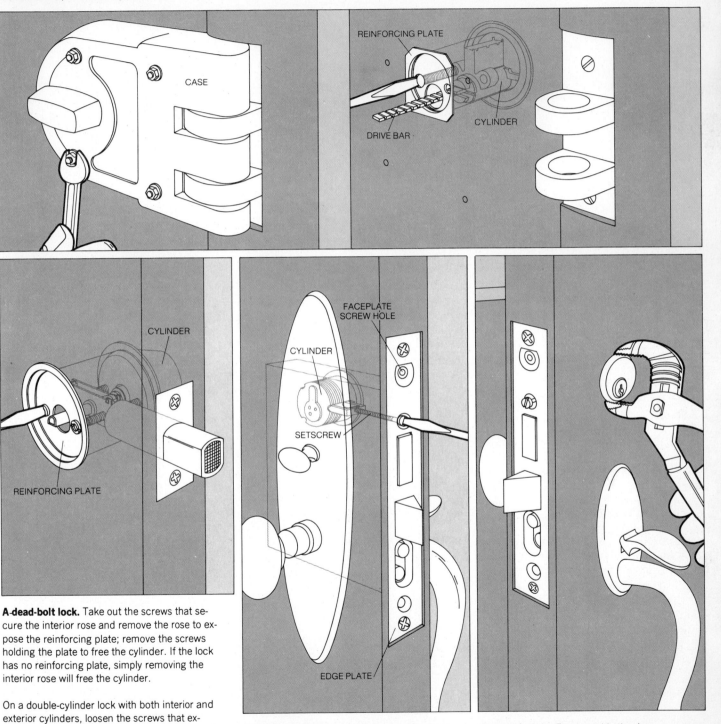

CASE

REINFORCING PLATE

DRIVE BAR

CYLINDER

CYLINDER

REINFORCING PLATE

FACEPLATE SCREW HOLE

CYLINDER

SETSCREW

EDGE PLATE

A dead-bolt lock. Take out the screws that secure the interior rose and remove the rose to expose the reinforcing plate; remove the screws holding the plate to free the cylinder. If the lock has no reinforcing plate, simply removing the interior rose will free the cylinder.

On a double-cylinder lock with both interior and exterior cylinders, loosen the screws that extend through the inside cylinder to free both cylinders. If these screws are nonreversible or if they have been deliberately damaged so they cannot be removed, you will probably need a locksmith to remove the cylinder.

A mortise lock. Find the small setscrew on the edge plate of the door, at the same height as the lock cylinder—if necessary, remove a decorative faceplate from the edge plate to expose the setscrew—and back the setscrew out three or

four turns (*left*). From outside the door, unscrew the cylinder; if it does not turn easily, grip its edge with channel-joint pliers, covering the teeth of the pliers with tape to prevent them from marring the cylinder (*right*).

Adding a Dead-Bolt

1 Marking the holes. Position the paper template on the edge and face of the door about 6 inches above the knob, making sure a lock in this location will not interfere with the inside handle of a storm door when both storm and main doors are closed; tape the template to the door. For maximum precision in boring straight, correctly placed holes, start each one by driving a finishing nail straight in ¼ inch through the marks on the paper template. To allow for variations in door thickness, some templates are marked with alternative locations for drilling the edge holes; be sure to use the mark specified for the size of your door.

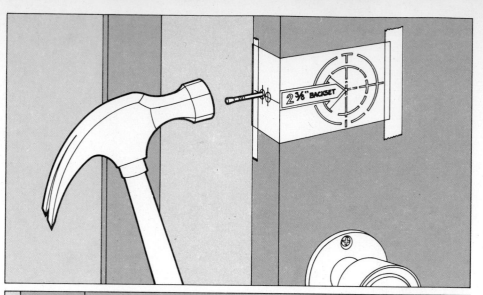

2 Boring the cylinder hole. With the door closed, or firmly wedged open, use a hole saw to bore a cylinder hole the size specified by the manufacturer. To avoid splintering the door face—on a flush door the veneer is very easily damaged—stop drilling as soon as the small bit of the saw breaks through; complete the hole from the opposite side of the door.

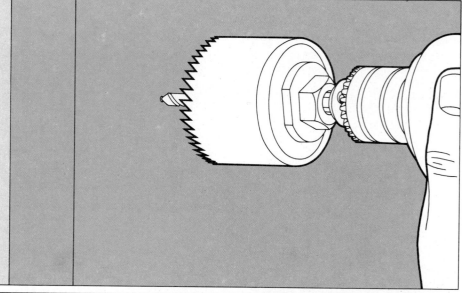

3 Drilling the bolthole. Wedge the door open with a shim. To help keep the drill bit level and straight when drilling the bolthole into the relatively narrow edge of the door, enlist a helper to guide you. While you watch the bit from above to direct it right or left, have your helper kneel so that his eye is level with the hole and he can tell when the bit wanders from true horizontal.

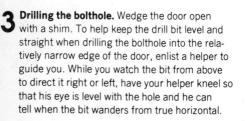

4 **Seating the bolt assembly.** Insert the bolt assembly into the bolthole and use a utility knife to scribe the outline of the faceplate—the score line left by a sharp knife is thinner and more precise than a pencil line. Chisel a mortise in the marked area for the faceplate and fasten the assembly in place with screws.

5 **Installing the lock.** For a dead-bolt with a thumb turn (*right*), assemble the cylinder, the drive bar and the reinforcing plate and ring as directed by the manufacturer. Then fit the assembly into the cylinder hole from outside the door, inserting the drive bar through the drive-bar hole in the bolt assembly. Screw the rear reinforcing plate, if any, to the cylinder hole from inside the door, then set the thumb turn against the door, fitting the drive bar into the thumb-turn hole. Insert mounting bolts through the thumb turn, the reinforcing plate and the bolt assembly and screw them into the back of the cylinder. For a double-cylinder lock, fit the drive bars of both cylinders into the drive-bar hole.

Test the dead-bolt action with both the key and the thumb turn. If the bolt will not move in or out, remove the drive bar from the cylinder, rotate the bar 180° and reassemble the lock.

6 **Marking for the strike box.** Coat the end of the bolt with lipstick or a grease pencil, close the door and use the thumb turn or key to press the bolt against the jamb, leaving a mark on it. Using the bit with which you bored the bolthole, bore a hole for the strike box into the jamb at the mark. If you hit a finishing nail, chisel around it until you can pull it out with pliers.

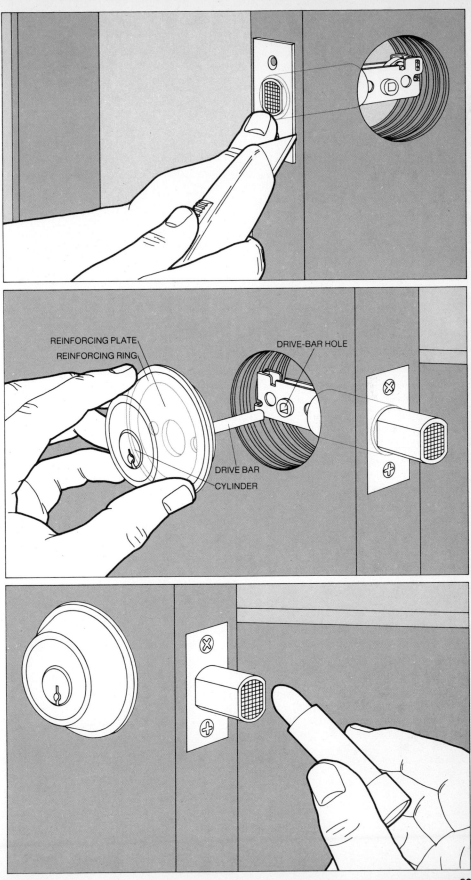

REINFORCING PLATE
REINFORCING RING
DRIVE-BAR HOLE
DRIVE BAR
CYLINDER

Installing a Spring-Latch

Fitting the lock. Drill a cylinder hole and a bolthole and mortise the latch assembly as for a dead-bolt lock *(pages 88-89, Steps 1-4);* then from the outside set the lock body in place, engaging the end pieces of the latch assembly *(inset).* From the inside, screw the inner mounting plate to the lock body. Finally, install the interior rose and knob, reversing the steps described on page 86. Install the strike plate in the same way as a dead-bolt strike.

LATCH ASSEMBLY

Installing a Rim Lock

1 Mounting the lock. About 6 inches above the doorknob, bore a hole for the cylinder. Insert the cylinder from the outside, screw the rear reinforcing plate to it and set the lock case against the door so that the drive bar fits into the thumb-turn slot of the case. If necessary, you can shorten the drive bar by breaking it with pliers at one of the grooves. Bore holes for the attachment bolts, using the lock case to locate the boltholes. Using carriage bolts and nuts, bolt on the lock case, placing lock washers and nuts on the inside.

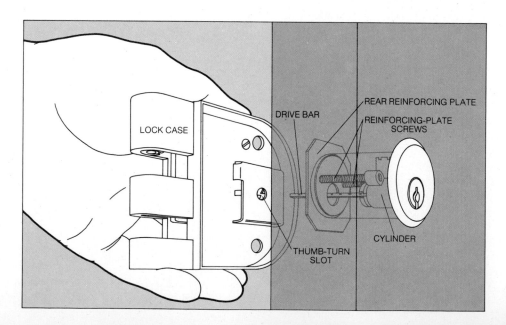

LOCK CASE

DRIVE BAR

REAR REINFORCING PLATE

REINFORCING-PLATE SCREWS

THUMB-TURN SLOT

CYLINDER

2 **Mortising for the strike.** With the door closed, score lines with a utility knife where the top and bottom of the lock case touch the door casing *(below, left)*. With the door open, hold the strike plate between these marks and score a vertical line in the casing along the outer edge of the strike *(below, right)*; mark a second line one strike-thickness farther out in the casing *(dotted line)*. Use a claw hammer to tap a sharp wood chisel, bevel side in, along the outermost marks made in the casing to cut right through it; then, holding the chisel bevel side down, pare out the wood within the marked area to create a uniform mortise the thickness of the strike. Take care not to dig too deeply and try to make the mortise

as flat as possible. For the jamb mortise, hold the strike in the casing mortise, mark the outer edges of the strike with a utility knife and chisel out a recess in the jamb in the same way the mortise in the casing was cut, again taking care not to chisel too deeply.

Test the strike mortises as you chisel recesses, paring away wood until the lock bolts slip easily into the rings of the strike. If you mortise too deeply, shim behind the strike with cardboard. Screw the strike in place, making sure that the fit is good; if the fit is imperfect, use the wood chisel or coarse sandpaper to smooth the casing or jamb mortises.

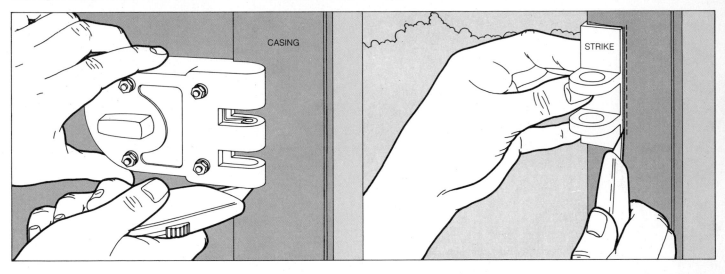

A Guide that Takes the Guesswork out of Drilling

A drill guide, which resembles its larger cousin the drill press, offers a sure way of drilling a hole straight and perpendicular—even into a door edge. The model shown here consists of a bracket to hold the drill, a pair of runners that slide along two steel rods, and a round base. When the guide is to be used, the chuck is unscrewed from the drill, the bracket is attached to the drill shaft, then the chuck is put back on.

When the rod ends are set flush with the base, the drill guide can be used on a door face; with the rods pushed partway through the base *(right)*, the guide can steady a drill bit on a door edge. A lock collar on one rod can be set to stop the drill when the bit has reached a predetermined depth.

To use a drill guide, hold the base

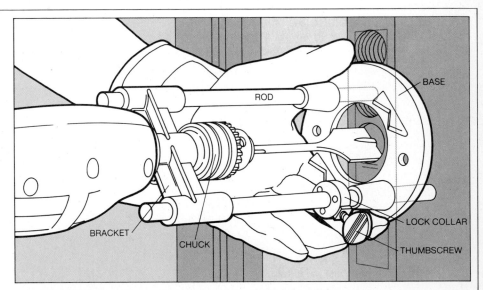

against a door edge with one hand pressing the rods against the face of the door. Since most doors have a beveled edge, hold the rods tight against the face of the door; one side of the

base plate then will ride about 1/8 inch above the beveled corner of the door. Use your other hand to operate the drill. The drill's torque will help lock the guide rods against the door faces.

Repairs for a Sliding Door

Like hinged doors, sliding glass units sometimes bind or jam—but for different reasons. The track in which the door glides may be dirty or dented, the rollers beneath it worn or broken.

Removing debris trapped in a track is simple enough: use a stiff brush and a vacuum cleaner. But to mend a dented track or replace broken rollers you must remove the door. You may have to lower it by turning roller-adjusting screws located on the face of the door or, as in the metal door shown here, on the edge. Lift the door out of the track and tilt it out of the opening.

For metal doors, remove the bottom rail (right) to get at the roller units, since rail and rollers are generally held in place by the same screws. Roller units of wooden doors can usually be replaced without removing the rail.

On both types, a slightly dented track can be easily and inexpensively fitted with a snap-on channel (below, right); replace a mashed track. When replacing a track or roller, you must match the original part exactly; you may have to write to the door manufacturer for the name of a supplier.

Replacing the Rollers

1 **Removing the bottom rail.** Lay the door on a flat surface, remove the bottom-rail retainer screws (inset) and, while a helper holds the door steady, tap a wood block against the top of the rail to free the rail from the door.

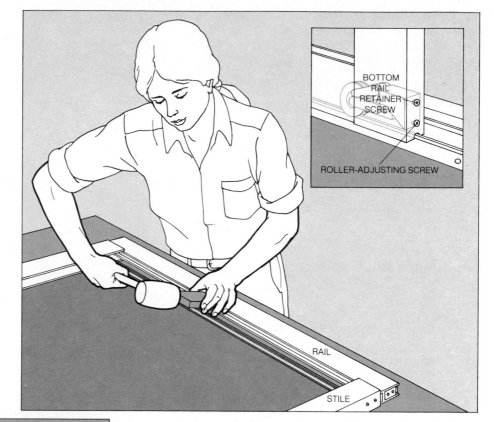

BOTTOM RAIL RETAINER SCREW

ROLLER-ADJUSTING SCREW

RAIL

STILE

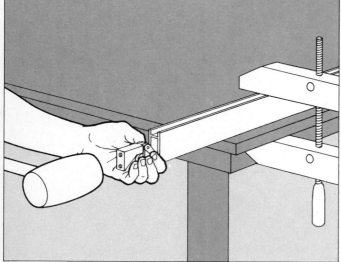

2 **Installing the rollers.** Clamp the bottom rail to a table and slide the worn or broken roller units out of the rail, prying with a screwdriver if necessary. Tap new units into each end of the rail, with the rollers facing the middle of the door.

A New Channel for an Old Track

Installing the track channel. With a hacksaw, cut a stainless-steel channel to the length of the dented track, then snap the channel onto the old track, pressing it down with a wood block. Readjust the rollers by turning the roller-adjusting screws.

Prescriptions for Screens, Blinds and Shutters

Screens, blinds, shades and shutters all help control air and light, and can improve the appearance and comfort of a house. They also wear out and must be repaired or replaced.

Of the two most common screening materials, aluminum is less likely to tear or sag; fiberglass will not corrode or oxidize. Whatever material your screens are made of, match the repair method to the nature and extent of the damage. Oxidized or dirt-encrusted aluminum screening, for example, needs only rubbing with a wire brush and a once-over with a vacuum cleaner. Loose joints on wooden frames can easily be reinforced with corrugated fasteners, angle plates or screws.

Holes in screening can be fixed in several different ways. Fixing a very small hole may mean simply pushing the wires of the screening back into line with the tip of an awl or ice pick. Other small gaps can be plugged with dabs of weatherproof glue or with patches glued in place. On metal screening you can also fasten patches by weaving the wires at the edges of the patch into the surrounding mesh, or you can use ready-made patches with edging wires prehooked to clip onto the screening. On fiberglass screening, iron patches in place: simply set an iron-on fiberglass patch over the hole, cover the patch with a cotton rag and run a hot iron over the rag, fusing the patch to the screening.

If the holes are so large that you cannot patch them, or so close to the frame that the screening sags, replace the screening completely. On all metal frames and some wooden ones, screening is secured with a spline—a thin flexible strip pressed down over the screening and into a channel at the inside edges of the frame. To replace the screening, you must pull out the old spline and screening, then put the spline (a new spline if the old one is broken or brittle) back in place over new screening. The only specialized tool you will need is a simple one—a double wheeled screen-spline roller as shown below.

On some wooden frames the screening is secured with tacks or staples that normally are concealed by molding. Professionals install new screening while the frame is slightly bowed by clamps; when the clamps are released, the frame itself tightens the screening as it straightens out.

A Spline for Screening on a Channeled Frame

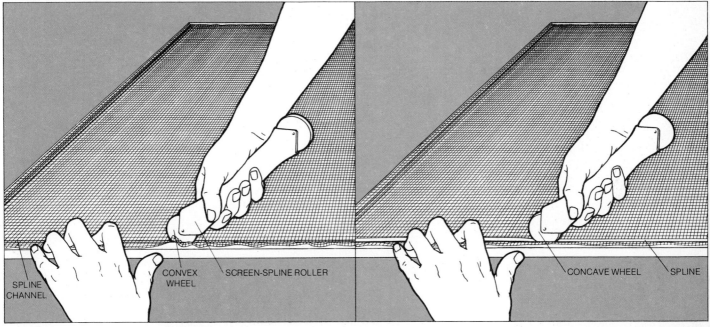

SPLINE CHANNEL   CONVEX WHEEL   SCREEN-SPLINE ROLLER   CONCAVE WHEEL   SPLINE

1 Securing a short side. Cut a piece of screening to the outer dimensions of the frame. If your screening is metal, crease it into the spline channel on a short side of the frame, using the convex wheel of a screen-spline roller (left); start at a corner and work in short back-and-forth strokes. With the concave wheel, force the spline into the channel over the screening (right). Fiberglass will not crease: roll the spline down over the screening in one step. New spline must be cut off at the corners of the frame and tamped into place with a screwdriver.

2 **Completing the splines.** Pull the screening taut at the opposite side of the frame, crease it if necessary and roll a length of spline over it and into the channel. If the frame bows inward, fit a temporary brace to hold the sides parallel. With the screening pulled flat across the frame, spline the two remaining sides.

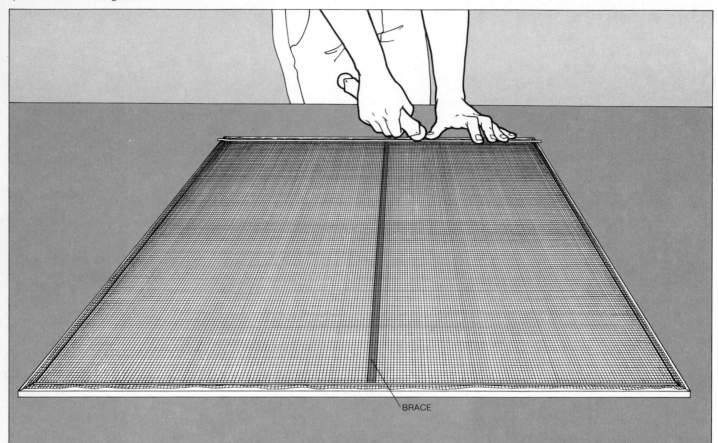

BRACE

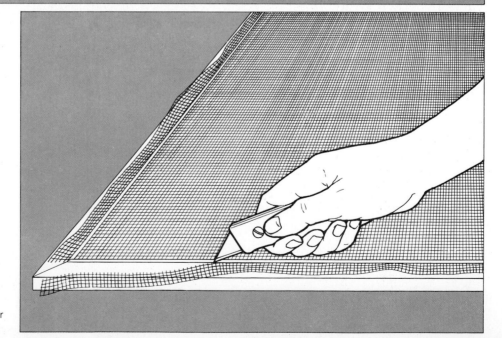

3 **Trimming the excess screening.** With a utility knife, cut through the screening along the outer edges of the spline channels. As you cut, slant the blade toward the outside of the frame, in order to avoid cutting into the spline.

Repairing Screens and Screen Doors

Giving a lift to a drooping door. To prevent a screen door from sagging, stretch wires with a center turnbuckle from the top of the hinge side to the bottom of the latch side. Open a 3-inch turnbuckle to nearly full extension, and attach 4 feet of woven wire to each of its eyes with a small wire clamp (*inset*). Drive a medium-sized eye screw into the door's face about 2 inches from the top corner of the hinge side, and attach one free end of wire to the eye screw with a wire clamp. Drive another eye screw about 2 inches from the bottom corner of the latch side, pull the other wire through, and hold the wire taut as you attach a wire clamp. Turn the center section of the turnbuckle, with pliers if necessary, tightening the wires to hold the door square.

WIRE CLAMP

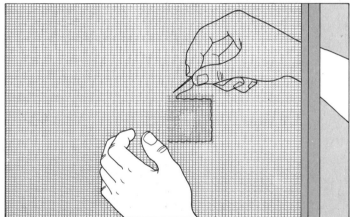

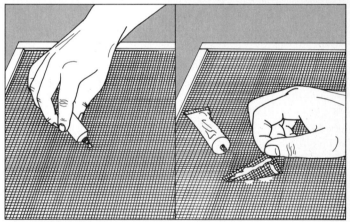

Patching an aluminum screen. To repair a small hole in an aluminum screen, cut away ragged edges, then use a needle and nylon thread to sew on a patch. Cut the patch from matching screening, overlapping the hole by ½ inch on all sides. Hold the patch over the hole and use a sewing needle to weave nylon monofilament sewing thread through both the screen and the patch, ¼ inch from the edge of the patch, passing through each square of mesh. When you have woven all around, weave a second border ⅛ inch from the edge. End this border about ½ inch past the starting point of the first.

If you cannot reach both sides of the hole at the same time, have a helper on the opposite side of the screen return the needle on each stitch, or use a curved upholstery needle and make at least three passes around the patch.

Fixing a fiberglass screen. Small holes in fiberglass screen are easily mended by laying the screen flat and sealing the hole with one drop of clear household cement capable of bonding vinyl or fiberglass (*above, left*). Apply the cement sparingly; otherwise the repair can become an unsightly mess.

This household cement is also handy for repairing a larger rip or hole; you will need a sheet of matching screening. First use scissors or a utility knife to cut a patch of screening large enough to cover the damaged area. Then, using an applicator, coat the patch and the area around the hole with a thin coat of the cement; for a neat repair, use the cement sparingly. Put the two glued surfaces together (*above, right*), matching the mesh weaving as closely as possible. Allow cement to dry and replace the screen. If the repair is made on a vertical surface, watch for cement drips and dab them before they dry.

Stapling Screening to a Wooden Frame

1 Fastening the first side. Cut metal screening 2 inches larger than the frame opening. Staple the screening to a short side of the frame at 2-inch intervals, starting at a corner. Angle each staple so that its prongs fit over two different strands of the mesh. Fiberglass screening must have a hem—a double layer at the edges—to keep the screening from tearing along the line of staples. Cut the screening ½ inch larger than the outer edges of the molding that will conceal the staples. To make the hem, fold the extra ½ inch over as you staple (inset).

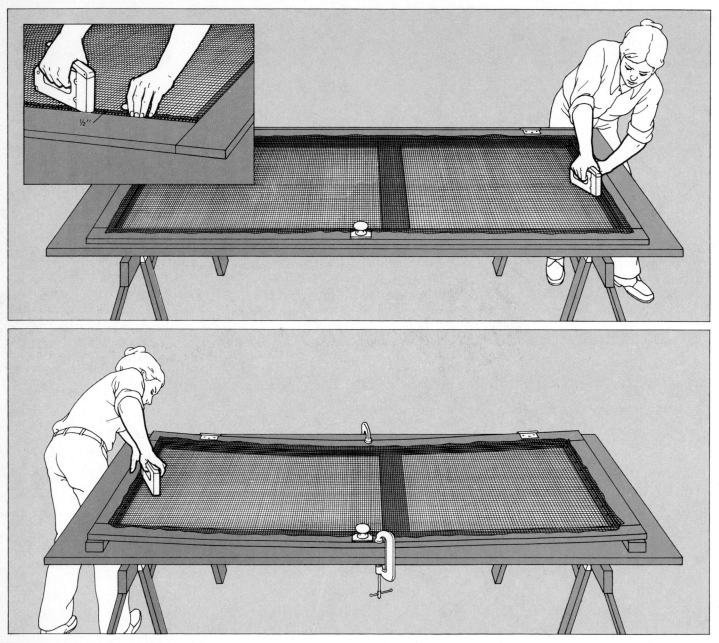

2 Bowing the frame. Set blocks of scrap wood under the short sides of the frame and use a pair of C clamps to force the centers of the long sides down about ¼ inch. Pull the screening taut along the unstapled short side, staple it there and release the C clamps. Staple the long sides, replace the molding and, on metal screening, trim off the excess screening with a utility knife.

The Anatomy of Blinds and Window Shades

A Venetian blind is a delicate affair, prone to frayed cords, torn tapes and bent or broken slats. You must dismantle the blind *(below, right)* to replace such parts with new ones from hardware stores; the dealer should also have replacement parts for the few mechanical components that occasionally do fail. Other repairs *(chart, right)* call for adjusting parts rather than replacing them.

The most common problems of a window shade—excessive or inadequate tension in the spring that rolls the shade up—are easily solved. To reduce the tension, raise the shade all the way and pull the flat end pin out of its bracket; then unroll the shade about halfway by hand and replace the pin in the bracket. To increase the tension, pull the shade halfway down, take the flat pin from its bracket and roll the shade up by hand. Repeat these procedures until the tension is satisfactory.

The works of a Venetian blind. Two cords regulate the tilt and height of the slats in a Venetian blind. The tilt cord, at the left side, is linked *(inset)*—by a pulley, a worm gear and a tilt rod—to the tapes at the front and back of the slats. Pulling the cord raises and lowers the tapes to change the tilt of the slats. In the metal blind shown here, the tapes are clipped to two short cylinders called tilt tubes, mounted on a metal tilt rod; in wooden blinds, the tapes are stapled to a wooden tilt rod.

The lift cord at the right side passes over pulleys in the headbox and is knotted under the bottom slat or bar. Pulling the cord straight down raises the bottom slat, stacking the others above it. An equalizer catch holds the ends of the cord in alignment to keep the bottom slat horizontal. The level of the bottom slat is fixed by a toothed lift-cord lock; when the cord is pulled diagonally, the teeth clamp it in place.

To dismantle a Venetian blind, remove the clamps or staples that fasten the tapes to the bottom slat or bar. Untie the knots at the ends of the lift cord and pull this cord free from the slats and pulleys. Pull the slats horizontally out of the tapes and detach the tapes from the tilt rod. For reassembly, reverse the procedure.

Diagnosing Venetian-Blind Troubles

Symptoms	Causes	Remedies
Bottom slats not horizontal	Lift cord misaligned	Raise or lower one side of lift cord until slats are level; set new alignment with equalizer catch
Slats do not tilt	Tilt cord not aligned in pulley	Rethread cord
	Tapes disengaged from tilt rod	Clip tapes to tilt tubes (metal blinds); staple tapes to tilt rod (wooden blinds)
	Worm gear sticks	Lubricate gear with light oil
	Worm wheel teeth disengaged from worm gear	Turn wheel by hand until teeth catch in gear
	Worm wheel or tilt rod is out of guides	Reposition wheel or rod
Lift cord does not lock	Incorrect operation of blind	Pull and release cord diagonally on one side, then the other to find position of lock
	Cord out of lift-cord lock	Rethread cord
Lift-cord lock catches too often or blind cannot be lowered	Incorrect operation of blind	Pull cord straight down and guide it straight up

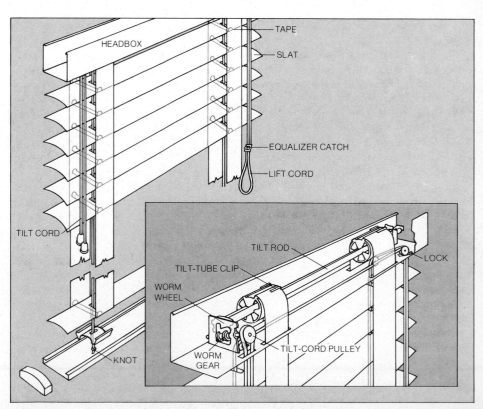

TAPE
SLAT
HEADBOX
EQUALIZER CATCH
LIFT CORD
TILT CORD
KNOT
TILT ROD
TILT-TUBE CLIP
WORM WHEEL
WORM GEAR
TILT-CORD PULLEY
LOCK

Common Shutter Repairs

Because they are constantly adjusted to regulate light and provide privacy, interior wooden shutters are chronic candidates for surgery—but the surgery is generally minor. For example, the job of refastening a loose louver to the rod that sets the tilt of the louvers can be done without removing the shutter from its hinges. If the U-shaped pin that holds the louver to the rod has worked loose and fallen off, a thicker replacement pin, available from hardware stores, can be driven into the old pinholes.

Repairing a sagging shutter is almost as simple. Take the shutter from its hinges, unscrew the hinge plate, and plug the screw holes with wood filler or a matchstick, then screw the hinge plate back into place. The only special tool you may need for repairs is a set of bar clamps—clamps that adjust for length by sliding along a steel bar or piece of pipe—if you must reglue loose joints.

Shutters can, of course, be improved as well as repaired. To give shutters additional support and prevent them from sagging, professionals fasten thin rubber bumpers to the bottom of each panel, so that the window stool as well as the hinges supports the closed shutters. Use white bumpers to avoid smudging the stool.

Exterior wooden shutters are simpler in every way: they rarely have movable louvers and generally are nailed to the exterior walls to serve a purely decorative function. If a hinged exterior shutter sags, fill the screw holes of the hinges as you would on an interior shutter; if it does not close securely, install a hook-and-catch lock on the shutter and stool.

Anatomy of an interior shutter. Each panel of this two-tiered set of shutters consists of a glued frame and a set of movable louvers; other types have fixed louvers. In each tier, the panels are hinged to each other; the panel at the edge of the window is also hinged to a hanging strip that is attached to the window jamb. Pegs fitted into holes in the shutter frame support movable louvers; compression springs in two peg holes (inset) hold the louvers at the angle set by a tilt rod, which is attached to all the louvers by a set of U-shaped pins.

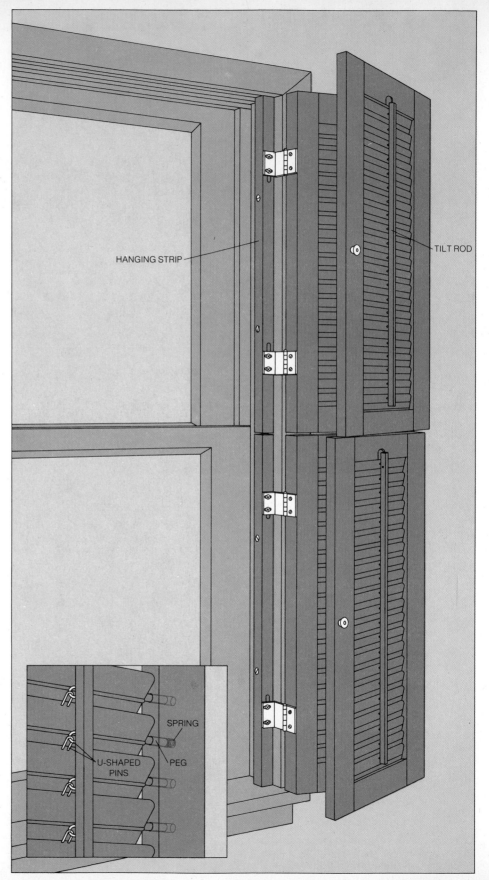

HANGING STRIP

TILT ROD

SPRING

U-SHAPED PINS

PEG

Fixing Pins, Pegs and Joints

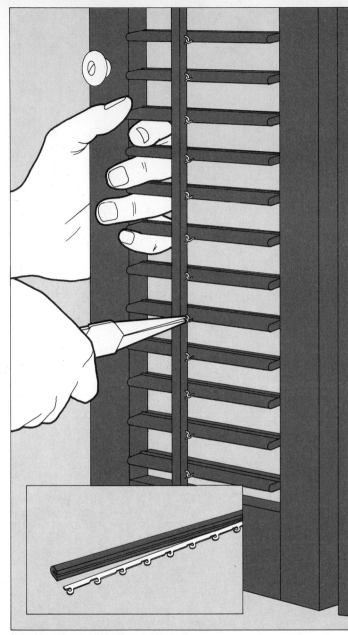

Replacing a broken louver peg. Unhook the louver from the tilt rod, pull it out of the shutter frame, and drill a ⅛-inch hole in the peg stub for the narrow end of a special replacement peg. Insert a spring and the new peg, wide end first, into the frame hole, holding the peg flush to the edge of the frame with a utility knife. Then slip the other peg into place on the opposite side of the frame, align the louver with the hole containing the spring and peg, and slide the knife out; the spring will push the replacement peg partway into the new hole in the louver.

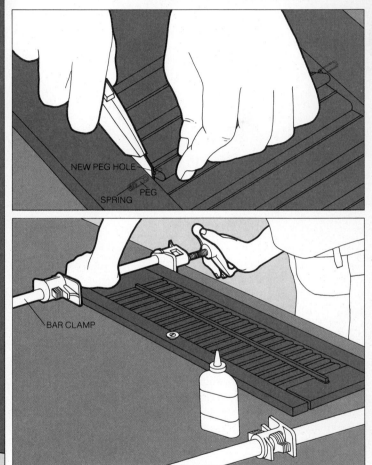

Attaching louvers to a tilt rod. Set the louvers individually to a horizontal position and hold the flat side of the tilt rod against them. If the rod is wood, hold the louvers in place with the fingers of one hand, then use long-nose pliers to push new U-shaped pins through the rod pins and secure them in the louver pinholes. Replace rod pins in the same way.

Your tilt rod may consist of a one-piece, looped aluminum strip set in a wooden shaft *(inset)*. If a loop snaps off or is badly bent, bend all the loops open with long-nose pliers and remove the tilt rod. Pull the strip out of its channel in the rod, slide a new strip into place and, one by one, bend the strip loops over the louver pins.

Gluing loose joints. With the panel off its hinges, clamp the end opposite the loose joint and check the fit of the louver pegs in the sides of the frame; the best tool for clamping is the bar clamp illustrated. Replace missing compression springs, then push the frame together, leaving just enough space for the tip of a glue dispenser, and coat both sides of the loose joint with glue. Clamp the frame tightly, using a second clamp at the glued end, and wipe off excess glue immediately. Leave the clamps in place until the glue dries—usually overnight.

The Glazier's Craft: Cutting and Setting Glass

Someday, by the law of averages, a budding Babe Ruth will drive a baseball through your picture window. If you learn a few tricks of reglazing, you will be able to easily replace the shattered pane. And using the same basic glazing techniques, you may even be able to refit your windows with insulated, or double-glazed, glass—two panes sealed at the edges, with an insulating air space between them. The insulated glass panes usually require a sash channel at least 1 inch wide; although they come in a range of precut sizes, panes generally must be custom-made. Single-glazed panes are cut to size by most hardware stores, but it may be more convenient and economical to cut your own.

Special tools for working with glass include a glass cutter (a carbide scoring wheel holds an edge better than a wheel of tungsten steel) and a pair of wide-nose glass pliers (page 103, Step 2). To install a pane in a wooden sash, you will need wedge-shaped fasteners called glazier's points to hold the pane in place, linseed oil to soften old putty and coat the inside of the frame (uncoated wood draws oil from new glazing compound and makes it brittle), and glazing compound to cushion the glass in the frame and make a watertight seal.

Use a latex-base compound to glaze insulated glass—though oil-base compounds are less expensive, they rot the sealant that holds the double panes together. For a metal sash, you generally need spring clips (page 105, top) rather than glazier's points; some models require gaskets or moldings.

Before you cut a windowpane, practice on scrap glass to get a feel for the amount of pressure needed to score the glass for a clean cut. Too much pressure will crack the glass; too little will not score it. A rasping sound as you draw the cutter across the glass indicates that the pressure you are exerting is right.

To determine the size of a replacement pane, measure the inside of the frame after you have removed the remains of the old pane and all old putty, then subtract ¼ inch from the width and ⅛ inch from the height to allow for expansion. Have a professional make any cut longer than four feet: Beyond that length, glass is difficult to handle.

Safety Tips for Working with Glass

Cutting and handling glass are not dangerous if you take the following precautions:

☐ Wear heavy leather work gloves when handling loose panes or fragments of glass.

☐ Wear safety goggles when removing broken glass or cutting glass.

☐ Work with a helper whenever you carry panes larger than 4 by 4 feet.

☐ Transport glass in several layers of newspaper on a padded surface (an old rug will do). Secure the pane by wedging a pillow at each side.

☐ Have a professional deliver any pane you cannot lay flat in your car.

☐ Before storing panes, mark them with a grease pencil or masking tape so they are easily seen.

☐ Cut glass on a padded surface.

☐ Immediately after cutting glass, brush fragments off the work surface.

☐ If the window is in a hard-to-reach location, remove the sash (page 67) and work on a flat surface.

Clearing the Frame

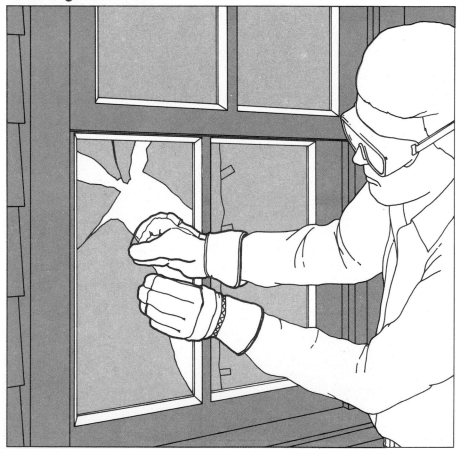

1 **Removing broken glass.** Tape newspaper to the inside of the frame to catch glass fragments; then, from outside the house, work the shards of glass back and forth to free them.

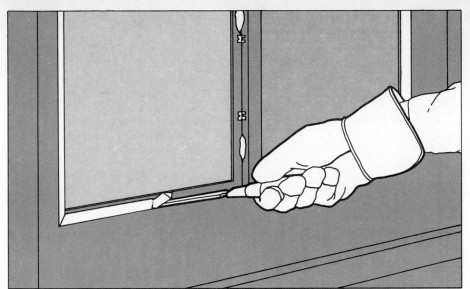

2 Removing glazing compound. Brush the old glazing compound with linseed oil, let the oil soak in for a half hour, then scrape off the softened compound with a wood chisel.

If oil does not soften the compound sufficiently, run the tip of a heated soldering iron lightly back and forth along the compound or heat the compound with a heat gun; then scrape the sash clean with the chisel. Caution: do not touch the tip of the iron to the sash. Do not use a blowtorch to soften the old glazing.

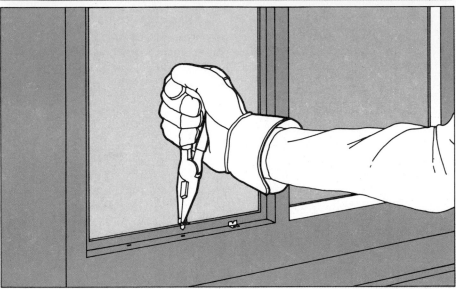

3 Smoothing the channel. Pull the glazier's points out of the frame with long-nose pliers and remove loose fragments of glass and glazing compound with a wire brush. Sand the channel smooth and brush it with linseed oil.

Cutting a Rectangular Pane

1 Scoring the glass. Lay the glass on a padded surface, such as a scrap of carpet or a sheet of thin foam rubber. Brush linseed oil on the area to be scored and set a straightedge along the cut line. Slanting the cutter toward you and holding it between your first and second fingers, pull it along the straightedge, starting about $1/16$ inch from the edge of the glass, to score the glass in one smooth motion. Caution: do not go back over the score line—a double score will cause the glass to break with an uneven edge.

2 **Deepening the score line.** While a helper tilts one edge of the pane up from the work surface, tap the glass lightly along the underside of the score line with the ball at the end of the glass cutter; the blows will deepen the score. Then proceed to Step 3 immediately.

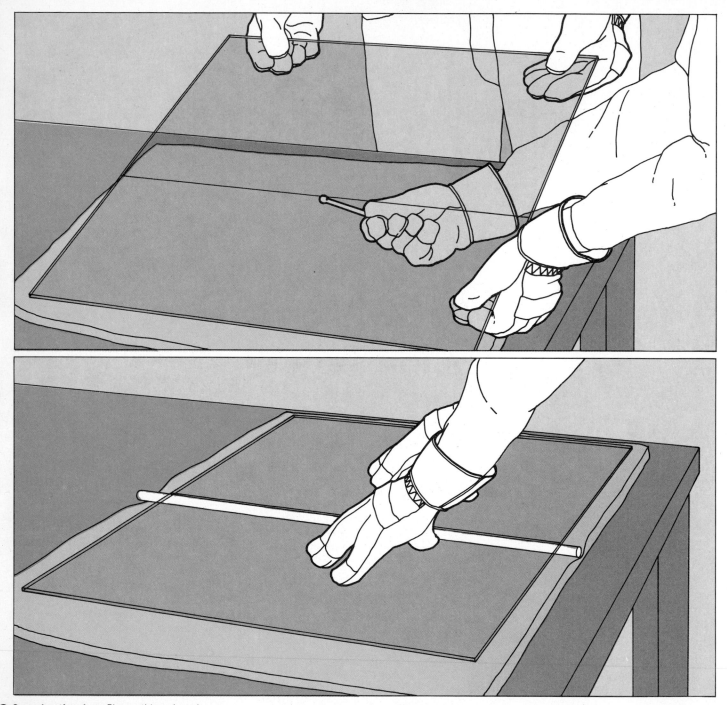

3 **Snapping the glass.** Place a thin rod, such as a dowel—at least as long as the score line—on the work surface. Position the score line directly over the rod and press down firmly on both sides of the score; the glass should snap cleanly. Use 240-grit silicon-carbide sandpaper or an emery stone to smooth the new edge.

A Template for a Curved Cut

1 Making the score. Cut a hardboard template to the desired shape of the pane and set it on the glass; for the most common type of curved pane, which has one straight edge, align the template's straight side with the edge of the glass. While a helper holds the template firmly with both hands, make the score in a single motion from one end of the curve to the other.

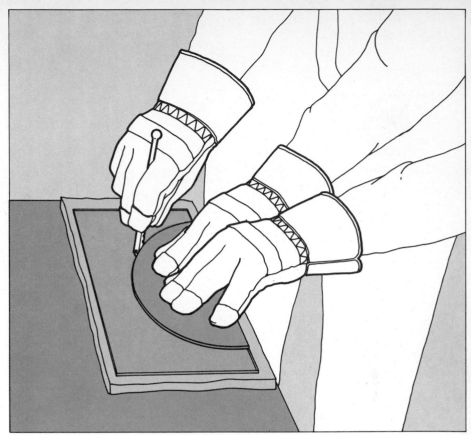

2 Snapping the curve. Scribe several radiating scores from the curve to the edge of the glass and tap under all the score lines *(opposite, Step 2)*; then hold one edge of the glass over the end of the worktable and snap off the scored segments with a pair of glass pliers. Smooth the edge with sandpaper or emery stone.

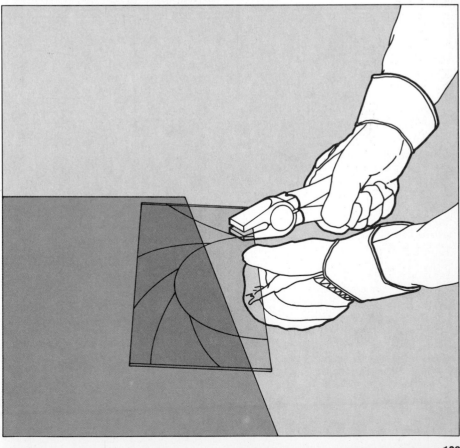

Setting Glass in a Wooden Sash

1 **Lining the frame.** Roll glazing compound between your palms into strips about ¼ inch thick and press the strips into the channels in which the pane of glass will rest. Add more compound until you have filled the channels completely.

2 **Securing the glass.** Press the pane of glass firmly into the glazing compound and scrape off excess compound with a utility knife or a razor blade; then fasten the pane securely in place with glazier's points pushed into the frame with a putty knife. Use two points on each edge for a frame up to 10 inches square, one point every 4 inches for a larger frame.

3 **Beveling the glazing compound.** Press additional strips of glazing compound around the frame, then smooth the strips with a putty knife into a neat bevel that runs from the face of a sash or a muntin (sash divider) onto the glass. As you work, dip the knife in water from time to time to prevent it from sticking to the compound. When the compound has hardened—in five to seven days—paint it to match the frame, extending the coat of paint 1/16 inch onto the glass for a weathertight seal.

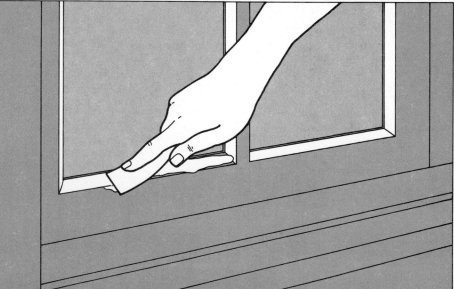

Three Ways of Glazing a Metal Sash

A set of spring clips. Some windows have flexible V-shaped metal clips to secure the glass, instead of glazier's points. With such a window, work on the inside of the frame; take out the old glass and glazing compound *(pages 100-101)* and remove the spring clips that secure the glass by pinching them and pulling them out of the holes in the frame. Paint the empty channel. When the paint has dried, lay a thin bead of glazing compound in the channel, then press the new pane firmly into the compound and replace the spring clips. Seal the pane with a bevel of glazing compound *(opposite, Step 3)*.

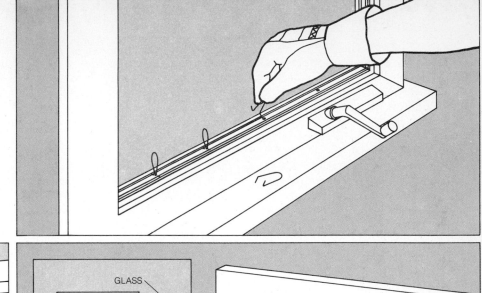

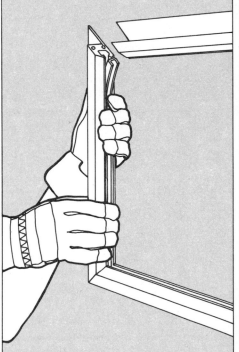

GLASS

MOLDING

CHANNEL

Rubber gaskets. In some metal windows, the glass rests in four rubber gaskets, U-shaped in cross section, and the sash comes apart for removal of the gaskets and glass. The model shown has screws at the top and bottom of one vertical edge of the sash. From outside the house, unfasten the screws and pull the side piece from the rest of the frame, remove the old glass from the gaskets, brushing out fragments with a wire brush, and pull the gaskets out of their channels. Fit the gaskets on the new pane, slide the pane into the frame and refasten the side piece. In another popular model, the gaskets are sandwiched between the halves of a split sash, and the retaining screws are at the corners of the sash face. In this type, replacement of the glass is done from inside. Remove the screws and pull the inner half of the sash away to get at the gaskets and glass.

Snap-out plastic moldings. Insulated glass is secured in a common type of metal window by four beveled moldings *(inset)* that snap into channels in the frame. When the glass must be replaced, put on gloves, remove any broken glass, then loosen the end of one piece of molding by inserting the tip of a putty knife where two strips meet; pull the strip from the channel with

your hands. Remove the other strips in the same way. Brush loose glass from the frame and set the new pane in place. Then push the beveled sides of the two short moldings into their channels, one at a time, pressing them into place with your fingers; fit the long strips last. If the moldings show even slight damage, install replacements, available at glass dealers.

Making Cloudy Glass Perfectly Clear

Washing glass can be one of the easiest of chores and often one of the most time-consuming. If the area is small, as with a tabletop or a mirror, cleaning is a simple matter of spraying on a commercial window cleaner and wiping it off with a lint-free cloth. Even a delicate crystal chandelier comes clean easily with a spray sold by lamp-supply stores *(opposite, bottom)*. This product spares you the tedium of dismantling and washing the fixture, crystal by fragile crystal.

Washing the windows in an average house is a much more formidable task, involving hundreds of square feet of glass. And, of course, every window has two sides—one of which is often hard to reach. In addition, the presence of storm windows doubles the work. Little wonder that cleaning women traditionally announce that they "do not do windows."

With the right tool, however—the squeegee used by professional window washers—the job is not all that difficult. A good-quality squeegee has two rubber blades locked in a metal housing. The blades have knife-sharp edges, which is what makes them so effective; professional window washers, who are rather particular about their squeegees, replace the blades for every house.

Squeegees come in various lengths. Choose one wide enough to cover 60 to 70 per cent of the window, so that only two vertical strokes are necessary to cover the entire surface *(below)*. Very large windows are squeegeed with a continuous sideways motion, without lifting the blade from the glass *(opposite, top left)*.

Corners and edges missed by the squeegee are cleaned with a chamois or a soft lint-free cloth, such as an old cotton T-shirt or cotton knit underwear. Discarded newspaper, crumpled up, does an excellent job of wiping glass dry without leaving streaks.

Many sorts of cleaning liquid can be used. All the traditional grease-cutting agents—rubbing alcohol, vinegar, baking soda, borax, even baby powder—are effective when mixed with water. Professional window washers generally prefer ammonia or trisodium phosphate. For a 2½-gallon bucket, they recommend 6 ounces of ammonia or 1 tablespoon of trisodium phosphate. To make the squeegee glide more easily, they sometimes add ½ teaspoon of automatic-dishwasher detergent. In freezing weather, they also add automobile window-washing solvent, mixed as specified on the label.

The toughest job, say professionals, is removing screen rust—tiny specks of oxidized aluminum deposited on the glass by rain filtering through old aluminum screens. This gritty residue must be removed before the window can be squeegeed. Oven cleaner, sprayed on a very fine steel-wool pad and rubbed on the glass immediately, will remove these stubborn particles. Paint spatters, another common problem, must also be removed in advance: Just scrape the window with a razor blade or with a wallpaper-trimming knife.

Washing the outside of upper-story windows is customarily done by leaning out the window or using an extension ladder. But both approaches are risky. A less hazardous alternative is a pair of telescoping poles that extend to reach 30 feet above the ground. Available at stores that specialize in janitorial supplies, the poles can be fitted with a sponge, a squeegee, a chamois or a scraper.

Skylights can be cleaned only by climbing on the roof. Although some are glass, many skylights are made of plastic, which is softer than glass. Before you wash a skylight, dust off loose dirt; it could scratch a plastic surface during cleaning. Then sponge on the cleaner and wipe it dry with a chamois.

Getting Windows Clean with a Rubber Squeegee

Cleaning small windows. Sponge on just enough cleaning liquid to wet the entire window, then pull the squeegee straight down over half of the window *(above, left)*. To clean the other half of the window, slightly angle the blade of the squeegee as you descend, so that the excess cleaning liquid is forced into the lower corner *(above, right)*. Then, using a chamois or a lint-free cloth, wipe off the edges of the glass and remove any drips from the window sill.

A clean sweep for large windows. After sponging cleaning liquid onto the glass, squeegee the window in a continuous side-to-side motion (*arrows*). Begin by placing the squeegee against the upper edge of the window, with the blade vertical. Pull it toward the opposite edge and, as the blade approaches that edge, reverse direction by pivoting the squeegee. Without lifting the blade from the glass, continue sweeping back and forth, from edge to edge, until you reach the bottom of the window. Then turn the blade so that it is horizontal, to carry the liquid down to the window's lower edge. Wipe off all the edges and the sill with a chamois or a lint-free cloth.

Extension poles for high windows. To reach windows between 7 and 30 feet above the ground, use adjustable aluminum extension poles, twisting the collars of the poles (*inset*) to lock them at the desired length. Use two poles, if possible, fitting one with a sponge attachment, the other with a squeegee, and enlist the aid of a helper to handle one of the poles. With a single pole, you will have to change fittings constantly, and the liquid may dry in the time it takes to switch from sponge to squeegee.

COLLAR

The Quick Way to Clean a Crystal Chandelier

Spraying dirt off glass crystals. Move furniture out from under the chandelier, and spread a plastic dropcloth over the floor. Turn off the electricity to the chandelier at the light switch and allow the light bulbs to cool; then tighten the bulbs in their sockets. Working from a ladder or step stool placed to the side of the fixture, spray a chandelier cleaner onto the glass pendants until the liquid begins to drip. Allow the chandelier to dry before removing the dropcloth.

Furniture Repair

Good, solid, everyday furniture seldom lasts a lifetime. It gets sat upon, dined upon, leaned against, and occasionally stood upon. Over the years, as one guest too many tilts backward on a dining-room chair, or the scuffs and wet glass marks become too numerous on a coffee table, the piece gets tucked away in the attic or basement and is seldom used again.

Thanks to today's modern materials and improved methods of joinery, most damaged furniture can be rescued. The repairs can range from simple tasks such as regluing loose joints or hiding a scratch to more complex and time-consuming projects such as adding a mortised brace or inserting a dowel to support broken wood.

The decision whether to do the job yourself or turn it over to a professional depends, of course, on how much you like the piece, the use you will get out of it when it is repaired and the nature of the work involved. Sometimes replacement of a poorly made piece of furniture outweighs its potential for failure in the future. However, if the piece is a true antique—defined by the U.S. Customs Service as anything made before 1830, and more loosely as anything more than 100 years old—it should be restored by a specialist, since any repair could reduce its value.

Choosing a Glue and Making It Stick

A proper glue joint has five layers, as illustrated below, and the weakest of them determines the strength of the joint. In earlier times the weakest layer was the glue, but more modern glues are so strong that the surrounding wood usually breaks before the glue or the intermediate layers of glue-soaked fibers.

In order to make a well-bonded joint, you must clean the two abutting wood surfaces of old glue, dirt and finish. If the wood is moistened in the process of removing old glue, allow it to dry. Shape the joint so the fit is tight, leaving no gaps.

In addition, apply only enough pressure to the joint to force the glue into the fibers of the wood; too much pressure will force the glue out and starve the joint. Usually you should preassemble the joint dry and clamp it, to make sure that the wood surfaces fit and that you have enough clamps. Then dismantle the joint and apply thin layers of glue to both surfaces—on end grain apply a slightly thicker layer than on side grain, which is less absorbent. Reassemble the joint, clamp it and wipe it clean—first with a damp cloth, then with a dry one. Immediately check the joint to make certain that the alignment is correct.

Choice of glue depends partly on the piece of furniture and where it will be used, and partly on preference—even professionals differ on which glues are best to use for furniture joinery. The following glues are most favored by furniture-repair professionals.

☐ WHITE GLUE, also known as polyvinyl acetate, is a good general adhesive for most indoor furniture but is not recommended for outdoor furniture. It comes ready to use and, once clamped, sets in 30 minutes, although it should remain undisturbed until it reaches full strength in two days. It need be applied to only one surface of the adjoining pieces unless the joint has gaps, in which case it should be applied to both of the surfaces.

☐ YELLOW GLUE, also called aliphatic resin, is an improved offspring of the white variety. Slightly stronger and more resistant to moisture, it is also more viscous and dribbles less when applied. But it begins to dry faster than white glue and thus requires swifter clamping. The clamps can be removed after 30 minutes, but the joint should remain undisturbed until it reaches full strength 18 hours later. Yellow glue has good gap-filling properties and is specially good for ill-fitting joints.

☐ HIDE GLUE is made from animal hides. As restorers of antiques are quick

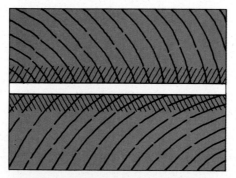

A proper glue joint. A glue joint has five layers: a thin film of glue, two areas (one on either side) consisting of wood fibers penetrated by glue, and the nearby wood that is unpenetrated. Chemical bonding between the wood fibers and the glue locks the wood pieces together.

to point out, the glue is reversible; steam and a sun lamp will undo the adhering properties of the glue, allowing a joint to be taken apart. In addition, liquid hide glue allows ample time—up to 20 minutes—for clamping before the glue begins to set. But it can be applied only at temperatures near 70° F., it stiffens in temperatures lower than 50° and thins in temperatures higher than 90°. Joints assembled with hide glue must remain clamped for six to 12 hours, and it cannot be used for outdoor furniture.

☐ PLASTIC-RESIN GLUE, sometimes called urea-formaldehyde, is very strong and is used on joints subject to unusual stress. It comes as a powder that must be mixed with water, but once it has dried, the glue is highly resistant to moisture. Plastic-resin glue must be applied at temperatures higher than 70° F. It starts to set in five to 15 minutes and, once clamped, it must be kept under pressure for five to 12 hours, depending on the temperature. It does not fill gaps well, so the joints must be tight.

☐ RESORCINOL GLUE is prepared by mixing a powder with a liquid catalyst. It is very strong, has the highest resistance to heat and moisture—it is even used in boatbuilding—and is the best glue for repairing outdoor wood furniture. It should be applied at room temperature and left clamped for 10 to 12 hours.

☐ OTHER ADHESIVES. The familiar epoxy glues work chemically to form a strong bond between pieces of wood as well as such nonporous materials as metal or glass. The contact cements, such as those used to laminate thin sheets of plastic to countertops, set almost instantly; they allow no time for adjustments when the joints are glued.

Restoring Separated Joints in Wooden Chairs

Chairs have more joints than most other kinds of furniture, and they are joints that have to work hard. Even a lightweight ballerina puts stress on a chair's joints when she sits. If a man tilts the chair back and hooks his heels over a footrail, the stress is multiplied. Sooner or later, a joint works loose or separates altogether.

A weak joint should be strengthened, and the sooner the better. One bad joint puts increased stress on the remaining good joints, and if too many joints loosen, the entire chair will have to be disassembled. This is a prospect to be avoided if possible, because pulling joints apart can sometimes lead to further damage. You should, in fact, break down a chair into as few subassemblies as the repair permits and, if you can, correct loosened joints without separating them.

Although innumerable joints are used in chair construction, the two most commonly encountered are dowel joints and mortise-and-tenon joints. For a dowel joint, one end of a chair member is fitted with a separate dowel or is lathed into a dowel shape. The dowel fits into a socket in a second member.

A mortise-and-tenon joint is the rectangular equivalent of a dowel joint. Here, too, there are two basic styles. In one, the rectangular member is the tenon and fits into a mortise cut into a larger member. In the other, one end of the rectangular member is cut smaller to form a tenon that is said to be haunched—and the haunch can be cut into any one or all four sides of the member, depending on the design of the chair and the whim of the woodworker.

Both dowel joints and mortise-and-tenon joints must fit tightly for the joint to be strong. Although glue alone ordinarily holds joints together, sometimes a wedge has been added to fill a gap, and in some cases a brad or dowel has been driven into the side of the joint to reinforce it further. All these supports must be removed when the joint is repaired, a job that is not always easy. In fact, you may have to balance your wish for a solid chair against the risk of damage during disassembly. For a prized piece that is intact, albeit wobbly, it may be best to settle for stopgap repairs, then go easy on the chair, instead of restoring the joint.

Glue, wedges and dowels also figure prominently in the repertoire of techniques used to fix joints that have failed. Tools for these projects are, for the most part, simple. A wooden mallet or a hammer and a block of wood with sheet cork glued to one face are needed for disassembly. Straps that tighten like seat belts, called web clamps, hold repaired joints in place while the glue dries.

A platform chair. In chairs of this design—an elaboration of a simple stool—the seat is the nucleus of the structure, and the back and leg assemblies are attached to the seat and are completely independent of each other. The leg assembly ordinarily consists of four leg stiles, fitted into sockets on the bottom of the seat and reinforced with horizontal members called footrails. In the back assembly of a platform chair, a back stile supports each end of a top rail, and intermediary spindle stiles fill in the back and further reinforce the top rail.

Chairs of this type are often assembled entirely with dowel joints that have the dowels turned directly onto the ends of the members. The joints between the footrails and the leg stiles are generally the most vulnerable.

A frame chair. In chairs of this construction, the seat is in effect suspended in a wooden frame and is not a critical part of the support structure. Instead, the design centers on the two main stiles that run from the top to the bottom of the chair back, forming the rear legs and the back of the chair. Usually each of these stiles is a single piece of wood. The seat is commonly a separate element, resting on four seat rails. The front legs are joined to the side seat rails, and may be reinforced with footrails on all four sides. The main stiles are joined with a top rail and one or more back rails. When there is only a single back rail, a flat wood member, called a splat, may be inserted between the top and back rails. In many chairs of this design, the seat is upholstered or made of rush or cane.

In addition to dowel joints, frame chairs often have mortise-and-tenon joints where the seat rails meet the legs. On some, screws are used to hold the parts together. Generally the joints at the back of the seat, where the side seat rails meet the main stiles, are most vulnerable.

Four Kinds of Joint Locks

Looking for obstacles. Before pulling a loose joint apart to make repairs, examine it to see if there is a fastener that you must first remove. Sometimes you must look for subtle clues. A dimple in the wood finish near the joint, for instance, may indicate that a brad is securing the end of a dowel *(near right, top)*. More obvious is a dowel that pins a mortise-and-tenon joint together *(far right, top)*, since its end is exposed.

Cracks around a joint often signal situations in which the joint should not be pulled apart. Hairline cracks on the sides of a dowel at the point where it emerges from its socket *(near right, bottom)* generally mean that the dowel has been wedged. Pulling such a joint apart may split the socket. In old furniture, cracks above and below a socket where a dowel enters an oval stile or rail are typical of a special joint called a shrink joint *(far right, bottom)*. In this older version of a dowel joint, a knobbed end of dry wood was fitted into a socket while the socketed member was still green. Since the socket then shrank around the knob as it dried, disassembling these joints probably will split the wood.

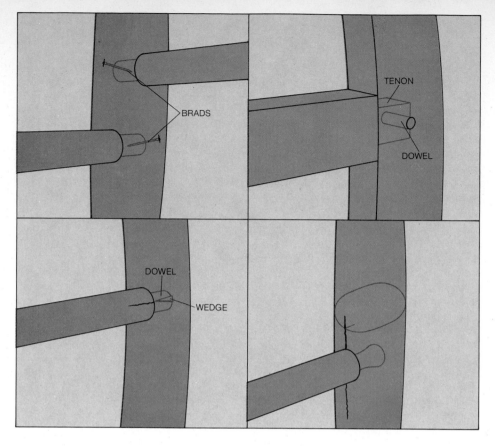

Regluing Loose Dowel Joints

1 Injecting glue. Pull the joint apart slightly and drill a perpendicular hole, slightly larger than the tip of a syringe-type glue injector, into the back of the dowel socket. Jam the tip of the injector into the hole, and squeeze the plunger until glue appears all around the dowel. You may have to drill and inject glue into a second hole if it is difficult to get glue into the first one or if the glue comes out on only one side of the dowel. Smear glue over the exposed section of the dowel, and press the joint back together again. Use wood filler to conceal the hole.

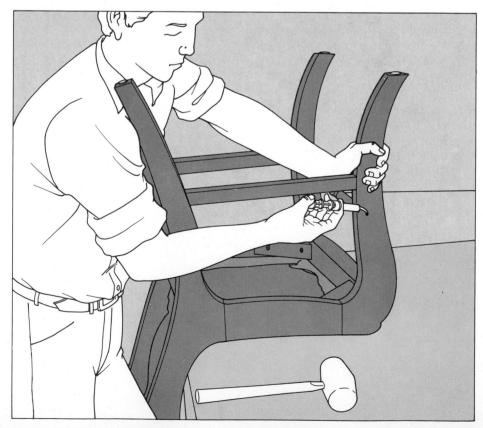

2 Using a web clamp. With the dowel in its socket, assemble a web clamp following the manufacturer's instructions, and loop it around the chair so that the loose joint will be forced together when the clamp is tightened. Rest sticks across rails or stiles as needed, to keep the web strap in place as the clamp is tightened (*inset*). Tighten the winch nut of the clamp with a screwdriver or a socket wrench; if you use a wrench, which is usually easier, tighten the nut only as much as you could if you were using a screwdriver. Tap the joint lightly with a mallet to make sure the dowel is completely seated. Let the glue dry before removing the clamp.

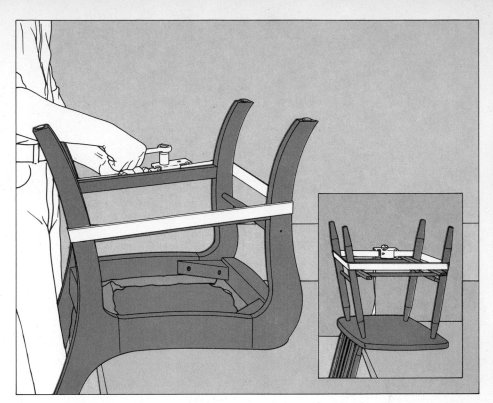

Wedging a Loose Mortise-and-Tenon Joint

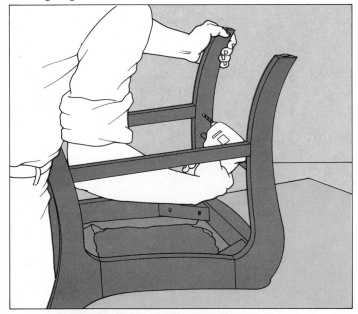

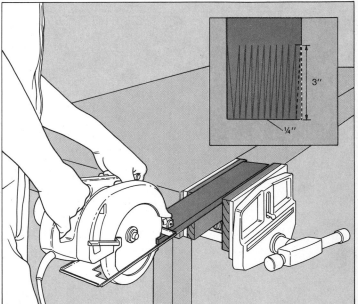

1 Drilling out a dowel pin. When a haunched tenon pinned with a dowel is loose, use an awl to make a starting hole for a drill bit in the center of the dowel. Then drill the dowel out, using a bit that has a diameter slightly greater than that of the dowel. If the tenon is not haunched, do not drill out the dowel; instead, fit wedges around the tenon to tighten it (*Steps 2 and 3*).

2 Making wedges. Use a table saw, radial-arm saw or portable circular saw to cut out hardwood wedges to fill the gaps around a loose tenon. If you use a circular saw, clamp the wood face up in a vise as shown here, and cut along the grain of the wood, not across it. Make wedges about 3 inches long, tapering from ¼ inch thick at the butt end to a sharp edge. For economical use of wood, alternate tapered cuts with straight cuts that square off the board again (*inset*).

3 Wedging the tenon. Pull the joint slightly apart, and trim thin wedges to fit the gap between the tenon and its mortise. For very loose joints, use wedges on all four sides to keep the mortise and tenon in alignment; for a joint only slightly loose, one wedge is sufficient. Inject glue into the back of the joint *(page 110, Step 1)*, and smear glue on the exposed part of the tenon. Coat both sides of each wedge with glue by sliding the wedge through a puddle of glue on a scrap of wood. Insert the wedges into the gaps around the tenon, and press the joint together to seat it. On a haunched tenon, as shown, the shoulders of wood will drive the wedges into place. On an unhaunched tenon, use a mallet and a small wood block to drive in the wedges. Clamp the joint *(page 111)* until the glue dries.

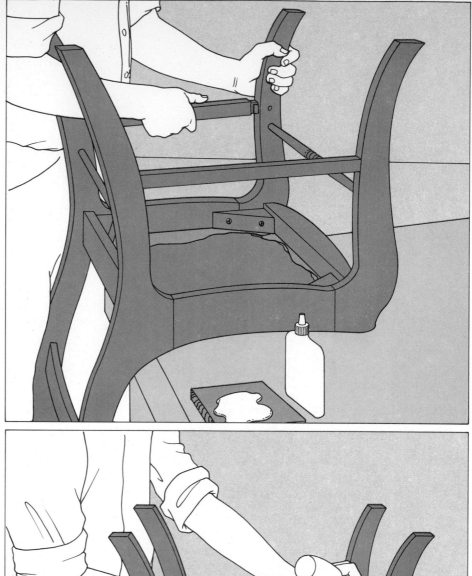

4 Pinning the joint. If you removed a dowel to release the joint *(page 111, Step 1)*, cut a new dowel of the same diameter as the drill bit you used but slightly longer than the depth of the hole. Bevel one end of the dowel to make it easier to insert. Use a stick to spread glue inside the hole; apply more glue to the dowel, and tap the dowel into the hole with a mallet. Let the glue dry, then sand the end of the dowel flush with the surrounding wood surface. Finish the end of the dowel to match the rest of the chair.

If necessary, use the same technique to add a dowel pin to a mortise-and-tenon joint that does not already have one. Drill the hole for the dowel after the glue in the wedged joint is dry.

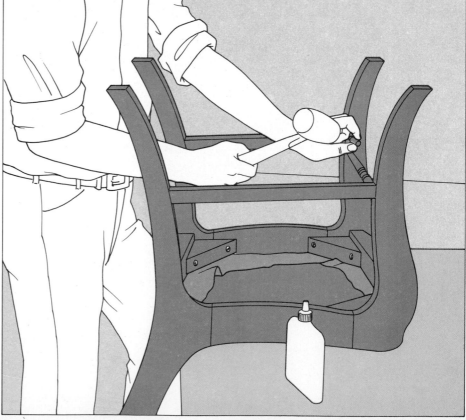

Techniques for Taking a Chair Apart

Using a mallet to loosen joints. With a mallet or hammer, break the bond of glue that holds the parts together. Label each part, as a guide for reassembly. Use a block faced with cork to protect the striking area, and lift that area of the chair slightly. Use blows of moderate force, then try levering (*below, right*) if necessary.

Separate the parts of a platform chair by first releasing the leg or back assembly from the seat, as shown below; then take apart the subassemblies as needed. On a frame chair, begin by separating the main stiles, as shown below, right, if they are loose; then proceed to the subassemblies. If the main stiles are not loose, separate only the parts with loose joints.

Using leverage to loosen joints. Cut two pieces of wood, the sum of whose lengths is slightly longer than the distance between the parts to be separated. Trim one end of each piece into a cup shape, to keep the pieces from slipping off the work, and cut a V and an inverted V in the other ends, to join the two pieces where they meet in the middle. Position this lever so that its outer ends are as close as possible to the joints that are to be opened, and place cork pads between the ends and the chair to protect the finish. Apply force gradually with your hand, to straighten the joint in the middle of the lever. To apply force over spans of other lengths, construct another two-part lever or recombine the halves of two different levers.

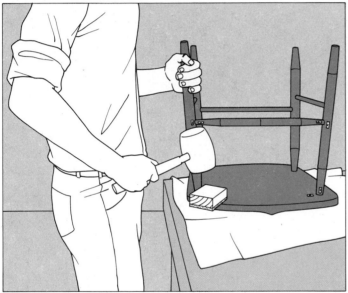
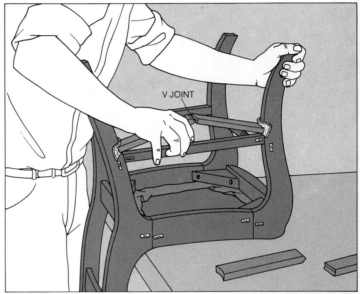

Refitting Dowels in a Disassembled Chair

1 Scraping glue from the dowel. Using a knife, paint scraper or rough textured file, scrape the old glue from the surface of the doweled end. If using a knife, hold it perpendicular to the wood, but tip the back of the knife slightly forward as shown, so that you will be dragging the blade across the surface of the wood. Use as much force as needed to remove the dried glue without digging into the wood.

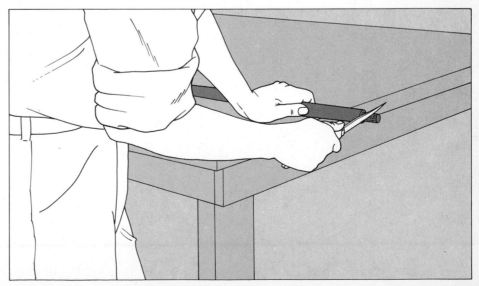

2 **Preparing the socket.** Wrap the socketed part of the chair in cork to protect its finish, and clamp it in a vise, socket up. Reach inside the socket with a ¼-inch chisel, held with the side of the blade against the side of the socket, and scrape out the old glue. Then enlarge the bottom of the socket slightly so that there will be enough room for the wedged dowel to expand.

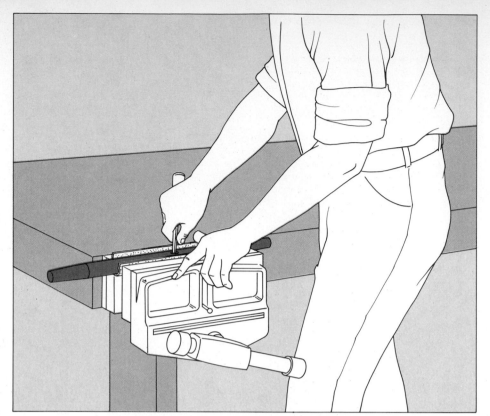

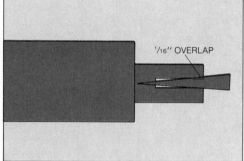

1/16" OVERLAP

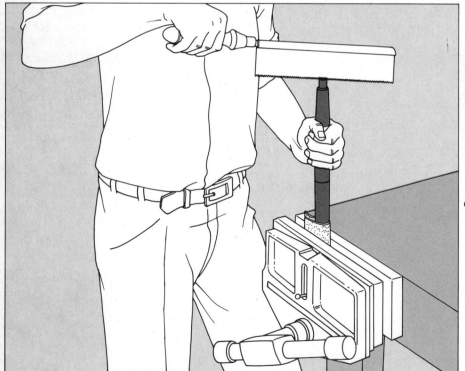

3 **Cutting a kerf in the dowel.** Use a dovetail saw or a small backsaw to cut the kerf, or slot, in the end of the dowel, stopping just short of where the kerf would be visible once the joint is assembled. Orient the cut so that the kerf will form a right angle with the grain of the socketed part.

4 **Wedging the dowel.** Cut a hardwood wedge (page 111), and fit it to the kerf in the dowel so that the end of the dowel will spread out slightly when the joint is assembled. First measure the depth of the socket and the length of the dowel to find the clearance between the end of the dowel and the bottom of the socket, usually about ⅛ inch. Then hold the wedge alongside the kerf, tapered end pointing toward the bottom of the kerf. Position the wedge so that its thickness where it passes the end of the dowel is no more than 1/16 inch greater than the width of the kerf; otherwise, you risk splitting the dowel.

Mark the wedge just beyond the end of the dowel; mark the other end of the wedge just short of the bottom of the kerf. Cut the wedge at these two marks. Temporarily secure the wedge to the dowel with a rubber band until you have dry-fitted the other joints and are ready to glue the chair back together (pages 116-117).

Replacing a Broken Dowel

1 **Drilling a hole for a new dowel.** To replace a broken dowel, saw off the broken end and sand it flush with the dowel shoulder. Dimple its center with an awl, then drill a hole for a new dowel. To drill, clamp the chair part (wrapped in a protective sheet of cork) in a vise, and, with a helper, align a $\frac{1}{16}$-inch bit to enter the wood at the same angle as the old dowel, which in most cases is parallel to the chair part. Drill a pilot hole with the $\frac{1}{16}$-inch bit, then use a larger bit to drill the hole to the same depth and diameter as the adjoining socket. Bevel a new dowel so it fits easily into the hole, and trim its extension to three quarters of the depth of the socket.

To replace a dowel that has broken off inside the end of the doweled piece, drill it out with progressively larger bits, starting with a $\frac{1}{16}$-inch bit, until the hole is the required size. If the broken doweled end of a part is simply a tapered extension of that part, it will probably be necessary to replace the whole part.

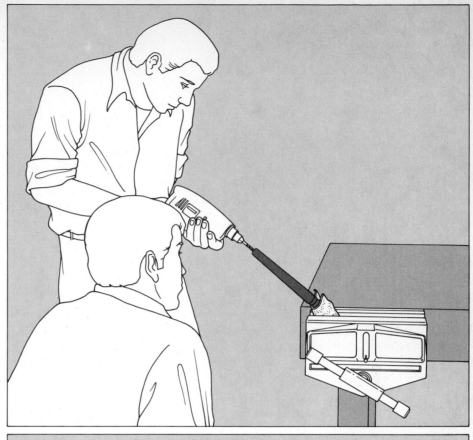

2 **Cleaning out the socket.** Saw, sand and drill out any broken dowel pieces left in the socket, using the same techniques and drill bits as in Step 1. Position the clamped chair part in the vise so that the socket is perpendicular to the top of the vise, regardless of the angle at which the dowel enters; to check the alignment, hold the joining piece—with its new dowel removed temporarily—in position against the socketed one.

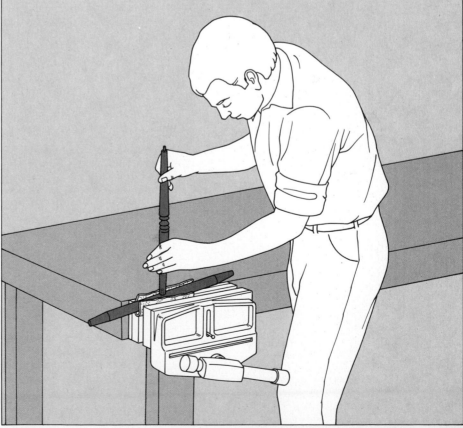

Using Shims to Enlarge a Loosened Tenon

Applying veneer shims. To refit a loose mortise-and-tenon joint, disassemble the joint and cut veneer shims to fit any or all sides of the tenon, depending on where the gaps fall; cut each shim slightly larger than the side of the tenon it will cover. Smear glue on the tenon and shim, and join the two; place a layer of wax paper over the glued shim, and clamp tenon and shim between two wood blocks until the glue dries. When attaching shims to opposite sides of a tenon, glue and clamp both sides as a unit. Remove the clamp and wax paper when the glue has dried, and trim off the excess veneer. Repeat for the tenon's opposite sides if necessary.

Test-fit the tenon in the mortise. If you cannot seat the joint using manual force, pull the tenon out and look for shiny areas where it is too tight. Sand and test again. Repeat as needed.

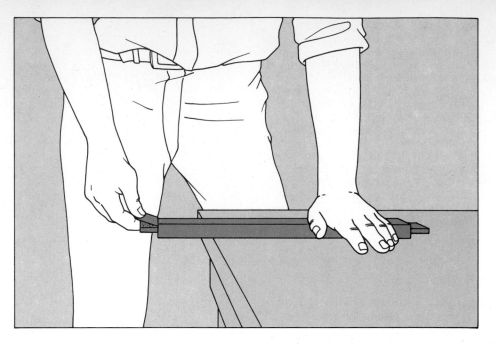

Reassembling a Platform Chair

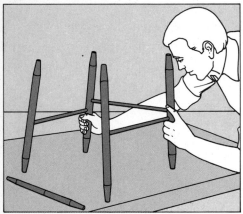

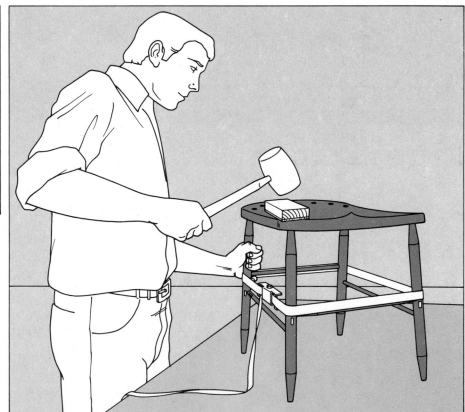

1 Assembling the legs and seat. Divide the reassembling of a platform chair into steps, and rehearse them first without glue or wedges, to prevent mishaps in the final assembly. If the chair has been completely disassembled, begin by reconstructing the legs and the seat. Make two H-shaped assemblies, each consisting of front and back leg stiles joined by a side footrail; then join the two Hs with front and back footrails. Next add the seat, and loop a web clamp around the assembly *(page 111)* to determine the best way to fit the clamp to the assembly.

Disassemble this portion of the chair and reassemble it in the same order, this time using glue and inserting wedges into any dowels that have been kerfed to receive them. Daub glue into sockets and mortises with a stick, smear it on dowels and tenons, and draw any wedges you are using through a puddle of glue poured onto a scrap of wood. Apply the web clamp, and proceed immediately to Step 2.

2 Leveling the chair. Place the assembled portion of the chair on a flat, level surface such as the top of a desk or a table saw. To check that the surface is absolutely flat, draw a metal straightedge across it twice, the second time perpendicular to the first, and look for gaps beneath the straightedge; there should be no gap greater than $1/16$ inch. Apply glue and, using a cork-faced block to protect the finish, strike the top of the seat over each leg with a mallet, to firm the legs in the sockets. Do the same for the joints between the rails and the leg stiles, tightening the web clamp around the legs as you go. Let the glue dry.

3 Attaching the back. Rehearse the back assembly of the chair without wedges or glue, as in Step 1, fitting the main stiles and spindle stiles into their sockets. Wrap two web clamps around the back and under the seat so that the clamp winches are behind the back. Then disassemble the back and repeat the procedure with glue, adding dowel wedges, if any. Alternately tighten the winches and tap the top rail with a mallet until all the stiles are set firmly in their sockets.

If the chair has arms, fit the horizontal arm members into the back stiles and the vertical arm members into the seat before joining the back assembly to the seat assembly. When you rehearse this final procedure, cut a temporary brace to fit exactly between the two arms near their front ends (*inset*). Wrap a web clamp under the seat and around the arms, just above where they join the seat, and use the brace to hold the arms apart while you tighten the clamp. For the back of the chair use a pair of web clamps, just as on an armless chair, but to avoid pulling the arms out of alignment position the winches in front of, not behind, the back.

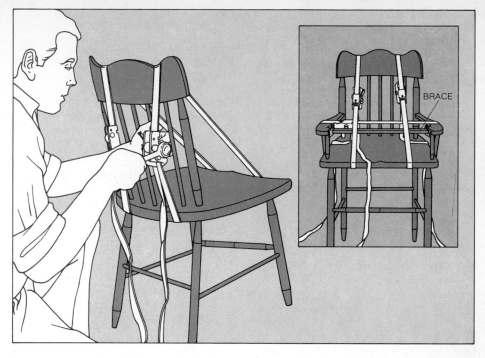

Reassembling a Frame Chair

Plotting the stages of reassembly. Rejoin the pieces of a frame chair into subassemblies, and test-fit them without glue or wedges; then repeat this procedure for the final assembly. Start gluing by joining the back stiles with their connecting rails, including the center splat, if there is one. Wrap one web clamp around this assembly just above the footrail and another just below the top rail. Alternately tighten the clamps and tap the joints with a mallet until they are firm. Lay the back assembly on a flat surface, and shift the parts until the back lies flat and the two diagonal measurements between the top of one main stile and the bottom of the opposite stile are the same. Allow the glue for this subassembly to dry before proceeding.

Assemble the front stiles and the rails that join them, then join the front and back assemblies with the side footrails and seat rails, and the arm parts if any. Position a web clamp around the legs of the chair halfway between the footrail and the seat rail. If the chair has arms, put a brace between the ends of the arms, and place a web clamp around the chair at arm level. If the arms consist of horizontal members joined to the vertical stiles with dowels or tenons, wrap another web clamp over the front ends of the arms and under the seat. Place the assembled chair on a flat, level work surface (*opposite, Step 2*). Tap with a mallet and tighten the clamps until all of the joints are firmly in place and all the legs touch the work surface. Allow the glue to dry before you remove the clamps.

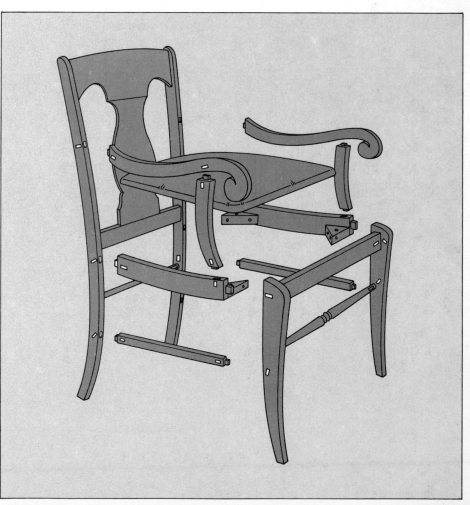

Restoring a Wobbly Table

Although a well-built table should last for many years, ordinary wear and tear frequently takes its toll, especially when the table is used for dining. The joints at the tops of legs are prime targets for trouble. Subjected to severe stress when the legs are kicked or the table is dragged across the floor, they may become loose or even break. Other commonly encountered problems are drop-leaf extensions that sag and sliding extension mechanisms that stick or break. Many of these flaws can be easily corrected.

Most tables intended for hard use are made with the top attached to an apron, a rectangular substructure of narrow boards permanently joined to the tops of the legs. In a few cases the apron is permanently joined to the top, and the legs are bolted to the apron. Simpler tables have legs attached directly to the underside of the top. These joints are held together by a variety of means, alone or in combination: glue, which may fail; tenons or dowels, which may break; clips,

screws or bolts, which may loosen. Glue bonds that fail are easily reglued—use techniques shown for similar chair joints *(pages 110-117)*— but in order to repair the more serious breaks in component parts, you may have to separate the joint and replace the broken parts. To complete the repair, you can reinforce joints by screwing on either metal corner plates or wood blocks.

Tables with moving parts that malfunction require other corrective measures. In most cases, you can treat a balky mechanism on an extension table by cleaning and lubricating the sliding parts, but if parts of the mechanism are broken, bent or missing, it may be necessary to replace them. The manufacturer or a hardware dealer can help you find new parts. For a sagging drop-leaf table, the simplest remedy is usually a wedge, which should be glued to the underside of the drop leaf to take up the slack.

For many of these repairs, it is helpful to have a glue injector to force glue into

a confined area. Clamps of one sort or another are also very important. You will need C clamps to close splits, while a pipe clamp—a pair of clamping devices mounted on a length of common iron pipe—is required to maintain pressure on glued apron-to-leg joints. Whenever you use clamps, pad their jaws with thin pieces of cork or other soft wood to avoid marring the surface of the piece you are clamping. Use only the minimum pressure needed to close the glued sections, since too much pressure may force out so much of the glue that you end up with a weak joint.

When the repair involves a broken joint that you intend to fix with a doweled butt joint *(page 120)*, you may want to invest in a doweling jig to guide the drill, and metal dowel centers; these tools, available at most hardware stores, ensure precise positioning and alignment of the dowel holes. Also helpful are specially grooved dowels, which make stronger glue bonds than smooth dowels.

Getting at a Damaged Substructure

Unscrewing the tabletop. To gain access to a broken joint, turn the table upside down atop several layers of cloth or a piece of rug, and remove the top. If the top is held in place with metal clips set into a groove, or kerf, in the apron *(right)*, remove the screws and clips to detach the top. If the top is attached with screws or bolts to the apron or to corner blocks, remove these fasteners *(insets)*. If the repair will require you to take the joints apart, use the disassembly techniques shown on page 113.

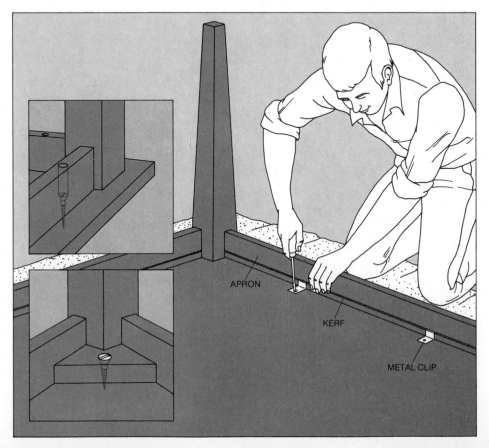

APRON

KERF

METAL CLIP

Analyzing the Leg-to-Apron Joints

Three types of joints. The most common permanent joint is a mortise and tenon, with a tenon (tongue) on the apron glued into a mortise (slot) on the leg (*left*). Possible damage includes a split at the mortise or a broken tenon.

Also common is a butt joint, which is usually reinforced with dowels that are glued into matching holes in each of the two pieces (*center*). These dowels may break; if they do, it will be nec-

essary to drill them out and replace them or to substitute a completely new dowel joint (*page 120, Step 2*). Butt joints with dowels are sometimes further reinforced by the addition of a corner plate or block (*page 121*); such a plate or block may also serve to strengthen a butt joint that is made without dowels.

If legs are connected to an apron by lap joints (*right*), the apron is glued and screwed to the out-

er face of each leg. The screwheads are sunk below the surface of the apron in counterbored holes filled with wood plugs or buttons. If the screws pull out of a leg, drill the plugs out of the apron, remove the screws, reglue the joint and use new screws of the same length but the next larger diameter. You may have to enlarge the upper parts of the holes counterbored for the screwheads, but do not redrill the lower parts, which are sized to fit the screw threads.

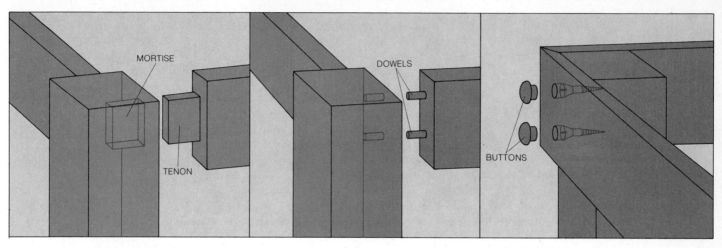

Closing a Split atop a Table Leg

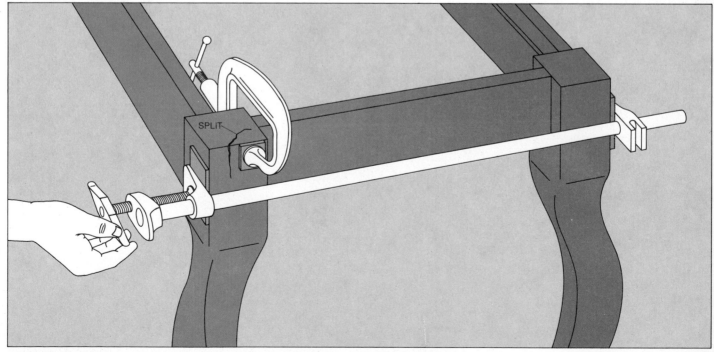

Gluing a split mortise. If a split occurs around the mortise at the top of a leg, inject yellow glue into the split as well as into the hairline opening between the mortise and tenon. Apply pressure with clamps. First put a C clamp across

the top of the leg to close the split; then put a pipe clamp across, extending from the outside of one leg to the outside of another, to hold the tenon in the mortise. Allow the glue to dry overnight before removing the clamps.

Repairs for a Broken Tenon

1 **Preparing for dowels.** When a tenon is badly cracked or broken, convert the joint to a doweled butt joint; first cut off the tenon and fill in the mortise. Use a fine-tooth crosscut saw—or better, a dovetail saw—to cut off the broken tenon flush with the end of the piece.

With a chisel, clear the mortise of glue and any pieces of broken tenon, then cut a wooden plug the same size as the mortise. Coat this plug with yellow glue and tap it into the mortise (*inset*). When the glue is dry, saw and sand away any wood protruding from the mortise.

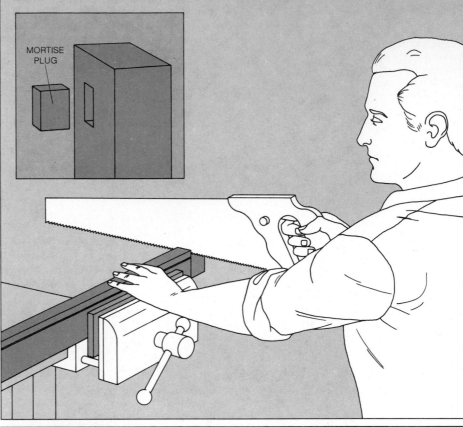

2 **Drilling and aligning dowel holes.** Mark two pencil lines across the end of the apron about one third of the way in from the top and the bottom. Center a dowel jig over one line and drill a $5/16$-inch hole $1\frac{1}{8}$ inch into the end of the apron. Repeat at the other line.

Insert the dowel centers into the holes, align the apron carefully in position at the top of the leg, and tap the other end of the apron with a rubber mallet, using enough force to push the tips of the dowel centers against the leg (*inset*) to leave marks. Use these marks to position the dowel jig, and drill two $5/16$-inch holes $1\frac{1}{8}$ inch into the side of the leg.

Spread a thin film of yellow glue on the end of the apron and on two $5/16$-inch dowels, each 2 inches long. Tap the dowels into the apron holes with the rubber mallet, then insert them into the leg holes and tap the apron into place. Apply pressure with a pipe clamp, as shown on page 119, until the glue dries.

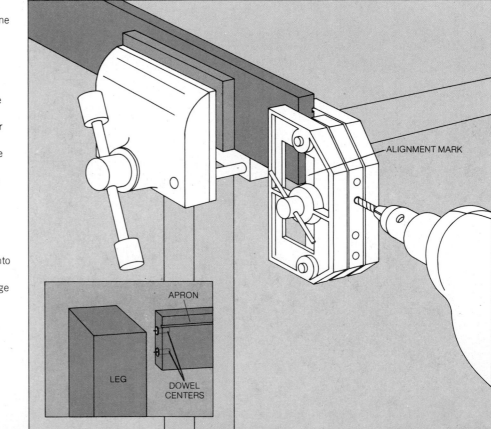

Two Joint Reinforcements

Bracing a corner. To attach a metal corner plate, *(below, top)*, position it across the leg and hold it temporarily in place against the apron by driving one screw on each side. Then drill a pilot hole into the leg through the center hole in the plate, using a drill bit slightly smaller than the diameter of the screw bolt. Remove the screws holding the plate and remove the plate. Screw the bolt into the leg, gripping the bolt in the center with pliers and turning it until all threads at the leg end are in the leg. Replace the plate, putting in all the end screws to fasten the plate to the apron. Then put a lock washer and wing nut onto the screw bolt and tighten.

To attach a wood corner brace *(bottom)*, cut a triangular block from hardwood, so that the grain runs from apron to apron, and notch it to fit around the leg. Attach the block to the apron with two No. 8 screws driven through the block and into the leg, perpendicular to the apron, one screw on each side of the leg.

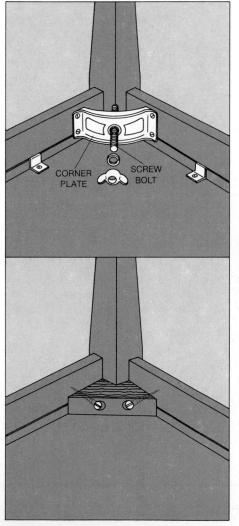

CORNER PLATE

SCREW BOLT

Leveling a Drop Leaf, Unsticking an Extension

Wedging a drop leaf. To level a drooping drop leaf, mark the outermost point where the supporting slide or gate leg touches the underside of the leaf, scrape away old glue or finish and attach a shallow wedge to the leaf. Cut the wedge from a scrap of hardwood, spread yellow glue on the upper face and push the wedge between the slide and the leaf, adjusting it until the leaf is level. Place a weight atop the leaf, to apply pressure until the glue dries.

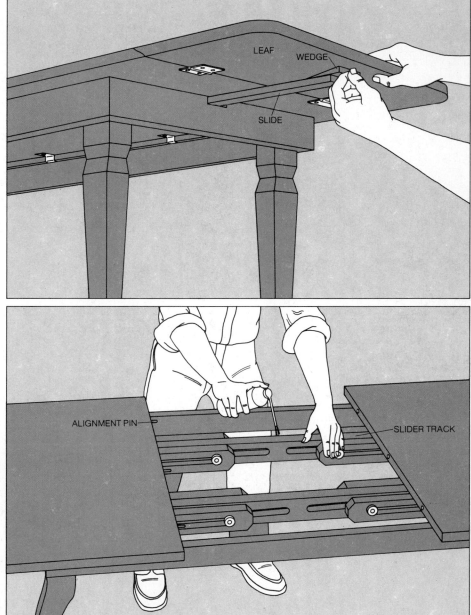

LEAF

WEDGE

SLIDE

ALIGNMENT PIN

SLIDER TRACK

Rehabilitating an extension table. To unstick an extension table that refuses to slide on wooden tracks, open it until it is fully extended and use a chisel to scrape away deposits of dirt and hardened lubricant from the insides of the tracks. Apply fresh lubricant to all accessible moving parts, using either a silicone spray or beeswax. If you are working on an extension table that has metal tracks, use a tapered dowel or stick to clean out the sliding parts. Then sprinkle them with powdered graphite.

If a wooden alignment pin on the edge of an extension leaf breaks, drill out the stub and replace it with a hardwood dowel. Glue one end of the dowel into the cleared hole and taper the other end to fit loosely into the alignment hole, sanding to round its end and reduce its girth.

Repairing Flawed Cabinets

Though cabinets come in many shapes and are constructed with a variety of joints, they do have some basic characteristics in common. Bureaus, vanities, armoires, desks and china cabinets all are boxlike structures *(below)* that are fitted with doors, drawers or both. Since cabinets are not built to support weight, the stresses on them are different from those on chairs or beds. It usually is the moving parts that wear out or break.

When drawers stick or doors do not latch, look for simple remedies first. A loose nail may be catching on a drawer guide; simply drive it back in. Door problems can often be traced to a loose hinge. Tighten the hinge screws. If the screw holes are enlarged, try a slightly larger wood screw, or plug the holes and redrill for the screws.

Some more serious problems, such as worn-out drawer guides, can be remedied without disassembling the frame. Most older cabinets have wood guides; frequently the bottoms of the drawer

sides serve as runners. Even if these pieces have been kept waxed, the rubbing wood surfaces can wear down or become rutted. Professionals restore the drawer sides by replacing worn edges with new wood.

A rutted drawer guide can be taken out and replaced, but an alternative is to attach drawer-glide buttons. These are vinyl-coated or metal disks—like large thumbtacks—with points on the bottom that are driven into wood. Positioned atop guides, the buttons lift the drawer up just enough to let it slide smoothly in the cabinet.

A drawer that is coming apart at the joints calls for some judgement in its repair. If all the joints are loose, knock the drawer apart with a mallet *(opposite)* and reglue. But if only one joint has worked free, it is easier to force glue into the joint and clamp it together, leaving the rest of the drawer intact. Open up sound joints only if you must; the force needed to separate a joint

can invite further damage to the drawer.

If the problem of an ill-fitting or warped door cannot be traced to loose hinge screws, the solution may lie in repositioning the hinges—"throwing the hinges." With this technique *(page 125),* you may be able to bring the protruding corners of a warped door back into line with the frame. With a similar technique *(page 125),* you can tilt a sagging door so it does not bump the cabinet frame. Trim a door edge only as a last resort, when problems of fit arise from a distortion of the cabinet's frame.

If a cabinet caster is broken or bent, it should be replaced immediately; a cabinet that is not relatively level is subject to stresses it was not built to withstand, and will be much more susceptible to joint failure. Replacements are available in many sizes and designs. You may need to increase the size of caster mountings *(page 127),* but select new casters of a style that complements the design of your cabinet.

Anatomy of a cabinet frame. Cabinets gain strength from a rigid boxlike construction. The carcass of a cabinet is composed of its top, sides and base. Most pieces are fitted together with rabbets and dadoes; others are mitered and the joints reinforced with splines *(bottom inset).* Like the bottom and sides of the cabinet at right, rabbeted on each side, many cabinet sections are assembled just with glue. Other parts, like this solid-wood top, are screwed to frames. Here, two hardwood cleats attached to the sides with glued rabbet-and-dado joints *(top inset)* anchor screws driven up into the top.

Most cabinet backs are thin plywood or hardboard nailed into rabbets in the cabinet sides. The back adds rigidity—it keeps the frame from twisting out of square. When you need to make repairs, remove the back by tapping it from the inside with a wood block and a mallet.

From the front, most cabinets are enclosed by drawer fronts or doors. Drawers rest on dust panels—thin sheets of plywood set in a dado on the inside edges of a simple frame. If dust-panel frames are dadoed into the sides of the cabinet, they also help to hold the carcass square. Doors are hinged onto a face frame that is glued (and sometimes nailed) to the front edges of the cabinet frame. The leg assembly at right has an apron and mortise-and-tenon joints, much like those of a table *(page 119).*

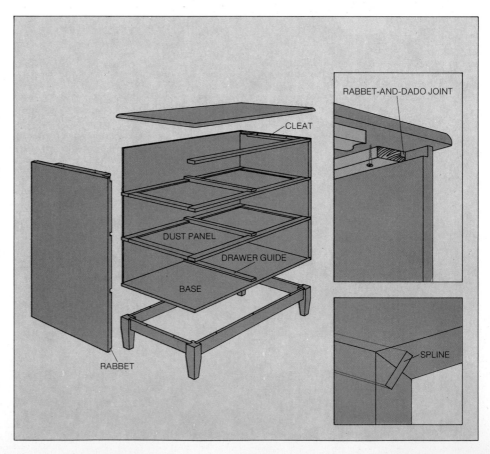

RABBET-AND-DADO JOINT

CLEAT

DUST PANEL

DRAWER GUIDE

BASE

RABBET

SPLINE

Gluing a Drawer Back Together

1 Knocking a drawer apart. To separate a loose dovetail joint, prop a block of wood inside the corner of the drawer and strike it sharply with a mallet or hammer. If the joint is very loose, a blow with your hand may be sufficient. Repeat at the other corners.

Two other common joints are shown in the insets; for each, an arrow indicates the correct direction of a mallet blow to separate the joint. The double-dado joint *(top)* is regularly found in older pieces. In dado-and-rabbet construction *(bottom)*, the drawer front hides the end grain

of the sides. On both drawers, the bottom rests in a continuous dado in the front and side pieces.

Scrape the joint edges with a chisel, cleaning them of dirt and old glue. Remove the drawer handles to facilitate clamping.

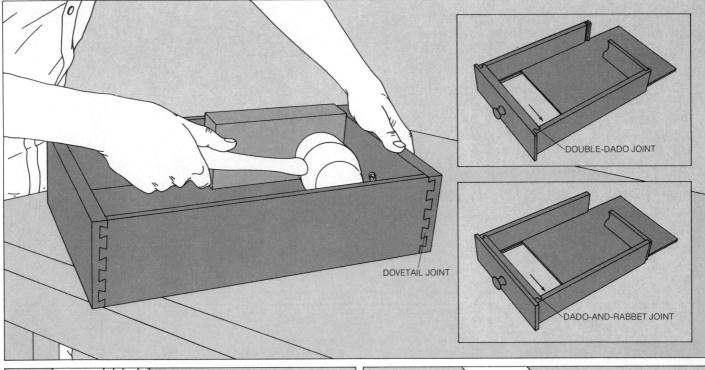

DOVETAIL JOINT

DOUBLE-DADO JOINT

DADO-AND-RABBET JOINT

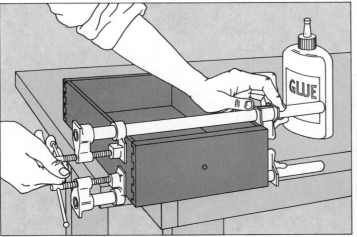

2 Regluing the joints. Apply white glue to all joining surfaces and reassemble the drawer. Attach pipe clamps on the top and the bottom, ½ inch behind the dovetails that join the sides and front of the drawer. Then rest the drawer on its front, and place a third pipe clamp across the back. Measure immediately to make sure the drawer is square: Diagonal measurements between opposite corners must be equal. Shift the clamps, if necessary, to square the drawer.

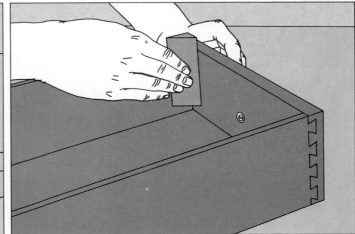

3 Adding glue blocks. To reinforce the joints of the drawer, cut four triangular blocks of wood as long as the drawer is deep , then glue one of them inside each corner. To set a glue block firmly without using a clamp, spread an even coat of white glue on two faces of the block and on the surfaces inside the corner. Press the block in place, and rub it up and down four or five times, until the glue begins to resist movement. The rubbing motion should cover only about ½ inch.

Easy Remedies for Drawers that Stick

Flipping a sagging drawer bottom. Using nippers to grasp the nailheads, pull the brads that fasten the warped bottom to the lower edge of the drawer back. Slide the bottom out of the dadoes in the drawer sides. You may have to use a chisel to pry off small glue blocks that join the bottom to the drawer front or sides. If the bottom also fits into a dado in the drawer back, the drawer will have to be disassembled.

Turn the bottom over and reassemble the drawer. If the bottom is split and cannot be mended, replace it with a new piece of thin plywood or hardboard.

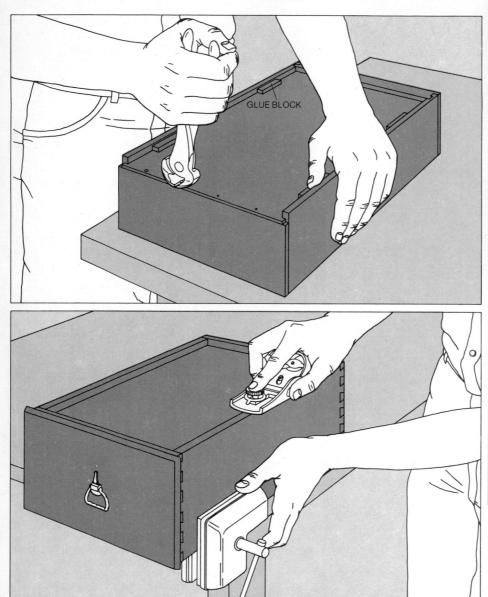

GLUE BLOCK

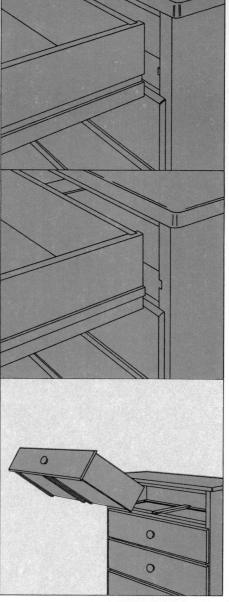

Reshoeing a drawer. If drawer sides that slide along wooden runners are so worn that the drawer does not move smoothly, plane the worn edges and rebuild them. Secure the drawer—or a side if the drawer is disassembled—upside down in a woodworking vise, then plane each worn edge to make it straight. Edges usually wear more at the front than at the back; to restore evenness, you rarely need to remove more than ⅛ inch of wood. If you are working on an assembled drawer and cannot plane to the ends of the edges, finish these areas with a chisel.

Cut strips of hardwood to the length and width of each side. Glue both strips in place, using straight-edged boards and large C clamps to secure them until the glue has dried. Then test-fit the drawer and, if necessary, plane or sand the new strips. Rub paraffin along the runners and the bottom edges of the drawer sides.

Replacing wooden drawer guides. Though there are several designs, most drawer guides made of wood consist of a cleat-and-groove assembly that can easily be replaced if the parts become worn. The drawer sides in the top drawing are dadoed to fit over cleats attached to the cabinet frame. At the center, the configuration is reversed: Cleats attached to drawer sides slide in dadoes in the frame. In the third design, directly above, two cleats on the bottom of the drawer form a groove that slides on a cleat in the center of the frame; the bottom edges of the drawer sides slide on cleats attached to the sides of the frame. To replace a cleat, trace its outline, remove it, then cut and install a duplicate. Use glue and screws to attach a cleat to a frame; use just glue to attach a cleat to a drawer.

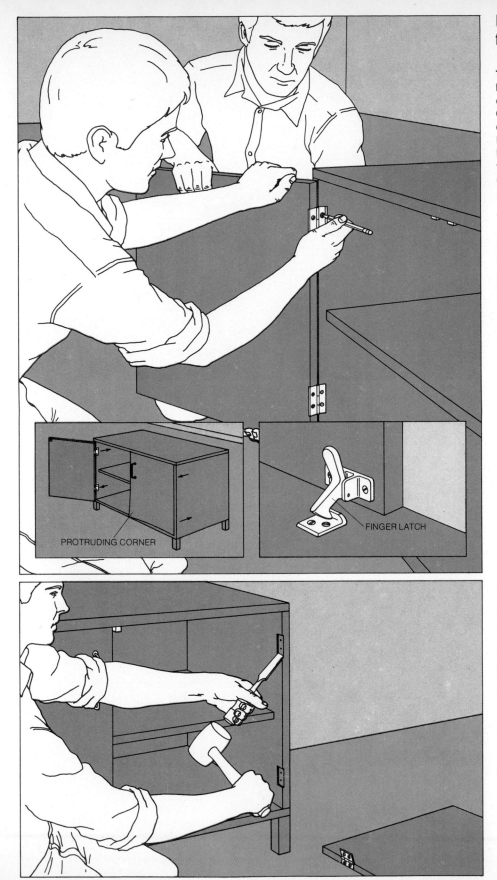

PROTRUDING CORNER

FINGER LATCH

Effective Fixes for Balky Cabinet Doors

Throwing the hinges. If one corner on the un-hinged side of a cabinet door protrudes when the door is closed, the door is probably warped. On a flush cabinet door hung with butt hinges, you can remedy this displacement with a process known as throwing the hinges: Unscrew the hinge leaves from the cabinet, plug the screw holes with glue and dowels and, while a helper holds the door in position, mark new screw holes to re-position the loose hinge leaves laterally.

To determine how much and in which direction to reposition hinges, measure the displacement at the protruding corner. You can compensate somewhat by moving just one hinge a distance equal to the amount of the displacement, but it is more effective to divide this amount equally between both hinges. In doing this, move the hinge that is directly opposite the protruding corner inward on the cabinet frame, then move the other hinge outward an equal amount.

If there is one warped door in a set of double doors that meet at the center, divide the displace-ment equally among all four hinges *(inset, far left)*. To determine which direction to move each hinge, follow the directions above for the door that is warped, but reverse the directions on the unwarped door. If both doors are warped, deal with each one individually.

On any double door, instead of moving hinges you can install a finger latch *(inset, near left)* in-side the cabinet to secure the warped corner.

Providing clearance for a sticking edge. If the unhinged edge of a cabinet door sticks as it closes—binding either just below the top cor-ner or along the bottom edge—first make sure the screws in the top hinge are tight. If they are, unscrew the hinge leaves attached to the cabinet, and remove the door. With a mallet and chisel, either deepen an existing mortise for the top hinge by $1/16$ inch, or cut a $1/16$-inch-deep mortise if there is none. Screw the hinge back in place, and check the swing of the door. On double doors whose edges rub together near the top, you can recess the top hinge on each door.

If this fails to clear a sticking edge, the prob-lem is probably due to a twisted cabinet frame. To remedy it, plane the door edges *(page 126, top)*.

125

Planing a door edge that sticks. After marking the spots that stick and removing the door from the cabinet, draw a line on the door's inside face ⅛ inch from the sticking point. Secure the door in a woodworking vise so the line is horizontal. On a lipped door, as shown, use a rabbet plane or a block plane to cut the inside lip down to the marked line. On a flush door, use a block plane to bevel the edge down to the line, being careful not to remove any more wood than is necessary where the edge meets the outside face of the door; if you shave away excess wood here, you will only increase the gap between the closed door and the cabinet's front frame.

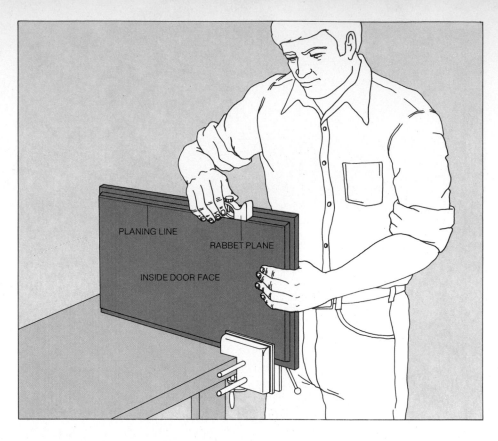

PLANING LINE

RABBET PLANE

INSIDE DOOR FACE

Analyzing Caster Troubles

Two basic designs. The commonly encountered types of caster differ primarily in the way they are attached to furniture. Plate-mounted casters are screwed directly onto the underside of the piece they support; they are quite strong and rarely require repair. They cannot, however, be mounted on small areas, such as the bottoms of narrow legs. Here stem casters are used. The roller of a stem caster is attached to a shaft that fits into a matching sleeve; the sleeve fits into a hole in the end of the leg. Though this design is more versatile, it is also more vulnerable to problems; the shaft may become loose in its sleeve, or the sleeve loose in its socket.

If the furniture design allows it, replace a faulty stem caster with a plate-mounted caster. Otherwise, repair it with the technique shown opposite. Both styles are available in various sizes, either with a wheel or with a ball-shaped roller.

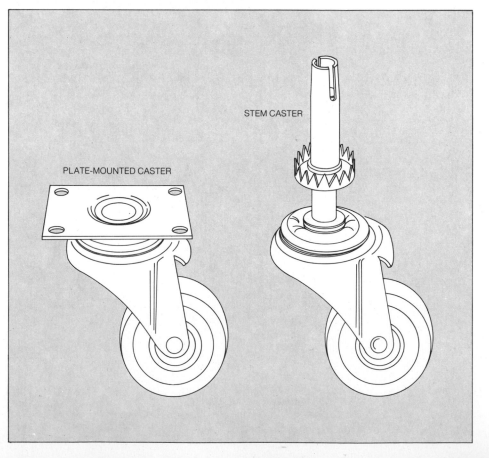

STEM CASTER

PLATE-MOUNTED CASTER

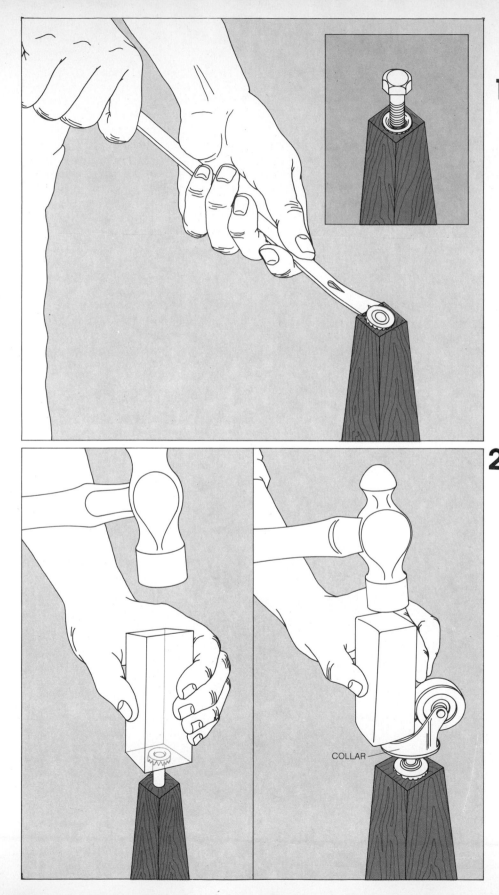

Replacing a Loose Stem Caster

1 **Removing the stem system.** After pulling out the roller and the shaft, try to work the clawed end of a small pry bar under the serrated flange of the sleeve so you can pry the sleeve out of its hole. If this fails, tap a threaded bolt of about the same diameter as the sleeve into the opening *(inset)*, just until it is wedged tight. Grip the bolt with pliers, and work the sleeve loose and out of its socket.

Use a drill to enlarge the old hole to fit the next larger size of stem caster. Wrap tape around the bit to mark the depth of the socket before drilling, and use a doweling jig *(page 120)* to center the drill bit. If the leg is too small for you to drill a larger hole, plug the old hole with a glued wood dowel, and drill a hole for a stem caster a size smaller than the old one.

2 **Installing a new stem caster.** Use a hammer and a wood block to tap the stem sleeve into its hole until the serrated flange bites into the wood *(far left)*. Push the stem shaft into its sleeve; if necessary, tap lightly on a wood block held against the stem collar just above the roller *(near left)* to force the stem into the sleeve. Repeat Steps 1 and 2 to put matching casters on the other legs of the cabinet.

COLLAR

Joints for Beds: Strong but Easy to Take Apart

Beds appear to be massive and sturdy but they are in fact fairly fragile. If you take away the mattress and box spring, all that remains is a rectangle of relatively thin wood parts, some of them designed to shift slightly to accommodate the changing positions of sleepers, and others designed to separate at moving time. Small wonder, then, that these parts can begin to deteriorate.

Some problems with beds have much in common with other furniture ailments—breaks, splintering and warping. Unique to beds, however, are problems found in or near the side rails (the long pieces that connect a bed's head and foot). One particularly vulnerable spot is the joint between the side rails and the bedposts. Here, special hardware—used so that the joint can be dismantled—can eventually become a source of trouble.

Metal fasteners for these joints fall into three categories. On modern beds the most common fastener is a pair of steel plates with interlocking parts; one plate is mounted on the rail, the other on the bedpost. The plates can be set into the wood or mounted on the surface. Such fasteners seldom break, but the wood around them may weaken and split. You can usually correct the problem by moving the fastener.

Most older beds have pin-and-hook fasteners. Flat metal hooks, much like the hooks on a modern fastener, are set into the end of the side rail and enter a slot on the bedpost, where they latch over metal pins. In some cases the pins are set directly into the bedpost, and wooden plugs cover their ends. Or the pins are set into a wooden block, which is inserted in a mortise in the bedpost.

When a pin-and-hook fastener fails, it is generally because the pins have weakened the wood around them. If pins inserted directly into the bedpost pose this problem, the old fastener must usually be abandoned and a new steel-plate fastener substituted. But with pins that are inserted in a wood block, it often is possible to salvage the fastener by replacing just the damaged block.

The last type of fastener, found on even older beds and reproductions, is a long bolt that penetrates the thickness of the bedpost and extends several inches into the end of the rail; the bolt is fastened by a nut embedded in the rail. The bolthead is sometimes countersunk in the bedpost and covered with a small disk; the nut is locked into place with glue, and the access hole to it, in the side of the rail, is commonly filled with a wood plug. When one of these joints works loose, it usually is because the bolthead has eaten into the wood or because the nut has broken away from its glue; both conditions are fixable.

Besides their joints with bedposts, side rails have other problem areas. They may bow outward under the weight of mattress and box springs. Or the narrow ledges attached to the rails, which support slats or box springs, may begin to sag. Mending a sagging ledge is a simple matter of refastening and reinforcing it, but straightening a bulging side rail calls for more elaborate techniques. A general rule to remember, however, is to avoid pulling the side rails too much; allow 1/8 inch of space between slat and rail on each side to assure a proper fit.

Anatomy of a bed. A bedframe is a rectangle that can be taken apart for moving. The headboard and footboard are permanently fastened to bedposts with glued mortise-and-tenon joints, but special hardware used at side-rail and bedpost joints allow them to be separated. To support box springs or the slats that hold a mattress, there is a wood strip (*the ledge*) on the inside of each rail and sometimes also on the inside face of the headboard and of the footboard.

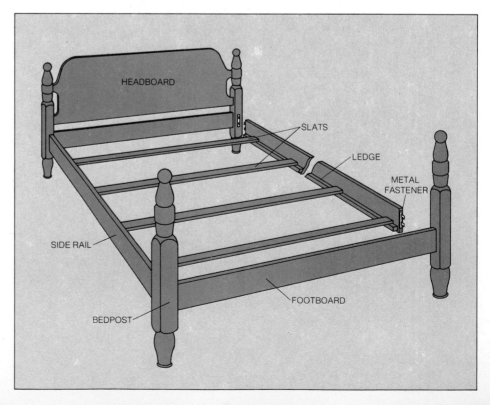

HEADBOARD
SLATS
LEDGE
METAL FASTENER
SIDE RAIL
FOOTBOARD
BEDPOST

Mending the Detachable Post-and-Rail Joints

Repositioning a steel-plate fastener. Disassemble a worn interlocking steel-plate joint *(top left)* and remove the fastener from the bedpost and the rail. Repair the damaged wood if possible; you can strengthen the end of the rail with a piece of plywood or hardboard, glued and screwed to the inside. Then remount the fastener parts in new positions on both the bedpost and the rail. To establish these positions, have a helper align the bedpost and rail while you hold the closed fastener against them, marking the new positions. Then separate bedpost and rail, and screw the fastener parts in place.

If the existing fastener parts are of the recessed type, replace them with a surface-mounted fastener *(bottom left)*. Fill in the mortises with blocks of wood *(page 120)*.

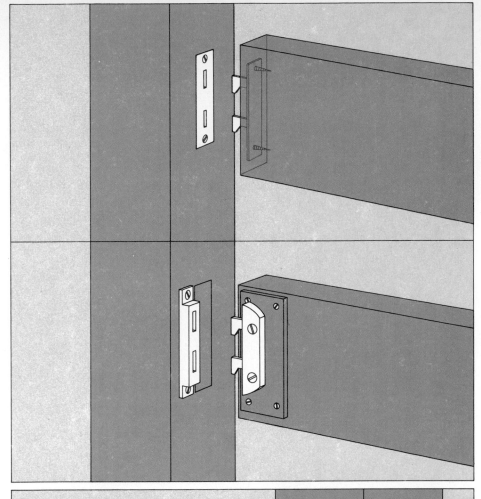

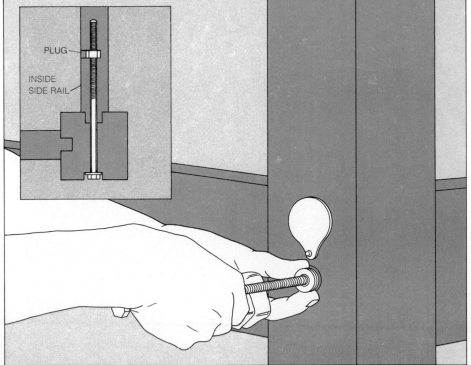

Tightening old-fashioned bolt joints. To tighten a bolthead that has eaten into the wood, remove the bolt and add one or two washers, then put the bolt back in its hole. If the nut inside the rail spins, so that the bolt cannot be tightened, drill or chisel out the wood plug that conceals the access hole *(inset)*.

Unscrew and remove the bolt and oil it lightly. Remove the loose nut from the access hole, clean the old glue from the hole, spread epoxy glue around the nut and replace it in the hole. Then, before the glue can harden, hold the nut in place with a screwdriver (or have a helper hold it), thread the oiled bolt into its hole and screw it just to the end of the nut; this will prevent the glue from hardening in the threads of the nut. Tighten the bolt only after the glue has hardened.

Cut a new plug slightly longer than the access hole. Apply glue, and hammer the plug into place until its end hits the edge of the nut. Trim off any part of the plug that protrudes, and refinish the area.

Repairing a pin-and-hook fastener. To replace a worn wood block, chisel out the old block, and clean the hole in which it rested. Cut a new block to fit the hole, and mark positions for the pins by holding the block against the side of the metal hooks and tracing their outline on the block. Make a slot wide enough and deep enough for entry of the hooks, either by drilling a row of holes the length of the slot and clearing them with a slender mortising chisel or by sawing a channel the length of the block. Then drill holes for the pins, put the pins in the block, and glue and clamp the block into the hole in the bedpost. If the pins are damaged, cut new ones from bolts of the same diameter.

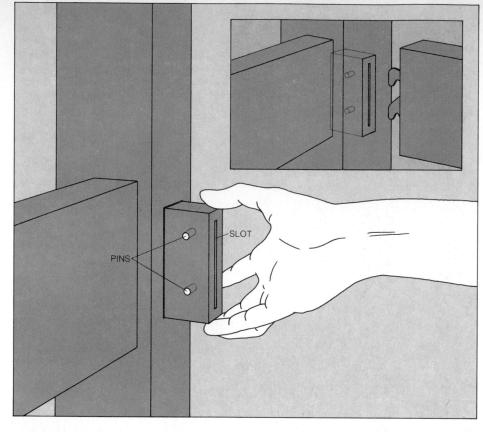

Strengthening a Loose or Sagging Slat Ledge

Adding reinforcement. Unscrew the ledge and gently pry it away from the rail with an old wood chisel, cleaning old glue from both ledge and rail. Fill in the existing screw holes in the ledge and rail with wood putty, then mark off and drill pilot holes for new screws along the ledge, using the distance between existing holes as a guide. Reattach the ledge to the rail, in the same position as before, with glue and screws. Glue and·screw several wood blocks against the underside of the ledge for added support, placing the blocks about 18 inches apart.

If the ledge is badly warped or if it cracks while you are removing it, replace it with a strip of hardwood you have cut to the same length. Prepare the strip as described above, reinforcing it with wood blocks if desired.

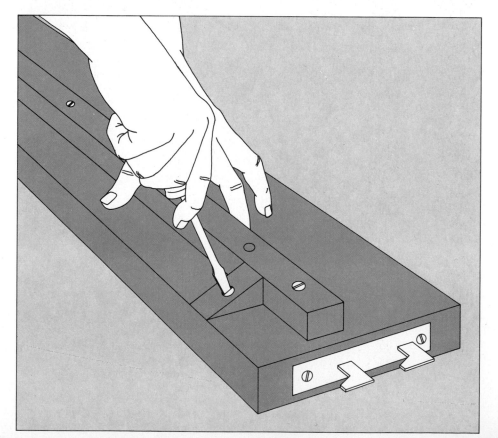

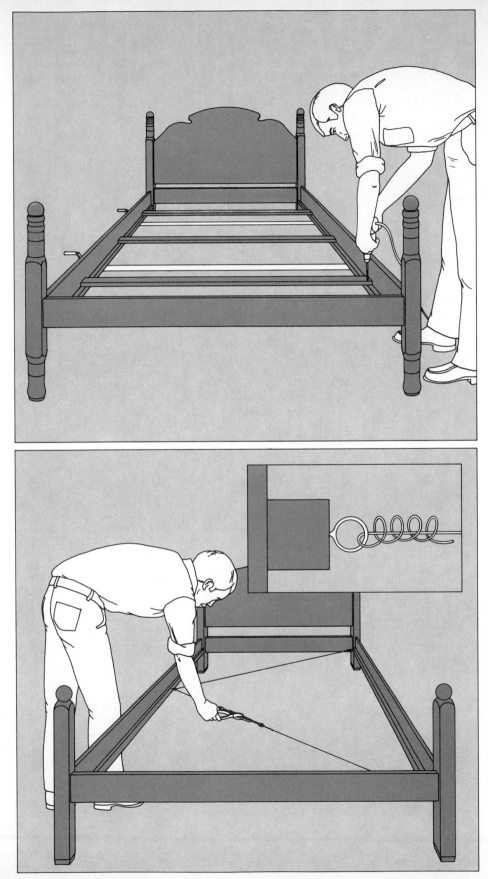

Repairing a Bulging Rail

Correcting slight warps. Using two bar clamps, pull the side rail back into line. Position three slats spaced evenly along the length of the rails, making sure that each end of each slat forms a right angle with the rail. Drill a $3/16$-inch hole through both ends of each slat and into the ledge below, leaving a $1/16$-inch gap between the slat ends and the inside face of the rail. Countersink the holes, then insert flat-head, $3/16$-inch-diameter bolts in the holes, add nuts and tighten. Place the rest of the slats on the ledges but do not fasten them down.

Using a turnbuckle for a bad bulge. Fasten eye screws to both bedposts on the side opposite the bowed rail, placing the eye screws at the height of the ledge. Attach a third eye screw to the ledge at the center of the bowed side rail; the eye screw should be long enough to penetrate the ledge and half the thickness of the side rail. Connect the three eye screws with two lengths of heavy picture wire, fastened at the bedposts by looping and twisting (inset), and joined with a turnbuckle that can be adjusted with pliers to pull the rail straight.

If the other side rail is also bowed, repeat the process on the opposite side.

Home Remedies for Bent and Bruised Wood

Furniture made of solid wood, for all its sturdiness, sometimes seems as prone to damage as a new car in a busy parking lot. It gets dented, gouged, scratched and nicked and, in addition, it may even be assaulted by the atmosphere—moisture present in the air can penetrate the wood and cause it to warp.

If the piece is very old and the injuries are minor, they are often left alone—in an antique, slight nicks and bends can be desirable signs of character. But greater damage should generally be repaired, using an appropriate cure.

Dents and warps can be steamed back into shape, and nicks and gouges treated according to the finish and the value of the furniture—the more precious the piece, the more painstaking the remedy should be. Whatever corrective measure is taken, the result should always be a piece at least as attractive and functional as before the damage occurred.

The simplest repair for slight nicks or scratches in solid wood is the wax-stick treatment, also used in repairing a damaged finish (page 143). If the nick or scratch is wide but not deeper than 1/4 inch, a quick and inexpensive repair can be made with wood putty. It dries rapidly, comes in tints to match many woods and

stains, and can be stained—although not always successfully. It should always be tested with the stain or finish that will be used over it.

A third, more elaborate, remedy for a scratch or gouge calls for patching the injured area with a new piece of wood (opposite). When you select the wood, check its age and color—as well as the pattern, shading and texture of the grain, which should be a near match with the wood of the furniture. Also test the planned finish on a scrap of patching wood before making a decision.

Most patches will have to be cut to fit, but for damaged areas less than 1/2 inch across, you can save yourself time by purchasing wooden plugs, called bungs, cut to show the side grain rather than the end grain of dowels. Bungs come in various woods and, like any patch, should be matched to the original surface. If you have a drill press with a plug cutter, you can save money by punching out the bung yourself.

For any of these spot repairs, begin by thoroughly cleaning the area of the damage, then sanding it with very fine sandpaper to remove the existing finish. But to flatten a warped surface, you may have to remove the finish from the entire

surface to get at the base of the trouble; you may also have to take the afflicted part off its frame. Warping usually occurs when one side of the board is finished and the other side is not; it can also occur when the board is not securely fastened to its understructure. Moisture enters the board's unfinished side, and it causes the edges of the finished side to curl.

Warping can sometimes be corrected if you place the warped board, concave side up and finish removed, on a flat surface, and iron it with an ordinary laundry iron over a damp cloth until the warp relaxes. Or, on a sunny day, you can place the board, concave side down, on a freshly watered lawn. Within a day, or perhaps two—weights speed the process—the warp should be gone. In either case, the board should be refastened to its support immediately and refinished when the wood is dry.

For more severe warping you may have to resort to more involved techniques. If moisture and heat do not eliminate the warp, you will have to cut shallow slots in the underside of the board and then attach hardwood battens across the slots to hold down the board's errant edges.

Removing a Dent with Water or Steam

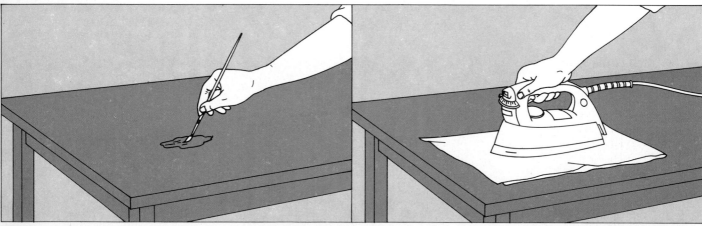

Raising wood fibers. Use an artist's brush or a finger tip to apply water to the crushed wood fibers (above, left), taking care not to moisten the surrounding area. On softwoods, repeat the applications of water until the fibers rise; on hardwoods, apply water, then place a wet cloth over the dent and hold an iron set at low heat against it for 15 seconds. Check the dent and re-

peat the steaming process if necessary. If the dent does not respond, prick the surface with a pin, making holes to channel steam into the fibers. Try to raise the crushed fibers slightly above the level of the surrounding surface.

For tiny dents or dents close to glue joints that might be loosened by steam, isolate the steaming

process. Cover only the affected area with a folded wet cloth, then place a bottle cap upside down on the cloth over the dent and hold the iron against the rim of the cap.

Allow the raised fibers to dry thoroughly. Then sand the area and refinish it.

A Custom Patch for a Solid-Wood Surface

1 Routing the grave. Join four pieces of wood to form a jig for a router, outlining the area to be patched, called the grave; clamp the jig in place—directly, as shown here, or, if the jig is not near the furniture edges, by clamping two boards atop the jig. The jig must be oriented over the damaged area so that its sides will lie at an angle of about 45° to the grain of the wood. The jig should be just large enough to allow the router to take out the damaged wood, leaving the undamaged wood alone. Rout out the grave to the depth of the damage, and square off the grave corners with a chisel. If you do not have a router, cut the grave with a hammer and a chisel. Make certain that the grave edges are vertical and that the bottom is flat.

2 Applying the patch. Tape paper over the grave, and trace the shape of the edges. Cut out this shape to make a pattern for the patch, and tape it to the patching wood, aligning the pattern so that the grain of the patch matches the grain surrounding the grave. Cut the patch slightly larger than the pattern.

With sandpaper or a plane, bevel the edges of the patch slightly inward (*inset*), testing the patch for fit frequently. When it fits snugly but lies slightly above the surrounding surface, apply white glue and fasten the patch into the grave. Cover it with brown wrapping paper or wax paper; weight it or clamp it overnight. Then sand it level with the surrounding surface, and refinish.

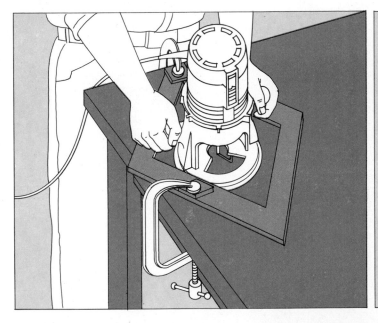
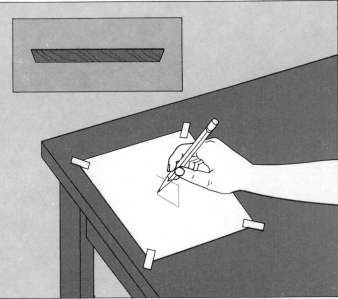

Wood Putty to Repair Edges

Filling in nicked edges. Rub paraffin or wax crayon on a scrap of wood that is long enough to span the area of edge damage, and clamp the waxed surface against the furniture edge, using edge clamps as shown, or C clamps with wood wedges to create the same effect. (The wax will keep putty from adhering to the scrap wood.)

With a spatula or a putty knife, force wood putty into the nick. If the nick is deeper or longer than ¼ inch, build up the putty in layers, giving each coat time to dry. Overfill the depression slightly, to compensate for shrinkage. When the putty has dried, remove the scrap wood, and sand the putty flush with the surface. Apply stain, if it is needed, then a sealer such as a coat of thinned varnish. Complete the repair with painted-on graining if necessary (*page 143*).

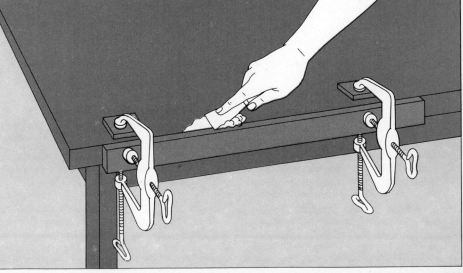

Molding a missing corner. Using wood putty and the same basic repair technique as for nicked edges *(page 133)*, rebuild a missing corner by constructing a three-sided mold *(inset)*. If a leg joins the piece of furniture near the corner, leave space for it. Wax all three sides of the mold that will touch the wood putty. Clamp the mold to the furniture, then fill in the damage.

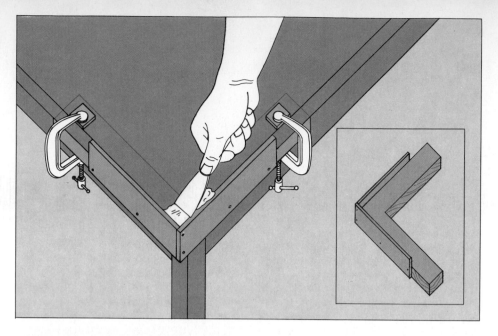

Reconstructing a Broken Corner with a Wood Block

1 Preparing the corner piece. Using a router or a mallet and chisel, prepare a smooth bed for the new corner by clearing away all the damaged wood on the existing corner. Then cut a wood patch to fit against the newly smoothed face of the corner, making this patch about ¾ inch longer and $1/32$ inch thicker than needed. Set the patch into place, and slide it back and forth until the grains of patch and of furniture are in the best alignment. Mark the patch in this position, then cut it down to size, leaving about $1/32$ inch of overhang at the sides.

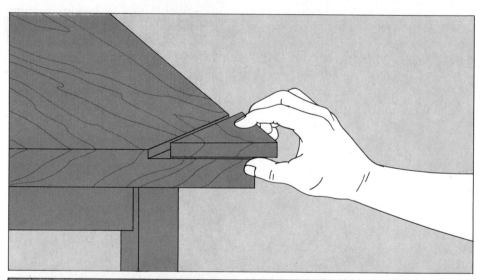

2 Clamping the corner. Apply glue to the horizontal and the vertical surfaces of the cleared corner, and set the corner patch in place. Slide a C clamp over the patch, and cock the clamp slightly off the vertical, until the swivel head atop the screw is ⅛ inch closer to the inner face of the patch than the top of the clamp is. In this position, pressure will be inward as well as downward against the patch. Tighten the clamp.

If the broken corner extends completely through the furniture, from top surface to bottom, construct a three-sided brace like the mold shown at top, coat it with wax or cover it with wax paper so glue will not adhere to it, then clamp it against the furniture. Wedge the new corner, coated with glue, into the brace. Or use two special edge clamps *(page 133, bottom)* to hold the new corner in place, but check periodically to make sure the corner has not slipped down.

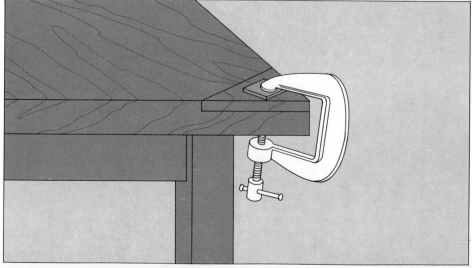

Pegs and Splints to Heal a Broken Part

A break in the supporting frame of a piece of furniture creates, in effect, a joint where none was intended, in an area originally designed to accept great stress. The repair of such a break must leave the broken part as strong as it was originally; at the same time it must be as unobtrusive as possible.

For certain breaks (below, center), glue alone will do an admirable repair job. But since wood that breaks is in many cases dry and brittle, a quantity of glue must be worked into the pores, so that as it soaks in enough will be left on the surface for a good bond. Some breaks need support from added wood—either dowels or rectangular bracing blocks. When inserted in or attached to the area of the break, these braces stiffen the joint by providing more surface for the glue to grip.

Dowels can be hidden within a broken part or inserted into a hole drilled from the outside; in the latter case, the end of the dowel will show. If a part is broken cleanly in two and its centers can be drilled to receive a dowel, a hidden dowel is the better repair. But if a break is at an extreme angle, or is located at a curve in the part, it is easier to insert one or even two dowels from the outside—and the repair will be just as strong. The di-ameter of the dowel should usually be half the thickness of the part being mended and its length usually twice that thickness, though it can be longer if more strength is needed.

Braces are used to mend breaks in flat, thin parts, such as chair-back splats or sofa frames. In a visible part a bracing block should be recessed into a mortise cut to span the break, but in a hidden area, such as one beneath upholstery, a brace can be mounted across the break without a mortise. The thickness of a brace should be half the thickness of the broken part and its length about twice the width of the broken part. Both dowels and braces hold best if they fit the broken part snugly but not tightly—a piece too loose will leave glue gaps and one too tight will force the break apart or even split the wood around it.

These reinforcements should be made of hardwood, cut along the length of the grain for strength and flexibility. You can purchase short hardwood dowels ready-made, or you can cut them to any length from a dowel rod of the right diameter. Hardwood to be used for braces can be purchased at a lumberyard or scavenged from old, unusable hardwood furniture. It is sometimes possible to obtain a piece of matching hardwood from hidden parts of the broken furniture piece itself, perhaps the glue blocks or the drawer runners.

Adequate clamping is crucial whenever glue is used. A clamp must be placed so its force is applied perpendicular to the line of the break, to draw the ends together without pulling them out of alignment. Since most furniture is not constructed with perfect 90° angles, and since breaks do not occur that neatly, you may have to use some ingenuity in devising a special clamping technique for each repair.

C clamps, for example, can be used to sandwich an extremely angled break or to press a bracing block into a mortise. A C clamp can also be attached to a curved part to serve as an anchor point for a pipe clamp, which runs from the C clamp to the end of the broken part, perpendicular to the break (page 138). A pipe clamp that cannot be placed so it applies force perpendicular to a break will tend to pull the broken pieces out of alignment, making the part bend at the break; by running a second pipe clamp from one end of the first clamp to another part of the furniture (page 137), you can shift the force so the joint dries straight.

Three Common Ways that Wood May Break

Three types of fracture. A wooden furniture part, held rigid by another part joining it or weakened by deep ornamental turnings, may snap cleanly (left). Since there is little surface area for glue to bond, glue alone probably will not mend this kind of break permanently. The repair should be strengthened with a brace or a dowel. Wood that breaks jaggedly (center) is said to have a lot of tooth, and it provides a large, irregular surface for an effective glue bond. This kind of repair becomes the equivalent of a tongue-and-groove joint. Wood that breaks along the line of the grain (right) produces a long, angled break that has a large surface area but not much tooth for the glue to grip. Depending on how heavily the piece is used, the repair for an angled break may need to be strengthened by the addition of a dowel or brace.

A Clean Break Rejoined with a Hidden Dowel

1 Drilling holes for a dowel. Place the piece of furniture (in this case a chair with a broken leg) at a convenient height, broken end up. Clamp the furniture to a workbench or sawhorses if it is unsteady and clamp the piece that broke off in a vise, also broken end up. If the pieces are broken cleanly enough that you can use a doweling jig, drill into their exact centers as shown. If a doweling jig is unusable because of the shape of the break or the piece, you will need to estimate the centers visually (*page 115*). Use a small bit to drill a pilot hole in each piece, then drill the final holes with a bit the exact size of the dowel to be used. Clean drill debris out of the holes with a vacuum, or turn the pieces upside down and tap the debris out.

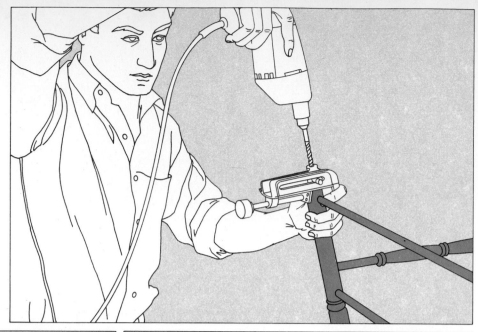

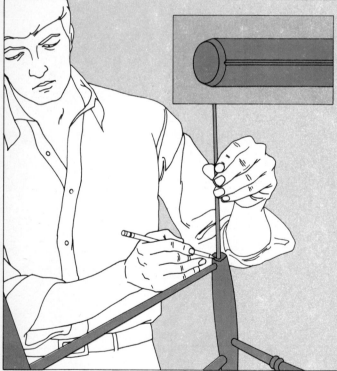

2 Making the dowel peg. Insert an undersized dowel or a pencil into each dowel hole and mark the depth on it. Cut a dowel of the right diameter for a snug fit to a length slightly shorter than the sum of the depths of the holes. Bevel the ends of the dowel slightly with a utility knife (*inset*) or sandpaper, and groove the sides of the dowel with the knife or with pliers to provide channels that will let the glue spread.

3 Joining the pieces. Put glue in one hole and on one end of the dowel and, with a mallet, tap the dowel into the hole as far as it will go. Then tap the other broken piece onto the protruding dowel, without glue, so you can check to see if the broken ends align precisely. If they do not, file down one side of the dowel or shave it a bit with a utility knife (*inset*) to allow the pieces to line up. When the pieces are aligned, put glue on the other end of the dowel, in the other hole and on the broken ends, then tap the pieces together securely. Wipe off excess glue.

4 **Clamping.** Apply a bar or pipe clamp extending from one end of the broken part to the other, running as nearly perpendicular to the break as possible (*near right*). If the clamp cannot be placed exactly perpendicular and tends to pull the pieces out of alignment, apply a second bar clamp connecting the first clamp with some part of the furniture opposite it, in order to pull the pieces back into alignment (*far right*).

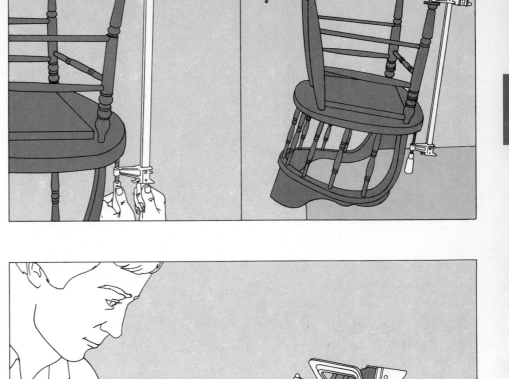

A Visible-Dowel Repair for an Angled Break

1 **Drilling the dowel hole.** Apply white glue to the broken edges and clamp the pieces together, using two strips of wood and two C clamps to hold them in place. At the least visible area, drill a pilot hole for the dowel hole through the first broken piece and partway into the second, at a right angle to the break. Using the pilot hole as a guide, drill a hole the same size as the dowel that is to be inserted. Clean the sawdust out.

2 **Inserting the dowel.** Use a dowel grooved as in page 136, Step 2, but in this case cut the dowel slightly longer than the depth of the hole. Put glue in the hole and on the dowel; tap the dowel into the hole with a mallet. Remove the clamps and the wood supports, and wipe off excess glue.

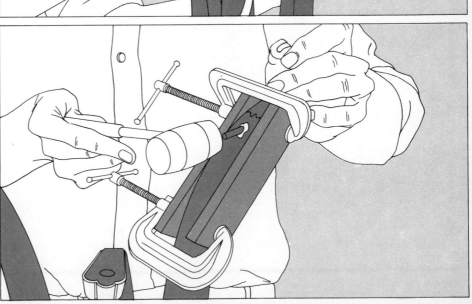

3 Clamping a curve. To apply force perpendicular to this break, you will have to attach a C clamp near the break to use as a bracket for applying force with a pipe clamp. Attach the pipe clamp in such a way that it runs from the C clamp to the end of the broken part, spanning the break and remaining perpendicular to it. When the glue has set, use a backsaw and sandpaper to trim the protruding end of the dowel flush with the surface of the broken part.

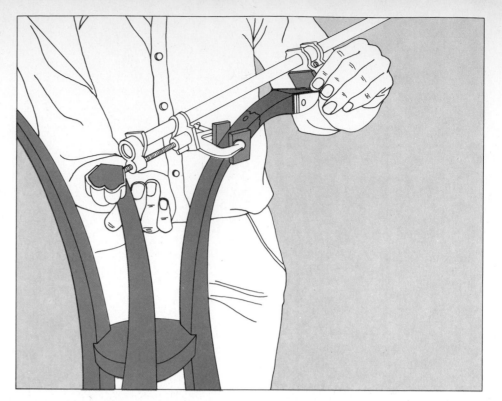

A Mortised Splint for a Flat Break

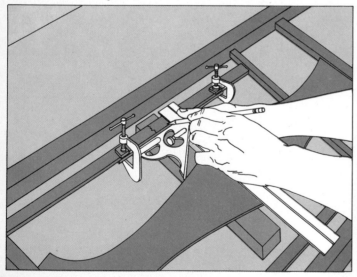

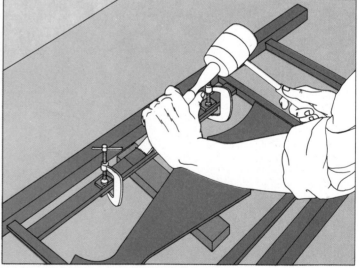

1 Getting into position. Clamp the furniture down on a bench or rest it on the floor with the back, or the least visible area, of the broken part horizontal and facing up. Apply glue to the broken edges and join them. Clamp the area of the break in position, using two C clamps, one on each side of the break, to secure a strip of wood spanning the underside of the break. Support the part from underneath with a second scrap of wood, if necessary, as shown. Guided by a combination square, mark where the ends of the mortise will fall on each side of the break, at right angles to the length of the part.

2 Cutting the mortise. Cut the mortise ends at the marks to the planned depth, using a backsaw. Or use a chisel, held vertically with its bevel facing the break as you tap it with a mallet. Then, keeping the chisel angled and the bevel side down, score the area between the cuts every ⅜ inch to a depth slightly less than that intended for the mortise. When you have scored the area, reverse direction in order to remove the chips, and then pare the bottom of the mortise smooth by shaving it with the chisel, still bevel side down. Smooth the bottom of the mortise with sandpaper or with a wood file.

3 **Clamping the brace.** Cut a hardwood brace to fit snugly into the mortise, then put glue in the mortise and on the back and ends of the brace. Insert the brace into the mortise, wipe away the excess glue and, without removing the original C clamps and strip of wood, clamp the brace into the mortise securely with additional C clamps. When the glue is dry, unclamp and sand the brace to match precisely the shape of the part.

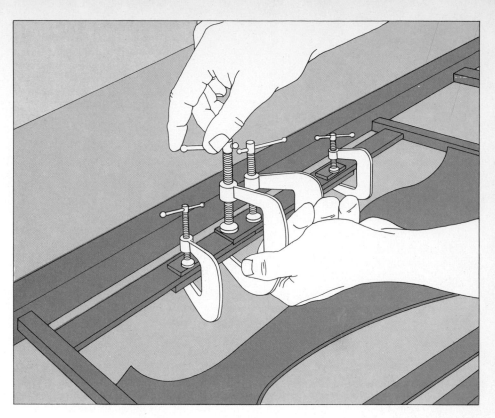

A Screwed-On Brace Concealed from View

A simple strengthener. Expose as much as possible of any concealed broken part; if the break is under upholstery, remove tacks or staples and fold back the fabric for several inches on each side of the break, without damaging the fabric. Apply glue to the broken edges and clamp them together with a pipe clamp running from one end of the framing member to the other. Drill pilot holes through the corners of a ½- to 1-inch-thick rectangle of wood that spans the break on the exposed side of the broken part. Spread the glue on this brace and attach it with screws. When the glue is dry, unclamp the piece and retack the fabric.

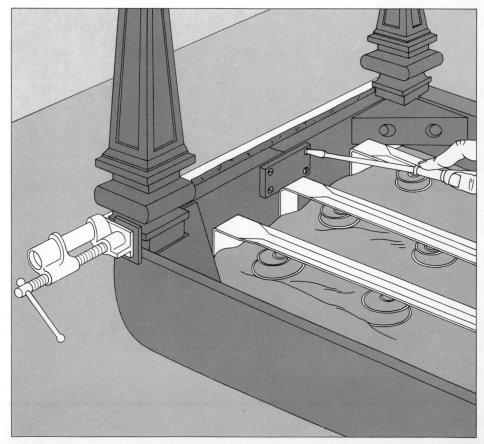

Saving a Damaged Finish with Minor Repairs

The original finish on a piece of furniture can sometimes be its greatest asset. It seals the wood against loss of moisture, prevents spills and stains from penetrating the wood pores and, with age, may take on a mellow patina that enhances the furniture's value. Therefore it may be preferable to correct a flawed finish instead of stripping it.

The corrective measures to be used will depend on the type of finish and the cause of the damage, and often the two are closely related. The white haze that clouds a tabletop, for example, is likely to be the result of a chemical interaction between the shellac or lacquer finish and moisture in the environment, which softens both finishes. (The white rings that form when wet glasses sit too long on a shellac or lacquer surface are localized versions of this same phenomenon.)

Both shellac and lacquer belong to a class of finishes called solvent-release coatings. They are solutions of resin in a solvent that evaporates, leaving behind a thin resin film. Solvent-release coatings have the special property of redissolving readily when the proper solvent is brushed over them. With care, it is sometimes possible to respread such a coating to a smooth new finish in a process that is called amalgamation.

A second major class of finishes, the chemically reactive coatings, harden through a much more complex process: They absorb oxygen from the air to change from liquid to solid. Two familiar examples of these coatings are varnish and enamel, which harden into a thin film; unlike shellac and lacquer, they cannot be amalgamated. Two other reactive coatings are boiled linseed oil and tung oil, both of which sink into the pores of the wood.

Distinguishing between these finishes requires no particular expertise. Application of the proper solvent (chart, opposite) in a hidden spot will cause shellac or lacquer to dissolve and quickly redry. If the finish does not respond this way it is probably varnish, enamel or paint, which will crinkle and soften when paint remover is applied. Indeed, the finish can in some cases be identified by its response to the materials used in the preliminary cleaning process. The simplest

of these cleaners consists of mild white soap and warm water, which are used to float away surface dirt. Water should be tested first on a small area, for it may tend to cloud a shellac or lacquer finish.

Alternatively, you can clean the surface with turpentine or mineral spirits, both especially useful for deep grime or built-up layers of wax. Mineral spirits may also remedy the flawed finish. If the finish is clouded by a smoky blue haze that disappears when cleaned with mineral spirits, the problem is one of incompatibility—the furniture has been oiled or waxed over a silicone polish, which repels the other coatings. The silicone, as well as oil or wax, is dissolved by mineral spirits.

In the normal course of repair, you will need two kinds of refinishing aids—abrasives and chemicals. The abrasives commonly used are extra-fine steel wool, grades 3/0 and 4/0, and silicon-carbide paper in grit sizes of 220 to 400, very-fine to superfine. Abrasive papers should be used with a sanding block (page 157).

Two other abrasives used in refinishing are rottenstone and pumice, both of which are mixed with mineral oil into a paste. Rottenstone is a very mild abrasive made of powdered limestone; pumice, which is much stronger, is powdered volcanic glass. It should be used only in fine grade, 3/F, or very-fine grade, 4/F, and be applied with a well-padded sanding block or a blackboard eraser so it will not mar the finish. In lieu of either of these two substances, a gentle but slightly abrasive car polish also makes an excellent abrasive for furniture finishes.

Chemicals useful in repair work include solvents, dyes, stains, oils and polishes. Solvents combine with the existing finish—as denatured alcohol amalgamates shellac, and lacquer thinner amalgamates lacquer—to remove hazing and to restore a crazed or crackled finish to its original smoothness. Dyes, stains, oils and polishes can improve the entire finish or be used for more localized repairs—they disguise scratches, scuffed areas and similar blemishes.

The simplest remedies for spot repairs are ordinary furniture oils and polishes, which have a wetting effect that may be sufficient to darken minor scratches to match the surrounding finish. When

these do not work, colored furniture polish or an oil-base stain may do the job. Two of the handiest products for disguising blemishes are dye-impregnated felt-tipped pens and small vials of dye with brushes attached to their lids, both available at furniture-refinishing shops.

Sometimes makeshift home remedies work almost as well as these professional products. A nutmeat rubbed over a scratch may darken it enough to hide it, and iodine will disguise a scratch in red-stained mahogany. Shoe polish in the right color will do for a scuffed table precisely what it does for scuffed shoes. With any of these coloring agents, begin with a lighter color and move to a darker one as necessary, since a scratch dyed too dark can seldom be lightened to match its surroundings.

For deeper scratches as well as other deeper blemishes, such as burns and chips, some sort of filler is needed. Sometimes it is possible to fill in a scratch by rubbing a child's crayon over it. On painted or varnished surfaces, a slight depression can be built up with successive coats of the same finish, layered on with a fine-tipped artist's brush. But the professional way to patch burned, chipped or gouged areas is with wax sticks or shellac sticks, both available at furniture-refinishing shops.

Whether you use a wax stick or a shellac stick, patching is done in essentially the same way: The stick is held against a hot knife and the wax or shellac is guided into the depression as it melts. But of the two, shellac-stick patching is much more difficult to do, and takes practice. The shellac hardens into a patch that is practically impossible to remove, so you may have to live with a mistake, whereas a patch made with a wax stick can easily be taken out and redone.

After any of these spot repairs, the area of the repair should be buffed with a fine abrasive to blend it into the surrounding finish, and then waxed or polished. A hard paste wax, the kind used on cars, provides the best protection and needs renewing only three or four times a year. An oil-base polish such as lemon oil imparts a lovely glowing shine, but the polish is not very durable and must be renewed about once a week.

Repairs at a Glance: Local Defects

Material / Problem	White rings or spots	Minor scratch	Deep scratch	Small burn	Small chip in finish
Furniture polish		Apply to entire furniture surface with clean cloth; rub well into scratch; buff.			
Colored furniture polish		Rub into scratch with cotton swab, and then, if desired, apply to entire surface with clean cloth.			
Furniture dye		Apply to scratch with brush or felt-tipped applicator; wipe away excess with a clean cloth.			
3/0 steel wool	Dip in mineral oil, rub over spot with grain in short strokes, wipe away excess with clean cloth.				
Rottenstone	Mix to creamy consistency with mineral oil, rub into spot with finger wrapped in clean cloth. Wipe off excess mixture with damp rag; dry with soft cloth.				
3/F pumice	Mix to creamy consistency with mineral oil, rub gently over spot with grain, using well-padded sanding block. Wipe off excess with damp rag; dry with soft cloth.				
Furniture-wax stick		Rub into depression to fill it, wipe away excess with a clean cloth.	Choose color that matches light grain of finish; melt wax into depression with a hot knife. Cool, scrape smooth. Paint in darker grain with artist's oil or watercolors; seal with spray varnish.	Scrape out all charred material with utility knife. Choose color that matches light grain of finish; melt wax into depression with hot knife. Cool, scrape smooth. Paint in darker grain with artist's oil or watercolors; seal with spray varnish.	
Polyurethane varnish or enamel			Using artist's brush, fill with successive coats of finish color. Build up higher than surrounding area, then smooth down with very fine abrasive paper on a sanding block.		Using artist's brush, fill with successive coats of finish color. Build up higher than surrounding area, then smooth with very fine abrasive paper on a sanding block.
Denatured alcohol (for shellac finish) / Lacquer thinner (for lacquer finish)	Wet a small, lintless pad with solvent, wring out. Stroke damaged area, remoistening pad, until spot disappears.				

Remedies for local damage. Listed across the top of this chart are local damage or spot defects that commonly afflict furniture finishes. Corrective measures for them use the materials in the far left column of the chart. The technique for using a specific material is described in the column beneath the problem. In most cases there are several alternatives, ranging here from mild at the top to more extreme at the bottom. Try the more conservative measures first; for example, to hide a minor scratch, try furniture polish before furniture dye.

Repairs at a Glance: General Damage

Material / Problem	Stubborn wax or grease, silicone haze	Scuffed, dull surface, multiple light scratches	White haze	Cracking, alligatoring
Furniture polish		Apply with a clean cloth; buff.		
Colored furniture polish		Apply with a clean cloth, working into marred surface to color it; buff.		
Turpentine or mineral spirits	Rub in with clean cloth, changing cloth as needed until all traces of coating are removed.			
Mixture of 3 parts boiled linseed oil to 1 part turpentine		Rub in along grain with lintless cloth, wipe away excess with dry cloth.		
3/0 steel wool		Dip in mineral oil, rub with grain over entire surface, giving special attention to scratched areas. Remove excess oil with clean cloth.	Dip in mineral oil, rub with grain in long strokes over entire surface. Remove excess oil with clean cloth.	
Rottenstone		Mix to creamy consistency with mineral oil. Apply with clean cloth, rubbing with grain, giving special attention to damaged areas. Wipe off excess mixture with damp rag; dry with soft cloth.	Mix to creamy consistency with mineral oil. Apply with clean cloth, rubbing with grain. Wipe off excess mixture with damp rag; dry with soft cloth.	
3/F pumice		Mix to creamy consistency with mineral oil and apply with padded sanding block. Rub along wood grain with an even touch. Wipe with damp rag; dry with soft cloth.	Mix to creamy consistency with mineral oil and apply with padded sanding block. Rub along wood grain with an even touch. Wipe off excess mixture with damp rag; dry with soft cloth.	
Denatured alcohol (for shellac finish) / Lacquer thinner (for lacquer finish)		Amalgamate, using varnish brush to apply in light strokes with the grain until scratches have melted away. Work horizontally.	Amalgamate, using varnish brush to apply in light strokes with the grain until haze disappears. Work horizontally.	Amalgamate, using varnish brush to apply in light strokes with the grain until cracks are smoothed out. Work horizontally.

Restoring a generally damaged surface. Across the top of the chart above are listed problems that typically affect the entire furniture finish. The materials that can be used to correct the damage are in the column at the left. The technique for using a specific material is shown in the column beneath the problem. The solutions range from mild at the top to more extreme at the bottom. You can save time and effort by trying the more conservative solutions first. For example, to remove a white haze, try fine steel wool before switching to quicker-cutting pumice.

Patching with a Hot Wax Stick

For this repair to be almost invisible, you need a furniture-wax stick the exact color of the lightest grain in the wood, and a tube of artist's color—either oil paint or watercolor—in the same color as the darkest grain. If you cannot find a matching wax stick, you can mix your own by melting and blending shavings of several colors in a spoon or a metal jar lid, then allowing the mixture to cool and harden.

Caution: Do not melt a wax stick directly over a flame or electric burner; it is a combination of paraffin, beeswax, oil and dye, and is dangerously flammable. Instead, heat the spoon or lid, take it off the fire, then drop the shavings into it; they melt quickly and can be blended before the spoon or lid cools.

Other supplies needed for the hot-wax patch are a curved knife, a sootless heat source, a fine-tipped artist's brush, spray varnish and 4/0 steel wool. Professionals use a curved knife called a burn-in knife, but you can substitute a grapefruit knife—or any knife with a slender blade.

Making an Invisible Plug

1 **Preparing the surface.** To repair a burned area, as shown here, first scrape away all charred material with a single-edged razor blade or a utility knife, then clean the depression with mineral spirits. To prepare gouges or deep scratches for filling, simply clean the blemish thoroughly.

2 **Forming the patch.** Warm the knife over an alcohol lamp or electric hot plate and, holding the end of the wax stick against the heated blade, guide the melting wax into the depression. Reheat the blade as necessary, adding wax to the patch until it is slightly higher than the surrounding surface; the wax will contract as it cools. When the patch is cool, pull a single-edged razor blade across it to level it, and give it a final smoothing with your fingertip.

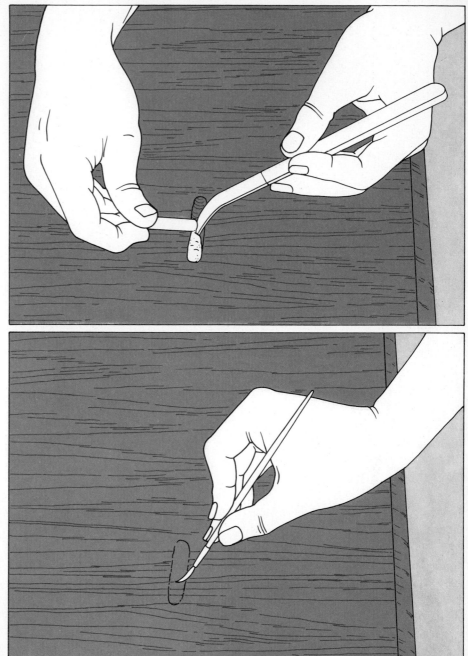

3 **Painting the grain.** Dip a fine-tipped artist's brush into artist's colors used undiluted, straight from the tube. Wipe the brush over paper, leaving the brush almost dry. Then paint feathery strokes over the wax patch with the nearly dry brush, blending them into the pattern of the surrounding wood grain. If the lines look too crisp, smudge the color lightly with a finger or a cloth for a more natural effect.

To fix the patch permanently, spray a light coat of clear polyurethane or acrylic varnish over the repair area and the surrounding surface.

Caution: Spray in a well-ventilated room, away from any open flame, and do not smoke. When the sprayed area is dry, buff with 4/0 steel wool to blend it with the texture of the finish. Wax or polish the entire surface.

2 PAINT AND WALLPAPER

Painting and Wallpapering Like a Pro

Almost everyone has painted or wallpapered at least one room—and finished the job convinced there must be faster and easier ways to achieve a better result. There are such ways. Every trade has its tricks, and painting and wallpapering are no exceptions. If you know these tricks, you will be able to save yourself time and effort and do the job right.

A painter's craft is not merely a matter of procedures and techniques. It begins with choosing the right product to apply. No one paint is right for every surface— and no paint of any kind will work well if you use the wrong tools to prepare the surface or apply the paint. The chart on pages 148-149 matches both interior and exterior paints to almost any surface that you are likely to find in your home. While you might select an interior paint chiefly to add life to a room, you choose an exterior paint also to help protect the outside of your house against the elements. The exterior choice is a bit more complicated because outdoor surfaces are more varied than those inside. Despite this range of materials, there is an exterior coating for every surface—and some that work on a great variety of surfaces.

On pages 154-155 and 176-177 you will find pictures and descriptions of all the tools you will need for any painting job. Pages 156-173 explain the techniques for painting your home's interior; pages 178-191 do the same for exterior painting, from diagnosing problems to how to spray paint. Keep in mind that it is as important to pick the right weather as it is to pick the right exterior paint. The best temperature range for the job is between 50° and 90° F., since no paint adheres well when it is very hot or very cold.

The once-arcane craft of paperhanging is today a routine job for the homeowner; according to one estimate, well over 60 percent of the wall coverings sold are hung by the men and women who buy them. Wall covering is no longer simply printed paper but plastic, fabric or a combination. These newer materials are tougher and generally easier to handle than older types. They do not tear as readily, and many of them offer such labor-saving features as pretrimmed edges, factory-applied adhesive and reinforced backings (which simplify removal the next time redecorating is necessary). The chart on pages 192-193 describes the types of wall coverings that are available, where they can be used and handling tips for the best result.

The hanging of any type of wall covering is simplified if the covering can be obtained prepasted—that is, with dry adhesive already on its back. You need only dip the paper into water to make the adhesive sticky and ready to put on the wall *(page 205);* you avoid the messy job of mixing and applying paste and setting up a table to work on. Most widely used wall coverings—vinyls, papers, foils and flocks—are available prepasted, but of course not all patterns in those types are supplied in this easy-to-use form.

Once you have chosen a material and a pattern, ask your dealer for a sample of the paper—a few square inches will do. Take it home and wet it by holding it briefly under a tap or by dunking it in water for a few seconds to simulate the conditions under which you will handle the paper after applying the paste. Test the sample to see how easily you can tear it; most paper will tear, but you should avoid buying those that tear too easily.

For a second test, rub the sample firmly with a damp sponge to see if the colors run; if they do—and they frequently will, especially in hand prints—you are dealing with an especially tricky paper. You will have to be extremely careful not to get adhesive on the patterned side of the paper because you will be unable to wash it off, and the standard practice of sponging off an entire strip after it has been hung must be omitted. After you have hung a paper that tends to run, you then can spray it with a transparent stain-resistant coating available at wallpaper stores; test the coating first on a large remnant to make sure that it will not smear the pattern.

If the sample passes these tests, buy enough paper for your needs, using the calculation described on page 199. You can make this estimate far more precisely than you can estimate paint needs— while the covering power of paint varies with the color, porosity and smoothness of a wall, a single roll of wallpaper will always cover about 30 square feet, whatever the condition of the wall. Do not stint on paper: The cost of an extra roll is small compared to the unsightly result of completing a job with paper from a different print run. You may be able to return unused rolls for a refund.

Washing Solutions for Paints and Wall Coverings

The solutions below are effective for removing dirt and various stains from walls and ceilings with washable finishes. In general, the stains that respond to washing are mildew, ink and substances with a greasy base— crayon, lipstick or food splatters. To remove mildew, add 1 cup of chlorine laundry bleach to 1 gallon of warm water, and sponge the surface. Wipe off with a clean, wet sponge.

FLAT PAINTS. For washing entire walls and ceilings, mix 2 tablespoons trisodium phosphate or powdered household detergent into a gallon of lukewarm water. For greasy stains, use a stronger solution of trisodium phosphate or a mixture of enzyme detergent and water. SEMIGLOSS AND GLOSSY PAINTS. When washing entire walls and ceilings, use a solution of 1 teaspoon washing soda per gallon of lukewarm water. Use the same solution for washable stains, except on painted wood, such as baseboards or a door frame. WASHABLE AND SCRUBBABLE PAPERS. To wash entire walls and ceilings, work as for flat paint, above; do not let water get behind seams. Rinse each section, then pat dry. For ink or grease, use a one-to-10 solution of enzyme detergent and water, or rub with a cloth dampened with isopropyl alcohol.

Doing the Right Things in the Right Order

Whether you paint a single room or the interior of an entire house, you will achieve the best results with the least fuss if you take the time to plan your work first. Doing the right things in the right order is the first essential. To begin with, you need to know how much paint to buy and how long the job is likely to take; these questions can easily be answered using the rules of thumb in the box below.

Next comes the choice of paint from among the dozens available. The chart on pages 148 and 149 lists the full range of interior and exterior paints; on pages 150-153, the advantages and disadvantages of interior coatings in the chart are described in detail.

From this point on the work falls into three stages: The preparation of surfaces, the painting itself and the final cleanup. Pages 156-159 discuss preparation. Pages 160-171 deal with paint mixing, rollerwork and brushwork, and also the correct sequence for painting a room. And pages 172 and 173 cover the final stage, in which a room is returned to its original condition and the painting tools are carefully cleaned and stored.

The most important part of a home-painting plan concerns the painter personally. If you have not painted for some time, you may become painfully aware of muscles you did not know you had. Painting probably requires more lifting, stretching and bending than most daily tasks. Plan the job to take into account your own capacities. If you schedule your work sensibly and allow for coffee breaks and lunch, you will finish in good condition, right through to the cleanup stage, and enjoy the results all the more.

How Much Paint? How Much Time?

The worst place to estimate how much paint you need for a job is at the paint store. Figure out the area you have to cover at home.

For a rectangular room with average-sized windows and doors *(below)*, first measure the length and width, round off each figure to the nearest foot, and add them together. Multiply that total by the room height and then double that result. The final figure is the area of your wall in square feet. From this total, subtract about 15 square feet for each of the windows and 21 square feet

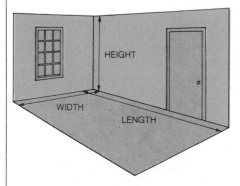

for each door. Ceiling area is the length times the width of the room.

If the room is an unusual shape, measure the height and width of each rectangular section to be painted. Multiply these figures to get the area, then add them together for the total area needing paint.

A stairwell often forms a triangular shape. For the area of the triangle, multiply the lengths of the horizontal and vertical legs and divide by two *(right)*.

If you plan to paint the trim with a different colored paint, figure these areas separately. Allow about 21 square feet for each side of a door and 15 square feet for the trim on an average window. A baseboard area is the product of its height times its total length, which is generally the same as the perimeter of the room.

When you know the total area you will cover, you have half the information you need to order paint. The rest depends on the covering capacity of your paint and the surface it must coat. If your walls are smooth, figure on covering 400 feet with a gallon of finishing paint. Divide your area figure by that amount to arrive at the number of gallons you need for a first coat. If you are using finishing paint on porous, rough or previously unpainted walls, the gallon will cover about 350 feet. You can count on more coverage for the second coat—about 450 feet per gallon for a smooth-surfaced wall and 400 feet per gallon for a rough wall.

One gallon of paint is generally ample for a 12-by-15-foot room with an 8-foot ceiling and smooth, previously painted walls; the ceiling of the same room would take 1½ quarts (if you must buy 2 quarts you can reserve the extra for repairs). Professional painters often

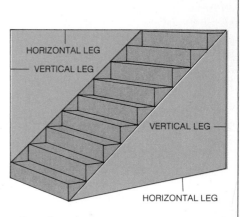

allow for about one quarter as much trim paint as wall paint, but you can make a more accurate and economical purchase if you calculate the trim area as suggested above.

Estimating time brings in a new set of variables. You are likely to cover about 120 square feet of an ordinary surface in an hour, or about 100 square feet of bare wood or plaster. Thus, you will probably be able to paint that 12-by-15 room with one coat in four to five hours —if you do not have much patching to do. Extensive repairs can more than double your working time. And if you apply two coats, you must allow time for the first coat to dry—a matter of two to 36 hours (check the label of your paint can). On a major job, however, the variables tend to cancel each other out. For example, you can safely figure on five or six days to paint seven rooms, including preparation and cleanup.

A Coating for Every Surface

There is a paint for every wall, but there is no single coating that can be used in every circumstance. Some finishes will not adhere to certain surfaces. No interior paint, for example, will last for very long on an exterior wall, because it cracks under the expansion and contraction caused by temperature changes. Oil paints will wrinkle and peel if they are applied to fresh plaster; as the plaster dries, the moisture and alkali it releases deform the film of paint. A finish such as varnish, which forms an impervious seal against water, soon blisters on a moist wall.

The wrong coating can actually damage a wall surface. Latex paint, which is thinned with water, promotes rust if it is applied directly to iron or steel. The thinners in other paints can dissolve glue; if paint containing such a solvent is used over wallpaper, both paper and paint could peel right off the wall.

To help to avoid such costly errors, the chart on these pages identifies finishing materials suitable for the common surfaces. The vertical columns at the left and right of the chart list the kinds of surfaces to be covered in four sections: raw wood, raw masonry, bare metal and previously finished surfaces. Major types of interior and exterior coatings are listed across the top. Suppose you want to paint a new plaster wall. Read down the left column under raw masonry to "plaster," then follow the horizontal row of boxes to the right. You will find dots or footnote numbers in the boxes beneath glossy and flat latex paint, rubber-base paint and alkyd primer, and beneath a whole sequence of other coatings. To learn more about these finishes—what they are made of, whether or not they are toxic, how fast they dry, if they are odor-free, what kind of painting tool to apply them with—turn to pages 150-155 for interior coatings, or pages 174-177 for exterior materials.

Surfaces	GLOSSY OIL PAINT (1)	GLOSSY ALKYD PAINT (1)	GLOSSY LATEX PAINT (1)	FLAT OIL PAINT (1)	FLAT ALKYD PAINT (1)	FLAT LATEX PAINT (1)	LATEX SHINGLE PAINT (1)	OIL OR ALKYD SHINGLE PAINT (1)	RUBBER-BASE PAINT (1)	CEMENT PAINT (1)	EPOXY PAINT (1)	URETHANE PAINT (1)	PORCH AND FLOOR PAINT (1)	MARINE PAINT (1)	MULTICOLOR PAINT
Raw Wood															
Wood, plywood or clapboard	•	•		•	•						•	•	•	•	
Particle board	•	•		•	•						•		•		
Hardboard	•	•	•	•	•	•					•	•	•		
Rough wood siding			•	•	•	•	•	•							
Wood shakes and shingles				•	•	•	•	•							
Exterior wood trim	•	•	•									•		•	
Raw Masonry															
Plaster			•			•			•						•
Gypsum wallboard			•			•									•
Concrete			•			•			•	•	3	3	3		•
Cinder block			•						•	•			3		
Brick			•		•	•			•	•	3		3		•
Stucco			•		3	•			•						•
Asbestos-cement shingles or board						•	•	•	3						
Ceramic tile or glass											•	•		4	
Bare Metal															
Steel or iron	5	5									•				
Galvanized metal															
Aluminum	5	5	5	5	5	5					•	•			
Copper or bronze											•	•			
Previous Surface Covering															
Wallpaper			•	•	•										•
Flat oil paint or primer	•	•		•	•				•				•		
Flat alkyd paint or primer	•	•		•	•				•				•	•	
Flat latex paint or primer	•	•	•	•	•	•	•	•	•				•		•
Glossy oil paint (2)	•	•		•	•								•	•	
Alkyd glossy paint or varnish (2)	•	•		•	•								•	•	
Glossy latex paint (2)	•	•	•	•	•	•							•		•
Epoxy paint or varnish (2)	•	•		•	•						•		4	4	
Polyurethane paint or varnish (2)	•	•		•	•							•	•		
Rubber-base paint			•	•		•	•		•				•		
Cement paint										•					
Zinc-dust primer	6	6													
Zinc-rich metal primers	•	•	•	•	•	•					•	•			
Aluminum paint	•	•	•	•	•			•			•	•			
Block filler		3	•	3	3	•	•		•	•	3	•	3		•
Wood filler	•	•		•	•			•			•	•	•	•	
Paintable wood sealer	•	•		•	•	•		•			•				
Paintable masonry sealer				3	•			•	•			3			•
Bleach	•	•		•	•		•	•				•	•	•	

1 These coatings include gloss and semigloss varieties, and are available in different compositions for exterior and interior painting; use the type appropriate to the job.
2 Sand glossy finishes before painting over them.
3 Use the type formulated for masonry.
4 Use the epoxy-paint type.
5 Use the type formulated for metal.
6 Use the type formulated for galvanized metal.

Table of paint/coating compatibility with surfaces. Columns are **Coatings**; rows are **Surfaces**. A dot (●) indicates a recommended combination; numbers refer to footnote references.

Surface	Latex Sand Paint	Latex Texture Paint	Dripless Paint	Fire-Retardant Paint	Alkyd Varnish	Polyurethane Varnish (1)	Epoxy Varnish	Moisture-Cured Urethane Varnish	Spar Varnish	Acrylic Lacquer	Shellac	Oil Stain	Water Stain	Alcohol Stain	Exterior Latex Stain	Varnish Stain	Bleach	Oil Primer (1)	Alkyd Primer (1)	Latex Primer (1)	Oil-Cement Primer	Zinc-Rich Metal Primer	Zinc-Dust Primer	Aluminum Paint	Wood Sealer	Masonry Sealer	Silicone Water Repellent	Block Filler	Wood Filler	Paintable Wood Preservative
Raw Wood																														
Wood, plywood or clapboard			●		●	●	●		●		●	●	●	●	●	●	●	●	●						●	●			●	●
Particle board			●		●	●		●	●		●	●	●	●	●	●	●	●	●						●	●			●	
Hardboard	●	●	●	●	●		●	●	●	●	●						●	●	●						●	●				
Rough wood siding												●		●	●		●	●	●						●	●	●			●
Wood shakes and shingles												●		●	●		●	●							●		●			●
Exterior wood trim				●	●	●	●	●	●			●			●	●	●	●							●	●	●		●	●
Raw Masonry																														
Plaster	●	●		●							●								3	●				●						
Gypsum wallboard	●	●		●							●									●										
Concrete	●	●		●															3	●				●			●			
Cinder block	●	●		●															3	●				●			●			
Brick	●	●		●			●	●			●							●	●					●			●			
Stucco	●	●		●															3	●				●			●			
Asbestos-cement shingles or board	●	●		●																										
Ceramic tile or glass							●	●																						
Bare Metal																														
Steel or iron					●			●										5	5	5		●	●	●						
Galvanized metal																		6	6	6		●	●	●						
Aluminum							●	●		●								5	5	5		●		●						
Copper or bronze							●	●		●								5				●								
Previous Surface Covering																														
Wallpaper																		●	●											
Flat oil paint or primer			●	●	●	●																		●						
Flat alkyd paint or primer			●	●	●	●																		●						
Flat latex paint or primer	●	●	●	●	●	●																								
Glossy oil paint (2)			●	●	●																			●						
Alkyd glossy paint or varnish (2)			●	●	●			●																●						
Glossy latex paint (2)	●	●	●	●																										
Epoxy paint or varnish (2)							●																							
Polyurethane paint or varnish (2)						●		●																						
Rubber-base paint				●																										
Cement paint																														
Zinc-dust primer																							●							
Zinc-rich metal primers																						●	●	●						
Aluminum paint				●	●																			●						
Block filler	●	●		●																●						●				
Wood filler				●		●	●	●	●			●	●	●	●		●	●	●										●	
Paintable wood sealer				●		●	●		●		●	●	●	●	●	●	●	●	●					●						
Paintable masonry sealer	●	●		●																							●			
Bleach				●	●	●	●	●	●		●	●	●	●	●	●	●	●	●					●			●		●	

A Guide to Interior Coatings

The chart on pages 148 and 149 can serve as a ready reference for matching interior and exterior coatings to almost every surface. Here and on the pages that follow, the interior coatings listed in the chart are discussed in detail.

In this guide, 20 types of interior coatings are grouped in four categories. First come general-purpose finishing paints for walls and ceilings—often the only paints you will need, especially if surfaces are in good condition. Next is a small group of special-purpose finishes that conceal uneven or damaged walls, or have other unique properties (one of these paints will not drip, another slows the spread of fire). The third category includes coatings that enhance the grains and colors of wood. The fourth is devoted to the undercoatings sometimes applied as a base for a finishing coat.

Finishing Paints

Color and gloss are usually the important factors in choosing a finishing paint. While color is a matter of personal preference, gloss affects both appearance and resistance to wear. The three major types of finishing coats—latex, alkyd and oil paints—come in versions labeled flat, semigloss and high gloss by manufacturers. As noted, however, high-gloss latex is somewhat less glossy than comparable versions of the other types.

High-gloss paints are the most wear- and moisture-resistant because of their relatively high proportion of resin, the ingredient that solidifies into the coating film as the solvent evaporates. The more resin, the heavier—and tougher—the film. The high-resin film of the glossy paints makes them ideal for areas subject to heavy use or frequent washing—particularly kitchens and bathrooms. Semigloss paints afford moderate durability with a less obtrusive shine for most woodwork. Flat paints provide a desirable low-glare surface for walls and ceilings that do not need frequent washing.

Along with latex, oil and alkyd paints, the most commonly used finishes include paints especially suitable for specific surfaces: Rubber-base and cement paints for masonry, and epoxy and urethane paints for surfaces that require the toughest and most moistureproof coating available.

Latex Paint
SIMPLIFIES CLEANUP
ODOR FREE
QUICK DRYING

Water is the solvent for latex paint, which is made of plastic resins—either acrylics or tougher polyvinyls. Its water solvent gives latex advantages that have made it the most widely used paint for walls and ceilings. Tools, spills and hands can be cleaned with soap and water while the latex is wet. Latex paint is almost free of odor and harmful fumes, and a coat is usually dry in little more than an hour.

Latex adheres well to most surfaces painted with flat oil or latex paints; it does not adhere to some alkyds, and tends to peel away from any high-gloss finish. Latex can be used over unprimed wallboard, bare masonry and fresh plaster patches that have set but are not quite dry; before applying it to new concrete, wash the surface with a good concrete etching solution recommended by your paint dealer. Use caution; wear goggles and rubber gloves.

The water solvent imposes certain limitations on latex paint. Although it can be applied directly over wallpaper, the water in the paint may soak the paper away from the wall. If latex is applied to raw wood the water swells the fibers, roughening the surface—a disadvantage where a smooth finish is desirable. Used on bare steel, it rusts the metal.

Flat latex is less resistant to abrasion and washing than either oil or alkyd paint, and so-called high-gloss latex is less shiny—and less durable—than comparable alkyds or oils. Any paint can be applied over latex.

Alkyd Paint
DURABLE
NEARLY ODORLESS

Any painted or wallpapered surface—or bare wood—can be covered with paint made from a synthetic resin called alkyd (often combined with other resins). This type of paint will not adhere to bare masonry or plaster, and should not be used on bare wallboard because it will raise a nap on the wallboard's smooth paper covering.

Alkyd is the most durable of the common finishing paints. It is also practically odor free. To take advantage of this characteristic, use low-odor solvents (usually listed on the manufacturer's label) for thinning and cleanup—but bear in mind that the fumes of these solvents, though nearly imperceptible, are flammable and toxic. Most alkyds are dry enough for a second coat in four to six hours.

Although some latex paints will not bond well to alkyd, most other paints can be applied over it.

Oil Paint
STRONG SMELLING

For many years paints based on natural plant oils, such as tung or linseed oils, dominated interior painting. An oil paint adheres well to bare wood and to surfaces previously painted with latex, alkyd or oil. In high-gloss and semigloss finishes, it stands up to repeated washing.

Oil paint has so many drawbacks, however, that it has largely been replaced by latex and alkyd mixtures and is now hard to find. In flat finishes, oil paint is less durable than alkyd. It does not adhere to wallpaper, bare wallboard or masonry. The oils in the paint give it a strong, unpleasant odor, and it must be thinned with strong-smelling turpentine or mineral spirits (tools and spills, however, can be cleaned with relatively odor-free solvents used for alkyd paints). An oil-base paint takes from 12 to 48 hours to dry sufficiently for a second coat, and from two to four days to dry thoroughly.

Although latex will not adhere well to a high-gloss oil paint, alkyds and other oil-base paints can be applied over it.

Rubber-Base Paint
GOOD FOR MASONRY
MOISTUREPROOF
VERY FAST DRYING

This moisture-resistant coating, a liquefied rubber, can be applied directly to bare masonry; bare brick, however, must first be sealed with a clear varnish, and new concrete should be washed with a good, safe concrete etching solution, then rinsed clean. (As always, when preparing masonry with any acid etch, exercise caution; wear goggles and rubber gloves). Rubber-base paint is truly waterproof and far more durable than latex, but it comes in flat and low-gloss finishes only and in a narrower range of colors, has a strong smell and is expensive. Because it is so tough, however, it is a good choice for basement floors. A coat normally dries in an hour. Rubber-base paints need special solvents; check the label carefully.

Any latex, oil or alkyd paint can be applied over a rubber-base paint, with one exception: A high-gloss oil paint will not adhere to this type of coating.

Cement Paint
RENEWS MASONRY SURFACES
APPLIED TO DAMP WALLS

This inexpensive coating gives a new surface to brick, stucco or concrete, adding a thin layer of cement to the old masonry. Some types also act as waterproofers—an advantage in basements. Two coats are necessary on new masonry.

The paint comes as a powder, which is a mixture of white Portland cement, pigment and, usually, a small amount of water repellent. This powder is mixed with water just before use and the paint is applied with a large brush. To help the cement set, the wall surface must be kept moist during the job and for at least 48 hours thereafter. Tools and spills must be rinsed off before the cement sets.

Cement paint forms a poor base for all other finishes.

Epoxy and Urethane Paints
VERY DURABLE INDOORS
TRICKY TO USE

Plastic paints are exceptionally elastic and resistant to abrasion, grease, dirt and most chemicals. Although they are expensive, they may prove to be the best coatings for surfaces that are subject to chemical and physical stress—floors and steps as well as the walls and woodwork of kitchens and bathrooms.

In some respects the two types of paint differ. Urethanes can be used on bare wood or over latex, alkyd or oil paint. Epoxies produce a slick, impervious coating on nonporous surfaces such as ceramic or metal tile, glass, porcelain or fiberglass; they can also be used on concrete or wood floors, but they will not adhere to latex, alkyd or oil paint.

The most durable epoxies and urethanes are two-part paints, which must be mixed

just before use because they dry and harden rapidly. Both types require special solvents, which are listed on the package labels, for cleanup.

Alkyd or oil paints can be used over an epoxy or urethane, but the surface must be roughened first by sanding.

Special Finishes

A number of unusual finishing paints are specifically designed to take care of special painting problems. They cost more and cover less than ordinary paints.

Multicolor Paint
DISGUISES FLAWED SURFACES
DISTINCTIVE AND DECORATIVE

These latex-base coatings contain two nonmixing pigments. Depending on the formulation, they produce a tonal variation or a flecked appearance that conceals uneven or slightly damaged surfaces. Multicolor paint can be used on any surface that takes latex paint. Choose a brand that can be brushed or rolled on and does not require spraying.

Any alkyd, latex or oil-base paint can be applied over a multicolor paint, but two coats may be needed to hide it.

Sand and Texture Paint
A COVER-UP FOR FLAWED SURFACES
ATTRACTIVELY ROUGH
DIFFICULT TO COVER

These paints dry to a rough rather than smooth surface that lends an unusual texture to walls and ceilings and also helps hide flaws. Sand paint is simply regular latex paint mixed with sand or a sandlike synthetic. It creates a fine-grained, glare-free texture that is attractive on ceilings but has a grittiness that limits its use to surfaces not likely to be touched.

Texture paint is an extra-dense flat latex or alkyd paint. To get an irregular, embossed texture, apply it to a small area at a time *(page 167)*.

These paints can be applied to surfaces compatible with their latex or alkyd base. The latex type is often used on wallboard ceilings since it adheres without a primer and helps conceal seams.

Painting over sand or texture coatings presents special difficulties; their rough surfaces require as much as 25 per cent more regular paint than usual.

Dripless Paint
GOOD FOR CEILINGS
EXPENSIVE

This alkyd coating is prepared in a consistency so thick that it will not drip from a brush or a roller, making it useful for painting ceilings and high, hard-to-reach places. The thick paint will usually cover any surface in a single coat, but it is considerably more expensive than conventional alkyds and more of it is required to cover a given area.

Though this paint will not drip, it will spatter if it is carelessly applied; and its thickness makes it somewhat difficult to remove. Be sure to clean up tools and spills while they are still wet.

Fire-Retardant Paint
A WORTHWHILE PROTECTION
AVAILABLE ONLY IN FLAT FINISH

This flat latex paint slows down the spread of fire inside a house by puffing up into a foamy insulating layer when exposed to high temperatures. The insulation helps to keep the paint film from flaring—as most paints will do—and also temporarily prevents flammable material underneath, such as wood studs and joists, from reaching the kindling point. Fire-retardant paint is particularly valuable in garages and basements.

Follow exactly the instructions supplied by the manufacturer, especially in controlling the thickness of the coating: If the coating layer is too thin, it will not provide adequate protection; if it is too thick, it may fall away in case of a fire. Some manufacturers suggest that their coatings not be washed because the puffing ingredients are water soluble; be sure to check the label.

Fire-retardant paints can be applied over any surface that is suitable for latex (and over bare wood, provided a perfectly smooth finish is not essential). Conventional paints should not be used over fire-retardant paint because they may impair its effectiveness.

Transparent and Natural Wood Finishes

The clear finishes and natural colorings described below are generally used to protect or tone wood materials without hiding their desirable natural grain or texture, although they are occasionally applied over other surfaces as an extra coating. Except for bleach, all of these finishes should be applied with a brush.

Varnish
MOISTURE RESISTANT
TOUGHER THAN MOST PAINTS

Interior varnish is used chiefly to form a clear, tough finish for wood, especially floors and steps. Because it is exceptionally durable, it is also used on painted surfaces to protect the finish. For the correct way to apply varnish, see page 165. Most varnishes dry in a day, but are ready for a second coating in six to eight hours.

The basic types of varnish, in order of increasing durability, are: Alkyd and phenolic, polyurethane, epoxy and moisture-cured urethane. The high-gloss versions are the most durable, but a medium-gloss varnish also provides good protection. Scratches can be hard to touch up, however, because new varnish forms a shiny patch on older varnish.

The alkyd and phenolic resin varnishes give a warm, glowing tone, but the others are much tougher; polyurethane varnishes are exceptionally resistant to alcohol and are useful for table and bar tops; epoxies can be applied to ceramic tile and other nonporous surfaces as well as raw or painted wood. Polyurethane and epoxy types come as ready-to-use liquids or in two materials, which must be mixed before use. In each, the two-part mixture is more durable.

Moisture-cured urethane is the toughest of all interior varnishes. It can be used on ceramic tile as well as wood and other surfaces. It is expensive, however, and hardens best if temperature conditions fall within a restricted range.

Most paints do not adhere well to varnish, but oil or alkyd paints can be applied if the varnished surface is thoroughly roughened, first by washing with a strong detergent and then by sanding.

Shellac
INEXPENSIVE
FAST DRYING
EASILY DAMAGED BY WATER OR ALCOHOL

Shellac is an alcohol solution of a resin derived from the lac insect of the tropics. Either clear or reddish brown (called orange), it is an inexpensive abrasion-resistant coating for bare, bleached or stained wood. It dries in two to three hours, depending on the weather, and it gives a mirror-smooth coating—brush marks disappear as the shellac dries. It is the traditional finish for wood floors.

These admirable qualities, however, are balanced by disadvantages. Shellac cannot be used over other coatings because the alcohol in its base tends to dissolve the existing surface. Furthermore, it is easily damaged by water, which causes whitish spots to form, and by alcohol, which dissolves the shellac.

Ready-mixed shellac, though convenient, soon loses its adhesiveness; check the date on the container to be sure it is not more than a month or two old. As an alternative, buy shellac in 4- or 5-pound "cuts" of natural shellac resin mixed together with 1 gallon of denatured alcohol. To thin this heavy material to a working consistency, add 1 gallon of alcohol to a 5-pound cut, or ¾ gallon of alcohol to a 4-pound cut.

Stain
CHANGES WOOD TONE

Stain enhances the grain of the wood by altering the color. Because it works by being absorbed into the wood pores, it must be applied to raw wood or to wood that previously has been treated only with sealer or bleach. After staining, the surface can be oiled, waxed or left bare, but generally it is coated with varnish in order to protect the wood and make it easier to clean and maintain.

Stains consist of varying amounts of pigment (the amount determines whether the final coat will be transparent or semiopaque) in oil, water or alcohol. Oil-base stains are most common. Stains with a water base penetrate more deeply than oil stains—an advantage if the surface is likely to be scratched—but the water raises the grain of the wood so that extra sanding is required. Alcohol-base stains dry faster than any other type—in only 15 to 30 minutes—but fast drying can produce a streaky finish.

So-called double-duty stains, a combination of stain and varnish, change the color of the wood and simultaneously provide a protective coating. Use these mixtures with caution, however: they streak easily and are not as durable as ordinary stain covered with varnish.

Any paint can be used over a surface of oil-, alcohol- or water-base stain. If a wax has been used over the stain, remove this finish with a commercial wax remover or sand the surface down to the bare wood. If you are covering a double-duty stain, see "Varnish," at left.

Bleach
LIGHTENS WOOD
REMOVES STAINS
CORROSIVE AND DANGEROUS

Raw wood that is too dark or discolored can be lightened with bleach. Bleach can also be used to correct a faulty staining job that has come out streaky or too dark. Caution: These chemicals are corrosive. Wear rubber gloves as well as protective clothing, protect eyes and be sure to wash away spatters immediately.

The most convenient bleach is simply undiluted liquid laundry bleach. Apply it to the wood with a rag or a stiff brush and scrub it in, then rinse it off thoroughly with warm water, sponging repeatedly to remove any trace on the bleach.

The bleaching and rinsing process raises the grain of the wood. After bleaching, let the wood dry, then sand it smooth and protect it with a coat of varnish.

Primers, Sealers and Fillers

A surface may be incompatible with the finishing coat of your choice. It may be so porous that the first coat will virtually disappear into it. On the other hand, it may be so uneven that no paint will give it a smooth surface. The solution to these problems is to apply an inexpensive undercoat of one kind or another. Fillers will smooth a wood surface that is uneven and sealers close the pores of wood or masonry. Most common of all undercoatings are primers, which not only serve as the first layer on absorbent materials but also as a bridge between a finishing coat and an incompatible surface.

The primer for a flat finishing paint can be the paint itself, thinned with solvent (epoxies and urethanes are their own best primers). In most cases, however, using paint as its own primer is needlessly expensive. Ready-mixed primers are usually made with cheaper pigments and cost less than quality finishing paints. The ready mixes are thinner than finishing paints to promote quick drying, and they have a flat finish to provide the rough surface, known as "tooth," needed for good top coat adhesion.

Latex Primer
QUICK DRYING AND ODOR FREE
EASY TO CLEAN UP

This water-base primer is especially valuable in preparing plaster, concrete, gypsum wallboard or concrete block. Such masonry contains alkalis that destroy oil or alkyd finishing coats; the latex primer forms a barrier between the alkalis and the finish. In addition, this primer serves as a bridge between incompatible types of paint, since any paint will adhere to it and it will adhere to almost any surface—even glossy oil paint if the surface is well sanded. Do not use on raw wood, however: It will roughen the grain.

A latex primer has many of the advantages of latex paint. It is virtually odor free, it dries in two to four hours, and painting tools can be cleaned up simply with soap and water.

Alkyd Primer
BEST UNDERCOAT FOR WOOD
GOOD FOR ALL PAINTS
NOT RECOMMENDED FOR WALLBOARD

An alkyd primer is the best undercoat for raw wood, because it does not raise the grain of the wood. Some primers of this type can be used on masonry. But it is not ideal as a first coat on gypsum wallboard because alkyd raises a slight nap on the wallboard's paper covering. Most finishing coats—including flat latex—adhere well to an alkyd base coat. Alkyd primers take overnight to dry; tools and spills can be cleaned with the odor-free solvents used for alkyd paints.

Metal Primer and Paint
PREVENTS PEELING AND RUST

In most homes, the metals commonly painted are steel and aluminum. Steel must be kept painted or it will rust away. Aluminum does not require painting, but it pits if it is left uncoated or exposed to weather. Either metal can be protected with a special primer plus a finishing coat or with a metal paint.

The best primer of steel is an alkyd or oil type containing zinc, which rust-proofs the metal. For aluminum, use a zinc-based oil or alkyd metal primer, or apply epoxy or urethane finishes directly to the bare metal as self-primers. Any compatible finish can then be applied over these primers. (When you apply a finish coat to a radiator, use flat instead of glossy paint, which blocks heat.)

Primer and top coat are combined in a single mixture in the so-called metal paints. These oil or alkyd paints come in high-gloss and semigloss versions and are available in a wide range of colors. They are applied by brush, and cleaned and thinned with the conventional solvents used for oil or alkyd coatings.

Copper, brass and bronze hardware are not normally painted; instead, the fixtures are usually lacquered at the factory to preserve their original appearance. If the coating wears away unevenly, clean the finish off completely with a lacquer remover. In the case of copper and brass, tarnish should be removed with fine steel wool and metal polish—or, for a mirror finish, metal polish alone—and a protective coating of polyurethane varnish or epoxy should be applied. Uncoated bronze develops an attractive patina that can be protected against abrasion with varnish; if bright bronze is desired, treat it like brass. To paint over these metals, use an alkyd metal primer containing zinc and any compatible paint.

All metal primers and paints must be applied to a surface that is absolutely free of dirt and grease as well as corrosion. Remove rust from steel with an abrasive such as fine grade steel wool and, if you are not using metal paint, be sure bare spots are touched up with metal primer. Clean off grease with paint thinner.

Sealers and Primer-Sealers
SEALS PORES OF WOOD AND MASONRY
PRESERVES NATURAL LOOK OF WOOD

These liquids, made of synthetic resins mixed with a high proportion of solvent, seal the pores of wood and masonry.

Transparent wood sealers sink into the pores, binding the fibers together and making them easier to sand. They protect wood against dirt and moisture but not abrasion. These sealers should not be confused with opaque primers or transparent shellacs and varnishes. They dry more rapidly than most primers, and unlike varnish or shellac, both of which leave a glossy sheen, they do not alter the appearance of the wood. Stain, oil or alkyd paints or varnishes may be brushed directly over a clear wood sealer, since the wood, even though it is sealed, can absorb liquid.

So-called primer-sealers are opaque wood sealers (usually white) designed to solve a special problem: Because they are resistant to wood resins, these sealers are brushed over wood knots to prevent the resin from seeping through a finishing coat. These sealers are often thinned with alcohol. Aluminum paint is also sometimes used as a stain sealer.

Clear masonry sealers—often tinted a translucent blue to make it easier to see the areas that have been coated—are used on concrete, concrete block or plaster to prevent chalking. Opaque masonry sealers are particularly effective at slowing unwanted water seepage through basement walls. All masonry sealers vary greatly in their composition; consult the label of the package for cleanup instructions and for compatible top coats if you intend to paint over them.

Wood Filler
SMOOTHS THE SURFACE
CAN BE MIXED WITH STAIN

Filling is an essential first step in attaining a really smooth finish on fine wood such as paneling. Though some painters skip this step when preparing paneling, a filler should always be used to smooth rough, damaged or irregular sections, and it will give good sections a satiny smoothness. Used alone, a filler preserves the natural look of the wood, but it can also be mixed with stain to fill and color wood in a single operation.

Filler, a combination of synthetic resins and a wood-toned pigment, comes in either paste or liquid form. The paste type is slightly thinned with turpentine (or with a special solvent recommended by the manufacturer) and the resulting thick liquid is brushed or troweled onto damaged surfaces or open-grain woods such as walnut, ash, oak or mahogany. Liquid filler, which is simply a prethinned paste, is generally applied to woods with a closer grain, such as maple or birch. Neither paste nor liquid filler protects wood; the filler should be supplemented by a coat of sealer and, in a surface subject to heavy use, a final coat of shellac, varnish or paint.

Tool Kit for Interior Painting

Like most jobs, painting requires both general-purpose tools and some that are more specialized. Have on hand a ruler, hammer, screwdriver, sanding block and clean rags. The more specific tools and materials shown here help you to do interior painting neatly, easily and efficiently.

☐ To protect furniture and floors from drips and spatters, use plastic or paper dropcloths. Lightweight plastic (½-mil to 2-mil gauge) will do for furniture; use a heavier gauge (up to 4 mils) for floors. Paper dropcloths are better than newspapers but not as good as plastic.

☐ For patching wallboard or plaster before painting, you will need both stiff- and flexible-blade putty knives, a 6-inch taping knife, a 10-inch smoothing knife and a roll of joint tape to close wallboard seams, and an ordinary beverage can opener to clean plaster cracks. Sandpaper smooths repairs, a sticky fabric called a tack cloth removes sanding and plaster dust, and a sponge cleans up dirt and washes down previously painted walls. For both painting and repairing you will need rubber gloves to protect your hands from solvents and caustic materials.

☐ Mixing paint calls for a medium-sized (one gallon) pail and either the mixing device that fits into an electric drill, or wooden mixing paddles.

☐ For the variety of painting situations you are likely to face, you need both rollers and several different brushes. Included here are a 3-inch flat brush with a beaver-tail handle for wide trim, flat areas, edges and corners; a chisel-edge brush; and angular and oval sash brushes for narrow trim and windows.

☐ Tools for rolling on paint include a roller tray, a grating for squeezing off excess paint, a roller cover, a 9-inch spring roller frame and an extension pole for ceilings and high areas.

☐ To protect nearby surfaces in precision painting, use masking tape, striping tape (used mostly for decorative work) and a triangular metal paint guard.

☐ Cleanup chores can be eased by a comb to clean and align brush bristles, a spinner to remove paint and solvent from rollers and brushes, and a window scraper to peel dried paint from glass.

SPONGE

TACK CLOTH

DROPCLOTHS

SANDPAPER

JOINT TAPE

CAN OPENER

1¼'' FLEXIBLE-BLADE PUTTY KNIFE

1½''-BLADE PUTTY KNIFE

6'' TAPING KNIFE

PAINT GUARD

10'' SMOOTHING KNIFE

MASKING TAPE

STRIPING TAPE

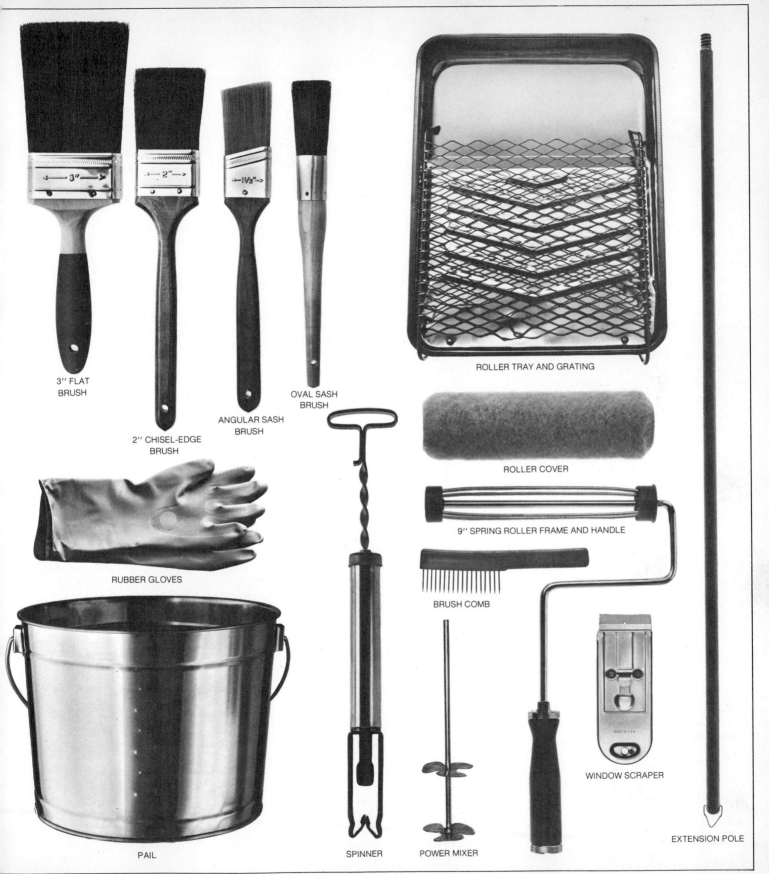

3" FLAT BRUSH

2" CHISEL-EDGE BRUSH

ANGULAR SASH BRUSH

OVAL SASH BRUSH

RUBBER GLOVES

PAIL

SPINNER

POWER MIXER

BRUSH COMB

ROLLER TRAY AND GRATING

ROLLER COVER

9" SPRING ROLLER FRAME AND HANDLE

WINDOW SCRAPER

EXTENSION POLE

Before You Paint: Preparing Interior Surfaces

The success of any interior paint job depends largely upon the care with which the surfaces of walls and ceilings have been prepared before you apply the first strokes of a brush or a roller. Rendering these surfaces free of dirt, dust, grease or flaking paint, repairing cracks or holes, and sanding surfaces smooth are chores that must be done, and done correctly. If they are not, your new finish cannot form a strong, long-lasting bond with the surface. Fortunately for the home painter, the tools and materials for these critical jobs are few and inexpensive, and the skills are easy to acquire.

Before starting any preparatory work, make the surfaces accessible by clearing the room as much as possible. Move portable objects such as lamps, end tables and chairs out of the room, then cluster the bulky furniture and heavy rugs in the center and cover them with dropcloths (plastic dropcloths are best, but even old sheets will do). Take down drapes, curtains, blinds and pictures and remove the rods, nails and hooks that support them. Protect the floor and carpet by spreading newspapers along the baseboards and covering the papers and the rest of the floor area with more dropcloths.

Now inspect the surfaces thoroughly to determine the work you must do, and draw up a list of the equipment you will need. First of all, look for structural damage or defects that may call for professional repairs. Bulges, stains and areas of chalky powder, for example, indicate serious leakage within a plaster wall or ceiling; large holes in wallboards may require the replacement of pieces of board or entire panels. If the surfaces have been previously wallpapered or painted, try to ascertain if the material beneath the paint or paper is wallboard or plaster, and, on a painted surface, the type of finish that was used. Such information will determine certain specific preparation treatments—deglossing paint, for example, or removing powdery coatings such as whitewash (box, right)—and will help you to select the proper under-coatings, primers and paints (chart, pages 148-149). You can paint over wallpaper, but any loose edges will show through the paint job. Since wallpaper is nearly impossible to remove once it is painted,

be sure to remove it first (pages 196-198).

To complete your checklist, go over the jobs that you must do. You may be lucky: If a surface is in good shape and the old paint is not loose or damaged, all that will be needed is a general cleaning (below). Far more often, however, surface preparation will include one or more of the following operations: Stripping old wallpaper (pages 196-198); patching damaged plaster (pages 13-14); repairing punctures, concealing nails and taping joints in wallboard (pages 15-21); and scraping or stripping old paint (page 158).

Some paint scraping and patching will be necessary in almost all cases, and these chores present a few special problems. Choose your patching materials with care. Some brands contain asbestos, a potential cause of cancer and lung disease, and particles of asbestos are released when the dry forms of these patching materials are mixed with water or when the materials are sanded. It is not likely that their limited use for small home repairs is dangerous, but to be on the safe side ask for an asbestos-free spackling compound, wallboard joint cement or patching plaster.

Be equally careful in sanding patched or repaired areas—though here the cau-

tion is more a matter of procedure than of materials. Electric sanders or commercial hand sanders with fittings that grip the sandpaper firmly can be used, but all that is required for sanding small areas on interior surfaces is a homemade sanding block and a supply of medium- and fine-grit flint sandpaper or—slightly more expensive, but longer lasting—aluminum oxide paper. Work in a well-ventilated room, wear a respirator (page 177) if you are not absolutely sure that your patching materials are asbestos-free, and follow all sanding with a thorough dusting and vacuuming of the surface and surrounding area.

With all the equipment on your checklist assembled, get to work. Surface preparation is a messy job, and cleansing agents, paint remover and sandpaper are either caustic or abrasive; therefore, wear old clothes, cover your head with a painter's hat or a scarf and protect your hands with gloves. Clean metal patching tools frequently so plaster or spackling compounds will not harden on them. Wipe them on newspapers, then wash with a wet cloth—do not rinse them off in a sink, because the compounds will clog the drains—and dry the tools thoroughly to prevent them from rusting.

The Importance of Cleaning

In every home, even the most immaculate, surfaces should be precleaned just before they are painted. Inevitably some dust or grease lodges on walls and ceilings—especially in bathrooms and kitchens—and such dirt-catchers as baseboards, doors and door tops, and window trim. Every bit of dirt on any of these surfaces must be removed, for even fingerprints can prevent new paint from adhering firmly.

A good washing down with a heavy-duty household detergent will usually suffice for wall and for painted woodwork; a ceiling (which is less accessible) or an area of virgin wallboard (which should soak up water like a sponge) can simply be dusted or wiped with a mop. Any traces of water washes, such as calcimine or white wash, should be scrubbed off with a stiff brush. An

extra-strong solvent for dirt and grease is trisodium phosphate, or TSP, but because phosphates can pollute water supplies, TSP solvents are banned in many communities.

In addition to these general procedures, solve special problems as they arise. New paint will not adhere properly to glossy surfaces; dull such finishes by raising a nap—or "cutting a tooth," in painters' jargon—with sandpaper or a commercial deglosser. If floor wax has adhered to baseboards, take it off with wax remover. Remove rust (page 185) from radiators, pipes and heat ducts, and clean mildew from damp places. When stripping wallpaper, wash off remaining bits of paper, paste and sizing. Finally, always be sure that precleaned surfaces are completely dry before starting to paint.

Two Ways to Use Sandpaper

1 **For a large, flat area.** Make a sanding block from wood or corkboard. A block about 3 inches wide and 4 or 5 inches long will fit most hands comfortably. Cut a piece of sandpaper large enough to cover one surface of the block, with sufficient overlap so the paper can be wrapped completely around the block, as in the drawing at right. Wrap the paper with the grit side out.

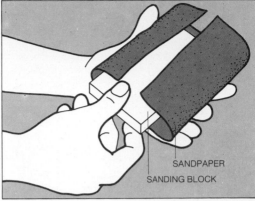

SANDPAPER

SANDING BLOCK

2 **Using the sanding block.** Make sure that all loose paint is removed from the area to be sanded, and that any patching compounds are completely dry. Grasp the block firmly, holding the sandpaper snugly around it, and sand with a gentle, circular motion *(arrows)*, "feathering," or blending, the edges of old paint or patching materials into the surrounding surface. Tap the sandpaper frequently on a hard surface to remove accumulated residue, and replace the paper when it becomes clogged. In sanding previously painted surfaces, start with medium-grit sandpaper; for an extra-smooth finish, sand again with fine-grit paper wrapped around the block. When sanding virgin wood, use only fine-grit paper and do not use the circular motion; instead, work in straight strokes along the grain.

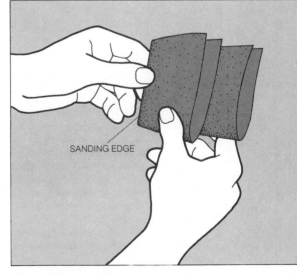

SANDING EDGE

3 **For a hard-to-reach area.** Angled or intricate places, such as corners, window trim or the indentations in moldings, are not easily accessible with a sanding block. To reach such spots, fold a 6-inch square of sandpaper into quarters to make a sharp sanding edge.

4 **Using the sanding edge.** Hold the folded sandpaper with the sharp main fold facing out, as in the drawing. Insert the fold into the area to be sanded—in this example, one of the wooden dividers in a window sash. Gently rub the paper over the surface, feathering the edges of old paint or patching material as you go. Refold the paper as necessary to make fresh edges.

Erasing Past Mistakes

A good paint job depends partly upon the care—or lack of it—exercised by previous painters. Careless painters leave heavy buildups of old, brittle finishes, many layers of incompatible paints, and surfaces that are badly scarred—and these defects, in turn, create additional problems such as alligatoring, blistering and peeling *(pages 178-181)*. These flaws must be corrected before you apply new paint, or the coating will not adhere and you will continue the cycle of failure.

To begin with, loose paint should be scraped off. If the process causes deep depressions in the scraped areas, the depressions must be filled in to level the surface *(far right)*. More serious paint problems call for a different procedure: if the area of damaged paint is extensive or if many layers of paint must be removed, the old paint should be stripped off completely with a chemical paint remover *(below)*.

Scraping Off Loose Paint

1 **Removing the paint.** For work on small areas, insert the edge of a 1¼-inch-wide, flexible or stiff-blade putty knife under the edges of loose paint *(drawing)* and, with a pushing motion, scrape off all the old finish that does not adhere firmly. For large areas, use a pull-type scraper *(page 176)* to save time. Be careful not to gouge the surface with either tool. (Caution: the pull-type scraper is comparatively difficult to control.) At the end of this phase, examine the surfaces to be repainted to be sure you have not overlooked any areas of loose paint.

PUTTY KNIFE

LOOSE PAINT

Stripping Off Old Paint

PAINT REMOVER

1 **Applying paint remover.** Use a water-washable, paste-type chemical paint remover for almost all surfaces. The exception to this rule is the surface covered with wood veneer, since a water wash may lift or buckle the veneer; use a solvent-based remover instead. All paint removers contain chemicals that are extremely caustic and can produce dangerous fumes; therefore, cover the surrounding area with a thick layer of newspaper, wear goggles, old clothes and rubber or plastic gloves, and be sure that the room is well ventilated.

Using a clean, inexpensive bristle paintbrush, spread a generous amount of remover on the area to be stripped *(drawing)*. Work with short strokes, brushing in one direction. Do not cover an area more than 2 feet square at one time.

2 **Filling in depressions.** A minor scraping job may leave a slight, almost invisible depression between a scraped area and the edges of adhering old paint. In this case, feather *(page 157)* the edges of the old paint with sandpaper to blend them into the scraped surface. If the depression is deep enough to be noticeable, fill the low place with vinyl spackling compound or wallboard joint cement *(page 16)*. Use a flexible-blade putty knife to apply the filler to a small depression; use a wide-blade wallboard taping knife *(page 154)* for extensive filling *(drawing)*. When the filler has dried, sand it even with the surface. Spot-prime *(pages 148-149)* all scraped or filled areas before repainting.

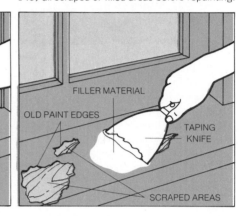

FILLER MATERIAL

OLD PAINT EDGES

TAPING KNIFE

SCRAPED AREAS

2 **Removing the paint.** When the paint begins to blister and wrinkle, peel it off with a taping knife *(drawing)* or stiff-blade putty knife. As you remove the paint, clean the knife frequently by wiping it on sheets of newspaper. Then apply the remover to the next area. If one application is not sufficient, brush on as many coats as necessary, but always peel off the loosened paint between coats of remover. When all paint is off, follow the instructions on the paint-remover label to clean the bare surface, using a wash of water or benzine as the label directs. Wait for the surface to dry, then smooth it lightly with fine-grit sandpaper.

OLD PAINT

A Room Wrapped Up and Ready for Painting

The room below indicates the wide range of repairs and preparation required before painting begins. Most of the repairs, such as patching cracks and holes or sealing wood joints *(pages 13-20 and 36),* will be necessary from time to time. Any properly prepared room, however, should bear some resemblance to this mosaic of swatches and patches.

A lot of the precautions you took before making repairs (such as covering the furniture with dropcloths) will serve equally well as protection against the inevitable splattering of paint. Minor paint splashes on hardware or glass are not serious; if you catch them before the paint dries they are easily removed with water or chemical solvent and a clean rag. If, however, you are a perfectionist—or you want to save some time when cleaning up—a few simple, last-minute tasks that will result in a neater job are suggested:

☐ OUTLETS AND SWITCHES. Unscrew the fuses or turn off the circuit breakers for the room. Remove the switch and receptacle plates, then group them together *(lower left);* paint the plates when you paint the walls. Sand off any chipped paint around the openings. Turn the electricity back on for illumination if necessary, but paint carefully around the openings and keep children and pets away.

☐ LIGHTING FIXTURES. Loosen the attaching screws of the mounting plates of the ceiling fixtures *(top center)* or the wall sconces *(right)* so that the plates stand away from the surface a bit. In painting, use a brush to cut in carefully around the rims of the mounting plates. Protect the fixtures by covering them with plastic bags or sheets of plastic fastened with masking tape, and do not turn on these lights while the plastic is in place.

☐ STATIONARY APPLIANCES. Use newspaper or plastic and masking tape to cover radiators *(below windows)* or thermostats *(beside light switch).*

☐ HARDWARE. Uninterrupted surfaces are always easier to paint, so some painters will remove as much hardware as possible—unless, of course, the objects themselves are to be painted. You may wish to take off items such as doorknobs, the plates behind them, cabinet handles and drapery hardware. Masking tape will protect parts not easily removed, such as door hinges, locks and striker plates. Window-sash locks can either be removed or masked.

☐ WINDOW GLASS. Many painters use the beading technique *(page 165)* on window sashes and dividers, but you may wish to protect the panes with masking tape, leaving a 1/16-inch gap between the tape and the wood or metal window parts.

Final preparations. After repairs are completed, you may find that the area to be painted looks worse than before, but the new paint will rapidly cover all of the patched surfaces. Before starting to paint, you may wish to attend to some of the protective measures suggested above.

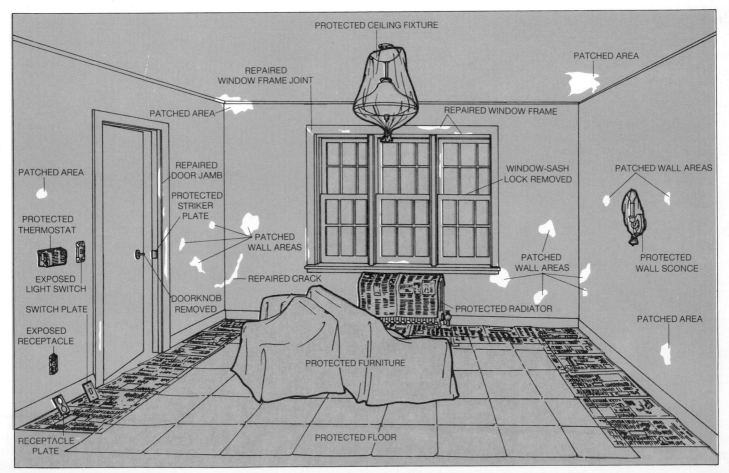

PROTECTED CEILING FIXTURE
REPAIRED WINDOW FRAME JOINT
PATCHED AREA
PATCHED AREA
REPAIRED WINDOW FRAME
REPAIRED DOOR JAMB
PATCHED AREA
PROTECTED THERMOSTAT
WINDOW-SASH LOCK REMOVED
PATCHED WALL AREAS
PROTECTED STRIKER PLATE
PATCHED WALL AREAS
EXPOSED LIGHT SWITCH
PROTECTED WALL SCONCE
SWITCH PLATE
REPAIRED CRACK
PATCHED WALL AREAS
EXPOSED RECEPTACLE
DOORKNOB REMOVED
PROTECTED RADIATOR
PATCHED AREA
PROTECTED FURNITURE
RECEPTACLE PLATE
PROTECTED FLOOR

Fine Points of Applying Paint

The basic rule for easy, efficient interior painting is simple: Use a roller whenever and wherever you can. In recent years even professional painters have been abandoning their cherished brushes for ceiling and wall work, and with good reason. A roller covers these areas more than twice as fast as a paintbrush and requires less skill and effort. Guidelines for picking a good roller and for matching a roller to a specific surface appear on the opposite page.

A roller alone, however, will probably not suffice for the whole job. Most interior painting calls for a combination of roller and brush; a single brush, as a matter of fact, may not be enough for the most efficient work. You need a brush for surfaces that a roller is not designed to cover—a delicate, ridged molding, for example, or the narrow divider between windowpanes. You also need a brush —not necessarily the same brush—to use in corners that a roller cannot reach. And you may turn to a brush to paint certain flat areas, such as the wall above a built-in cupboard, where working with a roller can be awkward.

Choose a brush of the right size and shape for the kind of work you are doing. Use as wide a brush as possible, to make the painting go faster, but not wider than the surface you are covering. A 1- or 1½-inch trim brush is good for window dividers, a 2- or 2½-inch sash brush for baseboards and window frames and

sills. For large, flat areas use a 3-inch or, at most, 4-inch brush. (Professional painters regularly use 4-inch or even 5-inch brushes, but it takes long practice and a powerful wrist and forearm to handle them with ease.)

Choose a brush shape that is tailored to the job, using the pictures on page 155 as a guide. The familiar flat brush with squared-off ends is a general-purpose brush; for precise edges and lines, pick a flat trim brush with a beveled, chisel-shaped working end. An angular sash brush, especially designed for certain hard-to-reach surfaces, cannot normally be used on flat surfaces but is ideal for the insides of window- and door frames or the louvers of a shutter. Round or oval brushes have the largest paint-carrying capacity and splay out when applied to a surface; they work best on thin, curved surfaces, such as pipes.

Finally, match your painting tools to the type of paint you are using. Latex paint, which is likely to be used for at least part of every job, calls for a brush or roller with synthetic bristles or nap. Natural bristles and fibers absorb water from latex paint and lose their resiliency. For oil or alkyd paints, which give a smooth gloss to trim, professionals have long preferred a finely tapered hog-bristle brush. However, a good synthetic-bristle brush will also do a fine job and can double as a cutting-in brush if you are using latex on the rest of the room.

Designed for flow. This cutaway shows the desirable elements to be found in a typical flat brush. The bristles, whether natural or synthetic, are "flagged"—that is, split or frayed—at the working end to provide greater area for holding paint. At the other end, the bristles are embedded in hard plastic. One or more "plugs," or spacers, made of metal, wood or hard rubber separate the bristles where they are embedded (you can see a plug by separating the bristles with your hand). The bristles along the sides of a plug "toe in" and meet at the tip in a firm, trim edge from which paint flows evenly. A metal band called a ferrule holds the bristle base to the heel of the handle.

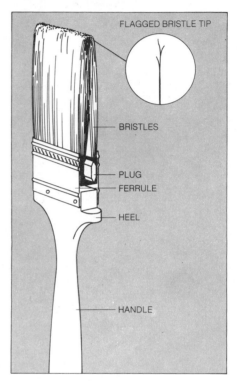

FLAGGED BRISTLE TIP

BRISTLES

PLUG
FERRULE

HEEL

HANDLE

What Makes a Good Brush Good?

When you are shopping for a paintbrush, carefully check the points that are listed below. These guidelines apply to both synthetic and natural-bristle brushes of any size and shape, and can help you to make a knowledgeable on-the-spot appraisal of quality.

☐ Grip the handle of the brush as you would for painting *(page 164)*. The shape and the weight should feel comfortable in your grasp. The metal ferrule should be attached solidly to the handle, preferably with nails. If the handle is made of wood, it should have a glossy or rub-

berized coating, which resists moisture and is easy to keep clean.

☐ Press the bristles against the palm of your hand. They should not separate into clumps but should fan out slightly in an even spread. When you lift the brush away from your hand, the bristles should readily spring back to their original position.

☐ Examine the bristles with care. They should be smooth and straight and the tips should be flagged, as shown in the drawing above. If you are comparing brushes that are the same width, select

the one with the longest, thickest bristles; it will hold the most paint.

☐ Part the bristles and examine the way they are set into the base. The plug or plugs should be no more than half the thickness of the setting.

☐ Slap the brush against the palm of your hand to shake out any loose bristles—any brand-new brush may have a few. Then tug on the bristles once or twice. No additional bristles should come out. If any do, be wary; badly anchored bristles will seriously hinder the efficiency of the brush.

Picking the right roller. Both the cover and the frame of the roller below have features worth looking for when you choose a roller. The cover wraps in a spiral around the central core (if it is not made this way, ridges will appear in the painted surface). The core itself is plastic; plastic-coated cardboard is almost as good, though less durable. The frame has a spring cage that holds the core firmly in place (cheaper models, with frames that do not support the middle of the cover, may quit working effectively long before a job is done). Nylon bearings at the end caps of the frame help the cover turn smoothly. The handle is contoured for a comfortable grip, and the end of the handle is threaded to accept an extension pole.

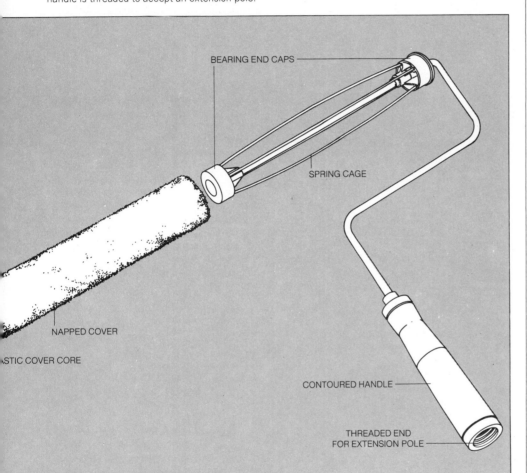

BEARING END CAPS

SPRING CAGE

NAPPED COVER

ASTIC COVER CORE

CONTOURED HANDLE

THREADED END
FOR EXTENSION POLE

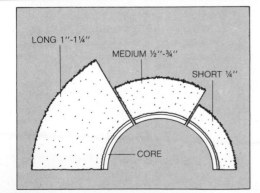

LONG 1″–1¼″

MEDIUM ½″–¾″

SHORT ¼″

CORE

Fitting a nap to a paint and a surface. Roller covers are sold in short, medium and long nap lengths. A short nap, generally about ¼ inch deep, does not hold as much paint as the others but is the best kind to use with glossy paint, since it leaves a thin, very smooth coating. The all-purpose medium nap, about ½ to ¾ inch deep, holds any type of paint well and produces a soft-looking, stippled effect. The deep pile of a long nap—about 1 to 1¼ inches—works a heavy load of paint into the irregularities of a textured, damaged or extremely porous surface, and can be used to create a deeply stippled effect on any surface.

Protecting Yourself —and Your Pets

Remember that when you paint you are using strong chemical mixtures, and must take proper precautions.

☐ Water-thinned paints, such as latex, are the safest, but like all coatings, they contain poisonous ingredients. Be sure to keep them out of the reach of children.

☐ Use special care in handling paints based on mineral spirits (oil and alkyd types); these paints are highly flammable and their fumes are toxic. Do not be misled by the fact that you may not smell any fumes; the new "odorless" types are just as flammable and poisonous as the ones you can smell. Do not use mineral-thinned paints in a poorly ventilated room, and do not drink alcoholic beverages when you paint with them; alcohol can so increase your body's susceptibility to some fumes that the inhalation of even a small amount may be fatal. Never rest a can of paint on a kitchen range; as an additional precaution, check the manufacturer's label to see whether a paint or thinner is so flammable that the pilot light of a gas range should be extinguished.

☐ When painting a ceiling or getting at a high spot on a wall, do not handle the roller or brush so that you risk getting paint in your eyes.

☐ Do not leave any coating on your skin longer than you must; wash up carefully every time you quit or take a break.

☐ The label on a paint can always lists specific antidotes. Keep the label on hand in the event that you need to call a physician.

☐ All too frequently, curiosity-prone pets find ways of getting into your painting area—and into your paint. The results may seem comical, but paint on an animal's skin or fur can do serious harm unless you remove it before the animal starts licking it off. Wash off latex paint with plain water. To remove oil or alkyd paints, soak a cloth with mineral oil or cooking oil and use it to slide the paint off the fur or skin. Never use turpentine or any other powerful paint solvent: It will burn the animal's skin and will be doubly dangerous if it is licked off.

Mixing and Straining

Most of a mixing job is generally done for you by the paint dealer, who will give paint a vigorous shake by machine when you buy it. Then if you use it within a day or so, all you have to do is give it a few turns with a mixing paddle.

If the paint you bring home has not been machine-agitated, however, you are likely to find a thin, colorless fluid on the surface and a thick layer of pigment at the bottom of the can. To restore such paint to its proper consistency turn it upside down, tightly sealed, and let it sit that way a few hours or, better still, overnight. Before you remove the lid, shake the can vigorously. Then open the can and follow the steps shown at right.

Plan to use a second container for the actual painting, especially if the original can is gallon-sized. Use a little paint at a time from this auxiliary pail, and keep the big can closed, so that the paint inside is less likely to dry out, get dirty or spill.

Manual mixing. Pour about one third of the thin paint at the top of the can into a second container. Stir the remaining paint to a uniform consistency, using a wooden paddle. Do not use a metal spoon or piece of wire; the inside of a paint can has a rust-preventing coating that might be damaged by metal scraping against it. Gradually add small amounts of the thin paint that was poured into the container back to the can, stirring as you add each portion *(below)*, until all of the original contents of the can have been returned to it. Pour the mixed paint from the can to the container and back again several times for a final, thorough blending.

Power mixing. A variable-speed electric drill with a two-blade mixing attachment like the one below stirs up a badly settled can of paint quickly. Submerge the mixer in the full can of paint until both blades are under the surface. Since power mixers are usually made of metal, which can scar the coating of a paint can, do not operate your mixer with the shaft near the sides or bottom of the can. With the drill off, lower the mixer until it touches bottom, then raise it to a position in which a couple of inches of paint-covered shaft show above the surface of the paint, and turn on the drill to a low speed. To avoid splatters, turn off the drill before withdrawing the mixer.

Removing paint skin. If a can of alkyd paint has been opened and then resealed carelessly a thick skin of hardened paint may form on the surface. Do not plunge a paddle or mixer into the skin; this tough layer never dissolves, and attempts to mix it with the rest of the paint will leave stray bits that show up on a newly painted surface. To remedy this problem, gently separate the skin from the side of the can with a paddle. Drape cheesecloth over a separate container and tie the cloth to the rim with string *(drawing)*. Pour all of the paint through this filter and then discard the cheesecloth and paint debris. Mix the remaining paint as described above; it is not affected by the loss of the material in the skin.

Mixing in color. Creating a special color for more than a gallon of paint is beyond the skills of most amateurs; you will find it almost impossible to match batches that are mixed separately. Rely instead on the wide variety of premixed colors, or ask your paint dealer to mix as much as you need in the shade you want. If you want to experiment with color-mixing, however, to create a new shade or match an old one, use the concentrated tint called universal colorant, which comes in many colors and works with all types of paint.

Do not mix the colorant directly into the full can of paint, for the smallest error can ruin a whole batch of paint. Instead, pour a small amount of paint into a clear plastic or glass cup. Using the proportion guidelines on the colorant label, add the tint to the sample of paint in the cup and stir *(above, left)*. The clear cup allows you to see whether any of the unblended color adheres to the sides.

When the color in the cup is thoroughly mixed, begin adding the tinted portion back to the original paint a little at a time, stirring slowly by hand until you have reached the exact shade you want. Remember that dry paint and wet paint vary in color, so test it first by preparing a sample and letting it dry. If you are adding color to sand paint, allow the paint to stand for about half an hour after you have added the color before using it.

Avoiding Lumps and Drips

Once the paint has been mixed and you are underway, time-consuming interruptions should be kept to a minimum. The best intentions and the steadiest hand cannot ensure against the drip that sticks to the newspapers on the floor, and that then sticks to the furniture or to your shoe. Stray bristles, dust and other debris find their way into your paint bucket and eventually onto what you hoped would be an unblemished surface. Correcting these little annoyances can take up more time than applying the paint. The following suggestions can help keep these distractions to a minimum, making the job neater and quicker and the results more satisfactory.

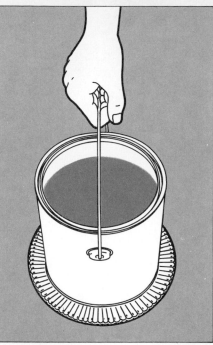

Drip-proofing the can. To cut down on paint splashes on your floor, make a drip guard for your paint can from a plastic-coated paper plate; attach it to the bottom of the can with masking tape, doubled over so it is sticky on both sides. The paper plate catches all of the drips from the edge of the can, and when you move the container the drip guard travels right along.

Keeping the paint clean. Stray bristles, hardened pieces of paint and bits of dirt that inevitably get into your paint can mar the work and are nearly impossible to fish out. Solve the problem another way. Before you begin to paint, cut several pieces of screen wire to the size of your paint-pail opening. Then, when something falls into the paint, drop a screen onto the surface. It will sink, taking debris to the bottom and trapping it there.

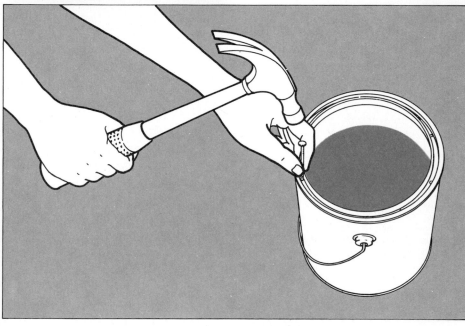

Preventing an overflow. The U-shaped rim of a paint can often becomes an overflowing reservoir of paint. To avoid drips from gallon cans, hammer a small nail several times through the bottom of the rim, making holes around the circumference. Paint that is caught in the rim will then drain back into the can, which can still be sealed for storage because the lid covers the holes.

Thick latex paints may clog the holes quickly, so keep a nail handy to open them up again. This draining technique cannot be used with cans smaller than a gallon because nailing holes through the narrow rim of a small paint can may skew it so badly the can cannot be resealed.

The Basics of Brushwork

The first step in brushwork starts before a drop of paint is deposited on a surface. To begin with, you must hold the brush correctly; your work will be neater and less tiring. A sash-and-trim brush like the one pictured at right is generally used for beading, cutting-in and a variety of jobs on flat surfaces such as doors. Its long, thin "pencil" handle is most effectively grasped with the fingers, much as you would hold a pencil or a fork. This grip provides the greatest control for careful work. A long-handled brush will enable you to adjust your grip for reaching into close areas, and to switch easily from one hand to the other.

Wider and heavier brushes for larger wall areas, like the one below, usually have stout handles, a type called "beaver tail." This handle provides balance for the heavier bristle bunch but is too thick to be gripped comfortably with the fingers, pencil-style. A beaver-tail handle is best held firmly with the whole hand, as you would hold a tennis racket. With all flat brushes, whatever their handle style, you may want to switch for a change of pace to the grip used for beading *(opposite, bottom),* with your thumb on one side of the ferrule and your other fingers on the other.

Painting in sections. When you paint an area considerably wider than your brush, such as the space above a built-in cabinet or below a window, work in rectangular sections. The size of a section depends largely on the setting speed of your paint and the capacity of your brush. With fast-setting paints, cover small sections, each about two brush widths across and two bristle lengths long; experiment with somewhat larger sections when you are working with medium- or slow-setting paint. Start a new section about two brush lengths below a completed one, and work toward and into the area of wet paint *(drawing).* Work vertically whenever possible; up-and-down strokes are the least tiring.

Loading the brush. Dip bristles into the paint one third to one half of the way up from the tip. Then tap the ferrule of the brush gently against the rim of the pail to remove excess paint. Do not wipe the brush across the pail rim because that removes too much paint. And do not overload the brush by dipping it in too far. The excess will drip off or run down into the heel and over the handle; if the paint collects and dries inside the ferrule, it will ruin the brush.

A fine, feathered brushstroke. If you are using the appropriate brush with the right paint, you need apply very little pressure as you paint. Each brushstroke should be about double the length of the bristles of your brush. The stroke begins with the flat side of the brush angled low to the surface (1). As you move the brush, the angle will increase gradually (2). Wherever possible, end each stroke in the wet paint of a previously painted section, drawing the brush up and off the surface with a slight twist (3); the brush should leave a thin, feathered edge of paint that will merge into a smooth layer of new paint.

Most initial brushstrokes are upstrokes, like the one shown below. Follow it with a downstroke over the same area or, if a single stroke covers the area satisfactorily, over the area at the immediate right or left. Continue brushing until you have covered a small section of the surface.

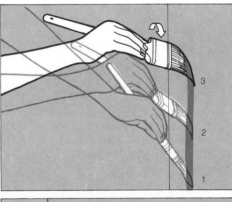

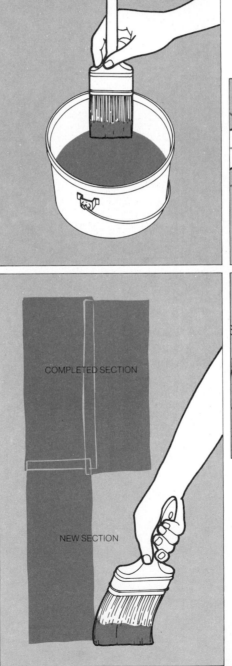

COMPLETED SECTION

NEW SECTION

PAINT SHIELD

Guarding as you go. A triangular metal or plastic paint shield, available for a few cents from paint dealers, is used by many painters to protect surfaces adjoining the area being painted. It works best on trim such as baseboards, where there is a fine crack separating the two areas. The guard can then be forced into the crack so that no paint gets on the edge of the shield, where it might cause smears. Hold the shield with one hand over the surface to be protected, push its edge into place and paint with the other hand. Wipe the shield clean frequently, or it will make more smears than it prevents; and do not use an improvised cardboard shield, which will soon become soggy and shapeless.

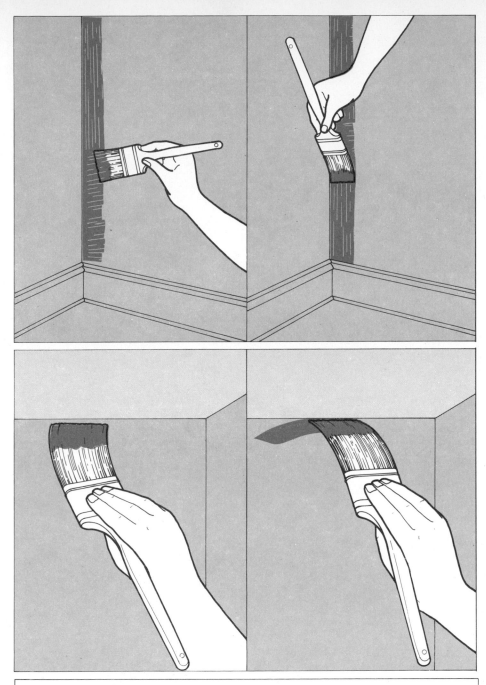

Cutting in. Even when you paint a room with a roller, you must first use a brush to cut in—that is, to paint a strip about 2 inches wide in corners between two surfaces of matching paints and colors. (Do not use the technique described here when you are painting ceiling and walls in different colors, or woodwork and walls in different colors or paints; instead, use the more precise beading technique shown below.) To cut in, take four or five overlapping brushstrokes perpendicular to the edge of the wall *(far left)* or ceiling, then smooth this strip with one long stroke that ends in an area of wet paint *(left)*. Leave a 1/16-inch space when you begin the perpendicular strokes near the baseboard, then smooth the paint all the way down when you begin your long stroke.

Beading. You can achieve a steady, straight edge where tow colors meet, or paint the narrow dividers between windowpanes without the bother of masking tape, once you master a brush technique called beading. Use a trim brush with a firm chiseled bristle edge *(page 155)*. Grasp the brush on the heel with your thumb on one side and all four fingers on the other. Press the brush flat against the surface, forcing a thin line of paint—the bead—to float along the bristle tips *(far left)*. Then, in one smooth, steady motion, draw this paint bead along a line about 1/16 inch from the edge of the surface you are painting *(left)*. The wet paint will spread out sufficiently in all directions—including the vertical one—so that it draws even to the line itself.

Varnish: A Clear Exception

The rules for applying varnish and other clear, fast-setting coatings are quite different from those for ordinary painting. Some manufacturers provide special instructions on can labels, but most clear coatings are applied by the following method:

Load the brush up more than you do with regular paint, dipping the bristles into the varnish for about half their length. With each brushload make one long, smooth stroke rather than several short, overlapping ones. (Repeated brushing creates bubbles on the surface that cannot be eliminated.) Instead of painting from a dry to a wet area, start each new stroke at the end of the previous stroke. Most jobs require at least three coats of varnish, with a light sanding between coats.

The Basics of Rollerwork

Rollers need no special preparation unless you are using glossy paint and a new, fluffy short-nap roller. In that case, prime the roller by sloshing it in soapy water to remove loose strands of material. Rinse thoroughly and make sure the nap is completely dry before you begin.

A roller pan can be used as it comes, but you will find it easier to saturate the roller evenly if you insert a specially made wire-mesh grating (right) over the sloped side of the pan. Cleanup is simplified if you line the pan before each use with a plastic tray liner or heavy-duty aluminum foil.

For most rooms, a 4-foot extension handle is all you will need to reach high places. Before you buy any extension, however, see if the threaded end of your push broom, mop or wax-applicator handle will fit into the roller handle.

Loading the roller. Crimp a sheet of aluminum foil securely around the rim of the pan. Fill the well of the pan half full and dip the roller in. It will be a little less than half submerged. Lift the roller and roll it down the sloped grating—but not back into the paint. Roll on the grating two or three times. Dip the roller into the paint once more and roll it on the grating until the cover has been saturated evenly. Do not overload the roller or it will drip and slide, producing an uneven coat.

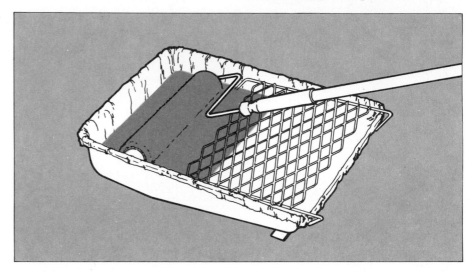

Starting with a Zigzag

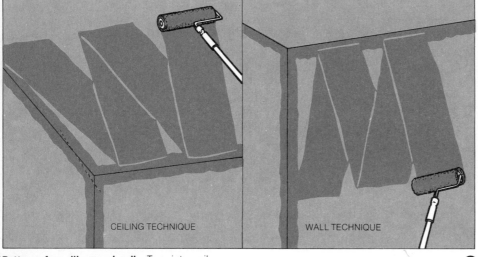

CEILING TECHNIQUE

WALL TECHNIQUE

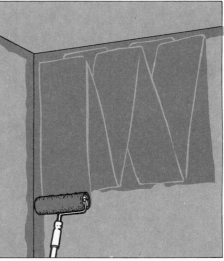

1 Patterns for ceilings and walls. To paint a ceiling, begin about 3 feet from the corner and roll toward the corner—the first stroke with a newly loaded roller should always be away from you. Then continue, without lifting the roller from the surface, to make a "W" pattern about 3 feet square, as in the drawing above.

To paint a wall, push the roller upward on the first stroke—away from you—and then complete an "M" pattern (center drawing). These initial strokes spread the heaviest part of the paint load evenly over the section you will now fill in (right) without removing the roller from the surface.

2 Filling in. After completing an "M" or a "W," begin filling in a 3-foot square by crisscrossing strokes of the roller without lifting it from the surface. Each stroke should be about 18 to 24 inches long. Use even pressure to avoid bubbles and blotches, and stop when the entire section is evenly covered with paint. Do not continue to roll once the paint on your roller has been used up; this will not make the paint cover a larger area, but it will affect your results. There is no need to finish up with uniform strokes all going in one direction. Move along to the next section, load the roller again and repeat the sequence by making an initial pattern and then filling in.

Creating a Texture Effect

Texture paint has the consistency of wet plaster and can be fashioned to produce a rough, rustic surface or more formal patterns. A similar product, called sand paint, is mixed with coarse granules that give it a gritty appearance. Both paints are usually used to cover walls and ceilings that have small cracks, bumps or poorly concealed wallboard joints.

Preparation of the old surface is still important, however. Peeling paint must be scraped off but you need not be so meticulous about smoothing over patches because the paint texture will obscure many of the irregularities.

Plain texture paint should be put on with a trowel, a wide brush or a wide sponge-rubber applicator like the one used here. Sand paint can be applied with a long-napped roller or a wide, stiff synthetic-bristle brush.

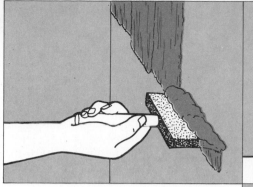

Stippling and swirling. To apply texture paint, smear it onto the surface as evenly as possible until you have covered a 3-by-3-foot section with about ⅛ inch of paint. Work your texture pattern on that area before covering another section. The sponge-rubber applicator shown here doubles as a texturing tool. When you pat the flat side of the tool over the surface, tiny peaks rise up that give a deeply stippled effect *(above, right)*. An ordinary sponge or a piece of crumpled wax paper produces a similar effect. For more formal patterns, draw a plastic whisk broom lightly over the wet paint in straight or wavy lines or, as in the drawing at right, in a series of overlapping arcs.

Taking a Break

When you suspend a painting project for more than a day you need the kind of major cleanup described on pages 172-173. When you break for a shorter time—a few minutes to overnight—take the following simple precautions.

☐ If you are certain to resume painting within 15 minutes or so, leave your brush on a support—never standing on its bristles in a can. The support at right is coathanger wire run through two holes in the top edge of a pail.

☐ For a longer break, wrap wet brushes or rollers in plastic wrap or aluminum foil *(right, below)*. Do not bind the bristles or nap too tightly. Set brushes on their sides or hang them by the handles.

☐ If you have paint left in your roller tray or in an open pail, cover it tightly with plastic or, better still, pour the contents into the original can and reseal by hammering the lid down.

☐ For an overnight break there is no need to clean the rim of a resealed can before you tap the lid in place. But to avoid splatters, toss a cloth over the lid before you tap.

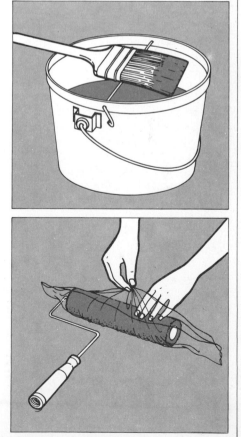

The Sequence for Painting the Parts of a Room

For the beginner, interior painting can become a blotched affair of smeared paint and drips on a newly finished surface. But it need not be. To avoid such problems, professionals have worked out an easy systematic approach.

Paint a room from top to bottom: The ceiling first, then walls, then windows, doors and other woodwork, and, finally, the baseboards. First "cut in" 2-inch-wide strips with a brush around the edges of the ceiling, using the technique described on page 165. Then switch to a roller with a 4- or 5-foot extension pole and, starting at a corner (drawing, below), paint a section about 3 feet square. Continue to cover the entire ceiling, working across its shortest dimension in 3-foot-square sections, covering each with one dip of the roller. With this technique you can do the job much faster and more easily from the floor than if you use the brush. Also, by overlapping each newly painted area with one that is still wet, you will avoid the lap marks made when the wet paint is laid over dry.

If the room is very small or the ceiling surface is heavily textured, you may decide to paint all of the ceiling with a brush. Paint small sections with each dip of the brush—the size of each section will depend on the size of the brush (page 164)—and continue across the room section by section. Once you have begun to paint the ceiling, either by brush or by roller, work steadily across the short dimensions as shown.

Walls are painted in much the same way. Starting at the ceiling, cut in with a brush. Use the brush also to cut in wall-to-wall corners and the edges of windows, doors, baseboards and cabinets. Then paint the walls in a way comfortable for you. Many people prefer to paint in vertical portions from top to bottom. However, if you are using a roller on an extension pole, you may find it easier to work horizontally across the wall in 3-foot-square sections; then remove the extension from the roller and continue painting across the room. This sequence saves the bother of removing and replacing the extension pole as you paint each strip down the wall. Paint each wall without stopping, then pause for a careful look at your work. As with the ceiling,

overlap each newly painted area with one that is still wet, avoiding lap marks. While the paint is still wet, cover missed spots with a thin layer of paint.

Painting double-hung windows in the sequence shown opposite will solve the tricky problem of moving the sashes to paint surfaces that are obstructed by the lower sash of the window. Paint the horizontal parts of the frame with back-and-forth strokes of the brush and the vertical parts with up-and-down strokes.

To minimize drips on the glass panes, hold the metal or plastic splash guard over the pane about $1/8$ inch away from the wood. Do not, however, rely on this shield for a straight edge; instead, use the beading technique shown on page 165, and apply the paint $1/16$ inch onto the glass to make an airtight seal. You can clean any paint smudges or drips, using a cloth

or the scraper technique described at the bottom of page 173.

Painting doors, cabinets and drawers is a relatively routine chore, although doors present a few special problems. There is one conventional rule: Paint the latch edge and hinge edge the same color as the room into which the edge faces when the door is open. Remember, too, that when you paint a brand-new unpainted door, you should take it off the hinges to get at the bottom edge to seal it and protect against warping. Remove the lower hinge first; otherwise the door may fall off the upper hinge and its full weight may ruin the bottom hinge. Tap the pin gently from below, using a punch and a hammer if necessary. When the pin has lifted a half inch or so, grip it just below the head with pliers and tap the pliers until the pin has been extracted.

Ceilings and Walls

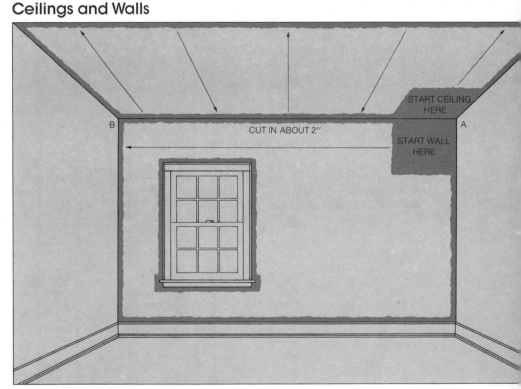

A basic pattern. Face the long dimension of a room, as in the diagram above, and start the ceiling at corner A or B. The arrows trace the paths to follow if you start at A; reverse their directions if you start at B. Shaded areas indicate where you must use a brush to cut in paint. When you reach a door or window, cut in the entire frame at once, rather than segment by segment.

Double-Hung Windows

1 Starting on the sashes. Raise the inside sash and lower the outside sash until their relative positions are almost completely reversed, as shown. To avoid getting in your own way, paint the inside sash in this order: inner strips (horizontals and then verticals), outer strips (horizontals and then verticals). Do not paint the top edge of the inside sash; you will use that surface to move the sash for the next step. On the outside sash, paint the same parts in the same order as far as they are exposed—but do not paint the bottom edge. Paint this edge when you paint the house's exterior.

2 Completing the sashes. Pushing against their bottom and top edges, move the outside sash up and the inside sash down to about 1 inch of their closed positions. In the same order as in Step 1, paint the surfaces of the outside sash that were obstructed; also paint the top edge of the inside sash. Now paint the wood framing of the window in this order: top horizontal, the two side verticals, then the sill. Wait until all of the paint is thoroughly dry before painting the wooden parts of the jamb (*Step 3*); in the meantime, if there is another window in the room, work on it.

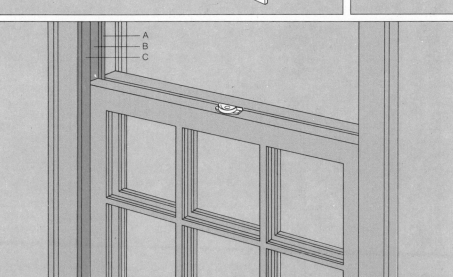

3 Finishing with the jambs. When the newly painted parts of the window are dry to the touch, move both sashes up and down a few times to make sure they do not stick. Then, push both sashes down as far as they will go to expose the upper jambs (*left*). Metal parts are never painted. Paint the wooden parts of the upper jambs in the order shown by the letters A through C. Use a light touch to prevent paint from flowing down into the grooves of the lower jamb. Let the paint dry thoroughly, then raise both sashes as high as they will go and paint the lower halves of parts A through C. Again, wait for the paint to dry before lubricating the channels with paraffin or silicone spray to ease opening and closing.

Casement Windows

Choosing a primer and paint. Casement windows may be made of aluminum, steel or wood. An aluminum window need not be painted at all, but to protect the metal against dirt and pitting, some owners coat it with a metal primer or a transparent polyurethane varnish. A steel casement should be coated with both a metal primer and paint, or with a paint especially suitable to metal, such as an epoxy or polyurethane paint. A wood window should be treated like any other interior woodwork. Before painting a wood casement, open the window. Working from inside outward and always doing horizontals first and then verticals, paint the parts in this order: inside strips, outside strips, hinge edge, frame and sill. Leave the window open until all the paint dries.

Door Frame and Jamb

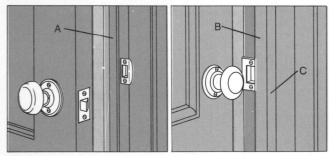

Opening in or opening out. Paint the top of the door frame, then the two sides. Next, paint the part of the jamb between the frame and the doorstop. If the door opens into the room you are painting (drawing, left) paint only the side of the doorstop that directly faces you (A). If the door opens into the next room, paint both the side of the doorstop that directly faces you (B) and the side that is adjacent to it (C).

Hinged Doors

Starting at the top. When repainting a door surface as part of a room renovation, open it wide to reach all of the parts to be covered. Always work from top to bottom. If the door is paneled, paint the panels first, the horizontal sections next, and finally the vertical sections. If the door opens into the room you are painting, use the same color on the latch edge that you have used for the rest of the door. If it opens into the next room, do not paint the hinged edge; it should be the same color as the other room. If the hinges have never been painted, it is preferable to leave them that way; to protect paint from spattering on the metal, cover the hinges with masking tape. The top and bottom edges of a door need be painted only once in its lifetime, to seal the wood.

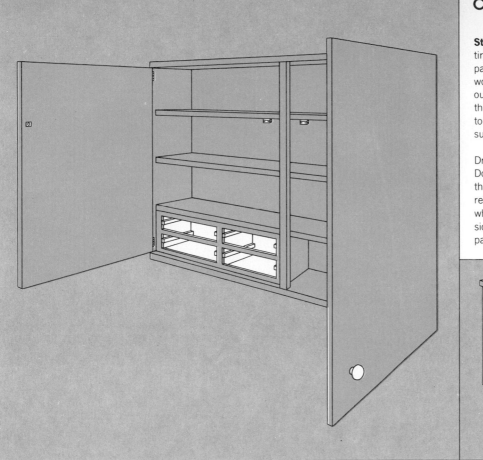

Cabinets and Drawers

Starting on the cabinet. Remove all drawers entirely before you begin to work; they will be painted later. Paint the cabinet (*drawing, left*) working your way systematically from inside to outside. Paint the walls first, then the shelves, then the door. When painting the shelves do bottoms first, then tops and edges. The outside surfaces are painted from top to bottom.

Drawers (*below*) need only their fronts painted. Do not paint the bottoms or exterior sides—paint there would prevent smooth sliding. For the same reason, do not paint the cabinet interior into which the drawers fit. If you wish to paint the insides of drawers for cleanliness or appearance, paint the sides first, then the bottom.

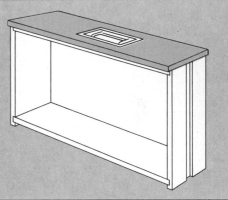

Sequences for Louvers

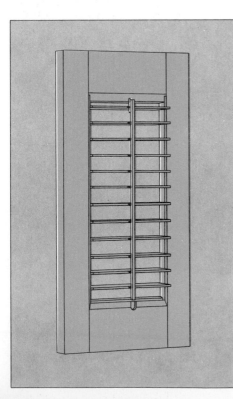

Solving the slat problem. The narrow slats of a louvered shutter or door are difficult to paint and call for special techniques. Use a ½-inch brush and a slow-drying alkyd paint, so that you have time to brush in and smooth drips on these slats. To avoid paint build up at the corners of a slat, start painting at one end of the slat, flowing the paint onto the wood in a long, smooth stroke. Start the next stroke at the opposite end of the same slat and flow the paint toward the wet area.

To paint an adjustable louver, open the louver wide and set the slats to a horizontal position. Cover as much of the slats as you can reach from the side of the louver opposite the adjusting rod, painting the slats first, then the frame.

Turning to the side of the louver with the adjusting rod (*drawing*), paint the inner edge of the rod, then wedge a small stick (a matchstick will do) through one of its staples to keep the rod clear of the slats. Finish painting the slats, one by one, smoothing out all paint drips as you go. Next, paint the outer edges of the frame, then the other parts of the frame. Complete the job by painting the rest of the adjusting rod. The slats of a stationary louver are set in a fixed, slanted position; therefore you will have to work the brush into the crevices between slats, then smooth out the paint with horizontal strokes. Follow the same sequence as for an adjustable louver, starting at the back so that you can catch and smooth out paint drips from the front.

Completing the Job: Cleanup and Storage

The correct cleanup for a paint job begins very early—in fact, before the first can of paint is opened. When you move furniture out of the way and cover floors with newspapers and dropcloths, you are spared the job of removing paint smears and spatters later. With these preliminary preparations done, the cleanup afterward is limited to removing paint from your tools and putting them away, storing leftover materials safely, and restoring order to the room.

Always clean paint from containers and applicators before the paint has a chance to dry. Begin by pouring unused paint from buckets and trays back into the original cans. Then wipe as much paint from the containers as possible with dry paper towels. Squeeze excess paint from brushes and rollers by drawing them across sheets of newspaper.

The procedure for removing the rest of the paint from your tools is relatively simple for water-thinned paints, somewhat more complex for solvent-thinned ones. If you have been painting with water-thinned latex products, simply rinse most of the paint with running water, then wash away the last traces with dishwashing detergent. A paintbrush comb like the one shown at right helps dislodge paint from the part of a brush near the ferrule. Use paper towels to dry buckets and trays; the inexpensive centrifugal device shown on the opposite page dries brushes and rollers much faster and more thoroughly than paper towels.

If you have been using a solvent-thinned paint, clean trays and buckets by wiping them with paper towels dampened with such solvents as turpentine, benzine or mineral spirits; the manufacturer's label will recommend a specific solvent for the paint you have used. Brushes and rollers must be agitated in a container of solvent to remove paint residue. Coffee tins make good containers for cleaning brushes; tennis-ball cans or loaf pans work well for rollers (if you have trouble finding an appropriate container for a roller, clean it in its own tray). Pour enough solvent to cover a roller completely or to reach the ferrule of a brush, then twist and pump the brush or roller to help dissolve paint lodged deep in the bristles or nap. Use a paintbrush comb at this stage to clear paint from the area near the ferrule.

Replace the solvent as soon as it becomes saturated; use two or three changes of solvent, if necessary, until the brush or roller scarcely tints the liquid. Remember that solvents are flammable and that their fumes are toxic. Do not smoke while using them, do not use them near an open flame and be sure that ventilation is adequate to disperse the fumes.

Blot up the excess solvent from your equipment with paper towels or by spinning the tools briefly, wash everything in warm, soapy water to remove the last traces of solvent and paint, then dry all containers and tools thoroughly. A brush should, if possible, be hung by a hole in the handle for this drying stage; a roller should be set on end.

After the final wash and dry, buckets and trays are stacked in a closet or under a workbench. Before a brush or a roller can be put away, however, it must be wrapped to protect the bristles or nap. A brush can be returned to its original package or folded in heavy kraft paper, such as a grocery bag, after a final combing to align the bristles, then either hung up or laid flat for storage. A roller should be rolled in heavy kraft paper or placed in a plastic bag—perforated so air circulation will prevent mildew.

After cleaning your equipment, seal up all the containers of paint and thinner and put them away—even small quantities of paint should be saved for future touch-up jobs. To keep air from spoiling the paint, each can must be cleaned around the lip and the lid must be hammered down to make an airtight seal. Paint will keep longest if there is little or no air at all in the container. You can make an air-free container for a small amount of paint by filling a glass jar with the paint (never use a plastic container), then capping the jar tightly; most paints preserved in this way will keep almost indefinitely. Thinners should also be tightly capped to prevent wasteful and potentially dangerous evaporation.

Paints and thinners should be stored out of reach of children and well away from the high temperatures and open flames of such devices as radiators and furnaces. Aerosol cans are particularly sensitive to heat; if they reach a temperature of 120°F.—which can happen if they are exposed to direct sunlight over a long period of time—they are liable to explode. Water-thinned paints, on the other hand, can be damaged by cold and should be protected from freezing.

The last step in a cleanup is to put the room back in order. First, discard disposable dropcloths and newspapers; if your dropcloths are re-usable, wipe off any large globs of paint and store the cloths with the buckets and trays. As soon as the paint on window frames is dry to the touch, straighten the line of paint that you applied to the panes to make an airtight seal and scrape any drips from the glass (opposite, bottom). Replace light fixtures, switch and outlet covers, hang curtains and blinds and arrange the furniture in the room. Take care to avoid scuffing the newly applied paint; it may not have hardened completely and until it does it will be quite fragile.

Care of Painting Tools

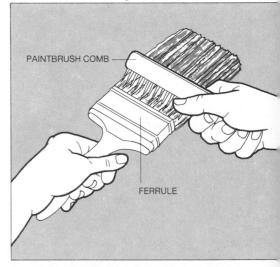

A comb for a brush. A paintbrush comb loosens stubborn, partially dried paint from the tightly packed bristles just below the ferrule of a brush and also from the spacer plug inside the bristles. The sharp wire teeth of the comb not only penetrate the bristles but also separate them slightly to help the solvent wash away paint residue. At a later stage of the cleanup process, just before the paintbrush is wrapped for storage, draw the comb through the bristles once more to straighten and untangle them. The brush will then be ready for a future paint job.

A spin-drier for brushes and rollers. This ingenious cleanup aid spins off excess solvent or water from paint applicators with a minimum of effort. A brush is secured to the drier by stiff spring clips *(drawing)*; alternatively, a roller can be slipped over the clips. When the handle is pushed in and out of the stationary tube, the brush or roller spins at high speed, throwing paint-laden solvent or water from the applicator by centrifugal force. To keep from spraying nearby objects, spin brushes and rollers inside a heavy paper bag or in a garbage can with a plastic liner.

Wrapping a brush. Cut a rectangle of heavy kraft paper—a section of a grocery bag will do— about twice the combined lengths of the ferrule and bristles and about four times the width of the brush. Crease the paper down the center of its longest dimension, place the brush on the paper so that the tips of the bristles are at the crease and roll the brush into the paper *(below)*. Fold the rolled-up paper toward the ferrule along the crease and secure the paper with a rubber band, making a wedge-shaped package that will preserve the taper of the bristles.

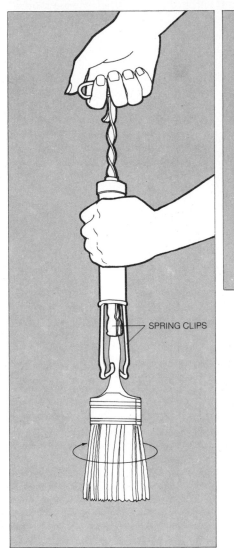

SPRING CLIPS

A Neat Edge for Windowpanes

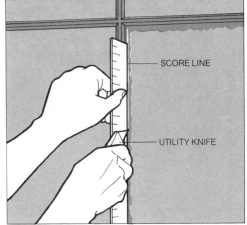

SCORE LINE

UTILITY KNIFE

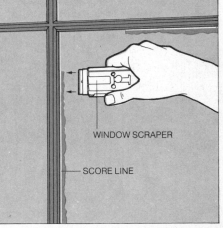

WINDOW SCRAPER

SCORE LINE

1 Scoring the paint. Unless you have used masking tape, you will need to straighten the irregular edges of the paint applied to windowpanes as an airtight seal. For the first step of the job, place the edge of a ruler on a section of glass and against a pane divider or sash. (Shorten the ruler, if necessary, to fit between parts of the window frame.) Score the paint with a utility knife, using the thickness of the ruler as a guide *(drawing)*. Repeat this step for all four edges of each pane.

2 Removing the paint. Lift the irregular edge of the paint from the glass with a window scraper. Position the scraper so that the edge of its blade is parallel to the score line cut by the utility knife, and carefully push the blade under the paint and toward the pane divider, stopping at the score. The paint will come off the glass easily, leaving a neat, straight line.

A Guide to Exterior Coatings

The same basic kinds of paint are used outside as inside—alkyds, latexes, epoxies and oils. But because outdoor paints must be more elastic and weather resistant than indoor coatings and often must adhere to rougher surfaces, they contain more plasticizers—agents that promote flexibility—and frequently have a higher proportion of resin.

No coating sold for residential use now contains more than a tiny, legally regulated amount of lead, a very hazardous poison that nevertheless once was a major ingredient of paint. Its absence was often blamed by old-time professionals for paint failures, but all authorities agree that the only loss attributable to the removal of lead is some covering power in a few deep colors; the durability and opacity that lead once gave is now provided by synthetic resins and by other pigments.

Even modern paints, however, might cause problems—partially because of the proliferation of types. Latex, the most convenient and versatile, may not adhere when applied over other types. Try to find out what you are painting over—keep a record or ask someone who might know. If you are unable to identify the existing paint layer, your best choice is an alkyd paint, which is least likely to react adversely with an unknown undercoat.

Finishing Paint

All the coatings listed here can be applied with brush, roller or sprayer, unless otherwise indicated. How long a properly applied paint job will last depends largely on when you think it begins to look drab and dull—bright colors fade faster than others, and a clear finish yellows somewhat after a couple of years.

Latex Flat
ODOR FREE
BEST FOR HUMID CONDITIONS

Latex flat is the most popular choice for most exterior siding surfaces because it is thinned and cleaned with water and is the fastest drying. It also allows water vapor to escape through the paint from underneath rather than expanding into a blister. This ability to "breathe" makes latex a good choice for a damp exterior wall. Unlike latex interior paints, exterior latex is often used on raw wood, since the grain exaggeration caused by water solvent is relatively unnoticeable outdoors. Like its interior counterpart, it can also be used on masonry. It does not cover as well as alkyd, however, and if your old surface is still chalking heavily, or is coated with an alkyd finish, latex paint may not adhere perfectly, or, if it holds at first, may not prove quite as durable as an alkyd-base paint.

Alkyd Flat
BEST FOR CHALKING SURFACES

Alkyd exterior paints adhere and cover all surfaces well except unprimed masonry or metal, but special solvents must be used for thinning and cleaning so that they are less convenient to use than latex. On damp surfaces alkyd paint may blister and peel more easily than latex, but alkyd adheres to chalking surfaces better than most water-thinned paints.

Oil Flat
SLOW DRYING

Oil-base flat paints have been outmoded by modern latexes and alkyds: they smell, dry slowly, require mineral spirits or turpentine and are less durable.

Glossy Trim
MORE WASHABLE THAN FLAT

Glossy paints contain more resin than flat ones, giving greater resistance to wear and washing and making them best for windows, doors and shutters. Both alkyd and latex exterior glossy paints wear well and are available in high and semigloss finishes, though latex high gloss is slightly less shiny than its alkyd counterpart. Latex gloss is thinned and cleaned with water and dries faster than alkyd—a big advantage in getting doors and windows back into service. It is also more weather and alkali resistant than alkyd paint. Oil-base trim paint is not as durable as either alkyd or latex, but if used with a zinc-based metal primer it is a good coating for exterior metals such as rain spouts or the undersides of roof gutters.

Marine Paint
VERY DURABLE
EXPENSIVE

These glossy paints are prepared with more epoxy, urethane, acrylic or alkyd resins in proportion to their pigment content than are ordinary exterior finishing paints. This resin step-up increases durability—marine paints were originally designed to protect boats against salt water and bruising weather. Their excellent wearing qualities have made them popular for outdoor wood or metal house trim, although they are expensive.

Porch and Floor Paint
HIGHLY ABRASION RESISTANT
FOR WOOD OR CONCRETE

Formulated to withstand bad weather and traffic on porches and outside steps, these abrasion-resistant alkyd, latex, urethane, rubber-base or epoxy paints are often used indoors also. Rubber-base floor paint gives a flat or semigloss finish and is limited to use on masonry floors. It is water repellent and highly resistant to scrubbing with detergents. Glossy alkyd, urethane and latex types of paint can be used on bare or previously painted wood floors or previously painted masonry floors. Epoxy will coat a smooth, bare floor or any epoxy-coated floor.

Before any floor paint is applied to new concrete, the surface must be carefully prepared to provide "tooth" *(latex, page 150)*. Latex, rubber, urethane or epoxy floor paint can then be applied directly to the concrete. Before an alkyd floor paint is used, however, the surface must be primed *(primers, opposite)*.

Shingle Paint
POROUS TO LET WOOD BREATHE
A UNIQUE TYPE FOR ASBESTOS

For an opaque finish on asbestos or wood siding shingles, use special flat shingle paints, which permit the escape of moisture that can accumulate behind shingles in damp weather. By allowing shingles to "breathe" as water vapor escapes, these paints help prevent wood rot and paint blisters. Latex, alkyd, or oil-base shingle paints work equally well on bare or most previously coated wood siding shingles. However, asbestos-cement shingles should be coated only with paints labeled for use on them. And wood shingles that are treated with creosote wood preservative should not be painted at all in less than eight years: the oily creosote will prevent the paint from bonding firmly to the wood.

Metal Paint
USED DIRECTLY ON METAL
METALLIC OR COLORFUL FINISH

Metal paints stop rust to greater or lesser degrees and are thinned with mineral-spirit solvents. Aluminum paint (powdered aluminum suspended in oil or alkyd resin) provides a shiny, metallic finish and is particularly durable. It is suitable for most primed metals and is the only paint that will bond to recently creosote-treated wood, providing a surface that usually can be painted over without danger that creosote stains will seep through to mar the finish.

Aluminum paint, however, is not recommended for shingles; it tends to seal in moisture and promote rot.

Glossy oil- or alkyd-base metal paints are available in an assortment of colors and are convenient to use since no primer coat is required. Before applying most of these paints, be sure that you clean the surfaces as you would before applying interior metal primers *(page 153)*.

Some of these oil- or alkyd-base metal paints contain penetrating, rustproofing agents and can be applied directly to rusty metal. Even with these so-called rustproofing paints, however, it is advisable to remove all rust and dirt before applying the coating.

Masonry Paint
LATEX EASIEST TO USE
RUBBER-BASE BEST FOR CINDER BLOCKS

The same types of paint meant for interior masonry also work outside the house: latex, cement paint, rubber-base coatings. In addition, special alkyds can be used on exterior masonry.

Rubber-base paint is the type that is generally recommended for exterior cinder block because the paint is waterproof; it thus prevents moisture from reaching the cinders and causing stains.

If exterior masonry has begun to crumble or if the painted surface is chalking heavily, first use a block filler *(below)* or a clear masonry-sealer *(page 153)*.

Stains and Clear Finishes

The natural materials your house is made of can be displayed yet protected by applying clear or semitransparent finishes rather than pigmented paints. Clear coatings rarely last as long as paint, however, because ultraviolet rays in sunlight penetrate them and alter the character of the surface they cover. This reduces the bond between surface and finish—sometimes in less than two years.

Stains
PROTECTIVE MATTE FINISH
REQUIRE MIXING

Exterior stains, usually used on wood siding and shingles to provide a matte finish, range from nearly transparent to nearly opaque, but all of them contain more pigment than interior stains and so must be mixed like paint before use. The water-base latex stains resist wear and retain their color longer than alkyd or oil-base stains. Latex stains are also more porous and are preferred in damp conditions that might cause an impervious finish to blister. Opaque stains last as long as most pigmented finishing coats.

Varnish
URETHANE TYPE IS TOUGHEST
SPAR VARNISH BEST NEAR SEASHORE

Exterior varnish is used almost exclusively on wood—to protect it from weathering while retaining the natural appearance and color. No exterior varnish lasts as long as an interior one; most have a life expectancy of no more than two years. The most commonly used varnish is spar varnish, which must be renewed every 12 to 16 months, although it provides excellent protection against salt corrosion if kept in good condition. Under most other circumstances, alkyd-base exterior varnish lasts slightly longer than spar varnish. Moisture-cured urethane varnish is the most resistant. An acrylic varnish is designed for ornamental metal.

Primers, Preservatives, Sealers

These special coatings provide raw wood, metal or masonry with extra protection against moisture and rot, and form a bridge when a surface and the desired top coat are incompatible.

Primers
EXTRA FLEXIBLE
A SPECIAL TYPE FOR GALVANIZED STEEL

Exterior primers, which are used under exterior paints, are extra flexible to adjust to wall expansion and contraction. Otherwise, these undercoats are essentially the same as those used inside the house *(page 152)*. A special kind of oil-base primer that contains Portland cement protects exterior steel. Since it has a zinc additive, it can be used on galvanized metal gutters and drains.

Wood Preservative
PROTECTS AGAINST INSECTS AND FUNGI
USED ONLY ON BARE WOOD

Raw wood exterior surfaces can be protected against insect and fungus damage with clear, paintable wood preservatives. Some are also waterproof and will deter warping. The preservatives will not work if the wood has been sealed, stained or painted; any finishing coat can be used over these preservatives.

Creosote, an oily black preservative, is still used because it is inexpensive. But it inhibits adhesion of other coatings for as long as eight years, kills vegetation near it and bleeds through any top coat unless it is first sealed with two coats of aluminum paint.

Block Filler
A MASONRY SEALER
AN UNDERCOAT FOR PAINT

Rough, porous masonry surfaces can be sealed and smoothed by these thick, white coatings that provide a good base for latex, alkyd or oil-base finishes. Block filler can be applied with a paint roller, but a stiff brush is more effective when the surface is rough.

Silicone Water Repellent
A BARRIER TO ALL OTHER COATINGS
PRESERVES APPEARANCE OF WOOD

These nearly invisible coatings reduce to a minimum water seepage through exterior wood surfaces. The silicone repels all topcoats for several years so this preservative should be used only to maintain the original appearance of the wood. Thin and clean up spills with the solvents recommended on the label.

Tool Kit for Exterior Painting

In addition to the standard tools you have on hand, you may need a selection of the specialized tools shown here to paint the outside of your home.

☐ If you face a difficult paint-removing job—a larger area or a section with a coating that is thick and hard to get off— the following tools can be helpful: a heavy-duty paint scraper, a power sander, an electric paint remover, and a power drill with a wire brush attachment. Simpler jobs of paint removal can be done by hand with a wire brush and steel wool, or with sandpaper and putty knives *(pages 157-158).*

☐ Special tools for making repairs before painting include a cold chisel and mallet for chipping out old caulking or crumbling mortar, a caulking gun for applying new caulking, and a trowel and jointer for laying in new mortar.

☐ Some safety equipment is essential: protective goggles that should be worn when working with power-driven brushes, chisels and corrosive cleaners; and a respirator when working with a power sander or paint sprayer.

☐ A 4-inch flat paintbrush is the standard tool for exterior painting. But a pad applicator may prove faster on some broad, flat surfaces; a mitten applicator simplifies the painting of pipes, metal furniture and out-of-the-way places where a brush cannot easily reach; and a rough-surface paintbrush is specifically designed for use on bricks and cinder blocks. (See page 190 for special equipment, generally rented, for spray painting.) The least expensive tool in the kit may be the handiest: an S hook to hang a paint bucket from a rung of an extension ladder.

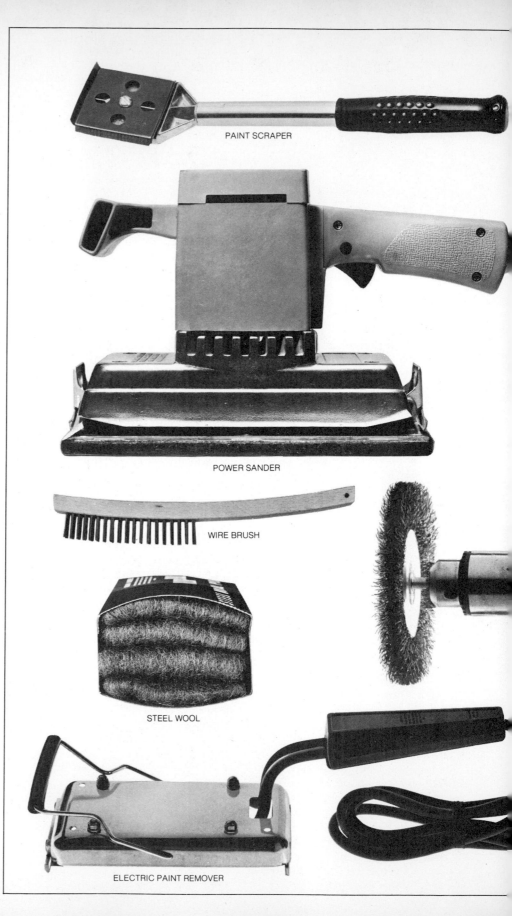

PAINT SCRAPER

POWER SANDER

WIRE BRUSH

STEEL WOOL

ELECTRIC PAINT REMOVER

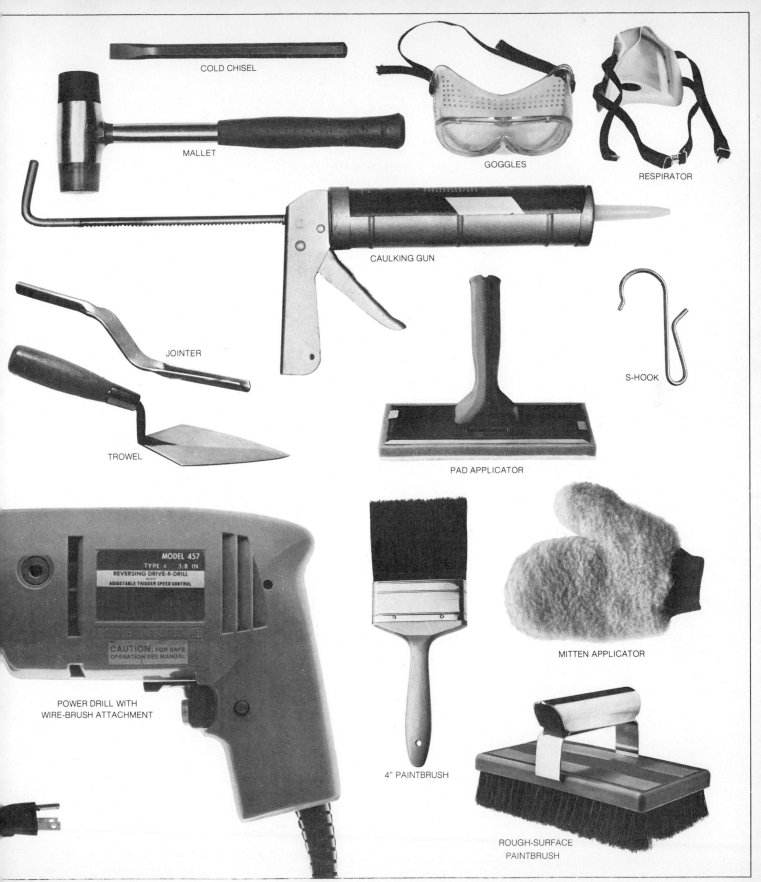

COLD CHISEL

MALLET

GOGGLES

RESPIRATOR

CAULKING GUN

JOINTER

TROWEL

PAD APPLICATOR

S-HOOK

MODEL 457
TYPE 4   3/8 IN.
REVERSING DRIVE-R-DRILL
WITH
ADJUSTABLE TRIGGER SPEED CONTROL

CAUTION: FOR SAFE
OPERATION SEE MANUAL

POWER DRILL WITH
WIRE-BRUSH ATTACHMENT

4" PAINTBRUSH

MITTEN APPLICATOR

ROUGH-SURFACE
PAINTBRUSH

Diagnosing Paint Problems

Before you paint the outside of your house, inspect it with the cool, unsparing eye of an appraiser. Wherever you see stains or signs that layers of paint have begun to pull away from the surface, try to identify the cause of the problem and fix it. The damage that you discover is rarely caused by the paint. More often it is the result of a defect such as faulty construction that traps moisture in the outside walls, incomplete surface preparation before the last paint job, incompatible paint, careless painting or a variety of other causes. If you ignore the underlying problem or simply repeat the same mistake when you put on the new paint, the same stains and peeling are likely to recur.

The photographs on these four pages help identify the problems that are most often encountered. All but one of these examples show the exteriors of homes, because paint problems develop more often with exterior coatings that are constantly exposed to changes in temperature than with interior paints. Nevertheless, the information about each problem applies to flaws that occur inside the house as well as out.

As you paint, you may yourself create the two kinds of unattractive paint problems illustrated on this page: blisters and wrinkles. These new-paint problems frequently appear soon after a new coat of paint is applied and should always be corrected immediately.

Blistering. Bubbles pop up when water or solvent vapor is trapped under the paint. Both kinds of blisters are more common with oil and alkyd paints than with water-base coatings. They can be diagnosed by cutting a bubble open. If you see bare wood inside, it is a moisture blister; scrape off the blistered paint, eliminate the source of moisture and let the wood dry thoroughly before repainting. If you see paint inside the bubble, it is a solvent blister caused by painting in the heat of direct sunlight, which dries the surface of the paint too quickly, forming a skin that traps solvent. Sand smooth and repaint.

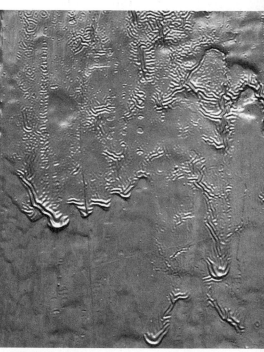

Wrinkling. Unsightly convolutions occur when oil or alkyd paints are applied too thick. At first a film forms quickly and smoothly across the surface. But as the excess paint under the film dries, it decreases in volume; the film cannot shrink enough to fit tautly, and droops down into wrinkles. To get rid of wrinkles, sand them smooth and repaint with a thinner coat.

Peeling from wood. Paint curls away from surfaces like the window frame at right because the coating was applied over dirt, grease or loose paint, or because the wood contained moisture. Before repainting a peeled surface, remove all loose paint *(page 186),* eliminate the source of dampness if possible and let the wood dry thoroughly. If you cannot prevent the wood from becoming damp because moisture is seeping through from inside the house or because of drainage problems, try repainting the stripped wood with thin coatings of latex primer and paint. They are more porous than oil or alkyd coatings and usually allow water vapor to pass through.

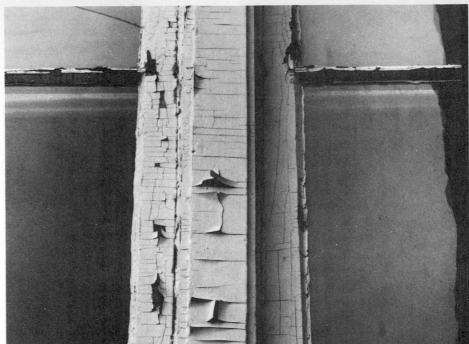

Alligatoring. The reptilian scales of paint on the window sash above are caused by the inability of the top coat to bond smoothly to the paint below. The paints may not have been applied according to the manufacturer's instructions or they may be incompatible with each other. Serious alligatoring allows water to seep through to the wood, and all the affected paint must be scraped off before new paint is put on. If the paint has not begun to flake and has simply developed a checkered pattern of small cracks that are not widening, clean the surface, sand it smooth and paint it again with a compatible coating.

Peeling from masonry. Paint flakes from stucco, concrete and brick not only for the same reasons that it peels from wood, but also because of chemical compounds called alkalis, found in most masonry, which destroy paint adhesion. Extensive peeling can best be remedied by having all old paint removed by sandblasting stucco or concrete or using a chemical stripper on brick. To prevent peeling, seal the masonry with sealer *(page 175)* and paint it with alkali-resistant coating.

Efflorescence peeling. The paint on the brick wall at right is disintegrating because of efflorescence, which can also affect concrete and other masonry. Alkali compounds in the masonry are dissolved by moisture and carried to the surface. When the water evaporates, the compounds crystallize under the paint, pushing it away from the wall. If efflorescence occurs on older masonry near pipes, gutters or downspouts, check for leaks.

To dissolve efflorescence, first scrub the rust off the bricks with a solution made with one part muriatic acid and 10 parts water. Caution: Always pour acid into water, never water into acid. If the deposits do not come off easily, make a solution of one part ammonia to two parts water to neutralize the acid. Then flush with a hose, directly into a drain, working down from the top of the wall. Both solutions used for this job are corrosive. Wear goggles and gloves, and use a long-handled scrub brush.

Rust-stained shingles. The dark vertical lines along the bottom of each of the shingles above are stains caused by rusting nails. This problem could have been avoided by using aluminum or stainless-steel shingle nails instead of galvanized steel ones. Removing rust stains from uncoated shingles like these is almost impossible. They probably can be hidden beneath a coat of paint, but the stains will soon reappear unless each nailhead is cleared of rust and then sealed with a rust-inhibiting coating *(page 148)*.

Rusted metal. The old steel gutters above are studded along the upper edge with rust pits that started when the paint deteriorated enough to let water through, probably because of inadequate preparation or neglect. Rust washing down from the pits has caused broad, vertical stains on the lower part of the gutter. These gutters should be replaced with more durable aluminum or plastic ones. Less extensive rust on steel can be arrested and painted *(page 187)*.

Chalk stains. The brick wall at right has been discolored by paint chalk that has washed down from the siding above it. Chalking paint helps keep the siding clean, but should not be used where the chalk can streak areas below. The only remedy for this situation is to wash the siding and repaint it with a nonchalking paint. The brick can be restored by scrubbing with detergent.

Bleeding knots. Knots in this siding are visible through the paint because the resin concentrated in them was dissolved by solvents in the paint. A new coat of paint will also stain, unless the knots are scraped down to bare wood, then coated with shellac or with primer-sealer.

Mildew. The dark discoloration near the porch of this house is caused by mildew fungus growing on the paint. These unsightly molds trap airborne dirt, and some varieties can eat through the paint. There is no lasting prevention for mildew; it will grow wherever conditions are right—usually in damp, shady areas. Mildew patches should be killed with a fungicide such as chlorine bleach before a house is repainted or fungus will grow through the new coat or cause it to peel.

Painting a House in Logical Order

Painting the exterior of a house calls for the same top-to-bottom strategy—as well as many of the same basic tools and techniques—as painting the interior. There are differences, of course. Scale is one of them. Painting the upper reaches of a house exterior is more perilous than any indoor job. And the variety of exterior construction details means that the painting sequence requires careful planning. There are also methods for applying paint, described on the following pages, that are more useful outdoors than in.

The safe ways to use extension ladders are described on page 389. Many houses have dormers, however, that can be painted only from a sloping roof. Use a ladder that reaches at least 3 feet above the edge. This enables you to step safely from the ladder onto the roof without standing on the top two rungs or climbing over the eaves. On the roof be extra cautious: Wear shoes with non-slip soles, use a ladder and ladder hook (often available at rental agencies) for foot- and handholds, and sit down as much as possible.

An exterior paint job has two major stages: First coating the sides of the house and then the trim. Start on the side that is not in direct sunlight *(page 184)*. If there are dormers on that side, paint them first, leaving the overhang, trim and windows for the next stage. Then continue down to the main section. Paint the siding in horizontal strips, moving the ladder as necessary to work safely. (If you paint in vertical strips, you will have to adjust the length of the ladder often.)

When the siding is complete, start on the trim. Again, begin with the dormers, then do overhangs, gutters and downspouts as you come to them. Next, do the windows, shutters and doors of the main part of the house. Door and window exteriors are painted the same way as their inside surfaces *(pages 169-170)*.

After painting the trim, do the porch railings, then the stairs and foundation. If stairs must be used before they have a chance to dry, paint all the risers but only alternate treads, and then do the rest after the first half has dried. The final flourish is a coat of tough polyurethane varnish on wooden thresholds.

SIDING

TRIM

RAILINGS

PORCHES AND FOUNDATION

The sequence of painting. This drawing shows most features that must be painted in a typical two-story house. Color (see key) is used here not to suggest a decoration scheme but as a guide to the order, top to bottom in each case, in which elements of the house should be painted.

Estimating the Paint You Will Need

The amount of paint needed for the outside of a house is calculated in much the same way as for a room *(page 147)*. The perimeter of the house multiplied by its height gives the total outside area. If you are using a different coating for trim, subtract from this figure the area of doors (approximately 21 square feet each) and window frames (approximately 15 square feet each for the average size). Then divide the resulting figure by the number of square feet one gallon of your paint will cover. The result will be the total paint requirement for one coat if you are using conventional brushes, rollers or exterior shingle pads; if you plan to use a sprayer *(pages 190-191),* you may have to double the size of your paint order since the sprayer applies the equivalent of two coats of paint at once. Remember as you figure out how much paint to buy that the coverage figures printed on the paint can label may be optimistic.

You will need a helper to correctly measure the perimeter of your house. Use a ball of twine tied to a stake or a steel tape and have the helper steady one end as you both move around the house. Or you can run a ball of string around the outside—again with your helper to keep the line in place—and then measure the length of the string.

Next figure the height of your house; climb a ladder to the eaves, drop a weighted string to the ground and measure the length. For a rough estimate, figure 10 feet for each story and add 2 feet if your house has gables. Or you can count the number of courses of clapboards and shingles and multiply by the height of a single course.

To estimate the amount of outside trim paint needed, measure one shutter or door (or one of each size if they vary) and multiply that area by the number of shutters or doors on your house. Then add about 15 square feet for the trim on each window. If you intend to paint gutters or edging, assume that each foot of length includes a square foot of area: For example, if you have 60 feet of metal gutter along your eaves, buy enough trim paint to cover 60 square feet.

Making these trim calculations will give you the most accurate estimate of how much paint you need. However, if this is inconvenient, use the following rule of thumb: Buy one gallon of trim paint for every six gallons of paint you buy for the siding. That should cover most needs—unless you have more shutters and doors than usual.

Estimating the Time It Will Take

You can paint the outside of an average house with a brush or roller in a week—or less—if the weather is fair. Small houses will take less time, larger ones a day or so more. Spraying cuts time on any house down to as little as a day. To calculate how long it will take to paint your house with a brush or roller, count on covering 120 square feet an hour on a smooth nonporous surface, and about 100 square feet of raw wood or 60 square feet of rough masonry or shingles per hour. Preparations take longer outside than they do inside, so do major repairs well in advance. Then, after calculating the time you need for actual painting, add one third more hours for the final preparation, such as masking fixtures and shrubbery. Double the time if you must make heavy repairs as part of the painting job itself.

Your own endurance is also a factor in making a time estimate. You cannot work as fast as the contractor who once painted your house in a day or two. He was used to the work, and he may have had an assistant. Get a helper yourself.

One of you can cover siding while the other trims. The gain in efficiency is so great that you may be able to cut job time as much as two thirds.

Your outdoor work time is also subject to seasonal change. The long days of late spring and early fall expand your work hours, and paint will dry quickly in the sunny warmth of these months. You should not paint in direct sunlight, however, for your own comfort and to prevent paint from drying so fast that you drag your brush over a drying coat. Your schedule depends on the sun for another reason: It is your guide to the place to start working. Observe where the sun hits the house in early morning. See where it moves as the day progresses. Then, when you are ready to paint, start on the side just abandoned by the sunlight and follow the sun around the house. The best temperature range for the job is between 50° and 90° F.

With more than one coat, paint drying time will be important in your planning. The following table lists the average times in which several coatings harden enough for a second coat on a surface such as prepainted clapboard. The drying times for latex also hold true when it is used on smooth, dry masonry, but latex may take up to 50 per cent longer to dry if it is applied to a damp surface. If you are painting on a very porous surface such as bare wood, cut the drying time about 20 per cent.

Alkyd flat house paint, 24 hours
Latex flat house paint, 2-4 hours
Alkyd glossy house paint, 12-48 hours
Latex glossy house paint, 4 hours
Alkyd trim paint, 12 hours
Latex trim paint, 4 hours
Alkyd metal paint, 12 hours
Oil metal paint, 2-4 days
Latex masonry paint, 4-12 hours
Alkyd primer, 24 hours
Latex primer, 2 hours
Zinc-rich metal primer, 24 hours
Opaque exterior stain, 8-10 hours
Semitransparent stain, 6-8 hours (interior) and 8-10 hours (exterior)
Silicone water repellent, 2-3 hours
Wood sealer, 2 hours

Before You Paint: Preparing Exterior Surfaces

Getting the outside of your home ready for a new coat of paint is essential because it makes the paint job not only look better but last longer. Even though outside paints are tougher than those made for inside use, they must have clean, solid and dry surfaces to bond to.

Most homes need no more than a hosing to remove minor accumulations of dirt. And small areas of deeply embedded grime can be cleaned with detergent. But your house probably has a wide variety of surfaces that may require special attention to get them ready for paint. The drawings and instructions on this and the following pages as well as in Section 6 will help you assess what needs to be done and guide you in doing the job right.

If larger areas on the outside of your house are dirty, consider renting a high-pressure water cleaning device, which does the work fast and removes not only dirt but peeling and loose paint as well.

Patches of mildew can also be cleared off the house by adding a household bleach to the power spray's water supply or by making a cleaning solution of one cup of chlorine laundry bleach to one gallon of warm water. Rust and other metal stains repel most paints so these deposits must be removed and prevented from recurring. If the stains are caused by leaks, stop them at the source: Seal joints with caulking, fix broken downspouts and gutters and repair damaged roofs. The steel nails in clapboard or shingle siding are a common source of rust streaks; scrape them and seal them from moisture *(below)* so that the problem will not recur. If screens or gutters are depositing metal stains on paint, scrape the metal clean with a wire brush and then paint it. Copper screens can be sealed with clear acrylic varnish.

If any of the old paint is damaged or loose—examples of typical deterioration are illustrated on pages 178-181—it must come off. Use hand sanders and scrapers *(pages 157-158)* to remove small patches from clapboard siding. Chemical paint removers *(page 158)* are efficient, especially around window trim and moldings, where it may be difficult to probe with a tool. While you are working on outdoor wood surfaces, seal any knots and oozing sap pores with shellac.

Peeling paint on exterior metal and masonry surfaces usually comes off easily with a stiff wire brush, although stubborn cases may have to be sandblasted by a professional. Brick, however, should not be sandblasted. Chemical paint removers usually work well on metals, but seldom work satisfactorily on brick. After you remove the paint you may have to follow some of the special procedures that are described on pages 187 and 436-437 to give the metal or masonry surface enough "tooth" to hold a coat of paint.

More than routine cleaning and paint scraping may be required before you start painting if you have not kept up with some basic outdoor maintenance tasks such as replacing split shingles, loose caulking around windows and doors and loose mortar in brick walls. These three jobs cannot be left till later because the repair will then mar your new paint job.

Eliminating rust stains. Use sandpaper or steel wool to take off stains caused by rusted nailheads. Clean the nailhead itself with the same material until bright metal appears. If you are working on clapboard or any other smooth wood, drive the nail ⅛ inch below the surface with a hammer and nail set *(page 39)*. Cover the nailhead with a rust-inhibiting metal primer. When it dries, fill the nail hole with putty or spackle; give this filler a chance to dry and then coat it and any bare wood with a primer. Flathead nails, which cannot be countersunk, should simply be sandpapered bright and coated with a primer.

If rust has worked its way into wood, as nailhead stains on textured shingles do, removing the stain would remove too much wood. The only remedy for this problem is to scrape and seal the nailhead, and then stain the shingle with an opaque stain, or paint it to hide the rust.

Removing Paint from Clapboard

If you have large areas of loose or peeling paint on clapboard, or places where layers of paint have built up an overthick coating, you will need something faster than a putty knife or a sanding block to get the paint off. Try the rigid-blade scraper or the power sander shown below, which can be rented from paint stores. Do not use a disk sanding attachment on a power drill; it leaves circular scratches that will show through paint. An orbital sander, which vibrates in a narrow radius, avoids such scratches. A belt sander also serves, but is hard to control and can damage wood.

Heat is an efficient paint remover for oil-base and alkyd paints, if just enough is applied to melt the paint and not burn the wood. Use an electric paint remover *(bottom)*, which is a heating coil mounted inside a protective shield. Do not use a propane torch; it can scorch wood and set a house afire. Take latex paints off with chemical removers or by sanding.

Scraping paint off. A rigid, hook-shaped replaceable blade makes this scraper a more efficient tool for removing paint from wood than a flexible-blade putty knife. The scraper will damage wood, however, if it is pulled across the grain with too much force; work carefully until you find the minimum pressure needed to take the paint off.

Sanding paint off. The most efficient power tool for clearing away large areas of damaged paint from clapboard is an orbital sander. Keep the sanding surface flat against the clapboard as you work, and keep the tool moving to avoid oversanding any spots. Caution: Always wear a respirator when you are using a power sander.

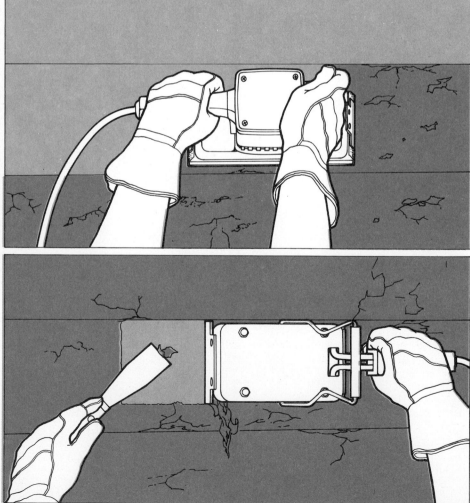

Lifting paint off with heat. Heavy deposits of paint can often be removed more quickly by heat than by sanding. Set the heating element of the paint remover over the painted surface. When the paint begins to sizzle, pull the remover firmly across the heated area, scraping the paint off as you go; keep a putty knife in your other hand to scrape off any paint that remains on the area, and to clean the device itself. Use the heating device with caution: do not touch the heating element, and wear gloves and heavy clothing to protect yourself from hot scraps of paint.

Brushing and Polishing Metal

Paint adheres best to metal when the surface is bright and bare, with all traces of finish and corrosion removed, but you can usually get a satisfactory bond by wire-brushing off loose or damaged paint and rust and painting over the sections where old paint still adheres firmly.

Wear protective goggles to keep grit out of your eyes. To prepare steel surfaces, scrape the paint and rust off by hand with a stiff wire brush, or with a wire-brush attachment in a power drill.

Prepare aluminum surfaces by wire-brushing off loose paint; then clean the metal areas with a commercial cleaning solution specifically made for aluminum. Both steel and aluminum should be given an undercoat of a primer paint made specifically for metals *(page 153)*.

To prepare ornamental brass fixtures such as doorknobs and knockers for fresh protective coating, remove all remaining traces of previous coatings with lacquer remover and then clean off tarnish with brass polish and a soft rag. Do not use steel wool or a wire brush; either will destroy the mirror-like surface of the brass. Then apply clear lacquer from an aerosol can or brush on polyurethane varnish.

Stripping metal by hand. Peeling paint and minor rust spots are easily removed from wrought-iron guard rails and outdoor furniture with a stiff wire brush. If the surfaces are badly rusted, do not try to get down to bright metal; just take off flakes and soft spots and brush off all powdered rust. To prevent rust buildup in the future, apply two undercoats of oil- or alkyd-base primer containing zinc *(page 153)*. Let the first primer coat dry thoroughly before applying the second.

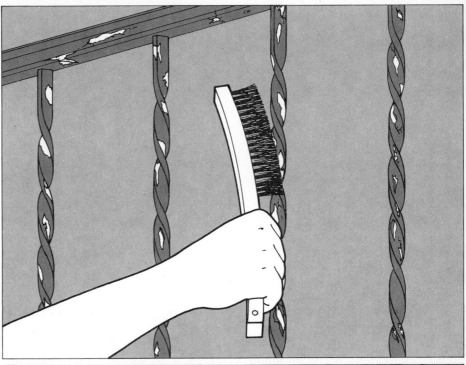

Fast stripping with a power brush. A wire brush attached to a power drill will shorten any metal cleaning task, and it is almost a necessity for such jobs as stripping down steel gutters and downspouts or taking peeling paint off large areas of aluminum. A cup-shaped brush, shown at right, covers a large area quickly. For tight spaces, such as the insides of a narrow gutter or a series of grooves, use the narrow-edged type shown in the inset. Make sure that you wear goggles and gloves when using either type of brush, and always keep the drill pointed away from you; if you tip the edge of the brush toward you, it may drive the grit straight at you.

Special Methods for the Outside

The basic tools for exterior house painting are the same kinds of brushes and rollers that are used indoors, with a few variations on how they are handled. For instance, there is a special technique, shown at right, for painting clapboard siding; the same technique can be easily adapted to painting shingles.

Be prepared for tiring work. The large, heavy 4-inch brush frequently used for painting outdoor surfaces, the side-to-side arm motions and the extensive area to be covered will inevitably result in fatigue, and there is no way of holding the brush that will avoid that problem. So grip the paintbrush like a tennis racquet, or flex your fingers on the ferrule and change from one grip to another—even on occasion from one hand to another—to rest your muscles as you work.

Conventional brushes and rollers work fine on exterior surfaces that are smooth or only slightly textured. But there are some rough surfaces such as stucco, cinder block or wooden shingles that these ordinary applicators might not be able to handle. On such surfaces, even a deep-pile roller may miss spots that you then must fill in with a brush. But avoid the temptation to poke at a rough surface with the tip of the brush to work paint into the pores and crevices, a practice that quickly ruins the bristles.

There are also a number of specialized applicators for certain kinds of outdoor work. The three most useful ones, shown on the opposite page, are a pad applicator for shingles, a rectangular paintbrush that looks like a pad with bristles for masonry and a mitten applicator for railings and pipes.

Painting clapboards with a brush. The bottom edges of four or five clapboards are coated first, then the faces. Using a brush about as wide as a clapboard and dipping only the tip in paint, apply paint to 3-foot lengths of the clapboard edge (*top drawing*). Next, with a fully laden brush, apply heavy dabs of paint to the face of one clapboard (*center*). Distribute the paint across the wood with horizontal brush strokes (*bottom*). Finish off each clapboard with a single long horizontal stroke to eliminate brush marks, then proceed to the next clapboard. Use the same sequence when painting shingles, but apply the paint with vertical strokes to follow the grain of the wood.

The pad applicator. Designed for painting or staining shakes and shingles, a pad applicator consists of a soft "rug" of short nylon bristles that are attached to a layer of flexible foam rubber so the bristles conform to the uneven surfaces of the shingles as pressure is applied. This replaceable pad is secured to a plastic handle by fold-over metal tabs, and can be reversed to prolong the life of the bristles. To use a pad applicator, dip the bristles into a tray of paint or stain and apply the coating first to the edge of a shingle with the edge of the pad. Then press the entire pad firmly against the front of the shingle (*drawing, below*) and pull downward with a single stroke. The applicator can also be used to paint wide clapboards and other flat surfaces.

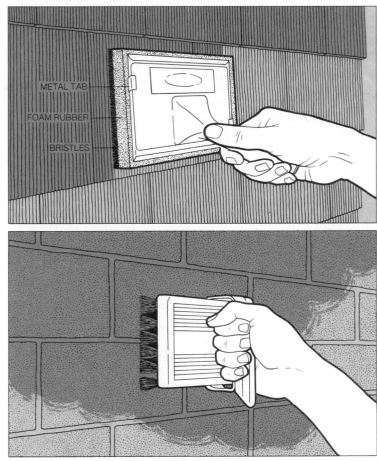

METAL TAB

FOAM RUBBER

BRISTLES

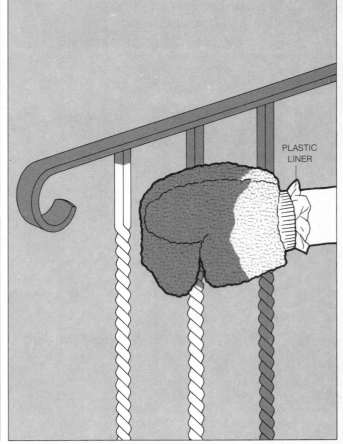

PLASTIC LINER

A rough-surface paintbrush. The stubby bristles of this brush are ideal for scrubbing paint, sealers or other coatings into the pores and crevices of cinder block, brick and stucco. Work the paint into the surface with a circular motion of the brush (*drawing*), then smooth it out with straight finishing strokes. This brush can also be used to paint shingles; the narrow row of bristles along the bottom is used to coat the edge of a shingle, and then the entire brush is used like a pad applicator to paint the face of the shingle.

A mitten applicator. Faster than any brush for coating pipes and railings, this applicator is a bulky mitten covered with lamb's wool on both sides so that it can be used on either hand. The palm of the mitten is dipped into a tray of paint, and then wiped onto the pipe or railing (*drawing*). A plastic liner, visible at the painter's wrist, keeps paint from seeping through the mitten onto his hand. The mitten can be cleaned and re-used just like any brush or roller.

Spray Painting: Fast but Tricky

Speed is the main attraction of spray painting. In less than a day an average-sized, two-story house with a garage can be sprayed with a coat of paint or stain that is almost the equivalent of two coats applied with a brush or roller. To get this double coating, a sprayer will of course use nearly twice as much paint as if it were applied in the conventional way. If you do not need a double coat, thin the paint with the proper solvent.

There are two kinds of sprayers in general use. The traditional type uses compressed air to atomize paint and deposit it on a surface. A newer type, the airless sprayer shown on these pages, is generally considered most efficient for house exteriors. It forces liquid paint directly through the spray-gun nozzle under extremely high pressure. The high pressure can be dangerous, however; note the cautions in the box at right. With any sprayer, always wear a respiratory mask, available at paint stores, to avoid inhaling paint or solvent mist.

You can rent spray gear by the day from many painting stores. But make sure there are no local ordinances that restrict outdoor spraying. Then, before you use the sprayer, prepare your house for painting as described on pages 185-187. Allot enough time—you may need a whole day—to mask everything that you want to protect from speckling. Park your car where a chance breeze cannot spatter paint over it. Once the house is masked, you can paint it on the first calm day.

Though airless equipment is surprisingly simple to use, make sure you receive written operating instructions—the manufacturer's instructions are best—when you rent the sprayer. Machines differ slightly in the way you set them up and clean them after the job.

The setup procedure is basically a matter of using the unit's pump to flush the sprayer with a solvent—water or mineral spirits—that is compatible with the paint, and then pumping paint through the hose to the gun. Cleanup is just the reverse. Pump remaining paint out of the hose, then flush the system with solvent.

For trouble-free spraying, make sure the spray tip has the correct size aperture for the coating you will be using. Thin liquids such as stains require a small-tip aperture; viscous fluids such as latex paint require a larger one. Ask for a tip that sprays a pattern about 8 inches high; this provides the best compromise between speed and accuracy of application.

To reduce the chance of the sprayer becoming clogged with foreign matter, strain the paint through two or three thicknesses of cheesecloth into a clean bucket. Then immerse the sprayer pickup tube in the paint and turn on the pump. Start with the pump set at its lowest pressure and test the sprayer against a large piece of cardboard or scrap plywood. Gradually increase the pressure, if necessary, until the gun produces an even pattern with no gaps.

To get the hang of actual spraying, practice on an inconspicuous part of the house where errors can be corrected with a paintbrush. After covering an area the size of a double-garage door, most people are proficient enough with an airless sprayer to do a professional-looking paint job on a house.

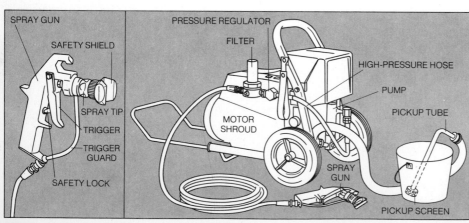

SPRAY GUN
SAFETY SHIELD
SPRAY TIP
TRIGGER
TRIGGER GUARD
SAFETY LOCK
PRESSURE REGULATOR
FILTER
HIGH-PRESSURE HOSE
PUMP
MOTOR SHROUD
PICKUP TUBE
SPRAY GUN
PICKUP SCREEN

The efficient airless sprayer. The heart of an airless sprayer is a hydraulic pump run by a powerful electric motor, which is concealed by a shroud on this model. The pump moves paint from a bucket through a pickup tube equipped with a coarse screen to trap foreign matter. The paint is then forced into a small-diameter, high-pressure hose, past a pressure regulator, which you adjust to produce an even spray pattern, and through a filter fine enough to capture particles that might clog the spray tip. Additional high-pressure hose, usually about 50 feet, carries the paint to the spray gun. The gun itself (inset) is equipped with a trigger guard and a safety lock to prevent accidental discharge and a safety shield to keep fingers from getting too close to the spray tip.

How to Spray

Spraying a uniform coat. The essential trick to spray painting is to hold the gun properly: perpendicular to the wall and 12 inches away. To maintain this constant angle and distance, crook your elbow slightly and bend your wrist (*drawing*), so that you can move the gun in a line exactly parallel to the wall. Never swing the spray tip in an arc as you would a garden hose—if you do, the spray pattern will expand and the coating will be uneven. For best results, do not spray a section wider than you can comfortably reach, no more than 36 inches for most painters.

Covering a wall. Spraying a series of smooth, overlapping strips is the most reliable method of achieving an even coat of paint over an entire wall. First spray a vertical strip down the edge of the wall, releasing the trigger at the end of the stroke. This strip keeps you from spraying past the edge and wasting paint when applying horizontal strips. For even coating, start the gun moving before depressing the trigger at the beginning of each stroke and keep it moving after releasing the trigger at the end. Each horizontal pass should overlap the previous strip and the vertical strip by about an inch to compensate for the thin coating at the ends of the spray pattern.

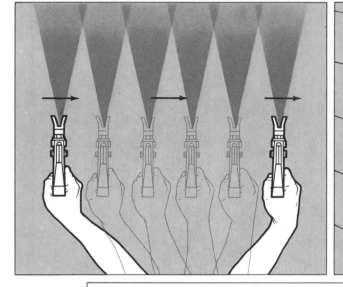

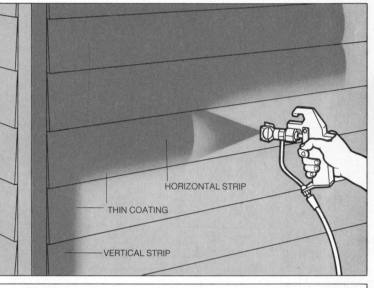

HORIZONTAL STRIP

THIN COATING

VERTICAL STRIP

Spraying the Wrong Way

The paint patterns illustrated at right are a tip-off that you are either holding or moving the spray gun incorrectly, producing coatings that are thicker in some places than in others. An hourglass pattern (*upper drawing*) results if you move the gun without bending your wrist to keep the sprayer the correct, 12-inch distance from the wall. As the gun arcs past the wall, it first moves closer to the wall and then farther away, leaving a wide thin coat at the ends of the strip and a narrow thick coat at the center.

Tilting the gun causes a different kind of unevenness (*lower drawing*). If the gun is pointed slightly downward, the resulting layer of paint will be denser at the top of the spray pattern than it is at the bottom; if the gun is pointed upward, the layer of paint will be applied too thickly along the bottom.

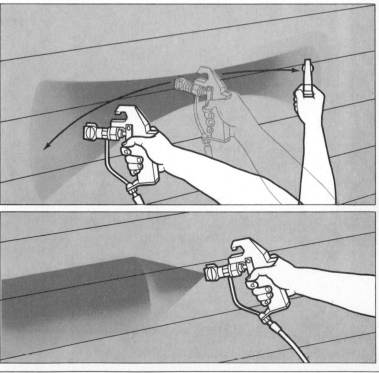

191

Choosing a Wall Covering

Hanging wallpaper is no more difficult than painting a room; the tools listed on pages 194-195 and the methods described on pages 196-221 will help you achieve professional-looking results even if you never attempted the task before. Your main problem, indeed, may be choosing the right type and pattern of wall covering for your needs. Both factors affect not only appearance but ease of hanging and long-range durability.

Great toughness characterizes some special wall covering materials—cork and leather for example—among the 13 types and 32 subtypes of wall coverings listed at right. But of the commonly used wall coverings, the most durable are those made of a sheet of plastic bonded to cloth, the so-called fabric-backed vinyls. They are more scuff resistant and can be scrubbed more safely than a painted surface. Un-backed vinyl is a close second, followed by vinyl-coated paper which, while less rugged than the others, is quite serviceable and somewhat easier to work with. Other types, from the textured grass cloths and common papers to the metalized foils and the fuzzy embossings of "flocked" papers, are considerably more fragile. These delicate coverings are less suitable for areas that are subject to heavy wear—such as kitchens, playrooms and children's bedrooms—and they also require extra care in hanging, since they are likely to tear or crease more readily than the vinyls.

Some of these types require special hanging procedures such as the use of lining paper (page 221), an inexpensive, unpatterned material that is applied to the wall and then covered over with the paper that is meant to be seen. It absorbs moisture quickly, protecting coverings like grass cloth that tend to separate from their backings when wet; and it provides a smooth surface, even on a rough wall, for hanging highly reflective coverings such as foils.

Type	Where to Use
Common Papers Untreated Vinyl-coated Cloth-backed	Areas of moderate wear, such as dining rooms and adult bedrooms
Vinyls Laminated to paper Laminated to woven fabric Impregnated cloth on paper backing Laminated to unwoven fabric	All-purpose, heavy-wear areas, such as kitchens, bathrooms and children's rooms
Foils Simulated metallic Aluminum laminated to paper Aluminum laminated to cloth	Decorative highlights; small alcoves or hallways
Flocks On paper On vinyl On foil	Decorative highlights and formal areas; dining rooms, hallways
Prepasted Coverings Papers Vinyls Foils Flocks	Same areas as similar nonprepasted coverings
Fabrics Untreated Laminated to paper Self-adhesive	Decorative highlights; dining rooms, bedrooms, hallways
Felt Laminated to paper	Decorative highlights; bedrooms; special effects
Textured Coverings Grass cloth Shiki silk Hemp Burlap	Living rooms, recreation rooms
Murals On paper On vinyl On foil	Special effects
Cork Laminated to paper Laminated to burlap	Small rooms; recreation rooms; decorative highlights
Laminated Wood Veneers Random patterns Matched veneers	Substitute for wall paneling; dens, around fireplaces
Gypsum-coated Wall Fabric	Covering for concrete blocks, masonry and damaged wall surfaces; basement recreation rooms
Leather	Special effects

Adhesives	Handling Hints	Special Comments
Wheat paste or stainless cellulose paste	Follow basic procedures *(pages 204-215)*; treat carefully to avoid rips	Susceptible to grease stains and abrasions; pattern inks may run if washed; strippable if cloth-backed
Mildew-resistant type; vinyl compound suggested	Does not stick to itself, double-cut all overlaps *(page 211)*	Most durable type currently available; may be scrubbed; almost always strippable
Mildew-resistant type; vinyl compound suggested	Hang over lining paper *(page 221)* to minimize wall defects; avoid wrinkles, which cannot be smoothed	Fragile and hard to handle; may cause glare in sunny areas; available in striking supergraphics
Same as for corresponding unflocked paper, vinyl or foil, but slightly thicker	Vacuum loose flock particles before applying adhesive; hang over lining paper to ensure smooth surface	Vinyl flocks washable; all may be damaged by excessive rubbing
Water-activated, applied at factory	Use water box *(page 205)*; follow manufacturer's instructions for soaking	Ideal for the inexperienced
Powdered vinyl adhesive or double-faced vinyl tape if fabric is untreated; wheat paste or stainless cellulose paste if laminated	Paint all woodwork before hanging; hang over lining paper; stretch fabric until taut, but not out of shape	Easy to clean with dry-cleaning fluids or powders
Wheat paste	Hang over lining paper; hang strips with nap in the same direction; avoid paste smears, which cause felt to pucker and fade when cleaned	May be vacuumed, but stains are hard to remove; some colors fade
Wheat paste or stainless cellulose paste	Reverse every other strip top for bottom to prevent abrupt changes of shading; avoid excess moisture, which causes fibers to separate from backing; hang over lining paper for faster drying	All available in either natural or synthetic fibers; Shiki silk, a fine grass-cloth type, also sold in overprinted designs
Same as for corresponding paper, vinyl or foil	Hang over lining paper *(page 221)* to ensure smooth surface	Muslin or unbleached cotton may be substituted for lining paper to create strippable mural
Wheat paste if laminated to paper; prepared vinyl adhesive if laminated to burlap	Hang over lining paper; requires no matching	Keep well vacuumed; all cork surfaces are washable; cork absorbs and deadens sounds within a room
Specified by manufacturer	Set room temperature to 70° F. or higher for fast drying; use manufacturer's recommended sequence when hanging matched veneers	Fire-resistant; allowed by strictest city codes where solid wood paneling is banned
Supplied by manufacturer	Set room temperature to 70° F. or higher for fast drying; reverse every other strip, top for bottom	Dries to plaster-like surface; available only in pastel shades, but may be painted in other colors
Mildew-resistant type; vinyl compound suggested	Cut into simple shapes such as squares, rectangles and triangles and arrange into an attractive pattern to fit the area; polish with paste floor wax	Expensive, handsome and durable; stains are difficult, but can be removed by brushing on rubber cement and peeling it off

Tool Kit for Paperhanging

Not every tool in the collection at right is used in every job—the water box, for example, is needed only for prepasted papers—and some, like the trimming knife and the cutting wheel, are interchangeable. Buy only what is necessary for the wall covering you choose.

☐ To remove an old covering from a wall, a paper stripper breaks the surface of a covering to prepare it for wetting. The flexible wall scraper finishes the job of removing the covering from the wall. You need a rigid putty knife if the walls must be patched before the new covering is applied.

☐ The tools for hanging paper make up most of the rest of the kit. Use a metal straightedge at least a yard long to take measurements and to guide long, straight cuts like those that trim edges. The cutting is done with scissors or a utility knife; for trimming, use a trimming guide and a cutting wheel or trimming knife (keep single-edge razor blades on hand for the knife, since the blades dull rapidly).

☐ You have to draw a precisely vertical line on the wall before hanging the first strip of paper and several times thereafter; the job is simplified by the plumb bob shown here, which has a pull-out string that automatically coats itself with chalk from a reservoir in the case.

☐ A metal or plastic paste bucket and a paste brush are used to mix and apply adhesive. Keep a second bucket for clear water, and a clean sponge to wash off excess adhesive after you have hung each strip. To fix the paper firmly on the wall, use a smoothing brush with ¾-inch bristles for a stiff vinyl or 2-inch bristles for a more pliable covering. A seam roller gives a final smoothing to edges.

☐ Fewer tools are needed for a prepasted paper: you can eliminate the paste brush and paste bucket, and a sponge is generally recommended for smoothing instead of the brush and seam roller. You will, however, have to buy a water box.

☐ Both the trimming knife and the seam roller may be needed for minor repairs on previously hung paper if its edges become loose. If you must eliminate an air bubble, use a thin artist's brush to apply adhesive or water under the paper.

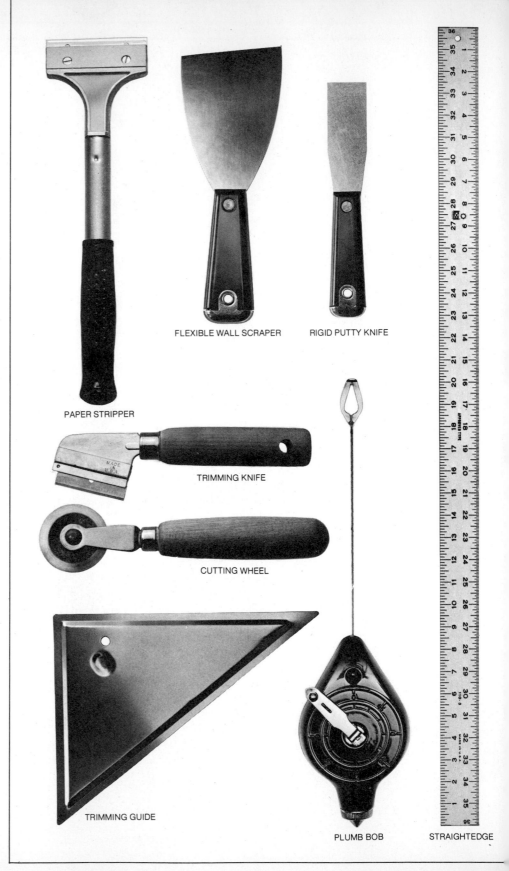

FLEXIBLE WALL SCRAPER

RIGID PUTTY KNIFE

PAPER STRIPPER

TRIMMING KNIFE

CUTTING WHEEL

TRIMMING GUIDE

PLUMB BOB

STRAIGHTEDGE

SPONGE

SMOOTHING BRUSH FOR VINYLS

SMOOTHING BRUSH FOR NONVINYLS

PASTE BRUSH

WATERCOLOR BRUSH

SEAM ROLLER

SCISSORS

PASTE BUCKET

UTILITY KNIFE

WATER BOX

The Three Ways to Remove Old Paper from the Walls

The first step in wallpapering a room is generally painting: if you plan to refinish the trim or paint the ceiling, complete this operation before starting anything else to avoid smudges on the walls. While it is simple to wipe wallpaper paste from woodwork, cleaning paint from new wallpaper is next to impossible. Next, clear the room, leaving space for a pasting table if you plan to apply wallpaper adhesive yourself.

Remove or loosen all objects attached to the walls exactly as if you were preparing to paint (page 156). You need not cover furniture as carefully as you would for a painting job, but be sure to spread several layers of newspaper over your work area to protect the floor from paste, water and sticky drips of old paper, if you are removing it before applying a new covering. To avoid having to drive new fastener holes for pictures or mirrors, insert a toothpick or a small nail in each hole as you remove the hook or screw. When you paper, these projections will puncture the covering and serve as markers when you rehang your decorations.

At this point, you have taken everything off the walls but old paint or paper. Paint presents no problem—you paper over it, though strippable paper should not be applied over latex paint—apply an oil- or alkyd-base coat for this type of covering. Most flat coats (except for calcimine or casein, which must be washed off) need no special preparation. Glossy finishes should be sponge-mopped or washed with a detergent (commercial floor-cleaning products are excellent) or a commercial deglosser to provide tooth—the roughness of surface needed for good adhesion. Because deglossers are usually strong solvents with toxic fumes, treat them as you would paint; let fresh air circulate in the room.

However, papering over paper, though possible, is risky: the water in wallpaper can loosen old layers so they pull away from the wall. Never attempt to paper over more than three layers of paper, no matter how well they seem to be attached. The weight of the additional layer, plus wet wallpaper paste, can pull away the whole sheaf of papers.

If you decide to paper over paper—because the wall beneath is too fragile to withstand paper stripping, or because the time you save by leaving the old paper on the wall is more important than the long-term durability of the finished job—make sure that the old covering is firmly attached to the wall and as smooth as possible. Tear away loosened strips of paper, feathering edges as for a repair job (page 218). Sand down lapped seams with coarse sandpaper; glue down curling corners with wallpaper paste. If you must paper over a shiny material such as vinyl or foil, either hand-sand or roughen the surface with a commercial liquid preparation that provides tooth.

In most cases, it is wiser to remove old paper; new coverings will always adhere better to a stripped wall. It is fairly easy to strip existing wall covering away if the material is vinyl-coated cloth or paper; these materials are easily identified by their rather smooth plastic texture. But if a test pull at a top corner gets no results, you are probably dealing with a nonstrippable material and will have to soak, steam or dry-strip the covering from the wall. The tools you will need are a paper stripper, a 3- to 4-inch-wide scraper or flexible putty knife, sponges, water, and possibly an electric wallpaper steamer, described on page 198.

The stripping method depends largely on the structural material of the wall beneath the covering. You can identify this material by drilling a small hole, not more than 1/4 inch wide and 1 inch deep. If your drill bit produces white dust and meets steady, moderate resistance, the wall is made of plaster. But to make sure the steady resistance is not caused by drilling into a stud, drill a second hole 6 or 8 inches away on a diagonal—it should give the same results. Brown dust and moderate resistance, followed by a sudden "pop" as the drill drives through to the hollow space within the wall, indicates wood or such wood products as particle board or hardboard paneling. White dust, little resistance and a quick pop of the drill are the signs of wallboard.

If the wall is made of plaster or wood, old wall covering can be soaked off (top, far right) or, if it resists soaking, steamed off (page 198). These methods will not work on gypsum board, because the moisture produced by soaking or steam-ing softens the kraft-paper covering of the board, and subsequent scraping to remove paper destroys the board's plaster core. Instead, use the stripping tool shown in Step 1 of the soaking process (top, right) to dry-strip the paper.

Once you have stripped the paper, prepare the walls so that the new paper will both adhere well and come off easily the next time you redecorate. First, repair damaged surfaces as described on pages 156-157. Then paint gypsum board, hardboard and particle board with a flat alkyd primer. Latex primer is least costly for priming wallboard, but foil, vinyl, mylar and most dry-strippable coatings will not adhere to it. Cover raw wood with lining paper (page 221) to prevent the grain of the wood, which the water in wallpaper paste can raise, from showing through the new coverings as a series of ripples and bumps.

Finally, seal unprimed or papered walls to prevent paste from being absorbed into them and to provide a surface that the paper will glide onto easily. The least costly sealer is the glue called wallpaper size, available in liquid or powder form. A quart of either type, mixed with water according to package directions, covers about 300 square feet. But glue-and-resin and straight resin sealers, designed especially as a base for wall coverings, are more versatile, though a quart will cover only about 150 feet. These sealers provide tooth without sanding on such slick surfaces as ceramic tile and glass and form a water barrier on gypsum board so that the paper you apply can later be soaked or steamed off without damage to the wall. They also seal plaster patches against the adhesion-destroying alkalis that rise to the surface of fresh masonry. (If you use glue size, locate and remove alkaline areas—"hot spots"—by the method shown on page 199.)

Apply size or resin sealer with a brush or roller just as you would paint, making sure that no patches of wall are left bare. When a wall is particularly absorbent or rough, glue size can be mixed with slightly less than the manufacturer's recommended amount of water for a thicker covering. Or apply two thin coats of size. Since appearance does not matter, the job will be done quickly.

Slitting and Soaking

1 Preparing the paper. Most papers can be wet through easily, but slick, nonporous coverings may need to be punctured before they can be soaked. Roughen them with coarse sandpaper or a wire brush, or pierce them with a stripper to let in water. Hold the blade of this tool perpendicular to the wall and, applying gentle pressure *(drawing)*, slit the paper horizontally at intervals of 8 to 10 inches. The same tool can be used to dry-strip paper from gypsum board. First slit the wall covering, then slide the blade into the slit at an angle and loosen a section of paper at a time. Tear the loosened sections off with your fingers.

2 Wetting the paper. Using a large sponge *(drawing)*, with a firm, circular motion, wet a strip of paper with warm water and detergent to soften the old paste. If the paste is especially water resistant, use a liquid paper remover—a solution of ethyl alcohol and other chemicals or a liquid containing enzymes that break down the organic materials in wallpaper paste. Use rubber gloves with liquid paper remover. Let the strip soak for five to 10 minutes. Then resoak it and give the adjoining strip a first soak. While waiting for water to penetrate the second strip, proceed to Steps 3 and 4 *(below)* on the first strip.

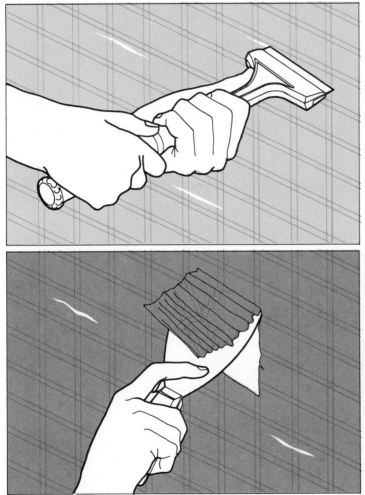

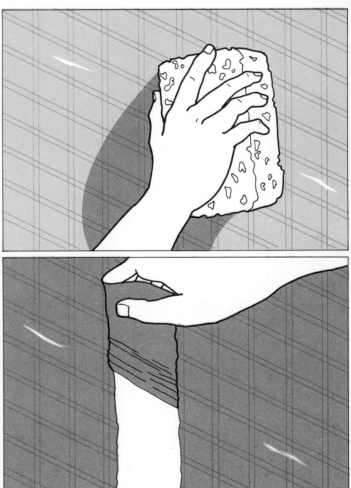

3 Scraping off the paper. Holding a flexible-blade, 3½-inch-wide wall scraper at about a 30° angle away from the wall *(drawing)*, firmly push the wet paper up from the bottom of the strip or from one of the horizontal slits made by a stripper. The paper should wrinkle in exactly the way that a wet jelly-jar label does when you push against it with a fingernail. If it does not, resoak and try again. If the paste is still resistant you will have to use a steamer *(page 198)*.

4 Stripping paper away. Grasp the loosened paper with your fingers and tear upward with a steady, firm motion *(drawing)*. Do not pull the paper outward: it may rip off in your hand before a sizable section has been removed. Paper that is uncoated will tear less evenly than vinyl-coated wall coverings, but both types of paper should peel away easily in long strips. After stripping off all the paper in the room, wash the walls down with warm water to remove any of the remaining scraps of wallpaper and paste.

Using an Electric Wallpaper Steamer

1 Starting the steamer. Some papers do not respond to the method shown on page 197. An electric steamer will probably do the job, for vapor·will penetrate where water cannot. A steamer, for rent at most wallpaper dealers, typically consists of a perforated plate connected by a hose to a water tank, heated by an electric coil in its base. To fill the tank, make sure the cord is unplugged and remove the stopper valve at the top. Set a funnel in the opening and pour in boiling water until the water-level gauge indicates full. Plug in the steamer; a pilot light shows when the unit is on. The steamer is ready to use when vapor comes from the steamer plate.

2 Using the steamer plate. When steam pours steadily from the perforations in the steamer plate, hold it firmly against the wall. Do not move the plate in any direction. In two or three minutes you will see the paper around the plate dampen and darken, and water droplets may start to run down the wall. Move the plate onto an adjacent area in the same strip of paper and repeat the steaming process. When you have steamed half a strip, proceed to Steps 3 and 4 of the removal procedure shown on page 197.

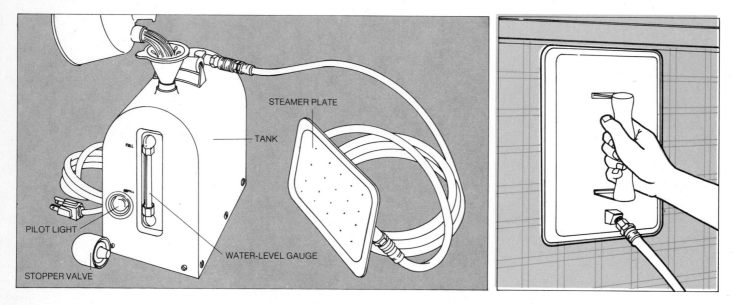

STEAMER PLATE

TANK

PILOT LIGHT

WATER-LEVEL GAUGE

STOPPER VALVE

Paper that Peels Off

Removing strippable wall coverings. Many vinyl and vinyl-coated coverings and some mylars and fabrics can be stripped from walls dry. Use a fingernail or a utility knife to pull away a corner of the covering at the top of a section, and carefully peel the covering downward, pulling it flat against itself. If you pull the covering outward and away from the wall, its paper backing may rip unevenly, leaving a rough surface. Do not remove any fuzzy residue that is left by the backing; it will help the next coat of paste stick better.

Hot Spots and Their Treatment

Neutralizing alkalis. Alkali patches—called hot spots by paperhangers—are present in all fresh plaster and many old plaster walls. Because they keep wallpaper paste from sticking, they must be found and treated with alkali-canceling acid. A plaster repair patch is easy to see; hot spots on larger areas become visible when glue size is applied—they turn pink, red or purple *(colored area in drawing at right)*. Neutralize spots with a solution of one part 28 per cent acetic acid and two parts water. Wearing rubber gloves, swab this mixture over the spot with a soft cloth. The color will fade gradually; when it disappears completely, the alkali is gone; finish by resizing the area.

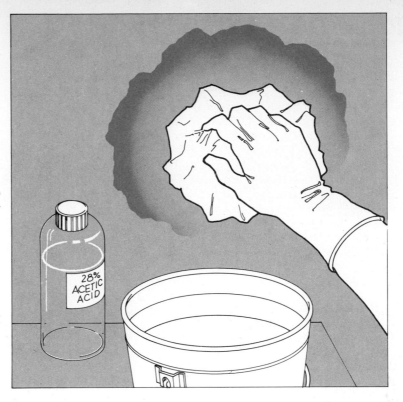

How Much Paper? How Much Time?

Wallpaper is manufactured in "runs"— long strips are painted from a single dye batch. Then the dye is replaced and another long strip—up to several thousand feet—is printed. This method may result in slight color variations from run to run. And because of these color variations, it is best not to hazard a guess at the amount of paper you will need. Rather than run short in mid-job and risk a bad match, buy all the paper you need at one time.

To calculate the amount of paper necessary to cover your room, find the room perimeter as you would for a paint job *(page 147)*. Multiply that figure by room height from the baseboard to the ceiling—or to a cornice, if you do not mean to paper above it—then subtract the exact area of doors, windows and other places you will not paper. The final figure will be a close estimate of the wall area of the room. If you plan to paper the ceiling as well, find the area of the floor; if it does not duplicate the ceiling (because of dormers or bay windows, for example), you may have to allow for cutbacks or extensions. Use a ladder to measure these areas and add them to the floor figure.

Wall coverings are measured in units called single rolls. Though the width of papers may range from 15 to 54 inches, a single American-made roll contains approximately 36 square feet of covering. Despite this standard unit of measurement, most papers are sold in double-length rolls called bolts and some are sold in three- or four-roll bolts.

You must expect to waste about 6 square feet per single roll on odd-shaped areas, on points where the wall ends before the pattern does, and in trimming excess paper from the top and bottom of a strip. Therefore, divide your total wall or ceiling area by 28-30 square feet to find the number of single-roll units you will need.

You should request that your paper be delivered in two-, three- or four-roll bolts cut in continuous, long strips. Working from a bolt of this length, you can cut as many as five or six floor-to-ceiling strips with ease and minimal waste. However, unless the actual number of rolls you need turns out to be an exact multiple of two or three, try to avoid paper that is sold only in bolts. If you should need to cover a small area calling for just one extra roll and you have only multiple-roll bolts, you could wind up wasting from one to three full rolls. But don't under-buy if you have no choice; it might be difficult or impossible to match your paper later.

If you are hanging on bare or painted walls in good condition, allow a full day to size and paper a 12-by-15 foot room. If the walls need substantial repairs, or if you must remove an existing coat of paper, double that estimate, especially if you are papering for the first time. But you need not feel that a papering job must be an extended and exhausting effort. Unlike painting, papering can be done piecemeal. If you are using pre-pasted paper there are no problems with paste preparation and cleanup; in any case, prepared paste can be saved till later *(page 204)*. If you must work in short spells, you can easily hang a strip or two and then leave the work—even for days if necessary—without harming the final effect.

Deciding Where to Start and Where to End

Because wallpaper must be hung in consecutive strips, with the pattern of each one matching a previously completed section, placement of the first strip governs the appearance of the finished job. Designs with narrow stripes and small random patterns do not cause matching problems; they can be started conveniently alongside any door or window. But before you begin to hang a complex pattern, you must choose your starting point carefully.

Complex patterns usually look best when the overall arrangement is symmetrical and the strips are placed so that the pattern draws the attention of a viewer to one part of a room: one wall, for example, or the space above a fireplace or the area surrounding one or more windows. When planning such an arrangement, it is wise to avoid having to hang strips narrower than 6 inches, because they may be difficult to align and affix. The instructions that follow explain how this problem can be minimized.

Keep in mind that a pattern may not necessarily be centered on the roll. In such cases, inspect the paper and note where the center of the pattern lies. But be aware that "drop-match patterns" *(page 209)* may not repeat horizontally until after two consecutive strips of the paper have been hung.

Make a light pencil mark on the wall where you want to center the overall pattern. Then, make a second mark to the left of the first mark at a distance equal to that between the center of the pattern on the roll and the left edge of the roll. You will want to hang the first strip with its left edge against this second mark; this will center the pattern precisely where you want it.

Unless the perimeter of the room is an exact multiple of the width of the pattern—an unlikely occurrence—there will probably be an unavoidable mismatch along one edge of the last strip that is to be hung. This will not happen in a room that has one surface interrupted by a floor-to-ceiling storage unit or a built-in corner cabinet. But in all rooms where four continuous walls are to be papered, you should plan ahead to locate the one inevitable mismatch so that you can contrive to have it happen in an inconspicuous place *(page 202)*.

Locating the First Strip

To center on a wall. With a pencil, mark the center of the wall. Using a roll of wallpaper as a yardstick, measure the distance to the nearest corner. Start by placing one edge of the roll against the mark, then move the roll toward the corner, one width at a time, until less than one roll width remains. If this remaining distance is 6 inches or less *(right, above)*, plan to center the first strip of paper over the mark *(right, below)*. If the remaining distance exceeds 6 inches, hang the first strip of paper where you started measuring—with the left edge of the strip against the pencil mark. To center the pattern above a fireplace, make the pencil mark above the center of the mantelpiece and proceed as for a wall.

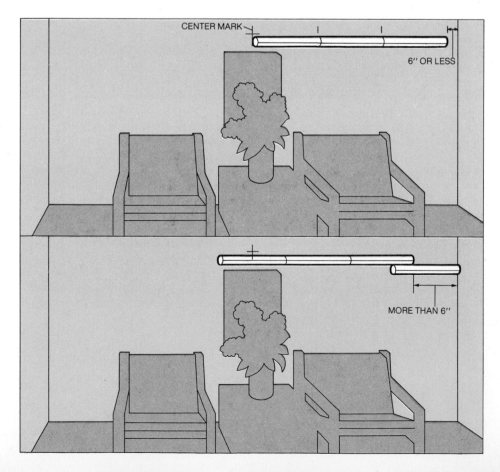

CENTER MARK

6" OR LESS

MORE THAN 6"

To center between two windows. The width of the wall between the windows will determine the placement of the first strip of wallpaper. With a pencil, mark a spot halfway between the windows and center a roll on that mark. If you find that centering the roll of paper on the mark would result in having narrow strips at each window edge (*left, below*), you may prefer to hang the first strip alongside the center mark (*right*).

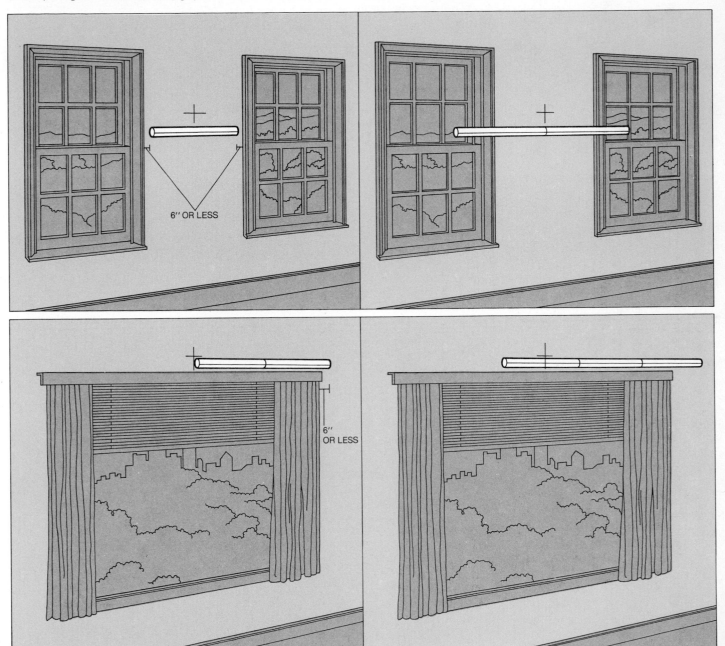

6″ OR LESS

6″ OR LESS

To center above a picture window. With a pencil, mark the center of the wall section above the window and measure as for walls (*opposite*), moving the roll toward the window's right upper corner. If the last full roll extends 6 inches or less beyond the corner of the window (*left, above*), plan to center the strip on the mark (*right*).

Locating the Last Strip

To end in a partly hidden area. You may find an unobtrusive corner where ending the wallpaper in mid-pattern will not be noticeable. In the room below, for example, the shallow corner where the fireplace meets the wall gets no direct light from the nearest window and is inconspicuous from most directions. Thus it is a suitable place to end. Another option might be one of the corners of the room itself—if it is hidden by furniture.

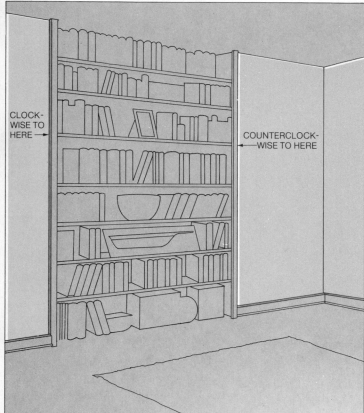

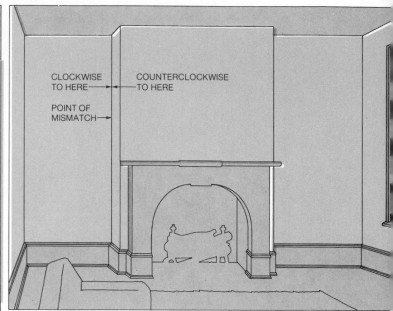

To end at a floor-to-ceiling interruption. If the wall you plan to paper is interrupted by a section of paneling, a fireplace or a built-in bookcase that goes from floor to ceiling, as in the illustration above, make this area the target of your final strip. Once you have chosen the location of your first strip *(pages 200-201),* work from there both clockwise and counterclockwise, ending at the left and right sides of the interrupted area. In this way, there will be no mismatched strip anywhere.

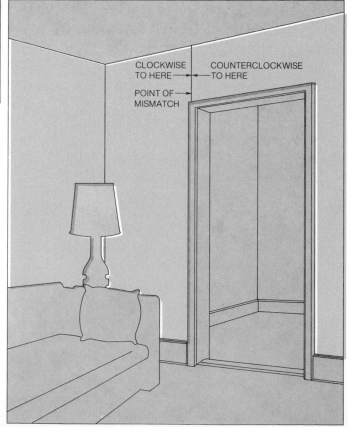

To end above a door. The narrow strip of wall above a door is often one of the least conspicuous features of a room. You should make the last two strips meet above the left or right side of the door, whichever is closer to the room's nearest corner *(right).* If, however, the door is centered on the wall, take into account the location of windows and lamps, and choose the side of the door that receives the least light.

A Plumb Line to Get the Pattern Straight

No house has truly vertical walls. If you hang successive strips of wallpaper while merely following the planes of the walls, the room may look tipsy by the time you finish the job.

You can avoid slanted strips by drawing a true vertical line against which to align the first strip. Also, recheck the alignment after hanging every few strips, particularly after turning a corner; doing so will enable you to correct the alignment before the adhesive dries. Two alternative methods of marking a vertical line on a wall are illustrated at right, one using a plumb bob and the other using a metal straightedge. If you own a carpenter's level, you can use it instead of the straightedge; read both the upper and lower vials to make sure that the level is truly vertical. Press the level firmly against the wall and draw a pencil line along the side of the level.

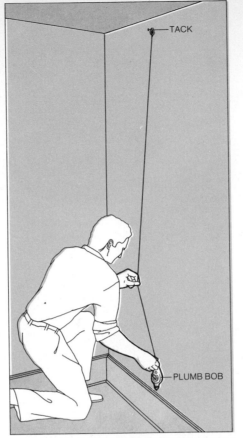

Plumb bob and chalk. Rub colored chalk on a plumb-bob string *(page 194)* and, with a thumbtack or small nail, attach the string to a point high on the wall. Wait until the bob stops swinging; the string will then be vertical. Without altering the bob's position, pull it slightly downward until the string is taut, press it firmly against the wall and snap the string with the other hand *(drawing)*. This action will deposit a lightly colored vertical chalk line on the wall.

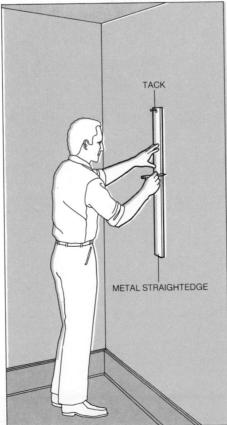

Metal straightedge. If your metal straightedge *(page 194)* has a hole at one end, tack it loosely to the wall through that hole. Let the straightedge dangle freely until it comes to rest; hold it firmly against the wall in that position and draw a light pencil line along its edge. The pencil line will be a true vertical *(drawing)*.

A Mess-Free Pasting Method

Unless you use prepasted paper and a water box *(opposite),* the proper choice of an adhesive and its correct application have much to do with the success of a wallpapering project. The wall covering you buy is frequently accompanied by the manufacturer's instructions for the adhesive to be used; if not, follow the recommendations of your dealer.

Adhesives, whether organic or synthetic, are available in both liquid and dry form. The liquids are poured directly into a bucket if you plan to use a paste brush, or into a roller tray if you use a paint roller. Dry substances must first be mixed with water; directions on the package indicate the amount of water required. About 30 minutes before use, pour the powder slowly into the water to minimize lumps. Mix thoroughly and make sure that all lumps are completely dis-

solved. Store the leftover adhesive in an airtight container for future use.

As you apply the paste, spread it evenly and cover the entire surface of the strip. Avoid getting paste on the pattern side—or on the table where the next strip of wallpaper would come in contact with it. One simple way of preventing this is to spread several layers of paper on the table, discarding the top layer after applying the paste to each strip. Avoid using newspapers, however, since printer's ink may rub off onto the pattern. Substituting layers of kraft paper solves that problem, though it is relatively expensive, since each layer is used only once. The method demonstrated step by step on these pages eliminates entirely the need for layers of paper, by keeping the brush well away from the table surface during the entire operation.

1 Pasting the lower left area. After you have measured and cut the wallpaper into strips *(page 206),* lay one strip with its pattern side down on the table. Allow the top end of the strip to hang over the table's edge. Slide the strip into position *(drawing);* the strip's left and lower edges now extend beyond the table by a quarter of an inch or so. Paste the lower left quarter.

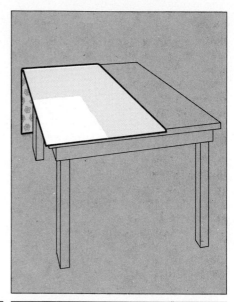

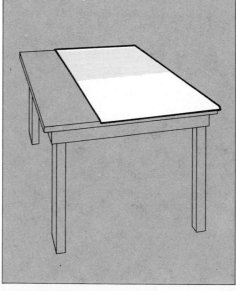

2 Pasting the lower right area. Shift the strip to the opposite long edge of the table with the strip's right and lower edges slightly over the edges. Paste the lower right quarter.

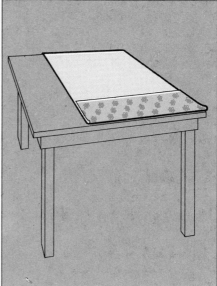

3 Making the lower fold. Pull the strip slightly toward you and gently fold the pasted section over on itself, pattern side out. Do not crease the fold. Make this fold somewhat shorter than the fold you will make at the top *(Step 6)* so that you will be able to identify the top when you are ready to hang the strip.

4 **Pasting the upper right area.** Slide the strip toward you until the upper edge of the paper barely overlaps the table. Make sure that the right edge of the paper still extends beyond the right edge of the table. The section of the strip that was previously pasted should now hang freely over the edge of the table. Paste the upper right quarter of the strip.

Using a Water Box

When using a prepasted paper, by all means get a special plastic container called a water box from your local wallpaper dealer. An inexpensive item, it will simplify your job.

Fill about two thirds of the box with water and place the box atop layers of newspaper, directly below each section of wall as you are working on it. After cutting a strip to the proper length, roll it loosely from bottom to top, with the pattern inside, then lay it in the box to soak for the length of time recommended by the manufacturer—usually 10 seconds to one minute. If the paper floats to the surface, slip an object without sharp edges —such as a wooden dowel—inside the rolled strip to weight it down.

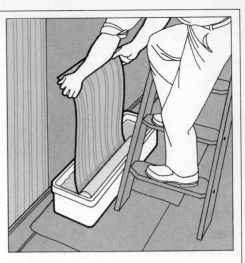

Pulling out the strip. Place your stepladder sideways in front of the water box. With the pattern facing you, draw the paper up as you climb the ladder. Hang the paper immediately.

5 **Pasting the upper left area.** Shift the strip to the opposite long edge of the table until the strip's left and upper edges hang slightly over the edges. Paste the upper left quarter.

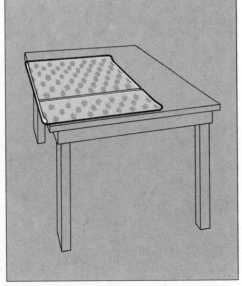

6 **Making the top fold.** After drawing the strip partly off the table, fold the upper section over on itself, pattern side out, so the top edge barely meets the bottom edge. Do not crease the fold. Set the pasted strip on a clean surface to cure for about 10 minutes; apply paste to additional strips while the first is curing. The strip will then be ready to hang (*pages 206-207*).

Putting Up the First Strip

After you have decided on placement of the first strip *(pages 200-201),* cut a length of wallpaper at least 4 inches longer than the height of the wall; the extra inches provide a trim allowance at the ceiling and baseboard. Apply paste and let it cure as explained on pages 204-205.

If the wallpaper has selvages—blank strips along both edges—remove them before wallpapering *(below, Step 1).* Usually, however, selvages have been trimmed off at the factory or the store. Some wallpaper is sold with perforations separating the selvages from the pattern; in such cases, you can simply knock the selvage off by rapping each end of the roll sharply against the edge of a table.

In hanging the first strip your primary concern should be to keep the strip rigorously vertical *(below, right).* Do not align the paper with the edge of a door frame or the corner line of room walls; such structural elements are almost certain to deviate from the true vertical in even the best-built house. Instead, mark a plumb line, as shown on page 203.

As you smooth the paper, avoid air bubbles—especially large ones; the brush strokes diagramed in Step 6 will eliminate all large bubbles and most small ones. The remaining small bubbles usually vanish as the paper dries (for any that persist, see page 220 for instructions on how to correct the problem).

As soon as the strip has been hung and trimmed—before the paste dries—use a clean sponge wrung in clear water to remove paste remaining on the ceiling, the baseboard and the face of the strip itself. Rinse the sponge often.

Although a smoothing brush is used to apply wallpaper in the steps that are illustrated here, a sponge or a paint roller works equally well.

The First Strip

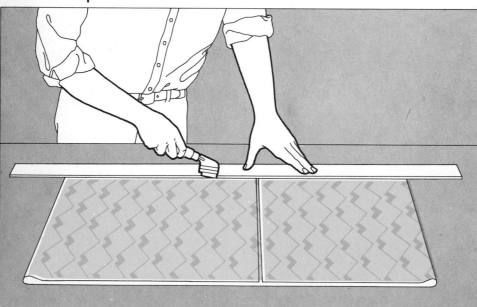

1 Trimming the selvages. If your paper has selvages, align the side edges of the pasted and folded strip, making sure that the visible portions of the selvages lie precisely over the hidden selvages on the underside of the folds. Exactly cover the visible selvage on one side with a straightedge. Using the straightedge as a guide, cut off the selvage with a firm, continuous stroke of your trimming knife or any sharp utility knife. Repeat the procedure on the other side of the strip.

2 Starting the alignment. Unfold the top section of the strip. Starting at the ceiling line, and allowing roughly 2 inches for final trimming along the ceiling, align one of the side edges of the paper with the plumb line *(drawing).* As you align the paper, pat the top section into place with your hand, just lightly enough to make it hold on the wall. Because wallpaper may stretch after it is dampened with paste or soaked in a water box, be careful not to pull the edges of the strip.

3 **Brushing at the ceiling line.** Use short, upward strokes of your smoothing brush to press the topmost few inches of paper against the wall, up to —but not beyond—the ceiling line. Work in this fashion across the entire width of the strip, pressing the paper firmly with the smoothing brush into the angle formed between ceiling and wall.

4 **Brushing on the top section.** With brisk, light strokes, press the entire top section of the strip against the wall, stopping an inch or so from the upper edge of the lower fold. Do not worry at this stage about occasional air bubbles. However, to avoid wrinkles, gently pull the lower part of the strip away from the wall up to the point where a wrinkle has formed and brush the paper smooth.

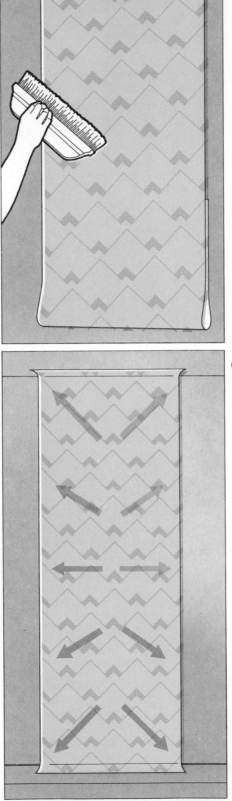

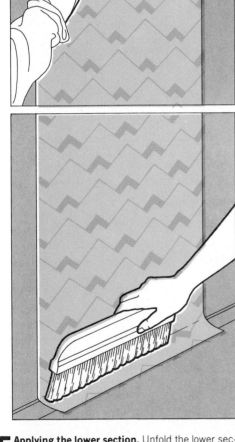

6 **Smoothing the strip.** Remove all air bubbles and ensure a firm bond between the paper and the wall with firm brush strokes—using both hands on the brush if necessary. Smooth the paper from the middle of the strip toward its edges, following the general direction of the arrows in the diagram and working from the top to the bottom. This technique will remove the air trapped in bubbles by forcing it out the sides of the strip. If any wrinkles appear while you are brushing the paper down or toward the edges, remove them as you did in Step 4. Finally, go over the entire surface of the strip with firm, vertical strokes.

5 **Applying the lower section.** Unfold the lower section of the strip and continue aligning it against the plumb line down to the baseboard. Apply this part of the strip to the wall as in Step 4, using light brush strokes and avoiding wrinkles.

Trimming the Strip

1 Creasing. Press the wallpaper against the upper edge of the baseboard with the blunt side of a pair of scissors (drawing). The pressure of the scissors creases the paper along the line where the paper is to be trimmed.

2 Cutting. Gently lift the strip away from the wall and use scissors to cut off the excess along the crease you have made in Step 1. Brush the paper down again with your smoothing brush. Repeat Steps 1 and 2 along the ceiling line.

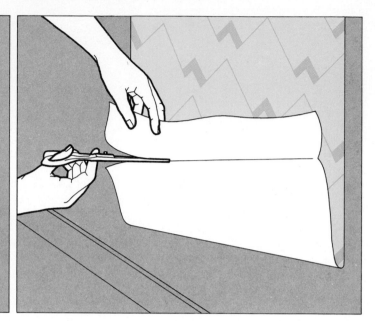

Other Ways to Trim

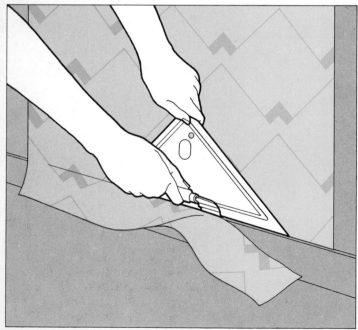

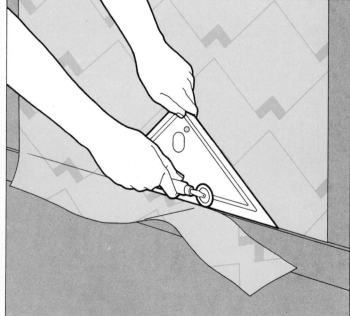

A trimming knife. Instead of using scissors, you may prefer to use a trimming knife, particularly in places where pulling the strip away from the wall would be awkward, such as around windows. Use a guiding edge such as a metal triangle (sold in paint stores) to ensure a straight cutting stroke and change the razor blade frequently.

A cutting wheel. For trimming fragile papers, which even a sharp knife might tear, use a cutting wheel. Handle the wheel as you would the trimming knife, rolling it along a guiding edge.

Matching the Basic Patterns: Straight and Drop

Except for those decorated solely with textures or stripes, wall-covering strips must be matched at their edges, and this requirement has to be taken into account in cutting every strip after the first. Patterns fall generally into two categories called "straight match" *(below, top)* and "drop match" *(bottom)*. The category is sometimes stamped on the back of the paper, thus alerting you to the matching sequence to follow. But even if there is no such indication printed on the wallpaper, there is a simple way to distinguish at a glance between the two types: If the parts of the same design on the left and right edges of the paper are directly opposite each other, the pattern is a straight match; all other patterns are drop matches.

Unroll a length of paper from the roll you started with and hold it against the wall alongside that first strip. Shift the paper up and down until the pattern matches along the adjacent edges of the two strips; there will almost always be a small element of the pattern along the edges of each strip to help you match two strips at a glance.

Allow 2 inches for trim both at the top and at the bottom of the second strip. However, before cutting the strip from the roll, repeat the matching operation with another roll to find out which of the two rolls will be left with the lesser amount of waste. Depending on the height of the wall and the length of the pattern, you may discover that much waste can be avoided by cutting the strips alternately from the two rolls.

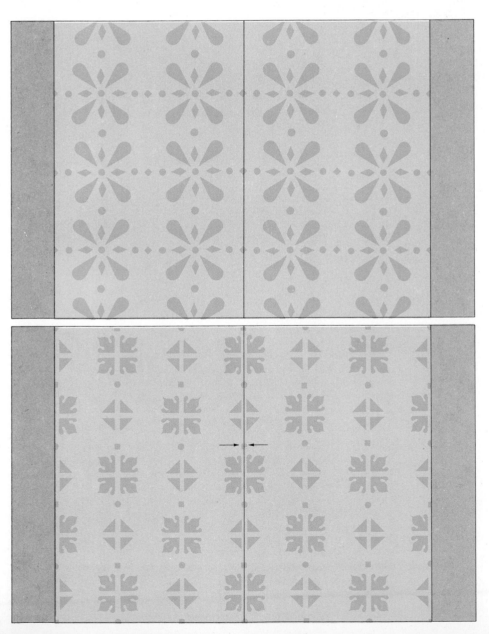

Straight-match pattern. In this type of pattern, the design stretches across the full width of a strip so that when strips are properly matched the design repeats horizontally from strip to strip. Some designs—such as plaids—may consist of small patterns that repeat horizontally several times between both edges of a strip. In either case, adjacent strips will be identical.

Drop-match pattern. This type of pattern is characterized by designs that extend beyond the width of a single strip. The most common variety *(left)* is drawn in such a way that the bottom half of the pattern on one strip fits exactly alongside the top half of the same pattern on the adjacent strip, and vice versa. This arrangement causes the design to repeat diagonally on the wall, hence the designation "drop match." Wallpaper designers usually incorporate a small element of the pattern along the edges of the paper *(arrows)* as a matching guide.

Joining Strips Together

All strips are hung and trimmed at top and bottom as demonstrated on page 208, but once the first strip is on the wall, all those that follow must be carefully joined together at their common seams. The joining procedure will vary depending on the type of wall covering you are using and the section of the room you are papering—a flat wall or corner, for example. Techniques for papering around corners are discussed on pages 212-213.

Because wallpapers are usually sold with their selvages trimmed off at the factory, the butted seam *(right, top),* in which edges just meet, has almost universally replaced the bumpy-looking overlapped edges still found in older wallpapering jobs. Only in special cases—such as turning corners or allowing for excessive shrinkage—will you need to resort to a lapped or a wire-edge seam, both of which are shown and described at right.

A vinyl wall covering—as opposed to a vinyl-coated paper—cannot be lapped because vinyl does not adhere to itself and the overlap would remain loose. When joining vinyl, you must almost always use the technique called "double-cutting," as explained on the bottom of the opposite page. There is, however, a vinyl-on-vinyl adhesive, carried by most wallpaper stores, that permits small overlaps when they are necessary.

Avoid stretching edges when you join strips of any kind of material and, except for very fragile coverings, use a seam roller to get a strong bond *(opposite page).* Because seam rolling works best after the adhesive has begun to dry, you will save time if you hang four or five strips before starting to roll the seams.

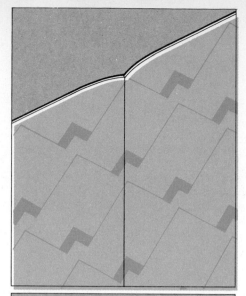

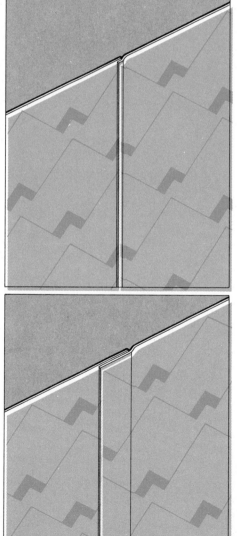

Three Types of Seams

Butted. Adjacent edges of two strips of wallpaper are brought firmly against each other until the edges buckle slightly. Because the paper shrinks somewhat as it dries, the buckling eventually flattens out against the wall. This is the best-looking seam and the one that is most frequently used in papering a flat expanse of wall.

Wire edge. In such a seam, the edge of one strip overlaps the adjacent edge by no more than 1/16 inch, hiding only a tiny portion of the pattern. This is the method that should be used if you have trouble butting your paper or if the paper shrinks so much the seams spread open.

Lapped. This type of seam, in which one strip overlaps the adjacent one by ¼ to ½ inch, was the most commonly used in earlier decades. It produces a noticeable ridge and is now used only in special cases—near corners, for example, where the alignment of the paper must be corrected because the walls are not perfectly vertical.

Making Seams

Positioning. Affix each new strip lightly on the wall, keeping it about ¼ inch away from the previous strip. Slide the new strip into position against the other strip. Keep your hands flat and well away from the edge of the strip to avoid stretching it. Move your hands about on the strip in order to get the pattern matched and the seam neatly butted. If you need a lapped seam, affix the strip about ¼ inch (¹⁄₁₆ inch for a wire-edge seam) over the previous one instead of away from it, and slide the new strip into place, using the same hand motions.

The roller method. When the adhesive is partly dry—10 to 15 minutes after you have hung a new strip—use a seam roller to press the edges of the seam firmly together and against the wall. Roll the cylinder against the seam with short up-and-down strokes until you have pressed the whole length of the seam. Do not use a seam roller on textured papers, flocks, foils or other fragile coverings, which would be marred by the rolling action; press the seam with a sponge instead *(far right)*.

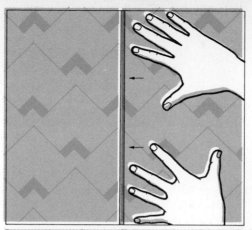

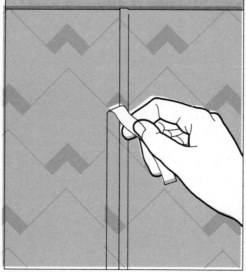

The sponge method. When hanging fragile papers, which a seam roller would damage, press the edges of each seam gently together with your fingers and a damp sponge. Manufacturers usually recommend using the same method for prepasted wallpapers.

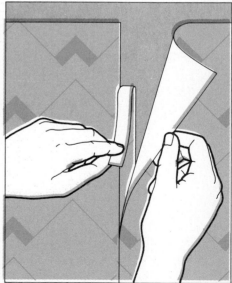

The Fine Art of Double-Cutting

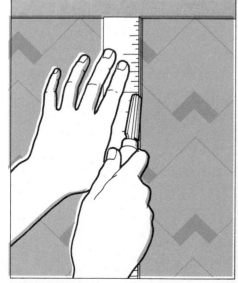

1 Cutting through the seam. Using a straight-edge to guide your trimming knife, slice through both thicknesses of the lapped seam approximately down the middle of the overlap. This will sever two narrow bands of paper, one clearly visible on the outside of the overlap and the other one hidden underneath.

2 Removing the outer band. Carefully peel off the outer band of the cut overlap. Use your trimming knife to deepen the cut if you find that the separation of the bands is not complete.

3 Removing the inner band. Now lift the edge of the strip from which you have just removed the outer band and peel off the band it covered *(drawing)*. Press both edges of the cut together with a sponge. Finish with a seam roller, unless the paper is the kind that rolling would damage.

The Ins and Outs of Getting around Corners

Corners are slightly more difficult to handle than a flat wall. But you can achieve a professional-looking job by observing a few simple rules.

Keep in mind that the two walls that form a corner are seldom precisely vertical. In order to re-establish the correct alignment of the wallpaper strips, you will have to draw a new plumb line *(page 203)* on the wall immediately after you have turned the corner.

Also—and again because the walls are not truly vertical—you cannot bend more than a few inches of a strip around a cor-ner without causing unsightly wrinkles. For this reason professionals prefer to slit the strip vertically into two sections to be hung separately, the first reaching just beyond the corner and the second lap-ping slightly over the first.

Slitting the strip also prevents a prob-lem that would arise if you used a full strip when papering an inner corner: be-cause most wall coverings shrink when they dry, the part of the strip that is pressed into the corner will eventually pull away; any pressure against the paper will then puncture it.

No such problems arise on an outer corner because drying merely tightens the strip against it. However, there is an-other hazard that must be avoided: if the lapped edge is placed less than ¼ inch or so from the corner, the edge will inevi-tably become frayed when people or furniture brush against it.

Note: The illustrations below and on the opposite page show the corners of rooms that are being papered from left to right; if you are papering your room from right to left, reverse the directions given in the instructions.

Inner Corners

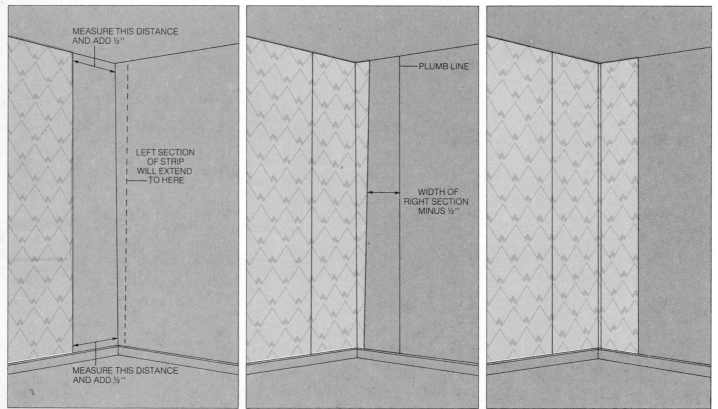

1 Dividing the strip. From the edge of the last strip that you have applied, measure the dis-tance to the corner, then add ½ inch. Make this measurement both at the top and at the bot-tom of the wall *(drawing)*. Cut the next strip lengthwise, using the greater of these two mea-surements as the width of the left-hand section of the strip. Hang this section to the left of the corner and trim it at the top and bottom.

2 Restoring the vertical alignment. After hang-ing and trimming the left-hand section of the strip, measure the right-hand section and sub-tract ½ inch. Measure off that distance on the wall, as shown in the above drawing, and trace a plumb line through that measurement.

3 Hanging the right-hand section. Hang the right-hand section of the strip against the plumb line, overlapping the first section near the corner. In nearly all cases, the overlap will slant on the wall because the corner is not truly vertical (the draw-ings exaggerate the slant to clarify this point). The slight distortion of the pattern resulting from this slant is usually quite inconspicuous. Make sure that you double-cut the seam *(page 211)* if you are hanging a vinyl covering.

Outer Corners

1 Dividing the strip. From the edge of the last strip that you have applied, measure the distance to the corner of the wall, then add 1 inch to the measurement. Make this measurement both at the top and at the bottom of the wall *(drawing)*. Then cut the next strip lengthwise, using the greater of these two measurements as the width of the left-hand section of the strip.

2 Turning the corner. To hang the left-hand section of the strip, smooth it on the wall as far as the corner, then slit the paper precisely as far as the ceiling line at the top, and precisely to the edge of the baseboard at the bottom. This will allow the paper to lie flat as you round the corner and smooth it on the other wall. Trim the strip at the top and at the bottom.

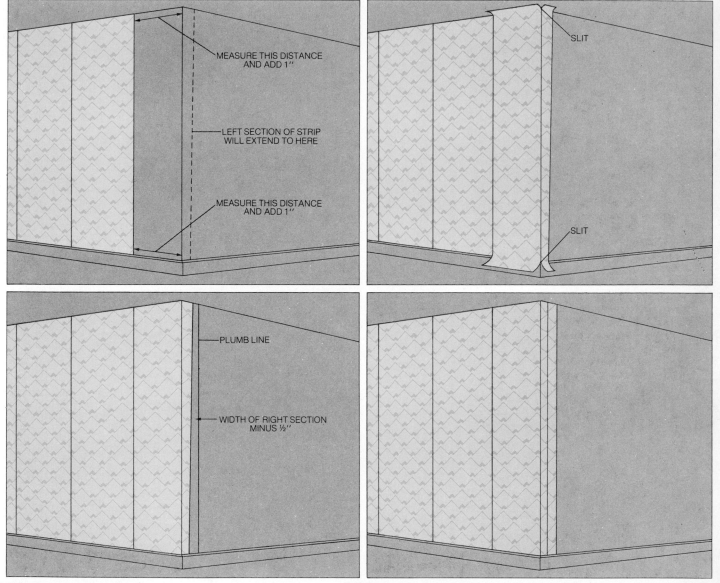

MEASURE THIS DISTANCE AND ADD 1"

LEFT SECTION OF STRIP WILL EXTEND TO HERE

MEASURE THIS DISTANCE AND ADD 1"

SLIT

SLIT

PLUMB LINE

WIDTH OF RIGHT SECTION MINUS ½"

3 Restoring the vertical alignment. After hanging and trimming the left-hand section of the strip, measure the width of the right-hand section and subtract ½ inch. Measure off that distance on the wall as shown in the drawing above, and trace a plumb line through that point.

4 Hanging the right-hand section. Follow the same procedures as for inner corners *(left, Step 3).* Double-cut the overlap if hanging vinyl *(page 211).*

Papering Doors and Windows

When you paper around doors and windows that are framed by moldings, you must slit the paper and ease it around the corners of the moldings *(right and opposite)* before smoothing it on the wall. Casement windows, which do not have moldings, are treated more simply if you use any wall covering except the vinyl type: Bring the wallpaper around the edges of the casement and cover the inner sides, lapping the wallpaper seams.

Vinyl coverings, which do not accept pasted lapped seams because vinyl does not adhere to itself, are trickier than other types. Every lapped seam must be double-cut *(page 211)* and the double-cuts must be away from the edges of the casement to keep the paper from fraying.

To a certain extent, a room with casement windows may restrict your choice of patterns. Some pattern mismatches are unavoidable at the casements, and the best way to keep them inconspicuous is to use a small overall pattern.

Double-Hung Windows

1 **Approaching the window.** Align the first strip that will reach the window as you would any previous strip, but smooth it onto the wall only as far as the window's vertical molding.

2 **Removing the excess paper.** With a pair of scissors, cut off part of the strip that overlaps the window molding, leaving about 2 inches of the overlap as a margin for final trimming.

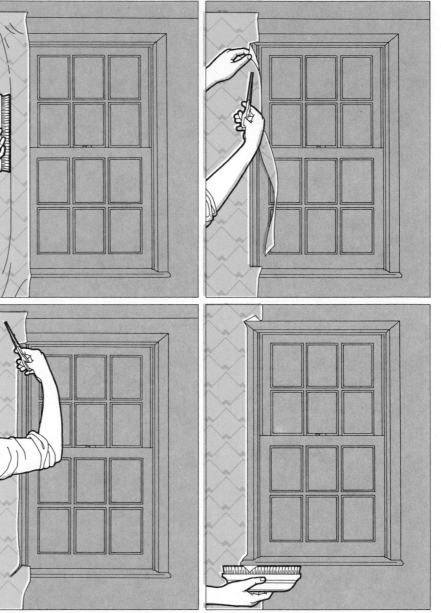

3 **Slitting the corners.** Cut the paper diagonally at the top and bottom corners of the window molding, as shown in the drawing above. Each cut should end against the wall, precisely where the wall meets the outer corner of the molding. These cuts will permit the paper to be smoothed against the wall around the corners of the molding.

4 **Smoothing the rest of the strip.** Smooth the paper to the wall above and below the window, pressing the paper firmly against the molding.

5 **Trimming the strip.** With your trimming knife and a trimming guide to steady it, trim the excess paper along the molding, at the top, side and bottom *(drawing).* When rounding corners, especially at the sill, make a few cuts into the trim allowance to ease the tautness of the paper so it will lie flat. Trim at ceiling and baseboard as you did on previous strips *(page 208).*

6 **Hanging the top and bottom strips.** Hang as many short strips as needed above and below the window until the remaining distance to the opposite vertical edge of the window frame is less than the full width of a strip. Match the pattern as carefully as you would for full-length strips, and trim as usual at the ceiling, the upper and lower moldings and the baseboard.

7 **Beginning to attach the last strip.** The final long strip, which will be fitted around the two remaining corners of the molding and along its right vertical edge, must be attached first above the window. Match the pattern precisely alongside the edge of the last short strip and then smooth the long strip on the wall only as far down as the outer corner of the molding.

8 **Papering down the second side.** With scissors, make a horizontal slit in the paper about 2 inches below the top edge of the molding, stopping about 2 inches short of the vertical molding's outer edge. This cut relieves the pull of the still-unattached portion of the long strip. Then slit the strip diagonally at the upper corner as described in Step 3 *(opposite).* Attach the paper along the right side of the window molding, pressing just enough to hold it in place.

9 **Matching the last seam.** Cut off the excess paper and make a diagonal slit at the lower corner as in Steps 2 and 3 *(opposite).* Slide the lower left edge of the strip against the edge of the short strip and check the matching of the pattern along the seam. If necessary, lift the strip off the wall, around the bottom and along the side of the window molding, and ease it back into place until the last seam matches to your satisfaction.

10 **Finishing the last strip.** With firm strokes of your smoothing brush, smooth the entire strip on the wall, pressing its edges neatly against the molding. Finish the trimming around the side of the window, the ceiling, and along the baseboard.

Allowing for Obstacles

The best way to paper around a fixture in a wall or ceiling is to paper under it—then the fixture will appear to rest against a surface design unbroken by any seam. To achieve this effect, you must remove the obstruction completely. For a receptacle cover or the switch plate shown on these pages, you need only detach a cover plate. For a wall sconce or ceiling fixture, you can hang a strip of wallpaper as close to the fixture as possible, then make a cut from the edge of the strip to the fixture, trim around the fixture, then smooth the seam to the outer edge of the strip. You can achieve a more professional-looking job, however, by detaching the fixture and disconnecting wires before you wallpaper. Never dismantle any electrical fixture without first removing the fuse or tripping the circuit breaker that controls current to it (page 297). This common-sense safety precaution is especially important in paperhanging: Wet wallpaper adhesive can be an excellent conductor of electricity, creating a dangerous shock hazard.

Switch Plates

1 Detaching the plate. After you have turned off power to the switch, remove the two screws in the cover plate. Then remove the plate.

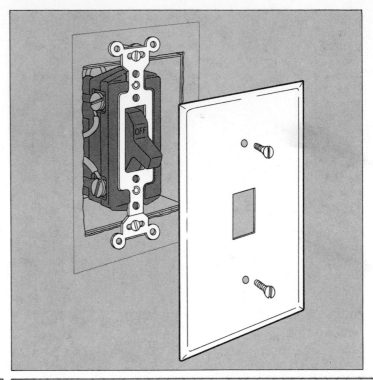

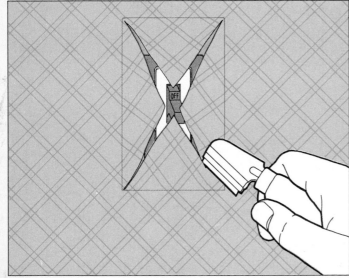

2 Cutting a hole for the switch. Paste and hang a strip of wallpaper in the usual manner, covering the recessed box. Split a small opening to uncover the toggle of the switch, and with a trimming knife or scissors, cut diagonally to each corner of the box. Enlarge the X cut into a rectangular hole, as big as the box, using the inside of the box as a guide. If you do not plan to paper the plate, screw it back on. To cover the plate with matching paper, follow the remaining steps.

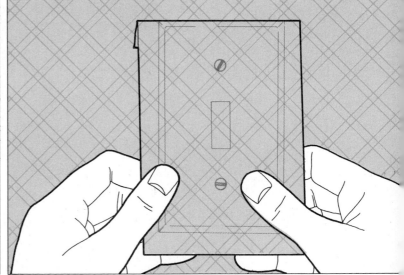

3 Matching paper for the cover plate. With two or three turns of the mounting screws, mount the cover plate loosely on the wall. (If the screws are too short for working behind the plate, use longer screws or a pair of nails for this temporary mount.) Cut a piece of paper larger than the plate, fold the top over the plate and match the upper fold of the paper to the wall above.

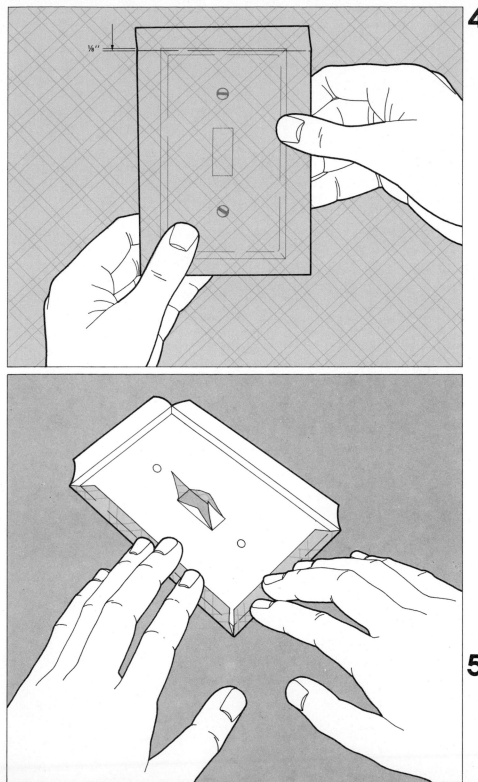

4 **Allowing for the bevels.** If the wallpaper has a small, intricate pattern that calls for close matching, you must allow for a slight increase in the size of the matching piece to cover the bulge created by the beveled shape of the plate. At this point in the job, the piece matches the paper on the wall perfectly at the top of the plate but poorly at the bottom. Move the paper about ⅛ inch downward *(arrow)*, then fold the top and bottom of the piece over the plate and crease these folds firmly. The piece should closely match the wallpaper above and below the plate.

To match the side edges, follow the same procedure. Fold one side of the paper over the plate, match the pattern at this edge of the plate, then move the paper about ⅛ inch away from the edge. Fold the paper over the left and right edges of the plate and crease these folds firmly.

5 **Papering the plate.** Remove the plate from the wall. Apply paste to the matching piece of paper and mount it on the front of the plate, using the creases you have made as a guide for exact placement. Cut off the corners of the paper diagonally with a pair of scissors, then fold the paper over the back of the plate and press it firmly to both sides of the plate. Cut a small X over the toggle slot of the plate and fold the flaps through the slot to the back of the plate. Remount the plate.

217

Repairing Damaged Paper

Days—or even years—after your wallpapering job is finished, problems may appear. Fixing a loose seam is easy: paste it down again. The only trick to doing a neat job is to use a small, long-handled artist's brush to apply the paste so that you do not stretch the paper. Simple tears, when the flap of paper is still intact and not crumpled, also pose no special problems. Use the same kind of artist's brush to apply paste and, when you smooth down the paper, stroke it gently in one direction only—outward toward the edges of the tear.

Holes and bubbles in the wallpaper, however, are more complicated to repair. Bubbles are generally caused by air trapped under the paper when it is applied. They may also appear hours or days later atop a spot that was not properly coated with adhesive.

If bubbles are near the ceiling or inconspicuously located, leave them alone. But if they are unsightly or in a place where an accidental puncture could result in a tear, use the method shown on page 220 to flatten them.

Holes have to be patched, and there are three ways to do that, depending on the kind of paper and the nature, size and location of the hole. If the damage is small or not noticeable, simply cut out a matching patch of wallpaper from a leftover roll or scrap and paste it directly over the damaged area. (Use vinyl-to-vinyl adhesive if you are patching vinyl or the patch will fall off.)

The second kind of patch is called a torn patch—one that is literally torn in a special way from a square piece of matching paper. The purpose of tearing rather than cutting is to get a section with tapered, or feathered, edges so that the entire patch can lie smoothly in place with no white edges showing. This technique, described below, works best when the paper pattern is small and busy, the color is light and the hole itself is no larger than about an inch.

The double-cut method described on the opposite page will give you an almost invisible repair on larger holes, dark papers, and vinyls and foils, which cannot be torn. A very sharp, pointed utility knife is the best tool to use to cut these patches. The squared-off ends of an ordinary trimming knife might dig into the paper and tear it.

The Torn-Patch Method

1 Tearing a neat patch. Practice tearing on a scrap of the same or similar wallpaper before you make the patch you will actually use. Grasp one edge of the paper with the fingers of both hands placed so that the index finger of one hand is on the section that will be the patch and the thumb of the other hand is on the section that will be discarded. Rotate the hand holding the patch section gently upward (*drawing*) and twist it slightly in toward the other hand. At the same time, the other hand pulls down and toward the patch. If you manipulate the paper correctly, you will have a patch with an intact design on top and a feathered edge on the underside. The entire patch should be no more than 3 inches wide.

2 Applying the patch. If you use adhesive, apply a thin layer of paste to the patch with an artist's brush, stroking outward from the center to the feathered edge. If your paper is prepasted, wet the patch and shake off excess water. Handle the fragile edge carefully as you position the patch over the damaged paper and match the top of the patch to the pattern below. Make the final pattern alignment when the whole piece is in place. The match may not be exact but the discrepancy is rarely great enough to be noticeable.

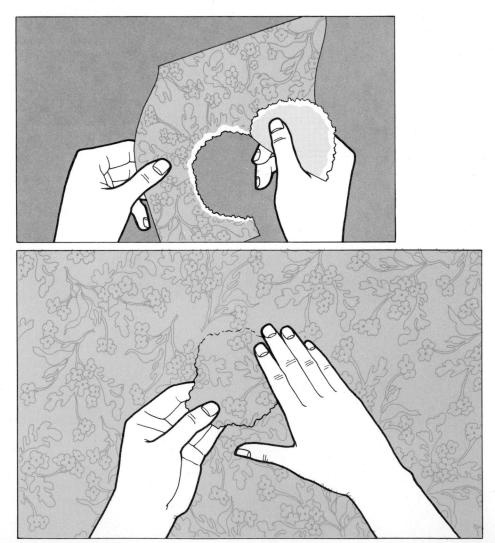

The Double-Cut Method

1 Before you cut. Your patch should be large enough to overlap the damaged area by about 1 inch. The patch will be hard to handle if you make it smaller than 3 inches square. Whenever the design permits, have the patch fall within an enclosed pattern such as a rectangle or a square. Cuts are better concealed when they coincide with existing lines, so if the damage is located in one corner of a pattern square, for instance, as in the example at right, your patch should include the whole square anyway. Position the wallpaper scrap over the damaged area, align it to the pattern exactly and secure it with masking tape or with thumbtacks if the wallpaper surface might be marred when you remove the tape.

2 Making the cut. With one hand, hold a metal ruler against one side of the section you are cutting (*drawing*). Using a sharp knife, cut cleanly through both layers of paper all around the section. Try not to cut past the corners. Carefully remove the patch and the scrap it was cut from. If any part of the patch is still attached to the scrap, do not tear it out; instead, place the paper on a work surface and cut neatly with the knife.

3 Making a space for the patch. Use the knife to go over the cuts on the damaged section of wallpaper to make sure that the edges have been completely separated. Then, with the blade of your knife, pry up one corner of the cut area. With vinyls and most heavy papers, the whole patch should come out in one piece. If it does not, pry all around the edge, using a putty knife if necessary (*drawing*). Then scrape any glue or lumps of paper off the wall.

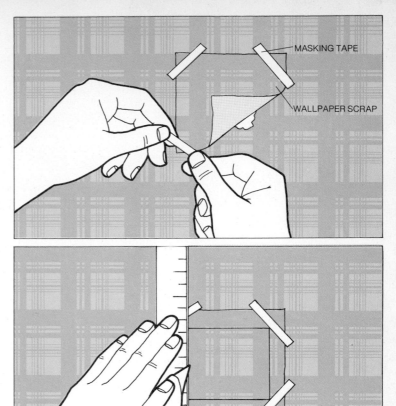

MASKING TAPE

WALLPAPER SCRAP

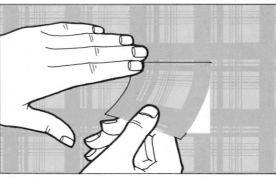

4 Inserting the new patch. If your paper is prepasted, wet the patch and shake off the excess water. If you use adhesive, apply it to the wall with a small artist's brush to avoid smearing any on the undamaged wallpaper. Hold the patch lightly with the fingers of both hands, taking care not to crease the paper. Insert the top edge into the cleaned-out section, pat it down lightly and then let the rest of the patch fall into place (*drawing*). Press it down lightly with a clean, damp sponge. After a few minutes press again with a clean sponge to be sure that the patch is firmly in place and that all corners and edges are down.

Cutting Flaps to Flatten a Bubble

1 Making the cuts. Most bubbles can be eliminated by making two crosswise cuts, which let air escape and create flaps so that adhesive can be applied to the underside of the paper. Bubbles pop up in a variety of shapes, three of which are shown by shaded areas in the drawing, along with the best pattern of cuts to make for each shape. Slash along a pattern line wherever possible.

2 Applying adhesive. Moisten the patterned surface of the wallpaper flaps with a clean, damp sponge to make them flexible. Lift each flap in turn, taking special care not to bend it back far enough to crease it. Using a thin artist's brush, apply a small amount of adhesive to the wall underneath. If the paper is prepasted, wet the underside of the flaps with the brush.

3 Folding down the flaps. Pat the flaps down gently in the sequence indicated, which evenly distributes any slack caused by stretching. Any overlap will disappear as the paper dries and shrinks. Sponge off excess adhesive after the flaps have been in place for a few minutes, but take care not to raise the flaps with the sponge.

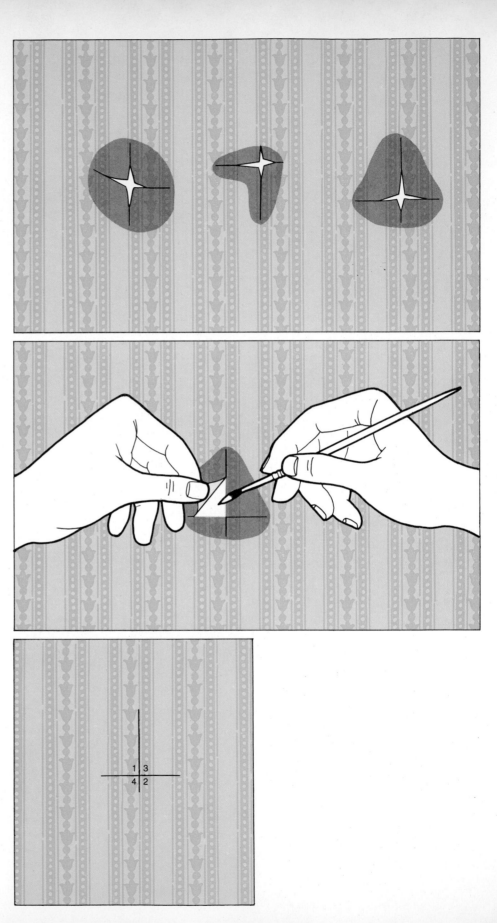

When and How to Use Lining Paper

Lining paper—also called blank stock or backing paper—is an inexpensive, unpatterned paper used as a final preparation of a wall covering, allowing the inexperienced wallpaper hanger to achieve professional looking results simply and easily. It speeds drying of adhesive after the final wall covering is hung, and it provides an exceptionally smooth surface on which to hang it.

Grass cloth, for example, tends to separate from its paper backing when it gets wet; lining paper quickly absorbs moisture from the backing and solves the problem. Foils laminated to paper present the same problem—and in addition, foils emphasize every surface defect of the wall because they reflect light readily. A coat of lining paper can also be useful when one wall covering is laid over another. If you plan to cover a dark pattern with a lightweight wall covering, lining paper will prevent the old pattern from showing through the new one. This method should be used only if the old paper cannot be easily removed.

Lining paper is hung like other wall coverings, but with many more simplifications (right) made possible by its lack of patterns and because it requires no trimming. Use exactly the same adhesive for lining paper that you use for the final covering to ensure the best bond between the two.

Hanging lining paper strips. Start hanging full-length strips of lining paper at a door (below) or at a corner. A plumb line is unnecessary because the lining paper is not patterned and the molding around windows and doors will provide a straight enough guide for this preliminary step in wallpapering. Cut a length of paper 1/4 inch shorter than the distance from the ceiling to the baseboard and hang it about 1/8 inch away from the doorjamb, the ceiling and the baseboard. These gaps will allow for a direct bond between final paper and wall surface. Continue hanging all the full-length lining paper strips that will fit on the wall area you are working on with 1/8-inch spaces between the strips and away from the ceiling, baseboard, and window or door moldings. Cut a strip lengthwise when turning corners of the wall. In the areas above and below the windows, and above the doors, you will save time and lining paper by hanging horizontal strips that are cut to fit these spaces. Again leave 1/8-inch spaces between these short strips and the surrounding long strips of lining paper, ceiling, window and door moldings to allow for direct adhesion between the final paper and the wall surface.

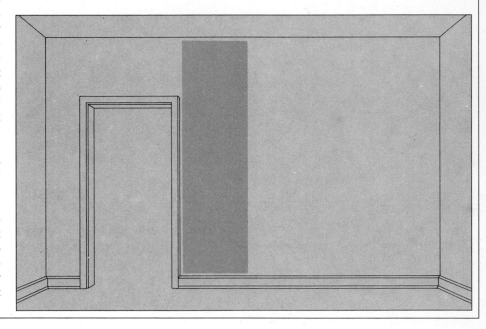

Cleaning and Maintaining Your Wallpaper

Most of today's wall coverings can be washed with mild soap and water. This is one job that, surprising though it may seem, is easier if you start at the bottom of a wall and work upward: if you work from the top, the dirty water flows down onto the dirt-clogged paper and leaves streaks that are very hard to remove. When you work from the bottom up, you can easily rinse off any water that runs down onto the clean section. Never use abrasive powdered cleansers on wallpaper, even on vinyls, and never use household woodwork cleaners that contain kerosene or other petroleum distillates. When the dirt is off, rinse the paper with clean water.

The material called cleaning dough, which works like a big eraser, can be used on nonwashable surfaces. Stubborn spots that do not come off with cleaning dough can be removed with a spray-can cleaner, or apply a paste made from carbon tetrachloride and cornstarch or fuller's earth. When the paste dries, brush it away. Whatever method you choose, test first on an inconspicuous spot because these cleaners change the paper's appearance.

Clear protective-spray coatings make nonwashable paper washable and add special protection over patched areas, which are more likely to hold dirt because of the cut or torn edges. Always use these coatings as soon as the adhesive is dry under the paper; otherwise dust may build up and be covered.

For minor repairs in the future, save unused powdered adhesive and wallpaper scraps. Keep the adhesive in a cool, dry place, making sure to label the container. Wrap leftover scraps in a sheet of brown wrapping paper and seal the ends. Store in cardboard mailing tubes to avoid crushing the paper.

3 HEATING, COOLING AND WEATHERPROOFING

A Home Climate Made to Order

To most people the systems that heat and cool their homes seem difficult and dangerous to tamper with. In fact, heating and cooling systems are fairly easy to comprehend, to control and even to improve. You need not accept less than adequate heating or cooling. The goal should be a comfortable climate in every room, with minimum expenditure of energy.

A good place to start looking for ways to improve a central heating system is at the point where fuel—gas, oil, or electricity—is turned into usable heat. Most heat sources are easy to get at and adjust. A gas burner, after all, is essentially only a pipe with holes in it; you can clean it with a stiff brush and a soft wire (page 236). An oil burner is no harder to tune up than a bicycle (pages 237-240), and by increasing its efficiency you may be able to cut your heating bills by as much as 10 per cent. Electric heaters seldom need more than an occasional vacuuming.

Once the heart of your heating plant is working properly, you can profitably examine its arteries—the ducts or pipes that carry hot air, hot water and steam around the house. The most common defect—too much heat in one place and not enough in another—may be corrected merely by adding a damper to a duct (page 227) if necessary. Cooling systems are as versatile as their heating counterparts: to keep them in good condition generally requires only an annual cleaning (pages 250-253) and very little maintenance.

With a few simple tricks—not one of them calling for work on a furnace or a boiler—you can greatly increase the efficiency of any heating system. Warm air, hot water or steam make their way through ducts or pipes to the rooms of a house. Once in these rooms, they release their heat—through a register in a warm-air system or through a radiator or a finned tube in a hot water or steam system called a convector. Working on these elements alone—the ducts, pipes, registers, radiators and convectors—you may get more heat, more evenly distributed throughout, for fewer dollars.

Start at the point where heat enters a room. Registers, radiators and convectors ought to be clean: Dust and dirt inhibit heat transfer, and can block the flow of air from a register. Vacuum louver-like vanes and fins, and remove a register face if necessary to get at small objects behind it. At the same time, check the air flow from the register. It should be completely unobstructed; if you must place furniture in front of a register, route the heat around the obstacles and into the room with a plastic deflector.

Radiators and convectors permit a greater variety of improvements. You can increase the heat they throw into a room by taping or tacking a sheet of aluminum foil to the wall behind them—cut the foil to fit from the floor to the top of the fixture. If convector fins are not straight, align them with pliers. A radiator cover can block air flow. Check for clear openings at the bottom to admit cool air, and at the top to release warm air—if necessary, cut small openings. In addition, metallic paint robs a radiator of heating power. You need not remove the paint, but you should repaint the radiator with nonmetallic paint—a dull black is preferable because it radiates the most heat.

To work efficiently, hot-water radiators and convectors must be completely filled with water. At least once a year, at the beginning of the heating season, purge these fixtures of air through their bleeder valves (opposite, bottom left); during the heating season, purge any individual fixture that runs cooler than normal. To keep a one-pipe steam radiator from hammering or losing heat, pitch it slightly toward its inlet valve with thin wood shims under a set of its legs (below).

Behind the scenes, yet still inside the rooms to be heated, you can make less obvious but even more effective improvements. One of them deals with the controls of the heating system. Modern thermostats are fitted with ingenious devices called anticipators, which prevent large swings of temperature in a heated room. At a setting of 70°, a thermostat might switch the heating plant on when the temperature of the room drops to 68°. The anticipator, which contains a tiny heating coil, raises the temperature of the thermostat faster than that of the room itself; the thermostat shuts the plant down before the room reaches 70°, but the heat already in the system carries the room temperature to the thermostat setting or a little beyond it. A faulty anticipator can be adjusted simply by working inside the thermostat (opposite, bottom right).

Simple Steps to Even, Economical Heat

Setting the tilt of a steam radiator. If your radiator is hammering or you suspect that it is losing heat, check its alignment with a carpenter's level. If the radiator tilts away from its inlet pipe, set a block of wood under the legs at the other end, under the air vent. The wood block should be just thick enough to reverse the tilt; normally, you will be able to drive the wood into place with a mallet, as shown above, after lifting or tilting the radiator slightly.

Finally, perhaps the most effective single improvement you can make in your heat-distribution system is insulating your system's ducts and pipes wherever they pass through an unheated basement, crawl space or attic. Inexpensive and easy to install, pipe and duct insulation blocks perhaps the most needlessly expensive of all heat losses—the heat that is squandered before it ever gets to a room at all.

While insulation is a one-time job, balancing a heating system may have to be done often—and done whenever you finish a new room or bring heat to a previously unused space. The object of balancing is not only efficiency, but comfort—the comfort of a house in which all the rooms are evenly heated or, sometimes even more importantly, in which individual rooms are brought to different temperatures for special purposes. In balancing, dampers or valves are individually adjusted to regulate the flow of air, water or steam through ducts and pipes. For the use of this technique in warm-air systems, see pages 226-227; for hot-water and steam systems, see pages 228-229.

As much as the climate in your home depends on your heating and cooling systems, it is also affected by the invasion of unwanted air, water, heat and cold from the outside. In winter, heat escapes from the house through the walls, roof, basement, doors and windows. In summer, heat can sometimes leak in by the same routes. Such losses, in either direction, have become intolerably expensive as energy prices have risen.

The battle against the elements is fought with a varied arsenal of materials and equipment. There are plugs and sealers, pumps and vents, insulation, awnings and tinted plastics. Few houses demand every weatherproofing remedy described in this section, but sooner or later most require one or more of them to remain sound and comfortable. Every few years, for example, new caulking (*pages 262-265*) and perhaps new weather stripping (*pages 254-261*) are needed to replace what has worn out and seal up gaps that appear as the house settles.

Once properly sealed, a house may have too little air entering to carry moisture away or to keep the furnace burning efficiently. In that case, install ventilators that take advantage of natural air currents or that create their own with electric ventilating fans. Intentional ventilation of this sort has a major advantage over the accidental air currents that come through odd cracks and crannies; it lets you control how much air gets in where.

Although ventilation removes airborne moisture, other measures are necessary to cure a house of leaks. More homes than ever have water in the basement. One cause is the proliferation of shopping-center parking lots, which, by reducing natural drainage of rainfall into the earth, send water into residential areas to flood basements that had never been wet before. In some cases, the key to a dry basement may be as simple as cleaning out the gutters or sealing cracks in foundation walls or leaks in the roof. When such routine steps are insufficient, you may have to lay underground pipe to carry water away, perhaps to a dry well, or take other waterproofing measures as described on pages 434-435, or even install a sump pump in the basement.

Depending on what part of the country you live in, your heating, cooling, insulation and weatherproofing needs may vary according to the nature of the climate in your particular area (*pages 286-287*). Your house may greatly benefit from as much as a foot of insulation in the attic (*pages 274-279*), for example. Storm windows and doors—a form of insulation you can also easily install yourself (*pages 266-267*)—are a definite necessity in all but the mildest climates as a finishing touch in making your house impervious to the ravages of the elements.

Bleeding a radiator. To release trapped air, small bleeder valves are mounted near the tops of radiators and convectors. Some have a slot for a screwdriver. Others, like the one above, have a head that can be turned with a key, sold at hardware stores. Holding a cup below the spout, open the valve slowly. Air will hiss out at first; then, when all the air is discharged, water will spurt out—fast. Close the valve immediately.

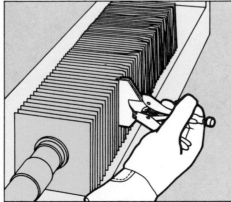

Straightening convector fins. The metal fins on convectors should provide straight, smooth paths for air rising through the fixture. If a fin is bent, twist the metal back into shape with a pair of pliers. The best tool for this job is the broad-billed pliers shown above.

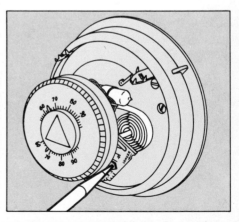

Adjusting a thermostat anticipator. Remove the thermostat cover. The anticipator, a movable pointer near the edge of the thermostat, is normally set for the amperage of the furnace. To correct wide swings of temperature above the thermostat setting, move the pointer down with the point of a pencil, .1 ampere at a time, and give the system a few hours to adjust before each change of the setting. If the furnace starts and stops too often, move the pointer to a higher setting, .1 ampere at a time.

How to Balance Your Forced-Air System

Your heating system is meant to give each room in your house the amount of heat you want in it. This does not necessarily mean keeping every room at exactly the same temperature; you may want some rooms warmer than others.

Adjusting a forced-air system is fairly simple if there are dampers—the movable metal plates in ducts that lead from the furnace to the outlets called registers, located in the rooms of the house. A damper regulates the flow of air into a room—but registers are relatively inefficient balanc-ing tools. Their movable vanes are primarily to direct or diffuse the currents of warm air supply in a room that will be empty for an extended period.

To work with dampers, you must iden-tify the duct that serves each room in your home, depending on the duct pattern *(below)*. An individual duct is wide open when the damper handle on its side paral-lels the duct path; it is closed when the handle is perpendicular to the duct path, and partially closed, or damped, when the handle is between these extremes. On some dampers, a locking nut holds the damper fast in any position.

Balancing is simple, but may take sev-eral days. Balance the ducts on cold days, when the heating system is in full opera-tion. Start by damping the duct to a room that seems too hot—preferably one that lies at the end of a relatively short duct run. (Damping at this point will send more air to rooms farther from the fur-nace.) Wait 6 to 8 hours, then check the temperature of the room, both by "feel" and with a thermometer held 4 to 5 feet above the floor surface. Then move on to the other rooms, one at a time, partially closing dampers or opening them wide for rooms that seem cold, until you have worked your way through the entire house; upstairs and downstairs.

When the major balancing job is com-plete, go through the rooms again, adjust-ing one damper at a time and observing the 6-to-8-hour waiting period after each adjustment. Finally, when the system is balanced, with each room getting the amount of heat you want in it, mark the damper settings with a felt-tipped pen.

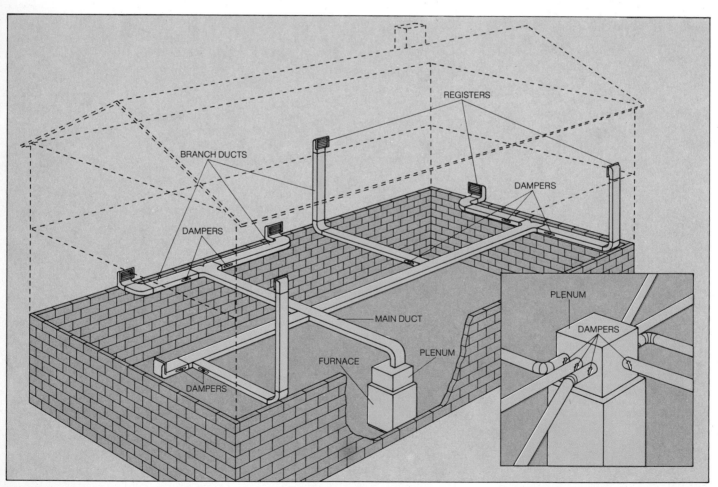

Where the dampers are. In all forced-air systems, duct runs begin at the plenum, a large cham-ber attached to the furnace and containing warm air under pressure. An extended-plenum sys-tem *(above)* has a main duct (or ducts) running from the plenum, and branch ducts running from a main to the registers in each room. You can usually detect the route and destination of a duct run by inspection; if necessary, close a damper to see which room turns cold. The dampers are set near the starts of the branches; to reach all of them while balancing a system, you may have to go from one end of a basement or crawl space to the other.

In a radial system *(inset)* all ducts run directly from the plenum to the registers. Dampers are near the furnace, readily accessible for balancing.

If your heating system is not fitted with dampers for the balancing job described opposite, put the dampers in yourself— they are inexpensive and easy to install. For round ducts, you may be able to buy a matching section that contains a factory-installed damper. To install such a model, turn off the furnace and, with a hacksaw or tin snips, cut out a length of duct 4 inches shorter than the damper section at the beginning of the duct run. Install the new section by joining a crimped to a plain end with sheet metal screws and sealing the connection with duct tape. Install a damper in an existing circular duct as described at right. Ready-made damper sections for rectangular ducts come in many sizes. But you can make and install your own damper, as shown below.

Installing a Damper in a Circular Duct

Adding a damper. Some dealers offer 2-foot duct sections equipped with factory-installed dampers. Alternatively, you can buy the damper separately and install it in an existing duct section near the furnace. In the common model shown at right, the damper is held in place by spring-loaded shafts. Drill or punch holes for these shafts in opposite sides of the duct, at least 6 inches in from the plain end. Retract the shafts in their slots, then set the damper in place, and release the shafts, threading them through the holes you have made. Finish by fastening the damper handle, following the manufacturer's instructions, and replacing the section of duct.

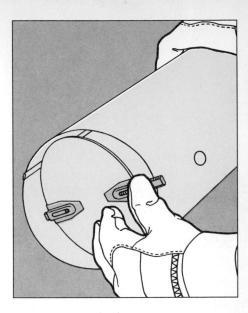

Installing a Damper in a Rectangular Duct

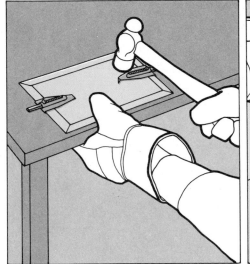

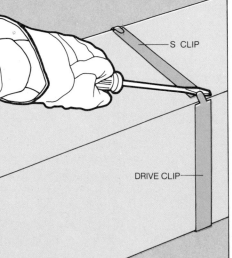

S CLIP

DRIVE CLIP

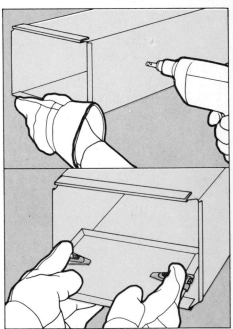

1 **Making the damper.** Measure the height and width of the duct. Wearing gloves, use tin snips to cut a rectangle of sheet metal 1 inch longer and wider than these dimensions. Mark the dimensions of the duct within this rectangle, snip off the corners at about a 45° angle and, with a bending tool or a pair of broad-billed pliers—used for duct work—fold the edges of the metal back along the marked lines to form rounded edges, two layers thick.

The hardware for the damper includes two spring-loaded clips, available at hardware and heating-supply stores; buy the type that does not require welding or riveting. Slide the clips over the short edges of the damper, lining them up at the exact center. Set the damper on a firm surface and drive the clip prongs through the damper with a hammer.

2 **Opening the duct.** Turn the furnace off and let it cool for an hour or so. Remove any duct tape, over a connection of the branch duct—just past the point where the branch leaves the main duct. Open this connection. Small ducts may simply snap together and can easily be pulled apart; more often, however, a rectangular duct is held together by horizontal S clips and vertical drive clips. Open the tabs at the tops and bottoms of the drive clips as shown above. Then pull the clips down and off the duct connections with pliers. Separate the duct sections by pulling them out of the S clips. Next, remove the hanger supporting the duct section that lies farther from the main duct; slowly and carefully lower the free end of this section until it is clear, support the section in this position on a convenient prop—a work bench or the rung of a ladder will do—until you have installed the damper.

3 **Installing the damper.** Mark dots on the sides of the duct at a distance from the edge equal to half the height of the damper plus 12 inches. Draw vertical lines through the dots, and horizontal lines along the centers of the sides of the duct. Where the lines intersect, drill holes the size of the bolts on the damper clips *(top)*. Wearing a long-sleeved shirt, compress the spring-loaded bolts, slide the damper into the duct *(bottom)* and release the bolts into the drilled holes. Install the damper and handle. To rejoin the ducts, slip their edges into the S clip. Fold the bottom tabs of the drive clips, tap these clips lightly into place with a hammer, then fold the top tabs. Cover the connection with duct tape.

Balancing Liquid-Heat Systems

Valves and vents take the place of dampers in heating systems that circulate water or steam, but the methods for tuning the temperatures of individual rooms are much the same as those of a forced-air system. The text on pages 226-227 describes these methods in detail; the major difference in practice is that water and steam do not permit the precision of forced-air balancing.

In a hot-water system, flow valves near the starting point of branch lines roughly correspond to warm-air dampers, inlet valves at convectors or radiators correspond to the movable louver-type vanes of registers. Few systems include both types of valve; use the flow valves for balancing if you have them, the inlet valves if you do not.

Steam systems are less flexible: Normally, their only balancing device is an adjustable air vent mounted on each radiator or convector. In the absence of such a vent you can make crude adjustments at the inlet valve at the other end of the radiator, but adjustable vents are inexpensive and easy to install.

At a higher price, you can substitute inlet valves with thermostatic controls to keep the system balanced in all weathers. This thermostatic valve is not set at a specific temperature but for a temperature range—65° to 70°, for example. A sensing device inside the valve regulates the flow of steam into the radiator or convector; when the temperature of the room is within the range of the thermostat setting, the inlet valve closes completely. Even if you choose to control the temperature with a valve control, however, the air vent should be cleaned periodically—and when balancing the system.

Adjusting Hot Water Flow

Where the valves are. No hot-water system would contain as many valves as the one diagramed below, but all systems resemble this one in certain major features. A furnace heats water, a circulator pumps the hot water through main and branch supply lines to convectors (or, in some systems, radiators), and return pipes carry cooled water back to the furnace to be reheated and re-cycled again. The diagramed system includes both balancing valves, installed in branch lines and opened or closed with a flat-tipped screwdriver (*opposite*, *top*), and inlet valves, mounted on convectors and turned by hand. To identify the branch lines that convectors and radiators are attached to, close all the balancing valves on a cool day and set the thermostat at 68°. Open a balancing valve and wait about an hour while the convector it serves heats up. Tag that valve with the name of the room, then open the others, one by one, until all the valves are tagged.

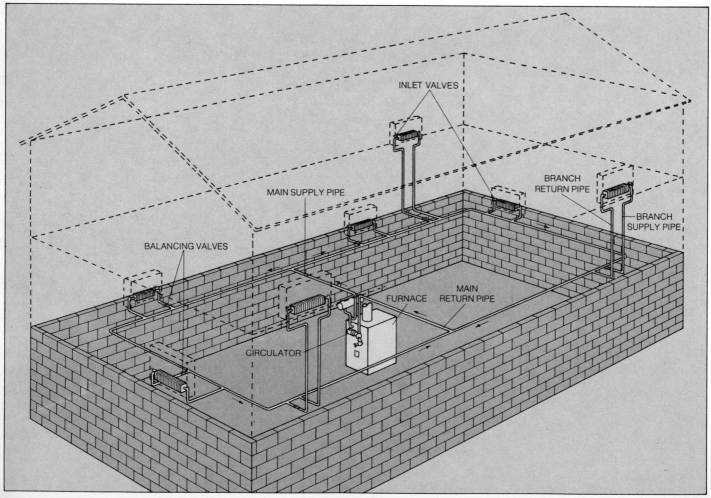

INLET VALVES

BRANCH RETURN PIPE

MAIN SUPPLY PIPE

BRANCH SUPPLY PIPE

BALANCING VALVES

MAIN RETURN PIPE

FURNACE

CIRCULATOR

Adjusting a balancing valve. The screwdriver slot that serves as a control device for this valve also indicates its setting: the valve is wide open when the slot is parallel to the path of the pipe, closed when the slot is perpendicular to the path. To regulate the flow of hot water to a convector or radiator, set the valve between these extremes and, when you have made all your balancing adjustments, mark the setting of the valve slot with a felt-tipped pen.

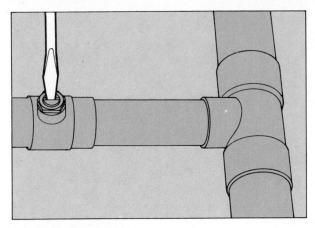

Setting the Warm-Up Time in a Steam Radiator

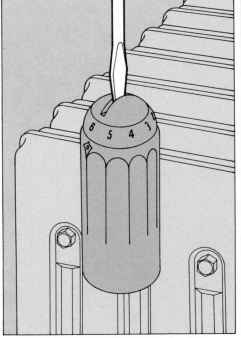

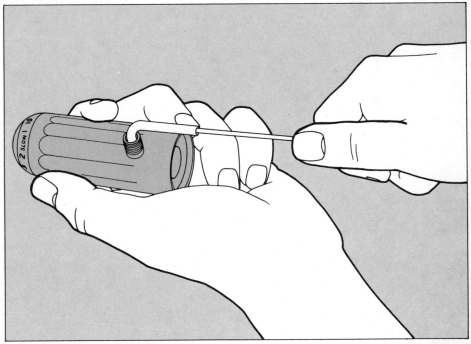

An adjustment air vent. The settings of this vent indicate exactly what you might expect—lower numbers mean less heat, higher numbers mean more. At the high-number settings, air leaves the radiator and hot steam enters it more quickly. Use the lower settings on radiators that tend to overheat a room—particularly those nearest the furnace—so that air leaves these radiators more slowly, while the others catch up. Some adjustable vents, like the one above, have a slot for a screwdriver; others have a locking nut. On the second type, loosen the nut and turn the movable cap to line up the setting number with an arrow on the vent body; then, holding the cap firmly, tighten the locking nut.

Cleaning an air vent. To keep dirt from clogging an air vent, clean the vent before balancing the system and whenever a radiator consistently runs cold. Turn off the furnace, wait an hour or so, and remove the vent. Let it soak in vinegar overnight; then rinse it off and ream the openings with a stiff wire.

The Thermostat: Key to Temperature Control

Most thermostats, whether they are the low-voltage models generally used in home heating and cooling systems or the 120- or 240-volt types that control some electric heaters and attic fans, consist of three sections. These are a cover, a middle section containing the temperature-control mechanism and a base with wire terminals and switches.

All of these—and even the cover—can cause trouble. If the cover is put on incorrectly or accidentally struck, it can jam the bimetallic coil that, by loosening or tightening as the metals expand or contract with temperature change, controls the system. Then the furnace or air conditioner may fail to start or to turn off. Often, you need only adjust the cover to get the furnace going. The base can give difficulty too. If it has slipped so that it is no longer level, the thermostat may not operate correctly. To fix it, remove the thermostat from the base and check that the base is level *(page 232)*.

Dust and dirt are more common problems. In an old type of thermostat—one having an external mechanical contact switch attached to the bimetallic coil rather than the newer sealed mercury vial switch—you may need to clean the switch contacts *(opposite, left)*. But in any thermostat, dust and lint on the bimetallic strip can reduce its sensitivity and cause room temperature to swing between too warm and too cool; dust it with a lens brush available at camera stores. To expose as much of the bimetallic coil as possible while you clean, turn the thermostat dial as far as it will go in both directions.

Wires near the coil can become loose and switches on the base that select heating, cooling or fan operation can become corroded. A fine-tipped screwdriver and a solvent-moistened swab will solve these problems *(opposite, below)*.

None of these repairs is difficult. Almost all thermostat covers snap off and the temperature-control section is screwed to the base for easy access. However, thermostats are delicate. When working on them, use a light touch to avoid bending the bimetallic coil or damaging other sensitive components. And turn off all power first.

While these simple repairs can keep any thermostat functioning for years, you may nevertheless decide to replace your old thermostat with a new one. This may be necessary only if you add central air conditioning, but you also may wish to replace an older, metal-contact unit with a newer, mercury-switch model *(page 232)*, or to install a fuel-saving programmable one. In most cases these are simple operations that call for removing color-coded wires from the old thermostat and attaching them to the color-coded terminals of the new one.

Releasing jammed parts. A thermostat cover, cocked during installation or inadvertently bumped afterward, can jam the thermostat and prevent it from turning the furnace on or off. If one of the metal support clips is bent *(inset)*, restore it to its original position. Rotate the thermostat dial to be sure that the parts move freely and that they turn the furnace on and off. If they do not—or if the thermostat no longer functions properly—replace the thermostat.

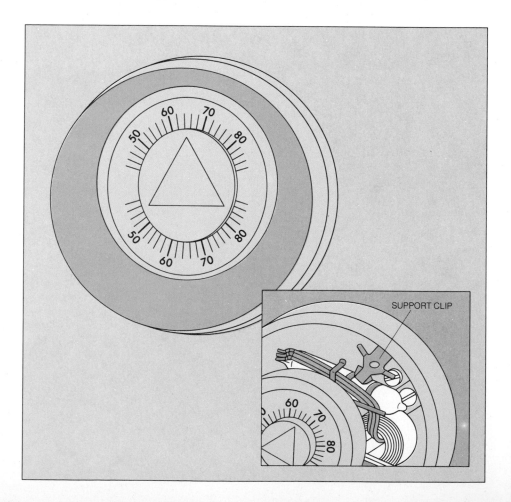

SUPPORT CLIP

Cleaning contact points. If you have a thermostat with an external contact switch attached to the coil, you may need to clean the contact points occasionally. Turn off power and remove the cover. Lower the setting to separate the points, and insert an index card between them. Never use an abrasive such as emery or sandpaper. Close the points by raising the setting. Move the card back and forth several times.

Tightening wire connections. Turn off the master switch on the heating-cooling system. Remove the cover and tighten any terminal screws that are accessible in the temperature-control section. In both the newer, mercury-switch type (illustrated below slightly rotated to show terminal screws) and the old external-contact type *(left)*, these small screws are more likely to loosen than the larger ones holding wires to the base.

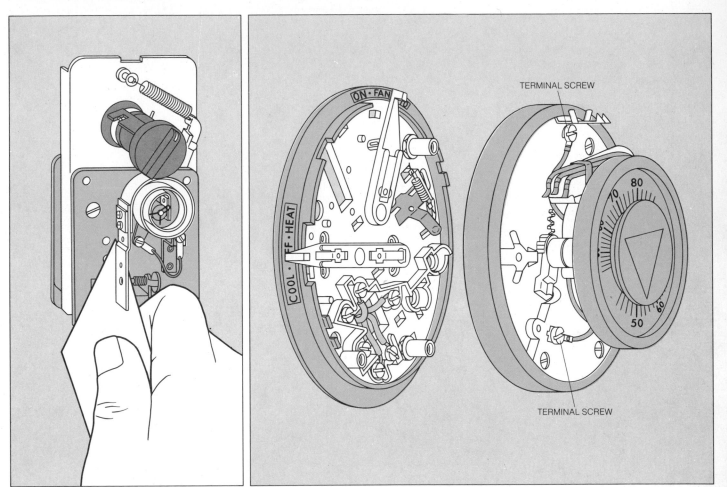

TERMINAL SCREW

TERMINAL SCREW

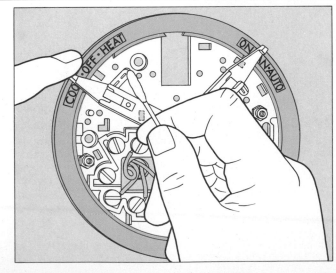

Cleaning thermostat switches. Take off the thermostat cover and, being careful not to bend the bimetallic coil, unscrew the temperature-control section from the base. Saturate a cotton swab with a nonsilicone tuner cleaner, available at electronics stores, or a strong vinegar-and-water solution, and clean the contacts near the switch levers. Move the levers from side to side to expose all the contacts. Remount the thermostat and attach the cover.

Replacing a Thermostat

Replacing an old thermostat with a new one that performs the same functions at the same location involves merely connecting the new one to your existing wiring (below, right). But if your replacement does something extra—automatically adjusts settings with a clock, for instance—you may have to run new wiring. And if you want to change the location of your thermostat in the course of putting in a new one, you will have to run wiring between the thermostat and furnace. Carefully follow the manufacturer's directions for making connections.

The best place to put a thermostat is on an inside wall, out of the way of drafts and near a return vent, where the air will best reflect the average house temperature. It should be about 3 to 5 feet from the floor for convenience and away from heavily traveled areas where vibrations can jar loose the components. Keep it away from a register, a television set, a stove or a dryer, direct sunshine, or an outer wall—in those locations temperatures are more extreme than anywhere else in the house, and the operation of the thermostat will be affected.

In replacing any thermostat, make sure the new unit is compatible with the primary controls on your furnace (page 237), that the power is off and that it is designed to carry the voltage and circuit to which it will be connected—most systems are controlled by low-voltages, generally 24 volts. Some systems, however, require 120 or 240 volts; working on these calls for a thorough knowledge of electricity.

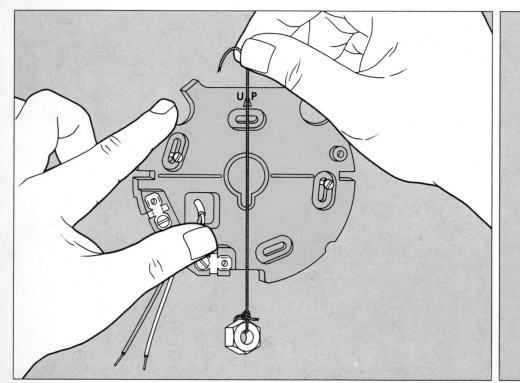

1 Mounting the base. Turn off all power to the heating and cooling systems. Pull off the thermostat cover. Disconnect the wires connecting the thermostat with the furnace. Depending on the kind of thermostat you have, you may be able to disconnect these wires before removing the thermostat; on some models, however, you must dismount the thermostat from the base to get at terminals on the back of the thermostat or on the face of the base. Remove the base.

Pull about 3 inches of cable through the wiring hole in the new base. Hold the base against the wall and trace the mounting holes on the wall. Plug old screw holes and the aperture around the cable to keep drafts from affecting the instrument. Attach the base, using a small spirit level or a plumb line to make sure it is level before driving the screws all the way in. Unless this type of thermostat is level, its fluid mercury temperature switch will respond inaccurately to settings.

2 Installing the unit. If the cable has two wires and the base two terminals, connect either wire to either terminal. If there are three wires but two terminals, connect the white wire to one terminal and the remaining wires to the other terminal. If the base has more than two terminals, match the colors of the wires to the color coding of the terminals. Check the anticipator setting (page 225). Then attach the thermostat to the base and slip on the cover.

Making a Hot Flame for Maximum Efficiency

The key to the efficient operation of any gas or oil heating system is the burner. In a gas furnace, the burner has the simple task of mixing one gas with another—natural gas with air—in the correct proportions for complete combustion. With no moving parts, a gas burner is much less complex than an oil burner, which has a pump and a fine nozzle to atomize liquid fuel oil so it can be mixed with air for burning.

Because of this complexity—and because oil has impurities that do not burn during combustion—oil burners need a yearly tune-up for efficient operation through the winter *(pages 237-240)*.

Gas burners, on the other hand, are less demanding, often operating for years without trouble. From time to time you may have to relight the pilot if it has blown out or if you have turned it off to conserve gas during the summer. Most furnaces have pilot instructions, which are basically the same as those below, near the control valve. Never light the pilot or make any furnace repair if there is a strong odor of gas; call the emergency service unit of your gas company. Furthermore, never try to light the pilot more than twice. If it fails to light the second time, replace the thermocouple *(page 234)* — a device that turns off gas to the furnace to prevent explosions—before trying again, or call a serviceman.

After a gas furnace has been in service for several years, rust and scale build up on interior surfaces of the furnace can flake off and fall into the burner area. Such residues can clog burner orifices, reducing the heat output of the furnace. The remedy is to unplug the openings and give the furnace a thorough cleaning with a wire brush and vacuum cleaner. The cleaning techniques shown overleaf for a gas forced-air furnace also apply to oil-fired forced-air furnaces, as well as to boilers heated by either fuel. The spaces inside boilers, however, are generally less accessible; a smaller wire brush or a piece of clothes hanger may be needed to poke out debris before vacuuming.

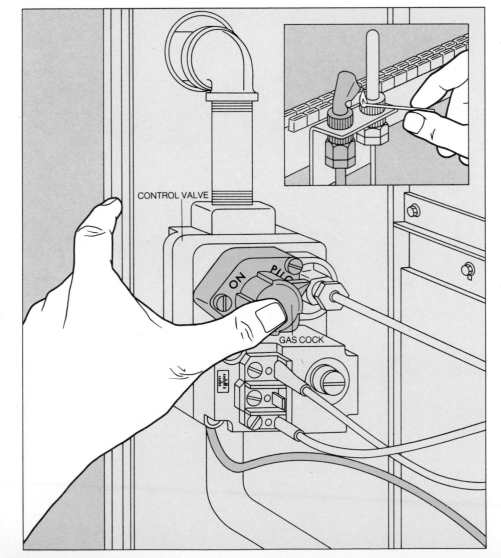

CONTROL VALVE

ON

PILOT

GAS COCK

Lighting the pilot. Remove the access panel from the front of the furnace. Examine the control valve. If it is a combination valve, it has a gas cock with a "pilot" setting *(left)*; be sure the manual shutoff valve is on *(page 234)*. If there is only a reset button on the control valve, turn off the manual shutoff valve and open the smaller pilot valve nearby. Check the service panel and emergency switch to be sure the furnace has electrical power, then turn the gas cock on the combination valve to "pilot." Depress the gas cock (or reset button) and light the pilot *(inset)*. Hold down the cock or button for 30 seconds, then release it. The pilot should remain lit. Check the pilot flame to be sure it envelops at least half an inch of the thermocouple *(page 235)*; if it does not, adjust the pilot *(page 234)*. Turn on the gas to the burners by rotating the gas cock to "on" or opening the manual valve.

If the light pilot fails to light, or to stay lit, wait five minutes for gas to dissipate. Then try again, depressing the gas cock or reset button for a full minute. If the pilot goes out again, replace the thermocouple or call for service.

Adjusting the pilot flame. A screw in the combination valve regulates the height of the pilot flame. On some valves, the adjustment screw is recessed and covered by a cap screw that you must remove; on others the adjustment screw is in plain view on the surface of the valve. Turn the screw counterclockwise to raise the flame, clockwise to lower it so that the thermocouple tip is well within the flame.

Adjusting the burner flame. Set the house thermostat at its highest temperature to start the furnace and keep it running. Then loosen the lock screw on an air shutter *(below)*. With your fingers, rotate the shutter open slowly until the blue base of the flame appears to lift slightly from the burner surface. Then close the shutter until the flame reseats itself on the surface, and tighten the lock screw. The flame should be blue and erect, with only occasional streaks of orange (due to impurities in the gas). Repeat this procedure for the remaining burners. Return the thermostat to its normal setting.

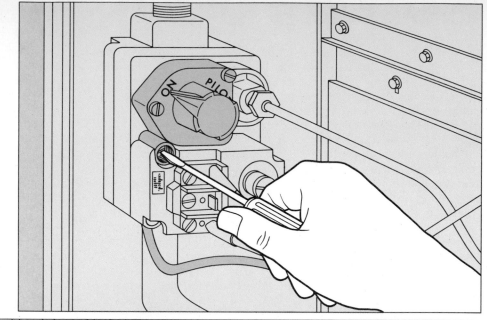

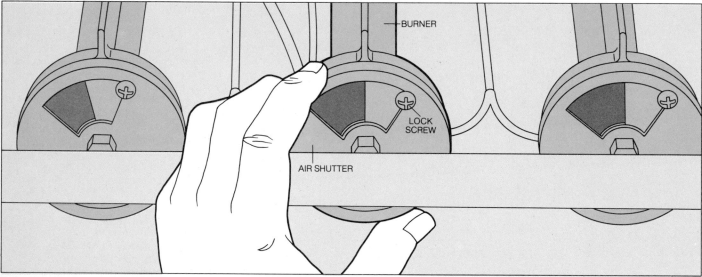

Replacing a Thermocouple

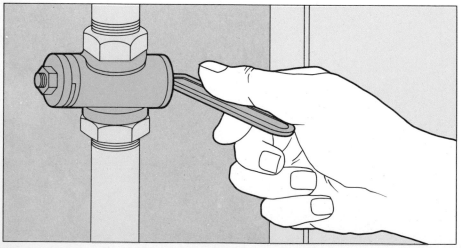

1 **Closing down the furnace.** Turn off the gas to the furnace by closing the manual shutoff valve. The valve is closed when the handle is at right angles to the gas line *(left)*. If there is a separate gas supply for the pilot, be sure to also close the manual valve on this line. Turn off the electricity: Turn off the furnace circuit breaker or, with the power off, remove its fuse. As an added close-down precaution, be sure to shut off the furnace's main electric switch.

2 Detaching the thermocouple. After turning off the supply of gas and electricity to the furnace, unscrew the nut which holds the thermocouple tube to the control valve *(below, left);* a faulty thermocouple tube should be cool. Unscrew the nut that holds the thermocouple and tube to a bracket next to the pilot *(below, right).* Connect a new thermocouple and tube to the bracket. Then clean the control valve's threaded connection with an old rag and fasten the other end of the tubing to it. You may have to bend the tube slightly to fit it properly in place; in that case be extra careful not to kink the tube. Tighten the connection nut gently with a wrench.

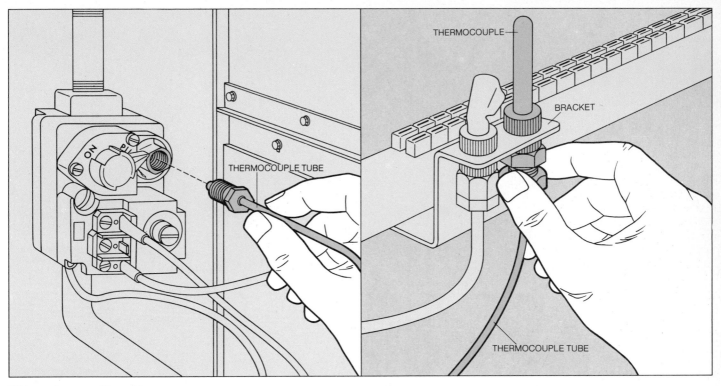

Cleaning a Gas Furnace

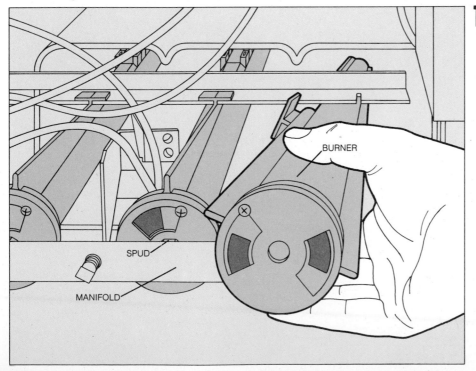

1 Cleaning the burners. Close down the furnace *(page 234),* then remove the access panel covering the burners. If the pilot and thermocouple are mounted on a burner, remove them by unscrewing the bracket. In most gas furnaces, the burners are removed one at a time by first sliding them forward off the spuds, which supply gas to the burners, and then twisting and lifting the burners outward *(left).* Some furnaces, on the other hand, have removable panels in the rear for taking out the burners.

Use a stiff brush to clean rust and dirt from burner surfaces and a soft wire—copper, for example—to unclog any plugged ports without chipping or enlarging them.

2 **Cleaning the spuds.** After the burners have been removed, run a soft wire through each of the spud openings to clear them of soot and dirt, as shown in the overview at right. Be careful not to damage or enlarge the openings. Spud openings are relatively large and easy to clean, but if a spud is so badly plugged that it cannot be cleaned in place, use a wrench to unscrew it from the manifold.

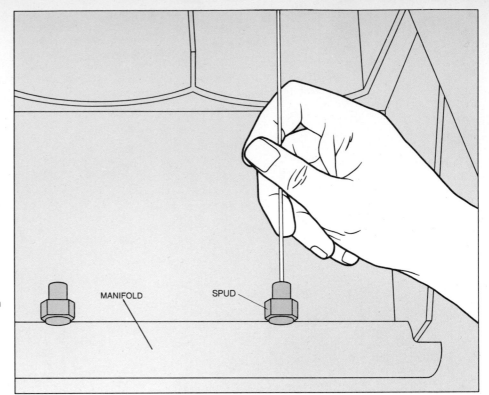

MANIFOLD

SPUD

3 **Vacuuming the furnace.** With the burners removed, use a wire brush to scrape scale, rust and soot from accessible surfaces of the combustion chamber. Unscrew the draft-diverter panel at the top of the furnace to expose the top of the heat exchanger (below). Remove the inserts inside the heat exchanger by pulling them out with your fingers (inset); some may be held in position with screws. Brush the inserts and as much of the exchanger surfaces as you can reach, then clean them with a vacuum cleaner. Replace the inserts, then vacuum the combustion chamber walls and the area below the burners. Finally, replace the draft-diverter panel.

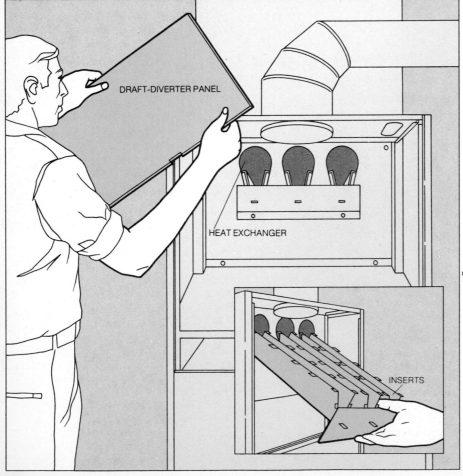

DRAFT-DIVERTER PANEL

HEAT EXCHANGER

INSERTS

TANG

SLOT

4 **Restarting the furnace.** Reinstall the burners, sliding them into the combustion chamber and onto the spuds, or directly onto the spuds from the back of the furnace. Some burners are supported by a tang-and-slot arrangement (above); others rest on the floor of the combustion chamber. Reconnect the pilot and thermocouple if you removed them earlier. Turn on the gas and electricity and ignite the pilot (page 233). Turn up the thermostat to ignite the burner, and adjust the burner flame (page 234) before replacing the access panel.

Tuning Up an Oil Burner

A morning's work on your oil burner before the heating season starts can help trim fuel bills, while extending the burner's life and cutting down on costly repairs and service calls. The process of tuning up the oil burner consists of first cleaning the unit thoroughly from the filter on the oil line to the nozzle on the firing assembly, then adjusting it for maximum combustion efficiency. You can undertake both of these chores safely because neither of them should involve adjusting the pump, the motor or the electric system.

Cleaning a burner calls more for patience than for any special skill. The work will take several hours and it is messy. You will want to be prepared with newspapers to protect the floor, an old pan to catch drips and a bucket for disposing of sludge and excess oil. You may also want to spread sand or cat litter in the pan to absorb oil and prevent splashing. Almost all burner parts can be cleaned with ordinary household brushes, rags and a carbon solvent such as kerosene. For parts that you need to replace such as gaskets or the filter cartridge in the oil line (right) be sure to get new parts of the same specification from your oil dealer or from a local heating and refrigeration supplier.

Checking the efficiency of the burner and adjusting the combustion is a trickier operation than a tuneup and requires the use of expensive instruments such as a draft gauge, carbon-dioxide indicator, sampling tube and stack thermometer. If you do not want to invest in the instruments, be sure to have a service person make the necessary tests for you. Instrument testing is the only way to safely adjust a burner for maximum efficiency.

Before you do any work on a burner always shut it down completely. Turn off the master switch—or switches, if you have one at the burner and another on a wall or beside the basement stairs. Also make sure to shut off the power in the circuit that governs the burner itself: Switch off the circuit breaker or, with the power off, remove the fuse. Then shut down the oil line at the valve between the filter and the storage tank. If your oil line is equipped with a special fire-safety valve at the pump, turn the handle clockwise to push the stem down. When the handle slips completely off the stem, give the stem a light tap with a wrench to make sure that the valve is completely closed.

Before you restore the power to the burner you must be sure to open the oil line first, to prevent the motor from drawing on an empty line and creating air pockets in the oil supply. If your burner refuses to start or misfires, see page 242.

Cleaning the Filter System

1 **Changing the oil filter.** After switching off the burner and shutting off the circuit and the oil line, set a bucket or pan under the oil filter. Then loosen the bolt on the cover above the filter bowl, pull down the bowl and upend it into a bucket. The gasket around the top of the bowl and the filter cartridge inside should fall out; if the gasket sticks to the cover, pry it loose. Wipe the bowl, put in a new cartridge and gasket, and bolt the bowl back into place.

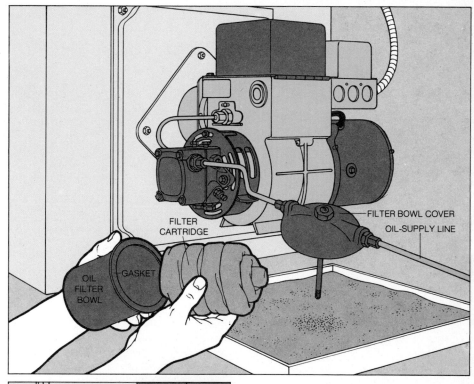

FILTER CARTRIDGE
FILTER BOWL COVER
OIL-SUPPLY LINE
OIL FILTER BOWL
GASKET

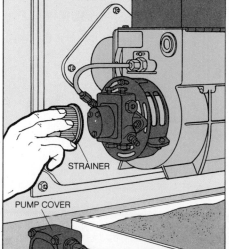

STRAINER
PUMP COVER

2 **Cleaning the pump strainer.** Check with your oil dealer to determine whether your pump has a strainer or a rotary-blade filter. If it has the filter, skip this step. If it has a strainer, unbolt the cover of the pump housing and lift off the cover. Discard the thin gasket around the rim of the pump. Remove the cylindrical wire-mesh strainer and soak it in solvent for a few minutes to loosen the sludge buildup. Then clean the strainer gently with an old toothbrush. If the strainer is torn or bent, get a new one. After reinserting the strainer, place a new gasket on the pump rim and bolt the cover back on.

Checking the Fan and Motor

1 Cleaning the fan. With power to the burner off, use a long, narrow brush to sweep out the air-intake vents on the fan housing. Expose the fan by unscrewing the transformer from the top of the burner and swinging it back out of the way. Clean the fan blades with the brush and wipe the interior of the fan housing with a rag.

To reach the fan on an old-style burner *(inset),* you must pull back the perforated bulk air band that surrounds the housing. First mark on the band and the fan housing the position of the band, then loosen the screw holding the band and pull the band back. After cleaning the fan, use the marks to set the band in its original location before you tighten the screw.

Dust on the fan and in the air-intake openings can drastically reduce your burner's efficiency, so clean them out every month or so.

2 Lubricating the motor. If your burner is equipped with small oil cups at each end of the motor, lift the lids or plugs from the cups. Then dribble four or five drops of 10- to 20-weight, nondetergent electric-motor oil in each cup and replace the lids or plugs. Lubricate the motor every two months, or at the intervals that are specified in the manufacturer's instructions. If there are no oil cups visible, the motor is self-lubricating and it is not necessary to oil it.

Cleaning the Sensor

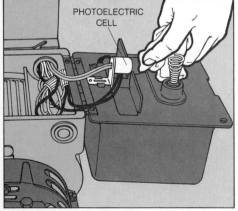

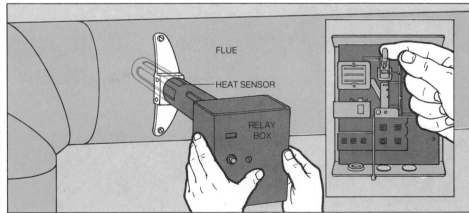

The light-detecting sensor. If the burner has a photoelectric cell that acts as a safety valve in the relay system and shuts off the motor when the ignition fails, the cell will be mounted at the end of the air tube—on the underside of the transformer or attached to the housing. Simply wipe the dirt off the cell with a clean rag.

The heat-detecting sensor. If the burner has a safety device that responds to heat to shut off the motor when the burner fails, it will be located behind the relay box on the flue. Mark the sensor tube where it meets the mounting flange. Remove the setscrew that holds the relay box to the mounting flange and pull out the box. Gently sweep the soot off the sensor with a soft-bristled paintbrush. Carefully replace the box and setscrew.

To ensure that the sensor is in contact with the shutoff mechanism, carefully remove the cover of the box. Pull the drive shaft lever toward you about ¼ inch *(inset),* then slowly release it. Do not handle other parts of the mechanism.

Cleaning the Firing Assembly

1 Removing the assembly. Turn off power to the burner, then mark the position of the firing assembly in the air tube. Using an open-end wrench, loosen the flare nut, then the lock nut at the junction between the pump oil line and nozzle oil line. Separate the two lines. Pull the entire firing assembly—the electrodes and the nozzle oil line—out of the air tube *(right)*. You may need to twist the assembly as you pull it, but be careful not to knock the electrodes or nozzle against anything.

To get at the firing assembly of an old-style burner *(inset)*, take out the bolts holding the rear plate and pull the plate off. Reach into the air tube and disconnect the electrode extension rods or cables from the transformer terminals with your fingers. With a felt-tip marker, mark the position of the nozzle oil line and disconnect it.

With the firing assembly off, clean the air tube with a cloth or brush. If there is a circular flame-retention device—metal, with louver-type fins or vanes—at the end of the tube, clean it also.

2 Cleaning the ignition system. Wipe soot off the electrodes and their insulators with a cloth dipped in solvent. Wipe off the electrode extension rods or cables *(right)* and the transformer terminals; the contact points between the rods or cables and the terminals must be absolutely clean. If the insulators are cracked or the cables frayed, take the entire assembly to a professional for repair. Examine and clean the electrodes. The electrode tips should be spaced exactly as specified in the manufacturer's instructions—usually about 1/8 inch apart pointed toward each other, and no more than 1/2 inch above the center of the nozzle tip and no more than 1/8 inch beyond the front of the nozzle *(inset)*. If necessary, loosen the screws on the electrode holder and gently move the electrodes into place.

3 Removing the nozzle. Use a pair of wrenches to grip both the nozzle body and the hexagonal adaptor at the end of the nozzle oil line *(right)*. Unscrew the nozzle carefully, taking care not to twist the oil line or alter the position of the electrodes. Examine the tip of the nozzle *(inset)*; the stamped specifications show the firing rate in gallons of oil per hour (gph), and the angle of spray, in degrees. The type of spray pattern is usually identified by a letter of the alphabet. If the nozzle has a firing rate of 1.50 gph or less, replace it with an identical nozzle. If the nozzle has a gph of more than 1.50, you can clean and reuse it *(Steps 4 and 5)*.

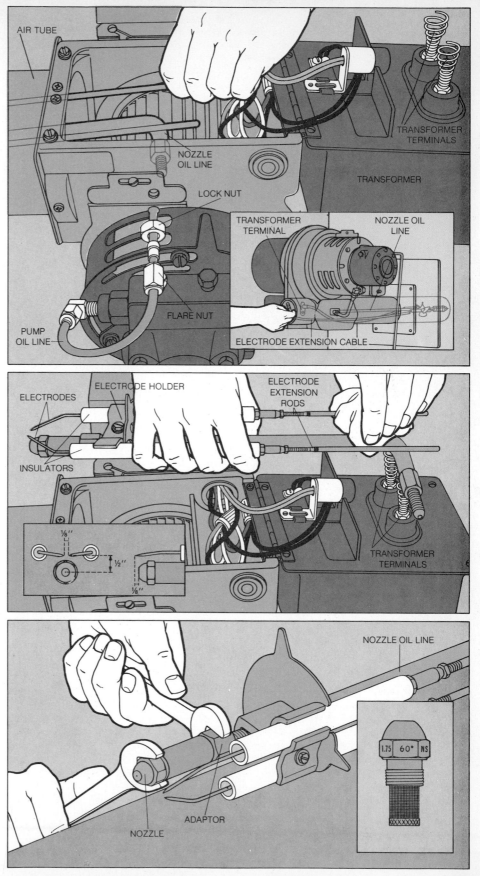

4 Dismantling the nozzle. With your fingers, gently unscrew the wire mesh or porous bronze strainer from the back of the nozzle. Then use a screwdriver to remove the lock nut that holds the distributor inside the tip of the nozzle. (On some nozzles, the lock nut and distributor may be a single piece.) Slide the lock nut and the distributor out of the nozzle body.

5 Cleaning the nozzle. Soak all the nozzle parts in solvent for a few minutes, then scrub them gently with a small toothbrush. Clean the slots in the distributor with a piece of stiff paper. Clear the nozzle orifice with compressed air or a clean bristle; never use a pin or wire that might scratch the nozzle and alter the angle or pattern of its spray. Finally, flush all of the parts under

hot running water, shake them, and allow them to air-dry on a clean surface.

Reassemble the nozzle on a clean surface with clean hands and tools. Screw the nozzle back onto the adaptor with your fingers, then tighten it with the wrenches. Do not force the parts together or use the wrenches too vigorously.

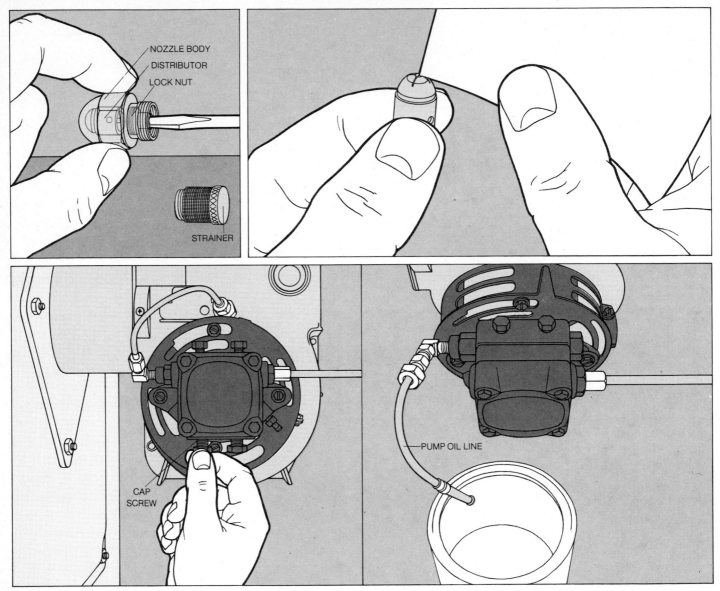

NOZZLE BODY
DISTRIBUTOR
LOCK NUT

STRAINER

CAP
SCREW

PUMP OIL LINE

6 Priming the pump. Loosen and remove the cap screw on the unused intake port of the pump opposite the port to which the oil line is attached *(above, left)*. When oil begins to flow, allow it to run into a pan for about 15 seconds before replacing and tightening the cap screw. (If you have an underground storage tank, the oil will not feed into the pump automatically so skip this step.)

Next, loosen the nut holding the pump oil line and feed the open end of the line into a bucket *(above, right)*. As a safety precaution, swing the transformer down or, on an old-style burner,

screw on the rear plate. Set the house thermostat several degrees above room temperature and restore power to the burner. Then station a helper at the burner master switch. When the helper throws the master switch, oil will gush out of the line with great force. Let the pump run for about 10 seconds, then turn off the motor and remove the fuse—with the power turned off—or trip the circuit breaker again.

Use the marks made in Step 1 to put the firing assembly back in the air tube, with the nozzle oil line centered in the tube. Connect the pump and

nozzle oil lines by tightening the lock nut and hexagonal nut with your fingers, then taking a quarter turn with a wrench. Screw the transformer down or, on an old-style burner, reconnect the electrodes and replace the rear plate. When you start the burner for the winter, some air may remain in the oil line. To prevent it from building pressure in the combustion chamber, partially open the chamber's observation door and turn the burner on at the master switch. Let the burner run for 10 seconds and shut it off. Repeat five times, or until the burner shuts down smoothly and instantaneously.

Cleaning and Sealing a Furnace

To obtain the best performance from your oil burner, you may have to clean or repair other parts of the furnace. An air leak, a dirty heat exchanger, soot in the flue and the chimney or crumbling and debris-filled combustion chambers all affect burner efficiency.

Most of these problems can be solved quickly and inexpensively. Leaks are sealed easily with furnace cement. The heat exchanger or boiler surfaces of an oil-fired furnace are cleaned in virtually the same way as those of a gas furnace *(page 236)*. To dislodge soot from a flue, simply dismantle the flue and rap each section against a floor covered with newspapers.

A combustion chamber usually gives years of trouble-free service. Eventually, however, intense heat combines with repeated expansions and contraction to crumble firebrick and molded linings; stainless steel simply burns up. If a firebrick lining crumbles in large chunks, you can use furnace cement to bond the pieces back in place. But the best repair for any combustion chamber is to reline it with a preformed, wet liner available from heating and refrigeration suppliers. This type of liner, made of flexible, heat-resistant fibers, is inexpensive and easy to install in any combustion chamber that retains its shape. In many cases, the liner will improve furnace efficiency because it heats up faster than conventional lining materials and reflects more heat.

Before buying a liner, check your furnace or boiler warranty to make sure that you will not void it by modifying your combustion chamber with the addition of a liner. To obtain a liner the right size for your combustion chamber, you will need its dimensions *(page 242, Step 2)*. You will also need the oil burner's firing rate in gallons per hour, and the spray pattern of your nozzle *(page 239)*. A heating supplier may recommend a different nozzle to compensate for the increased flame intensity caused by the liner.

Stopping Leaks

1 Locating the leaks. In the drawing below, the colored outlines indicate seams where leaks may occur; at the combustion-chamber cover plate, the burner-mounting flange, the fire door and the flue joints. Leaks may also occur in rusted flue sections. Check for rust by pressing on the flue with your finger. To detect leaks in seams, fire up the burner and move a lighted candle along each seam. The flame will be deflected inward wherever there is a leak.

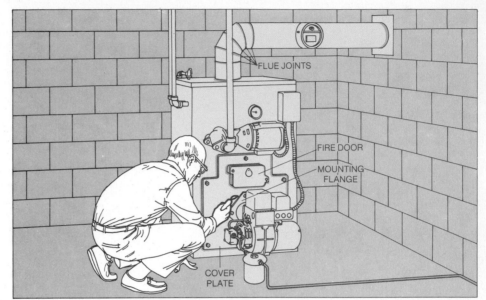

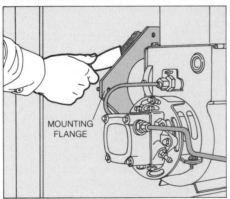

2 Sealing a leak. Turn off the burner and allow the furnace to cool. Clean off the surfaces around the leak with a wire brush and use a putty knife to fill leaks with refractory furnace cement. If a flue section is badly rusted and perforated with small holes, replace it. To seal a leak around the burner-mounting flange *(left)* unscrew the bolts around the edge and pull the flange back a fraction of an inch. Scrape away any old gasket material under the flange and apply a thin layer of cement around the edges. Screw the flange back in place.

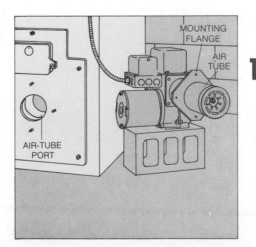

Relining Combustion Chambers

1 Removing the burner. Shut down the burner at the master switch and service panel, then close the oil-supply valve. Mark the air tube so that you can insert it the same distance into the combustion chamber when you reinstall the burner. Unscrew the bolts on the mounting flange and pull the burner away from the combustion chamber. If you cannot do so without bending the oil-supply line, disconnect the line at the oil-burner pump. As you pull the burner from the air-tube port make sure that any gasket material encircling the air tube does not fall off and break. Set the burner down on its own pedestal or support it on a cinder block.

2 Measuring the combustion chamber. Inspect the chamber by looking in through the air-tube port and by reaching inside and feeling the chamber walls and floor with your hand. Pull debris out through the air-tube port, then vacuum the chamber. To measure the inside length and width of the chamber, hold a tape measure as shown below—with one arm through the fire door and the other holding the tape measure at the air-tube port. If the fire door is too small for you to get your arm in or if it is located so that you cannot reach into the chamber through it, measure the chamber length by inserting a yardstick through the air-tube port. Calculate the chamber width by measuring the width of the furnace and subtracting twice the thickness of the combustion-chamber walls, measured at the air-tube port. Take your measurements to a heating supplier and buy a liner to fit.

3 Preparing the liner. Remove the liner from its plastic bag—it comes wet, so it can be molded—and spread it open. Measure the height of the combustion chamber and the height of the liner. If the liner is taller than the combustion chamber, mark the height of the chamber on the liner and use scissors to cut flaps 4 or 5 inches wide around the top. If the liner does not have a hole for the air tube, measure from the top of the combustion chamber to the top of the air-tube port. Then, the same distance below the top of the liner (or below the flaps if you have had to cut them), cut out a circle slightly smaller than the diameter of the air tube.

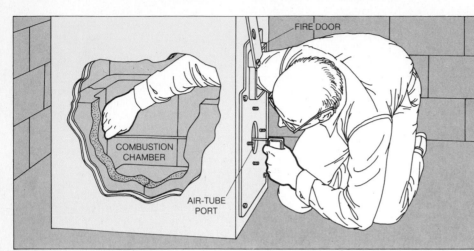

FIRE DOOR

COMBUSTION CHAMBER

AIR-TUBE PORT

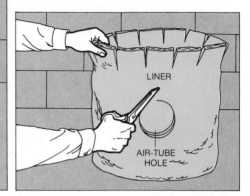

LINER

AIR-TUBE HOLE

4 Lining the chamber. Roll up the liner and push it into the combustion chamber through the air-tube port. Reach through the fire door and the air-tube port and unroll the liner. If you cannot reach through the fire door, you will have to position the liner with one hand. Turn the liner so that the air-tube hole coincides with the air-tube port. Then, working from the back of the chamber to the front, press the liner into place against the walls and the floor of the chamber. Make sure the top of the liner adheres firmly to the top of the combustion chamber. Pat the liner smooth and fold any flaps at the top of the liner over the top edge of the combustion chamber. If you tear the liner, simply press the torn edges back together. You can also patch torn sections with scraps from the air-tube hole.

Partially dry the liner with a propane torch or a light bulb of at least 100 watts until it has the consistency of stale bread. Then, with a sharp knife, trim the air-tube opening in the liner so that its edge is flush with the air-tube port.

Push the air tube into the port up to the mark made in Step 1. Screw the mounting flange to the furnace; reconnect the oil line, if you disconnected it earlier. Open the oil valve and restore power to the burner. If you disconnected the oil line, prime the pump *(page 240)*. Then turn on the burner at the master switch and allow it to run for three minutes and shut it off for three minutes. (You may see a little smoke and detect an unfamiliar odor; both are normal.) Repeat this procedure twice to set the liner.

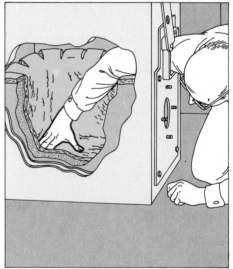

What to Do When Your Burner Won't Start

An oil burner can be balky, stopping unexpectedly or not firing when it should. Before calling a serviceman, try these remedies. In many instances, you can get the burner going yourself.
☐ Check the thermostat setting and reading to make sure it is higher than the temperature in the room.
☐ Make sure you have turned on the master switch—or switches.

☐ Check for a blown fuse or tripped circuit breaker.
☐ Check the storage tank to make sure it is not empty; if it has no gauge, insert a long stick through the filler pipe. Make sure the oil-line valves are open.
☐ Press the restart button on the ignition safety relay; it may be located at the burner or the stack. If you have a stack-mounted relay, open the cover and realign the contacts *(page 238)* before pressing the button. Do not press the restart button more than once.
☐ Press the restart button on the unit's burner motor.
☐ Remove the firing assembly and check the ignition system *(pages 239-240)*. If the burner still does not start—or starts but shuts off within 60 seconds—call for professional service.

Servicing Your Forced-Air System

In a forced warm-air system, the blower—or fan—that distributes the heat is spun by a motor that may be attached to the fan shaft *(page 245)* or connected to the shaft by a belt running between pulleys *(below)*. Belts wear out and pulleys get out of alignment, but because they and the motor are outside the fan housing, this system is easy to work on. On the direct-drive system, the motor is inside the fan and less accessible, but repairs are seldom needed.

With either type, the principal problems are noise, too little or too much air flow, and—rarely—a burned-out motor. Vibration noises are often quieted simply by tightening the screws holding the blower housing and the motor, and—with a belt-driven motor—correcting belt tension and pulley align-

ment. Also check lubrication of the bearings on the blower and motor. Some bearings are permanently lubricated and sealed, but most require oiling or greasing once a year before the heating season starts—and again at the end of the season if the blower also distributes cool air from a central air conditioner. If air velocity gets so high you hear a siren-like sound from the ducts, cut down the speed *(page 244)*.

If the system fails to deliver enough heat, the problem may be too low a blower speed; speed it up. Sometimes, though, the lack of warm air may be caused by dust and lint. If the blower wheel gets dirty, clean it with a vacuum cleaner and brush. If a glass-fiber type filter gets clogged, replace it; if a plastic or aluminum filter gets clogged, wash it off.

When a motor burns out, you usually can replace it with one of the same size. If you have added air conditioning to an old system, however, the new motor probably should be at least a size larger than the burned-out one. To disconnect a motor for replacement, turn off power to the heating system at the service panel, check to be sure it is off, then simply undo the motor wires and remove the bolts holding the motor to its brackets.

Besides keeping the motor and blower running smoothly, you also may want to improve your forced-air system by adding a humidifier or by installing an electrostatic filter. Whatever the addition or adjustment you plan to make, always shut down the power completely before you tackle the job. Be sure to leave the power off until you finish working.

Belt-Drive Blowers

Lubricating the motor and blower. Unsnap or unscrew the access panel in front of the blower unit. If the bearings have no oil cups or grease fittings, lubrication is not needed. If you see cups, lift the lids or pull the plugs one at a time at both ends of the motor and blower. Dribble six to eight drops of 10- to 20-weight nondetergent electric-motor oil, available at hardware stores, into each cup. If you see grease fittings—the hexagonal nipples ending with flattened balls that are common on blower bearings—use a hand-operated grease gun to lubricate them with two full pumps of automotive lubrication grease.

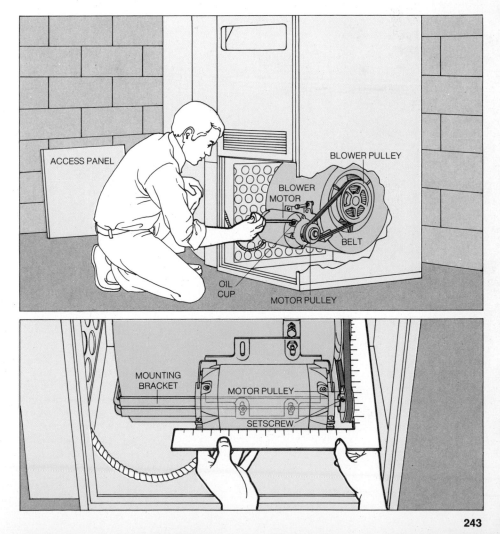

Aligning the pulleys. Set one edge of a carpenter's square against the outside faces of the motor and blower pulleys to make sure they are positioned in a straight line and at right angles to the motor shaft. If the pulleys are less than ½ inch out of alignment, use a hex wrench to loosen the setscrew holding the motor pulley to the motor shaft, and slide the pulley back or forward as necessary. Retighten the setscrew. If the setscrew is rusted or if you need to move the pulley more than ½ inch, loosen the bolts holding the motor to the mounting bracket. Slide the motor along the bracket until the pulleys align, then retighten the bolts.

Checking the belt. With your hand, press on the belt midway between the motor and blower pulleys. If the belt deflects more than about ¾ inch up or down, use a wrench to turn the motor adjustment bolt clockwise to increase tension. If the belt deflects less than ¾ inch, turn the bolt counterclockwise to decrease tension.

Replace a frayed, stringy or cracked belt immediately—if it breaks it may cause damage. Any A-type V belt of the correct length will do, whether from a heating-supply dealer, an auto-supply store or a garage. Turn the motor adjustment bolt counterclockwise until the belt slips easily off the pulleys. To attach a new belt, loop one end around the motor pulley. Slide the edge of the other end of the belt onto the blower pulley. Rotate the blower pulley by hand until the belt feeds into the slot. Correct the tension when you put the belt on and check it again in two weeks; new belts often stretch.

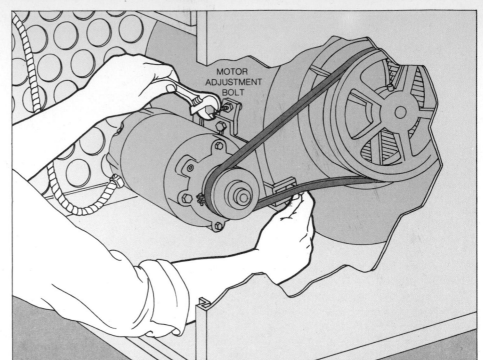

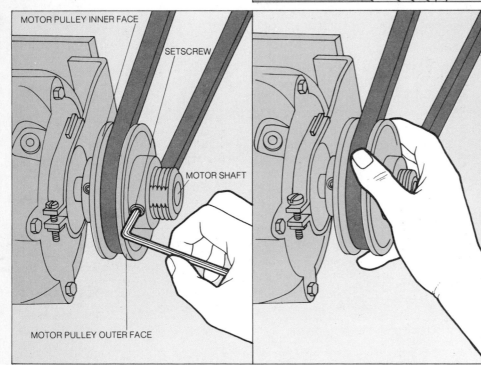

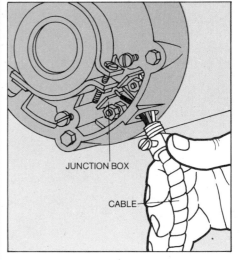

Changing blower speed. With a hex wrench, loosen the setscrew locking the two faces of the motor pulley together *(above, left)*. To increase blower speed, turn the outer pulley face clockwise in increments of 180° to bring it closer to the inner face *(above, right)*. In some cases you may need to release the belt tension to rotate the face of the pulley. If adjusting the pulley until the faces touch does not provide enough speed, replace the motor pulley with another adjustable one of the next larger diameter. To decrease

blower speed, turn the outer pulley face 180° counterclockwise to separate it from the inner face. Retighten the setscrew against one of the two flat spots on the outer end of the shaft; readjust the pulley alignment and belt tension.

Caution: Increasing the speed raises the amperage, or amount of current, going into the motor and may burn it out. About an hour after you adjust the pulleys, check the motor. If it feels unusually hot, decrease the speed.

Removing the motor. With the power off, slide off or unscrew the plate covering the junction box at the end or side of the motor. Detach the wires from the electrical terminals inside the box, taking note of which terminals they attach to; unscrew the lock nut holding the armored cable that covers the wires and pull the cable and wires away from the motor. Loosen the lock nut on the motor adjustment bolt, turn the bolt counterclockwise to release the belt tension and slip the belt off. Remove the bolts holding the motor to the mounting bracket and lift off the motor.

To replace the motor with the same or a larger model, fasten the new motor to the old bracket and slip the belt over the pulleys. Then attach the cable to the motor junction box and secure the wires to the terminals in the original arrangement. Cover the box and adjust the belt.

Direct-Drive Blowers

Oiling the motor and blower. With the power off, remove the access panels from both the blower and furnace compartments. Use a screwdriver to loosen the two front screws in the metal strip between the compartment openings. Slide the blower partway forward by pulling the metal shelf below the unscrewed strip. If the wires are too taut to permit the blower to slide easily, unclip the wires from along the side of the furnace opening or detach or unplug them at the blower or furnace junction box. Look for oil cups *(inset)* at the visible end of the blower motor; if there are none, lubrication is not needed. If you find oil cups, lift the lids or pull the plugs and drip six to eight drops of 10- to 20-weight nondetergent electric-motor oil into each cup. Slide the blower back in place, reattach the metal strip and put back the access panels.

Adjusting a multispeed motor. Whether the motor has a blower-mounted junction box *(right),* an exposed terminal strip, or a junction box beside the furnace box, only one or two of the terminals on the board inside the box or on the strip will be wired with hot lines from the main power source. One hot line (usually red) will be connected to the low or medium-low terminal that powers the blower when the surface is in operation; the other hot line (usually black) will control the high and medium-high terminals only used for central air conditioning. The neutral line (usually white) will be wired to a neutral terminal. To increase or decrease blower speed, first make sure the power to the furnace is off, then unplug the appropriate hot line and attach it to the adjacent terminal. Finally, replace the junction box cover and access panel. Restore the power to test your work.

Replacing the motor. Turn the power off and check to be sure it is off, then disconnect the wires to the blower by unplugging the box or the hot and neutral lines. Then slide the blower and attached shelf onto the floor. Remove the bolt assemblies holding the motor mounting bracket to the blower housing *(near right)* and loosen the bolt that connects the opposite end of the motor shaft to the blower wheel. Ease the motor out of the blower *(far right).* Remove the nut and washer at the ends of the bracelet-like ring of the mounting bracket. Slip off the bracket and save it. Fit the bracelet around the new motor approximately as far from the ends as it was on the old motor. Slide the motor into the blower, reattach the mounting bracket and tighten the bolt against the flat spot on the motor shaft. Rotate the blower wheel by hand; if the wheel rubs the housing, loosen the bolt and shift the wheel sideways until it rotates freely. Slide the blower back in place and reconnect the wires. Reattach the access panel.

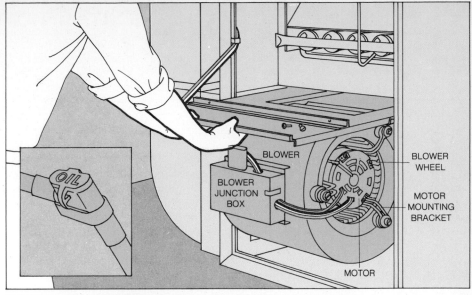

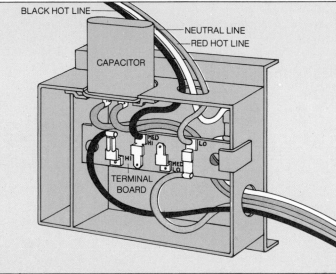

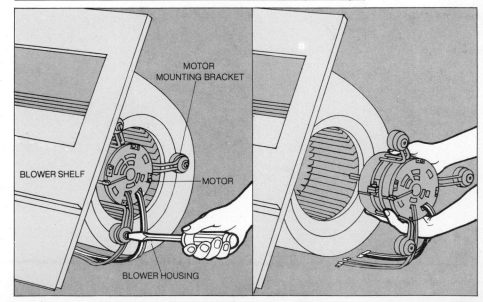

Hot-Water Heat: Easy to Maintain and Modernize

Keeping a forced hot-water system running smoothly takes only a minimum of regular service. And bringing the system up to date by adding new valves *(page 248)* or replacing radiators with convectors *(page 249)* is simple piping work.

Once a year, before the boiler starts up, bleed the radiators or convectors *(page 225)*. At the same time lubricate the pump that circulates the water through the system by putting a few drops of 20-weight nondetergent electric-motor oil into the oil cups at both ends of the motor and on the top of the bearing assembly between the motor and pump body.

During the heating season make periodic checks of the water pressure in the system by examining the combination gauge mounted on the side or front of the boiler. Depending on the size of your house, pressure can safely range from as little as 3 pounds per square inch, when the water cools and contracts, to about 30 pounds when it heats and expands.

If the movable "pressure" pointer on the gauge drops below the stationary "altitude" pointer, you need to increase the pressure in the system. How you do this will depend on the type of expansion tank you have *(page 248)*. The tank, which provides a cushion of air for the expanding and contracting water, may be a conventional one, with a top layer of air in direct contact with a layer of water, or it may be a diaphragm tank, with the air layer at the bottom, separated from the water by a rubber membrane. With the conventional expansion tank, you increase the pressure by adding water to the to the system; with the diaphragm tank, you recharge the air in the tank instead.

If there is too much pressure—i.e., when the movable pointer nears the 30-pound mark—the pressure should be lowered. You can recharge a conventional tank with air *(page 248)*, but call for professional service if you have a diaphragm type tank.

With care you can keep the repair jobs few. Components rarely fail, but when breakdown occurs it most likely involves one of these units: the pump motor, the coupler holding the motor to the pump shaft or the pump seal. Remove the burned-out or broken part *(opposite)* and take it to the heating-supply dealer so you can be sure to get an identical replacement. If you must replace the pump seal, or change the valves or heating elements, first drain the system and then refill it *(below)*.

Draining and Refilling the System

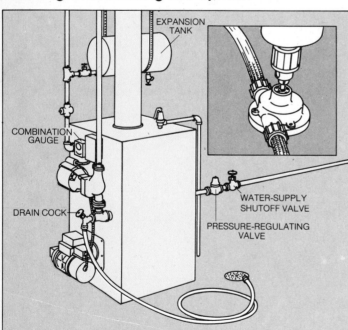

EXPANSION TANK

COMBINATION GAUGE

DRAIN COCK

WATER-SUPPLY SHUTOFF VALVE

PRESSURE-REGULATING VALVE

PRESSURE-RELIEF VALVE

1 Draining the water. Cut off the boiler at the master switch and service panel. When the water in the system cools to lukewarm as shown on the combination gauge, close the water-supply shutoff valve. Attach one end of a garden hose to the boiler drain cock and run the other end of the hose to a floor drain (or use an electric-drill pump such as the one shown in the inset to lift the water to a sink or an open window). Open not only the boiler drain cock but also the bleeder valves of all the radiators or convectors on the upper floor of the house.

2 Adding water. Close the drain cock. Unscrew the pressure-relief valve and pour rust inhibitor into the opening. Replace the relief valve. Close the radiator or convector bleeder valves. Then open the water-supply valve. If there is a pressure-regulating valve on the line, the flow will stop automatically when the system if full. Otherwise, fill until the movable pointer corresponds to the position on the stationary pointer. Bleed all of the heating units on the upper floor. If you do not have a pressure regulator, have someone bleed each unit while you watch the gauge.

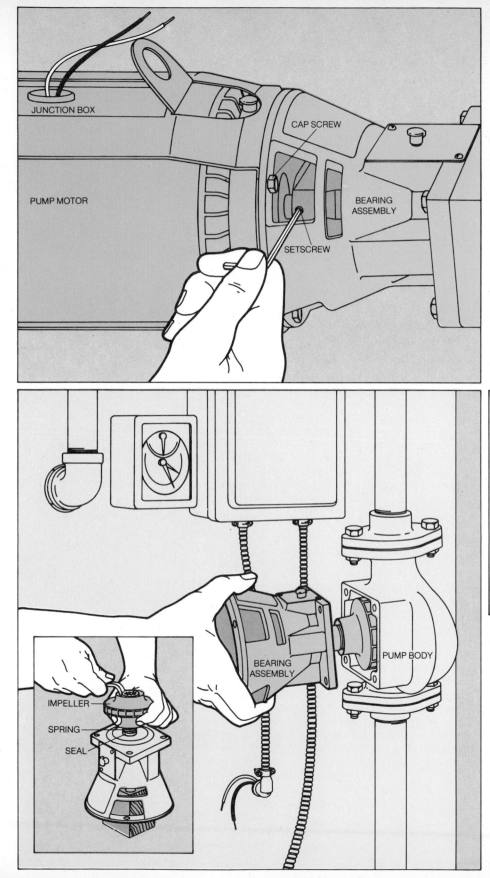

Replacing Pump Parts

Replacing the motor. After turning off the power, and checking to make certain it is off, remove the junction-box cover from the pump motor and disconnect the wires. Use a hex wrench to remove the setscrew holding the coupler to the motor shaft *(left)*. Then, gripping the motor in one hand , use an open-end wrench to loosen the cap screws that hold the motor to the bearing assembly. Back the motor out, leaving the coupler attached to the pump shaft.

To install the new motor, fit the free end of the coupler onto the motor shaft with the flat on the motor shaft aligned with the setscrew. Hold the motor against the bearing assembly, reinsert the cap screws and secure the coupler setscrew.

Replacing the coupler. Remove the motor and use the hex wrench to loosen the setscrew holding the coupler to the pump shaft *(below)*. Slide the coupler off. To install the new coupler, secure one end to the pump shaft with the setscrew. Then replace the motor and attach the other end of the coupler to the motor shaft. The setscrews should bite into the flats on both shafts.

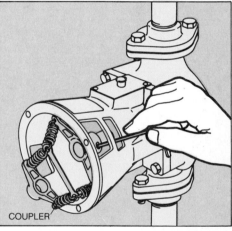

COUPLER

Replacing the pump seal. With the power to the furnace off, drain the system *(opposite, Step 1)* or turn off the power to the burner and then cut off the water to the pump by shutting the valves above and below it. Remove the motor and coupler, then undo the cap screws holding the bearing assembly to the pump body. Pull the assembly out *(left)*. Standing the bearing assembly on a wood block to support the pump shaft *(inset)*, turn a box or socket wrench clockwise to loosen the nut holding the impeller to the pump shaft. Slide off the impeller and spring, and save them. Pull off the brass seal.

To install the new seal, slide it onto the shaft and press it tight. Attach the old spring and impeller with the nut and washer. Reassemble the pump. Refill the system *(opposite, Step 2)* or open the valves at the pump. Restore the power.

Recharging an Expansion Tank

Recharging the expansion tank. If your system has a conventional tank, run a garden hose from the combination valve at its base to a floor drain or sink. Then close the shutoff valve on the line between the tank and the boiler and open the combination valve until the tank is emptied. If there is no combination valve, open the drain and let the water empty into buckets; if you do not have a shutoff valve, drain and refill the entire system *(page 246)*. If your system has a diaphragm tank *(inset)* check the pressure by attaching a tire gauge to the air-recharge valve. If air is needed, use a bicycle pump to add it.

If you want to install a combination valve do so while the tank is empty. Close the shutoff valve. Then use a hacksaw or tubing cutter to cut the vent tube of the valve to two thirds the height of the expansion tank. Using a pair of open-end wrenches, remove the plug or drain cock from the base of the tank and screw the combination valve into the opening. Open the shutoff valve.

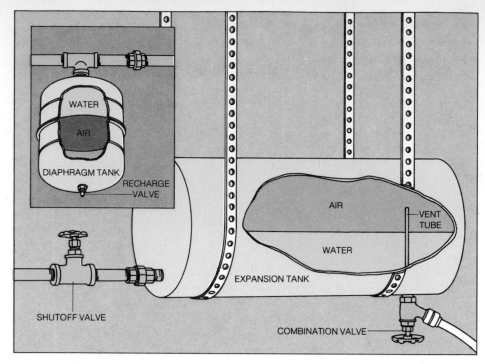

Adding a Shutoff Valve

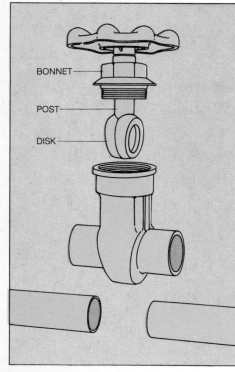

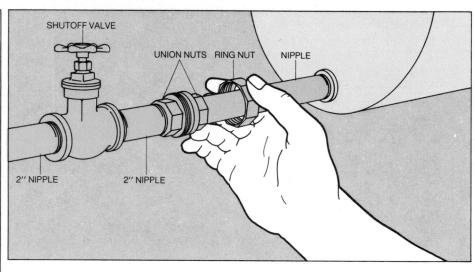

A sweated fitting of copper. Drain the system *(page 246, Step 1)*. Working on the line between the expansion tank and the boiler, use a tubing cutter or hacksaw to cut out a section 1 inch shorter than the length of the gate-type shutoff valve. Before sweat soldering it in, use a wrench to unscrew the bonnet from the valve and lift out the disk assembly; otherwise the soldering heat may warp the disk or post.

A threaded fitting of steel. Drain the system *(page 246, Step 1)*. Hacksaw through the line near the inlet to the expansion tank. Unscrew the pieces of cut pipe from their fittings at both ends of the section. Attach a 2-inch nipple—a short pipe with threads at both ends—into one existing fitting. Then attach a gate-type shutoff valve and another 2-inch nipple. Screw on an assembled union and measure from the union to the remaining existing fitting to determine the length for the third nipple. Undo the ring nut of the union and lift off the free union nut. Then attach the third nipple to the existing fitting, slip the ring nut over the nipple and attach the remaining union nut. Slide the ring nut over the union nuts and tighten it. Refill the system *(page 246, Step 2)*.

New Convectors for Old Radiators

The old-fashioned radiator, which warms partly by radiation (by giving off heat rays) and partly by convection (by warming cold air that flows up over it), is being largely replaced nowadays by the less obtrusive convector, which, as the name indicates, works mainly by convection. Both kinds of units have a pipe at each end, connecting to the supply and return main from the boiler. One pipe, which is called a supply riser, brings water into the unit; the second pipe, called a return riser, carries water back to the main. Because the piping systems for both are identical, you can take an old radiator out and use its risers for the installation of a new convector.

Convectors come in either upright or baseboard models, in either copper or steel, and with either aluminum or cast-iron fins. Copper with aluminum fins is easiest to install and comes in a wide range of sizes to suit your heating needs (pages 286-287). Because metals heat and cool differently, however, mixing even one or two copper units with existing iron ones may make some areas too hot while others are too cold.

The piping required for substituting convectors is minimal. Some upright units, such as the one shown at right, may align so exactly with old risers that you can connect them with unions and nipples (inset). For most uprights and all baseboard convectors you can zigzag new stretches of pipe to the joints downstairs where the risers elbow up from the main. Where codes allow, copper is the easiest piping material to use—Type L or M rigid tubing for straight stretches and flexible convectors for turning corners. Where the new copper meets the old steel piping or the threaded ends of the pipes on upright convectors, install steel-to-copper adapters or transition fittings.

Upright convector pipes come fitted with tappings for bleeder valves. To vent a baseboard unit, use an elbow with a vent tapping to connect the baseboard pipe to the return riser. Similarly, use an angle valve at the supply riser so you can balance the heat of the baseboard (pages 228-229). For the upright convector, you can install a shutoff valve (page 248) on the supply riser line.

Removing a radiator. Drain the system (page 246, Step 1) and open the radiator's air vent. Pull back any carpeting, then cover the floor with heavy tarpaulin or plastic. Set a pan nearby to catch the residual water—usually ink black—that will drip from the radiator when you disconnect it. Using a pipe wrench, loosen the union between the radiator and the elbow at each side of the unit. To break tight joints, fit a length of pipe over the wrench handle for extra leverage. Plug the openings of the radiator with rags, tip it onto an old rug turned pile-side down, and drag it out. Then disconnect the elbows from the supply and return risers.

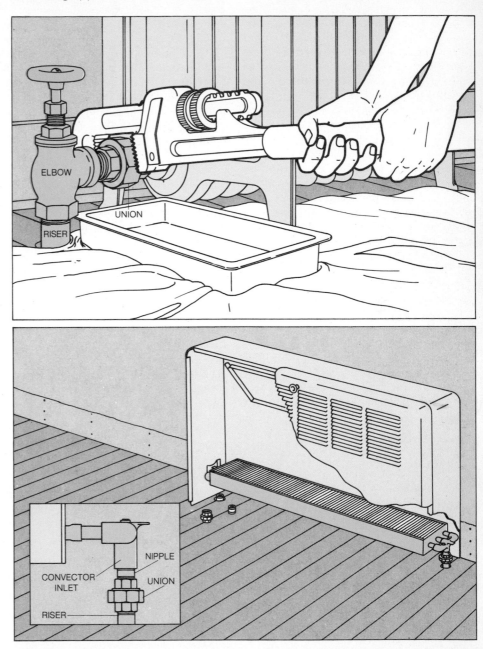

Connecting an upright convector. If the inlet and outlet of the convector align with the existing radiator risers, set the unit in place and center the inlet and outlet above the risers. Screw an assembled union onto each riser tip—using a reducing bushing in the union if the convector is smaller than the riser pipe. Measure from the top of each union or bushing to the convector inlet or outlet above it and add 1 inch to determine the length for each nipple you will need to connect the convector to the risers. Attach the nipples and half unions to the convector and the other halves of the unions to the risers (inset), using the technique for making a threaded fitting shown on the opposite page. Remove the plug from the tapping over the return riser and screw in a bleeder valve. Then trace the supply riser down to the basement or crawl space and add a shutoff valve at a convenient place on its line. Refill the system (page 246, Step 2).

Repairs for Air Conditioners

Room air conditioners, central air conditioners and heat pumps—simply reversible air conditioners *(page 252)*—are remarkably trouble-free. The principal maintenance needed is cleaning. Replace disposable filters and wash reusable ones about once a month. Owners of older units that are not permanently lubricated should oil fan and blower motors and bearings once a year.

Meticulous homeowners, aware that dirt on refrigerant coils and fans reduces efficiency, start each season by cleaning the air conditioner. More often, however, no attention is paid to an air conditioner or a heat pump until something goes wrong.

As the troubleshooting chart on page 253 shows, there are minor ailments you can cure yourself. Dirty components are often the problem, and cleaning restores efficient operation. The more serious difficulties in a central unit most often occur in the thermostat and blower—the parts it shares with the heating system.

Before repairing an air conditioner or a heat pump, unplug it or turn off its electrical power at the service panel. Then remove the access panels that cover the interior components. A central unit has a cover for the evaporator, or A-coil, and another for the blower, both of which are in the furnace. Outdoors, the grilles over the condenser either unsnap or unscrew. Room air conditioners may have similar panels, but many large units can be slid partway out of their casings and into the room for easy access.

Cleaning an air conditioner or a heat pump requires both a gentle touch and a firm hand. Fins on the cooling coils are delicate; for them, a soft brush and a vacuum cleaner are the best tools. Fans and blowers, however, become encrusted with hard-to-remove dirt; you may need to use a wire brush or putty knife.

Before switching the unit on after you have repaired it, be sure it has been off at least five minutes; unless you give it time to dissipate excess pressure you could overload the compressor. Conversely, leaving a central air conditioner or heat pump (not a window unit) disconnected from all power for a considerable time—three days or more—also causes a problem: refrigerant in the compressor may liquefy, and in this state it can damage a working compressor. To avoid such harm, wait at least 24 hours after you restore power to the unit before turning on the operating switch. During this waiting period, an automatic heater in the unit will vaporize any refrigerant that has liquefied.

Cleaning the condensate box and pump. Unplug the pump motor, and take off the box cover. Remove the screws at the base of the pump impeller shaft *(below, left)* and lift out the pump, complete with its motor switch and float assembly. Remove the motor housing screws and lift off the housing with the switch-float assembly attached. Clean the fan on top of the motor with a brush and a kerosene-soaked rag *(below, right)*, and oil the motor, following the directions that are on the plate attached to its cover.

Scrub the inside of the box, then scour the float rod so it can move freely. After you replace the motor housing and mount the pump on its base, check that the float ball and rod do not bind, and the power cord does not dip below the motor.

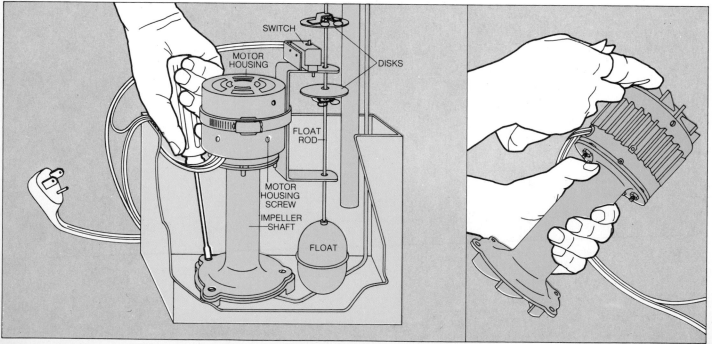

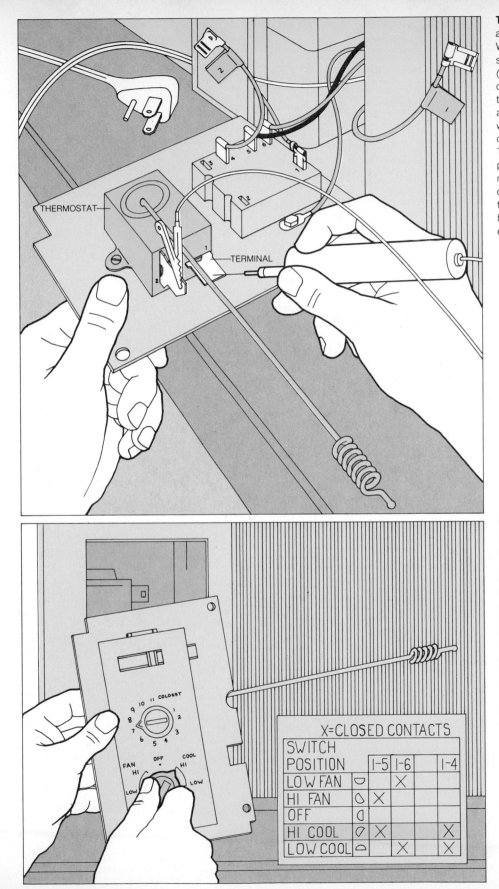

Testing a window-unit thermostat. Unplug the air conditioner and unfasten the control panel. With masking tape, label each of the two thermostat wires with the number next to its terminal *(left)*. Remove the wires and attach the alligator clip of a continuity tester to one terminal. With the air temperature near the unit between 70° and 80° and the temperature control at its warmest setting, touch the tester probe to the other terminal; the tester bulb should not light. Turn the thermostat to its coldest setting and repeat the test; the bulb should glow. If the thermostat fails either test, replace it with an exact duplicate and connect the two wires. Reattach the control panel; if the thermostat has a sensor bulb, position the new bulb in the air stream exactly where the old one was.

THERMOSTAT

TERMINAL

Testing a selector switch. Unplug the unit and unfasten the control panel. Pull the wires from the switch terminals, and label each one.

Find the wiring diagram—it will be somewhere inside the unit—and note the small chart *(inset)* showing terminal numbers and switch-shaft positions for each switch setting. At each setting, test all the terminal combinations shown in the chart—1-5, 1-6 and 1-4 in this example—by attaching the alligator clip of a continuity tester to terminal No. 1 and touching the tester probe to each of the other terminals. Combinations marked by Xs or a similar symbol should light the tester. With the switch shown here set at HI COOL, the tester should light for the combinations 1-5 and 1-4, but not 1-6. If the tester lights when it should not or fails to light when it should, replace the switch.

COLDEST
FAN HI · COOL HI
LOW · LOW

X=CLOSED CONTACTS

SWITCH POSITION		1-5	1-6	1-4
LOW FAN	◡		X	
HI FAN	◠	X		
OFF	◖			
HI COOL	◗	X		X
LOW COOL	◡		X	X

A Unit that Heats and Cools

A heat pump is essentially an air conditioner that not only draws heat from indoor air and transfers it outdoors, like other air conditioners, but can also reverse itself by means of a special valve, and draw heat from the outdoor air to the interior of a house (even cold outdoor air contains much heat energy).

Heat pumps have the same servicing needs as air conditioners and a few special needs of their own too. Almost all have mechanisms that permit them to operate under freezing conditions and that sometimes need attention.

When outside temperatures approach 32°, the outdoor coil of a heat pump frosts up like the freezer compartment of an old-fashioned refrigerator as water vapor in the atmosphere condenses on the coil. An icy sheath blocks the flow of outdoor air through the coil and prevents the coil from picking up enough warmth from the air for transmission to the house. If the heat pump is functioning properly it will defrost itself by switching automatically from the heating to the cooling mode; then heat from the house is transferred to the refrigerant, which warms and defrosts the outside coil.

At the same time, the unit automatically switches on a supplemental electric-resistance heating unit inside the house to provide warmth there until the heat pump has defrosted itself and gone back to work. Occasionally it may fail to defrost or, once started, may fail to stop defrosting. In either case, the supplemental heater keeps working, and unless you notice and correct the malfunction promptly you may incur an unexpectedly large electric bill from the continued running of that heater.

The signs of such trouble are visible on the outdoor coil. It should show frost, at least periodically, when the outdoor temperature is near or below 32°; if it stays warm and dry, the unit is defrosting continuously and you should call a serviceman. On the other hand, you may find the coil covered with a heavy coat of ice; if it shows no sign of defrosting, try setting the thermostat below room temperature to shift the unit into the cooling mode. (Some units have an additional switch you must set to select cooling.) After 10 minutes, switch the thermostat to emergency heat for 10 minutes, to keep the house warm, then back to cooling. If your problem is a sticky valve this operation may cure it.

If the unit does not defrost within an hour or so, call a serviceman. If the unit does defrost but immediately ices up again, try cleaning the sensing device that controls defrosting, as shown below or in the picture at right.

Clearing an air-flow sensing tube. Heat pumps like the one below have a tube at the top connected to an air-pressure-activated switch. As long as the fan freely sucks air in over the coils, pressure in the tube keeps the switch open. When ice buildup on the coils blocks the flow of air, pressure in the tube drops; the switch closes, turning on the defrost circuit. Spiderwebs or other foreign matter may block the tube and keep the unit from switching to defrost. Turn off power to the heat pump, remove the access panel and unscrew the nut that holds the tube to the switch. Then thread a wire through the tube, attach a bit of cloth to the wire and pull it through the tube. Refasten the tube to the switch.

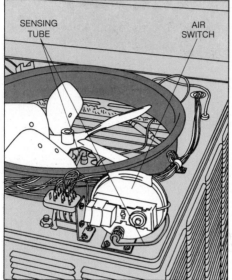

SENSING TUBE

AIR SWITCH

Cleaning a sensing bulb. Heat pumps like the model at right have a thermostat at the end of a thin copper tube that is either held by a clamp to the pipes along one edge of the coil or is located inside a sleeve attached to a refrigerant pipe. When the coil temperature drops below 32°, causing frost to collect, this thermostat switches on the defrost circuit. Corrosion may interfere with its sensitivity. Clean the bulb with sandpaper and the sleeve with a thin, spiral metal brush.

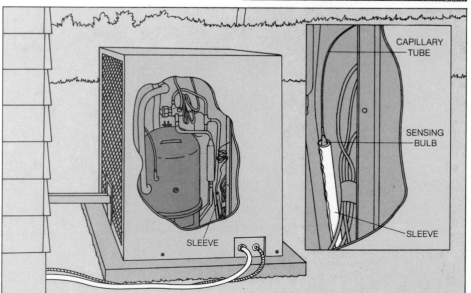

CAPILLARY TUBE

SENSING BULB

SLEEVE

SLEEVE

Troubleshooting Air Conditioners and Heat Pumps

Symptoms	Causes	Remedies
Air conditioner does not run	Defective cord or plug (room unit)	Replace cord and plug
	Dead circuit	Check circuit breaker or fuse.
	Faulty thermostat (room unit)	Test thermostat; replace if necessary (page 251).
	Inoperative switch (room unit)	Test switch and replace if necessary (page 251).
Air conditioner operates continuously or goes on and off repeatedly	Faulty thermostat (room unit)	Test thermostat; replace if necessary (page 251).
	Sensor bulb out of position (room unit)	Reposition sensor bulb (page 251).
	Thermostat improperly located (central unit)	Reposition thermostat (page 232).
Air conditioner works ineffectively	Dirty filter*	Replace disposable filter; wash reusable filters and coat with light oil.
	Clogged grilles and dirty blower or fan*	Loosen dirt with a stiff brush or putty knife and then clean up dirt with a vacuum cleaner.
	Blower drive belt too loose (central unit)	Tighten belt (page 244).
	Faulty thermostat (room unit)	Test thermostat; replace if necessary (page 251).
	Other problems	Call for professional service.
Frost on evaporator coil	Unit turned on when outdoor temperature is below 60°*	Do not operate when temperature is below 60°; severe ice build up can break refrigerant lines.
	Dirty filter*	Replace disposable filter; wash reusable filter and coat with light oil.
	Bent coil fins*	Straighten fins with special fin comb available from refrigeration-supply dealers.
	Blower drive belt too loose (central unit)	Tighten belt (page 244).
	Faulty thermostat (room unit)	Test thermostat; replace if necessary (page 251).
	Coil clogged with dirt	Clean coil with vacuum cleaner.
Water leaks into a room	Air conditioner tilted (room unit)	Lay a level on top of the unit, directly above each support bracket. Adjust the leveling screws until the level bubble is half off its center line, tilting the unit slightly downward towards the outside.
	Condensate drain hole plugged (room unit)	Clean drain with a coat hanger.
	Condensate box and pump clogged (central unit)	Clean box and pump (page 250).
Blower motor overheats	Motor needs lubrication (central unit)	Oil motor (pages 243 and 245).
	Drive belt too tight (central unit)	Adjust belt tension (page 244).
Excessive noise or vibration	Loose grilles or access panels*	Tighten screws or secure with tape.
	Thermostat sensor bulb touching coil (room unit)	Bend sensor bulb away from coil; replace rubber washer that secures sensor if worn.
	Incorrect drive belt tension (central unit)	Adjust tension (page 244).
	Drive pulleys misaligned (central unit)	Realign pulleys (page 244).
	Blower motor loose on mount (central unit)	Tighten mounting bolts (page 243).

*These causes and remedies apply both to room and central units.

Weather-Stripping to Block the Drafts

The cracks around doors and windows are the main cause of air leakage in most homes. Weather-stripping those cracks can reduce heating and air-conditioning costs as much as 30 per cent.

In many houses, window sashes and doors are grooved to interlock with metal flanges around the frames. If your house lacks this sort of built-in weather stripping, the illustrations on these and the following pages will show you how to install other types of protection.

There are some simple tests to determine your weather-stripping needs. On a cool, windy day, feel for air leaking in by placing your hand on several places along door and window cracks. Another method is to hold a tissue next to the crack to see if it flutters. Or, shine a flashlight along door and window edges from the outside at night while someone inside watches to see if light penetrates.

Once you know your trouble spots you can select the weather stripping best suited to the job. Materials suitable for both doors and windows come in flexible rolls of metal, felt, plastic foam, rubber or vinyl *(below)*. Types designed for the sides and tops of doors are rigid strips edged with foam, felt or plastic *(page 258)*. Several varieties of door bottoms also can be purchased *(page 260)*.

All come prepackaged with nails or screws, and include enough stripping to cover at least one door or window. Another type fits a channel routed into the door jamb or window frame. It should be installed by a professional.

All weather stripping is installed so the resilient part seals out air by pressing against the door or window. Do not make the seals too tight or windows and doors will not open and close smoothly.

Before beginning, make sure the doors and windows work properly. Doors that do not hang straight may have to be shimmed or sanded to eliminate binding *(page 259)*. Sometimes windows will not shut all the way: the top rail of the lower sash and the bottom rail of the upper sash should meet evenly across the center of the window. If they do not, scrape paint or dirt off top and bottom rails and their channels. It may be necessary to sand the top or bottom of the window.

For double-hung windows, the best easily installed seal is the springy metal stripping shown on these pages. Such strips are nailed only along one edge; the other edge springs out to block leaks. Metal stripping is installed so it cannot be seen when the window is shut.

Felt, rubber and vinyl weather stripping *(page 256)* are easier to install, but not as long lasting and must be mounted in full view on the sash or frame.

Casement and gliding windows are more difficult to seal and require special solutions *(page 257)*.

A Choice of Materials

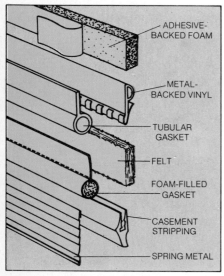

ADHESIVE-BACKED FOAM

METAL-BACKED VINYL

TUBULAR GASKET

FELT

FOAM-FILLED GASKET

CASEMENT STRIPPING

SPRING METAL

Selecting flexible weather stripping. The materials shown above can be used on doors or windows. Durable spring metal is hidden when doors or windows are shut. Metal-backed vinyl or felt is difficult to install, and the vinyl, though applicable to exteriors, may pull away in cold weather or stick when it is warm. Tubular and foam-filled gaskets of vinyl or rubber can be mounted outside. Adhesive-backed foam may come loose on movable surfaces. Felt strips are inexpensive, but they attract dirt, tear easily and must be installed inside. Special vinyl stripping will seal casement windows snugly.

Spring-Metal for Windows

UPPER SASH

BOTTOM RAIL

LOWER SASH

BOTTOM RAIL

CHANNEL

1 Measuring the strips. On double-hung windows, spring-metal weather stripping is installed in the side channels of both upper and lower sashes, on the bottom rails of the upper and lower sashes and on the top rail of the upper sash.

To determine the length of the four side channel strips, raise the lower sash, then measure from the base of one channel to a point 2 inches above the bottom rail of the upper sash. Use tin snips or wire cutters to cut the strips. Finally, measure the bottom rail of the lower sash and cut three strips to this length.

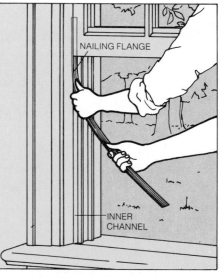

NAILING FLANGE

INNER CHANNEL

2 Installing bottom-sash channel strips. Each metal strip must be installed so the nailing flange lies flush against the inside edge of the frame. Open the lower sash as far as possible and remove any loose paint or dirt from the channels. Slip the end of a strip into the narrow slit between sash and channel, and slide the strip upward until it fills the bottom of the inner channel. Repeat on the other side. If you cannot readily slip the strips into place, scrape out the slits with a thin-bladed knife and try again.

3 **Securing the channel strips.** Fasten the strips by nailing through the holes near the edge. Secure the lower portion of the lower-sash channel strips first; then drop the lower sash and fasten the portion that extends above the top rail.

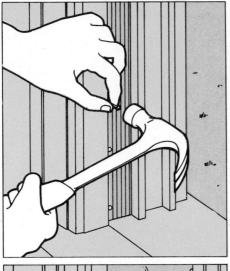

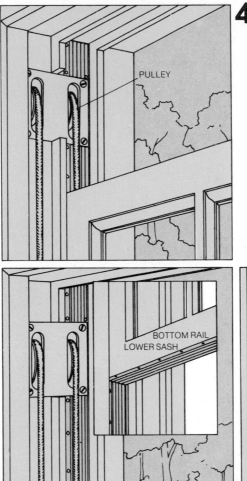

PULLEY

BOTTOM RAIL
LOWER SASH

TOP RAIL
UPPER SASH

4 **Installing outer-channel strips.** If the window lacks rope or chain pulleys, lower both sashes as far as possible and install the strips in the tops of the outer channels as you did in the bottoms of the inner channels in Steps 2 and 3.

If the window has pulleys, as shown here, proceed as follows. Cut the metal into two pieces —one to fit the space above the pulley and one to extend from the pulley to a point 2 inches below the top rail of the lower sash. Install the short piece above the pulley, and fasten extra tacks across its bottom edge. With the top and bottom sashes still all the way down, carefully pull the rope or chain out of the way and feed the long strip into the outer channel below the pulley. Nail the strip in place, then push both sashes all the way up and fasten the end that protrudes below the upper sash's bottom rail.

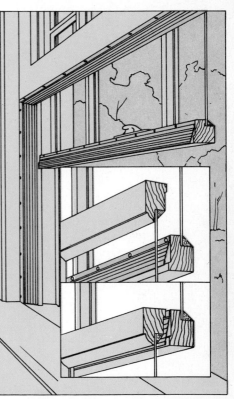

5 **Tightening the seal.** Once the channel strips are nailed in place, use a wide-bladed tool like a putty knife to bend out the unfastened side about ¼ inch, or until the window holds position but does not bind. This increases the spring action and provides a better seal.

6 **Installing top and bottom cross strips.** Metal strips should extend across the full width of the window on the top side of the top rail of the upper sash, and also on the underside of the bottom rail of the bottom sash. The flange to be nailed should be positioned along the inside edge of the window. (Hammer gently or you may crack the glass.) Once in place, pry out the two crosspieces as shown in Step 5.

7 **Mounting the center cross strip.** Install the last metal strip on the inner side of the bottom rail of the upper sash (*above*). The nailing flange should extend across the top edge of the rail. After fastening the strip, sink the nails well into the metal by hammering them again with a nail set or with an inverted flathead nail; this ensures that the sashes will move smoothly yet maintain a tight seal when closed (*inset*). Complete the installation by bending this strip as you have the others.

Using Gaskets and Strips

1 **Installing gaskets.** While weather-resistant vinyl or rubber gasket strips cannot be hidden away like metal weather stripping, they can be applied to the outside of a window where they are not visible. To ensure a straight, tight seal, maintain tension in the strips while nailing them to the window frame. Their thickened edges should fit snugly against the sides of the sashes. Nail additional strips to the bottom edge of the bottom sash rail and the top edge of the top sash rail, making sure that both gaskets press tightly against the frame when the window is shut.

2 **Sealing the meeting rails.** Complete the installation of vinyl or rubber gaskets by securing a strip under the bottom rail of the top sash (*below*). Placed against the inside edge, it will seal the crack between the two halves of the window.

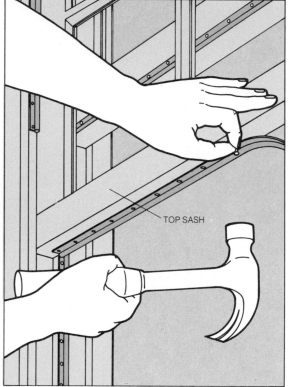

TOP SASH

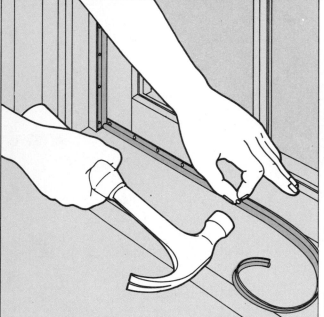

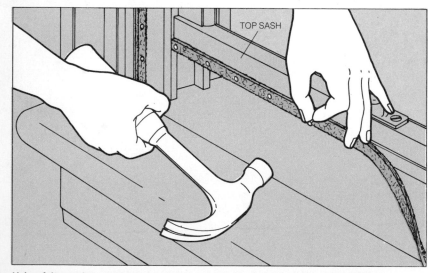

TOP SASH

Using felt weather stripping. Install felt strips as shown for gaskets (*above*), but place the strips on the indoor side of the window sashes and frame. Seal the meeting rails by applying a strip of felt to the interior side of the bottom rail of the upper window sash, positioning the felt as you would spring metal (*page 255, Step 7*).

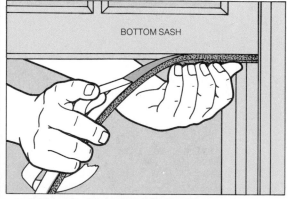

BOTTOM SASH

Installing adhesive-backed stripping. Press the adhesive side of the strip to the clean surface with your fingers as you slowly pull off the protective backing (*above*). Since opening and closing a double-hung window could cause this material to come unstuck from frame edges, use it only on the friction-free areas—the underside of the lower sash's bottom rail and the top side of the upper sash's top rail.

Casement Windows

Weather-stripping metal casements. Metal casement windows can be weatherproofed by a special vinyl gasket with a deep groove that easily slips onto all four edges of the frame. First, apply a vinyl-to-metal adhesive to the frame, then install the vinyl gasket so that the window closes against the flat side of the strips.

Sealing wood casements. Many new styles of wood casements have their own built-in weatherproofing. If yours do not, nail spring metal stripping of the type described on page 254 to the frame. For casements that open outward *(below)*, the nailing flange should be placed along the outside edge of the frame. Reverse the position of the nailing flange for windows that open inward.

You can also install felt or adhesive-backed foam stripping on the inside of the frame, but such materials tend to loosen after a few months of frequent opening and closing of the windows.

These same procedures apply to awning-type windows, which are really sidewise casements.

Gliding Windows

Weatherproofing gliding windows. Most new types of wood gliding windows come with weather stripping built in between the frame and the sash. Older types, however, may need sealing. If both sashes move, treat the window as if it were a double-hung window turned on its side.

For windows with one gliding sash, treat only the movable part. Install a strip of spring metal in the side channel that receives the movable sash, lining up the nailing flange along the inside edge. Then nail vinyl or rubber gasket along the exterior top, bottom and outer edges of the gliding sash. The outer strip will fit snugly against the rail of the inside sash where the window sections meet.

Most metal gliding windows have rubber weather stripping in the tracks of each sash but, like wood gliders, should be sealed where the sashes meet. Attach the gasket with vinyl-to-metal adhesive.

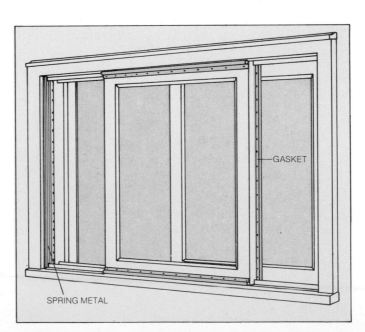

GASKET

SPRING METAL

Weather-Stripping Doors

The big leaks in most houses are around doors. They lack the twofold edge enclosures of double-hung windows, so an open crack is inevitable. Any of various types of weather stripping can fill the crack, but it cannot do so effectively unless the door fits properly. If weather stripping is attached to a binding door, it may make the door impossible to open or close. So the first step in weatherproofing a door is to adjust hinges, and sand or plane edges until it opens and closes smoothly, leaving a narrow, uniform space between edge and jamb.

Generally you can see how the door fits by looking at the edges all around. To find invisible binds, slide thin cardboard between the closed door and the jamb, or rub colored chalk on the door edge—it will rub off on the jamb at binds. Most often a door sticks because loosened hinge screws made it sag. Tighten the screws. If the screws will not hold, replace them with longer ones or stuff the screw holes with toothpicks. If screw-tightening does not solve the problem, try shifting the door by spacing hinge leaves with thin material *(opposite, top)* or plane off the door edge at the binds. If the entire latch side binds, remove the door and plane the hinge side—so you will not have to move the lock—then reset the hinges.

Once you have fixed the door so it operates smoothly, one of the weather-stripping materials illustrated below will stop up the cracks at the sides and top. The crack at the bottom of the door is sealed differently, with any of several devices described overleaf. For sliding doors, follow the instructions given for gliding windows *(page 257)*.

Types of weather stripping. Most durable and effective of weather strippings intended for do-it-yourself installation is the so-called V-strip. A doubled-over strip of springy metal, it fits between door edge and jamb, filling the crack. Other types attach to the doorframe—or the doorstop molding—so that their flexible edges press against the door face when it is closed. Some are rolls of felt or plastic foam backed with adhesive so that they can be stuck on. Sturdier and less obtrusive are wood, metal or plastic strips, edged with plastic tubing or foam, that look like extra decorative trim on the doorstop.

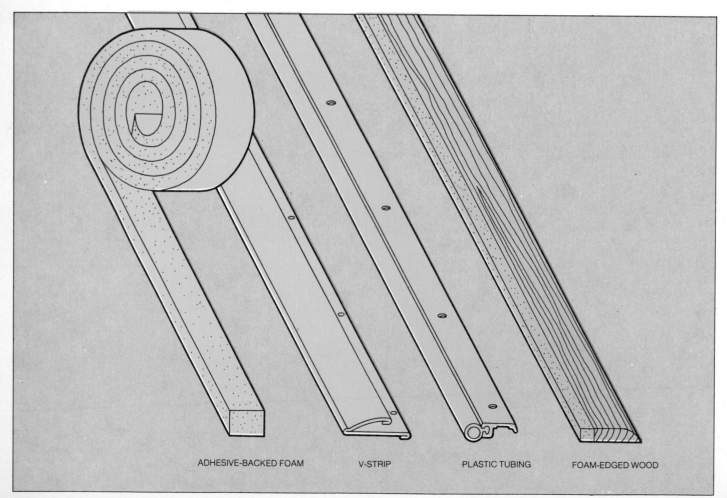

ADHESIVE-BACKED FOAM   V-STRIP   PLASTIC TUBING   FOAM-EDGED WOOD

Straightening a door. If the bind is on the top or bottom edge of the door, plane or sand wood from that edge until the door fits easily. If a door binds on its leading edge—where the lock is installed—it is not necessary to remove any wood. Instead, insert a shim—a piece cut from a plastic bottle—under the jamb leaf of one hinge. For binds near the top of the leading edge, shim out the lower hinge; shim out the upper hinge for lower binds. Simply open the door, put a piece of wood under the bottom for support, unscrew the leaf and add shims until binding is eliminated. For binds on the hinge side, shim the hinge nearest the bind.

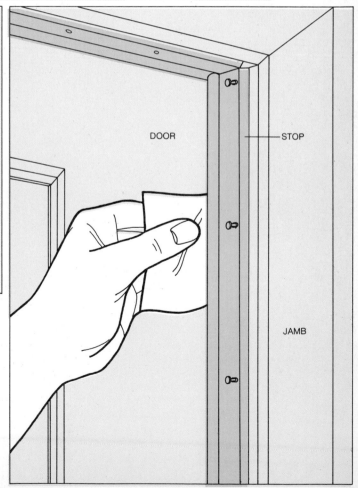

Installing V-strip weather stripping. Cut strips to run along both sides and the top of the door, trimming away sections that would cover hinges and the lock. With the nailing flange against the doorstop and the point of the V facing the door, nail each strip to the jamb.

Attaching doorstop weather stripping. Cut the strips to the lengths of the top and side doorstop moldings. With the door closed, position the top piece against the top stop, pressing the flexible edge lightly against the door face. Attach the strip to the stop with nails or screws but do not drive the fasteners all the way. Install the side strips the same way. Test the positioning by sliding a piece of paper between the door and the flexible edge; it should barely slide all around. Do not position too tightly or the door will not close. Adjust strip positions, resetting fasteners as necessary, then drive the fasteners all the way.

Seals for the Bottom

Door bottoms. A number of devices are made to plug the most troublesome door crack, that at the bottom. Those called sweeps drag a flexible strip against thresholds; special thresholds press flexible material upward against the bottom edge. All come in many shapes and sizes, and most adjust to fit any door. Plain sweeps (*top, far right*) attach to the bottom outside edge of the door; one has a spring to raise it as the door opens and lower it when the door is shut. Bottom sweeps of the type shown at bottom, near right, slide onto the underside of doors. Like the plain sweeps, bottom sweeps can be installed without removing the door. Threshold weather strip fastens to the sill, replacing the existing threshold. For overhead garage doors, plastic or rubber stripping adds a flexible bottom edge.

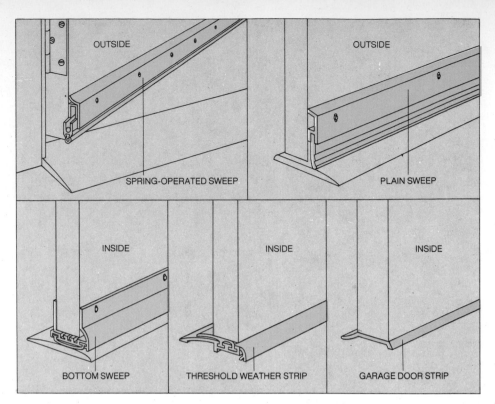

SPRING-OPERATED SWEEP

PLAIN SWEEP

BOTTOM SWEEP

THRESHOLD WEATHER STRIP

GARAGE DOOR STRIP

Installing Sweeps

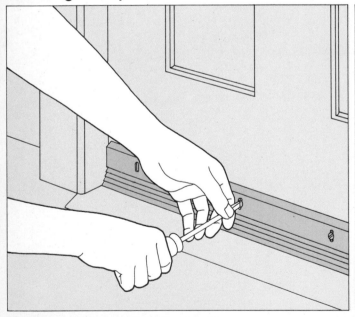

Attaching a plain door sweep. Cut the sweep to door width and screw it across the bottom edge on the outdoor side so it fits snugly against the threshold when the door is shut, yet allows the door to open and close smoothly. Most sweeps have slots, so positioning is easily adjusted.

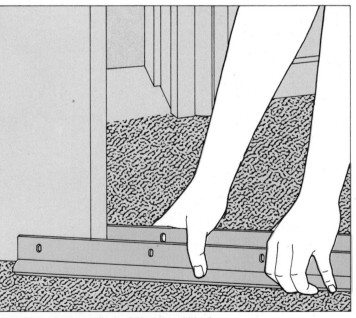

Attaching a bottom sweep. Adjust the width of the sweep to the thickness of your door by slipping the movable piece into the appropriate groove on the channel base. Cut the sweep to the width of the door. Then swing the door open and slide the sweep under the bottom of the door. Close the door, let the sweep drop against the threshold, then drive the attachment screws in their slots partway. Adjust positioning until the sweep drop is snug, but not so tight that the door will not work smoothly. Tighten the screws.

Installing Weatherproof Thresholds

1 Removing the existing threshold. Shield the floor or carpet around the door with pieces of cardboard secured by masking tape. Try to remove the threshold with a pry bar. If it does not lift up easily, cut through at each end with a backsaw (*below*) and force up the center piece.

2 Knocking out end pieces. If the new threshold is the same height as the old one, tap out the ends with a mallet and chisel as shown below. Otherwise, saw through the door stops to heighten the opening and release the end pieces as well. Clean the sill with turpentine.

3 Installing the new threshold. Cut the threshold to fit tightly against both sides of the doorjamb. Position the threshold so that the flap side of the plastic seal is toward the outdoors. Lift the plastic flap and insert screws through the holes in the strip underneath.

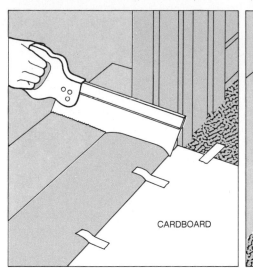

CARDBOARD

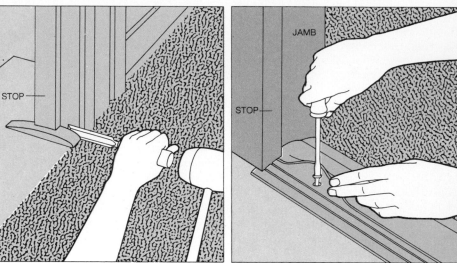

STOP

JAMB

STOP

Strips for Garage Doors

Sealing wood overhead doors. Paint the garage door bottom to protect it against moisture. Then cut stripping of thick rubber or plastic to length with wire cutters. Pull the door partway down so the bottom edge is accessible. Brace the door against a 2-by-4 and fasten the weather stripping with heavy nails so that the thickened edge of the channel is on the outside of the door. The material has enough resiliency to adjust for a tight seal against uneven concrete floors.

2-BY-4

Plugging Up All the Cracks and Crannies

Houses are built of a number of different materials working together to keep out drafts, dust, moisture and insects. Because these varied materials expand and contract at different rates with changing temperatures, cracks and gaps are bound to appear wherever two different materials meet. Traffic vibrations, the closing and opening of windows and doors, even the pressure of wind against the roof and walls widen these openings. If you add together all these unintentional vents in an average house—around the windows and doors, at the spots where the pipes and wires enter the house, and in a surprising variety of other places (drawing, opposite, top)—the total space would equal a hole 2 feet square.

You can choose among dozens of sealant materials to caulk these gaps. All are air- and watertight. The easiest way to use them is to get handy 11-ounce drop-in cartridges that fit a caulking gun (page 264). Each of these available sealants in the table below has been assigned to one of three performance groups. At the lowest level, in the basic group, are ropes, cords and sealants based on natural oils and resins. These have the least durability. The intermediate group, consisting mainly of natural or synthetic rubbers, adheres better to most building materials and is elastic enough to accommodate moderate movement in a crack. Advanced synthetic materials make up the high-performance group—the most costly of the three, but in most cases worth the additional investment. These are the most versatile of all sealants and the easiest to apply as well as the longest lasting.

In fact, silicone rubber sealant is so durable that its working life has yet to be determined.

All sealants work best when applied to joints that are about the same width as depth. If a joint is too deep, it can be filled with a compatible filler material or plumber's rope oakum. Joints that are too shallow should be raked out.

Foam caulk, which is not covered in the table, comes in handy aerosol cans. On application, it expands rapidly to fill large voids with insulating foam.

Soap and water or a damp cloth is the recommended cleanup for most sealants—before they have been cured; mineral spirits may be used with butyl rubber caulk. A fully cured bead of caulk can usually be trimmed with a knife; be careful not to undercut the seal.

A Sealant for Every Surface

	Special uses	Sealant	Durability (years)	Adhesion	Shrinkage resistance
Basic performance	glazing	oil and resin caulks	3 to 5	fair to good	poor
	very wide gaps	polybutane cord or rope	1 to 2	none	excellent
Intermediate performance	indoor and protected surfaces	nonacrylic latex; PVA	3 to 5 or more	good, except to metal	fair
	indoor and outdoor	acrylic latex	3 to 10	excellent, except to metal	fair
	metal-to-masonry	butyl rubber	4 to 15	excellent	fair
	concrete	neoprene; nitrile	15 to 20	good	good
High performance	anywhere	siliconized acrylic latex	15 to 20	good	excellent
	anywhere	polysulfide	10 to 20 or more	excellent	excellent
	anywhere	polyurethane	20 to 30	excellent	excellent
	anywhere	silicone	20 to 50	good, excellent with primer	excellent
	anywhere	ethylene copolymer	10 to 20	excellent	excellent
	anywhere	solvent-based acrylic	10 to 25	excellent	excellent

Finding gaps and cracks. The house at left is highlighted in dark green at the points where caulking is generally needed. If your chimney rises along an outside wall, caulk the line at which it meets the siding. One trouble spot is not shown in the drawing: The point at which the pipe or wire enters from an unheated attic, basement or crawl space; always caulk that entry point.

Judging a sealant. All the sealants in this chart are general-purpose caulks for wood, masonry, metal and glass, but many have areas of special usefulness, as listed. Use the other columns to match a specific sealant to your needs. Keep in mind that new sealant products are often introduced to the market, and that manufacturers' trade names rarely indicate the composition of a sealant or of a cleaner to use at the end of the job—read the fine print on the label to find the generic names shown here.

Adhesion is a measure of a sealant's ability to bond to a surface; shrinkage resistance measures its ability to stay there under changing conditions. A sealant is tack-free when it loses its initial stickiness; in the curing stage, it hardens and dries to its final form. For sealants that need primers, follow the manufacturer's instructions.

Tack-free (hours)	Cure (days)	Primer	Paint	Comments
2 to 24	up to 1 year	needed on porous surfaces	should be painted	lowest initial cost; may stain unprimed surface; shrinks with aging
remains moist and pliant		none needed	should not be painted	often used for temporary or seasonal caulks
¼ to ½	3	none needed	optional	tub-and-tile caulk; not for outdoor use
¼ to ½	3	needed on porous surfaces	optional	easy to apply in cool weather and on relatively damp surfaces
½ to 1½	7	none needed	optional	high moisture resistance; relatively difficult to make into a neat bead
1	30 to 60	none needed	optional	toxic; apply only when ample ventilation can be provided
2	5	prime porous surfaces	optional	relatively easy to apply; must be applied at temperatures above 40° F.
6 to 72	14 to 60	neoprene primer needed	optional	nontoxic when cured, but may irritate skin when it is applied
24	14 to 30	recommended	optional	relatively easy to apply; nontoxic when cured
1	2 to 5	prime porous surfaces	some can be painted	high moisture resistance; can be applied at low temperatures; nontoxic when cured
2	14	needed on asphalt, some plastics	optional	may be applied at low temperatures; do not use on plastics
1 to 7	14 to 21	none needed	optional	super-adhesive; apply only above 60° F.; usually must be heated for application

Five Ways to Seal Cracks

Most of the newer and more efficient sealants are usually applied with a caulking gun. The most popular type uses individual cartridges *(top, right)* that are thrown away when empty. Getting a smooth flow of sealant—a proper bead—may require practice. So if you are doing the job for the first time, make a few trial strokes.

While a caulking gun is best for most jobs, some small repairs are more conveniently done in other ways *(opposite):* caulks that are squeezed like toothpaste from a collapsible tube, glazing compound that is pressed into cracks with your fingers, ropelike strands that are pushed into place and filler that must be tamped into openings. Whatever you use, thoroughly clean the area around a crack, removing old sealant and chipped paint with a wood chisel or putty knife. Wipe the crack with turpentine, then use a stiff brush to get rid of remaining dirt. Do not try to caulk when temperatures are below 50° F.—the sealant will be too hard to handle easily and it will not stick to the cold surfaces.

Using a caulking gun. Hold the gun at a 45° angle to the surface and squeeze the trigger with a steady pressure. Keep the gun slightly slanted in the direction you are moving and draw it along slowly so that the sealant not only fills the crack but also overlaps the edges.

To get a smooth bead, fill a single seam in one stroke if you can. Pressure inside the cartridge will keep pushing out the sealant after you release the trigger; to avoid getting a lumpy bead, where several strokes are necessary, release the trigger quickly at the end of each stroke and continue to move the gun as you slowly squeeze the trigger for the next stroke. When you want to stop the flow of sealant altogether, disengage the trigger by turning the plunger so that the teeth point upward and then pull the rod back an inch or so.

The Versatile Caulking Gun

Caulking manufacturers package their products in standard cartridges that fit interchangeably into a caulking gun. The gun pushes caulking out of the cartridge with a trigger-activated plunger. To load a caulking gun, turn the plunger rod so that the teeth face up and pull it back as far as you can. Insert the cartridge in the top opening and press the nozzle firmly into the slot at the front end. Turn the plunger rod so that the teeth face down and engage the trigger mechanism. After loading the cartridge, snip off the sealed tip of its nozzle at a 45° angle. The nozzle is tapered so you can make an opening for a thin, medium or heavy bead. Next, insert a nail through the tip to puncture the seal at the base of the nozzle. After use, plug the nozzle with the nail.

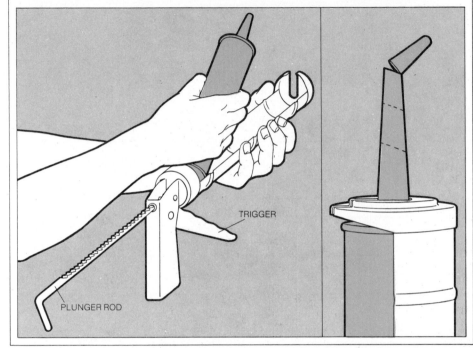

TRIGGER

PLUNGER ROD

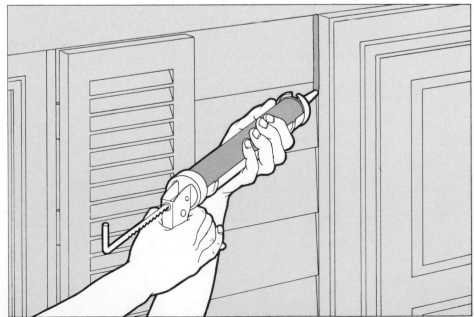

Using a roll-up tube. For sealing around outside water faucets (below), vents and other small areas, use a squeeze tube. Snip the tip off the nozzle in the same way as for a gun cartridge (opposite, top right) to give a bead of the desired size. Apply the sealant by squeezing the tube from the bottom—much as you would a toothpaste tube—and draw it slowly across the crack.

Sealing with glazing compound. To keep cold air from leaking around the joint between glass windowpanes and their frames, press this soft, sticky material along the edge of the glass with your fingers. Then smooth it with a putty knife. Turpentine can be used with the knife in order to make a smoother finish and it can also be used with a rag to clean off excess compound.

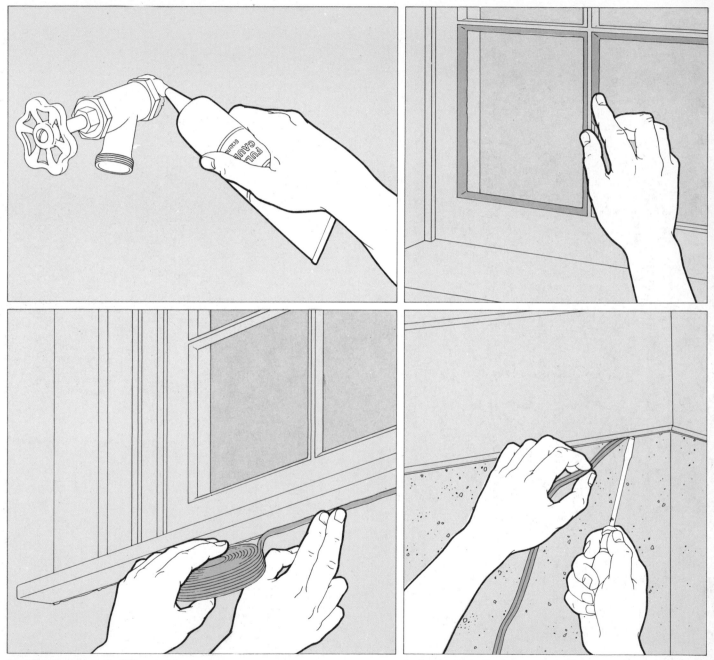

Applying ropelike caulk. This material, especially useful for temporary seals and hard-to-reach corners, can be unrolled in single or multiple strands, depending on the size of the crack. Press it in with your fingers—wetting them will make them less likely to stick to the sealant.

Sealing large cracks. For a crack more than ½ inch deep—common at the joint between siding and foundations (above)—first plug the crack with sponge rubber or oakum. The latter is durable but very oily. Push the filler into a crack with a screwdriver or putty knife. Then apply one or more beads of sealant with a caulking gun.

Storm Windows that Fit Inside

One way to weather-tighten a house is to install storm windows that mount on the inside. These seal off most air leakage that slips past aging window sash and trim, are easy to install and do not detract from the windows' inside appearance; you can also work comfortably no matter what the weather.

A set of inside storms can be fitted even to off-sized windows. Made of rigid clear plastic, they are available in kits that include a plastic frame *(right),* or they can be made at home from scratch in a version that screws directly to the window molding *(bottom).* Either type does almost as effective a job as an exterior storm window. Because of the interior location, however, condensation can form on the inside of the pane facing the existing window. Since the water can damage both paint and wood, the plastic pane may have to be taken out periodically to remove the condensation.

Assembling and Installing a Ready-Made Window

1 Cutting the pane. For a tight, draft-free seal, the framed storm window should be wide enough so that its edges overlap flat areas on the existing window molding. Measure the width between flat areas. Measure the height the same way unless there is a sill. In that case measure to the top of the sill. From these measurements subtract twice the width of the mounting frame, and use the results as dimensions for the pane.

Use a grease pencil to mark these dimensions on the plastic sheet for cutting. Place the sheet on a nonabrasive surface and, with a straight length of board as a guide, use a sharp knife to score each cutting line several times from edge to edge. Snap the sheet along the scored lines.

2 Making the frame. Cut four pieces of frame material to fit around the panes, making side pieces longer than top and bottom pieces. If the window has a sill, cut the bottom piece from the sill framing *(inset)* supplied in the kit. Snap the pieces of frame material to the edges of the glazing.

Strip the protective tape from the frame's adhesive backing. Center the bottom of the new window on the sill or bottom molding of the existing window and press firmly. Working upward, position the frame so that it sticks to the window trim. Once the frame is attached, the pane can be removed by snapping open the frame.

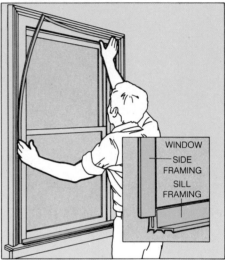

Custom-Building a Window

Cutting the pane. Cut ¼-inch-thick rigid clear plastic to the dimensions of the window trim as measured in Step 1 at top; do not allow for a frame. If the existing window has no sill, drill pilot holes for 1-inch wood screws around the entire perimeter of the pane, ½ inch from the edge and 8 inches apart. If the window has a sill, drill holes only along the top and sides of the pane.

If there is no window sill, stick adhesive-backed weather stripping around the entire back of the pane, alongside the edges. If the window has a sill, attach weather stripping along the top and sides; for the base, stick it to the bottom edge so the cushion fits between pane and sill *(inset).* Hold the pane against the window molding and screw it to the molding with 1-inch wood screws. When the window is removed for the summer, fill the screw holes with wood furniture plugs, available in most hardware stores. The plugs can be painted the color of the window trim.

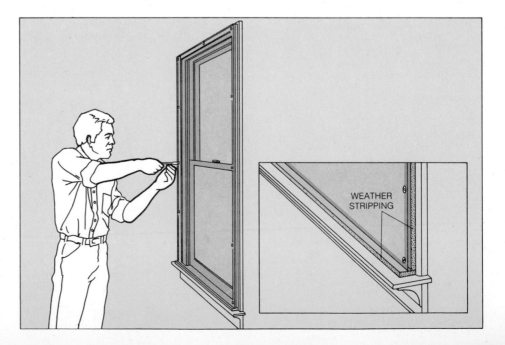

Replacing a Storm Door

Even though a storm door was tight when new, it can develop leaks as it ages; the appearance may also deteriorate faster than the door's weather-sealing ability. Although a wide selection of replacement storm doors is available, the simplest models to install come hinged in an aluminum door frame. To install this variety, remove the old door and its hardware, then caulk and screw the new storm door in its place. New storm doors are available hinged on the right or on the left. To facilitate passing through, it is best to hinge a new storm door on the same side as the door it replaces.

If your door frame is not a standard size, buy a storm door slightly smaller than the frame and build out the jamb with strips of wood. These are best glued and screwed to the old frame using an outdoor caulking-cartridge construction adhesive; door bottoms often adjust longer or shorter.

1 **Measuring the door frame.** To find the size door you need, remove the old storm door and its hardware, measure the width of the doorway from the jamb, then measure the height from the threshold to the head jamb. Storm doors are available in sizes that fit standard doorways, generally 2½ to 3 feet wide and 6 feet, 8 inches high. After buying the door assembly, check its fit before going further: The shape of the threshold may interfere with the fit of the frame base. If necessary, cut the rear corners of the frame with a hacksaw so that it fits flush with the threshold (inset).

2 **Caulking the door frame.** Once the storm door and frame assembly correctly fit the existing opening, remove them and set aside. Where the doorjamb and doorstop of the existing frame meet, apply a line of butyl rubber caulking around the entire frame. Apply a line of caulking around the extreme outer edge of the doorjamb (inset).

3 **Installing the storm door.** Set the door and frame assembly into the existing frame so the back fits into the frame where the jamb and stop meet. Press it firmly into place to spread the caulking, then screw the side of the frame to the doorjamb through the holes provided.

Where to Insulate a House

Although houses come in a wide variety of shapes and sizes, all of them incorporate some of the elements of the dwelling at right. Using this drawing as a simple guide, make a check list of the walls, ceilings and floors that should be insulated in your own home to reduce your heating and air-conditioning bills.

The overall rule for insulating a house is simple: insulation should be present at any surface separating living spaces from unheated areas, since that is where heat loss occurs—and also where the sun's heat can make unwelcome entry in the summer. All exterior walls should be insulated, not neglecting any wall of a split-level house that rises above an adjacent roof. Any wall between a heated room and an unheated area such as a garage, utility room or open porch also demands insulation, as do floors separating living spaces from such unheated areas. And be sure not to overlook the overhanging portion of a room that projects out from the rest of the house.

If the house has an unheated cellar or crawl space, the floors above must be insulated. In the case of a finished basement, the below-ground walls require insulation. Similarly, the floor of an unheated attic calls for insulation, whereas a finished room in a heated attic must have an insulated ceiling and knee walls as well as protection for the ceilings and walls of all dormers.

Where insulation goes. Because heated air rises and is lost through the roof, the most critical insulation sites in this house are the floor of the unfinished attic *(far right)* and the roof above the finished attic *(right).* To complete the envelope protecting the heated interior from the unheated exterior, the exterior walls and foundation should be protected. Then come the ceilings of the unheated basement, garage and crawl space. Not to be neglected are such heat escape routes as dormers and overhangs, which should be blanketed with insulation.

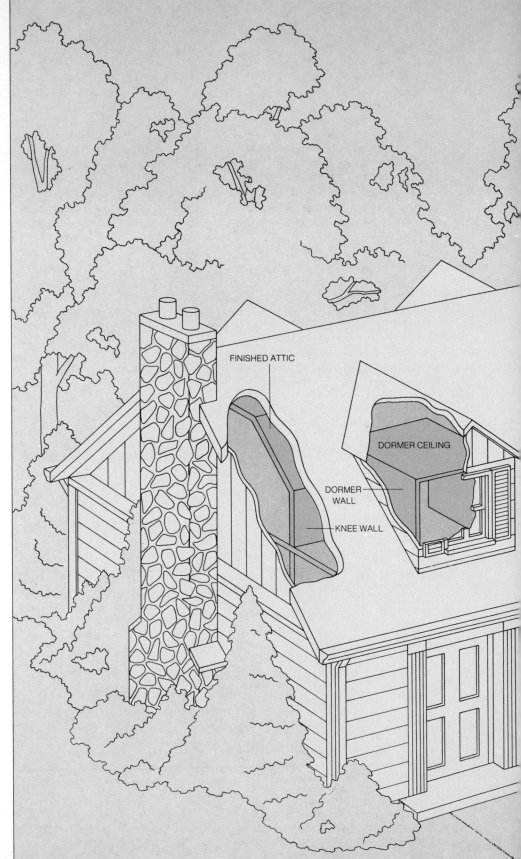

FINISHED ATTIC

DORMER CEILING

DORMER WALL

KNEE WALL

UNFINISHED ATTIC FLOOR

OVERHANG

UNHEATED GARAGE

FINISHED BASEMENT

CRAWL SPACE

A Guide to the Complexities of Insulation

All popular home insulating materials have certain features in common. Light for their bulk, they are fluffy or foamy—even rigid insulation boards have the feel of congealed foam. They have these qualities because they consist mainly of tiny pockets of trapped air.

The air pockets resist the flow of heat out of or into a house. Heating engineers rate the resistance on a scale of R-values, based on the amount of heat that will pass through a material. The R-value depends on both the composition and thickness of the material (chart, below).

By far the most common material used for insulation consists of fibers—fibers of glass; rock-wool fibers, made by blowing steam through molten rock; and cellulose, or plant fibers. There are two common ways of packaging this material: In long rolls that are called blankets, or precut flexible rectangular sections which are called batts (opposite, top).

Fibers can also be used as loose-fill insulation, poured or blown onto attic floors or into hollow walls. Besides fibers, loose fill may consist of pellets or granules, usually made of vermiculite (a form of mica) or perlite (volcanic ash).

The remaining insulating materials are man-made synthetics. One type comes in rigid boards or sheets and is widely used to insulate masonry walls, such as those found in basements. Another, called foamed-in-place, consists of plastic foam that flows around obstructions to fill a space completely, then hardens to a rigid mass.

By blocking heat flow, insulation solves one problem but introduces another. It increases the temperature difference between inside and outside wall surfaces. And temperature determines how much vapor air can hold; moisture that is vapor at the interior temperature turns into liquid at the lower exterior temperatures reached somewhere between the inside and outside of the wall. The condensed water makes insulation worthless, and damages paint and wood.

The solution to the problem is a vapor barrier—a layer of impervious material on the inside of the wall that prevents water vapor from reaching a section cold enough to make it condense. Most blankets and batts are sold with vapor barrier already installed as a backing. When using loose fill you can install a separate vapor barrier or cover the interior of an insulated wall with oil-base enamel paint and a top coat of alkyd paint.

Types of Insulation

Material	Approximate R-value per inch of thickness	Form	Advantages	Disadvantages
Vermiculite	2.08	Loose fill	Especially suitable for the spaces in hollow-core blocks	Low insulation efficiency; moisture-absorbent
Perlite	2.70	Loose fill	Easily poured into hollow spaces	Comparable to vermiculite
Fiberglass	3.33	Blankets, batts loose fill	Relatively inexpensive; fire-resistant	Particles can irritate skin; gives off odor when damp
Rock wool	3.33	Blankets, batts loose fill	Comparable to fiberglass	Particles can irritate skin
Polystyrene Foam	3.45	Rigid boards	Moisture-resistant; useful for below-grade floors and exterior walls	Combustible; easily dented
Cellulose	3.70	Blankets, batts loose fill	Fine consistency permits loose-fill installation through small access holes; does not irritate skin	Flammable unless chemically treated
Urethane Foam	5.30	Foamed-in-place, rigid boards	Highest insulation efficiency	Foam requires professional installation gives off noxious gases if ignited

Comparing insulation materials. Although insulation is marketed under a bewildering variety of trade names, almost all of it uses one of the basic materials listed by their generic names on this chart. Fiberglass and rock wool account for more than 90 per cent of all insulation sold in the United States and Canada, but the others have distinctive forms or properties, listed in the last three columns, that make them preferable to fibers in some applications.

The materials are ranked in an ascending order of resistance to heat flow, or R-value. The R numbers, given here as R-value per inch, cannot be simply added or multiplied for greater thicknesses—a glass fiber batt 6 inches thick, for example, does not have exactly six times the R-value of a 1-inch batt. The exact rating, however, is printed on all blankets, batts and boards (the 6-inch fiber batt will be rated R-19—the value recommended for exterior walls in most of the United States and Canada). When you buy loose fill, look for bags that indicate the R-value of the insulation at different thicknesses.

How Insulation Is Packaged

Blankets. These rolls of insulation are sold in thicknesses of 1 to 7 inches, lengths of 16 to 64 feet, and widths designed to fit snugly between standard stud spacings. Blankets usually have thin marginal strips, called flanges, for stapling, and a vapor barrier of paper or foil, but they also come without a barrier. Blankets are difficult to cut and are best for long runs of unobstructed space: between floor joists in an unfinished attic or between rafters in a roof.

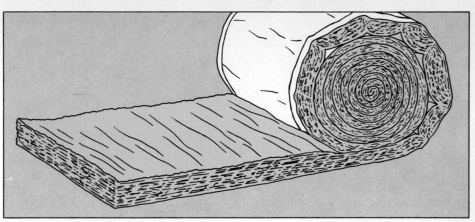

Batts. These are simply short blankets, cut into uniform lengths of 4 or 8 feet for easier handling—the 8-foot length fills the space between studs in a standard wall; an 8-foot batt plus a 4-foot one completes a common joist run of 12 feet. Batts without attached vapor barriers can be squeezed between joints without fasteners.

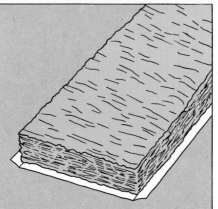

How a Vapor Barrier Works

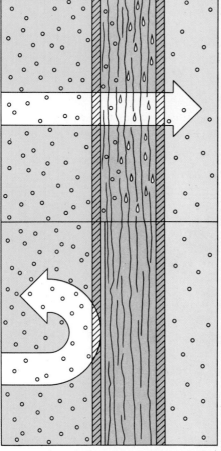

Rigid boards. Constructed from lightweight plastic foam, rigid insulation is supplied in sizes from 8-inch squares to 4-by-12-foot sheets. They provide relatively high insulation in thicknesses of ½ to 1 inch, and are often used as sheathing beneath aluminum or plastic siding. Because the plastic boards are flammable, they should not be left exposed or covered with wood paneling—on a basement wall, for example—but should be protected with gypsum wallboard, which resists fire.

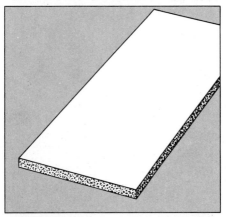

Loose fill. This type is easy to spread into open, flat spaces, such as unfloored attics, or to blow inside covered walls and floors through access holes. But it requires a separate vapor barrier, and unlike other forms of insulation, it settles, especially in walls or sloping areas. This can result in a loss of heat resistance over the years unless the fill is replenished occasionally.

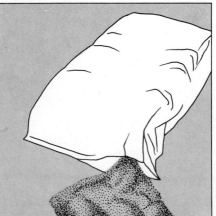

How a vapor barrier works. In winter, when the interior temperature of an insulated building is much higher than that of the air outside, warm, moist interior air releases its moisture as it passes through the insulation *(top)*, condensing into water inside the insulation and on the cold inner surface of the exterior wall.

A vapor barrier of aluminum foil, heavy plastic sheeting or waterproof paint *(bottom)* prevents water vapor from passing beyond the interior surface of the insulation—it never reaches a cold region and cannot condense.

How Much Insulation Do You Have?

Before you can estimate how much additional insulation your house needs you must find out how much and what kind it already has. A good place to begin your survey is in unfinished areas such as the attics, basements, crawl spaces and garages. If there is insulation in these areas it will be visible between joists, beams and studs; its thickness can be readily measured with a ruler.

Insulation inside finished walls can often be checked through existing openings. The most convenient are those for switches and receptacles *(below)*. If the wall has no outlets, look for less obvious openings. Remove the louvers of forced-air ducts and peek along the edge of the duct, or pry off a section of baseboard and chisel a small peephole through the wallboard; the hole will be concealed when the baseboard is replaced. As a last resort, drill or chisel a small opening directly into the wall; you can easily reseal the opening afterward.

Another important area of hidden insulation is the flooring of a finished attic. If the boards are simply butted alongside each other, you can pry one up for a look underneath it *(opposite)*. Tongue-and-groove boards are difficult to separate; instead, drill a small hole through one of the boards and the subflooring underneath, then use a pencil to measure the thickness of the underlying insulation *(opposite, far right)*.

To measure the thickness of insulation through an opening on the heated side of a wall or floor, you may have to make a fairly large tear in the vapor barrier. You can patch it with duct tape, metal foil or plastic sheeting before resealing the wall. If a check at an outlet box shows that the insulation in your wall is in the form of a blanket or batt, do not open a large tear for measurement purposes at that point; batts and blankets are usually compressed where they pass over and around electrical outlet boxes, so that any measurement is likely to be misleading. If you think the insulation does not fill the 3½-inch depth of most wood-frame walls, you will have to open a hole in the wallboard or plaster to verify your suspicion.

Once you know the thickness and type of your existing insulation, you can estimate its approximate R-value by mul-tiplying the thickness in inches by the R-value per inch as shown in the table on page 270. For example, if you find that you have about 3½ inches of fiberglass, multiply 3.5 by 3.33—the R-value of an inch of fiberglass—for a total R-value between R-11 and R-12. If you find that the stud cavities are filled with perlite loose fill, the R-value is 3.5 times 2.70, or between R-9 and R-10; similarly, 3½ inches of urethane foam translates into an R-value between R-18 and R-19. Once you have determined the R-value of your existing insulation, you will be able to calculate how much you must add to reach the optimum R-values for your areas, as illustrated on page 286.

Sometimes, however, simply adding insulation to the right R-value is not enough. If you find that your existing insulation has been soaked by moisture or partly melted by fire, it is best to remove it if you can and substitute new material.

You may have even more unpleasant surprises awaiting you when you peer behind walls, ceilings and floors of an old house. Sawdust and rags—both highly flammable—have been used as insulation in the past. So have stacks of bricks, which have almost no insulating value at all. Adobe and sod were the insulation in many Western homes, and solid wood planks and corncobs filled that role in early New England dwellings. All of these materials should be removed, if possible, and replaced with modern insulation.

Measuring Inside a Wall

1 Cutting an opening. To check the insulation of a finished wall, use the existing openings around electrical outlet boxes. First turn off power to the circuit serving that outlet; if you are not sure of the circuits, turn off the main electric switch at the service panel. Then unscrew the cover plate to expose the metal box. You will usually find a crack between the sides of the box and the plaster or wallboard. Widen this crack to about ¼ of an inch with a cold chisel and a hammer.

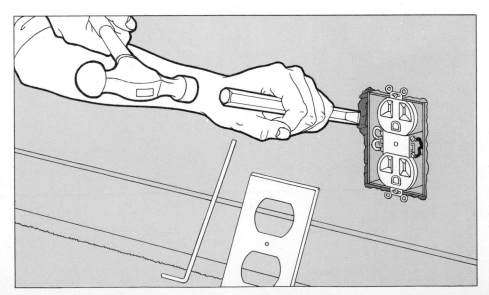

2 **Determining the type of insulation.** Use a flash-light to see if any insulation is visible inside the crack. If you find a vapor barrier *(pages 270-271)* just inside the opening, you probably have blanket or batt-type insulation. The only way to add more insulation is to remove the wall completely or to blow in loose fill through holes in the exterior wall.

If you find insulation without a vapor barrier, you probably have loose fill or foamed-in-place insulation. To identify the type of loose fill, insert a hooked length of stiff wire into the wall cavity and pull out a sample. To find out whether the fill has settled in the wall, leaving uninsulated gaps near the ceiling, place the palm of your hand against the wall every 3 feet, starting at the baseboard and working toward the ceiling; for a more precise test, use a thermometer, with its bare bulb pressed against the wall and the back of the bulb insulated from the heat of the room by two or three layers of tape. If you notice a sharp temperature drop (i.e., 10° or more) toward the ceiling, the fill has settled; the cavity should be refilled.

Measuring Under a Floor

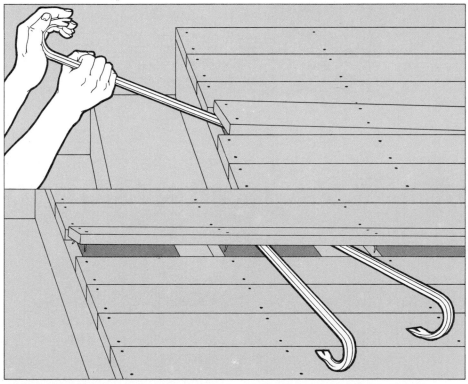

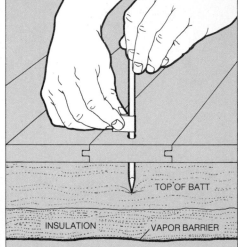

Butted floorboards. If your attic floorboards are simply nailed alongside each other, use a pair of pry bars to free a board without damaging it. At the attic entrance, work one of the bars under the board and pry the end up as far as you can. Move to a new position from which you can insert the second bar underneath the raised side of the board and pry the board upward slowly but

firmly. Repeat the process until you have raised the entire board from the joists below it. The insulation can now be identified and measured with a ruler. Afterward, nail the board back in its original position.

Tongue-and-groove floorboards. Do not attempt to raise a board of tongue-and-groove flooring. Drill a ½-inch hole in the middle of a board between two joists; insert a sharpened pencil into the hole, point first, until you feel resistance as the pencil touches the top level of the insulation. Use masking tape to mark the pencil level with the floor surface. Then push the pencil down through the insulation until the point reaches the vapor barrier. (If the vapor barrier is not flush with the ceiling below, you will feel additional resistance as the point penetrates the barrier.) Mark the pencil again at floor level and withdraw the pencil; the distance between the marks is the thickness of the insulation. Use a hooked length of wire to remove a piece of material for identification. Plug the hole with a dowel.

273

The Attic: Where Insulation Pays Off Most

Attic insulation is the most important in the house, not only because heat is lost up through the attic in winter, but also because attics build up heat in summer. So insulating your house begins here, whether your attic is simply an unfinished, unheated, unused space without a floor *(below)*; an unfinished, probably unheated, storage area with a floor *(pages 276-277)*; or a finished room, heated and perhaps even occupied. And do not forget the stairway or access hatch; in most homes, it acts as a gaping hole for heat transfer. However, do not seal your attic space completely; adequate insulation must be combined with adequate ventilation to be most effective.

The most practical insulation for the attic is batts of glass fiber or mineral wool *(page 271)* that come with an attached vapor barrier. Loose fill is often spread into the spaces between floor joists, but it requires the addition of a separate vapor barrier. Batts are more convenient to handle than blankets in the confined spaces under the roof, since they are pre-cut to maneuverable lengths. Batts are also used as an extra layer over existing floor insulation; for this application, slash any vapor barrier to avoid trapping moisture between insulation layers. Remember that the packages of batts appear compact, but they will expand more than four times their thickness once opened; unwrap one package at a time.

If your attic is unfinished and unfloored, you will probably need to install temporary lighting and flooring. Hang one or more safety lights, set walkway boards across several joists (the exposed ceiling will probably break if you step on it) and lay down other boards to support the insulation. You will need a serrated knife or dull handsaw to cut the batts, and a staple gun. Wear gloves, a breathing mask and goggles, and consider a hard hat: you might hit protruding roofing nails under the eaves.

Batts for an Unfinished Floor

Installing a vapor barrier. If you use loose fill or batts or blankets lacking a vapor barrier, you must also install strips of polyethylene plastic to block moisture. For the joist spaces in an unfinished floor, cut strips a few inches wider than the floor joists. Lay them into the spaces before installing the insulation. Staple them to the sides of the joists without gaps or bulges. Do not lay a continuous sheet up and over or across the joists. Patch gaps and tears with masking tape 2 inches wide. Separate vapor barriers can be similarly installed between wall studs or rafters.

1 Laying batts between joists. Start at the eaves on one side of the attic, pushing the batts just far enough in between to cover the top plate *(inset)*. Do not jam the batts tightly against the eaves because that would block the flow of air through the attic space. Install the batts with vapor barrier side down, toward the heated part of the house. Fill several rows at a time while working toward the attic center. Repeat, working in from the opposite eaves. When the batts meet in the center of the attic, compress their ends to butt tightly together.

2 Cutting batts. Set the batt on scrap plywood or boards to provide a working surface. Compress the batt as shown below, putting a 2-by-4 or long straightedge tool along the line of the cut. Cut with a sharp serrated knife or dull handsaw.

3 Fitting batts around obstacles. Cut the insulation to fit snugly around protruding objects and compress it to slide under wires. Batt ends should butt against each other at cross braces; separate the layers to slide below and above the braces. Wrap a chimney with heavy-duty aluminum foil and add noncombustible insulation.

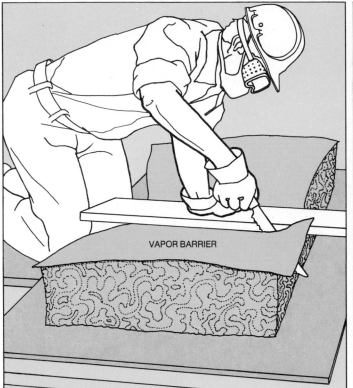

VAPOR BARRIER

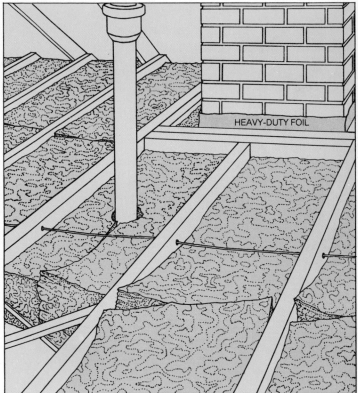

HEAVY-DUTY FOIL

An Extra Layer for Extra Protection

Adding insulation. Top the present layer with loose fill or batts with no vapor barriers; if they have vapor barriers, slash them with a knife so moisture is not trapped within insulation layers. If the existing insulation is level with the tops of the joists, nail 2-by-6 supports to the sides of the joist every 4 feet along two middle rows. These supports, which should stick up about 6 inches above the joists, will support a new walkway over the new insulation. Lay the new batt at right angles to the joists, following the preceding instructions for laying, cutting and fitting batts.

Insulating an Attic Ceiling

An unfinished attic with a floor can be insulated simply by stapling batts between the studs on the end walls and also between the rafters of the roof *(right)*. But it is more effective to hang insulation below the roof peak, if necessary installing "collar" ceiling beams to support the batts. The space between the beams and the peak of the roof, when combined with vents, will act as a channel to remove excess heat in summer and water vapor in winter. The collar beams can be 2-by-4s nailed across rafters, but if you use 2-by-6s, with ends that are beveled to match the slope of the roof, you will be one step closer to finishing your attic.

Insulating without collar beams. Fit batts between the rafters with the vapor barriers facing you. Do not push the batts all the way to the roof, but leave some air space between the batt and the roof for ventilation. Staple flanges to the edges of the rafters every 6 inches, and butt the ends at the roof peak, overlapping the flanges. Insulate end walls as in Step 3 *(opposite)*.

VAPOR BARRIER

Batts for a New Room

1 Installing the beams. Cut 2-by-4s to span each pair of rafters across the attic at a convenient ceiling height, making them long enough to reach the roof sheathing at both ends. Drive nails through the beams into the sides of the rafters.

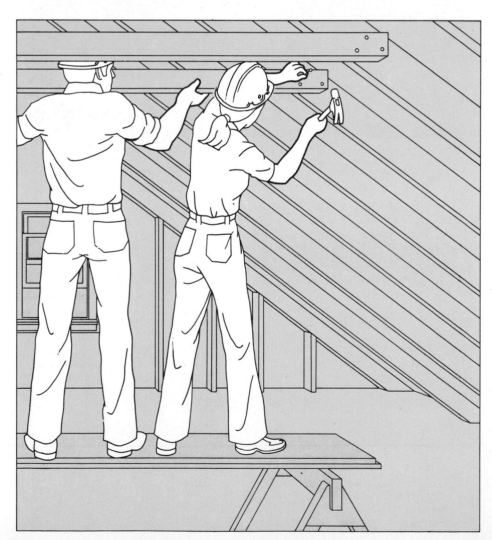

2 **Installing roof and ceiling batts.** Staple batts of insulation to the edges of the collar beams, with the vapor barriers facing you. Space staples at 6-inch intervals. Then staple batts between rafters from the collar beams down to the floor. Do not try to run continuous batts up the rafters and across the beams; they will gap. Tape the edges of insulation where the collar beams and rafters meet, to make a continuous vapor barrier.

3 **Insulating the end walls.** Install batts between the wall studs with the vapor barrier facing you. Trim the batts to fit all angles, and wedge pieces of batts around windows or louvers.

VAPOR BARRIER

VAPOR BARRIER

VAPOR BARRIER

Insulating an Attic Access

Access to an unfinished attic—whether it is an open stairwell or just a hatchway—can be a major hole in the swathing of insulation that holds heat in or out, undermining the hard work you put in packing batts between floor joists, collar beams and rafters.

If there is a stairway, make sure it has a door, and glue a rigid insulation board to the back. If possible, fill the spaces under and around the treads of the steps with loose fill (right). Hatchways present more of a challenge. The best way to seal cracks around the opening is to build an insulated box in the attic that encloses it as well as any stairs or ladder it contains. The top of the box is provided with a hinged lid you push up as you climb.

TOP TREAD

LOOSE FILL

Insulating stairs. Pry up the top tread and pour loose fill to fill the cavity under the stairs. Spread the insulation with a long-handled rake as you proceed. If the wall studs on either side of the staircase are exposed and uninsulated, fit batts between them; if there is a door, glue rigid insulation boards to its back (page 284).

A Box for a Hatchway

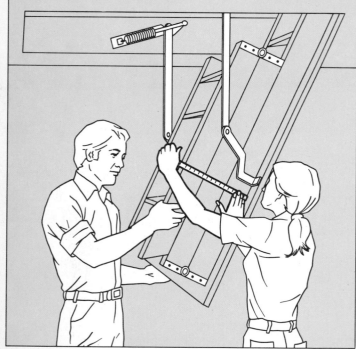

1 Measuring the stairway depth. If the hatchway contains pull-down steps, lower them but do not unfold the folding type. Measure the thickness to determine how much clearance the stairs need when they are raised into the attic.

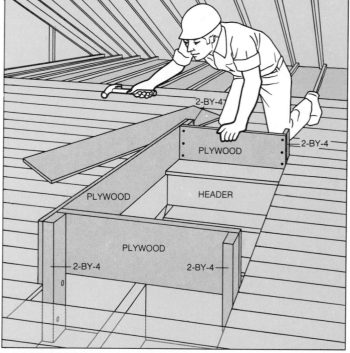

2-BY-4

2-BY-4

PLYWOOD

PLYWOOD

HEADER

PLYWOOD

2-BY-4

2-BY-4

2 Building the box frame. Remove flooring and insulation from around the stair opening. Saw 2-by-4 uprights long enough to rise above the floor joists 2 inches more than the measurement made in Step 1. Nail an upright to each joist behind the corners at the ends of the hatchway. At the top of the stairs, place the uprights 10 inches back from the opening, to provide a step in the attic. Then nail ½-inch plywood to the uprights. Replace any removed flooring.

3 **Finishing the box.** Cut a length of 2-by-4 to match the height of the plywood; nail it through the plywood into the upright at two corners of the box on the side where the lid will be attached. Then nail to each upright another 2-by-4 that projects 8 inches higher, so that the lid can rest against them when it is open.

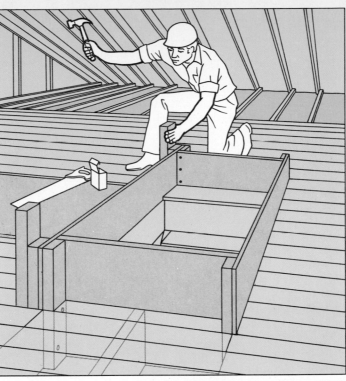

4 **Covering the frame.** Saw a lid from ¼-inch plywood, big enough to extend to the outer edges of the four original uprights. To prevent warping, put a 2-by-4 down one long edge of the lid, nailing through the plywood into the 2-by-4. Attach the other side of the lid with bolt-held hinges to the outside of the frame on the side of the box with the uprights (*Step 2*). Attach a door handle to the inside of the lid at a point that allows you to conveniently pull the lid down.

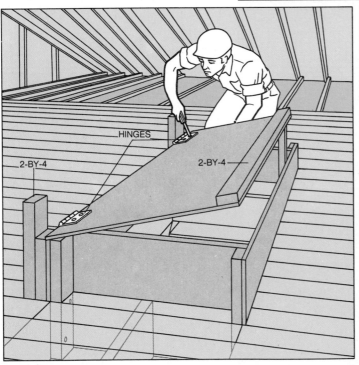

5 **Insulating the box.** Cut two batts slightly longer than the short sides of the box and compress them snugly between the end uprights, with their vapor barriers against the plywood. Trim two more batts to fit the long sides of the box and staple their flanges to the sides. Place another batt or batts, vapor barrier down, on top of the lid and staple the flanges to the lid.

Down Below: Barriers to Stop Cold, Conserve Fuel

Because warm air rises, some homeowners assume that a well-insulated attic is all they need to keep it in . But an insulated basement or crawl space is an expensive nuisance. If it is heated, it needs insulation as much as any outside room. If it is both unheated and uninsulated, it may make the floors above it cold, wasting expensive fuel and causing chills.

The worst offenders are spaces with unfinished dirt floors. Cover such floors with plastic sheeting—preferably 6-mil opaque polyethylene. Then, if the space is unheated, install vents in the walls to prevent condensation from occurring on basement beams and ground-floor walls. Finally, apply the insulation itself.

In a heated basement or crawl space, lay the insulation against the walls *(pages 283-285)*. In an unheated space, it goes against the ceiling *(below)*, in batts or blankets pushed, vapor-barrier side up, between the floor joists overhead and held in place with wire braces.

This ceiling insulation does not meet all the problems of an unheated space. All heating and air-conditioning ducts should also be insulated. You may be able to buy duct blankets 2 inches thick for this purpose. If you cannot get them, cut your own from the same insulation you used between the floor joists, cutting sections to fit around the ducts, not along them. For minimum waste in cutting, use blankets rather than batts. Make sure the vapor barrier faces you, that all exposed duct surfaces are covered and that seams are completely sealed with duct tape. If ducts hang so low that they might be bumped into, wrap them with 15-pound building paper to protect the vapor barrier against damage and punctures.

In cold climates, water pipes in an unheated basement or crawl space may also need insulation to conserve heat on hot-water lines. (Insulation will not prevent freeze-ups in cold-water lines.) Use preformed pipe insulation, which is sold in precut lengths and in a wide range of diameters, and apply pipe-insulating wrap. If you use preformed insulation, be sure to tape the joints with duct tape for a complete seal. Insulate the fittings, too *(page 282)*, so that no part is exposed.

Insulating the Unheated Spaces

Working with batts and braces. Push a batt of insulation, vapor-barrier side up, into the spaces between the floor joists overhead. The barrier should just touch the subflooring. Every 16 inches or so install wire braces—cut from wire clothes hangers a bit longer than joist spacing—so that they barely touch the blankets; crushing insulation reduces its effectiveness.

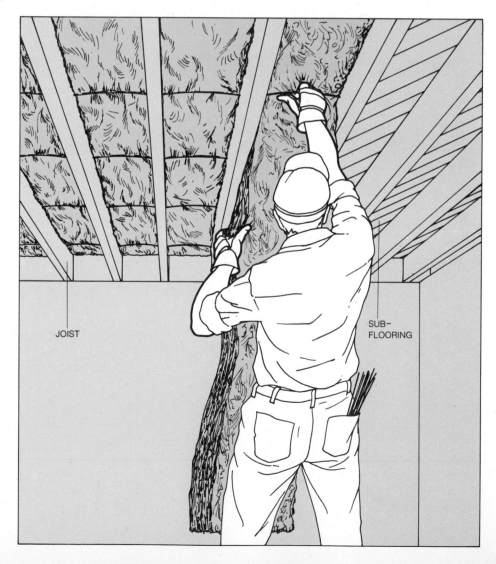

JOIST

SUB-FLOORING

Wraps for Ducts

1 Working with blankets and tape. To cover a duct, use sections of insulation cut from long blankets and wrapped crosswise around the duct. To find the length of each section, multiply the thickness of the insulation by four and add the circumference of the duct. To find the number of sections you need, divide the length of the duct by the width of the blanket. Wrap the sections around the duct, vapor barrier out, and seal the seams between the sections with duct tape.

2 Cutting the section for the duct end. Before finishing the horizontal duct, lay a patch of insulation against the furnace side of the vertical duct that rises into the floor overhead. Cut a final section of insulation to fit around the bottom and sides of the horizontal duct end and extend beyond the end to a distance half the width of the duct. Tape this section in place and cut the insulation beyond the end of the duct along the dotted lines shown in the drawing below.

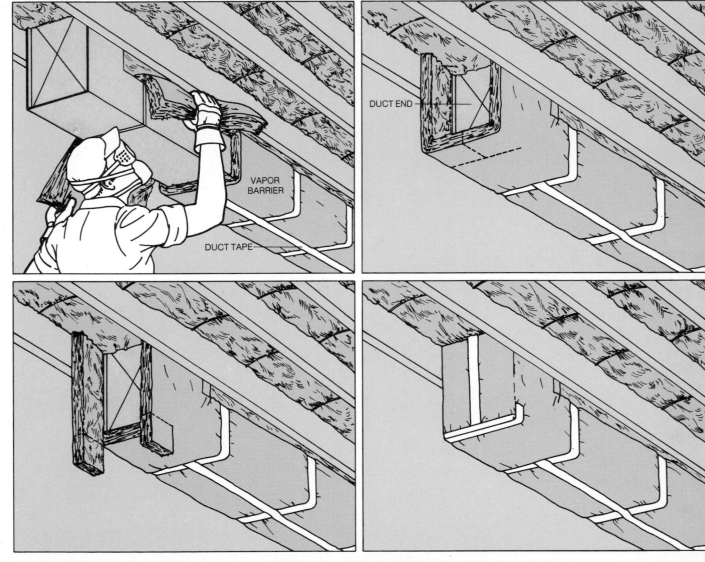

VAPOR BARRIER

DUCT TAPE

DUCT END

3 Trimming the tabs. Cut off the excess insulation at the end of the duct—two tabs hanging down from the bottom of the wrapped portion —as indicated by the dotted lines (*above*).

4 Sealing the end of the duct. Fold the flaps of insulation beyond the end of the duct to cover the front of the vertical duct. If the final section does not fit the duct, so that the flaps do not meet, cut a piece of insulation to fill the gap. If the flaps are too wide, trim them to meet. Seal the last seams with duct tape and, if the insulated ducts hang below the top of your head, cover them with 15-pound building paper.

Insulating a recessed duct. To insulate a duct nestled between two joists, cut blanket sections long enough to reach the outside edges of the adjoining joists. Push the insulation an inch or so back from the ends of each section, leaving the vapor barrier intact. Wrap the insulation around the bottom of the duct with the vapor barrier out, and staple the exposed barrier to the bottoms of the joists. For the part that enters the floor overhead, cut a section that extends beyond the edge of the duct for a distance equal to the thickness of the insulation; cover the end of the duct with a patch of insulation and seal all seams with duct tape.

Sleeves for Piping

1 **A close-fitting sleeve.** Clean the pipes, scraping off any rust and sealing all leaks, however small. Cover the pipes with lengths of cylindrical pipe insulation and glue any lap down tightly. To make short sections of insulation, cut the insulation with a utility knife or a handsaw.

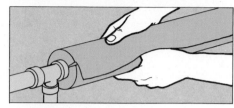

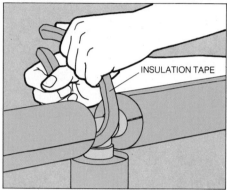

2 **Taping the fittings.** Cover the pipe fittings with insulation tape ¼ inch thick. Be sure to cover the fittings completely: no part should be exposed to air. To complete the job, wrap both the pipe and the fittings in aluminum foil.

A Vapor Barrier for a Dirt Floor

Laying plastic strips. Cover an unpaved basement or crawl-space floor with strips of 6-mil polyethylene plastic, with overlaps of about 6 inches. Strips about 3 feet wide are easiest to work with. Use duct tape to fasten the end of each strip to the wall 2 inches above the ground, and tape the plastic down where the wall meets the ground. Trim off excess plastic and weight the overlaps with bricks or stones.

Floors in older houses and in houses where air conditioning is used frequently have some moisture content; in these cases, cover only about 70 per cent of the soil area in order to avoid a sharp drop in the moisture content, which would cause the floors to shrink or warp.

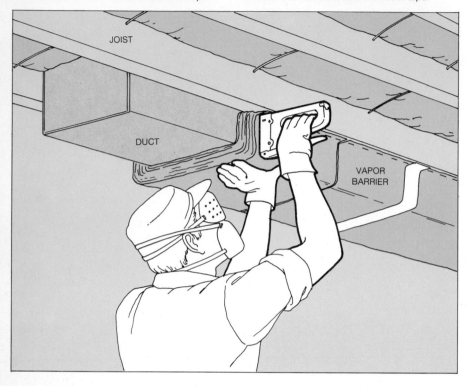

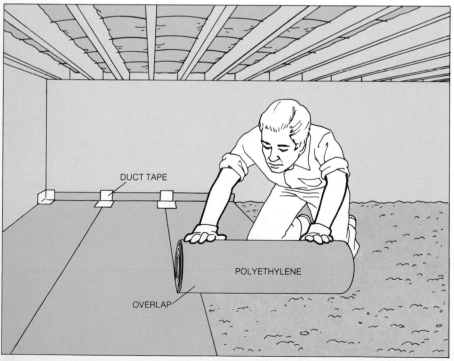

Insulating the Warm Spaces

Since their functions are dissimilar, heated basements and heated crawl spaces are not insulated alike. A heated unfinished basement, potentially part of the living area of a house, must be insulated with compact materials in a way that makes finishing the space easy. A heated crawl space in a one-story house can never be lived in, of course, but it can be part of the house heating system. In some houses it serves as a huge duct, called a plenum, through which heat passes on its way to the living area above. Even a well-insulated plenum is relatively inefficient. Before insulating a heated crawl space, consider the advantages of ducts to carry the heat from its source to the living area—the ductwork may save enough fuel to compensate for its cost. If ducts cannot be installed, you can greatly reduce heat loss by covering the ground with a polyethylene vapor barrier, and by draping the walls and part of the ground with insulation blankets as shown on page 285.

For insulating the walls of a heated basement, the material commonly used is rigid foamed plastic. It is installed between furring strips, to which gypsum wallboard (not wood paneling) is nailed, covering and protecting the flammable plastic from fire. Be sure to get board with a Class A fire-rating stamp; it has the lowest rate of combustion. The space between the top of the wall and the subflooring is filled with flanged blankets.

Heated Basements

1 **Attaching furring strips.** Cut 1-by-2-inch furring strips to frame each window and load a caulking gun with construction adhesive. Then run a bead of adhesive around the window and press furring strips into the adhesive. In the same way, apply furring strips in all corners and at the tops and bottoms of walls. Within this framing, mount additional furring strips in a grid pattern to fit the panels of rigid insulation board—often 4 by 8 feet. If necessary, use a carpenter's level (below) and a plumb bob to check the horizontal and vertical alignment of the strips.

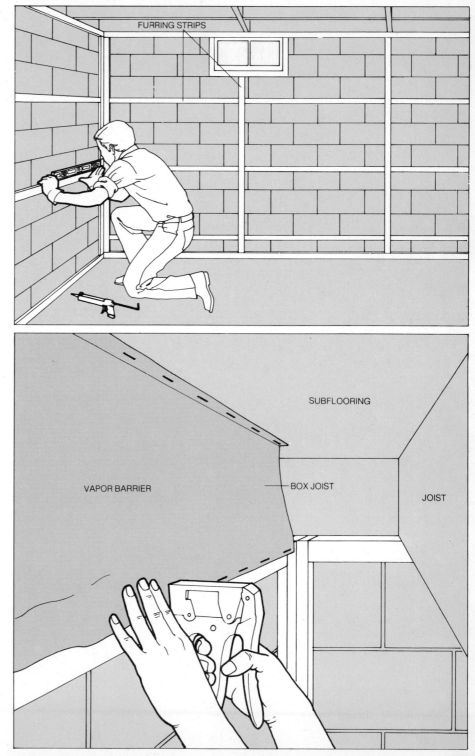

FURRING STRIPS

SUBFLOORING

VAPOR BARRIER

BOX JOIST

JOIST

2 **Insulating the box joists.** On walls that run in the same direction as the joists, the spaces between the top of the wall and the subflooring are called box joists. Use one-piece strips of flanged blanket for insulation. Install the blankets with the vapor barrier facing you and the insulation tucked into the contours of the space. At 6-inch intervals, staple one flange to the subflooring, the other to the top of the furring strip frame.

3 **Insulating headers.** The spaces enclosed by the ends of joists, the top of the wall and the subflooring, called headers, are insulated with sections of insulation blankets cut with a 1-inch overlap over the top of the furring-strip frame. Fit the sections between joists and staple the existing flanges to the joist sides. At the bottom of each section, push the fluffy insulation back an inch or so to form a bottom flange and then staple this flange to the furring frame.

4 **Fitting the rigid insulation.** Apply a compatible below-grade construction adhesive to the backs of the insulation boards in the amount and pattern specified by the manufacturer—a common pattern is shown below. Mount the insulation on the wall between the furring strips, cutting the boards to size with a utility knife or a handsaw. The boards must fill the spaces between strips snugly.

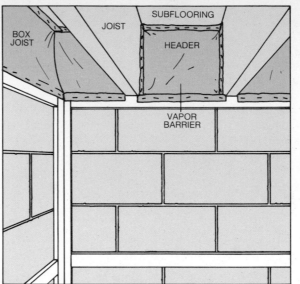

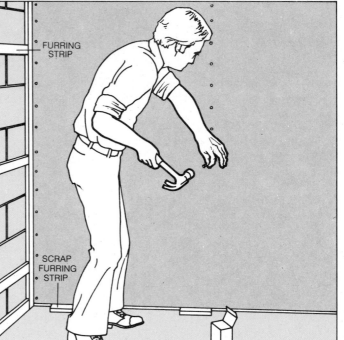

5 **Covering the insulation.** For fire protection, nail to the furring strips ½-inch-thick panels of gypsum wallboard. The wallboard should be used even if you plan to cover it with wood paneling. When attaching the wallboard, support the bottom edges temporarily on scraps of furring strip. When you pull the scraps from under the panels, the ¾-inch space left will protect the wall from any moisture that accumulates on the floor.

Heated Crawl Spaces

1 Insulating the box-joist walls. Lay single strips of polyethylene vapor barrier *(page 282)* along the ground next to the box-joist walls—the walls that run parallel to the joists. Then insulate these walls with sections of insulation blankets cut to the height of the crawl space from the ground to the subfloor. Fasten the sections to the walls, with vapor-barrier side facing you, by setting narrow strips of scrap wood along the top of each section, and nailing through the wood and the insulation to the box joist.

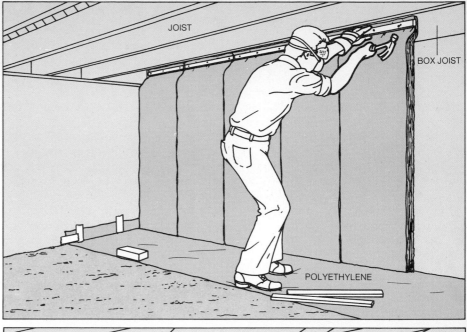

2 Insulating the corners. Starting at the end of the crawl space farthest from the exit, install corner blankets with one side butting against the box-joist insulation and the top flush to the subflooring. Trim the blankets to fit around the joists and fill in the corners with scrap insulation. Run these blankets down the walls and along the plastic strip to meet in the middle of the room. At the meeting point and at the bases of the walls, weight both strips of insulation down with bricks *(drawing, Step 3).*

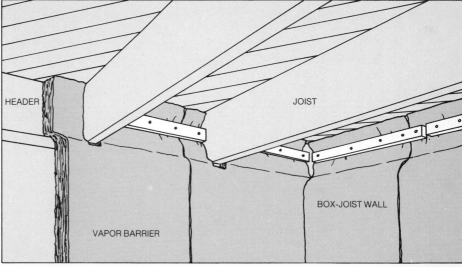

3 Completing the header walls. Lay a second strip of polyethylene vapor barrier on the ground and install a second width of insulation blankets to the header walls; in these and succeeding widths, run the insulation only 2 feet onto the floor. Continue laying polyethylene and installing insulation toward the exit until you reach the opposite box-joist wall; there, install two blankets *(Step 2)* extending across the polyethylene to meet midway.

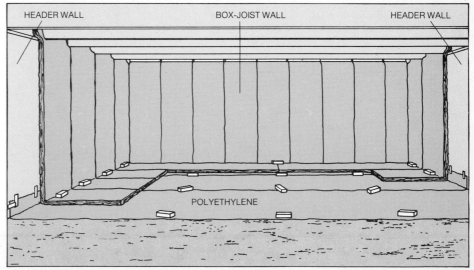

Calculating Your Cooling and Heating Needs

How big a furnace—oil, gas or electric—do you need for your house? How big an air conditioner? The answers, whatever the size, condition or location of the house, can be derived from a few simple observations plus some simple arithmetic. First you must take into consideration where you live and the quality of your weatherproofing (below): geography determines not only your primary heating or cooling needs but also the insulation and weatherproofing you should have; tighter weatherproofing can lower the cost both of buying and of running your new equipment.

The capacity of heating and cooling equipment is generally rated in British thermal units per hour, abbreviated as BTUH. (A single BTU is the amount of heat needed to raise the temperature of one pound of water by one degree.) For a gas or oil furnace, the BTUH rating is usually given as one of the basic facts of the unit; for an electric furnace, which is generally rated in watts, multiply the wattage by 3.4 to get the BTU equivalent; and for an air conditioner, multiply the tonnage by 12,000 for the same purpose.

The calculation of your own BTUH needs begins with the climatic maps opposite. The summer cooling map is zoned for typical maximum temperatures, the winter heating map for typical minimum temperatures and the effects of winter winds. In both maps, the zone numbers form the basis for BTUH calculations.

The numbers on the summer cooling map (opposite, top) indicate the area in square feet that can be cooled by 12,000 BTUH of equipment in a house with average weatherproofing. The BTUH requirements for a house with tighter or looser weatherproofing must be adjusted with a correction factor.

Determining BTUH for heating (opposite, bottom) is more complex. Once you find the base BTUH figure, and adjust it if necessary for a tight or loose house, additional calculations give a BTUH figure for a gas or an oil heater. A final calculation gives the BTUH for a furnace used to heat water as well as space.

The tightness or looseness of your weatherproofing depends upon factors of construction and quality. By far the most important of these factors is the amount of insulating material in the walls, floors and ceilings; others have to do with the sealing of chinks and cracks. A tight house has vapor barriers, tight storm doors and windows, new weather stripping and caulking, and more insulation than the average for its climatic zone, as listed in the insulation chart below. An average house has vapor barriers, somewhat loose storm doors and windows, and the average insulation listed in the chart. A loose house—typically, one built before 1930 and not insulated since—has no storm doors or windows, no weather stripping, caulking or vapor barriers, and little or no insulation.

Determining Your Insulation

Meeting a variety of conditions. The zones on this map reflect insulation practices ranging from those of Alaska, where temperatures may drop to -50°, to those of Florida, where the thermometer may rise above 100°. Used with the chart at right below, these zones indicate the average insulation needed for both cooling and heating. In northern regions, minimum winter temperatures and wind-chill factors determine insulation needs: the insulation works to hold heat within the house. In the South, high summer temperatures determine the needs: insulation works to keep heat from flowing into the house.

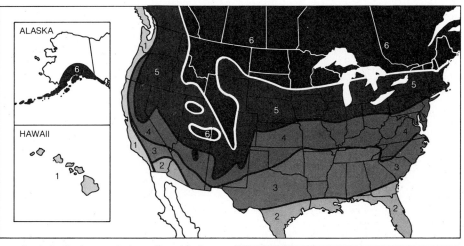

Average amounts of insulating material. The chart at right lists the actual R-values—a measure of a material's resistance to heat flow—of the insulation materials generally installed in well-built houses 10 to 30 years ago. Numbers in brackets indicate R-values for newer homes. To use the chart, determine the R-value of the insulation in your home, and check it against your zone number on the map above to see if it is above or below average. If you live between two zones, choose the zone with the higher value. Insulation is installed only within certain ceilings, walls and floors: in a ceiling below a roof or an unheated attic; in an exterior wall; and in the floor over an unheated basement or crawl space.

If you do not know the R-value of your insulation, check unfinished attics, basements or crawl spaces. If the insulation consists of batts or blankets, their R-values are printed on the surface. Inside walls there is no simple way to look for R-value markings. Poke around the outer edge of an electrical outlet box to pull out a sample of the insulation; take it to a building-supply dealer and ask its R-value, assuming the thickness is 3½ inches, sufficient to fill the wall space.

Zone	Ceiling or roof	*	Exterior wall	*	Floor	*
1	R-9	(R-19)	R-9	(R-11)	R-7	(R-11)
2	R-11	(R-26)	R-9	(R-13)	R-9	(R-11)
3	R-13	(R-26)	R-11	(R-19)	R-9	(R-13)
4	R-19	(R-30)	R-11	(R-19)	R-11	(R-19)
5	R-19	(R-33)	R-13	(R-19)	R-11	(R-22)
6	R-22	(R-38)	R-13	(R-19)	R-13	(R-22)

* Homes built in the last 10 years.

Summer Cooling Zones

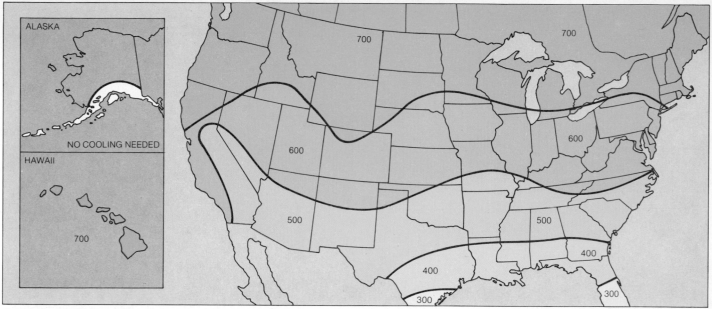

Calculating BTUH for cooling. Find your zone on the map. To determine the tons of refrigeration you need, divide the number of square feet that you wish to cool by your zone number; to convert the tonnage figure to BTUH, multiply it by 12,000. Thus, a house with a 500 zone number and 2,000 square feet of floor space needs 4 tons, or 48,000 BTUH, of refrigeration.

This figure is for a house with average weatherproofing *(opposite, top)*. A house with tight weatherproofing will require less refrigeration; a house with loose weatherproofing will need more. If your house is tight, multiply the base figure by 0.85—giving, in this example, an actual requirement of 40,800 BTUH. For a loose house, multiply the base figure by 1.3 to get the actual requirement—62,400 BTUH.

Winter Heating Zones

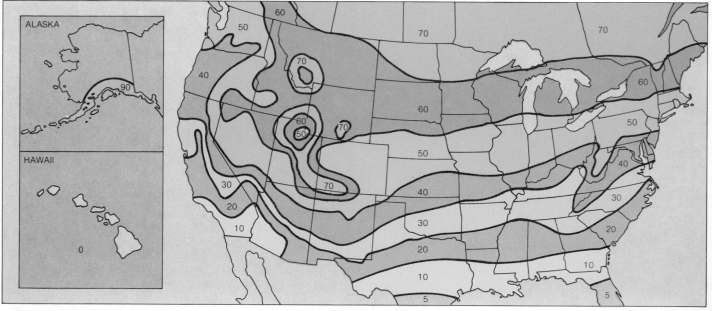

Calculating BTUH for heating. Find your zone on the map. Multiply your zone number by the square feet of floor space to be heated to find the base amount of BTUH. For a tight house *(opposite, top)*, multiply this figure by 0.7; for a loose house, multiply it by 1.5. For example, an electrically heated house in Zone 30 with 2,000 square feet and average weatherproofing needs 60,000 BTUH of equipment. If tight, the house needs 42,000 BTUH; if loose, 90,000 BTUH. To calculate the requirements for a gas or oil furnace, you must raise the adjusted case capacity. For gas, multiply the adjusted base capacity by 1.25; for oil, by 1.3. (In the example above, the loose house requires a 112,500-BTUH gas furnace, or a 117,000-BTUH oil furnace.) If the heating system also heats the water supply, multiply the required capacity by 1.2. The loose house in the example would require a 108,000-BTUH electric furnace, a 135,000-BTUH gas furnace, a 140,400-BTUH oil furnace.

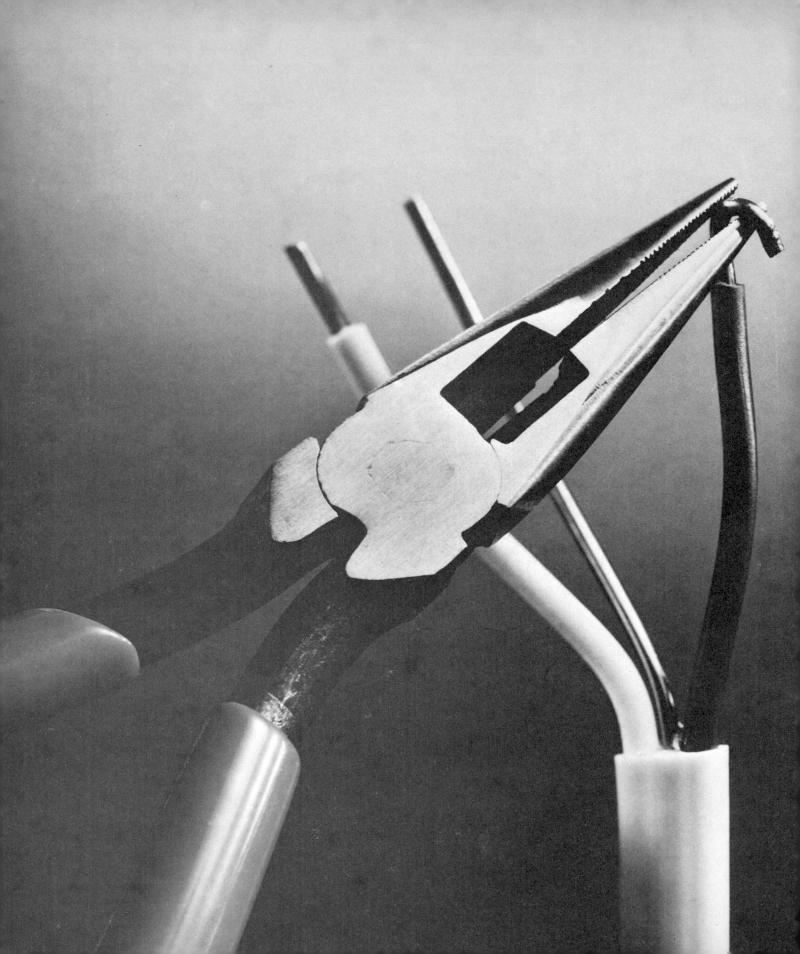

4 ELECTRICITY

The Multiple Pathways of Electric Current

Working with wiring is something that many homeowners are unwilling to do for themselves; electrical jobs seem to hold an aura of danger. Like many other misconceptions, this belief is built up from grains of truth—or no truth at all.

Many electrical jobs are in fact straightforward, orderly and, in the great majority of cases, surprisingly easy. Procedures and equipment are standardized and repairs are safe—providing you start your work by observing these two electrical safety rules: Always turn off the power before working on your wiring *(page 297)*. Before touching any wire, test *(page 301)* to make absolutely sure you have turned off the power.

Electricity originates as a stream of negatively charged particles called electrons. These particles are carried by a variety of materials—called conductors; metals conduct electricity, for example, so does the human body. Other materials, like plastic and rubber, are nonconductors or insulators because they do not carry electrons.

Electricity always travels from high pressure to low pressure. Since the earth is a zero-pressure point, electrons attempt to reach the earth—or ground. Anything that touches ground or is at the same electrical pressure as the ground is said to be "grounded," attracting the highly pressurized electrons in a wire. People must be particularly careful around electricity: Electrons will travel through any conductor that leads to ground, including the human body.

Two voltages—240 and 120 volts—usually enter the house via three service-entrance wires. Two of the wires are called hot wires; the third wire—called a neutral—is grounded. Located at the house service entrance, an electric meter *(page 293)* accurately measures how much power flows into your home. Nearby, a main service panel contains fuses or circuit breakers that protect against overload.

Fuses or circuit breakers are sized according to the gauges of wires in the circuits they serve. If too much current flows in a circuit because of an overload, a short circuit or a ground fault *(page 296)*, its fuse or circuit breaker instantly cuts off the power.

From the service panel, electricity travels around your home in insulated wires. House branch circuits are usually wired with cables, each containing three or four wires inside a protective metal armor or plastic sheathing. Colors of insulation or wires identify wire functions. Black- or red-insulated wire—called the "hot" wire—delivers 120 volts of current to lamps and appliances. White- or gray-insulated grounded wire carries the electrons at close to zero volts back to the service panel; this wire is called "neutral."

Green-insulated or bare copper grounding wire safeguards the system by providing a second path for electricity to return to the service panel *(page 298)*.

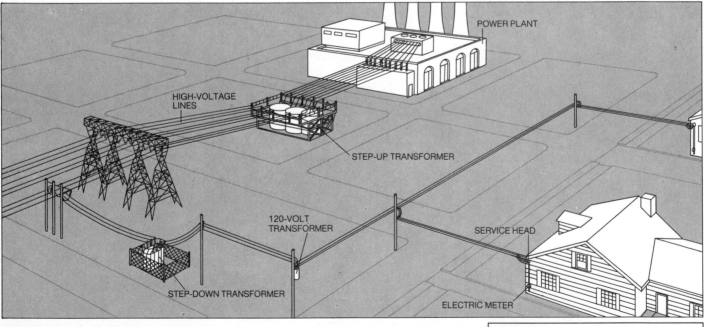

From power plant to home. On its way to your home, electricity generated at the power plant first flows through transformers that step up the voltage to as much as 765,000 volts—less energy is lost when it is transmitted at high voltage. Lines then carry the current cross-country. At points along the way, lines branch off and feed the power to step-down transformers that lower the voltage for local distribution. A final transformer lowers the voltage to 120 volts.

Electrical codes. The NEC (National Electrical Code) sets strict safety standards for electrical procedures and equipment. Before undertaking any electrical work, consult your local building authority to find out about national and local code requirements.

290

A variety of voltages. In most houses built in the last 50 years, electricity enters the house through the service head which is fed from the utility company's power lines. Electrical circuits, then directed by the service panel, create a round-trip path for electricity. In 120-volt branch circuits for lights and general purpose outlets, power goes out through a black (hot) wire and returns through a white grounded (neutral) wire. In 240-volt circuits, which power heavy appliances such as a water heater or clothes dryer, power exits the service panel through a cable's black and red hot wires. A combination 120/240-volt circuit, such as that used for the electric range, uses black and red hot wires and a white grounded (neutral) wire.

In all 240- and 120/240-volt circuits, the black and red wires are fed from opposite hot sides of the incoming service panel. Most house branch circuits serve eight to 10 outlets each, often located in adjoining rooms as shown below. A circuit begins its run from the service panel as a single cable. At a typical "middle-of-run" outlet, like that next to the television set, the incoming cable's three wires provide two current-carrying wires and an equipment-grounding wire. Another set of three wires in the outgoing cable continues the branch circuit to the next outlet. Other outlets, such as the one shown at the switch near the bedroom door, may be the junction point for three or more cables, each containing two

current-carrying wires and one equipment-grounding wire. These wires branch off in different directions. An "end-of-run" outlet—where the shaver is plugged in—is connected to a single cable because no other outlets are served beyond it. The two ceiling fixtures and their switches are connected to the circuit in different ways. The bathroom light is wired like a middle-of-run outlet with current-carrying and equipment-grounding wires entering and leaving its outlet box; its third cable is a switch loop that carries current only to and from the switch. The living room light, however, receives its power like an end-of-run outlet, with its black (hot) wire attached to the switch terminal.

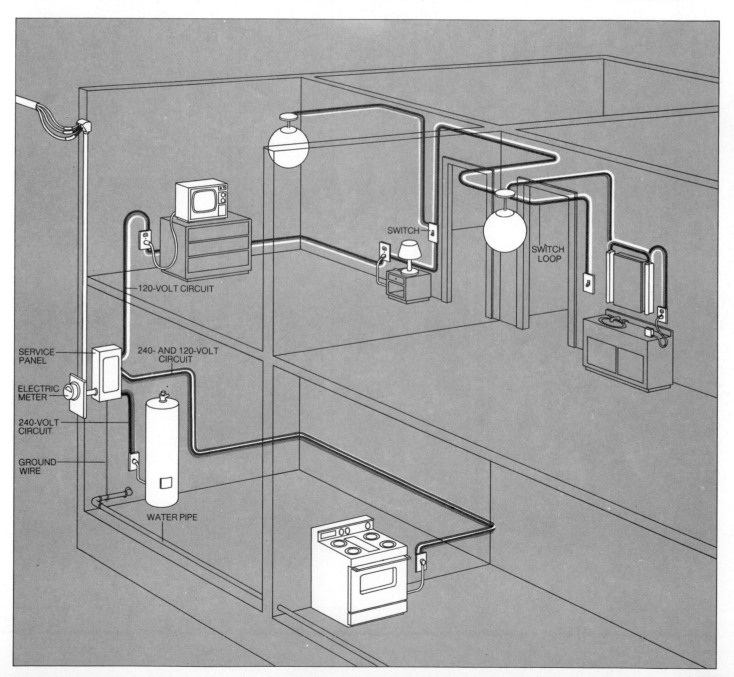

120-VOLT CIRCUIT

SWITCH

SWITCH LOOP

SERVICE PANEL

ELECTRIC METER

240- AND 120-VOLT CIRCUIT

240-VOLT CIRCUIT

GROUND WIRE

WATER PIPE

An Electrical Safety Checkup

A thorough electrical safety inspection of your house and grounds can pay off in home safety and peace of mind. Follow the guidelines below and take immediate action if you find any faults in your electrical system.

☐ Inspect all lamp and appliance cords. They should be routed where they cannot be stepped on; replace any frayed or otherwise damaged cords. For maximum safety, every cord should be fitted with a polarized cord *(page 298)*.

☐ Plug extension cords into polarized outlets, and do not nail or staple them in place, or wrap them around furniture.

☐ Read the tag on each extension cord to determine its rating, which should not exceed the power use of the lamp or appliance it serves. Note: If any extension cords are used daily, more outlets are needed.

☐ See that all outlets and switches work properly. Each should have a faceplate so that no wiring is exposed. Test whether plugs fit tightly into outlets, and whether they are cool to the touch; a hot plug may be a sign of loose plug connections.

☐ Place appliances such as television sets where air can circulate around them.

☐ Do not use portable electric heaters in a bathroom or around combustibles; position these appliances out of the path of traffic. *Caution: Make sure an electric heater has a power cutoff switch, in case it is tipped.*

☐ Check countertop appliances; when not in use, they should be unplugged. Keep appliances away from the sink and route the cords away from hot surfaces. For maximum safety, countertop outlets should have GFCI protection *(page 299)*.

☐ If you are shocked while touching an appliance, repair it—or have it repaired—immediately.

☐ If a major appliance vibrates greatly, it probably does not have a level, secure footing; adjust it accordingly.

☐ If your home has fuses, make sure that each one is the correct rating for the wires in its circuit *(page 297)*.

☐ Inspect all outdoor outlets; they should have weatherproof covers and GFCI protection *(page 299)*.

Installing dead-front plugs. Because older plugs with exposed terminals often cause short circuits when used with metal-faceplate outlets, the National Electrical Code now requires that all 15- and 20-ampere plugs be of the "dead-front" type (with no current-carrying parts except the blades exposed in front of a built-in cover). Always replace plugs with the dead-front variety; a three-pronged model is shown below. For maximum safety, convert all older plugs.

Checking fixture rating. The rating stamped on a lighting fixture tells you the maximum-size bulb to be safely used in it; if there is no rating, the fixture is designed to accommodate a maximum of 60 watts. If the bulb is rated higher than the fixture, replace the bulb with one of lower wattage. Caution: This is particularly important for recessed ceiling fixtures where cooling air circulation may be limited. If a fixture is overloaded, it can heat up and become a fire hazard.

Testing major appliances for ground. Set a multitester selector to "Rx1 Ohms." With the two test probes touching, set the Ohms scale to zero. Insert a long jumper wire into the D-shaped grounding hole of an outlet with the power turned off. Connect the free end of the jumper to one test probe and touch the other probe to the appliance body. The reading should be 0 Ohms; a higher or infinite reading indicates incorrect grounding; call for service.

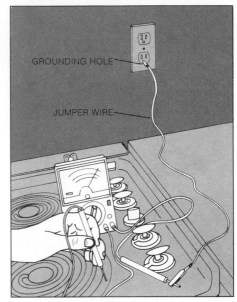

GROUNDING HOLE

JUMPER WIRE

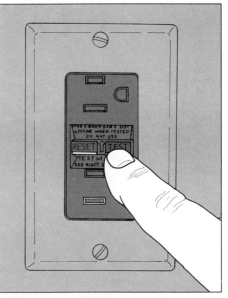

Testing GFCIs. Ground-fault circuit interrupters (GFCIs), commonly used in bathrooms, protect you against shock caused by electrical defects in tools and appliances, and should be tested approximately once a month. On a GFCI receptacle *(above)* or circuit-breaker GFCI, push the "test" button; it should trip the power off immediately. Press the "reset" button to restore electricity to the GFCI. If it fails to trip, replace it.

How the Electric Meter Works

As a water meter measures gallons or cubic feet of water used, an electric meter measures thousands of watt-hours, called "kilowatt-hours" (kWh). One kWh is the same as 1000 watts of electricity used for one hour—or 1 watt used for 1000 hours. For example, a 100-watt bulb burning for 10 hours consumes 1 kWh of power.

While lights and appliances operate, current supplying them flows through the electric meter. Meanwhile, a small motor inside the meter measures the power being consumed. Geared to a set of dials, the motor records current flow over time.

Many residential electric meters have five dials which—in order from left to right—show readings for 10,000 kWh, 1,000 kWh, 100 kWh, 10 kWh and finally 1 kWh. To read such a meter, start with the left dial and write down the number its pointer has just passed. (Note: Depending on the dial, the pointer may rotate clockwise or counterclockwise; numbers from 0 to 9 indicate in which direction each pointer turns.) Next—still working from left to right—record the remaining dial readings. If a pointer rests directly over a number (as the fourth pointers from the left in both examples below), its reading is affected by the dial immediately to its right. On the meter below (top row, right), for example, the pointer has just passed zero; the last two digits should be read as 50. On the meter below it, however (bottom row, right), the pointer has not yet reached zero; the last two digits here should be read as 49.

To make any electric meter reading meaningful, it must be compared with the previous reading. Subtract the previous reading to find how much power was used between readings. In the examples below, the top reading is 17650; the bottom reading is 18349. During the period between readings, 699 kWh was used. If the utility company charges 10 cents per kWh for electricity, this basic electric bill would be $69.90.

You can also use your electric meter to calculate how much it costs to run a major appliance such as an air conditioner or electric heater. When very little electricity is being used elsewhere in your home, turn on the appliance and take a meter reading; note the time. An hour or several hours later, take another reading. Pay special attention to the 1 kWh dial. Subtract the initial reading from the later one and divide by the number of hours between readings. Finally, multiply the result by your local electric rate per kWh; you can get this figure by calling your utility company, or calculate it from a recent bill. This is the appliance's running cost per hour.

The power usage of small appliances can also be found using the meter's horizontal dial (right, below); have all other power uses in the house turned off or unplugged for this test. Start the appliance being tested, for example a fan. Watch the dial to see how many seconds it takes for the black mark on the dial to make a complete revolution. Divide this into 3.6 times the meter's calibration constant—the number found on the meter face, typically 7.2 as shown at right, which indicates watt-hours of power usage. (If no such number appears on the meter, your utility company can probably give you the information.) Then multiply by the electric rate per kWh. This tells you the fan's running cost per hour and where consumption can be cut.

Common Electrical Terms

☐ **Amperes:** The amount of current passing a given point at a given time. Each electrical device has an ampere rating; each circuit is rated for a total number of amperes it can safely deliver.

☐ **Circuit:** A continuous path for electrical current. In a household electrical system, a branch circuit begins at the service panel, runs to various switches, outlets and fixtures and returns to the service panel.

☐ **Circuit overload:** Occurs when the combination of lights and appliances draws more amperage than the circuit can handle. Normally, a fuse blows or a circuit trips, interrupting the flow of electricity to the circuit.

☐ **Ground wire:** The bare copper or green-insulated wire that drains off current that escapes its normal path.

☐ **Hot wire:** A wire that carries current forward from the source. Often identified by black (or red) insulation.

☐ **Neutral wire:** Used to complete the circuit by carrying current back to the source. Identified by white insulation.

☐ **Short circuit:** When an exposed hot wire touches a neutral wire or a grounded metal box, the circuit will heat up suddenly. The fuse or breaker will shut off the power immediately.

☐ **Volts:** The strength, or pressure, of an electrical current is measured in volts. Household circuits are usually 120 volts, 240 volts or low-voltage.

☐ **Watts:** The rate at which electrical devices consume energy. Usually marked on the lamp or appliance.

A Tool Kit for Basic Wiring

Tools for the electrical repair and improvement jobs in this book are few in number and require only a modest investment; some of them may already be in your home tool kit. Buy only those extra tools necessary for the specific job you are about to undertake. In addition, you will need the general-purpose tools common to most households, such as an electric drill, cabinet-tip screwdriver, saws, a hammer and a nail set.

☐ TESTERS. Essential to any kind of wiring job are two inexpensive testers. The voltage tester has a neon bulb and two insulated wires that end in metal probes. Its main purpose is to check that the current is off before you begin a job. It is also used, with the power on, to test for proper grounding and, in some special circumstances, to check that voltage is available in wires. Standard voltage testers can be used on circuits carrying from about 90 to 500 volts. There is also a low-voltage tester that looks similar, so be sure to check the rating on the package before you purchase one. The continuity tester has its own source of power, a small battery, and is used only with the power off to pinpoint malfunctions in a removed wiring component—a broken switch or light socket, for instance.

☐ MULTIPURPOSE TOOL. Preparing wires to be attached to electrical devices is accomplished efficiently with a multipurpose tool that both cuts the wires and strips insulation from them. Wire gauges printed on the tool indicate which hole to use for stripping insulation without damage to the wire. Other uses include cutting small bolts and crimping special kinds of wire connectors.

☐ PLIERS. Two kinds are needed for electrical work. Long-nose pliers have striated jaws that hold wire firmly while you shape it for attachment to a terminal. A useful model is about 7 inches long and has a wire cutter near the pivot. Lineman's pliers are used for pulling wire, bending heavier wire and twisting out removable parts of certain electrical components. These pliers also have a wire cutter and striated jaws.

☐ FUSE PULLER. If your service panel contains cartridge fuses *(page 297)*, removing them for testing or replacement is done simply and safely with a fuse pul- ler, which looks somewhat like pliers but, for insulating purposes, is made entirely of plastic. Fuse pullers come in one size for cartridge fuses up to 60 amperes, and another for larger fuses.

☐ METAL SHEARS. Metal shears, or aviation snips, do a fast, neat job of cutting cable, and may also be needed to trim off metal flanges from certain components. Straight-cutting blades are preferable to cutting blades.

☐ FISH TAPE. Two fish tapes are necessary for pulling new electrical wiring through walls. Long fish tapes are wound around a metal reel, as shown; short ones come without reel.

☐ DRILL BITS. A ¾-inch spade bit drills a hole in wood through which cable can be run. Other sizes of spade bits may be needed for specific projects. To drill holes for running cable through masonry, use a ½-inch carbide-tipped masonry bit, the largest masonry bit that will fit a ⅜-inch drill. An 18-inch extension attachment is essential if you have to drill through thick or widely spaced beams.

☐ TAPE AND WIRE CAPS. The fasteners of electrical wiring, wire caps (also called wire nuts) and electrician's tape are used for making and securing wire connections. Buy an assortment of wire caps, sized according to the gauge of the wire you are working with. If you are extending or adding a circuit, you will also need cable staples to fasten cable to wood studs and joists. Buy the appropriate staple for the kind and size of cable to be used.

For extending wiring outdoors, you may need a conduit bender and perhaps a star drill, which is actually a special kind of chisel. Use it with a ball-peen hammer to make round holes for conduit in masonry. For chipping box-sized holes in masonry, use a forged-steel cold chisel; wear eye protection.

If you plan a large wiring project, such as wiring an addition to your house, you may want to consider a couple of special tools that make the work go faster. One is an automatic wire stripper, which with one motion cuts and strips insulation. Another is a cable ripper that makes a lengthwise slit in plastic sheathing without slicing the wires and their insulation. The sheathing is then folded back and cut off with scissors or a utility knife.

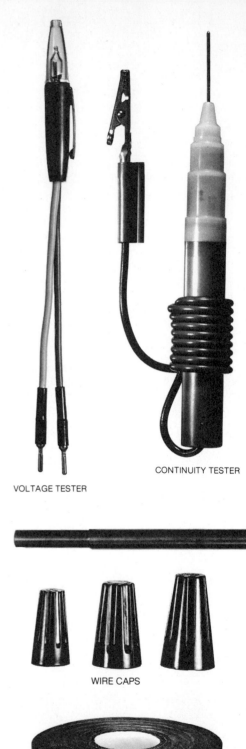

VOLTAGE TESTER

CONTINUITY TESTER

WIRE CAPS

ELECTRICIAN'S TAPE

FISH TAPE

LINEMAN'S PLIERS

LONG-NOSE PLIERS

MULTIPURPOSE TOOL

SPADE BIT

EXTENSION ATTACHMENT

MASONRY BIT

FUSE PULLER

METAL SHEARS

UTILITY KNIFE

Safeguards that Shield Against Dangers

Although overcurrents—in the form of overloads, short circuits or ground faults—are potentially dangerous, every home is protected by either fuses or circuit breakers. An overload occurs when a circuit draws more power than its wires are designed to handle continuously—for example, too many lights or appliances operating at the same time or a motor overworked because of lack of lubrication. A short circuit results when two current-carrying wires contact each other metal-to-metal; this can happen if a wire connection comes loose. A ground fault occurs when a hot wire comes into contact with something that is grounded or can conduct to ground—for example, the body of a tool or appliance. This type of overcurrent brings electrons outside insulated wiring, and can cause shocks to the device's user.

Because all overcurrents cause heat, they should be cut off immediately—before equipment is damaged, a fire starts, or someone is seriously shocked. While an overload can safely continue for a short time, a short circuit and ground fault must be stopped immediately. This is the function of fuses or circuit breakers—depending on your electrical system.

Fuses and circuit breakers clear an overloaded circuit after a short period of time and turn off the power to short circuits and ground faults within a fraction of a second—before any harm can occur. A fuse protects by a metal strip which melts; a circuit breaker protects by tripping its switch-like contacts. After the cause of a power interruption has been corrected, a blown fuse must be replaced; a circuit breaker is simply reset by pressing its toggle to "on" or, in some cases, to "off," then "on."

An overload can be diagnosed by figuring the load on the circuit; plug any excess loads into a circuit that is not overloaded. If your home has fuses, do not try to solve an overload problem by using a fuse with an amperage rating higher than the one that blew it—it can cause dangerous overheating of the wires. Should the problem persist, you may want to consider upgrading your home electrical system. Short circuits or ground faults that recur often could be a sign of wiring defects; in either case, call for professional advice.

Besides protecting your home's circuits and wiring, circuit breakers and fuses perform another all-important safety function. Because fuses can be removed and breakers switched off, you can turn off the power to a circuit and make repairs without any danger of shock.

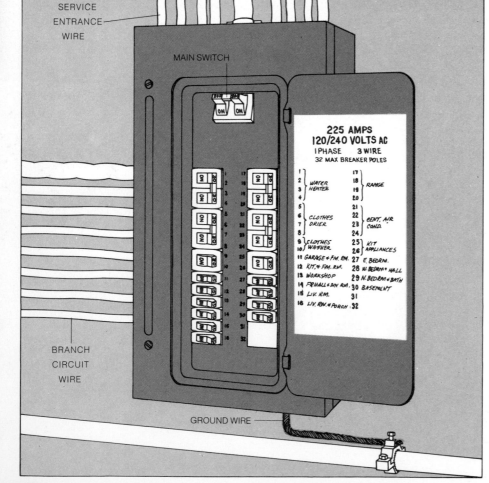

SERVICE ENTRANCE WIRE

MAIN SWITCH

ON ON

225 AMPS
120/240 VOLTS AC
1 PHASE   3 WIRE
32 MAX BREAKER POLES

1	17	
2	18	RANGE
3 WATER HEATER	19	
4	20	
5	21	
6 CLOTHES	22	CENT. AIR COND.
7 DRIER	23	
8	24	
9 CLOTHES WASHER	25 KIT APPLIANCES	
10	26	
11 GARAGE + FM. RM.	27 E. BEDRM.	
12 KIT.+ FM. RM.	28 W. BEDRM + HALL	
13 WORKSHOP	29 N. BEDRM + BATH	
14 FR HALL + DIN RM.	30 BASEMENT	
15 LIV. RM.	31	
16 LIV. RM. + PORCH	32	

BRANCH CIRCUIT WIRE

GROUND WIRE

Main service panel. Every home has a main disconnect where power to the whole house may be turned off. In the circuit-breaker type panel at left, a pair of heavy-duty 200-ampere circuit breakers at the top serves as the main disconnect. Moving these toggles down turns off power to the whole house. These main breakers also protect the service-entrance wires when all house branch circuits demand high power at the same time.

The panel's other circuit breakers protect branch circuits. Some breakers are linked to serve 240-volt branch circuits for appliances such as a water heater, kitchen range or clothes dryer. Since a 240-volt circuit is served by two hot wires from the incoming power, both breakers serving 240-volt appliances must be switched off simultaneously. Smaller single breakers (usually 15 to 30 amperes) are located at the bottom of the service panel and protect 120-volt circuits. The empty space shown at the bottom right of this panel permits the addition of new circuits and their breakers if necessary. A general description of the breakers and the locations they serve is usually entered on the service panel.

Turning off power. Fuses and circuit breakers enable you to turn off the power so you can work without getting shocked. To cut the power in a circuit served by a breaker, simply move the toggle to "off" as shown below. If the breaker is mounted vertically, turn it off in the downward direction.

Fuses must be removed to turn off the power in circuits served by them. Whenever handling fuses, the main disconnect should be off at the service panel.

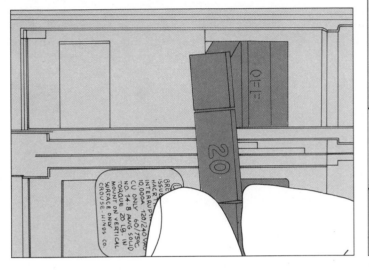

Removing a cartridge fuse. To replace a cartridge fuse, turn off the main power. Then open the box by throwing the switch lever to "off." Using an insulated fuse puller, grasp the middle of the fuse; pull firmly to release it from the spring clips. Do not touch the metal ends of the fuse; they may be hot. Push the replacement fuse into the spring clips with the fuse puller. When replacing a fuse in a panel block, pull the block out first.

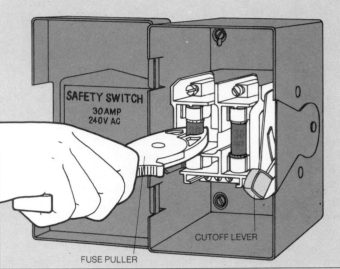

FUSE PULLER
CUTOFF LEVER

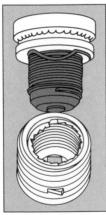

Type S fuse. Since type S fuses, also called nontamperable fuses, are required by the National Electrical Code for new fused installations, it is a good practice to replace older plug-type fuses with Type S fuses. Buy fuses and matching adapter bases that are correctly suited for the current-carrying capacity of each circuit in the fuse panel. No. 14 (AWG) copper wires use 15A fuses; No. 12 wires use 20A fuses; and No. 10 wires use 30A fuses. Lower-rated fuses than these may be used, but higher-rated ones may not. Fuses and adapters are screwed into fuse sockets in place of the old plug fuses, and, thereafter, will accept only the correct Type S fuses. Nontamperable fuses come in both standard (for lighting and other loads) and time-delay, used for motorized loads.

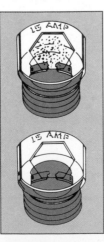

Detecting trouble. A glance at a blown plug fuse often reveals the cause of a circuit's failure. The high power draw of a short circuit or ground fault melts the center of the metal strip rapidly, vaporizing the metal and leaving a discolored window *(top)*. A lower-current overload melts the strip but leaves a clear window *(bottom)*. If you cannot tell the trouble from looking at a fuse, you may have to calculate the load when the fuse blew to tell whether an overload or a short circuit/ground fault caused it to blow.

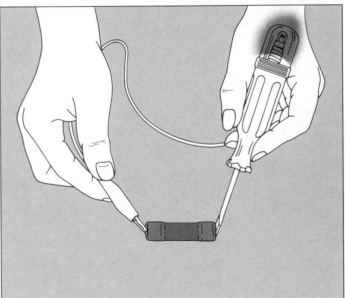

Testing a cartridge fuse. When a cartridge fuse blows, there is no visible sign. If an appliance on a circuit protected by a cartridge fuse fails, test the fuse to see if it has blown or the appliance has failed. Remove the fuse *(top),* and test it by touching a continuity tester's probes to each end. If the bulb lights, the fuse is good; the trouble is elsewhere. If the bulb does not light, the fuse is blown. Replace the fuse. If the appliance still does not work, call for professional repairs.

Grounding and Polarization for Safety

Because any deviation from the normal path of electricity is dangerous, a home electrical system is designed to ensure that path; it prevents hazardous shock in a number of ways. Insulation on wires protects you against being shocked by wayward electrons seeking ground; the grounding system, ground-fault circuit interrupters (GFCIs) and polarization work along with overload protection *(page 296)* for maximum safety.

A ground connection must run without interruption from every receptacle and box on a circuit to the service panel. There, along with the grounds from all other circuits, it is connected to a metal strip called the neutral bus bar *(opposite)*. The neutral wires from all the circuits—the normal return paths of current—are also connected to the bus bar. From a terminal on the bus bar a bare copper or green-insulated grounding wire provides the connection between the service panel and the grounding system beneath the earth.

If your home has older two-slot receptacles and a means of grounding is available, you can make your wiring safer by replacing the old receptacles with the three-slot variety. In some older systems that use two-slot receptacles, however, no means of grounding is available. In that case, you can increase your safety by replacing the old outlets with new GFCI receptacles *(opposite)*.

In addition, the National Electrical Code requires that the wiring in your home be color coded—or polarized—with the hot wire colored (usually black) and the neutral wire white. The use of polarized outlets and plugs maximizes this safety system, providing one continuous path for hot wires and one continuous path for grounded (neutral) wires throughout the home *(below, left)*. In a polarized circuit, the hot terminal (identified by its brass or dark color) on each receptacle and socket is connected to the circuit's hot wire; switches interrupt only the hot wire, ensuring that when a switch is turned off, no current flows to the appliance or lamp plugged into the receptacle. Likewise, the neutral terminal on each receptacle and socket connects with the neutral—grounded—circuit wire. Since the white wire is not interrupted by switches, it remains a continuous path to ground.

Polarized plugs—with one blade wider than the other—ensure polarization of lamps, radios, televisions, tools and many appliances. Grounding plugs, which have three prongs, are automatically polarized because the hot and neutral prongs are properly positioned in the outlet by the third (grounding) prong. These plugs must be used in a three-slot outlet, as shown below.

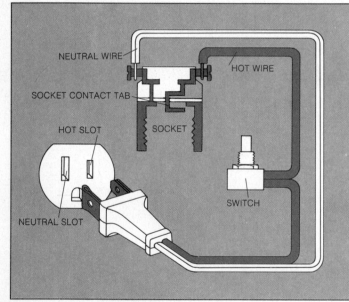

Polarization at the switch. In a properly wired lamp or lighting fixture, the switch interrupts the hot wire that carries current forward, ensuring that no electricity flows through the lamp or fixture when the switch is turned off. If polarity is reversed, an exposed socket can give a shock even though the switch is off. Polarization in a lamp *(above)* begins at the wall outlet. The narrow slot of the outlet is hot; when a polarized lamp cord is plugged into the outlet, power enters the plugs through the narrow prong and is transmitted through the hot, unmarked wire to the brass- or dark-colored socket contact tab.

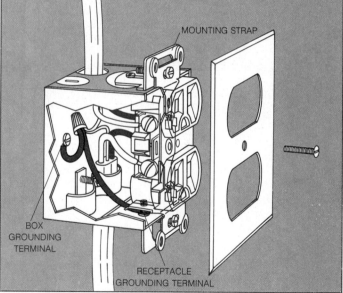

How a receptacle is grounded. Three-slot receptacles provide equipment-grounding protection for tools and appliances. All metal parts of an outlet and box that should not carry current, but might if something went wrong, are given emergency routes to a ground through the bare wire of the plastic-sheathed cable. This wire is spliced to short green-insulated or bare jumpers. One of these goes to the box grounding terminal which is part of the mounting strap. A three-pronged plug also contacts the mounting strap, grounding the equipment. A second jumper reaches to the box grounding terminal in a metal outlet box to ground the box.

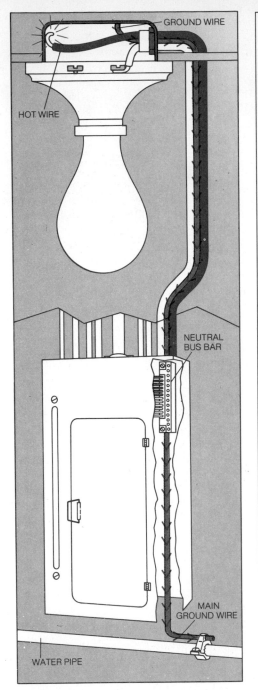

Grounding at the service panel. The main grounding wire is connected to a grounding system which may include underground water piping and a driven rod, providing excess current with a direct path to ground. In the house, a grounding wire provides an alternate path for leaking current; this protects the circuit from damage and the user from shock. In the example above, the hot wire has become disconnected from its terminal. Since the circuit cannot be completed via the neutral wire, the metal box would become electrified and dangerous. But the grounding wire picks up this leaking current and returns it to the service panel, where it will trip the breaker or blow the fuse.

The GFCI – A Lifesaving Device

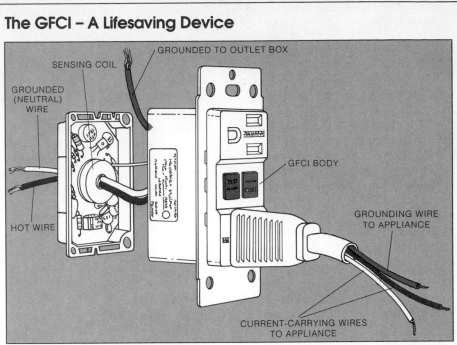

After mowing a damp lawn, a man stoops to unplug his electric lawn mower from an extension cord lying in the grass. As he picks up the plug, he is jolted by a severe electrical shock. Yet the mower cord was properly grounded and the circuit breaker in the service panel was in good condition. What happened?

In this imaginary—but quite possible—incident, the man was the victim of an electrical leakage too small to trip the circuit breaker but large enough to cause harm under certain conditions. A tenth of an ampere—about half the current required by a 25-watt bulb—can kill a person if it passes through the body for as little as two seconds. Usually this small current is difficult to maintain in the body. But on damp earth, the man in the example provided a good path from the leaky connection to ground, and when he picked up the plug, current flowed through his body into the earth.

Using a defective tool or appliance with the tiniest ground fault *(page 296)*—which may not even trigger the fuse or circuit breaker—can be dangerous. As protection against this kind of serious or fatal shock, the National Electrical Code now requires ground-fault circuit-interrupter (GFCI) outlets in bathrooms, garages, basements, swimming pools, spas and outdoors. They are also recommended in workshops, laundry rooms and other damp locations. For maximum safety when working outdoors, always use extension cords that are GFCI-protected *(page 300)*.

A GFCI protects the circuit—and you—by tripping instantly when it detects a leak in current. Even when the leakage is not enough to trigger the fuse or circuit breaker, the GFCI takes immediate action. A GFCI uses a sensing coil *(exploded view above)* which measures current in—and out of—the device through the hot and grounded wires. As long as the current in and out are equal, no ground-fault leakage is taking place. But if the in-current exceeds the out-current, some current is leaking away through the ground fault. Switch contacts inside the GFCI body open within 1/40 second—less time than it takes for a human heartbeat—turning off all power before a person can be seriously shocked.

GFCI outlets are widely used and can be purchased inexpensively to take the place of standard receptacles found in the home; connect each GFCI according to the instructions that come with it. You can use a replacement GFCI to protect any single outlet, or install one in the first outlet box in the circuit, protecting all outlets along that circuit; the instruction sheet will tell you how to identify the first box. Make sure each GFCI outlet in your home works properly by testing it approximately once a month *(page 292)*.

Working Safely with Electricity

When you work with electricity, you are dealing with potentially dangerous current. But, by taking the appropriate safety measures and precautions, most repairs can be rendered safe.

Before beginning any repair on a branch circuit, always turn the power off by flipping the circuit breaker or pulling the fuse affecting the circuit you plan to work on. (When handling fuses, the main switch should be off.) To ensure long-term safety of the work after it is done, follow standard electrical procedures exactly—take no shortcuts—and test the finished job with the power on: Use a voltage tester to check from the black wire to the grounded metal box and to the white wire; the voltage tester should light. Check from the white wire to the grounded metal box; the voltage tester should not light.

Whenever you do an electrical repair, keep yourself and your home safe by following the applicable safety tips below.

☐ Always shut off the power before you begin work. If you are working on a branch circuit, turn off the circuit breaker or pull the fuse. Be sure to take basic safety precautions: Dry any water on the floor; protect your body from making a circuit to the ground (below, left); have a plastic flashlight stocked with fresh batteries at a convenient spot near the service panel so that you do not have to change a fuse in the dark.

☐ After you have turned off the power, label or lock the service panel so no one will restore the power by mistake.

☐ Do not touch a service panel that is sparking, blackened or rusted; call an electrician. Do not remove the panel cover to expose the service cables; even if you have turned off the main breaker or pulled the main fuse block, parts of the box may remain charged with current.

☐ Before you begin work, check to make sure the power is off (opposite). If you find voltage or notice wires with damaged insulation, call an electrician.

☐ Never work with or near live power. If you drill or saw through a wall, for example, turn off power in the vicinity; remember, most wiring is invisible, hidden in walls.

☐ Make sure your body is dry. Working with wet hands, feet or hair, for example, makes you susceptible to serious shock.

☐ Avoid being grounded: Do not touch a metal pipe or any other potential conductor while working on electricity.

☐ Use protective equipment when necessary. Depending on the location of your electrical work, consider wearing eye protection and nail-free rubber-soled shoes; if a hard hat is needed wear a nonconducting plastic one. In some cases, a wood or fiberglass ladder may be more advisa-

Staying ungrounded. When handling fuses or circuit breakers, stand on dry boards to put additional insulation between you and the ground or a concrete floor, or wear dry rubber boots and heavy rubber gloves. Work with one hand only, keeping the other in your pocket or behind your back to avoid touching anything metal.

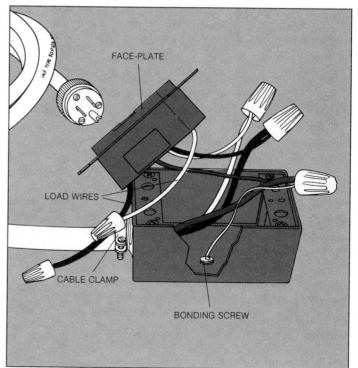

FACE-PLATE

LOAD WIRES

CABLE CLAMP

BONDING SCREW

Making a GFCI extension cord. To make a ground-fault-protected extension cord, use an ordinary three-wire extension cord with its outlet cut off and a weatherproof outlet box with a cable clamp threaded into one knock-out hole to clamp the cord's end. Strip about 6 inches of outer covering from the cord and connect a GFCI outlet's grounding and "line" leads as described in the unit's instructions. Use wire caps to insulate unused load wires. Finally, install the GFCI face-plate.

ble than a metal one, and a flashlight should be made of nonconducting plastic.

☐ When working outdoors with power tools, be sure they are properly grounded or GFCI protected. Never remove the grounding prong from a three-prong plug.

☐ Be careful not to touch overhead power lines when working on your roof or siding. Call the power company to locate any underground power line before digging in the yard.

☐ Unplug a lamp or appliance before working on it. Pull the plug itself; do not pull the cord.

☐ Never venture into a flooded basement to turn off the power at the main circuit breaker panel or fuse box; call the utility company.

☐ Use only replacement parts of the same specifications as the original, or upgraded according to federal and local codes. Look for the UL (Underwriters' Laboratories) or CSA (Canadian Standards Association) logo on replacement parts; this will tell you that the electrical device you are planning to use has been tested and listed.

☐ For safe electrical repairs and installations, follow the requirements of the National Electrical Code, usually available in most public libraries, and use only materials permitted by local electrical codes. If you are doing extensive electrical work, it may be a good idea to have it inspected by a qualified electrician.

Two Ways to Test Voltage

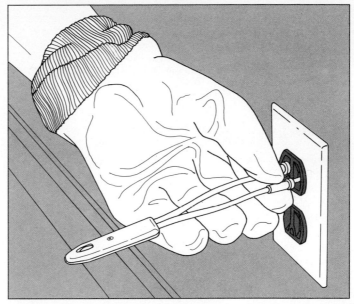

Making sure the power is off. After the power has been turned off, use a voltage tester to confirm that it is indeed off. Insert one tester probe into the wide (neutral) slot and the other into the narrow (hot) slot. Then insert one tester probe into the D-shaped grounding slot and the other into first the narrow slot, then the wider slot. The tester should not glow in any test. If it does, return to the service panel and pull the right fuse or flip the right circuit breaker.

In some cases the voltage tester is used with the power on to locate a hot (current-carrying) wire or to test the grounding at an outlet. Work with

care when performing a live voltage test. Hold the tester probes by the insulated handles or use one hand only as shown. For additional protection against shock, wear a heavy rubber glove.

Buy a voltage tester rated for both 120- and 240-volt household current. Always hold the two probes by their insulation—never touch the bare metal ends. Before using the voltage tester, check to make sure it works. Plug a lamp into a working outlet. If the lamp lights, unplug it and insert the probes of the voltage tester into the slots of the outlet. If the bulb glows without flickering, the tester is good.

Testing for voltage with the power on. A bar-meter voltage tester (right) is used to check the wiring of 240-volt circuits; it may also be used to make sure power has been shut off at a panel or a circuit. More expensive than the voltage tester shown above, this type uses two probes properly spaced for easy one-handed testing.

The tester also loads the circuit it is testing; this identifies a circuit with a poor connection. In addition, it is always ready for testing powered circuits; other testing tools, such as a multitester, must be properly set. For live voltage tests, use only a tester that is UL-listed.

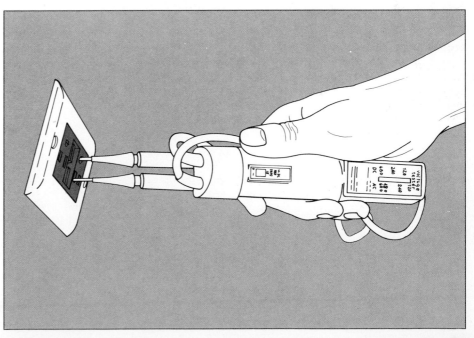

Electrical Emergencies

When your electrical system is properly inspected and maintained, electrical emergencies should be rare. Most emergencies begin at points where electrical equipment is handled—in the form of frayed cords or cracked plugs. Periodically inspect your appliances, lamps, lighting fixtures and power tools. Replacing any worn or damaged parts immediately can prevent emergencies later.

If a receptacle or switch snaps or sparks when being used, for example, cut all power to it and replace the defective device before restoring power. If a fire occurs, call the fire department as soon as possible, even if the fire has been put out. If there are flames or smoke coming from the walls or ceiling, leave the house to call for help. Snuff an accessible fire as shown opposite. Even when the fire has been extinguished, watch carefully for "flashback," or rekindling, and be prepared to spray the fire extinguisher again. Find the cause of the fire and replace damaged wiring and devices before restoring the circuit to use.

Water can turn a small ground fault into a deadly hazard by making your body a convenient path for electrical current. Do not handle electrical devices—even switches or power tools—in wet conditions. When a washing machine runs over with water, do not touch it and do not stand in the water. Unplug the appliance until the area is thoroughly dry; if necessary, call for service. In any case, check to be sure it is grounded *(page 292)*. If a basement is flooded and an electrical appliance is submerged or partially submerged, stay out of the water. Before entering the water, make sure power to the house is cut—from the service panel if you can reach it, or by calling the utility company. After the power is off, wear dry rubber boots and avoid touching anything that is grounded, such as wiring, plumbing or gas and heating systems.

If a nearby line is down, do not go near it or touch it with anything. Call the utility company to cut the power immediately. If you must rescue someone stuck to a live current—at an outlet or toaster, for example—do not touch him; follow the procedures at right.

Freeing someone from a live current. In most cases, a person who accidentally touches a live current will be thrown back from the electrical source. But if the victim is stuck to the wire or appliance, do not touch him. If the source is an appliance or lamp, pull its plug. For a switch or outlet source, shut off power at the main service panel. If the power cannot be cut immediately, use something nonconductive—a wooden broom handle or chair—to knock the person free, as shown below.

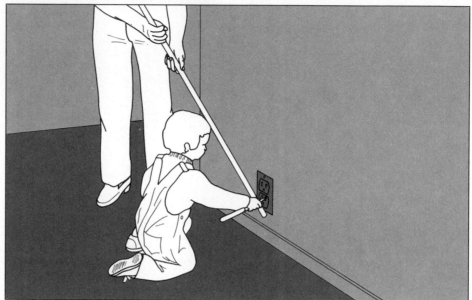

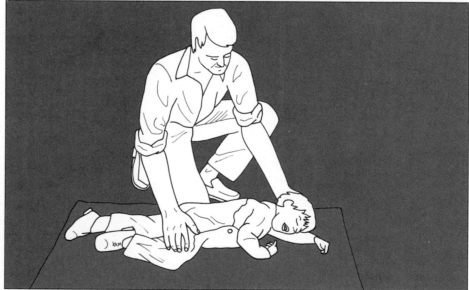

What to do about electrical shock. If the victim is burned or unconscious, call for help immediately. Check for breathing and heartbeat; if the victim is breathing and shows no signs of back or neck injury, place him in the recovery position *(above)*. Tilt the head back, the face to one side and the tongue forward to maintain an open airway. If there is no sign of breathing or heartbeat, give mouth-to-mouth resuscitation or cardiopulmonary resuscitation only if you are qualified to do so.

Removing a hot cord. If an electrical cord smells burned, smokes or even feels hot, unplug it. Caution: If the floor or counter is wet, or the outlet itself is sparking or burning, do not touch the cord, lamp or appliance. Instead, turn off power to the circuit at the service panel. To disconnect a hot plug, protect your hand with a thick, dry towel or a heavy work glove. Without touching the outlet, grasp the cord with one hand several inches from the plug, as shown, and pull it out.

Tools for fire prevention. A multipurpose dry-chemical extinguisher rated ABC *(below)* should be installed along with either an ionization or photoelectric alarm near kitchens, in central hallways and in garages and basements. Check alarms and extinguishers monthly; have extinguishers recharged professionally after any discharge or loss of pressure and change alarm batteries whenever if necessary.

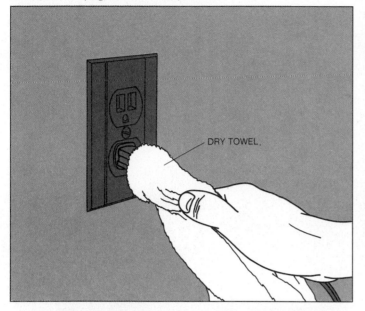

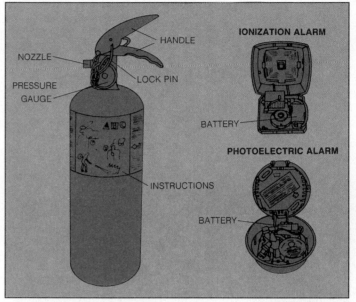

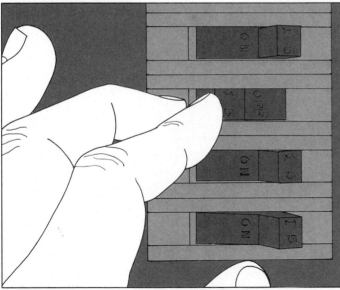

Restoring the power. When a short or overload occurs *(page 296),* find the cause before restoring power to the circuit. In the case of an overload, unplug the appliance that produced it and move its plug to an outlet on another circuit. Then replace a fuse or flip the circuit breaker *(above)* to restore the power. If the circuit goes dead regularly with no apparent cause, your house may need more circuits; call an electrician.

Snuffing a small electrical fire. If a fire at an appliance, outlet, switch or light fixture is accessible, use an extinguisher (above). Stand near an exit, 6 to 10 feet from the fire. Pull the lock pin out of the extinguisher handle and, holding the unit upright, aim the nozzle at the base of the flames. Squeeze the two levers of the handle together, spraying in a quick side-to-side motion. You may also have to turn off power at the service panel to remove the source of heat.

Emergency supplies. A basic, well-planned supply kit will keep you out of the dark—and warm—in case of an electrical emergency. Perhaps the most important item is a first aid kit. Next, if you have ever experienced a long-lasting power outage, you know how valuable candles can be—as well as a supply of matches and a nonconductive flashlight with fresh batteries. Finally, be sure to have a fuel-fired lantern and heater with spare fuel on hand; when using these devices indoors, always provide ample ventilation by opening a window.

A portable generator. During an extended power outage, one of the most useful things you can own or rent is a portable gasoline generator. Providing from 1500 to 2500 watts of power, a generator can be used for powering a food freezer and refrigerator or keeping a sump pump running. It can also light the house and even operate a television. Place a generator outdoors where there is direct ventilation, and power it by running an extension cord inside the house. For permanent hook-ups call an electrician.

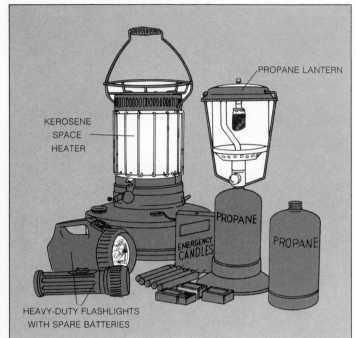

KEROSENE SPACE HEATER

PROPANE LANTERN

PROPANE

PROPANE

EMERGENCY CANDLES

HEAVY-DUTY FLASHLIGHTS WITH SPARE BATTERIES

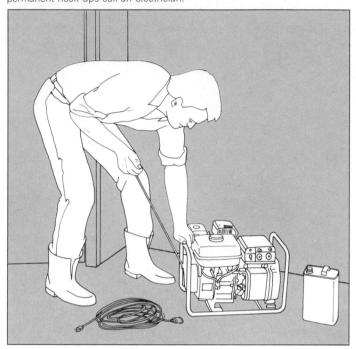

Special Precautions for Aluminum Wiring

Because of the rising cost of copper, many houses built or enlarged between 1965 and 1972 have branch circuits of old-design aluminum wiring. Over a 10-year period, some 500 fires, causing at least 12 deaths, were attributed to this type of wiring, which was installed before new, safer devices and wiring methods were developed.

Two factors make old-design aluminum wiring potentially hazardous: Corrosion of the aluminum wire ends can cause high resistance to current at the terminals, generating a great deal of heat. In addition, since heating and cooling causes aluminum to expand and contract, this wire tends to wiggle loose from terminals. This looseness adds to resistance, which can also generate heat. If the electrical system in your home uses old-design aluminum wiring, however, you can use it successfully and safely—provided you take the following precautions.

☐ Since aluminum wire is less conductive than copper, use a large size: No. 12 for 15-ampere branch circuits and No. 10 for 20-ampere branch circuits; both must be marked CO/ALR.

☐ If a device is marked "CU and CU-clad wire only," do not use it with solid-aluminum wire. This marking means copper-clad aluminum wire, a copper-coated version rarely used in home branch-circuit wiring.

☐ Make wire loops for aluminum terminals carefully; give screws an extra one-half turn after making full contact with the wire.

☐ All wire caps used for splicing must be marked CU/AL, and are suitable only for dry locations—indoor wiring that is located above ground.

☐ By splicing short copper jumper wires onto aluminum circuit wires inside an outlet box, you may use switches and receptacles not listed for use with aluminum wire. Caution: only the copper jumper wires may be connected to these devices.

☐ Protect any aluminum wire connections from corrosion by applying an antioxidant paste—widely sold by electrical supply dealers.

Make sure you are alert for danger signals: uncharacteristically warm cover plates, switches or receptacles; mysteriously inoperative switches or receptacles; or smoke. If you notice any of these telltale signs, call an electrician.

How to Check Your Work

Two inexpensive devices—a voltage tester *(right)* and a continuity tester—are all you need to check wiring connections described in this book. (The bar-meter voltage tester shown on page 301 is used for more advanced work involving live voltage tests.) The voltage tester is primarily a safeguard against shock, used to make absolutely sure that there is no voltage in the circuit you are working on. The continuity tester helps diagnose electrical faults.

The voltage tester has no source of power built into it; it lights when its probes are touched to anything that is charged with electricity. The probes are designed to fit into the two slots of a receptacle, making it possible to check whether the power is off or on without first removing the cover plate. In some instances, the voltage tester is used very carefully with the power on, to locate the feed cable bringing electricity from the service panel. The most useful tester is designed for about 90 to 500 volts.

The continuity tester has its own power source, a small battery that lights a bulb when a continuous path for current lies between the probe and alligator clip. The device must be used only when power to an appliance or a circuit is turned off. The alligator clip is attached to one point and the probe touched to another; if the bulb does not light, there is a break in the path of the current between the two points.

By this method, a continuity tester can detect interruptions in a circuit caused by a break in a cord, a bad connection, or a defective socket or switch. It can also check the soundness of a cartridge fuse *(page 298)* and the operation of a toggle switch *(page 323)*. When the tester is not in use, insert the probe in the plastic sleeve provided for it; otherwise, the probe may accidentally touch the alligator clip, lighting the bulb and wearing out the battery.

Using a Voltage Tester

Testing a receptacle. After removing the cover plate of a receptacle, set the prongs of the voltage tester against the bare ends of the black and white wires at the points where they are attached to the receptacle. Be sure to test both sets of wires on a receptacle that, like this one, has wires at all four terminals. The bulb should not light during the test, indicating that the power is indeed off. If it does light, return to the service panel to find the fuse or circuit breaker that controls the receptacle and turns off the circuit. A switch is tested in a similar manner *(page 322)*.

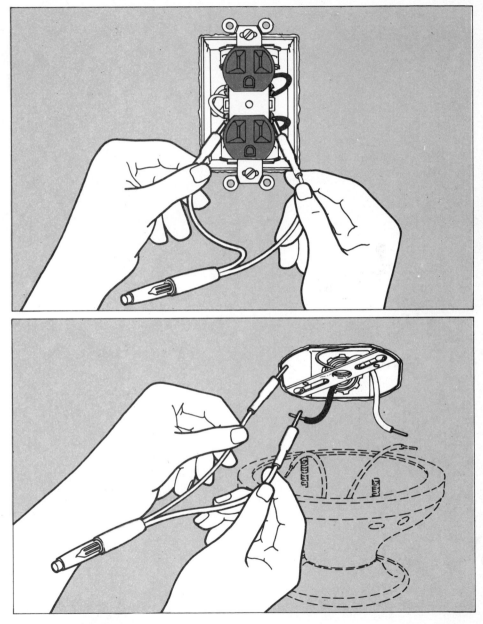

Testing for voltage at a light. Turn off power at the service panel and set the wall switch that controls the light to the "on" position. Then check to make sure the power is off by removing the screws or nuts that hold the fixture to the ceiling or wall, and pull the fixture out of the box to expose the wires. Remove the wire caps with one hand keeping any connections apart; hold the fixture with the other. Grasp the wires by the insulation only and untwist them while supporting the fixture. Set the fixture aside. Set one probe of the voltage tester on the bare end of the black cable wire and the other against the metal box, which should be grounded. Then test from the same black wire to the white cable wire. Finally, test from the white cable wire to the grounded box. The tester bulb will not light during these tests if the power is indeed off.

305

Checking a receptacle's ground. Test the grounding of a newly installed receptacle by inserting one probe of the voltage tester into the semicircular ground slot and the other into each of the elongated slots successively. The tester should light when the probe is plugged into the hot slot (in modern receptacles, this slot is slightly shorter than the other slot). If neither slot lights the tester, the receptacle is not grounded and the wiring must be corrected

Checking the cover-plate ground. A newly installed receptacle should also be checked to make sure that the cover plate is properly grounded. Set one probe of the voltage tester against the mounting screw of the plate and insert the other probe into each of the straight slots successively. The tester bulb should light when the second probe is placed in the hot slot. If it does not light in either slot, the cover plate is not grounded and the wiring must be corrected.

Testing for incoming power. Occasionally you will need to know which of two or more black wires is the feed connecting a box to the house service panel. Turn off the power and check to make sure it is off *(page 305)*. Pull the device from the box and test for power again; there should be none. Disconnect the black wires and pull the wires apart so that they are not touching one another or any other equipment. Hold one probe of the voltage tester against a black wire and the other against the grounded metal box; have a helper turn the power back on. Caution: Do not touch the wires or box with your hands, and do not push the black wire against the box. If the tester lights, you have located the incoming wire. If it does not light, have your helper turn off the power; repeat with another black wire. When you find the feed wire, have your helper turn off the power; use the voltage tester to make sure that it is off. Identify the feed wire and mark it. (If the outlet box is plastic, test between a black wire and the ground wire.)

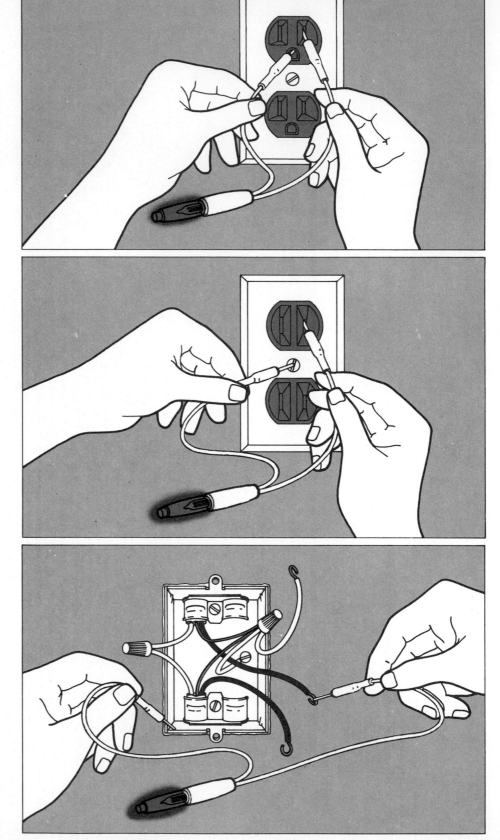

Using a Continuity Tester

1 Checking a lamp socket. When a bulb is good but a lamp does not work, the fault may be an open circuit in the socket. Unplug the lamp, remove the bulb and take the socket apart *(page 312)*. Then clamp the alligator clip of a continuity tester to the threaded metal tube and touch the probe to the silver-colored, or neutral, screw terminal. The threaded tube and the terminal should both be neutral and the tester should light; if it does not, the socket has an open circuit and should be replaced.

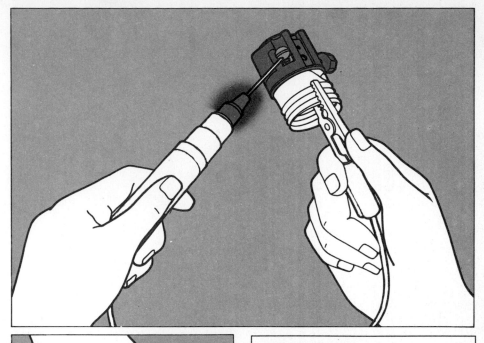

2 Checking a lamp switch. Clamp the alligator clip to the brass, or hot, screw terminal and touch the probe to the rounded contact tab at the center of the socket. Turn the switch off, then on. If the switch is faulty—a common problem in lamp sockets—the tester will not light; replace the socket with a new one. If the tester lights when the switch is on, but the socket still does not work with a bulb you are sure is good, the problem may be that the contact tab does not make proper contact with the bulb. Raise the free end of the tab slightly with the screwdriver tip. If the lamp still does not light, the fault is not in the switch; check the cord and plug *(pages 312-313)*.

Check the switch of a three-way socket *(right)* in the following sequence. Clamp the alligator clip on the brass screw terminal. Test the four switch positions, touching the probe to the small vertical tab in the base of the socket and then to the rounded tab as you turn the switch. In the first "on" position, the tester should light when the probe touches the vertical tab but not when it touches the rounded tab. In the second "on" position, the tester should light only when the probe is touched to the rounded tab. In the third "on" position, the tester should light at either tab, and in the fourth position—"off"—at neither tab.

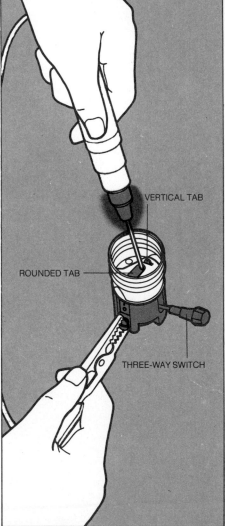

VERTICAL TAB

ROUNDED TAB

THREE-WAY SWITCH

Cutting Down on Electricity Bills

☐ Dimmer switches *(page 327)* reduce power consumption by allowing decreased lighting levels that conform to varying needs.

☐ Switches with pilot lights *(page 326)* warn when an out-of-the-way light or appliance has been forgotten.

☐ A timer *(page 326)* turns off your air conditioner when you leave home and turns it back on before you arrive.

☐ Use a single bulb of higher wattage rather than several low-watt bulbs. Two 60-watt bulbs produce less light than one 100-watt bulb though they consume about 20 per cent more energy.

☐ Use long-lasting bulbs only when the extended life is an advantage, outweighing the fact that they produce less light per watt than standard bulbs.

☐ Turn off incandescent lights when not in use. Although frequent switching shortens a bulb's life somewhat, it is a false notion that switching, in itself, uses power. However, you do not necessarily save by switching fluorescents off for a short time.

☐ Before you buy a large appliance, see how much energy it consumes; this information usually appears on an appliance's data plate, expressed in watts. Compare this wattage with that of appliances made by other manufacturers.

Working with Wire

In house wiring, there are two kinds of connections: wires are either attached to terminals such as those on switches or receptacles, or they are spliced to other wires. For safety reasons, a wire splice must be made only inside an outlet or junction box—never in the wires running between the boxes or in conduit. Before attempting any wire connections, shut off power to the circuit and test to be sure it is off *(page 301)*. Remove plastic sheathing from the cable *(right)* and prepare the end of the wire by stripping off the insulation *(right, bottom)*.

To attach the stripped wires to a receptacle or switch, either wrap the wire around a terminal screw or insert it in a self-gripping slot, depending on which type of terminal the device has *(opposite, top)*. Only one wire can be attached to each screw or push-in terminal. If you need to connect more than one wire—as may be the case with ground wires or switch-controlled receptacles—use a jumper wire. A jumper is an extra piece of wire of the same diameter and with the same color of insulation as the wires to which it is attached. Strip both ends of the jumper, splice one end to the other wires with a wire cap and attach the other end to the terminal. The jumper should just reach from the wire cap to the terminal.

To make splices, use a pair of pliers—twist the stripped wires around each other clockwise, then secure them with a wire cap. The most practical type of wire cap is the one shown on the opposite page. It consists of a cone-shaped insulating shell of hard plastic with a spiral of copper inside. When the cap is twisted clockwise over the ends of bared wires, the copper spiral grips the wires tightly together. Another type has a rounded shell of soft, instead of hard, plastic. It is less susceptible to breakage, but unlike the hard-shelled type, it cannot be removed. To correct a faulty splice or to add a new wire, snip the wires below this type of cap and start again.

Wire caps are manufactured in several sizes. To determine the size appropriate for the job, consult the table on the container; for the wire size and the number of wires that the cap is designed for.

Stripping Off Insulation

Removing sheathing. Place the cable on a steady surface and with your thumb indicate on the cable a distance of about 8 inches from the end. Insert a utility knife into the sheathing near your thumb and cut down the middle of the cable a shallow groove to serve as a guide for cutting the sheath. Then follow the groove and cut as deep as the ground wire *(below, left)*. Be sure to avoid touching the insulated wires with the knife; if you mar the copper conductors, cut away the cable and begin again. Peel back the plastic sheath to the beginning of the cut, tear off the paper that is wrapped around the wires and snip off the loose section of sheathing *(below, right)*.

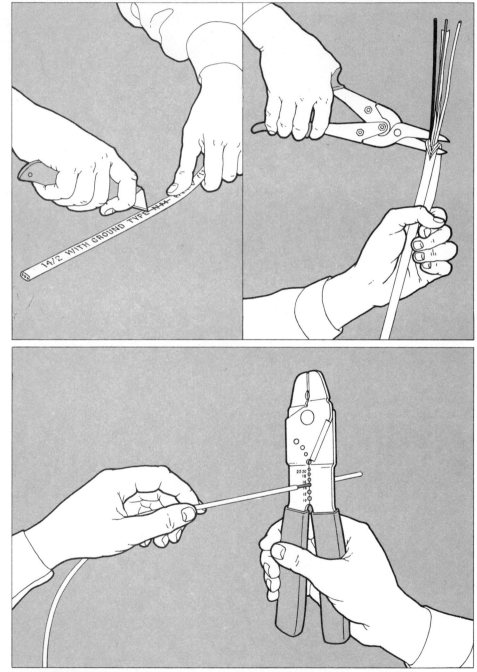

Stripping insulation. Remove wire insulation with a special stripping tool or with the part of an electrician's multipurpose tool *(above)* that is designed for that purpose. Place the wire in the hole sized for the wire, close the tool over the wire and twist the tool back and forth until the insulation is cut through and you are able to pull it free. Do not attempt to strip insulation with a knife. It endangers fingers and generally nicks the wire metal, creating an electrical hazard.

Two Kinds of Terminals

Screw terminal. Strip only enough insulation to allow the bared end of the wire to be wrapped three quarters of the way around the terminal screw. With long-nose pliers, twist the bare end into a loop, loosen the terminal screw, and hook the loop clockwise around the screw so that when the screw is tightened it will help close the loop.

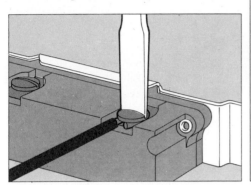

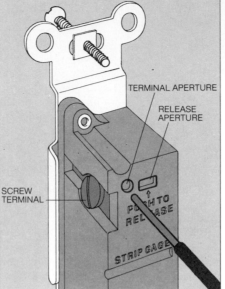

TERMINAL APERTURE

RELEASE APERTURE

SCREW TERMINAL

PUSH TO RELEASE

STRIP GAGE

Push-in terminal. Some switches and receptacles are designed so that you can loop the wire around a screw terminal or insert it through an aperture that automatically grips for a solid connection. To attach a wire to such a push-in terminal, strip insulation as indicated by the strip gauge marked on the device—usually about ½ inch. Insert the bare wire into the terminal aperture (*drawing, left*), and push it in up to the insulation; a spring lock will grip the wire in place. To remove a wire from such a device, insert the blade of a small screwdriver or the end of a stiff piece of wire into the release aperture next to the push-in aperture, press the spring lock and pull the wire free.

Making Connections with Wire Caps

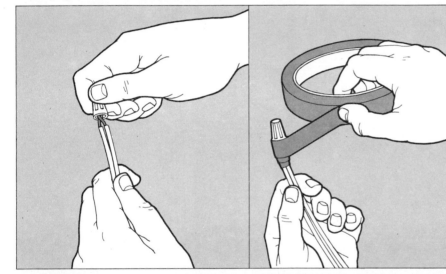

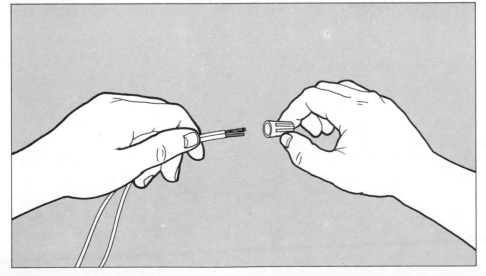

Solid wires. Strip about ¾ inch of insulation from the wires to be joined and hold them parallel. Slip a wire cap over the bare wire ends; twist the cap clockwise around the wires, pushing them hard into the cap (*far left*). If any bare wire remains exposed, remove the cap, cut the wires to the proper length, then twist the wire cap back on.

To make certain that the wire cap will not jar loose when the wires are pushed back into the box, many electricians secure the cap with insulating tape (*left*). Wrap the tape around the base of the cap, then once or twice around the wires and finally around the base of the cap again.

Stranded wire to solid wire. Strip about ¾ inch of insulation from the solid wire and about ¾ inch from the stranded wire. Hold the two bared ends parallel, push a wire cap over the two of them and twist the cap clockwise until it is tight. Then wrap the wires and cap as above.

Replacing Plugs and Cords

Servicing a faulty 120-volt plug or cord is usually a fast and easy job that can eliminate a fire hazard. When lamps and small appliances are plugged in and unplugged often in the course of everyday use, their plugs begin to show signs of wear and tear. A plug with a cracked casing, bent prongs or other damage should be replaced immediately.

Most lamps use standard gauge No. 18 zip cord, while appliances which draw more electricity for their heating elements require No. 16 or No. 18 HPN heater cord. Grounded power tools and appliances use a sheathed round cord containing three color coded wires: usually black for hot, white for neutral and green for ground. Connect the hot wire to the brass terminal screw, the neutral wire to the silver terminal screw and the ground wire—if any—to the green terminal screw inside the plug.

When buying a replacement *(below)*, look for a polarized plug, with one prong wider than the other, and polarized cord, which is ridged or otherwise marked on one side. These plugs are designed to fit into the slots of modern—polarized—wall outlets and ensure that when the switch is turned off, no power flows to the lamp or appliance.

Quick-connect plug. Because wires do not require stripping, this is the easiest type of plug to install. However, its connections are not as sturdy as other types of plugs; the quick-connect variety should be used only for lamps that are not plugged in and unplugged often.

Flat-cord plug. Often used for lamps and other electric devices, this is one of the most common types available. It separates into two parts; the shell and the core. After wires are attached to terminal screws on the core, the shell is snapped back on.

Polarized plug. With one wide (neutral) prong and one narrow (hot) prong, this type of plug helps ensure maximum safety *(page 298)*. A polarized plug can only be used in a polarized outlet. To ensure polarization—continuity with your house's electrical system—the marked side of the cord should connect the wide plug prong and the silver terminal screw; the unmarked side of the cord should connect the narrow prong and the brass terminal screw. Appliances containing elements, such as irons and toaster ovens, do not require polarized plugs.

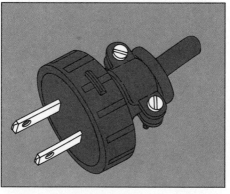

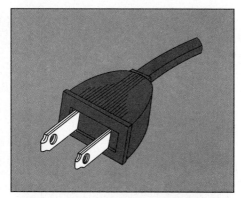

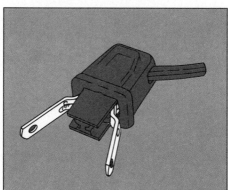

Round-cord plug. For use with round shielded cable where there is strain on the cord, this plug is commonly used for swag lamps that hang by their cords. For secure connections, a clamp is tightened after the cord is attached and the shell is snapped back on.

Three-prong plug. This plug features a third—D-shaped or round—prong which grounds power tools and appliances if equipment malfunctions. Connect the third prong attachment to the green wire inside the sheathing insulating the wires. *Caution: Never cut or pry off the third prong.*

Removing and Replacing a Damaged Plug

Servicing a damaged plug. A melted or otherwise damaged plug poses a serious fire and shock hazard and should be replaced with a new plug—available at hardware and electrical supply stores. Using wire cutters, cut the damaged plug from the appliance cord. Remove the shell from the new plug and feed the wire through it. Unless you are using a quick-connect plug, part the cord along its groove for 1½ inches, then strip ½ inch of insulation from the ends of both wires. (Tie an Underwriters' knot—shown on page 312—if the plugshell is big enough to accommodate it.) Twist the wire strands, then hook each wire end clockwise around a terminal screw; be sure to connect a polarized plug properly *(opposite)*. Then tighten the terminal screws, as shown, making sure there are no stray ends. Close the plug by snapping the core into the shell.

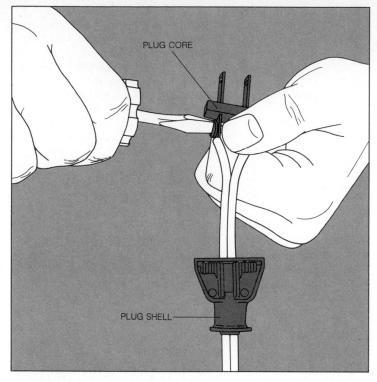

PLUG CORE

PLUG SHELL

Replacing a Damaged Appliance Cord

BACKPLATE

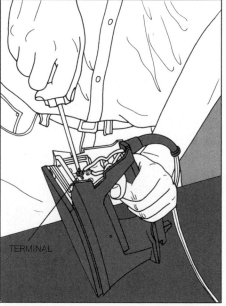

TERMINAL

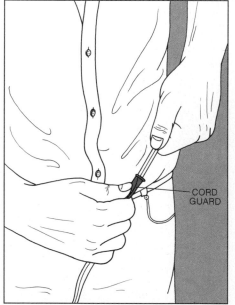

CORD GUARD

1 **Accessing the internal connections.** Cords of small appliances often require replacement because they are used frequently. For maximum safety, when an appliance cord deteriorates, always replace it; avoid quick-fix patches with electrical tape. Access the internal connections by removing the screw or screws on the appliance housing or backplate, as shown.

2 **Disconnecting the cord.** Remove the housing or backplate, then locate the connection terminals—where the cord is attached; unscrew the terminals to free the end of the cord.

3 **Attaching the new cord.** Buy a new electrical cord the same length, gauge and type as the old cord. Small appliances with heating elements—such as the iron shown—use HPN heater cord. Feed the new cord through the rubber cord guard and part the cord along its groove. Then strip ½ inch off the wire ends, twist the strands and hook each wire end clockwise around a terminal. Tighten the terminal screws, replace the housing or backplate and attach a new plug *(top).*

How to Rewire a Lamp

Despite the great variety of lamp shapes and sizes, the electrical components and the way they are wired together are much the same in all. The components consist of one or more sockets, a switch, a plug and a cord, all of which can easily be replaced. Usually the supporting skeleton is a threaded pipe, invisible in the center, that holds the socket, lamp body and base together, and also guides the cord from the base to the socket. The socket cap may fasten the lamp body to the pipe. If you take the cap off, make sure the lamp is supported while you work on it or the base and body may slip apart.

The part of the lamp that most often fails is the switch. If it is a separate unit in the base, replace it with a new one. Most lamps, however, have switches in their sockets (which also may need replacement if they corrode). Standard sockets are almost always interchangeable, although they may use either a pull chain, push button or rotating switch. Even the special socket used with a three-way bulb is hooked up in exactly the same way as the standard one-way socket shown below. Rewiring a lamp fitted with two sockets (opposite) involves a few additional connections.

A plug should be replaced if its casing is cracked or if its prongs are so loose that they no longer make a good connection at the receptacle. For safety, all new plugs should be of the dead-front type (opposite)—and polarized if the receptacles in your home are polarized (page 298). In a standard plug the cord wires must first be stripped of insulation, tied in an Underwriters' knot and then screwed clockwise to the plug's terminals. Other plugs clamp directly to the cord, eliminating the need to strip the wires or screw them down. However, because no Underwriters' knot or terminal screws are used in quick-connect plugs, their connection to the wire is not as strong as in the standard plug. They are not recommended for lamps that are unplugged often.

If a lamp cord is damaged, buy a new cord instead of splicing the old one—a safe splice is more work than it is worth, and sloppy splices are a hazard. When buying a new cord, specify SPT 16- or 18-gauge lamp cord, called zip cord because the insulation is grooved between the wires so they can be pulled apart.

The Simplest Lamp: A Switch-and-Socket Combination

1 Socket. Be sure to unplug the lamp and remove the light bulb (below) before starting repairs. On the outer shell of the socket is a point marked "press"; push against this point with a screwdriver to separate it from the socket cap. Pull off the shell and the insulating sleeve. Remove the socket assembly by loosening the terminal screws and taking the cord wires off the terminals. If only the socket is being replaced and the socket cap is not bent or corroded, leave it in place and reuse it, attaching only the new socket, sleeve and shell as explained in Step 4. If the socket cap is damaged, untie the knot in the cord, loosen the setscrew in the cap, unscrew it from the top of the center pipe and replace it.

2 Putting in a new cord. Untie the knot in the end of the cord resting in the socket cap and pull the old cord out through the center pipe. Untie the knot in the cord at the channel in the bottom of the lamp and pull it free of the lamp. If the old plug is reusable, save it to attach to the new cord according to the procedure in Step 3. Push the new cord through the channel in the lamp base and knot it just inside. Make sure you will have enough cord to reach the socket cap with about 4 inches to spare. Snake the cord up through the center pipe and work it through the socket cap.

3 Tying an Underwriters' knot. Separate the two wires of the cord you have pulled up through the socket cap, parting them gently 2 inches along the grooved insulation. Strip ½ inch of insulation from the end of each (page 26) and tie the cord ends into an Underwriters' knot (below). Tighten the knot and pull the cord back into the center tube so that the knot nestles in the neck of the socket cap. If you are installing a plug with screw terminals, insert the cord end through the neck of the plug and tie a second Underwriters' knot. After tying it, pull back on the cord so that the knot rests in the neck of the plug.

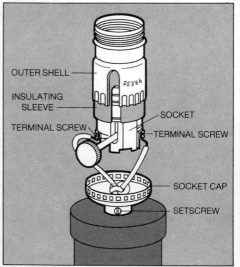

OUTER SHELL
INSULATING SLEEVE
TERMINAL SCREW
SOCKET
TERMINAL SCREW
SOCKET CAP
SETSCREW

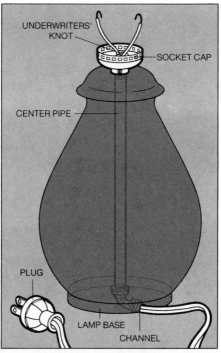

UNDERWRITERS' KNOT
SOCKET CAP
CENTER PIPE
PLUG
LAMP BASE
CHANNEL

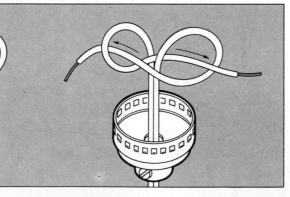

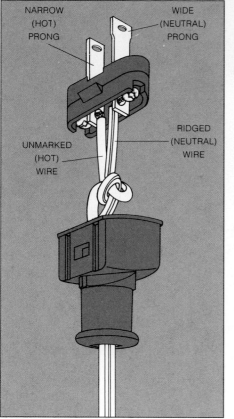

Attaching a polarized plug and socket wires.
Polarization of lamps, radios and many appliances
is ensured by polarized plugs *(page 298).*
Three-prong plugs are automatically polarized;
the location of the third (grounding) prong
establishes the location of the other two.

Check your home for old-style unpolarized plugs
with removable insulating disks covering the
plugs' screw connections. They are potential
hazards and should be replaced with polarized
"dead-front" plugs like the one shown above.

To replace an unpolarized or damaged lamp plug,
clip off the old plug with a pair of wire cutters
and feed the wires through the opening in the new
plug shell. Then, pull the two wires apart until there
is a 1½-inch separation between them; strip ½-
inch insulation off the wire ends *(page 308).* Tie an
Underwriters' knot *(opposite, bottom)* with the
wires if the plug shell is big enough to accomodate it.
Wrap the identified—ridged or marked—wire clockwise around the neutral, silver-colored, terminal and
the unmarked wire around the hot, brass-colored
terminal. Snap the plug pieces together.

At the socket cap, loop the stripped and twisted
tips of wire clockwise around the terminal screws
of the new socket. Attach the hot wire to the brass-
colored terminal and the neutral wire to the silver-
colored terminal. Tighten the terminal screws, then
fit the new shell and sleeve over the socket;
push them down until they snap into the socket cap.

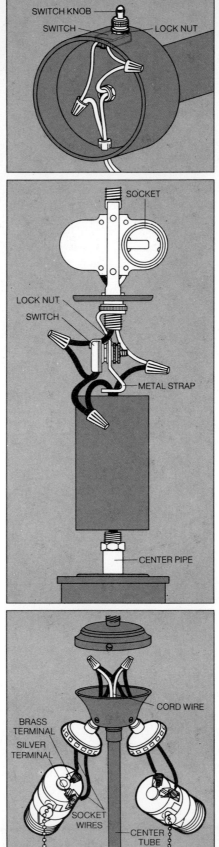

Separate Switches and Twin Sockets

One socket with a separate switch. To replace a
separate switch mounted in the base of a single-
socket lamp, unplug the lamp, then remove the
knob and unscrew the lock nut. If the lamp base is
sealed, remove the bottom cover, pull out the switch
and remove the wire caps holding switch wires to
the cord. Reattach the wires of the new switch to the
cord, place the switch in its mounting hole in the
base and reverse the disassembly procedure.

Two sockets with a separate switch. In this arrangement, a single assembly includes both
sockets. One black wire and one white wire serve
both sockets and are permanent parts of the
unit. A single switch located below the sockets
controls both. To replace the socket assembly or
the switch, first unplug the lamp, then remove the
switch knob. Remove the socket, switch and
wiring by turning the socket assembly counterclockwise until it is free of the center pipe. Remove
the wire caps holding the two socket wires.
Unscrew the socket from the metal strap and
remove it. Reverse the procedure to put in a new
socket. (When replacing the switch, remember
it should always interrupt the hot wire.)

To replace only the switch, remove the socket
and switch assembly. Unscrew the lock nut holding the switch to the strap and pull the switch from
the strap. Disconnect the old switch wires from the
cord and socket wire; in a properly wired lamp,
these should be the hot wires. Reattach these wires
to the new switch and refasten with the lock nut.

To remove only the cord, unscrew the wire
caps holding the cord wire to the white wire
and the other cord wire to the switch wire.
Reverse the procedure to attach the new cord.
If the plug is polarized, connect the hot wire to
the switch. All other steps are the same
as for a single-socket lamp.

Two switch-and-socket combinations. In this
lamp, as in the single-socket lamp opposite, each
socket is served by two wires and each has its
own switch. The socket wires branch off from the
main cord at the top of the lamp's center pipe.
Replace the sockets, following the same procedure that was used for a single-socket lamp.

To replace only the cord, unplug the lamp and
remove the cover at the top of the lamp and unscrew
the wire caps holding the socket wires to the cord
wire. Replace the cord wire using the same method
as for a single-socket lamp, but after stripping ½
inch of insulation from the separated cord ends,
attach the socket wires to the cord wires with
wire caps. Be sure to attach the wires from the
brass-colored socket terminals to the plain cord
wire and the wires from the silver-colored socket
terminals to the ribbed or marked cord wire.

Removing and Replacing Fixtures

Whether you want to check the connections in a faulty lighting fixture, remove a fixture to paint behind it or replace an outmoded model with a new one, chances are you will one day see how a fixture is mounted. Wiring is essentially the same for all fixtures, whether they use incandescent bulbs or fluorescent tubes, but the hardware needed for mounting varies. These variations, which apply to most wall and ceiling fixtures, are shown at right and below. The method used for hanging a chandelier is shown on page 316; fluorescents appear on page 319.

Before starting the job, turn off the power to the fixture circuit at the service panel, then check to make sure it is off (page 305). Merely turning off the wall switch is not sufficient, since in certain situations (page 291) the switch may not turn off power to all wires in the box.

With the power off, remove the screws or nuts holding the fixture in place, pull it away from the box and hang it from the box with a hook made from a wire coat hanger. Do not let the fixture hang by the wires; a dangling fixture may pull the wire connections loose before you are ready to remove them. Detach the connections to the fixture. Do not tamper with any of the other wires.

If you are connecting a new fixture, strip 1/2 inch of the insulation from its wires, then connect them to the house wires in the box, black to black, white to white. If the new fixture is the same size, shape and weight as the one being replaced, you can probably reuse the same old hardware in mounting it. If a different-sized fixture is being installed, however, you may need other hardware to attach the fixture to the box. Either remove the old fixture first, examine the box and buy the necessary parts from an electrical supply store or hardware store, or buy a package of parts in assorted sizes. If the new fixture is equipped for a grounding connection, make sure that connection is made between the fixture and the box for maximum safety.

A simple fixture. The single-bulb fixture, usually made of porcelain and often used in garages and basesements, has no wiring of its own. The holes in its canopy are spaced so that they line up with the screw holes in the box tabs for direct mounting. The black house wire is attached to the brass-colored screw terminal, and the white house wire to the silver-colored terminal. When remounting the fixture, fold the wires neatly into the box, then the fixture is screwed on.

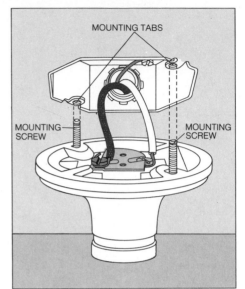

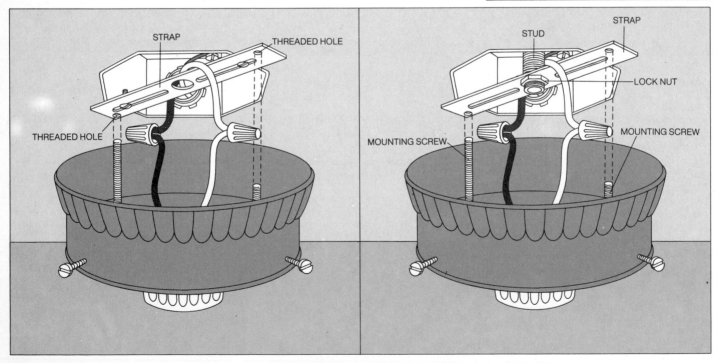

A strap-mounted fixture. If the base of a fixture is so large that the canopy screw holes will not line up with the box tab holes, the fixture is mounted with an adapter called a strap. If the box has a stud projecting from its middle, the strap's center hole is threaded onto the stud and secured with a lock nut (above, right). When remounting the fixture in a studless box, insert screws through the strap slots into the box tabs. Connect the fixture and wires to the house wires with wire caps—black to black and white to white—and fold them into the box. Screw the fixture to the holes in the strap.

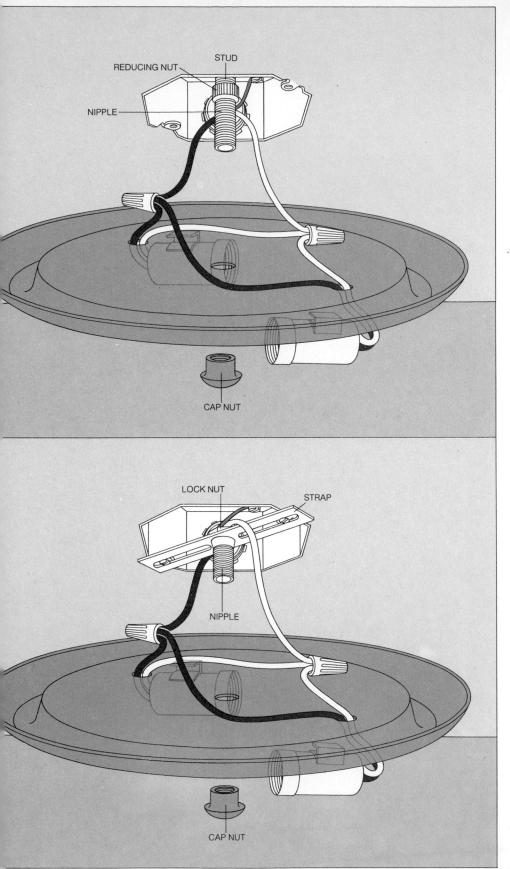

A center-mounted fixture. This type of fixture uses a reducing nut which is threaded to fit the stud at one end but threaded differently at the other end to fit a smaller threaded metal tube, called a nipple *(left).* When remounting this fixture, insert the nipple into the reducing nut and screw it in tightly. If the box has no stud, fasten the nipple into the center hole of a strap and screw the strap to the box tabs *(bottom).* Connect the two wires from the sockets of the fixture to the white house wire. In the same way, connect the two black socket wires to the black house wire. Place the fixture over the box so that the nipple protrudes through the center hole of the fixture. Then fasten the fixture to the nipple with a cap nut.

Chandeliers

A chandelier that weighs less than 10 pounds can be attached to the tabs of a ceiling box with a strap and nipple *(page 315)*. But a chandelier of 10 pounds or more requires some special hardware and can be safely attached only to a ceiling box equipped with a stud *(right)*. Therefore, if you want to replace a lightweight chandelier with a heavier one and the present ceiling box has no stud, you will have to substitute a new box equipped with a stud. Before removing the old box, shut off the power to that circuit and make sure it is off *(page 301)*, then refer to the drawing on page 314.

Rewiring a chandelier is similar to rewiring a two-socket lamp *(page 313)*, but the number of steps varies, depending on the number of sockets and whether the sockets are prewired or not. Both types of sockets are shown on the opposite page. With either type, however, the basic connections are the same. Each individual socket is served by two branch wires. The branch wires from the hot, or brass-colored, terminal on each of the sockets are attached with a wire cap to one of the chandelier's two main-cord wires. The branch wires from all the neutral, or silver-colored, socket terminals are attached to the other main-cord wire. Then the main wires are connected to the house wiring, hot wire to the black house wire and neutral wire to the white house wire. If there is a grounding wire, it is attached to the metal outlet box using a green bonding screw. Use a continuity tester—with added wire from the alligator clip to a connection, if necessary—to check your work.

Never let a chandelier hang by its wires. Either have a helper hold the chandelier or suspend it from the box with a hook made from a wire coat hanger.

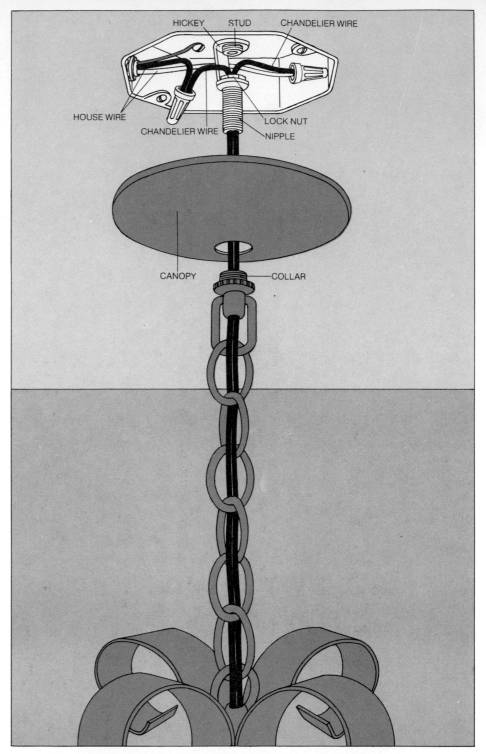

How a heavy chandelier is mounted. On a ceiling box with a stud, as shown above, a large adapter called a hickey is threaded onto the stud; a nipple is attached to the chandelier. When hanging the chandelier, screw the nipple into the hickey far enough so that when the chandelier's collar is in place it will hold the canopy of the fixture snugly against the ceiling. Secure the nipple with a lock nut. Push the chandelier wires through the collar, canopy, nipple and the lower part of the hickey. Using wire caps to secure the connections, attach the chandelier wires to the house wires in the ceiling box—neutral to the white wire, hot to the black wire. If there is a third—green —grounding wire, attach it to the green bonding screw on the metal outlet box. Raise the canopy and secure it against the ceiling by screwing the collar onto the end of the nipple.

Rewiring a Chandelier

1 **Replacing the main cord.** Shut off the power, test to be sure it is off, then remove the chandelier from the ceiling box and detach its main-cord wires from the house wiring. Locate the branch wires connecting the main-cord wires to the chandelier's sockets. On some chandeliers, the connections are clearly visible on the outside of the fixture; more often they are concealed. In the drawing at right, for example, they are hidden in a caplike recess at the lower end of the chandelier's main tube. Open the part of the fixture where the wire connections are made and disconnect the socket wires from the main-cord wires. Pull out the old main cord. Using a length of 16-gauge stranded zip cord for a new main cord (one side plain and one side ribbed), snake the cord through the chandelier's center tube, as shown. Strip ½ inch of insulation from both ends of the new main-cord wires and twist the exposed strands. If the chandelier is equipped for a grounding connection, make that connection.

2 **Replacing socket wiring.** Many chandeliers have sockets, like lamp sockets, with terminal screws *(near right)*. To replace wires, slip the insulating sleeves off the sockets and detach the wires. Replace them with 16-gauge stranded wire of the same length, the ends stripped ½ inch and twisted. The wire attached to the brass-colored terminal is hot; code it with black tape. If terminals are not color-coded, the wire connected to the base terminal should be marked black.

Some chandeliers have sockets with preattached wires *(far right)*. This type must be unscrewed from the threaded tube in the chandelier arm and replaced. Snake the wires of a new prewired socket back through the chandelier and screw the socket to the tube. Code black the free end of the wire connected to the brass-colored terminal visible inside the base of the socket.

3 **Hooking up the new wiring.** Take the unattached ends of the socket wires you have coded as hot and twist them together with the end of the main-cord wire that you have coded with black tape. Twist together the neutral socket wires and the other main-cord wire. If you had to open a part of the chandelier to make the connections, conceal joined wire ends there and close it. Reattach the fixture to the ceiling box following the directions on the opposite page. Connect the black-coded main-cord wire to the black house wire and the other cord wire to the white house wire.

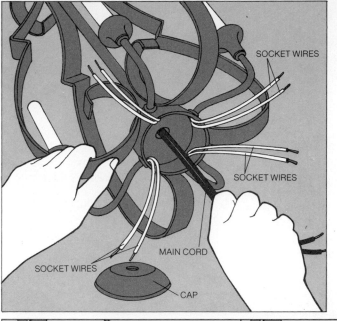

SOCKET WIRES

SOCKET WIRES

SOCKET WIRES

MAIN CORD

CAP

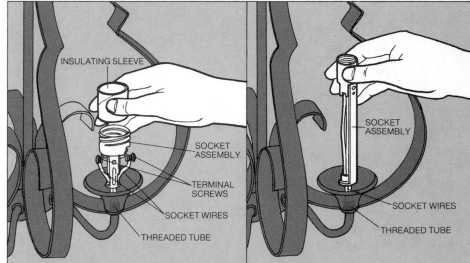

INSULATING SLEEVE

SOCKET ASSEMBLY

TERMINAL SCREWS

SOCKET WIRES

THREADED TUBE

SOCKET ASSEMBLY

SOCKET WIRES

THREADED TUBE

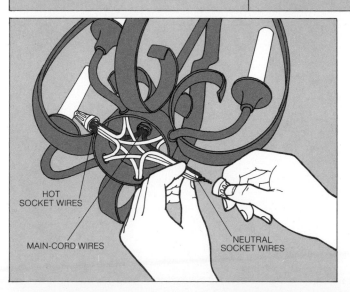

HOT SOCKET WIRES

MAIN-CORD WIRES

NEUTRAL SOCKET WIRES

Fluorescent Light Fixtures

A fluorescent tube works when a switch starts an electric current in a gas, causing it to emit light waves that are not readily perceived by the human eye; these waves strike chemicals coating the inner surface of the tube, "exciting" these phosphors so that they emit visible light.

To start the process, a device called a ballast provides a momentary extra surge of voltage. In older types there is also a starter, which helps the ballast produce high initial voltage; such lights may take several seconds to glow brightly. Rapid-start or instant-start fluorescents produce sufficient initial voltage without a starter; their tubes light up almost immediately.

A malfunctioning fluorescent fixture with either a straight or a circular tube is simple to repair because its major components—tubes, tube holders and ballast—are easily removed. Diagnose problems by referring to the troubleshooting chart below. If the cause of the problem is not obvious, you still may be able to diagnose it yourself by substituting new parts, one at a time. Before starting any work, shut off power in the circuit *(page 297)* and test to make sure it is off*(page 301)*. Use new parts of the same wattage as those you are replacing. First replace the tube. If that does not solve the problem and the lamp has a starter, replace the starter.

Put in a new ballast, the most costly replacement part, only as a last resort. To install a new ballast in a straight-tube light, remove the lid from the metal box, called the channel, that holds the light to wall or ceiling; the ballast is either mounted on the inside of the lid or on the channel itself. The ballast in a circular fixture can be reached only by removing the entire fixture from the ceiling box. Transfer the wiring connections one at a time, checking against the diagram printed on the new ballast.

Troubleshooting Fluorescent Fixtures

Problem	Possible Causes	Solution
Tube will not light	Fuse blown or circuit breaker switched off	Replace fuse or reset circuit breaker.
	Tube worn out	Replace tube.
	Dirt on tube	Remove tube and clean it with damp cloth: let dry before replacing.
	Tube pins not making proper contact with lamp holders	Rotate tube in holders for starter and rapid-start types. For instant-start type, make sure pins are fully seated in sockets.
	Incorrect tube for ballast	Check that tube wattage is same as that shown on ballast.
	Incorrectly wired ballast	See diagrams opposite or check wiring diagram on ballast. Rewire if necessary.
	Defective starter	Replace starter.
	Defective ballast	Replace ballast.
	Low voltage in circuit	Have power company check house voltage.
	Air temperature below 50°	Install low-temperature ballast.
Ends of tube glow but center does not light	Defective starter	Replace starter.
	Incorrectly wired ballast	See diagrams opposite or check wiring diagram on ballast. Rewire if necessary.
	Inadequate ground (especially in rapid-start type)	Check attachment of fixture's ground wire.
Tube flickers or blinks	Normal with new tube	Should improve with use—if not, replace starter.
	Tube pins not making proper contact with lamp holders	Rotate tube in holders for preheat and rapid-start types. For instant-start, make sure pins are fully seated in sockets.
	Tube worn out	Replace tube.
	Air temperature below 50°	Install low-temperature ballast.
Fixture hums or buzzes	Ballast wires loose or incorrectly attached	Tighten connections and check wiring against diagram on ballast.
	Incorrect ballast	Replace with ballast of correct type and wattage.
Brown or grayish bands about 2 inches from ends of tube	Normal	
Dense blackening at ends of tube	Tube worn out	Replace tube. If tube is new, replace starter instead.
Slight blackening at ends of tube	Tube nearly worn out	Replace tube.

The Three Types of Fluorescent Lights

Rapid-start. This type, the most popular fluorescent fixture for home use, requires no starter and lights up without the few seconds' delay of the starter type. If a rapid-start malfunctions, the cause may be improper grounding. For proper operation, the tube should be no more than ½ inch from a grounded metal strip, usually the channel or a metal reflector attached to the fixture. A rapid-start tube may also malfunction if it is turned on frequently but only for brief periods at a time. Such operation interferes with key electrical mechanisms inside the lamp and it may take several seconds to light. If such a tube does light up, let it run for several hours. If it continues to work properly, the malfunction has cured itself and no replacement parts are needed.

Starter type. Many low-wattage fluorescent lights, as well as larger ones of an older type, contain starters, a small canister in a socket near one lamp holder. To replace a worn-out starter, turn off the power, remove the fluorescent tube, turn the starter counterclockwise and pull it from its socket. Be sure the new starter matches the wattage that is printed on the tube.

Instant-start. This type is relatively trouble-free, but when it does malfunction the trouble often arises because of the high voltage needed to start it. Even when the tube is partially burned out and blackened at one end, the high voltage will allow it to operate—producing brilliant orange flashes—but it should be replaced immediately or the ballast may be damaged. Failure to operate at all may be due simply to improper insertion of the tube in the lamp holders. As a safety measure, one holder has a spring-operated switch that shuts off current if the pin at the end of the tube is not fully inserted. To make sure the pins are seated, jiggle the tube in its holders.

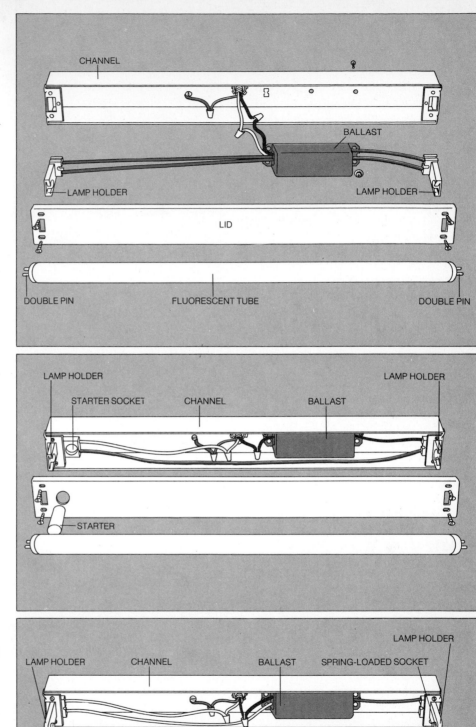

Switching Switches

The wall switch that turns a light or appliance on and off is one of the sturdiest devices you will ever own—under normal use, a good one lasts at least 20 years. Long before a switch breaks down, however, you may decide to replace it with a newer, more sophisticated model. If your house has aluminum wiring, you should look for a switch that has the CO/ALR designation. Other switches have special grounding terminals that are designed to prevent shocks from switch parts and cover plates. Or you might prefer one of the special-purpose switches—a mercury switch, which is completely silent and lasts a lifetime; a switch that turns itself on and off at preset times; a rocker switch; a push-button switch; or a dimmer switch, which simultaneously matches the light level to your mood and saves money.

No matter what switch you choose —and even if you are only replacing one that has gone bad—the installation procedure is essentially the same. Turn off the power, disconnect the old switch and buy a new switch of the right type —the rules of thumb on this page will enable you to identify the four basic types. Check the data stamped on the mounting strap of the new switch to be sure that it matches the old in voltage and amperage ratings and meets modern safety requirements (opposite, bottom). The replacement switch may have terminals of different types or in different positions; the information at the top of the opposite page will help you choose the best switch for your needs.

If the new switch is identical with the old one, you need only hook up the same wires to the same terminals. Even if it is not, standardized color-coding of wires and terminals makes it easy to connect switches correctly.

The Four Basic Switches

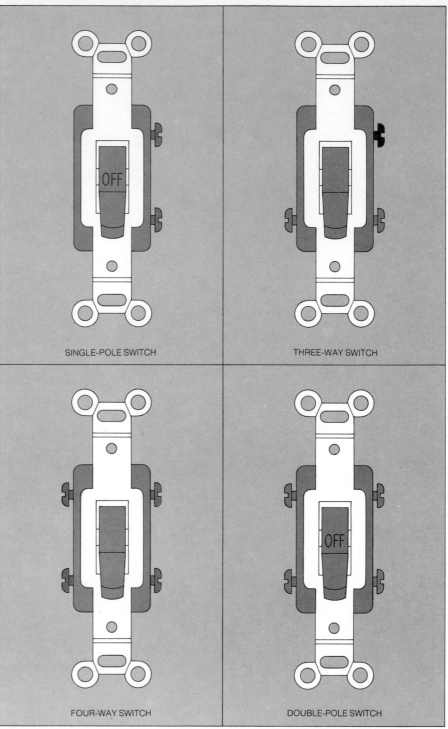

SINGLE-POLE SWITCH

THREE-WAY SWITCH

FOUR-WAY SWITCH

DOUBLE-POLE SWITCH

Telling the switches apart. A single-pole switch, the commonest of all switches, controls a light or receptacle from one location. It has two brass-colored terminals and "on" and "off" markings on the handle, or toggle. Three-way switches, used in pairs to control a light or receptacle from two locations, have three terminals: one black or copper-colored and two brass- or silver-colored. There are no "on" and "off" markings. A four-way switch works with three-way switches to control a light or receptacle from three or more locations. It has four brass-colored terminals and no "on" and "off" markings. A double-pole switch, sometimes used to control 240-volt appliances, can be mistaken for a four-way switch—both have four brass-colored terminals—but the double-pole switch has "on" and "off" markings.

Terminals for Convenience

A range of choices. Though all switches are standardized in operation and fit standard-sized outlet boxes, they vary widely in the placement and type of their terminals. The single-pole switches at right illustrate these variations. All work in exactly the same way, but you can choose the terminal type that you find easiest to wire and the terminal positions that permit you to arrange the wires conveniently in the outlet box.

Screw terminals, the commonest, are usually located on one or both sides of the switch housing, but may be on the top and bottom ends or recessed in the front. Push-in terminals, always located on the back of the housing, eliminate the need for a fastening loop since they secure the wire with spring clamps when it is inserted into the hole. A rectangular release slot is used to disconnect the wire *(page 309)*. Push-in terminals can be used only with solid copper or copper-clad wire; aluminum or stranded wire should always be connected to a screw terminal. Many switches come with both push-in and screw terminals.

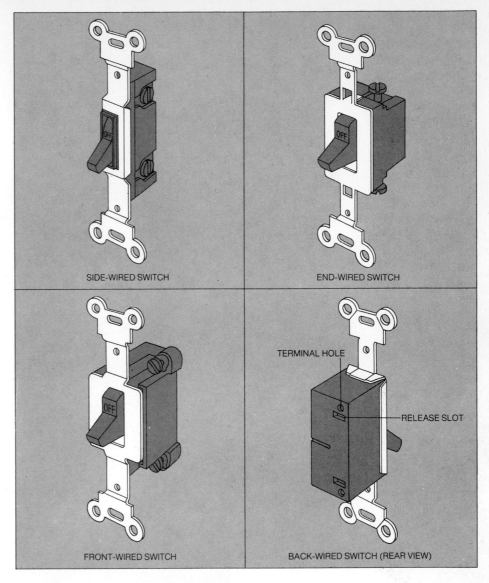

SIDE-WIRED SWITCH

END-WIRED SWITCH

FRONT-WIRED SWITCH

BACK-WIRED SWITCH (REAR VIEW)

TERMINAL HOLE

RELEASE SLOT

Reading a Switch

Facts to look for. The mounting strap of a switch is stamped with data on safety tests and operating characteristics: The Underwriters' Laboratories, Inc. listing (abbreviated UND. LAB. INC. LIST.) or, in Canada, the symbol of the Canadian Standards Association (a CSA logo), which indicates that the switch has met standardized tests. The maximum voltage and amperage at which the switch may be used is indicated (15A-120V means the switch can control up to 15 amperes of current at voltages up to 120 volts). An AC ONLY stamp, or an AC designation in the rating (for example, 15A-120VAC), indicates the switch can be used only in the AC systems that now are almost universal. And, if the switch can safely be used with aluminum wiring, the mounting strap will have a CO/ALR stamp.

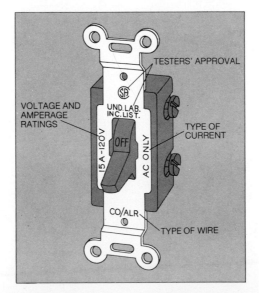

TESTERS' APPROVAL

VOLTAGE AND AMPERAGE RATINGS

TYPE OF CURRENT

TYPE OF WIRE

The Single-Pole Switches

Single-pole switches are the basic type most frequently used in the home—and therefore, the ones most frequently replaced, either because a switch has failed or because you want to substitute a newer type. Before finally deciding that a switch has failed, however, check the light bulb it controls and the fuse or circuit breaker that controls it.

Most single-pole switches are replaced as shown below and on the following page—a job requiring one screwdriver, pliers and two inexpensive testers. The replacement may be fitted with a special grounding terminal, a protection against shock that most older switches do not have, and this extra connection requires an additional step in installation *(page 323)*. And some special devices such as time-clock and pilot-light switches require a neutral wire connection and must be installed as shown on page 326.

When you begin the replacement of any switch, turn off power to the switch, unscrew the cover plate and loosen the two screws holding the switch in the box until you can pull the switch out without touching the switch terminals or bare wire ends. The screws should not come out of the mounting strap (fiber washers hold them in the slots). Grip the ends of the mounting strap and pull the switch out of the box until the wires are fully extended.

2 **Identifying the wiring.** With the wires exposed, you will find one of the two wiring variations that determine how the new switch is to be hooked up. In one variation, called middle-of-the-run wiring *(near right),* at least two cables enter the box. Two black wires, or one black and one red wire, are the hot wires attached to the switch terminals; you will also see white wires and generally bare copper wires connected with wire caps. The white wires are neutral, the bare ones are ground wires; neither should be disconnected or pulled out of position for this job. In the second variation, called a switch loop *(far right),* only one cable enters the box, and one black and one white wire are connected to the switch. Here, the white wire is not neutral; it is hot and should be marked as such with black electrical tape or black paint near the end of the insulation. If the wire has not been so identified, code it before replacing the wires.

Replacing a Switch

1 **Removing the switch.** To be sure the current is indeed shut off, touch one probe of a voltage tester to the metal shell of the outlet box and the other probe to each of the brass terminals in succession *(right).* If the switch has push-in terminals, inset the probe into the release slots. The tester should not glow on either terminal. If it does, you have not disconnected the fuse or turned off the circuit breaker that controls the circuit; return to the service panel and find the right one. When you are certain that the power is off, loosen the terminals with a screwdriver and remove the wires, using long-nose pliers to open the loop on the end of each wire. (The method for disconnecting push-in terminals is described on page 309.)

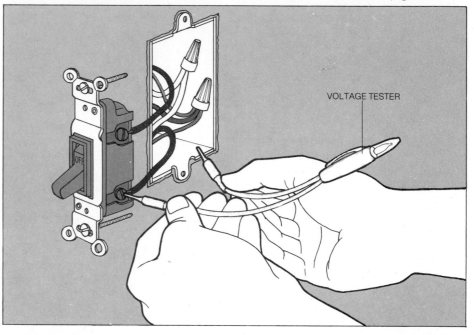

VOLTAGE TESTER

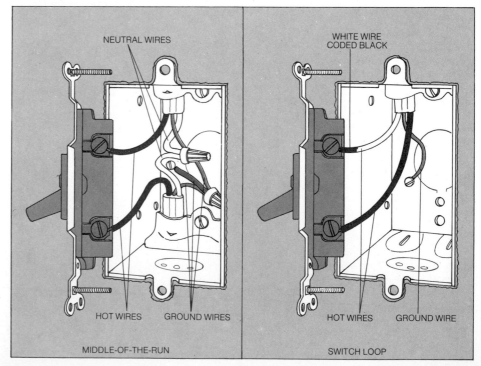

NEUTRAL WIRES

HOT WIRES   GROUND WIRES

MIDDLE-OF-THE-RUN

WHITE WIRE CODED BLACK

HOT WIRES   GROUND WIRE

SWITCH LOOP

3 **Testing the switch.** If you are replacing the switch because you think it faulty, use a continuity tester for two checks on the internal wiring of the switch. First, apply the alligator clip and probe of the tester to the switch terminals. Move the switch handle back and forth between the "off" and "on" positions. On a good switch, the tester will light at "on," but not at "off." Second, fasten the alligator clip of the tester to the metal mounting strap of the switch and touch the probe to each of the switch terminals in succession, moving the handle from the "off" to the "on" position at each terminal. On a good switch, the tester will not light in any position. If the switch fails either of these tests, it must be replaced.

4 **Installing the new switch.** Align the replacement switch vertically. A single-pole switch should be off when the handle is down and on when it is up. Connect the two hot wires to the terminals, either wire to either terminal. Push the switch back into the outlet box, folding the slack wire behind the switch, and fasten it with the mounting screws.

If the box is slightly tilted—as it generally is— change the position of the screws in the wide mounting slots to get the switch straight. If the box is recessed in the wall, circular tabs called plaster ears, located at the corners of the mounting strap, will keep the switch handle flush with the wall. If the box is flush and the ears get in the way of the cover plate, take them off with pliers.

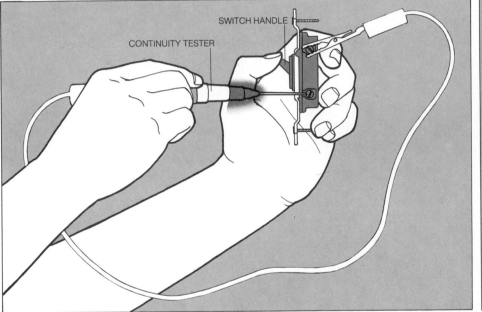

CONTINUITY TESTER

SWITCH HANDLE

PLASTER EARS

MOUNTING SCREW

MOUNTING SLOT

Grounding Switches

A safer grounding scheme. In the past, the metal parts of switches were grounded only by mounting screws that fastened them to grounded outlet boxes. Switches are now available with a more reliable ground connection: a separate grounding screw terminal, which is identified by a green screwhead or by the letters GR next to the screw hole. Ask your dealer to order such switches and use them as replacements. To ensure a good ground, the switch harness should contact the metal box.

To ground one of these switches in an outlet box wired with plastic-sheathed cable, run a short length of bare or insulated green wire from the green grounding terminal to the wire cap linking the bare ground wires of the cables and box. If armored cable serves the box, you may find no separate ground wire; run the wire from the green terminal directly to a grounding screw in the box.

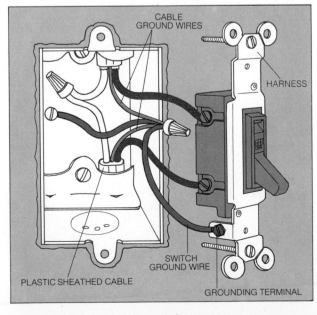

CABLE GROUND WIRES

HARNESS

SWITCH GROUND WIRE

PLASTIC SHEATHED CABLE

GROUNDING TERMINAL

Replacing a Three-Way or Four-Way Switch

If you are replacing a three-way switch because it is defective, you must first determine which of the two switches is the faulty one. Check three-way switches with a continuity tester as shown in the drawings at bottom.

However, when a four-way switch is used in conjunction with a pair of three-way switches *(shown opposite),* you will have to remove all of the cover plates to determine which of the devices are three-way switches and which is the four-way. A three-way switch has three terminals: a dark-colored one, the common terminal, and two lighter-colored terminals for traveler wires. (On back-wired three-way switches the common terminal is marked COM. or COMMON.) A four-way switch has four brass terminals for traveler wires connecting it to three-way switches. If both three-way switches check out satisfactorily, then you will know that the four-way switch is defective and should be replaced.

Before you put a new switch in, pay close attention to the way the wires are connected to the old switch. Like single-pole switches, the three- and four-way switches interrupt only the hot wire. You may find black, red and white wires connected to either type of switch, but all of them are hot wires regardless of color. A white wire that is connected to a switch should be coded black as shown in the drawing opposite. Other wires passing through the box go to other electrical devices and should not be disconnected when replacing the switch.

Quiet-action and mercury types are available as replacements for both three- and four-way switches, and there are also three-way switches equipped with lighted handles, dimmer controls *(page 327)* and pilot lights *(page 326).*

Replacing a three-way switch. Shut off the power to the circuit and without disconnecting the wires remove the switch from its box. Double-check that power is off by touching one probe of a voltage tester (page 322) to each of the three switch terminals in turn, while the other probe is touching the grounded box. Before disconnecting the wires, use a piece of masking tape to designate the wire that is attached to the common terminal—it is usually black or copper-colored, darker than the brass- or silver-colored traveler terminals. Disconnect all three wires. Then connect the wires to the new switch, attaching the marked wire to the dark-colored common terminal. Either traveler wire can be connected to either traveler terminal.

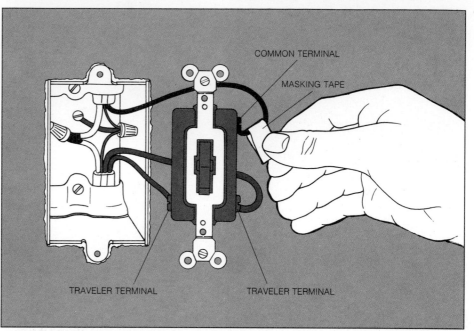

Testing three-way switches. To find which of a pair of three-way switches is faulty, shut off the power, disconnect one switch *(drawing, top),* and attach the clip of a continuity tester *(page 323)* to the common terminal. Place the tester probe on one traveler terminal *(above, left)* and move the switch toggle up and down. The tester should light when the toggle is in only one position, either up or down. Leaving the toggle in the position that showed continuity, touch the probe to the other traveler terminal *(above).* The tester should not light in this position, but should light when the toggle is flipped to the opposite position. If the switch passes both these tests it is good; reconnect it, then remove and check the other switch in the same manner.

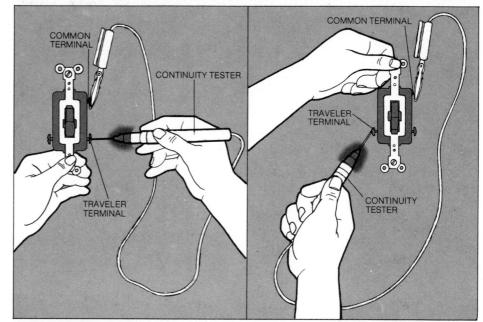

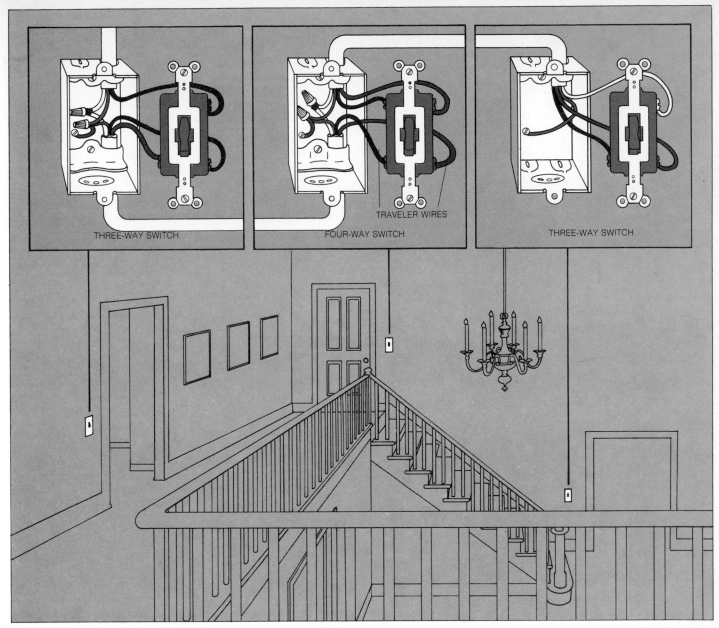

THREE-WAY SWITCH

FOUR-WAY SWITCH

TRAVELER WIRES

THREE-WAY SWITCH

Replacing four-way switches. To replace the four-way switch used with two three-way switches, shut off power and remove the cover plates from all three switches to make sure which is the four-way device. The hot traveler wires to the four-way switch must be black or red. Disconnect the traveler wires from the terminals at the top of the switch and transfer them to the terminals at the top of the replacement switch. (Either traveler wire can be connected to either terminal.) Then repeat the procedure for the wires on the bottom terminals.

If the replacement switch does not work properly when wired as shown in the center inset above, it may have a switching mechanism requiring a different wiring configuration. In that case, shut off power, loosen the two wires on either side of the switch and reverse the connections.

Time-Clock and Programmed Switches

1 Preparing the box wires. A wall-mounted time-clock switch can replace a single-pole switch only in middle-of-the-run wiring *(page 322, Step 1)*, where a neutral wire is available for the clock motor. If this requirement is met, turn off the power and remove the existing switch. Observing the precautions described on page 306, turn the power back on. Use a voltage tester to determine which of the two black wires in the outlet box is now hot; this is the incoming wire from the service panel. Turn the power off again. Mark the incoming wire with tape and remove the wire cap from the neutral wires.

2 Connecting the switch. If a special mounting plate is used (not all switches need one), attach it to the box. Straighten out the wire loops at the ends of the black cable wires. Using wire caps, connect the incoming black wire to the black wire of the switch, the outgoing black wire to the red (or other color, according to the instruction sheet) switch wire and the two white cable wires to the white switch wire. Fasten the switch to the mounting plate, restore power and follow the manufacturer's directions to test (and program if necessary) the switch.

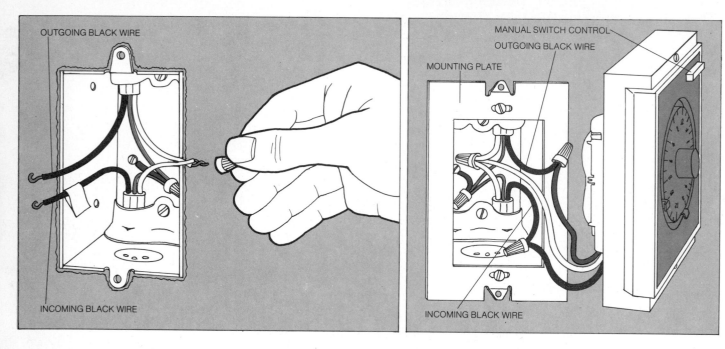

Pilot-Light Switches

Connecting the switch. Like time-clock switches, pilot-light switches can replace ordinary single-pole switches only in middle-of-the-run wiring where a neutral wire is available, in this case for the pilot-light bulb. Turn off the power and remove the old switch; prepare the box wiring as you would for a time-clock switch *(Step 1, above)*. Most pilot-light switches have three brass terminals and one silver one, with two of the brass terminals joined by an exposed brass strip. Connect the outgoing black cable wire to either of the joined terminals and the incoming black wire to the brass terminal on the opposite side. Connect the silver terminal to the white cable wires with a white jumper.

Some pilot-light switches have a bulb in the handle, and two rather than three brass terminals. Connect each brass terminal to one black cable wire. If the pilot light stays on when the switch is off, reverse the black-wire connections.

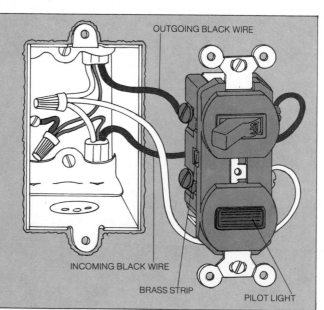

Incandescent Dimmer Switches

Dimmers provide a convenient way to adjust lighting levels to suit a particular activity or mood. They also save electricity and make light bulbs last longer (a dimmed filament operates at a lower temperature, slowing the burn-out process). Dimmers can be used to control only lights, not appliances or the receptacles into which appliances or motor-driven tools might be plugged. A dimmer switch also must be matched to the type of lighting it will control; incandescent dimmers cannot be used on fluorescent lights, which require their own devices. Finally, the total wattage of lights connected to the dimmer must not exceed the capacity listed on the front of each switch.

Wall-mounted dimmers like the ones shown here are designed for use only with permanent light fixtures and are available in both single-pole and three-way types. (Other types are available for use with table and floor lamps; check your electrical supply store for sockets with built-in dimmers and for dimmers that can attach to lamp cords or plug directly into wall receptacles.) Three-way dimmers are designed so that only one of the two three-way switches *(page 324)* is replaced. Thus, a light on such a three-way switch circuit can be turned on and off from two locations but it can be dimmed at only one of those points.

Most wall-mounted dimmers are full-range controls that provide completely variable light settings, from a faint glow to full brightness. These switches usually have a 600-watt capacity—more than enough for normal household lighting. When a full-range light control is not needed, a less expensive high/low dimmer can be used. These switches are usually controlled by toggles rather than rotary knobs and provide only two levels of illumination: full brightness and about 30 per cent brightness. High/low switches generally have a 300-watt capacity.

The electronic components of dimmers sometimes cause interference on television sets and AM radios that are plugged into the same circuit or located nearby. Most dimmers have a built-in filtering device. If the problem persists in spite of the filter, move the radio or TV as far away from the dimmer as practical or, if possible, plug it into another circuit. If no other circuit is available, a power-line filter will have to be used. These devices, available at radio and television supply stores, are attached between the appliance cord and the receptacle to trap interference coming through the house wires.

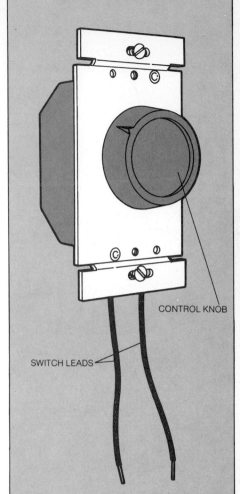

SINGLE-POLE DIMMER SWITCH

CONTROL KNOB

SWITCH LEADS

Wall-mounted dimmer switches. Single-pole dimmer switches *(top right)* are installed in the same manner as regular single-pole switches *(page 322)*. The only difference you may find on some is the presence of wire leads instead of screw terminals; fasten the leads to the cable wires with wire caps. Most dimmers have rotary control knobs that are pushed onto the knurled shaft after the cover plate has been installed.

If you want to provide dimming control on a three-way switch circuit, use only one dimming switch; the other switch in the circuit remains unchanged. Decide which three-way switch you wish to replace. Shut off power to the circuit and remove the switch *(page 324)*. Be sure to tag the wire on the common terminal with tape *(right)*. Connect this wire to the black switch wire and the red switch wires to the traveler wires.

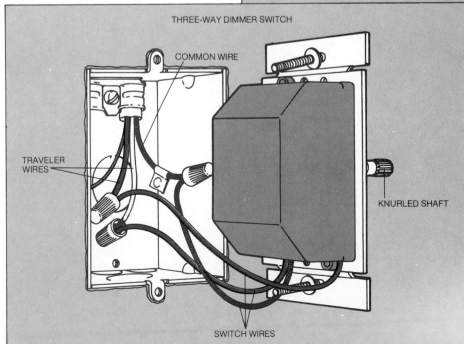

THREE-WAY DIMMER SWITCH

COMMON WIRE

TRAVELER WIRES

KNURLED SHAFT

SWITCH WIRES

Substituting New Plugs and Receptacles for Old

Plug-in receptacles and the plugs that fit into them are easy to install, whether to replace a defective one or to provide extra usefulness. A great variety of specialized receptacles are available to do the job of an ordinary one while adding safety or convenience. There are devices that combine a receptacle with a light fixture or a switch, nestle a receptacle below a floor, hide the cord of a clock, prevent children from poking into the holes or lock the prongs of a plug so it cannot be pulled out accidentally.

To connect a new receptacle, turn off the power and use a voltage tester to make certain it is off *(page 301)*. Follow the wiring patterns on pages 330-331. If the replacement is identical with the old one, you will probably hook the same wires to the same terminals—but be sure the old one was wired correctly. Some old installations may be improperly grounded or not grounded at all. More often, the replacement will differ slightly from the old one. For maximum safety, install a GFCI receptacle *(page 299)*.

Always replace a 120-volt outlet with the same kind; three-slot with three-slot, two-slot with two-slot. But if a ground is available in the box, three-slot grounding replacements should be used. Many 120-volt outlets now come with easy-to-use push-in terminals *(opposite)*. In the United States, 120/240-volt plugs usually use the neutral white wire for grounding an appliance; in Canada a fourth grounding wire is used, with a fourth prong and slot.

Plugs are available in two types. Molded plugs have the cord permanently attached; terminal types are attached to a separate cord. If a molded plug breaks, replace the plug-and-cord unit or cut the plug off and install a terminal plug as shown on page 313; do not splice a cord to a molded plug.

120-volt, grounded. The modern 15-ampere receptacle, as well as the 20-ampere receptacle for heavy-duty kitchen circuits, has an inverted U-shaped grounding slot for a matching grounding prong on the plug. The 15-ampere plug shown here will fit both 15- and 20-ampere receptacles. A 20-ampere plug has one prong angled so it fits only a 20-ampere receptacle.

120/240-volt, 30-ampere. Designed especially for clothes driers, this large receptacle supplies 240 volts for the heating coils and 120 volts for the motor and accessories such as the timer and the pilot light. In Canada, this circuit requires a fourth grounding wire, fourth prong and fourth slot.

Types of Slots and Prongs

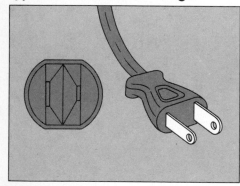

120-volt, 15-ampere, ungrounded. This receptacle is found in older homes without equipment grounding. In many receptacles, one slot is longer than the other. When the receptacle is correctly wired, the shorter slot is hot, the longer slot neutral. All 120-volt plugs fit such a receptacle. But almost all new lamps and appliances have plugs with similarly polarized prongs. These plugs can be inserted only one way, since the appliance circuits require a foolproof match of hot and neutral wires. To install the receptacle and plug, connect black wires to the terminals for the short slot and narrow prong, and white wires to the long slot and wide prong *(page 298)*.

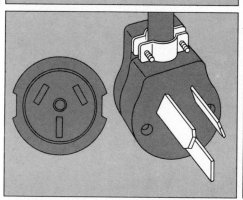

15 AMPERE

20 AMPERE

120/240-volt, 50-ampere. Electric ranges require the combination of voltages provided by this receptacle. High oven and burner settings work on the 240-volt circuit; the low burner settings, the timer and pilot lights run on 120 volts. Canadian codes require a four-wire plug and receptacle to accommodate a ground wire.

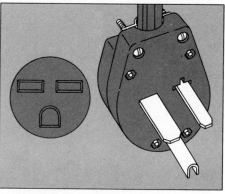

240-volt, 30-ampere, grounded. This receptacle, which supplies only 240 volts to appliances, is used mainly for small hot-water heaters and 240-volt air conditioners. The plug in the drawing above is a type that may be purchased separately if a replacement is needed. It is attached to the appliance cord.

The Two Kinds of Terminals

Side-wired receptacles. Two brass-colored terminal screws for black or red wires and two silver-colored terminal screws for white wires are located on the sides of this type. A green screw for the ground wire is at the bottom.

Back-wired receptacle. In this type, wires are attached by inserting them into holes at the back of the receptacle and detached by pressing the tip of a screwdriver into a release slot *(page 309)*. A green screw terminal for the ground wire is at the bottom. Some back-wired receptacles also have screw terminals like those at left.

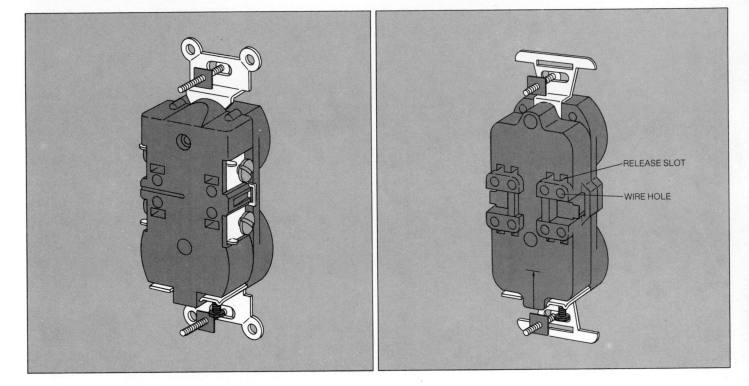

RELEASE SLOT

WIRE HOLE

Reading a Receptacle

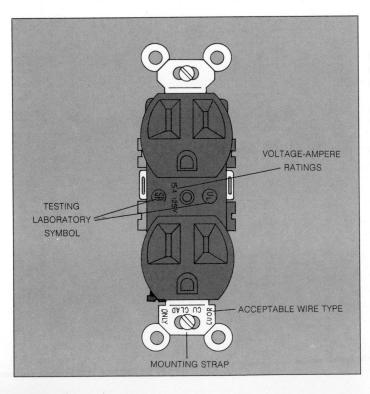

VOLTAGE-AMPERE RATINGS

TESTING LABORATORY SYMBOL

ACCEPTABLE WIRE TYPE

MOUNTING STRAP

Facts to look for. A receptacle like this one should be stamped with data on safety tests and operating characteristics: the UL logo of the Underwriters' Laboratories, Inc., or CSA of the Canadian Standards Association, which indicates that the receptacle has met standardized tests; the maximum voltage and amperage at which the receptacle can be used; and an abbreviation indicating the metal of the wires that can be connected to it. The abbreviation CU OR CU CLAD ONLY, indicates that either copper or copper-clad wire may be used. If solid aluminum wire is acceptable, the abbreviation reads CO/ALR, CU/AL or AL/CU. In this example 15A/125V means the receptacle can carry up to 15 amperes of current at voltages up to 125 volts, and CU or CU CLAD ONLY indicates that uncoated aluminum wire is not to be attached.

Replacing 120-Volt Receptacles

Middle-of-the-run with plastic cable. In middle-of-the-run wiring two cables enter the box, each containing a black, a white and a bare copper wire. Connect each of the black cable wires to a brass terminal of the new receptacle; connect each white cable wire to a silver receptacle terminal. Attach one 4-inch green jumper wire to the back of the box and another to the green receptacle terminal. Connect both jumpers to the bare cable wires with a wire cap.

Middle-of-the-run with armored cable. Connect each black cable wire to a brass receptacle terminal and each white cable wire to a silver terminal. Attach a 5-inch green jumper wire to the back of the box with a machine screw and connect this jumper to the green terminal.

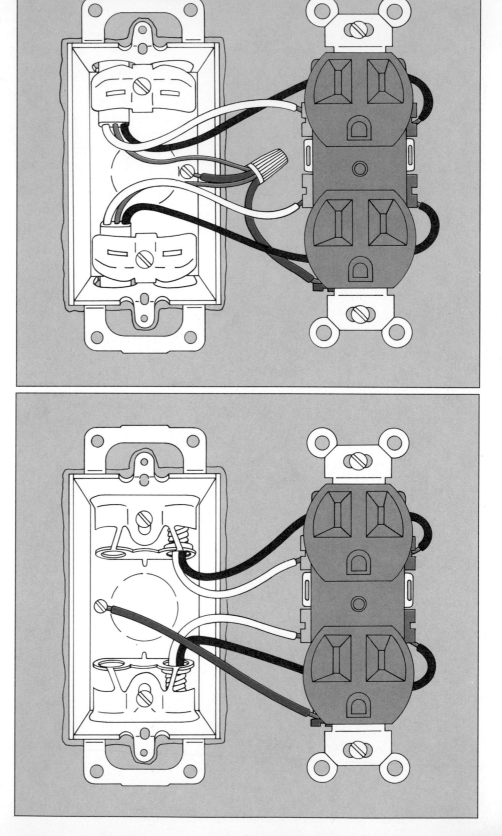

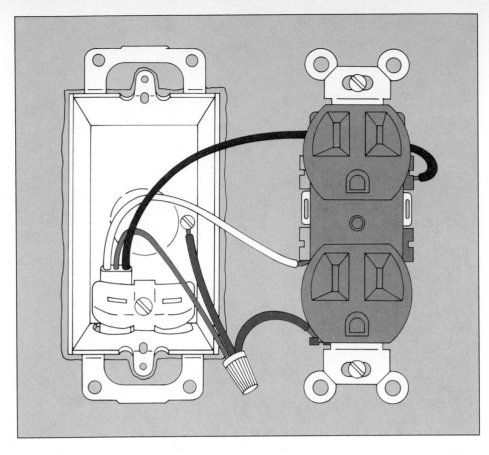

End-of-the-run wiring. In end-of-the-run wiring a single cable enters the box. If the cable is plastic-sheathed, it contains a black, a white and a bare copper wire. Connect the black cable wire to a brass terminal on the new receptacle and the white cable wire to a silver terminal. Attach one 4-inch green jumper wire to the back of the box with a machine screw and another jumper to the green receptacle terminal. Then join both jumpers to the bare cable wire with a wire cap.

Armored cable has no bare wire inside the box. To ground the installation, use a 5-inch green jumper wire and attach it to the back of the box with a machine screw. Then connect the jumper wire to the green screw on the receptacle.

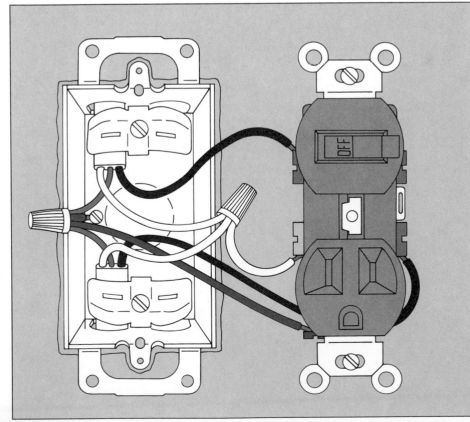

From Switch to Switch-Receptacle Combination

Installing the switch-receptacle. This installation, which combines a single-pole switch with a receptacle that is always hot, is possible only if the switch to be replaced is middle-of-the-run (*opposite*), because a white neutral wire must be available for the receptacle. Connect the incoming black cable wire to one of the pair of brass terminals linked by a metal tab. Connect the outgoing black wire to the brass terminal on the opposite side of the switch-receptacle. Attach a 4-inch white jumper wire to the silver terminal and connect it to the two white cable wires with a wire cap. Attach one 4-inch green jumper wire to the back of the box with a machine screw and another jumper wire to the green terminal of the switch-receptacle. Connect both jumpers to the bare cable wires with a wire cap.

Repairing Doorbells and Chimes

Doorbells and chimes are among the simplest electrical devices in the home. Consisting of three main components—the sounding unit, transformer and push button—they faithfully announce the arrival of guests for years without breaking down. Some chime units use modern electronics, and can be programmed to play a variety of tunes. Less costly and more common, however, is the mechanical chime that works when a plunger hits a sounding bar. Also popular is the familiar doorbell, which sounds when a metal clapper hits a gong.

When a doorbell or chime fails to sound, first check for a blown fuse or tripped circuit breaker. Otherwise, the problem is usually at the push button, where the weather and constant use can eventually take their toll. With only a regular screwdriver, you can easily take apart a push button and clean, dry and adjust the contacts. If the button is badly worn or damaged, replace it.

Next, inspect the wiring between the transformer, push button and sounding unit; make sure all connections are secure and that nothing has punctured the wire insulation. Use a cotton-tipped swab dipped in alcohol to clean around the small moving parts inside the chime unit, or between a doorbell's clapper and gong. (Electronic chime units use more complicated electronics and cannot be cleaned in the same way; however, they generally require less service.)

Since chimes and bells operate on very low voltage, repairs to them present little danger of electrical shock. However, to be sure, turn off the power to the doorbell system while working on the bell wires at the push button, chime and transformer. And, of course, when handling the connections between the transformer and the 120-volt house wiring, turn off the power and test to be sure that it is off.

Single push-button systems. At its simplest, this system consists of three main components as shown below: the transformer, which steps down high-voltage house current to anywhere between 10 and 20 volts, the push button that—when pressed—allows electricity to travel to the bell unit, which sounds when a clapper strikes a gong.

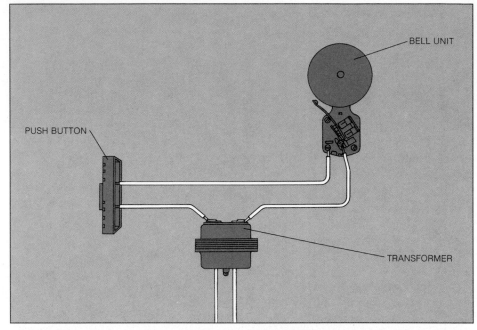

Two push-button system. Connected to the two doors in the same house, this system allows the bell or chime to be activated from two locations. The chime unit cover is easily removed for cleaning and lubrication of the plungers inside. Use a cleaning fluid that won't leave a residue on the moving parts.

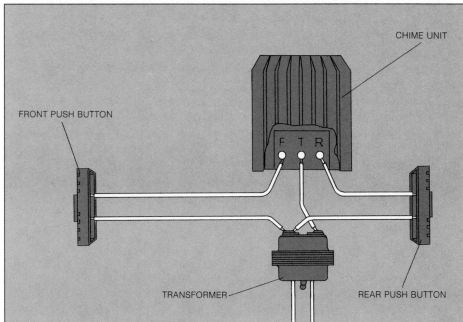

Servicing the Push Button

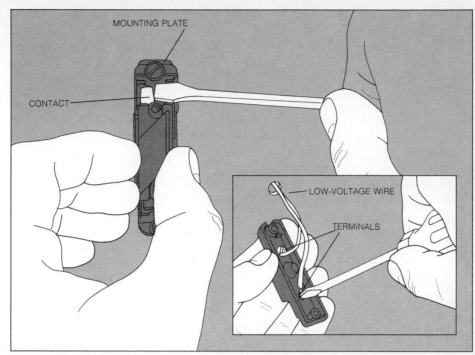

MOUNTING PLATE

CONTACT

LOW-VOLTAGE WIRE

TERMINALS

1 Inspecting the contacts and connections. With the power to the doorbell turned off *(page 297)*, remove any screws holding the push-button assembly together or securing it to the door frame. Check for any apparent corrosion on the contacts and clean them with fine sandpaper or steel wool. Next, use a screwdriver to bend the contacts, as shown. Remove the mounting, if any, and check that the low-voltage wire connected to the terminals is firmly screwed in place. If not, clip back and strip the wire end; wrap and screw it clockwise around the terminals *(inset)*. Reassemble and remount the push button, turn on the power and try the doorbell. If the doorbell keeps sounding even when the push-button is not pressed, the contacts have been bent too much. Bend them back after turning off the power. If the doorbell does not work when the push button is pressed, turn off the power and test the wiring *(below)*.

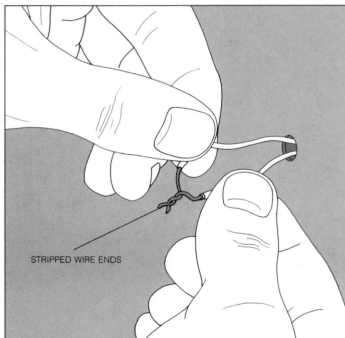

STRIPPED WIRE ENDS

2 Testing the wiring. Turn off the power *(page 297)* and remove the push-button assembly from the door frame; unscrew the low-voltage wire from the terminals and twist the stripped wire ends together. Turn on the power. The doorbell should sound; if it does not, the low-voltage wiring between the push button, transformer and chime or bell unit may be faulty; turn off the power and replace it with wire of the same type and gauge as the original wire. If the doorbell or chime unit works when the wires are twisted together, turn off the power and replace the push button *(right)*.

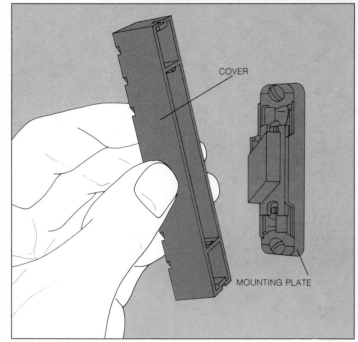

COVER

MOUNTING PLATE

3 Replacing the push button. With the power turned off to the chime or bell unit *(page 297)*, untwist the stripped wire ends and screw them to the terminals on the back of the push-button mounting plate, if any. Screw the mounting plate to the door trim and snap the cover in place, as shown. Turn on the power and press the push button to test it.

Outdoor Lighting

Outdoor fixtures may be permanently wired to a house circuit or temporarily plugged into an outdoor outlet. Regardless of how they are wired, these fixtures must be protected from the elements and accidental grounding by means of waterproof covers and insulation. The bulb,

too, should be weatherproof to prevent shattering from contact with rain or snow.

Depending on local codes, outdoor 120-volt fixtures are served by heavy, sheathed cable buried in the lawn, or by wiring fed through plastic or metal conduit. The wiring usually taps into an indoor circuit at a porch light or through the foundation or eaves of the house.

Regular maintenance can lengthen the life of your outdoor lighting system significantly. Periodically remove leaves, dirt and other debris from the fixtures.

Wipe cool bulbs and fixtures with a damp cloth to remove dust and insects. Replace burned-out standard bulbs with weatherproof ones; long-life bulbs are useful in hard-to-reach fixtures.

When repairing any part of an outdoor lighting system, seal all connections by wrapping the wire caps with electrical tape. At the same time, inspect each housing and gasket for signs of damage. If any part is cracked, corroded or broken, replace it before the wiring inside is affected. Any joint between the fixture

Porch Light

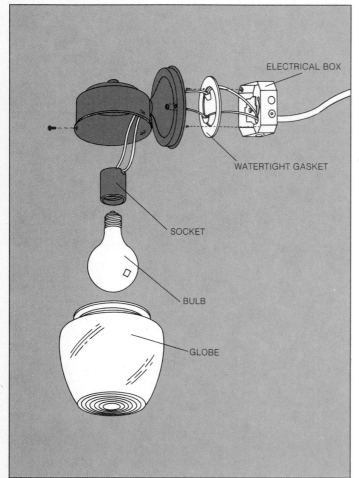

ELECTRICAL BOX

WATERTIGHT GASKET

SOCKET

BULB

GLOBE

Servicing a faulty porch light. When your porch light does not work, the cause may be a blown fuse or tripped circuit breaker—or a loose or burned-out bulb. Otherwise, check next for a faulty indoor wall switch *(pages 322-325)*. If the switch is working, the problem may be at the socket. Remove the globe and inspect the socket. Clean a dirty contact tab or adjust a bent one; check for loose or dirty socket connections and clean or tighten them as necessary. Test the socket *(page 307)* and replace it if faulty. Also replace a cracked or worn gasket.

Post Light

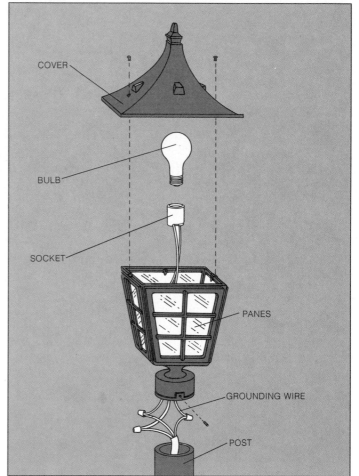

COVER

BULB

SOCKET

PANES

GROUNDING WIRE

POST

Troubleshooting a non-working post light. A typical post light is mounted on a post ranging in height from 3 to 8 feet and anchored in concrete or stone; a grounding wire is attached to the base of the fixture. The bulb is usually protected by glass or plastic panes and a weatherproof cover, as shown above. When a post light flickers or does not light, check the possible causes described at left for a faulty porch light. If you still cannot identify the problem, the cause may be a faulty outdoor circuit; have an electrician check the circuit and run a new one if necessary.

and the wall should also be made water-tight with a water-resistant caulking compound such as silicone.

Before working on permanent outdoor fixtures—or even changing a light bulb—turn off the power to the circuit by unscrewing the fuse or tripping the circuit breaker at the main service panel *(page 297)*. Then confirm the power is off by testing for voltage *(page 301)*. Unplug a plug-in patio light and, when working on a low-voltage system, unplug the transformer from the 120-volt house current.

For maximum safety outdoors, stand on a wooden plank or rubber car mat when working on wet or damp ground *(page 300)*; be sure to use a wooden ladder for hard-to-reach fixtures.

When an outdoor fixture does not work, first check for a loose or burned-out light bulb. The next most likely causes are loose connections and corroded sockets. A low-voltage fixture's transformer could be faulty or require a new fuse. Also inspect the low-voltage wiring between a transformer and the lights it

serves. Low-voltage wiring is generally less durable.

A less commonly damaged part of your outdoor system is underground 120-volt cable or conduit. If your wiring is severed by a shovel or backhoe, or otherwise damaged, you can splice it—according to local and national codes—if the repair site is flagged and easily accessible. Otherwise, replace it or call an electrician. If more than one fixture—or the entire system—does not work, chances are the circuit is damaged and needs repair.

Plug-In Patio Light

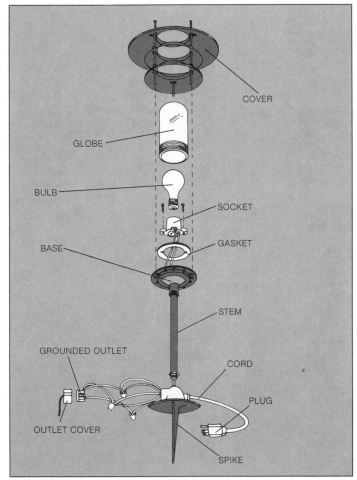

Fixing a plug-in patio light. Like the fixture shown above, many plug-in patio lights have one cord leading to a grounded outlet, and another attached to an exterior-grade plug which connects to the next patio light in a series. The base—protected by a waterproof gasket—houses the outlet and wire connections. A spike secures the light in the ground. In addition to the possible causes described for porch lights *(opposite)*, check a plug-in patio light for loose or dirty outlet connections, a faulty outlet and a damaged plug or cord *(page 328)*.

Low-Voltage Patio Light

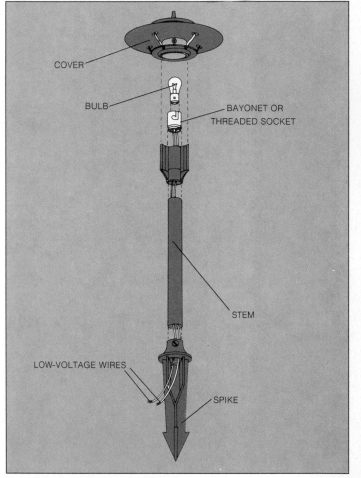

Repairing a low-voltage patio light. The low-voltage patio light may also be planted in the ground with a spike. Low-voltage wires are connected to the next patio light in a series or to the transformer. 12- to 16-gauge wire is buried 6 inches underground or simply run across the lawn. If one light is not working, the problem could be a loose or burned-out bulb, faulty socket and wires, or faulty wiring between lights. If more than one light is out, the transformer connections may need tightening or cleaning. Otherwise, the fuse or transformer probably needs replacement.

5 PLUMBING

A Guide for the Home Plumber

Most people fix dripping faucets as a matter of routine. Yet today a whole list of tasks once done by professionals can be handled by amateurs. Economy is one reason, but perhaps more important is the revolution in plumbing techniques; new materials are light in weight and many are assembled simply by tightening nuts or applying glue.

Every family can keep its water—and plumbing—bills down by a regular program of repairs and minor alterations. For example, repairing a drip *(pages 348-358)* while it is still in the drop-by-drop stage saves an amazing quantity of water —a trickle wastes a bathtubful of water a day. Inexpensive aerators—easily fitted into sink and lavatory spouts *(pages 359-360)*—deliver a splash-free stream and will pay for themselves many times over in water savings.

Using the right tools and methods, you can meet the crises and increase the conveniences of your plumbing system— thaw a frozen pipe *(pages 382-383)* or unclog a stopped-up main drain *(pages 346-347)*. Standardized plumbing materials and fittings have made these tasks simpler; some varieties of copper tubing and the increasingly popular plastic pipe are flexible and easy to install.

At one time or another, a plumbing repair may require shutting down the plumbing system. And when you leave a house empty and unheated for the winter, you must also weatherproof the system.

In order to drain your system efficiently follow this checklist:

☐ Cut off the house water supply by closing the main shutoff valve.
☐ Turn off the gas or electricity to the boiler and the water heater.
☐ Siphon water out of the clothes washer tub.
☐ If you have hot-water heat, open the toilet drain faucet and let the water flow into the floor drain. Next open all of the radiator valves. Then remove an air vent from a radiator on the top floor so that air will replace the water as it drains into the boiler.
☐ Working floor by floor, starting at the top, open all hot and cold water faucets— indoors and outdoors—and flush all toilets.
☐ Open the water heater drain faucets and water treatment equipment, if you have any.
☐ Finally, open the drain faucet on the main supply line to release any water that may remain in the pipes.

At this stage, your plumbing system will be adequately drained for repair or remodeling work. If you are closing the house for the winter months, be sure to take additional precautions.

For cold weather protection, the water remaining in your plumbing system must be replaced with antifreeze solution; this will keep the traps from bursting while still functioning as a barrier against sewer gases. Get the nontoxic propylene glycol antifreeze sold for recreational vehicles; the ethylene glycol antifreeze used in automobiles is toxic and alcohol-based products evaporate fast.

Mix the antifreeze with water, as directed on the label. Prepare the lavatory, sink and tub traps first. Remove all accessible cleanout plugs, drain the water from each trap into a pail and discard it; replace the plug. Pour at least a quart of the antifreeze solution into each trap. With traps you were unable to empty, pour the solution in very slowly so that it will push the existing water ahead of it.

Next, wipe up any water remaining in the bottom of toilet bowls with rags or newspapers. Pour at least a gallon of the antifreeze mixture into each toilet tank, and then flush it.

To complete the winterizing, remove either the inlet or outlet plug of the main house trap if you have one, and siphon out the water left in the trap. Pour about a quart of antifreeze into the trap and replace the plug. If you have your own well system, drain the water tank and dry off all parts of your pump—unless it is a submerged one, which requires no special precautions.

Plumbing Codes

Codes protect public health and safety by regulating the use of materials, placement of fixtures in relation to the stack and vent, slope and location of pipes, and anything pertaining to alterations, additions or repairs of the plumbing system. Seven regional codes serve the U.S. Local codes vary to meet the conditions of a particular area, especially for drainage and septic systems. Most plumbing repairs do not call for a permit, but to be safe, check first with local authorities.

Minimizing Water Damage if a Leak Floods You Out

Often the first sign of a leaking pipe will be a spreading stain on a wall or ceiling or a puddle on the floor. To prevent further damage, shut off the water supply immediately, before trying to trace and repair it.

You can sometimes anticipate water damage and keep it to a minimum. Where leaking pipes are concealed above the ceiling and a water stain is visible, place a waterproof dropcloth on the floor and position a catch basin under the wet area. If water is leaking from a ceiling light fixture, shut off the electricity *(page 297)* and confirm that it is off *(page 301),* then drain the fixture by removing its cover. Poke a hole through the ceiling or remove a section of it to let any remaining water drain out. Stand out of the way!

During a plumbing freeze-up, take precautions against leaks until you can be certain the pipes have suffered no damage. Since the leaks will be frozen until the pipes thaw, waterproof the suspect area with plastic dropcloths like those used by painters.

If you spot a crack, patch it *(page 376).* And be ready with a few extra pails in case undetected leaks reveal themselves suddenly.

If you arrive on the scene too late to avert a flood, you can still construct a makeshift dam from sandbags or rolled-up rugs to prevent the flood from spreading. For a bad flood, you may need a pump with a submersible motor, usually available from rental agencies (check under "pumps" in your phone directory). If the situation is desperate call the fire department— which is usually prepared to help.

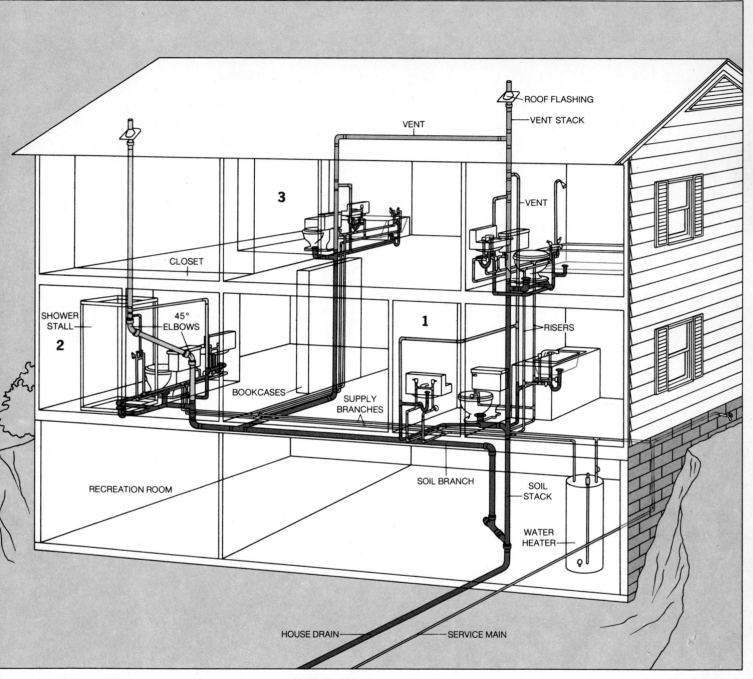

ROOF FLASHING
VENT STACK
VENT
VENT
CLOSET
3
SHOWER
STALL
45°
ELBOWS
2
RISERS
1
BOOKCASES
SUPPLY
BRANCHES
RECREATION ROOM
SOIL BRANCH
SOIL
STACK
WATER
HEATER

HOUSE DRAIN —————————— SERVICE MAIN

Pathways for pipes. In this two-story house, the existing plumbing core consists of two systems of pipes running from the basement to a first-floor kitchen and a second-floor bathroom. Supply pipes *(dark blue)* carry cold water from the service main and hot water from the water heater. Drains *(light blue)* and vents *(grey)* run to a soil stack that vents gases through the roof and carries wastes down to the main drain.

Three newer installations—a powder room next to the kitchen and full baths on the first and second floors—illustrate ways in which new plumbing was later added to the existing system.

In the powder room—labelled 1—all the newly installed fixtures were close enough to the existing plumbing core to be tied directly into it. An added drain runs across the open ceiling underneath the powder room to the existing stack, and another vent is connected to the existing vent. The supply lines are short extensions of nearby hot and cold vertical lines, called risers.

The first-floor bathroom—labelled 2—uses supply branches and a soil branch (the large horizontal drain) which run across the basement ceiling to and from the added bathroom. The pipes that cross the finished ceiling in the recreation room

can be concealed by a soffit or a dropped ceiling. The vent, too far from the existing vent for a direct connection, is a newer vent, offset with 45° elbows to carry it into the closet of a second-floor bedroom and onto a new roof outlet.

In the second-floor bath—labelled 3—an even larger run of supply piping and drainpiping runs to the second floor across the length and width of the basement and up along a first-floor wall. There, it is concealed by floor-to-ceiling bookcases. The vent, however, is close enough to the existing stack to be connected to it by a pipe running up through the wall and across the attic.

Tool Kit for Plumbing

A few specialized tools will help you meet most plumbing emergencies as well as install and replace pipes and fixtures.

☐ For unclogging blocked drains you will need a plunger—the "plumber's friend." A fold-out cup extension converts the plunger so it can be used on either basins or toilet bowls. A drain-and-trap auger (also called a plumber's snake) hooks and draws out blockages from sink drains. For toilets, use a closet auger; its curved end gets the tool started inside the toilet bowl passage.

☐ For loosening and tightening many different plumbing parts, several specialized wrenches are helpful. A pipe wrench has teeth that bite and hold. You need two, one for holding a part, another for turning. Get a 12- to 14-inch pipe wrench for supply pipes and an 18-inch one for drainage pipes. A basin wrench turns faucet nuts in tight places up behind sinks. Its swiveling jaw is turned one way for loosening, the opposite way for tightening. The toothless jaws of a spud wrench open wide for turning the large nuts on sinks and some toilets. Although cast iron pipe is no longer commonly used, its sections are secured using a torque wrench.

☐ For cutting copper water tubing, use a tube cutter. A coiled tube bender lets you form tubing without kinking. To join copper tubing by sweat soldering, you'll need a propane torch, emery cloth, low-lead solder, soldering flux and a flux applicator. A flameproof pad or piece of sheet metal is handy to protect nearby framing. A tube flaring tool lets you make flared joints in water supply tubes. A flame spreader attachment for your torch is helpful when thawing frozen pipes.

☐ Working with plastic water supply and drainage pipes requires no specialized tools, just some solvent cement and a fine-toothed saw. (With some kinds of plastic you need only the saw.)

☐ To fix leaks caused by worn faucet seats, you need a seat wrench, which has a square tip at one end and a hexagonal tip at the other end. It will grip either of the two common types of faucet seats. A faucet seat dresser with assorted cutters and guides is used for refacing older nonreplaceable faucet seats right in the faucet body.

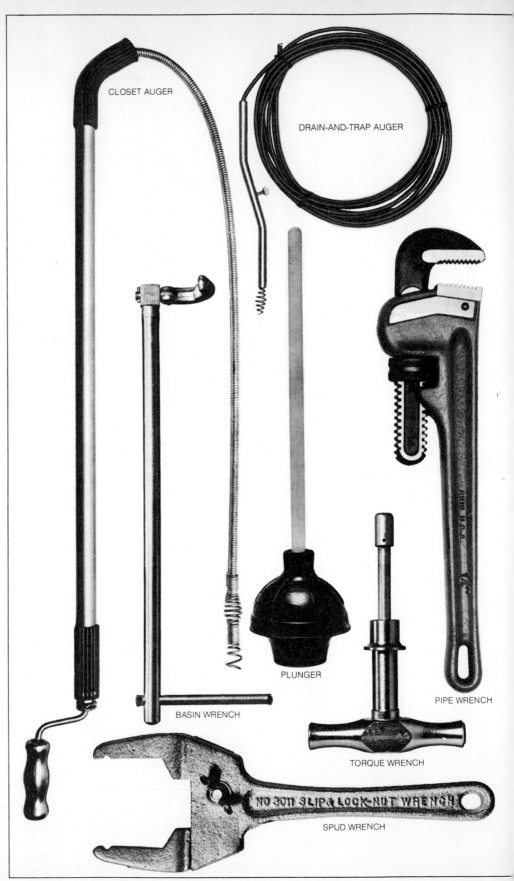

CLOSET AUGER

DRAIN-AND-TRAP AUGER

PLUNGER

BASIN WRENCH

TORQUE WRENCH

PIPE WRENCH

NO 3011 SLIP & LOCK-NUT WRENCH

SPUD WRENCH

FLAME-SPREADER
ATTACHMENT

FLAMEPROOF PAD

SEAT WRENCH

SEAT
DRESSER

TUBE CUTTER

LOW-LEAD SOLDER

FLUX

FLUX APPLICATOR

TUBE-FLARING TOOL

PROPANE TORCH

EMERY CLOTH

TUBE BENDER

Time-Tested Methods for Unclogging Drains

A drain blockage may be in the trap under the fixture, in a branch line carrying waste from several fixtures to the main drain, or in the main house drain or its connections to the sewer. If only one fixture is blocked or sluggish, start by cleaning its trap. If several fixtures are clogged, follow the techniques on the opposite page and pages 346-347 for cleaning branch and main drains. When you are working with branch or main drains, turn off the water at the main shutoff valve to avoid accidental flooding if someone should turn on a faucet elsewhere in the house.

A common force-cup plunger and a drain-and-trap auger are not only the easiest unclogging tools to use, but also the most effective and the safest. Devices that use compressed air often impact the blockage and may loosen or blow apart fragile pipes such as lavatory traps.

It is not advisable to use a chemical drain cleaner in a fixture that is completely blocked. The most powerful cleaners contain lye, a caustic compound that is dangerous and can harm fixtures if left too long in them. If the chemical cleaner does not clear the drain, you will be exposed to the caustic when you open a cleanout plug or remove a trap.

After a drain has been cleaned, chemical cleaners do serve a useful purpose. When used regularly—every two weeks or so—they prevent buildup of debris that could lead to a future blockage.

Lavatories and Sinks

1 Using a plunger. Remove the sink strainer or pop-up drain plug *(pages 367-368)*. If there is an overflow opening—most kitchen sinks have none—plug it with wet rags. Any air gap provided for a dishwasher also must be plugged. Be sure there is enough water in the basin to cover the plunger cup completely. Coat the rim of the cup evenly with petroleum jelly and center the cup over the drain hole. Without breaking the seal between the drain and the cup, pump down and up with short, rapid strokes 10 times, then jerk the plunger up from the drain quickly. Repeat the procedure several more times if necessary. If the drain still remains clogged, try Step 2.

2 Using an auger. With strainer or pop-up stopper removed, feed a drain-and-trap auger into the drain by cranking the handle clockwise. As you push the auger wire farther into the drain, alternately loosen and tighten the thumbscrew on the auger handle. When you hook something move the auger backward and forward slowly while cranking, then withdraw the auger wire slowly while continuing to crank in the same direction. Pour hot water and detergent through the trap to clear away residual grease or oils. If the auger does not clear the trap, try Step 3.

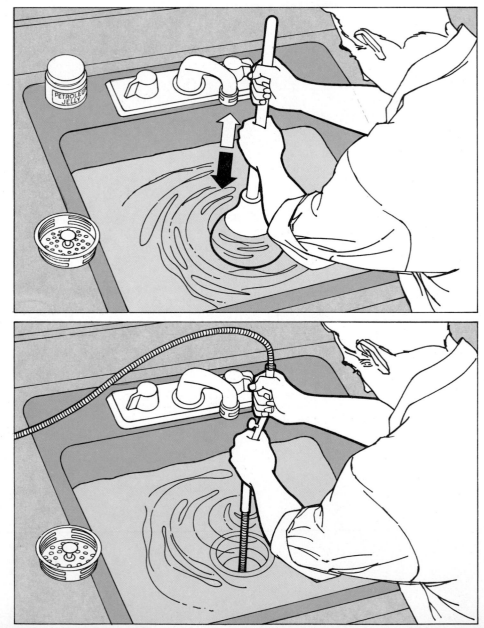

3 **Working through the cleanout plug.** If the trap under the clogged fixture has a cleanout plug, place a bucket under the trap and remove the plug. After water has emptied from the trap, straighten a wire coat hanger, form a small hook in one end, and probe through the trap. If the obstruction is near the opening, you should be able to dislodge it or hook it and draw it out. If not, feed a drain-and-trap auger first up to the sink opening, then through the back half of the trap. If the blockage is not in the trap, try Step 5.

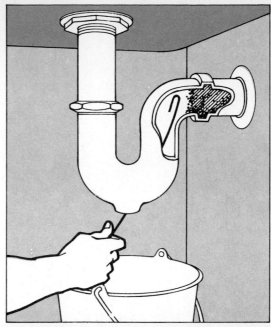

4 **Removing a trap for cleaning.** A trap may not have a cleanout plug. If the blockage cannot be cleared by a plunger or an auger inserted through the sink drain, shut off the water, wrap the jaws of a wrench with tape to protect the chromed slip nuts at either end of the trap, unscrew the nuts and detach the trap. Clean it with detergent and a bottle brush. Replace the trap and turn on the water. If the drain is still clogged, try Step 5.

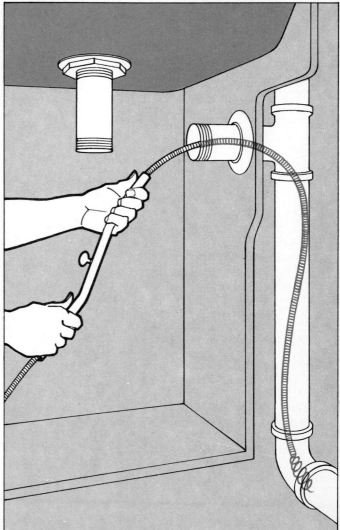

5 **Cleaning beyond the type.** With the trap removed, crank the drain-and-trap auger into the exposed end of the drainpipe that goes into the wall. The blockage may be in a vertical pipe behind the fixture or in a horizontal pipe—a branch drain—that runs through the wall or floor to connect to the main drain-vent stack serving the entire house. If the auger goes in freely through the branch drain until it hits the main stack, the blockage is probably in a section of the main drainage system (pages 346-347).

Drains below Floors

A hose instead of an auger. For floor drains like those in showers or basements, a garden hose often is more effective than an auger if the blockage is far down. Remove the strainer from the drain. Attach the hose to a faucet (a threaded adapter is needed for a sink or lavatory faucet). Push the hose into the drain and pack rags around it. While you hold the hose—and the rags —in the drain, have a helper turn the water alternately on full force and abruptly off. The surges of pressure should clear the blockage.

To get increased pressure you can buy, at plumbing-supply stores, an inexpensive rubber device *(inset)* that resembles a hose nozzle and seals the hose in the drains better than rags. When the water is turned on, the device expands against the drainpipe so that the full force of water is directed into the drain. Caution: Never leave a hose in any drain. If water pressure should drop suddenly and drastically—a rare but not impossible occurrence—sewage could be drawn back into the fresh-water system.

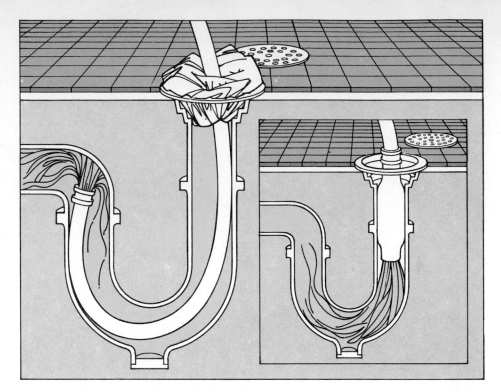

Bathtubs

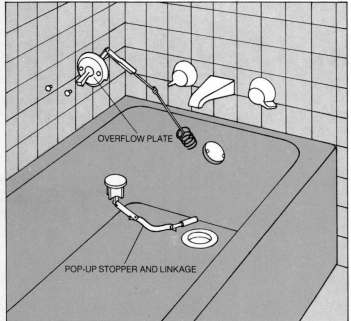

OVERFLOW PLATE

POP-UP STOPPER AND LINKAGE

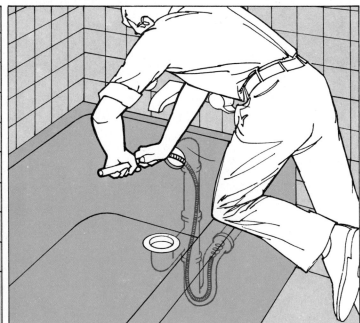

1 **Gaining access to the drain.** To unclog a bathtub, unscrew the overflow plate and lift it up and out. Draw out the stopper and its linkage. (Note how the parts line up so that you can put them back in the same way—there is a detailed view of the linkage on page 370.) Close the overflow opening with rags or masking tape, then use a plunger to open the clog. If that fails, try an auger as explained in Step 2.

2 **Unclogging a bathtub with an auger.** Run the auger through the tub overflow opening to reach the P trap, which serves both tub drain and overflow. Use the cranking and back-and-forth movements of the auger described on page 342.

A different type of bathtub trap. Instead of the common P trap, bathtubs in older houses and apartments may have a so-called drum trap located at floor level alongside the tub. To get at it, unscrew the cover of the trap counterclockwise with an adjustable wrench. Remove the rubber gasket. Using a drain-and-trap auger, first search for a blockage in the lower pipe inside the drum. If you find no obstruction there, insert the auger in the upper pipe, which goes to the main drain.

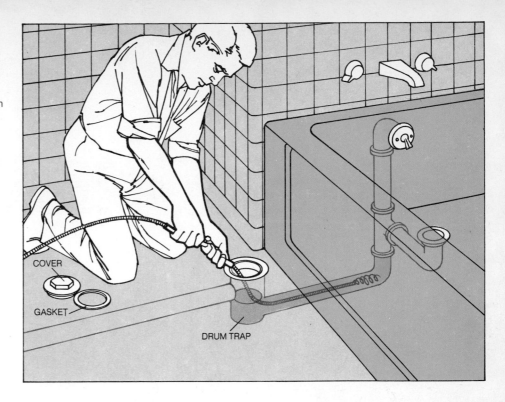

COVER

GASKET

DRUM TRAP

Toilets

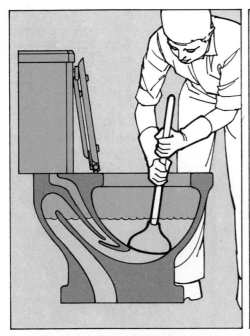

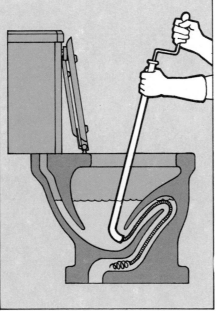

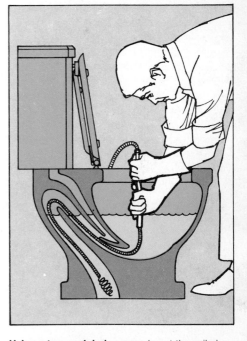

1 Using a plunger. If the clogged toilet bowl is full to the rim, empty out half its contents. If the bowl is empty, add water up to the normal level. Fit a rubber plunger, which has an extended lip to fit into the drain, over the large opening near the bottom of the bowl. Pump 10 times with short, rapid strokes, then lift the plunger quickly. If water rushes out, you may have cleared the blockage; test by pouring in a pail of water. If the plunger does not work, go on to Step 2.

2 Using a closet auger. Add or remove water as in Step 1. The type of auger shown above—designed specifically for unclogging toilets—has a cranking handle attached to a long sleeve shaped to guide the auger hook directly into the trap. Hold the sleeve firmly near the top and crank the auger hook slowly clockwise into the trap until you hook the obstruction. The closet auger above is being used on a bowl that has the drain opening toward the front; it also works well with the models that have rear drain openings.

Using a trap-and-drain auger. Insert the coiled-spring end into the drain opening. To avoid chipping the fragile vitreous china of the bowl, you must guide this auger carefully past projections of the trap. Crank the auger handle clockwise until you break through the obstacle or hook onto it and can pull it out. When the drain seems clear, test with a pail of water.

Unclogging the Main Drains

If all the waste from the fixtures in a bathroom backs up into the tub, or water from the clothes washer floods the basement, the trouble probably lies in the main drain and its branches, which channel waste into the sewer. When the clog forms in any part of the major drainage system, all the fixtures above the blockage stop up. When a clog forms in the stack vent, which keeps air flowing through the system, waste drains sluggishly and odors may be noticeable in the house.

Before you start work, track the pipes and connections in your own, perhaps unique, drainage system and try to pinpoint the cause of the trouble. If the clog seems to be in a branch drain, you can clean it out with a drain-and-trap auger, working at the fixture closest to the soil stack and following the instructions on page 343, Step 5. In order to make the job easier, you can rent an electrically powered auger up to 50 feet long from a tool-rental dealer.

Even an electric auger, however, will not work effectively if you push it around too many bends in the pipes. So if the problem seems to be beyond a branch, take the straightest possible route to the clog. To clear the main stack, the vertical pipe to which branches are attached, feed the auger down from the vent on the roof; to clear the basement or below-floor-level drain connected to the bottom of the stack, work through the main cleanout or—if you have one—the house trap. When you suspect that the problem is in the sewer line, somewhere between the house and the street, you will most likely have to enlist the services of a professional plumber.

In most plumbing repairs speed is essential, but unclogging the main drain calls for patience. The column of water trapped by the blockage may extend above the cleanout, and it will gush out, adding to the existing flooding, as soon as the plug is removed. If possible, wait for at least two or three hours after you spot the trouble to permit dispersion of whatever waste can seep past the blockage. Even then, you will need to arm yourself with mops, pails, rags and old newspapers for soaking up up the overflow.

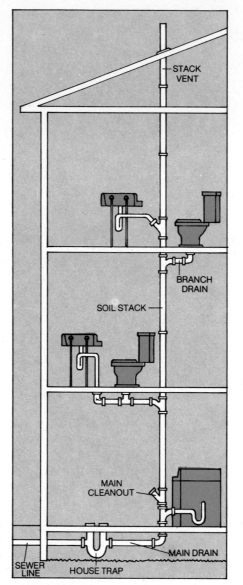

Locating the clog. Since waste flows downward and toward the sewer, any clog in a major drain is always below the level of the lowest stopped-up fixture and above the level of the highest working fixture. In this example, if the fixture at top left drains freely while the one at top right is blocked, the blockage is in the branch drain at right. If all top floor fixtures clog and the main floor and basement fixtures drain freely, the blockage is in the upper soil stack. If the main floor and top floor fixtures are stopped up while the basement ones drain freely, the blockage is in the lower soil stack. Clear the stack from the roof (above, right). If everything clogs, the blockage is in the main cleanout or house trap, (opposite).

Clearing the Soil Stack and Stack Vent

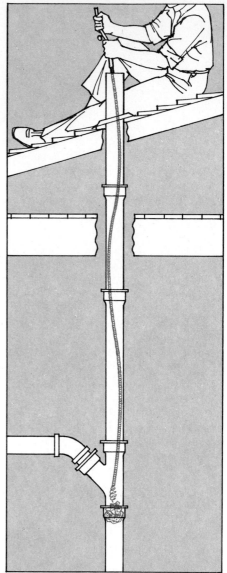

Running an auger down the stacks. Choose a trap-and-drain auger that is long enough to reach to the bottom of the soil stack. Position yourself securely on the roof beside the vent opening; use extreme caution when working on a roof. Feed the auger down the stack, using it as described on page 343; then flush out the stack with a garden hose.

Getting at the Main Drain from the Cleanout

1 Opening the main cleanout. Look for this Y-shaped fitting near the bottom of the soil stack or where the drain leaves the house. Set a pail underneath the cleanout plug and lay rags around to catch the flood that may occur. Use a pipe wrench to unscrew the plug counter-clockwise. If the plug does not turn, first try working penetrating oil into the threads, then slide a section of pipe over the wrench to increase your leverage. As a last resort, nick the plug's edge with a cold chisel and—keeping the blade in the nick—hammer the plug around.

2 Working from the main cleanout. Remove the plug completely and mop up the flood. Using a drain-and-trap auger long enough to reach the sewer outlet, probe and remove the obstruction, then flush with a hose. Coat the plug with grease or pipe compound and recap the cleanout.

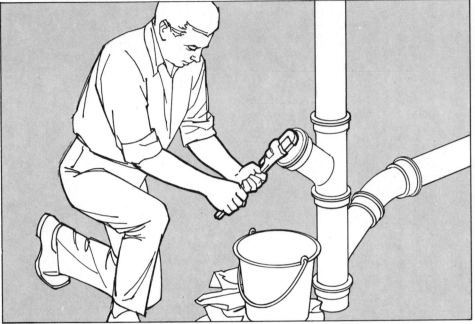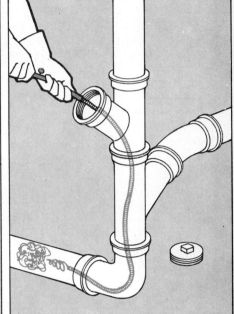

Getting at the Main Drain from the House Trap

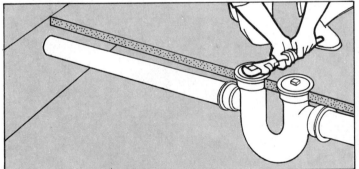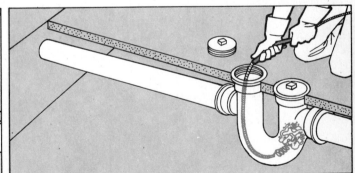

1 Opening the house trap. Locate this fitting by its two adjacent cleanout plugs, visible at floor level if the main drain runs under the floor. Spread heavy rags or stacks of newspapers around the trap to prepare for flooding, then slowly loosen the plug closest to the outside sewer line.

If no water leaks out as you unscrew the plug, the clog is in the trap or the main drain between the trap and main cleanout and may be fairly easy to remove (*Step 2*). If water seeps out, probe the drain beyond the house trap with an auger. Unless you can remove such a blockage quickly, recap the plug and call the plumber.

2 Working from the trap. Unscrew the trap plug completely and feed an auger through the trap toward the main cleanout, but probe gently. Do not attempt to free the blockage all at once, as you would when working from above, but poke a small hole in it. Wait for water to drain gradually, then break up the blockage with repeated jabs of the auger. After the flow subsides, open both house trap cleanouts and scrape out any remaining sludge with a wire brush. (If the clog is not in the trap but in the main drain between the trap and the cleanout, remove the second trap plug and feed the auger toward the cleanout, following the same precautions.) Recap the house trap cleanouts and insert a hose into the main cleanout to flush the main drain. Replace the cleanout plug.

Repairing Faucets

A dripping faucet is not only annoying but stains and erodes a sink or lavatory and wastes water—25 drops a minute may consume one gallon a day. Faucet trouble usually announces itself as a steady drip, drip, drip from the spout, or as a slow leak from around the handle or collar. To solve the problem, you must first identify what kind of faucet you have so that you can buy the exact replacement parts. In most cases, this means disassembling the faucet, then comparing it to those illustrated in this section.

Compression faucets, always double-handle, have a washer that rests on a seat at the bottom of the stem. When a compression faucet is turned on, the washer rises to allow water to flow to the spout.

(When a reverse-compression faucet is turned on, the stem lowers to create a space between the washer and seat, allowing water up.) Simply changing the stem washer will often stop the spout from dripping, but on older faucets the seat may also need replacement. Replacing the O-ring or packing in the stem will usually stop leaks from the handle.

A *diaphragm* faucet, another type of double-handle faucet, is easily repaired. A change of O-ring stops most leaks from the handle. Replacing the diaphragm, which controls water flow, stops leaks from both the spout and the handle.

A *disc* faucet, double-handle or single-lever, has a pair of plastic or ceramic discs that move up and down to regulate the volume of water, and rotate to control temperature. The disc assembly rarely needs changing, but the inlet ports can become clogged, and the seals can wear out.

A *cartridge* faucet regulates water flow by means of a cartridge controlled by a single lever. Repairs involve changing the O-rings or replacing the entire cartridge.

A *rotating-ball* faucet, another single-lever faucet, employs a slotted plastic or brass ball set atop a pair of spring-loaded rubber seats. The handle rotates the ball to adjust water temperature and flow. When this faucet leaks from the spout, its springs and seats probably need replacing. Seepage around the handle points to worn O-rings or an adjusting ring that should be tightened.

Double-Handle Faucet

Single-Lever Faucet

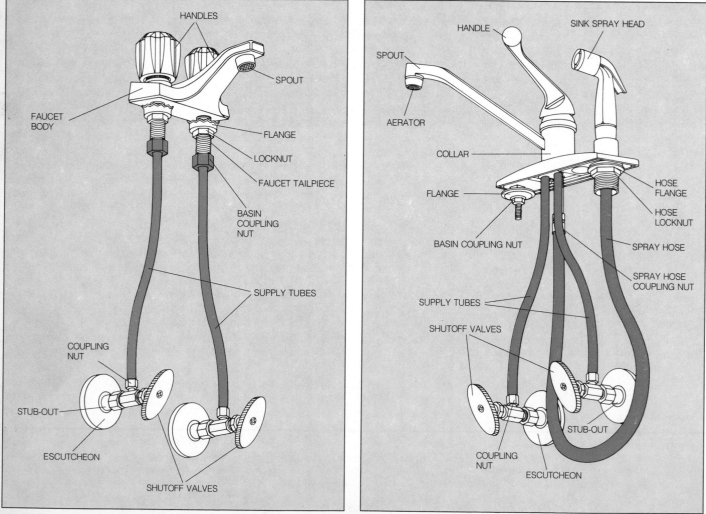

Stem Faucets

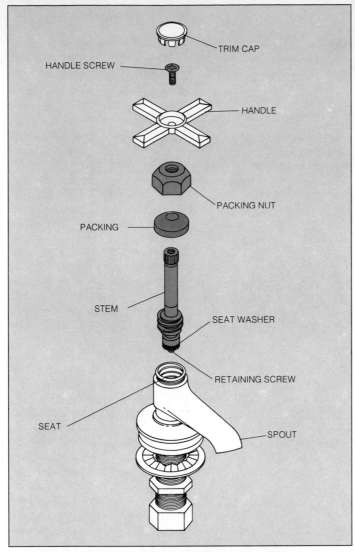

- TRIM CAP
- HANDLE SCREW
- HANDLE
- PACKING NUT
- PACKING
- STEM
- SEAT WASHER
- RETAINING SCREW
- SEAT
- SPOUT

2 Removing the old packing. Use an adjustable wrench to unscrew the packing nut from the faucet body *(below)*. Pry off the old packing washer or unwind old packing string. Scour the base of the stem thoroughly with steel wool to remove mineral deposits, and replace the packing *(Step 3)*. If the spout drips, also change the washer at the base of the stem.

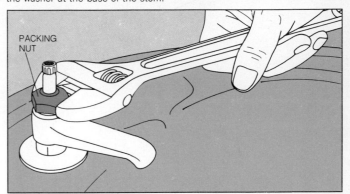

- PACKING NUT

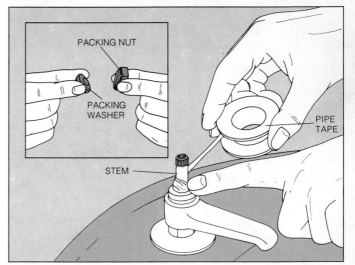

- PACKING NUT
- PACKING WASHER
- PIPE TAPE
- STEM

3 Changing the packing. Insert a replacement packing washer into the packing nut *(inset)*; replace packing string with pipe tape *(above)* or packing string. Wrap the tape or string several times around the base of the stem, stretching and pressing it down as you go. Thread the packing nut back on, but do not overtighten. The nut will compress the packing when you screw it down. Reassemble the handle and test the repair.

- TRIM CAP
- HANDLE SCREW
- STEM
- PACKING NUT

1 Opening up the faucet. To stop leaks around the handle, try tightening the packing nut by turning it clockwise with an adjustable wrench, its jaws taped to protect the chrome finish. (Be careful not to overtighten the nut, however.) If this has no effect, turn off the water and carefully pry off the trim cap with a small screwdriver *(above, left)* or knife. Then unscrew the handle screw *(above, right)* and pull off the handle.

Double-Handle Compression Faucets

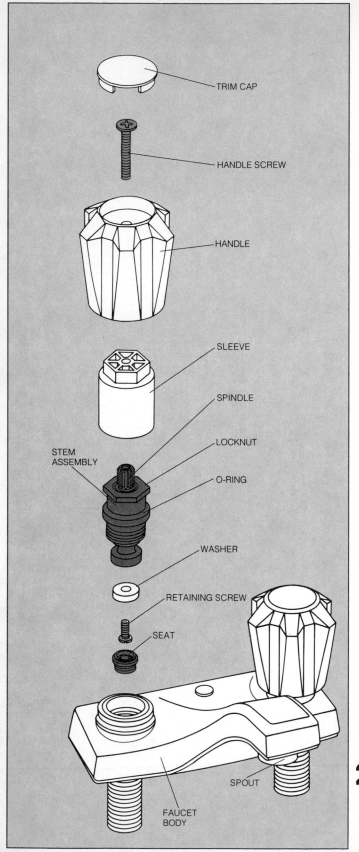

- TRIM CAP
- HANDLE SCREW
- HANDLE
- SLEEVE
- SPINDLE
- LOCKNUT
- STEM ASSEMBLY
- O-RING
- WASHER
- RETAINING SCREW
- SEAT
- SPOUT
- FAUCET BODY

1 **Opening the faucet.** To find out which handle needs servicing when the spout drips, turn off one shutoff valve under the sink. If the leak stops, the problem is with that handle; otherwise, the other handle is at fault. If there are no individual shutoff valves, service both. Turn off the water supply, open the faucet and close the drain to prevent loss of parts. Pry off the trim cap with a knife or small screwdriver (*below*). Remove the handle screw (*inset*).

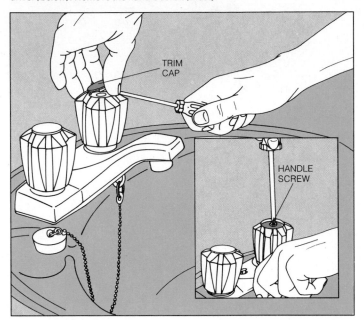

TRIM CAP

HANDLE SCREW

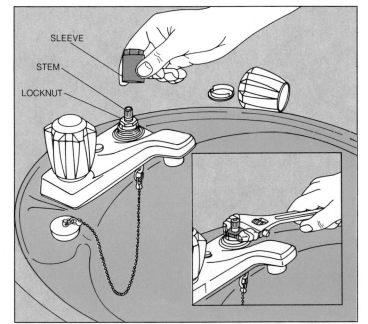

SLEEVE

STEM

LOCKNUT

2 **Getting at the stem.** Lift off the faucet handle and sleeve (*above*). If it will not budge, apply penetrating oil and wait an hour before trying again. Never strike the handle sleeve with a hammer; you might damage the soft brass stem. Open the faucet one-half turn, then unscrew the locknut that secures the stem to the faucet body (*inset*).

3 Replacing the O-ring. Grasp the stem spindle with taped pliers and lift it out of the faucet body. To stop leaks around the handle, pinch off the O-ring *(below),* lubricate a new O-ring with petroleum jelly, then roll it onto the stem until it is firmly seated. Reassemble and test the faucet.

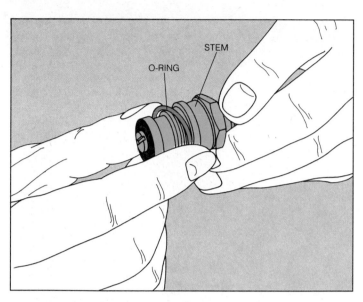

4 Replacing the washer. A dripping spout points to a worn stem washer. Carefully remove the retaining screw *(below)* and pry the washer from the stem with the tip of a screwdriver or knife. (If the screw is tight, reinstall the faucet handle for better leverage.) Replace with an identical washer, its flat side facing the stem. With the washer in place, tighten the retaining screw until it presses the washer squarely into the stem. Reassemble and test the faucet. If the spout still leaks, replace or dress the seat *(Step 5).*

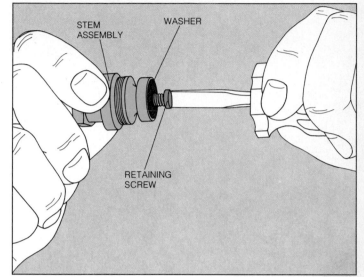

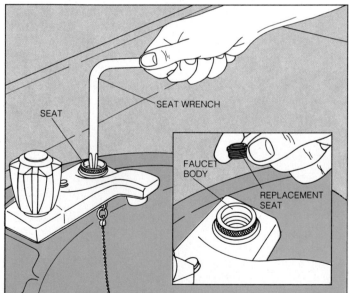

5 Removing the seat. Use a hex wrench or special faucet seat wrench *(above)* to unscrew a leaking seat by turning it counterclockwise. If the seat will not budge, apply penetrating oil, wait overnight and try again. Once the old seat is free, fit an identical replacement seat into the faucet body by hand *(inset)* or with a pair of long-nose pliers. Screw it in tightly with the hex wrench or seat wrench. If the seat cannot be removed—it may be built into the faucet—it must be ground smooth with a valve-seat dresser *(next step).*

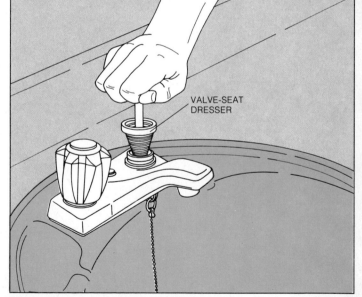

6 Dressing the seat. Buy or rent a valve-seat dresser with the largest cutter that fits the faucet body, and screw on a guide disc that fits the valve seat hole. Slide the cone down snugly into the faucet body. Turn the handle clockwise several times to grind the seat smooth *(above).* Wipe off the filings with a damp cloth, and reassemble the faucet.

Double-Handle Diaphragm Faucets

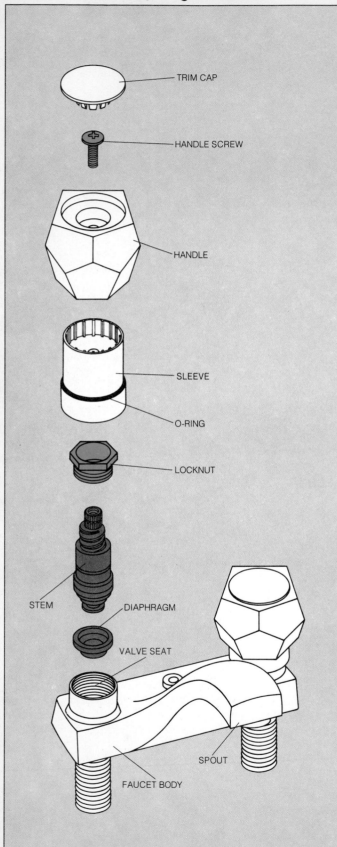

TRIM CAP

HANDLE SCREW

HANDLE

SLEEVE

O-RING

LOCKNUT

STEM

DIAPHRAGM

VALVE SEAT

SPOUT

FAUCET BODY

1 **Opening the faucet.** Turn off the water supply, open the faucet one half turn and close the drain to prevent loss of parts. Carefully pry off the trim cap with a knife or small screwdriver. Remove the handle screw and pull off the handle *(below)*. To stop water leaking from the handle, replace the O-ring. Roll it off the sleeve *(inset)*, lubricate a new O-ring with petroleum jelly and roll it into place. Reassemble and test the faucet. If the leak persists, replace the diaphragm *(next step)*.

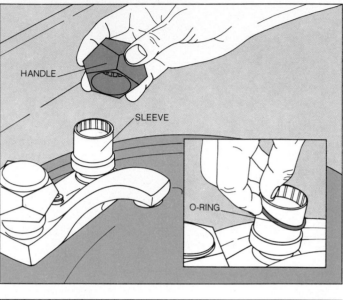

HANDLE

SLEEVE

O-RING

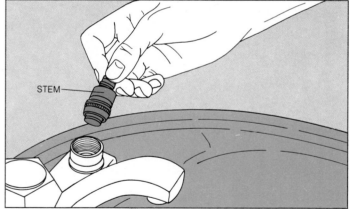

STEM

2 **Replacing the diaphragm.** To stop the leaks from the handle or spout, replace the hat-shaped diaphragm. Lift off the chrome sleeve with tape-covered pliers, exposing the locknut. Unscrew the locknut with a tape-covered adjustable wrench and lift the stem from the faucet body *(above)*. Pry off the diaphragm by hand.

Double-Handle Disc Faucets

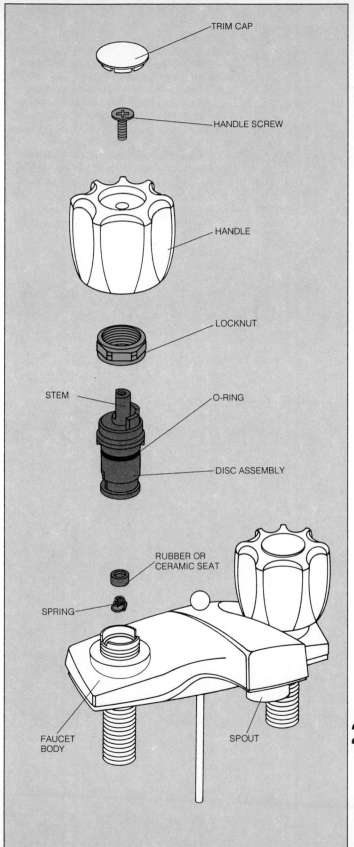

TRIM CAP

HANDLE SCREW

HANDLE

LOCKNUT

STEM

O-RING

DISC ASSEMBLY

RUBBER OR
CERAMIC SEAT

SPRING

FAUCET
BODY

SPOUT

1 Replacing the O-ring. Turn off the water, open the faucet one half turn and close the drain to prevent loss of parts. Carefully pry off the trim cap with a knife or small screwdriver. Remove the handle screw and pull off the handle. Unscrew the locknut with a taped adjustable wrench. Lift the cartridge from the faucet body *(below)*. Water leaking around the handle may be caused by a cracked or pitted disc assembly. If so, buy a new assembly and O-ring. Insert the assembly, lining up its slots with those on the faucet body. If only the O-ring is worn, pinch it off the assembly *(inset)*, lubricate an exact replacement with petroleum jelly and slip it on. Reassemble the faucet.

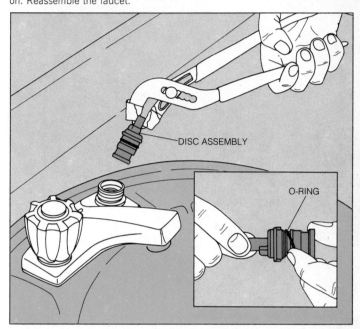

DISC ASSEMBLY

O-RING

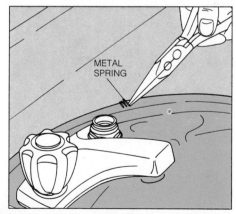

METAL
SPRING

2 Servicing the seat and spring. To stop water dripping from the spout, use long-nose pliers to pick the rubber seat and spring out of the faucet body *(above)*. (Instead of a seat and spring there may be a ceramic seal and O-ring.) Replace these with parts from a repair kit for the same make and model of faucet. Then insert the disc assembly, lining up its slots with the faucet body, and reassemble the faucet.

Single-Lever Cartridge Faucets

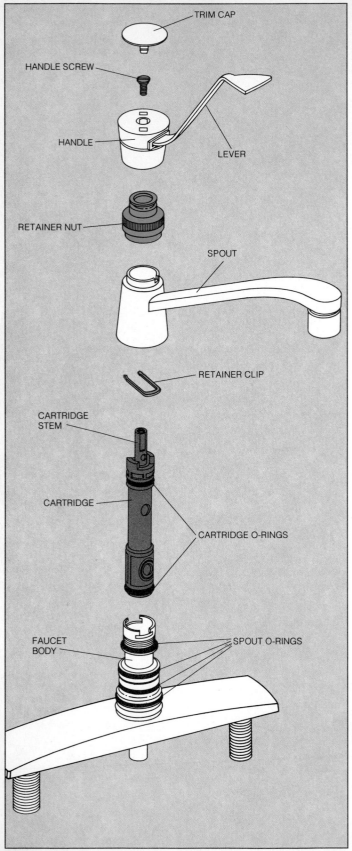

TRIM CAP

HANDLE SCREW

HANDLE

LEVER

RETAINER NUT

SPOUT

RETAINER CLIP

CARTRIDGE STEM

CARTRIDGE

CARTRIDGE O-RINGS

FAUCET BODY

SPOUT O-RINGS

1 **Removing the handle.** Turn off the water supply, lift the handle several times to drain the faucet and close the drain to prevent loss of parts. Carefully pry off the trim cap with a small screwdriver *(below)* or knife. Remove the handle screw that secures the handle assembly to the cartridge *(inset)*.

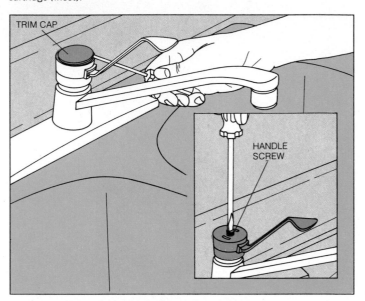

TRIM CAP

HANDLE SCREW

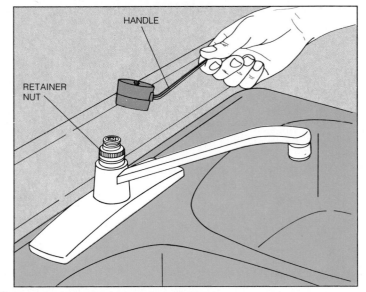

HANDLE

RETAINER NUT

2 **Removing the handle.** The faucet handle attaches to the lip of the retainer nut much like a bottle opener to a cap. Tilt the handle lever up sharply to unhook it from the nut, then lift it free as shown.

3 **Removing the retainer nut.** Unscrew the retainer nut with taped channel-joint pliers *(below)* and lift it off the faucet body. To stop a leaking handle or a dripping spout, replace the O-rings or the entire cartridge *(Step 4)*. To stop leaks from the spout collar, replace the spout O-rings *(Step 6)*.

4 **Freeing the cartridge.** Locate the U-shaped retainer clip that holds the cartridge in place in the faucet body. Using long-nose pliers or tweezers, pull the clip from its slots *(below)*, being careful not to drop it down the drain.

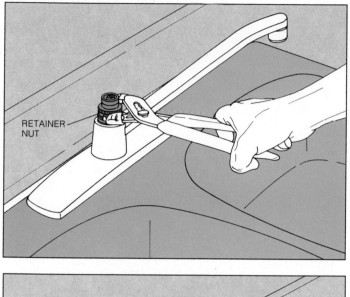

RETAINER NUT

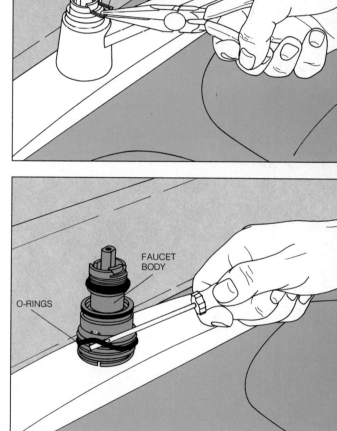

CARTRIDGE STEM

RETAINER CLIP

CARTRIDGE EARS

CARTRIDGE STEM

CARTRIDGE

O-RINGS

FAUCET BODY

O-RINGS

5 **Servicing the cartridge.** Grasping the cartridge stem with taped pliers, lift the cartridge out of the faucet body. Examine the O-rings and replace them if they are worn or cracked. Pry the old rings off the cartridge with the tip of an awl or other pointed tool. Lubricate the new O-rings with a dab of petroleum jelly and roll them down over the cartridge until they rest in the appropriate grooves. If the cartridge itself is worn or damaged, replace it with a new one. Reinsert the cartridge, align it properly in its seat, and replace the spout and retainer nut. Attach the handle by hooking its inside lever on the lip of the retainer nut. If the hot and cold water are reversed, remove the handle and rotate the cartridge stem one-half turn.

6 **Replacing the spout O-rings.** If water leaks around the spout collar, replace the spout O-rings. Lift off the spout and pry off the cracked or worn rings *(above)*. Lubricate new O-rings with petroleum jelly and roll them into the grooves on the faucet body. Replace the spout and reassemble the faucet, hooking the inside edge of the handle lever onto the lip of the retainer nut.

Single-Lever Rotating-Ball Faucets

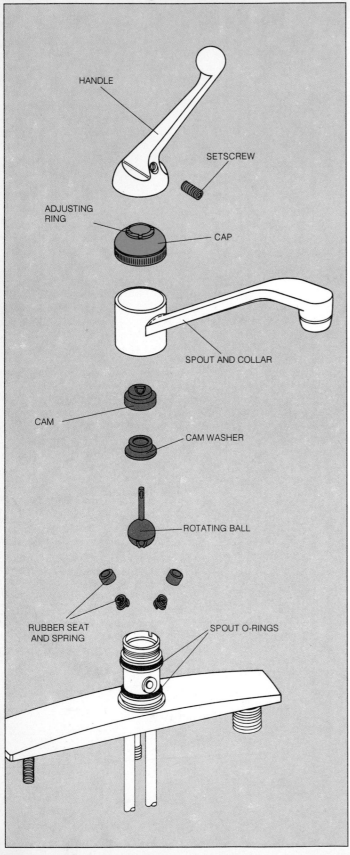

HANDLE

SETSCREW

ADJUSTING RING

CAP

SPOUT AND COLLAR

CAM

CAM WASHER

ROTATING BALL

RUBBER SEAT AND SPRING

SPOUT O-RINGS

1 **Removing the handle.** The setscrew that secures the handle to the faucet body is underneath the handle. Use a small hex wrench to loosen the screw *(below),* but leave the screw in the handle since it is small and easily lost. Lift off the handle to expose the adjusting ring.

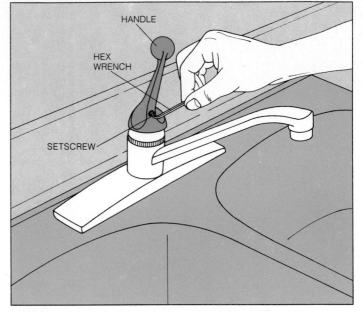

HANDLE

HEX WRENCH

SETSCREW

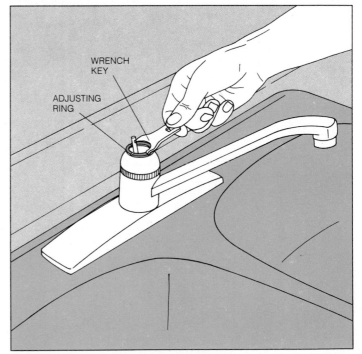

WRENCH KEY

ADJUSTING RING

2 **Tightening the adjusting ring.** To stop water leaking from the faucet handle, use the edge of an old dinner knife or a special wrench included in the repair kit to tighten the adjusting ring clockwise, as shown. (The ball should move easily without the handle attached.) Reassemble the handle and test for leaks. Tighten the adjusting ring again, if necessary. If the leak persists, go to Step 3.

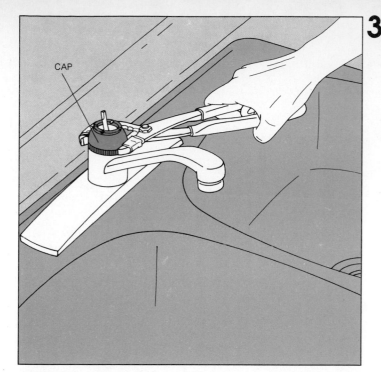

CAP

3 **Removing the cap.** Service the cam-and-ball assembly if the handle continues to leak after you have tightened the adjusting ring, or if the spout drips. First turn off the water supply, open the faucet and close the drain to prevent loss of parts. Unscrew the cap by hand or with a pair of channel-joint pliers taped to protect chrome parts *(left)*. Lift off the plastic cam exposing the cam washer and rotating ball. Buy a repair kit that includes replacement parts for your make and model of faucet. Service worn or damaged parts individually *(Step 4)* or replace all of them while the faucet is disassembled.

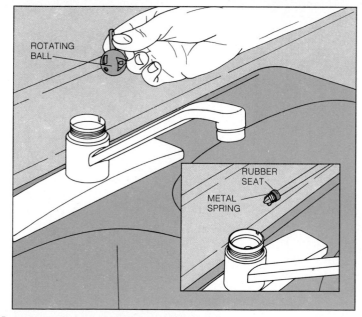

ROTATING BALL

RUBBER SEAT

METAL SPRING

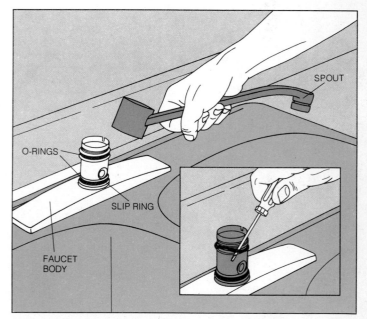

SPOUT

O-RINGS

SLIP RING

FAUCET BODY

4 **Replacing the seats, springs and ball.** Lift the rotating ball from the faucet body *(above)*, then reach into the faucet body with long-nose pliers or the end of a screwdriver and remove the two sets of rubber seats and metal springs *(inset)*, or two seats of ceramic seals and O-rings. Replace these parts from the kit, making sure they are properly seated in the faucet body before reassembling the faucet. If the cam-and-ball assembly appears damaged, replace it at the same time.

5 **Replacing the spout O-rings.** If the water leaks from the spout collar, twist off the spout *(above)* to expose its O-rings. Slip the end of a small screwdriver under the O-rings to pry them off the faucet body *(inset)*. Lubricate the new O-rings with petroleum jelly, and roll them into place. Lower the spout straight down over the body and rotate it until it rests on the plastic slip ring at the base. Reassemble the faucet.

Single-Lever Ceramic-Disc Faucets

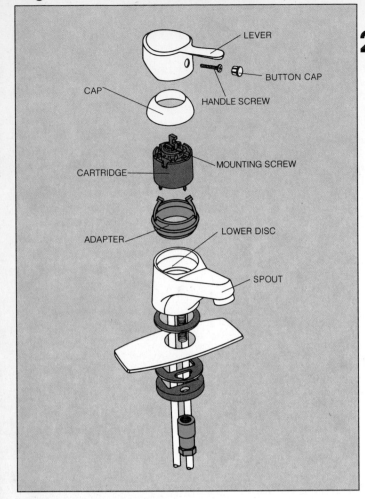

LEVER

BUTTON CAP

CAP

HANDLE SCREW

CARTRIDGE

MOUNTING SCREW

ADAPTER

LOWER DISC

SPOUT

2 Freeing the cartridge. Pry the cap off its plastic adapter (below) or, on some faucets, unscrew it from the faucet body. Loosen the two or three brass screws holding the cartridge to the faucet body (inset), and lift out the cartridge.

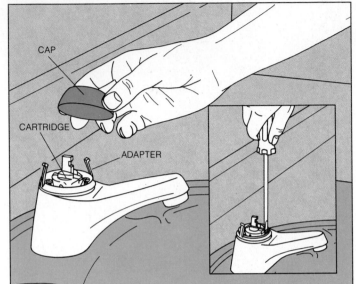

CAP

CARTRIDGE

ADAPTER

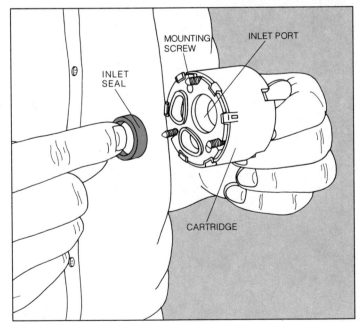

MOUNTING SCREW

INLET PORT

INLET SEAL

CARTRIDGE

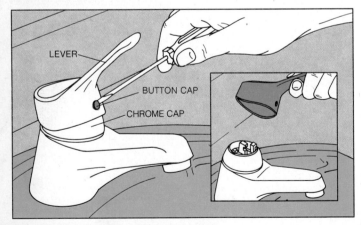

LEVER

BUTTON CAP

CHROME CAP

1 Removing the lever. Turn off the water supply and drain the faucet by lifting the lever to its highest position. Close the drain to prevent loss of parts. Pry off the button cap at the base of the lever with a knife or small screwdriver (above), and remove the handle screw. (On some models the screw is underneath the lever body and there is no cap.) Lift off the handle (inset).

3 Servicing the cartridge. First check to be sure that the leak is not caused by a piece of dirt caught between the ceramic discs. Clean the inlet ports and the surface of the bottom disc. If the upper disc is cracked or pitted, buy a replacement cartridge for the same make and model. Insert the new seals in the disc, position the cartridge in the faucet body and screw it in place. Check that the three ports on the bottom of the cartridge align with those of the faucet body.

Beyond the Faucet: Spouts, Stoppers and Drains

Water that is released by a faucet makes a circuitous journey. It pours out of a spout, shower head or kitchen-sink hose, sometimes going through an aerator. There, it mixes with air to produce a splashless stream, then flows past a stopper or pop-up plug, onward through a strainer at the base of the bowl or tub into a water-filled trap below. Finally, it enters the house drain system.

Compared to the faucets that get the whole process going, these flow-and-drain fixtures are relatively simple. Locating a trouble spot is easy and the jobs that must be done are usually straightforward repairs or replacements. You do not have to shut off the water supply for these jobs—just close the faucets tightly.

The difficulty of the jobs, when difficulty arises, is in getting at a fixture and reassembling its components in the correct order. Some of the fixtures between are nestled under sinks, basins and tubs, where work space is cramped and special tools may be needed to unscrew fasteners. Others consist of intricate combinations of small parts, which must be fitted together precisely.

The combination of sink spout, aerator and spray shown here presents the full range of these problems. An aerator unscrews easily from the end of a spout and should be removed periodically for cleaning, because minute amounts of grit in the water supply will quickly clog it. But an aerator will not do its job if its internal parts are replaced incorrectly.

The spray head also contains an aerator; here, clogging can block the action of the diverter valve that switches water from spout to spray. Concealed in the base of the spout, this valve is the most delicate component of the entire assembly. Like aerators it can clog up, though far less often, and even a clean valve will not work if its covering fills with grit or dirt. If you have cleaned both aerators and still have problems—low or uneven water pressure, or a failure to switch smoothly from spout to spray and back again—go to work on the diverter valve.

The sturdiest, simplest component of all—the spray hose—is, paradoxically, the hardest to work with. Replacing the hose calls for tight maneuvering under the sink, often between two adjoining faucet pipes. In these closed quarters the plumbing tool called a basin wrench may offer the only way of getting at the nut that holds the hose in place.

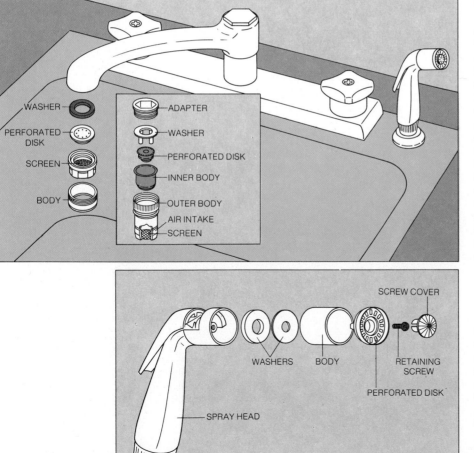

Cleaning a Spray Nozzle

An array of small parts. Unscrew the aerator from the end of the spout with tape-wrapped pliers. Disassemble the parts inside the aerator body and set them aside in the correct order and orientation: A part reassembled upside down will keep the aerator from working. Whatever its design, your aerator will contain a plastic or rubber washer, a disk perforated by tiny holes or a sawtooth edge, and one or more screens. A more complex model (inset) may also have a disposable adapter for internal and external spout threads, and air-intake holes in the outer shell. Clean the screens with a small stiff brush; use the brush and a toothpick to clean out the disk and intake holes. Replace badly worn or misshapen washers, and flush out all parts by holding them upside down in a full stream of water before reassembling the aerator.

Spray nozzle repair. On some models you can unscrew the tip of the spray nozzle by hand. More often it is secured by a Phillips screw and the screw may be concealed by a cover. Pop the cover out with a screwdriver or penknife, remove the retaining screw and disassemble the internal parts. Clean or replace these parts as you would those of an aerator; before reassembling them, run water through the spray head at full force for a minute or two. Do not try to repair the mechanism inside the spray head. If defective, the sealed unit should be replaced with an identical model from the manufacturer.

Removing the Hose

1 **At the spray head.** If a hose leaks or blocks water, detach it for possible replacement, starting at the spray head. Unscrew the head from its coupling, then free the coupling from the hose by prying off a retaining snap ring with the tip of a screwdriver or penknife. Replace the hose washer if necessary, and try to clear a blocked hose by running water through it at full force (with the spray head removed, opening a faucet will send water to the hose rather than the sink spout). If the hose still leaks or is permanently obstructed, go on to Step 2.

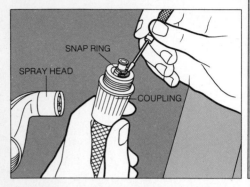

SNAP RING

SPRAY HEAD

COUPLING

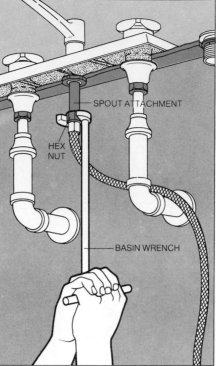

SPOUT ATTACHMENT

HEX NUT

BASIN WRENCH

2 **At the spout.** Only a single hex nut secures the hose to its attachment at the base of the spout, but this nut is often hard to get at. If you cannot unscrew it with an ordinary wrench or a pair of locking pliers, use a basin wrench *(page 340)*, a plumber's tool especially designed for working in close quarters. Lie on your back under the sink as you unscrew the nut, and illuminate the work area with a work light or a flashlight.

Replace the hose with a new one, preferably of vinyl with nylon cord reinforcement. Be sure to take the hex nut with you when you get the new hose; if your plumbing supplier does not have a model that matches your spout attachment, ask for an adapter.

Working on the Diverter Valve

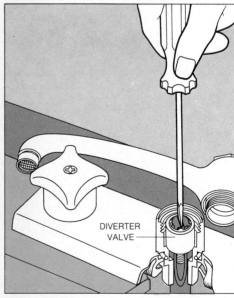

DIVERTER VALVE

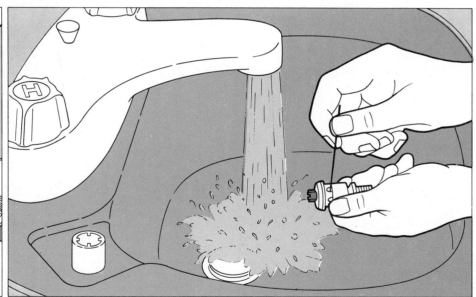

1 **Getting into the spout.** In some sinks the spout is secured to the faucet body by a grooved ring, in others by a nut atop the spout. These chrome-plated fasteners are easily scarred; remove them carefully with a tape-wrapped wrench or pliers. Inside the faucet body you can now see the tip of the diverter valve, usually capped by a brass screw. The screw is an integral part of the valve: turn it just enough to free the valve from the valve seat inside the faucet body, then pull out the screw and valve together. A valve without a screw top can simply be pulled straight out with pliers.

2 **Cleaning the valve.** The valve will have a distinctive pattern of small outlets and channels and may come as a removable inner body sliding in a sleeve. Take it apart, if possible, and clean all its openings and surfaces with a sharp, soft object, such as a toothpick. Do not use a metal tool for this job; the valve is easily nicked or scratched. As you work, flush the valve frequently with water at full force from a working faucet. Reassemble the valve and spout, and try the spout-spray mechanism. If switching is poor or pressure uneven—and if you have already checked out the aerators, the spray head and the hose—replace the diverter valve. Take the old valve with you to your plumbing supplier to be sure of getting a perfect match.

Some Special Twists for Tubs and Showers

The valves and spouts for tubs and showers are serviced like those on lavatories —with two exceptions. The diverter valve, which directs water to tub or shower, is special. And you may encounter an access problem repairing leaks from a wall-mounted stem valve.

To remove a wall-mounted faucet or diverter valve, you will have to unscrew a bonnet nut that is recessed. In some fixtures the out-of-the-way nut offers enough purchase to permit the use of locking-grip pliers or a basin wrench. If not, you will need a socket wrench to slip over the protruding faucet stem and the nut. Inexpensive sets of long sockets designed explicitly for this sort of job are available at plumbing-supply stores. Alternatively, your own tool kit may hold a socket that will suffice, although an unorthodox turning technique will be necessary because of the length of the faucet's stem (right).

Unlike faucets and wall-mounted diverter valves, the working parts of a tub-spout diverter—a knob on top of the tub spout that controls a diverter gate within —are not replaceable. Failures can be remedied only by installing a new spout. Most problems with shower heads, however, are easily cured. Replacement of washers or O-rings will generally take care of leaks. And erratic or weak pressure from the shower head can usually be traced to a buildup of minerals from the water supply. Proper flow can be restored by disassembling the parts and giving them a good cleaning; soaking in vinegar loosens mineral deposits.

Wall-Mounted Faucets

Removing the bonnet nut. The recessed bonnet nut of a wall-mounted fitting is generally plastered in place to keep splashing water from leaking into the wall. Chip away the adjacent plaster with a hammer and cold chisel so that the socket wrench—a type designed for plumbing jobs (below)—can be slipped over the faucet stem and bonnet nut. Insert the socket wrench's handle through the holes at the socket's outer end and turn to loosen the nut. After the repair has been made, replaster as necessary.

Shorter sockets that are normally used for work on engines can also be used to unscrew a recessed bonnet nut (inset), since the faucet stem will fit through the hole meant for the tool's ratchet handle. In lieu of the handle, simply turn the socket with a pipe wrench.

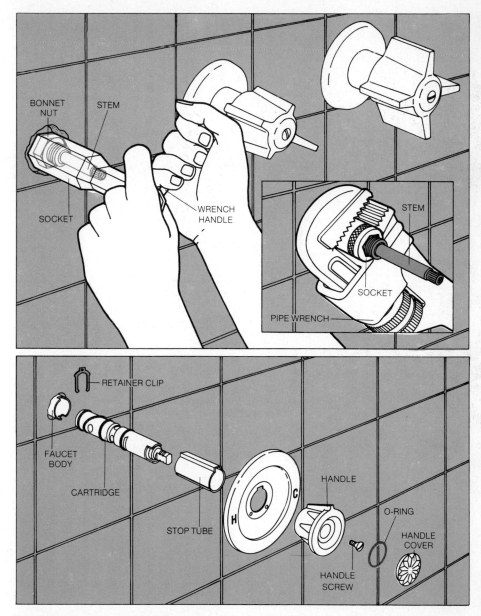

Fixing the faucet. The single-handle controls found on many modern tubs and showers work in exactly the same way—and are repaired the same way—as the single-lever faucets on sinks or lavatories (pages 354-355), although the exterior portions may be quite different in appearance and assembly. To get at the mechanism of this particular faucet, pry off the handle cover with a small screwdriver. Unscrew the handle screw, remove the handle and escutcheon, then draw out the retainer clip with long-nose pliers, noting its position. Pull out the cartridge and replace it (page 355) with a new one, then reassemble the faucet. Stem-type tub and shower faucets are also repaired like their deck-mounted equivalents, as described on pages 349.

Tub-Shower Diverters

Repairing a diverter valve. A tub-shower diverter valve functions like a faucet. A clockwise turn moves the stem into the valve seat, closing the pipe to the tub spout and forcing the water instead through a hollow plastic housing and up into the shower head. A counterclockwise turn of the handle moves the stem back to open the pipe to the tub spout. If the valve leaks, disassemble it by the same steps used for the stem faucet on page 349. Replace worn washers, O-rings, packing, or badly worn metal parts. If the hollow housing has worn out so that the flow of water is incompletely diverted to the shower head, replace the whole diverter valve assembly.

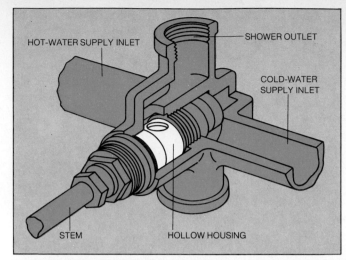

Replacing a tub-spout diverter. The knob of a tub-spout diverter raises an internal gate that closes the pathway to the tub spout, forcing the water up to the shower head. If the mechanism fails to work properly, the entire spout must be replaced. To remove the old spout, place a piece of wood, such as a hammer handle, in the spout and turn it counterclockwise. Buy a replacement that is the same length as the old spout.

If a spout of the same size is unavailable, get a nipple—a short length of pipe that will make the connection to the pipes behind the wall *(inset)*. Use pipe-joint compound and lampwick or plumber's tape to seal the nipple. When screwing the spout into the nipple, hand tighten it only. If alignment cannot be completed by hand, use the makeshift wood tool *(right)* or— provided the spout comes with a pad to protect the finish—use a wrench.

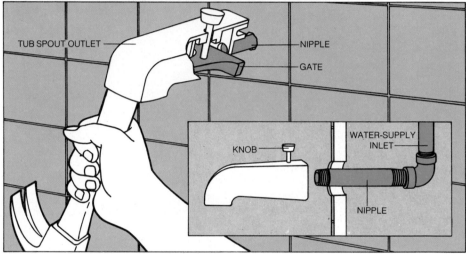

Shower Heads

Keeping a shower head showering. If dripping occurs where the shower head swivels, replace the O-ring or washer that fits between the swivel ball and the outer part of the head. On this model, you must first unscrew the collar.

If the flow of water is blocked, unscrew the head with tape-wrapped pliers and disassemble the shower head. Most have a screw that secures a face plate or a screen cover. The adjustable type shown here has a handle operating a cam that moves the nozzles in and out of the face-plate holes to adjust the spray. As you remove parts, line them up in order for easy reassembly. To clean off mineral deposits, soak the parts in vinegar. Use a toothpick to clear the holes of the spray adjusters or screen, and scrub the other parts with a wire brush. Before reassembling, lubricate the swivel ball with petroleum jelly. When screwing the shower head back into the arm, hand-tighten it only. Seal the joint with pipe-joint compound.

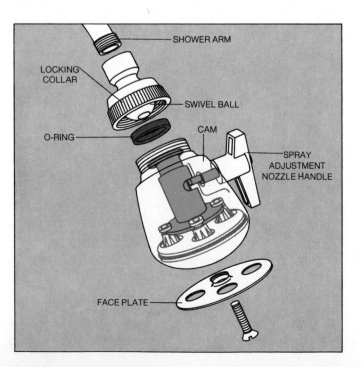

Replacing Traps and Tailpieces

The curved traps beneath kitchen sinks and lavatories are vital but vulnerable. Some of the water that flows off through the sink or lavatory drain remains in the trap as a seal to keep odors and gases from backing into the house from drain and sewer lines. But traps are often made with comparatively thin walls because they are not subjected to the high water pressure of supply lines. In time, they corrode and leak, and must be replaced.

The traps shown on these pages, called P traps, are the ones commonly found in most homes. They may be made of brass, galvanized iron, steel or (where plumbing codes permit) PVC or another type of plastic. The best—and most expensive—are chrome plated for looks and relatively heavy for long wear. Choose heavy traps; they are a better buy, particularly on fixtures that get substantial use. As a general rule of thumb, choose a matching material and weight for the pipes that accompany the trap; mixing metals can cause corrosive galvanic action. PVC, however, can be used with brass, galvanized iron or chrome plated piping using special adaptors.

The trap you choose may be either a swivel or fixed type. A swivel trap can be turned in any direction on a drainpipe by adjusting a separate slip nut—a useful feature when you want to replace a tailpiece without first removing the trap, or when you must make a connection between a drainpipe and sink that are not in perfect alignment.

Fixed traps, which screw directly onto the drainpipe, are less adaptable. You can, however, replace a tailpipe on a fixed trap without removing the trap by using a professional plumber's tactic (*page 364, bottom right*). Plumbers "roll the trap"—that is, they free the tailpiece and drop it neatly into the trap; then loosen the trap and roll it to one side to get at the tailpiece. The procedure may seem tricky, but it is easy to follow, making a tailpiece replacement as simple on a fixed trap as on a swivel. Replacing drainpipes, however, remains a tougher job: you must remove traps completely to get at the drainpipe.

Three Trap-to-Drain Connections

Removing a one-piece swivel trap. Set a pail beneath the trap and remove the cleanout plug, if there is one, to drain the trap. With a tape-wrapped pipe wrench or a monkey wrench, unscrew the nuts that attach the trap to the tailpiece and drainpipe. If the drainpipe must be replaced, pull the escutcheon from the wall and unscrew the slip nut that fastens the drainpipe to the drain outlet. Discard all the nuts and washers and clean the drain outlet threads.

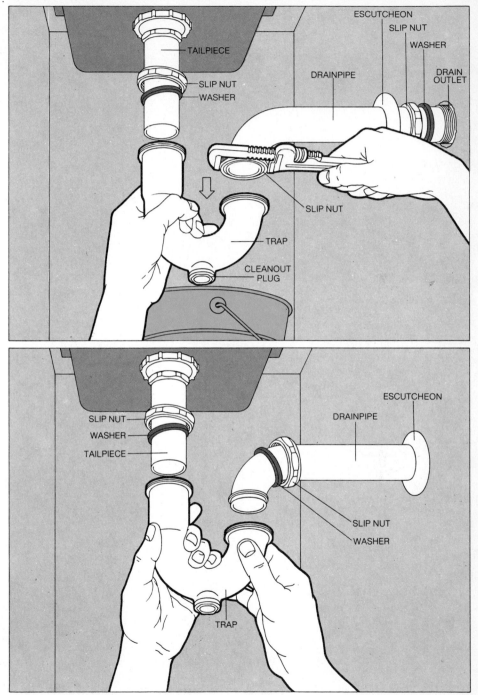

Installing a new trap. If you are replacing the drainpipe, slide the escutcheon, a slip nut and a washer—in that order—onto the end of the new pipe that will face the wall. Screw the slip nut tight to the drain outlet and push the escutcheon against the wall. Slide the slip nuts and washers that come with the new trap onto the tailpiece and the drainpipe, slip nuts first.
Fit the trap in place against the tailpiece and drainpipe, and tighten the slip nuts.

A two-piece swivel trap. Remove the U-shaped section of a two-piece trap by unscrewing the slip nuts at the ends, and sliding them back onto the tailpiece and the trap. The elbow screws directly onto the pipeline; remove it by turning it counterclockwise. To install a replacement, first separate the elbow from the U-shaped section. Coat the threads of the drainpipe with pipe-joint compound or plastic joint tape and screw the elbow onto it. Slide a new slip nut and a washer onto the tailpiece, set the trap in place against the tailpiece and the elbow, and tighten the trap and tailpiece slip nuts.

A fixed trap. A slip nut fastens a fixed trap to the tailpiece; at its other end the trap screws directly onto the drainpipe. Before removing the trap, you must disengage the tailpiece running between the trap and the sink or lavatory drain. Unscrew the slip nuts that fasten the tailpiece to the drain and trap, push the tailpiece into the trap, then turn the entire trap counterclockwise with your hands or a wrench until it comes off the drainpipe. Transfer the old tailpiece to your new trap and coat the drainpipe threads with pipe-joint compound or plastic joint tape before making a replacement.

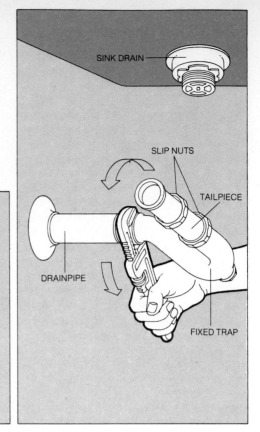

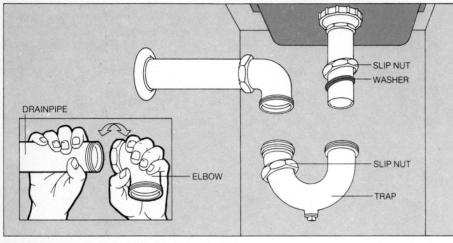

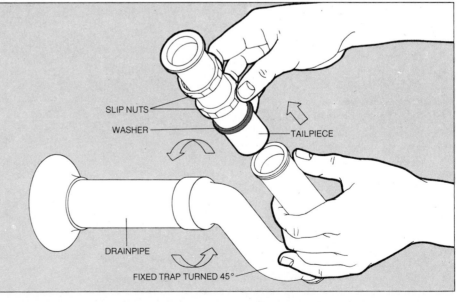

Removing a Tailpiece: Two Shortcuts

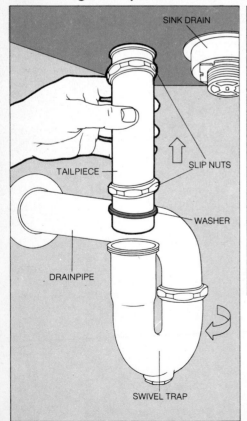

On a swivel trap. Unscrew the slip nuts that fasten the tailpiece to the trap and the sink drain, and push the tailpiece down into the trap. Loosen the slip nut that fastens the trap to the drainpipe or an elbow, and swivel the trap away from the sink drain, then lift out the old tailpiece and insert the new one. To complete the installation, lift the new tailpiece up to the sink drain and tighten all slip nuts.

On a fixed trap. Free the tailpiece as you would on a swivel trap (*left*) and push it down into the fixed trap. Then, using your hands or a tape-wrapped wrench, turn the entire trap counterclockwise about 45° on the drainpipe. You can now pull the old tailpiece out of the trap and insert the new one. Complete the installation by retightening the trap on the drainpipe and fastening the slip nuts on the tailpiece.

Replacing Sink Strainers

If you notice a leak around a sink drain hole, you may be able to fix it by simply loosening the strainer from underneath and applying fresh plumber's putty under the lip. Often, however, the strainer itself is corroded—it may break apart as you pry it up. Replacement is simple and inexpensive. There are two kinds of basket strainers: one secured by a lock nut, and the other held by a plastic retainer and three screws. The lock-nut type is generally used for stainless-steel sinks because the lock nut tightens against the sink without bending the sink metal.

To remove an old strainer, first detach the tailpiece *(page 364)*. Then remove the lock nut or detach the retainer screws and pry the old strainer out.

Installing a Lock-Nut Strainer

1 **Sealing the opening.** Turn off the water supply. Remove all old putty from around the drain opening in the sink and dry it completely. Apply a ⅛-inch bead of plumber's putty to the flange of the strainer and place the strainer body through the opening, pressing down firmly so that the putty spreads evenly.

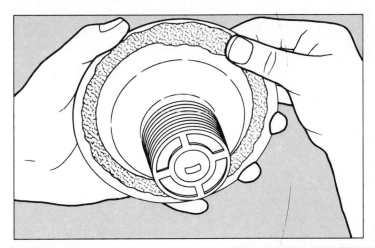

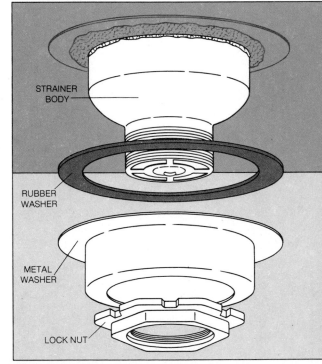

STRAINER BODY

RUBBER WASHER

METAL WASHER

LOCK NUT

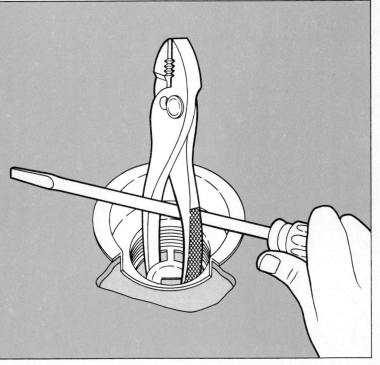

2 **Securing the strainer.** Place the rubber washer and the metal washer onto the strainer body. Then screw on the lock nut finger-tight *(above)* to hold the strainer while you work underneath the sink. Place the handles of pliers into the crosspieces of the strainer and slide a screwdriver between the handles *(right)*. Have a helper hold onto the screwdriver to immobilize the strainer while you tighten the lock nut.

3 **Tightening the lock nut.** Tighten the lock nut several turns more, using a spud wrench or a hammer and wood dowel as shown below. Brace the dowel against one of the grooves of the lock nut and tap it with the hammer. Do not over-tighten the lock nut because you may distort the metal parts or crack the ceramic.

4 **Connecting to the trap and tailpiece.** If the tailpiece is worn or corroded, replace it *(page 364)*. Otherwise, fit the strainer sleeve over the existing one, and secure it by tightening the coupling. Then tighten the trap couplings. Wipe away excess putty with a soft cloth. Turn on the water and make sure there are no leaks.

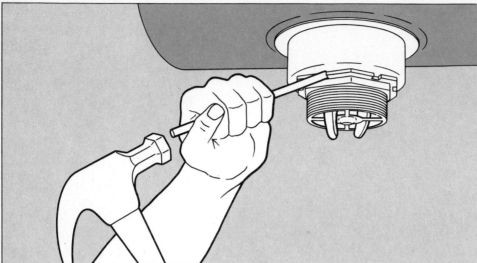

STRAINER SLEEVE

STRAINER COUPLING

TAILPIECE

TRAP COUPLING

Installing a Retainer-Type Strainer

Attaching the retainer. Put the puttied strainer body into the opening, then attach the rubber and metal washers from underneath as for the lock-nut strainer *(page 365, bottom)*. Fit the retainer onto the strainer body and turn it until the ridges on the side of the drain fit into the grooves of the retainer. Twist to lock it in place, then tighten the retainer screws. Connect the tailpiece as you would for a lock-nut strainer.

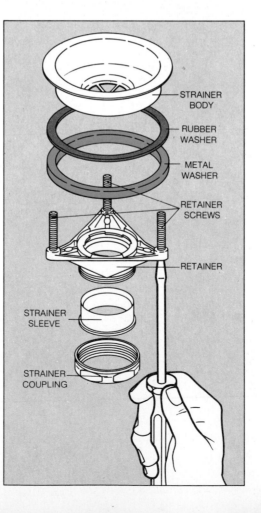

STRAINER BODY

RUBBER WASHER

METAL WASHER

RETAINER SCREWS

RETAINER

STRAINER SLEEVE

STRAINER COUPLING

Adjusting and Replacing a Lavatory Pop-Up

The seal of some pop-up drains—a metal plug closing upon a metal flange, or ring—is never quite as watertight as that of an old-style rubber stopper. Moreover, the pop-up mechanism has several moving parts and needs periodic adjustments. But the pop-up's convenience has made it almost universal, and a homeowner must learn to cope with its malfunctions. They are, fortunately, few in number: a plug that fails to open or close properly, and the two enemies of all drainage systems—clogs and leaks.

Pop-up problems are usually caused by faulty connections. The control knob atop the lavatory is part of a three-section linkage: a vertical lift rod; another vertical rod, flat and pierced by holes, called a clevis; and a seesaw-like horizontal rod that pivots on a plastic ball inside the drain to raise and lower the plug. Adjusting the mechanism calls for two simple settings on the lift rod and clevis.

Loose hair and similar lavatory debris are the usual causes of clogging. To clear the drain you must remove the plug, either by lifting or twisting it out of the lavatory bowl, or by disassembling the pivot rod (page 368, top). When you have freed the plug, clean it thoroughly, then clear out the drain below with a brush or piece of cloth wrapped around stiff wire, such as a length of coat hanger.

There are two kinds of leaks. Water that drips or trickles from the mechanism beneath the bowl is leaking around the pivot ball. Tighten the retaining nut that holds the ball in place; if that does not work, remove the nut and then replace the pivot-ball washer. Water that seeps down the outside of the drain is a more serious matter. The thudding of the plug against the flange may have broken a putty seal beneath the flange; by loosening a lock nut under the bowl you can lift the flange slightly and renew the seal. More often, this type of leak is due to corrosion of one of the parts of the drain —a sure signal that the drain will soon fail completely. To fix the leak properly, you should replace the entire drain assembly (page 368, bottom).

1 Setting the lift rod. If the pop-up plug does not make a good seal in the closed position, begin your adjustment with the lift rod—the vertical shaft that runs down from the control knob and through the top of the lavatory. Free the rod by loosening the clevis screw with a pair of tape-wrapped pliers. Press the pop-up plug down to seal the drain (the clevis rod will rise). Pull the knob as far up as you can, then lower it ¼ inch and retighten the clevis screw. You may find that the pop-up mechanism is now slightly jammed and difficult to operate; if so, go on to Step 2.

2 Setting the pivot rod. With your fingers, squeeze the spring clip that holds the pivot rod in the clevis rod completely out of the clevis. Reset the rod in the next higher clevis hole, threading it through the spring clip on both sides of the clevis. Try the pop-up mechanism and, if necessary, repeat Step 1.

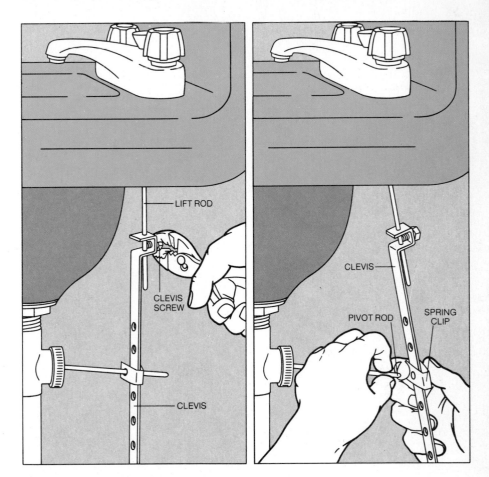

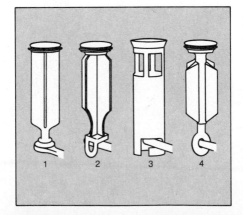

A medley of pop-up plugs. These four common types of pop-up plugs all do the same job, but the methods of installing and removing them differ widely. Numbers 1 and 2 rest on the inside end of the pivot rod; to remove either of them, raise the plug to the open position and lift it out of the drain. Number 3 engages the rod in a slot, and comes free of the rod with a quarter turn counterclockwise. If you cannot remove your pop-up plug by lifting or turning, it must resemble Number 4, which engages the rod in a loop like the eye of a huge needle. To disengage this plug, you must free the pivot rod and pull it partly or completely out of the drain T underneath the basin

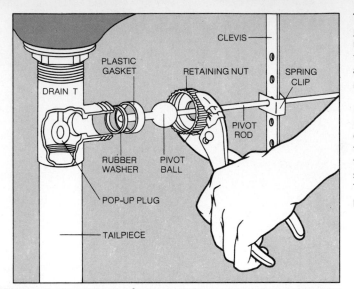

The pivot-rod assembly. With a tape-wrapped adjustable wrench or pliers, unscrew the retaining nut that secures the pivot-rod assembly inside the drain T. Squeeze the spring clip on the clevis and back the pivot rod out of the T. You can now pull the plug out of the drain for cleaning.

Follow the same procedure as the initial step in dismantling a pop-up drain, either to stop leaks or to install a new assembly. A leak at the retaining nut may be stopped simply by tightening the nut, but check the gasket and washer inside the pivot ball and, if necessary, replace them. The remainder of the disassembly and installation procedure is described below.

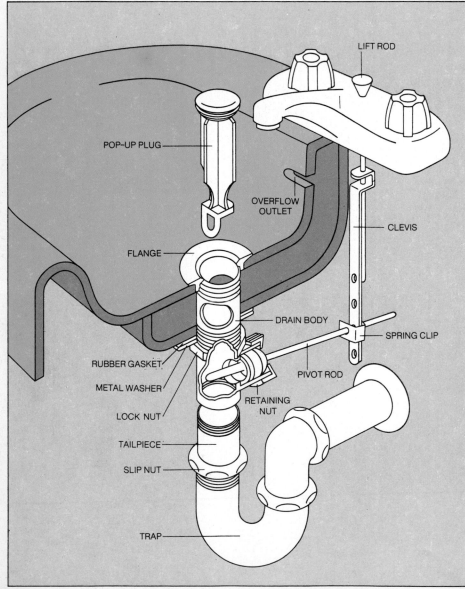

Replacing the drain. Start a replacement job by freeing the pivot rod from the drain T (*above*). Unscrew the slip nut that fastens the tailpiece to the trap, then unscrew the tailpiece from the drain body and push it down into the trap, out of the way. Loosen the lock nut that secures the drain body underneath the basin, and unscrew the drain body from the flange. An old, corroded body will be hard to budge at first; do not hesitate to apply pressure with the wrench, even if you flatten the body a bit. Inside the sink pry up the flange with a dull-bladed knife or the tip of a screwdriver; be careful not to scar the sink surface. Scrape away the putty at the mouth of the drain and wipe the drain clean with a dry cloth. Discard the old tailpiece (a new one will come with the new drain assembly) but keep the slip nut that fastened it to the trap; replace the slip-nut washer if it is badly worn.

Use tape-wrapped wrenches for all steps of the installation job. Start by setting a slip nut and a washer on the new tailpiece and pushing the piece down into the trap. Apply a ⅛-inch bead of plumber's putty under the rim of the flange, and press the flange into place in the mouth of the drain. Coat the threads of the drain body and tailpiece with pipe-joint compound, screw the drain body into the flange and the tailpiece into the drain body, and tighten the tailpiece slip nut onto the trap. Finally, tighten the lock nut against the washer and gasket with an adjustable wrench. Caution: Do not overtighten this nut or the porcelain above it may crack.

If you are replacing the pop-up mechanism as well as the drain, feed the pivot rod into the drain T and tighten the retaining nut. Insert the lift rod down through the faucet body or the top of the basin and fasten its lower end to the clevis with the clevis screw. Feed the pivot rod through a clevis hole, making it fast with the spring clip. Try the mechanism and, if necessary, reset the lift rod and clevis (*page 367, top*).

Adjusting Bathtub Drains

Modern bathtub drains, controlled by a lever on the overflow plate, operate in large part from a position of concealment. Hidden in the bathtub overflow tube is a so-called lift linkage that, rising or falling in response to the control lever, opens or closes the drain in one of two ways. A pop-up drain utilizes a metal stopper at the tub outlet, while a trip-lever drain regulates the outflow of water with a plunger at the intersection of the overflow tube and the drain.

A common problem of bathtub drains is clogging caused by the accumulation of hair on the trip-lever drain plunger or on the spring at the end of a pop-up drain lift linkage. To remove the hair, the lift linkage must be removed from the overflow tube. This is done by unscrewing the overflow plate and pulling on it. The same procedure is sometimes necessary in order to adjust the length of the lift linkage; improper adjustment—perhaps caused by faulty installation, perhaps by wear and tear—can result in a leaky drain or one that fails to open fully.

The various conduits of the drain—the overflow tube, outlet pipe and trap—are less likely to suffer problems than those of lavatories or sinks. They are usually made of heavier pipe with sturdy cast-brass fittings that strongly resist corrosion. And their hidden position protects them from accidental knocks.

A trip-lever drain. The key element of a trip-lever drain is the brass plunger suspended from the lift linkage. When lowered by the control lever, the plunger sits on a slight ridge below the juncture of the overflow tube and the drain, blocking outflow of water via the main tube outlet. However, any water that spills into the overflow tube can pass freely down the drain because the plunger is hollow. If a drain of this type leaks, the cause may be wear on the plunger due to repeated impact against its rigid seat. Lift out the whole mechanism, and slightly lengthen the linkage, as shown opposite at top. At the same time, check the cotter pins of the assembly; if they are corroded, they should be replaced.

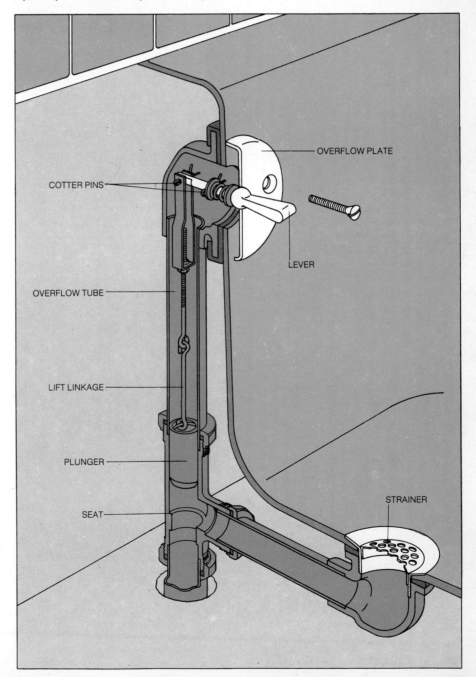

OVERFLOW PLATE

COTTER PINS

LEVER

OVERFLOW TUBE

LIFT LINKAGE

PLUNGER

STRAINER

SEAT

Adjusting the lift linkage. The upper segment of the lift linkage consists of a brass yoke from which a threaded rod is suspended; a lock nut secures the threaded rod in place. To adjust the length of the linkage, loosen the lock nut with pliers, turn the threaded rod the desired amount, then tighten the lock nut again. Try slight adjustments at first. A trip-lever lift linkage that has been lengthened too much will work fine when the drain is closed, but will fail to lift the plunger clear of the drain when the control lever is in the open position. Similarly, an excessively long lift linkage in a pop-up drain will prevent the stopper from completely shutting.

A pop-up drain. The lift linkage of a pop-up drain resembles that of a trip-lever drain, except that the lower end of the linkage is shaped to form a stiff spiral spring. This spring rests on the end of a separate horizontal linkage shaped like a rocker in the middle and leading to the metal stopper. When the spring presses downward, the stopper rises, seesaw fashion.

Because the pop-up drain lacks a screen at the tub outlet, the stopper has a cross-shaped base that prevents small objects—such as the top of a shampoo bottle—from passing down the drain. Householders sometimes try to cure sluggish drainage during a shower by entirely removing the plug, but this merely invites a more serious blockage. The proper solution to a persistent clogging problem is described on page 344.

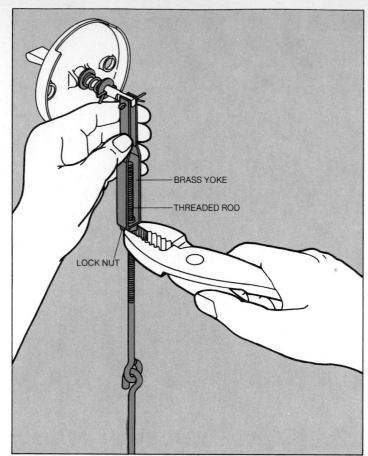

BRASS YOKE
THREADED ROD
LOCK NUT

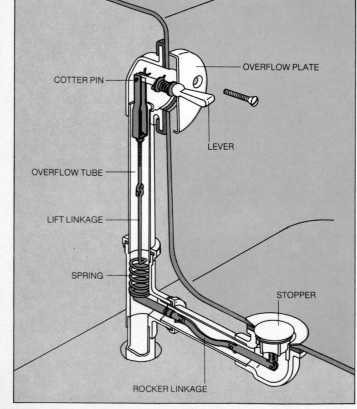

COTTER PIN
OVERFLOW PLATE
LEVER
OVERFLOW TUBE
LIFT LINKAGE
SPRING
STOPPER
ROCKER LINKAGE

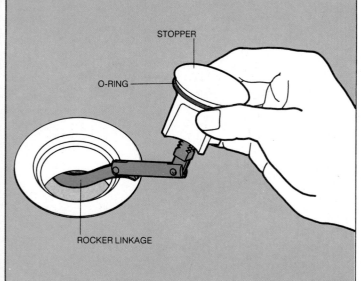

STOPPER
O-RING
ROCKER LINKAGE

Pop-up repairs. If a pop-up drain leaks, the O-ring below the metal stopper may be worn. Open the drain and pull out the stopper and the rocker linkage. Clean these parts of accumulated hair. Slip on a new O-ring, then replace the stopper, working it sideways or back and forth until it clears the bend in the pipe. Make sure that the bottom of the curve in the linkage faces down.

Toilets: Simple Repairs for Complex Machines

Considering that nearly half the water that is used in the average household flows through toilets, it is remarkable that these virtually automatic devices give such trouble-free service with so little attention. Repairs and adjustments are usually minor and within the capabilities of an inexperienced home plumber.

Although the mechanism of the tank toilet, by far the most common type in houses, remains a mystery to many, no householder need be finicky about removing the tank top and poking around inside. The water there is as pure as it is anywhere in the rest of the house, and the valves, levers and floats move so slowly so that it is easy to observe the way they interact and control the flushing cycle.

Leaks and noises are the most frequent problems with tank toilets, and the two are often interrelated. An intermittent gurgle of water from tank to bowl, for example, indicates a faulty toilet valve *(below, top)*. A high whine or whistle accompanied by a continuous run of water is a sign that the ball cock—the device that starts and stops the toilet's refill cycle—needs attention *(pages 373-374)*. Learning to diagnose such problems is a big step toward correcting them.

Another kind of toilet, the pressure flush valve type, has no tank but uses a pressurized flow of water to achieve the flushing action. Although rare in houses, pressure valves are common in apartments and other multiple-family dwellings because some models use less water than tank toilets. For the same reason, they have in recent years been recommended and sometimes required for new buildings in areas with chronic water shortages. While the valves are somewhat intricate in design, they are on the whole easier to adjust and maintain than tank toilet mechanisms.

Stopping Leaks from Tank to Bowl

1 **Adjusting the tank ball.** Water seeping past an imperfectly seated tank ball is the commonest cause of a continuously running toilet. Shut off water to the tank and remove the lid. Flush the toilet and watch the tank ball as it drops with the water level. If it does not fall straight into the outlet valve—the large opening at the bottom of the tank—loosen the thumbscrew that fastens the guide arm to the overflow pipe. Reposition the arm and the lower lift wire so the tank ball will be centered directly over the outlet valve. Straighten both of the lift wires if necessary.

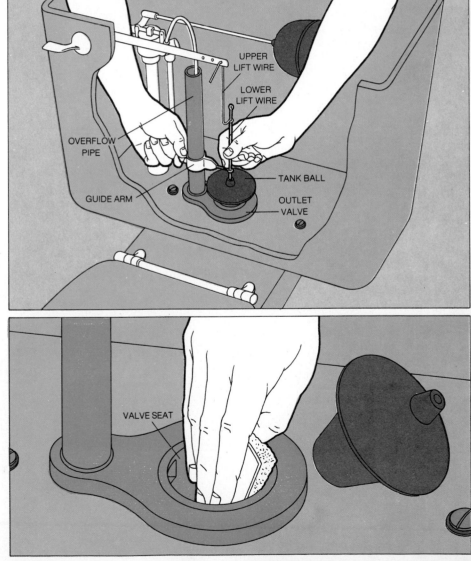

2 **Cleaning the tank bowl and the valve seat.** If the tank ball seems to seat properly but water still escapes, the problem may be a build-up of mineral deposits. Unscrew the ball counterclockwise from its lift arm and wash it with warm water and detergent. If the ball is damaged or feels mushy, replace it; an improved type is shown on page 372, top. Before replacing the ball, gently scour the seat, or rim, of the outlet valve with fine steel wool or a soap-impregnated plastic cleaning pad *(right)*.

Installing a hinged flapper ball. A flapper tank ball, which has no guide arm and lift wires, is easier to install and less prone to misalignment than the conventional type. The model shown is recommended by most plumbers because it has a semirigid plastic frame that keeps the ball from being jostled out of position by outrushing water.

Drain the tank and remove the old guide arm and lift wires. Slip the collar of the frame to the bottom of the overflow pipe, align the ball over the outlet valve and tighten the thumbscrew on the collar. Hook the chain from the ball through a hole in the trip lever directly above, leaving about ½ inch of slack. Turn the water on, then flush the toilet and see if the tank drains completely. If it does not, lessen the slack or move the chain one or two holes toward the rear of the lift arm. Do not forget to reposition the refill tube aiming down into the overflow pipe.

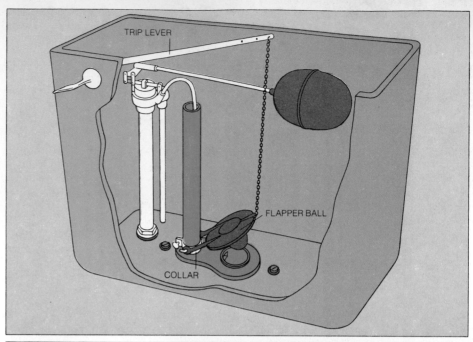

Tightening the handle and trip lever. A loose linkage between the tank handle and the trip lever will cause an incomplete or erratic flush cycle. Use a screwdriver or wrench to tighten the handle on its shaft. If this does not solve the problem, remove the tank lid and tighten the lift lever on the inside of the handle shaft. The model at right has a bracket that lifts the lever; use an adjustable wrench to secure the retaining nut so the bracket does not wobble but still moves freely when the handle is turned. With the wrench or pliers, tighten the trip-lever setscrew against the flattened surface of the handle shaft.

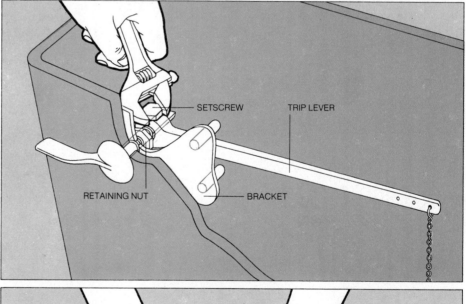

Adjusting the water level. When water cascades into the overflow pipe, the likeliest cause is a defective float ball or one that does not rise high enough to actuate the valve that cuts off incoming water. Unscrew the float ball counterclockwise and shake it; if water has leaked into the float, replace it. If it is sound, grasp the float rod with both hands (*right*) and bend it ½ inch downward. (If you find this difficult, unscrew the rod with pliers and bend it slightly over a rounded surface.) Flush the toilet. The water should stop rising about ½ inch below the top of the overflow pipe. If the water does not reach this level, bend the rod upward.

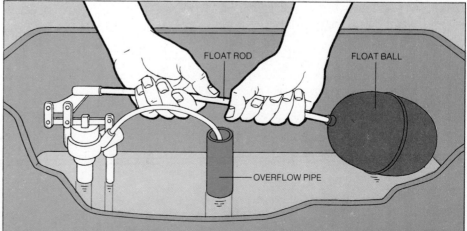

Stopping Ball-Cock Leaks

1 **Removing the plunger.** Check the action of the ball cock by lifting the float rod as high as it will go. If incoming water does not stop, the plunger washers probably are worn. Turn off the water. Unfasten the two retaining pins that hold the float assembly and, with your fingers or pliers, pull the plunger up and out of the ball cock.

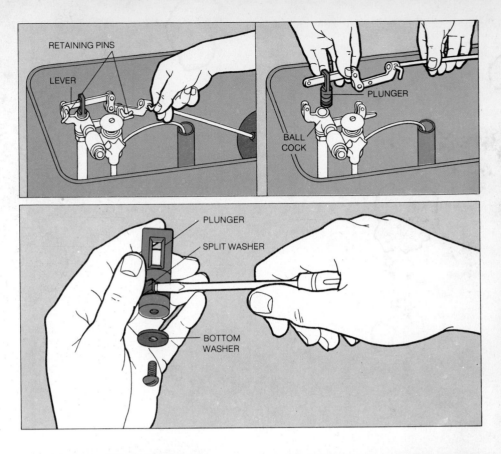

2 **Replacing the washers.** Plungers like the model shown at right have a screwed-in bottom washer; on the other models, this washer is press-fit and can be lifted out. Pry out the split leather washer (sometimes called a packing washer) from its groove on the side of the plunger. Use a screwdriver to remove the other washer from the bottom of the plunger. Scrape any residue or mineral build-up from both grooves with a penknife or the tip of a small screwdriver, taking care not to scratch or gouge the metal. Install new washers. Larger pre-packaged kits of assorted washers often include some for a ball cock. If you have none, ask for a ball-cock washer kit—or, for a perfect fit, take the plunger to your plumbing-supply dealer.

Replacing a Ball Cock

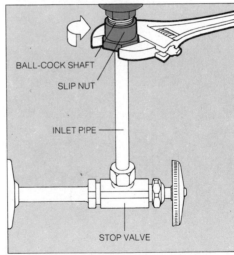

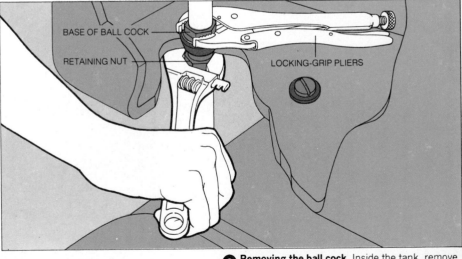

1 **Starting the disassembly.** A ball cock that still leaks after the plunger washers are renewed should be replaced—further repairs are impractical. Washers and gaskets that form a watertight seal on the tank should also be replaced; these are supplied with the new ball cock. Turn off the water and flush the tank. Sponge out the remaining water. With an adjustable wrench, unscrew the slip nut on the underside of the tank that holds the inlet pipe to the ball-cock shaft.

2 **Removing the ball cock.** Inside the tank, remove the float mechanism from the top of the ball cock and attach locking-grip pliers to the bottom of the ball-cock shaft. The pliers will wedge against the side of the tank and free your hands. Returning to the underside of the tank, use an adjustable wrench to unscrew—counterclockwise—the retaining nut that holds the ball-cock shaft to the tank. Use firm but gentle pressure to avoid cracking the vitreous china of the tank. If the nut resists, soak it with penetrating oil for 10 or 15 minutes and try again. Once the nut is removed, lift the ball cock out of the tank.

3 Installing the new ball cock. The ball cock shown here fills faster, is quieter and has a diaphragm valve instead of a plunger, but is installed in the same way as conventional models. Insert a new washer in the slip nut and place the slip nut washer over the pipe. Put the shank of the ball cock through the gasket and through the hole in the tank. Screw the retaining nut onto the ball-cock shaft. Grip the base of the ball cock with locking pliers and, under the tank, tighten the retaining nut against the tank. Screw the slip nut to the bottom of the ball-cock shaft. Attach the float rod and ball, and the overflow pipe.

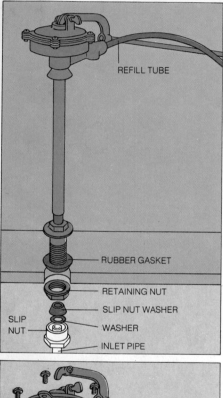

REFILL TUBE

RUBBER GASKET

RETAINING NUT

SLIP NUT WASHER

SLIP NUT

WASHER

INLET PIPE

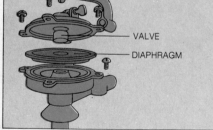

VALVE

DIAPHRAGM

4 Servicing a diaphragm ball cock. If your water supply contains a high concentration of minerals or other impurities you should occasionally clean the moving parts of a diaphragm ball cock. Turn off the water, remove the screws in the top of the ball cock, lift out the parts and clean them—and the inside cavity—with a plastic scouring pad. After several years of use you may need to replace the diaphragm valve. These parts are available as an inexpensive kit from your plumbing-supply store.

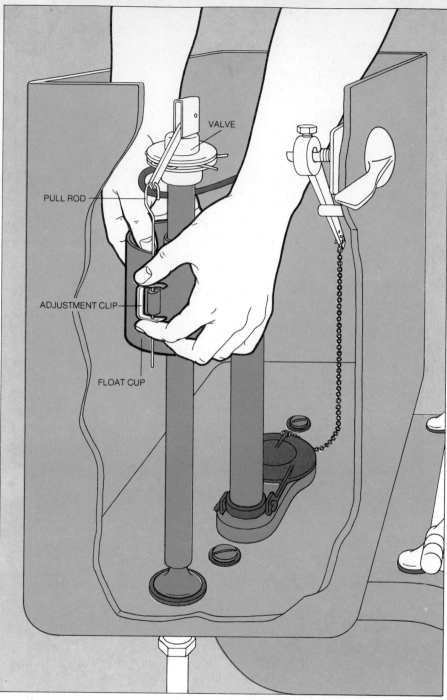

VALVE

PULL ROD

ADJUSTMENT CLIP

FLOAT CUP

A New Type of Ball Cock

Installing and adjusting a float cup. Many homeowners prefer to replace a worn ball cock. To install a float-cup ball, follow the procedure for a conventional ball cock; the fittings are identical. To raise the water level in the tank, simply pinch (*drawing, above*) the spring clip in the pull rod and move the cup higher on the shaft. To lower the level, move the cup down.

Stopping Leaks at Bolts and Gaskets

Tightening the hold-down bolts. Seepage around the two bolts that hold the tank to the toilet bowl is often mistaken for condensation. To make a sure diagnosis, pour laundry bluing into the tank and hold a piece of white tissue over the tips of the bolts. If the tissue turns blue, you have a leak. In most cases tightening the bolts will stop the leaks. Drain the tank and hold the head of the bolt—or have a helper do it—with a screwdriver. Use an adjustable wrench, or better, a socket wrench with an extra-deep socket, to tighten the nut below the tank. Caution: Do not overtighten or the brittle finish of the tank will crack. If the leak persists, you will have to remove the bolts and replace their washers.

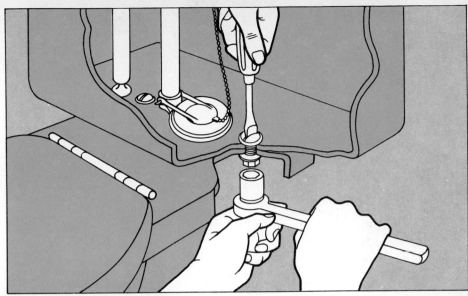

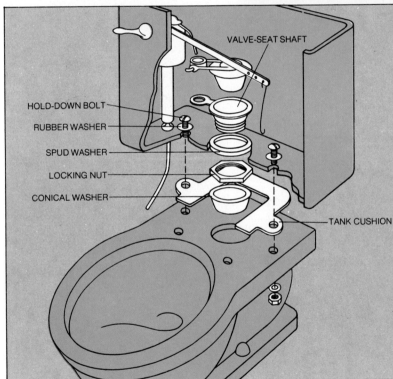

HOLD-DOWN BOLT

RUBBER WASHER

SPUD WASHER

LOCKING NUT

CONICAL WASHER

VALVE-SEAT SHAFT

TANK CUSHION

SLIP NUTS

Replacing flush-valve washers. If a leak occurs around the flush valve—the large opening between the tank and the bowl—you must remove the tank. After draining the tank, unscrew the two hold-down bolts and disconnect the supply pipe to the ball cock as explained on the preceding pages. Carefully lift the tank upward and off the bowl, and set it on its back. Remove the large locking nut on the threaded valve-seat shaft that protrudes from the bottom of the tank. Pull the shaft into the tank and replace the spud washer on the shaft. Also replace the large conical washer that covers the threaded shaft of the flush valve. Remount the tank.

Leaks from wall-mounted tanks. Older toilets have a tank suspended on the wall and connected to the bowl by an exposed L-shaped pipe. Leaks often occur around the pipe fittings because of shifts in wall or floor. Use a larger pipe wrench or a spud wrench to unscrew, counterclockwise, the large slip nuts at the tank and the bowl. Wrap the exposed threads with self-forming packing: Untwist the packing strands and wrap it in layers around the threads. Retighten the slip nuts.

Emergency Pipe Repairs

Pipes have a disconcerting way of springing a leak on Saturday night, after your friendly plumber has left for the annual union banquet. Fortunately, some simple fixes, easy to cobble together from the junk box on a workbench, will tide you over until you can make (or commission) a permanent repair.

When you first discover a leak in a supply pipe, the first thing to do, of course, is shut off the water. This will reduce pressure on the damaged section so you can proceed to plug the hole.

An application of epoxy glue or plastic tape is the quickest emergency procedure. Various "bandages" or plugs are even better. But before trying any remedy, make sure the pipe surface is dry enough for adhesives or sleeves to hold.

In the case of a leaking supply pipe that is not frozen, completely drain and dry the affected section if possible—an electric hair dryer does a quick job. Damaged pipes that are frozen should be left unthawed and undrained until patching is completed. Drainpipes, unlike supply pipes, are not under pressure and normally contain no water unless a fixture is in use.

A Patch for a Larger Leak

A hose patch. An effective temporary patch can be made by splitting a section of rubber hose lengthwise so that it will fit around the pipe. There are several ways to secure the hose. Strong, flexible wire such as that used for hanging pictures will serve—make a series of loops along the patch, spaced about an inch apart, and twist each loop tight with pliers (right). An automobile hose clamp (far right, top) holds more uniformly and can be adjusted to fit virtually any diameter of fresh-water pipe; it is best to install at least three clamps over the patch. To guarantee uniform clamping pressure, cut a section out from a tin can wide enough to cover the leak and long enough so the top rims of the sheet metal extend above the pipe when fitted around the hose patch. Bend the top rims at a right angle to the pipe so they fit closely together. Drill holes through both rims and fasten with bolts and nuts.

A Patch for a Tiny Leak

1 **Plugging a hole with a pencil.** One of the best emergency plugs for a small leak in a supply pipe is a pencil point jammed into the hole and broken off; the soft graphite point will conform to the shape of the opening and seal the leak.

2 **Securing the plug.** Dry the surface of the pipe after the leak has been plugged, then roll heavy tape over the damaged area to hold the plug in place. Wrap the tape several inches to the left and the right of the leak.

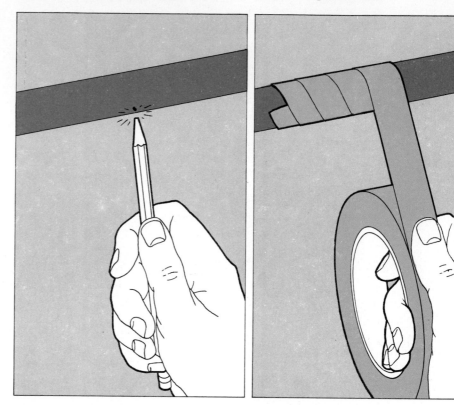

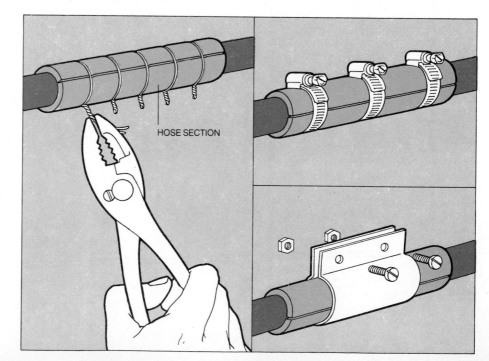

HOSE SECTION

Pipe Repairs

Copper is today's standard for supply pipes. However, its cost is high and there is danger of lead pollution from the solder used to join copper pipes and fittings. (Consider low-lead or silver solder.) Galvanized steel is best suited for pipes that will be exposed to damage or vibration. It is prone to corrosion, however, and it must be joined with threaded fittings. If local codes permit, two types of plastic — chlorinated polyvinyl chloride (CPVC) and polybutylene (PB) are light, inexpensive and easy to use. Cast-iron is used solely for drains. Polyvinyl chloride (PVC) and acrylonitrile butadiene styrene (ABS) are used for drainage where codes permit.

Galvanized Steel Pipe

1 **Removing the broken pipe.** Threaded joints make galvanized pipes easy to assemble but complicated to remove. Once in place, a threaded pipe cannot be unscrewed as one pipe; loosening one fitting will tighten it at the other. Close the main shutoff valve and drain the supply lines. Look for a union near the damaged section and, if there is one, unscrew the pipe from it. Unscrew the other end from its coupling. If there is no union, cut through the pipe with a fine-tooth hacksaw or mini-hacksaw and unthread the two pieces from their couplings. To unthread pipe, grip the coupling with one wrench and turn the pipe with another so that the rest of the run will not be twisted or strained. The jaws of the wrenches should face the direction in which force is applied (below).

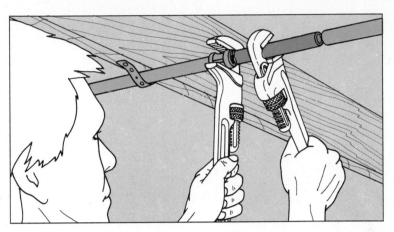

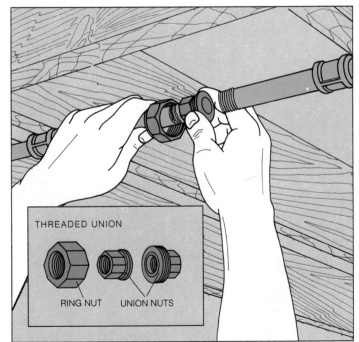

THREADED UNION

RING NUT   UNION NUTS

2 **Preparing the new pipes and union.** Buy two lengths of new pipe and a union whose combined length, when threaded together, is the same as the broken section. Wind 1½ turns of pipe tape over the threads of the new pipe, tightly enough so that they show through. Thread one of the pipes into the nearest coupling using the same double-wrench technique described in Step 1. Then thread the other pipe into its fitting, leaving a slight gap in the run. Disassemble a threaded union (inset). Slide the union nuts onto each pipe end (above).

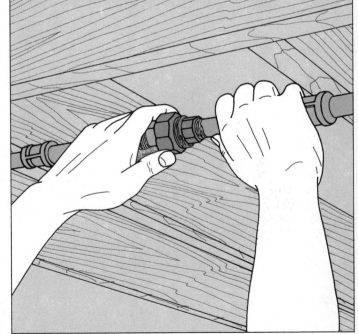

3 **Connecting the union.** Slide the ring nut to the center of the union and screw it onto the exposed threads of the union nuts (above), joining the two pipes. Grip the exposed union nut with one wrench and tighten the ring nut with a second wrench.

Copper Pipe

1 **Cutting copper pipe.** Close the main shutoff valve and drain the supply lines. If the broken pipe is hard to reach, cut it with a hacksaw. If it is accessible, you can use a tube cutter. Fit the jaws of the tube cutter around the pipe at one end of the defective section. Screw the knob clockwise until the rollers and the cutting disc grip the pipe firmly, as shown below. Give the knob another quarter-turn so that the disc bites into the pipe. Rotate the cutter once around the pipe, then tighten the knob and rotate again. Continue tightening and turning the tube cutter until the pipe is severed. Loosen the knob, slide the cutter down the pipe, and cut through the other side of the broken section.

2 **Measuring and deburring copper pipe.** If you are using standard couplings, fit them on the ends of the old pipe, hold the new pipe against the gap *(below, top)* and mark it at the coupling ridges. (If you are using slip couplings, mark the new pipe flush with the old pipe.) Cut the replacement pipe to length with the tube cutter. Use the triangular blade attached to the cutter (or a round metal file) to ream out the burrs inside the old and new pipes *(below, bottom)*. Next, prepare the joints for soldering *(Step 4)* or bend the pipe first if necessary *(Step 3)*.

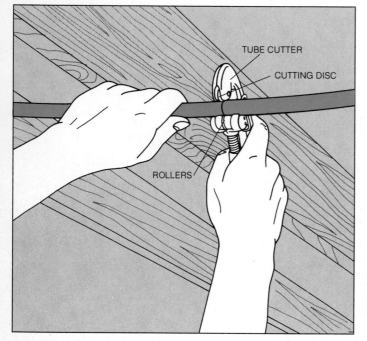

TUBE CUTTER

CUTTING DISC

ROLLERS

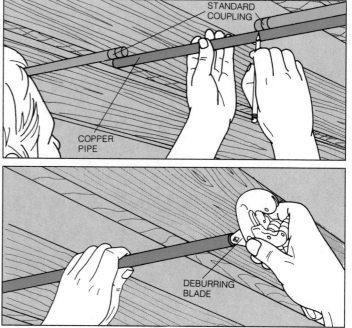

STANDARD COUPLING

COPPER PIPE

DEBURRING BLADE

3 **Bending copper pipe.** To prevent kinks in a replacement pipe that must be bent, slip a coiled-spring pipe bender onto the pipe using a clockwise, twisting motion. If the pipe is flexible, bend it with your hands or form it over your knee. Overbend the pipe slightly, then ease it back to the correct angle. If the pipe is rigid, clamp the pipe bender in a vise and bend the pipe with both hands *(right)*. Or, for greater leverage, slip a rigid pipe into the slot of an electrical conduit bender and push down on the handle.

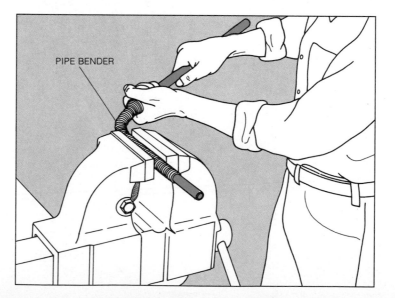

PIPE BENDER

4 **Preparing the joints.** Rub the inside of the couplings and the ends of the old and new pipes with emery cloth or fine steel wool until they are brightly burnished *(right, top)*. Remove any grit left on the surfaces with a clean, dry cloth. With a small brush, spread a thick, even coat of soldering flux on all of the pipe surfaces *(right, bottom)*. Brush a small amount of flux inside the couplings.

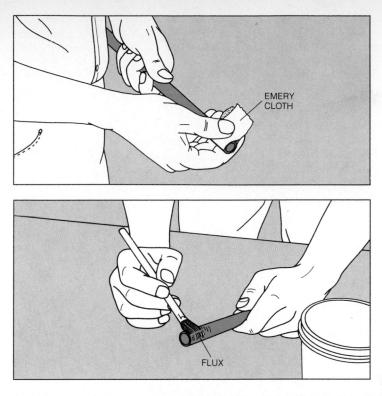

EMERY CLOTH

FLUX

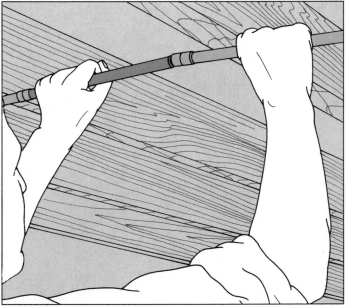

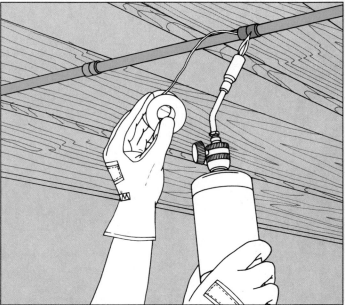

5 **Fitting the couplings and replacement pipe.** Fit a coupling onto each end of the old pipes; give a quarter-turn to evenly spread the flux. If water drips from the standing pipes, the joint cannot be properly soldered. (A plumber's trick: ball up some white bread and plug the pipe before soldering to absorb moisture. The bread will dissolve.) If using standard couplings, fit one end of the new pipe into the coupling until it bottoms out. Pull the pipes toward you until you can slip the other end into the second coupling *(above)*. For slip couplings, hold the new pipe in place, then slide the couplings over the joints. Give the new pipe a quarter-turn to evenly distribute the flux.

6 **Soldering the joint.** Wear safety glasses and work gloves, and protect flammable materials with a fireproof shield. Light the propane torch and play the flame over the fitting and nearby pipe, heating them as evenly as possible. Touch the top of the wire solder to the joint *(above)* until it melts into the fitting, but do not let the flame touch the solder. When the joint is properly heated, the flux inside draws molten solder into the fitting to seal the connection. Feed solder into the joint until a bead of metal appears around the edge.

CPVC Pipe

1 **Cutting the replacement pipe.** Close the main shutoff valve and drain the supply lines. Cut out the damaged pipe section with a hacksaw or plastic tube cutter. Measure the gap, then cut the replacement with a tube cutter or miter box.

2 **Deburring and beveling CPVC.** The ends of a sawed-off CPVC pipe must be deburred (but not a pipe cut with a plastic tube cutter) and beveled. Using a sharp knife *(below),* trim the inside edge to aid water flow and the outside edge to improve the welding action of the solvent.

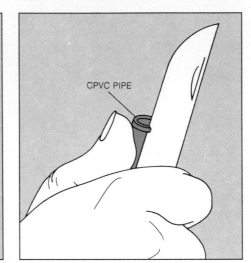

3 **Preparing the joint.** Clean the ends of the standing pipes and two coupling sockets with CPVC primer. Apply a liberal coat of CPVC solvent cement to the couplings and pipe ends *(right)* to the depth of the socket. Push the couplings onto the pipes, give them a quarter-turn to spread the cement, and hold the pieces together for about 10 seconds. (Caution: Solvent cement fumes are extremely flammable—avoid inhaling them.)

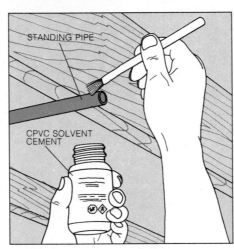

4 **Inserting the section of replacement pipe.** Clean and prime the exposed coupling sockets and both ends of the replacement pipe as shown in Step 3, then apply cement. Working quickly, push one end of the replacement pipe into a coupling, then gently bend the pipes toward you until there is just enough room to slip it into the other coupling as shown at right. Give the pipe a quarter-turn to spread the cement and press the pieces together for about 10 seconds. Wipe off any excess cement around the pipe or fittings with a clean, dry cloth. Do not run water in the pipe until the CPVC has cured. (This takes approximately two hours at temperatures above 60° F.)

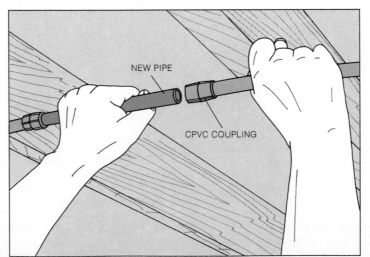

Polybutylene Pipes

1 **Cutting flexible PB pipe.** Close the main shutoff valve and drain the supply lines. If the damaged pipe is in an awkward location, cut it with a mini-hacksaw, then file the ends square with a metal file. (Otherwise, use a tube cutter.) Deburr both ends of the standing pipe *(page 380)*. Measure the gap in the copper pipe and transfer that measurement to the PB pipe. Hold the PB pipe against a flat surface and press down squarely with a sharp knife *(below)*. Once the knife bites into the surface it will easily slice through the pipe.

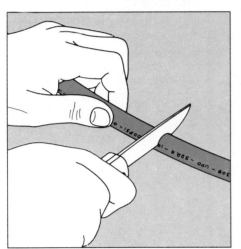

2 **Fitting the adapters.** Disassemble a compression fitting *(inset)*, used to join unthreaded pipe without solder or cement. Slide a coupling nut onto one end of the PB pipe, then a metal gripping ring and plastic sealing cone *(below)*. The end of the PB pipe should protrude ¼ to ½ inch from the cone. Other compression fittings may simply slide onto the two pipes to be joined.

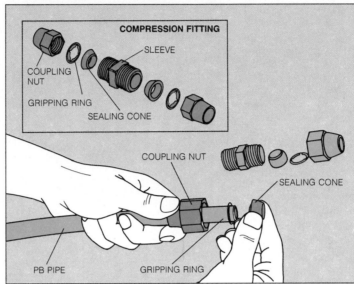

COMPRESSION FITTING

SLEEVE

COUPLING NUT

GRIPPING RING

SEALING CONE

COUPLING NUT

SEALING CONE

PB PIPE

GRIPPING RING

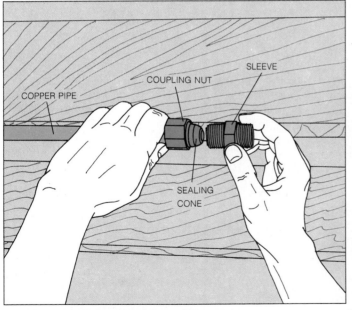

COPPER PIPE

COUPLING NUT

SLEEVE

SEALING CONE

3 **Adapting copper to PB.** Fit the second nut, gripping ring and sealing cone onto the end of the copper pipe. With one hand, hold the sleeve against the sealing cone on the copper pipe *(above)*. With the other hand, screw the nut to the sleeve *(above)* and tighten by hand. Then fit the PB pipe, with its half of the fitting, onto the other end of the sleeve and tighten by hand.

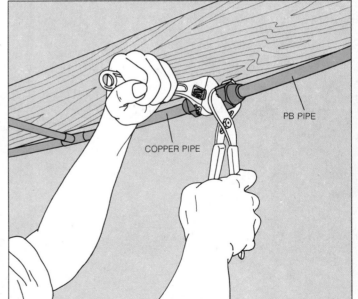

PB PIPE

COPPER PIPE

4 **Tightening the fitting.** Use two adjustable wrenches or channel-joint pliers to tighten the compression fitting. Grip the sleeve nut with one wrench and tighten the coupling nut one-half turn (but no more) with the second wrench *(above)*. Do not overtighten. Connect the other end of the PB pipe to the copper pipe with a second compression fitting. Turn on the water; if a joint leaks, reassemble the fitting rather than tightening it further.

First Aid for Frozen Pipes

A properly constructed and heated house is safe from plumbing freeze-ups even during the most severe cold snap—unless the heating system breaks down or is knocked out by a power failure. Then no home is immune. If heat is not restored promptly, indoor temperatures will drop precipitately and you must act quickly to keep pipes from freezing and bursting *(right)*. Even in an otherwise well-built house, pipes that run through an unprotected crawl space, basement, laundry room or garage can freeze during exceptionally cold weather, especially if the room tends to be drafty.

If pipes do freeze, the first sign may be a faucet that refuses to yield water. But all too often, the freeze-up is announced by a flood from a break. Water expands about 8 per cent in volume as it begins to freeze, generating pressure that splits pipes, especially where expansion is impeded by joints or bends. Ice may form throughout a long straight section of supply line before it meets an obstruction and cracks the pipe; thus, the entire length of pipe that supplies a stopped faucet should be considered suspect, both for ice blockages and leaks.

When you prepare to thaw a section of pipe, keep the affected faucet open to let vapor and melting ice run out. Then turn off the water supply once you have located the leaks and marked them for repairs. After temporary patches have been applied to the damaged areas *(page 376)*, open the main shutoff partway; the movement of water through the frozen section of pipe will aid the thawing process. The surrounding area should be guarded against water damage *(box, page 338)* in the event that any other leaks have gone undetected.

Electrical heaters are generally safest for thawing. However, freeze-ups often occur during power failures and in such a case you are likely to have to use hot water poured over rags or—with caution—the flame from a propane torch.

Electric heating tape. Wrap the tape in a spiral around the frozen pipe, allowing about six turns per foot, and leaving at least half an inch between each turn. Secure the spiral with masking tape about every 4 inches. Some electric heating tapes come with built-in thermostats and can be left plugged in: when the temperature drops toward the freezing point, the thermostat automatically activates the tape and warms the pipe to prevent freezing.

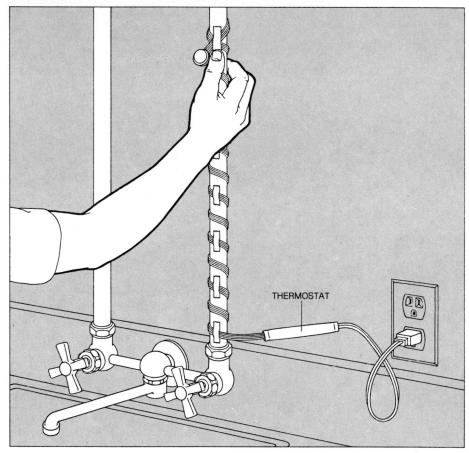

THERMOSTAT

How to Keep Pipes from Freezing

There is only one sound way to prevent freeze-ups in an unheated house: drain the entire plumbing system as described on page 338.

For pipe protection in other circumstances, you can choose from several methods—both electrical and nonelectrical, temporary and permanent.

☐ If power is available, plug in an electric heater or heat lamp, or hang a 100-watt bulb near vulnerable pipes.
☐ Keep a door ajar between a heated room and an unheated room with pipes so that the unprotected area will receive heat.
☐ Set an electric fan on your furnace to blow warm air over basement pipes.
☐ Insulate exposed pipes. In addition to the thermostatic heating tape, there are wrap-on and snap-on varieties of pipe insulation that will retard freezing.
☐ If no commercial insulation is at hand and pipes must be protected immediately, wrap several layers of newspaper loosely around the pipes and tie with string.
☐ If the temperature suddenly drops and you have no time to install insulation, turn faucets on to a trickle; this will prevent freezing.

Propane torch. Equipped with a flame-spreader attachment, a propane torch can thaw a pipe rapidly and effectively, but use it cautiously. Place metal sheeting between the pipe and nearby framing. Apply heat near the open faucet first, and then work gradually back along the pipe, feeling frequently to make sure that you are not overheating it. Caution: the pipe should never become too hot to touch; if water boils inside, steam can cause a dangerous explosion.

Hair dryer. If you have electricity, an appliance that blows warm air—a hair dryer or a tank-type vacuum cleaner with the hose set into the outlet end—can be used in the same fashion as a propane torch, although it will work more slowly.

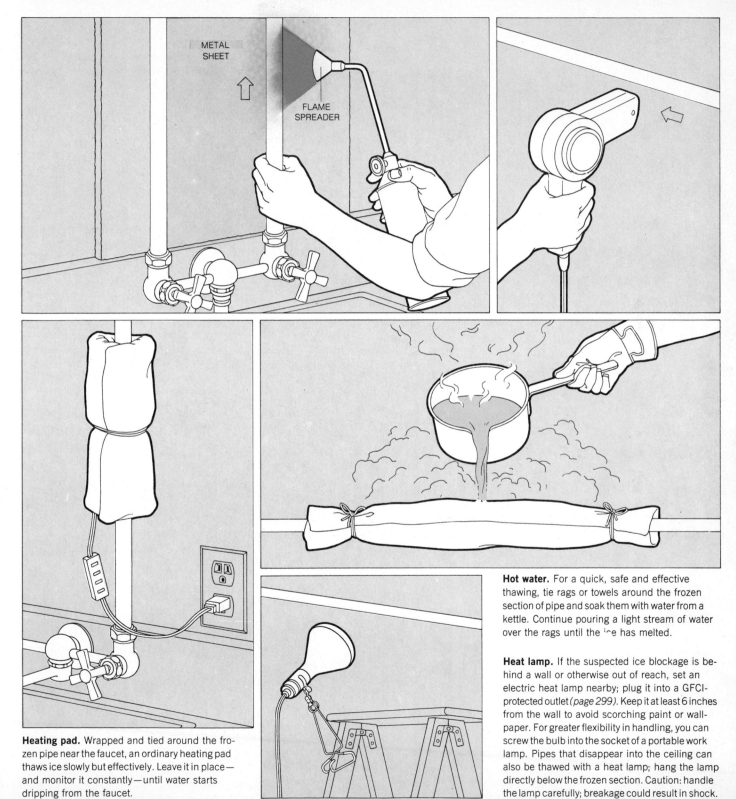

METAL SHEET

FLAME SPREADER

Heating pad. Wrapped and tied around the frozen pipe near the faucet, an ordinary heating pad thaws ice slowly but effectively. Leave it in place—and monitor it constantly—until water starts dripping from the faucet.

Hot water. For a quick, safe and effective thawing, tie rags or towels around the frozen section of pipe and soak them with water from a kettle. Continue pouring a light stream of water over the rags until the ice has melted.

Heat lamp. If the suspected ice blockage is behind a wall or otherwise out of reach, set an electric heat lamp nearby; plug it into a GFCI-protected outlet *(page 299)*. Keep it at least 6 inches from the wall to avoid scorching paint or wallpaper. For greater flexibility in handling, you can screw the bulb into the socket of a portable work lamp. Pipes that disappear into the ceiling can also be thawed with a heat lamp; hang the lamp directly below the frozen section. Caution: handle the lamp carefully; breakage could result in shock.

6 EXTERIOR REPAIRS

The Surfaces and Structure of Roofs and Walls

For everyday purposes, the exterior of a house can be adequately described by naming the materials that cover the walls and roof—a wood clapboard wall, an asphalt shingle roof. But anyone who undertakes an extensive repair needs a larger vocabulary. The skin of a house is a web of interlocking parts, broken at dozens of points by windows, doors, vents and roof projections, and supported by a hidden framework of rafters, joists, studs and beams. Each part has its precise name, and to discuss your plans with an architect or building inspector or to order materials from a supplier, you should learn some of the language of the trade.

Though roofs are made in dozens of styles and covered by a variety of materials *(page 388),* most roof shapes are variations on two types: the gable roof and the hip roof *(right).* The gable roof, sloping on two sides, is named for the triangular wall section, or gable, formed by the slopes at each end wall. The horizontal upper edge of the roof, where the two slopes meet, is the ridge; the horizontal lower edges are eaves; and the sloping edges that frame the gable are rakes.

A hip roof has slopes on all four sides and eaves all the way around; the roof is named for the raised corners, or hips, at which slopes intersect. The fourth slope on the hip roof at right has been eliminated to illustrate a valley—the V-shaped channel or trough formed at the intersection of two slopes.

Different roof styles are, of course, often combined in a single building. A gable-roofed home may have an extension covered by a flat roof or an enclosed patio with a single-slope shed roof. But these differing styles remain variations of the basic ones: a flat roof is one with no slope at all; a shed, or lean-to, roof is actually half of a gable roof; a gambrel roof *(not shown)* is a gabled roof with a steep lower slope and a flatter upper slope on each side of the ridge; and a mansard roof, which has two slopes on each of its four sides, is essentially a gambrel roof with hips.

Roof slopes are broken not only by intersections with other slopes but also by projections that admit light and air to an attic or release smoke, fumes and hot air from the house. Dormers—

roofed projections designed to house vertical windows—are described by their roof style: gable, hip or shed. Ventilation openings are named for their locations on a roof: ridge vents, for example, provide a continuous opening along the ridge line, gable vents are mounted high in an end wall and roof vents are set into the slope of the roof. Chimneys may be set into the roof slope or built into a gable wall; a stack vent—a 3- or 4-inch pipe that releases gases from the plumbing system—usually rises from one of the main slopes near the ridge.

Any substantial interruption in a roof—the joints around projections or the seams where roof slopes meet or where a roof meets a wall—must be waterproofed with metal flashing. Flashing comes in various forms, including a collar that fits around vent pipes, a wide strip that runs along the full length of a valley and a double-layer pattern, called counter-and base flashing, used at seams where roof slopes meet walls or chimneys.

At their eaves, most roofs project well beyond the building wall to carry rain away from sidings and foundations. The projection, called the overhang or cornice, usually consists of a fascia board nailed to the rafter ends and a soffit board that forms the underside of the overhang. Many gable roofs also overhang at the rakes: the underside, like that of an eave, is a soffit; the outer face is called a rake board or rake fascia. Rain gutters usually hang from the eaves fascia, and metal drip edges along eaves and rakes direct runoff away from the fascia boards. In colder climates, snow guards mounted above the eaves prevent frozen snow from sliding off the roof in sheets.

Because it is protected by overhangs and gutters from the direct attack of sun, wind, rain and snow, siding is less trouble-prone—and less complex—than roofing. The chart on page 408 lists a variety of available siding materials; the drawing at right shows one of the most common: overlapping horizontal boards, called clapboard or lap siding.

The structural terms and features of siding are also few and relatively simple. The gap between the siding and the soffit is finished with a frieze board, and the lower edge of the siding extends below

the top of the foundation wall. Siding edges are covered by corner boards at outside corners and butted against corner strips or moldings at inside corners. Metal drip caps over door and window frames protect the casings from water damage, and door- and window sills are sloped outward for drainage.

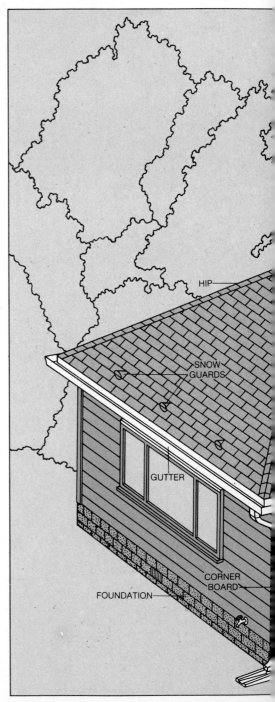

An unlikely exterior. This improbable house is a composite of clashing styles and features; it is not intended to represent a real house, but to illustrate the exterior parts defined and described in the text at left. Every detail, however, is accurately rendered, and mastering the names of these parts is an essential first step in repairing or in dealing with home repair professionals.

Repairing Roofing

Over its lifetime, an asphalt-shingle roof is drenched by more than a million gallons of water weighing almost 5,000 tons, baked by 50,000 hours of direct sunlight, stretched and squeezed by changes of temperature totaling a half a million degrees and swept by two million miles of passing wind. Only then—after 20 years—is this type of roof ready for replacement. Roofs of slate and tile do even better; they can shrug off nature a century or more.

Putting up roofs to withstand such punishment used to be the exclusive province of a skilled professional, who pieced each roof together from small, irregular units, locally made and individually fitted. No longer. Over the years the job has been made easier for both professional and amateur by standardized roofing materials designed especially for easy installation and repair. Asphalt shingles, for example, come with dabs of adhesive that automatically seal the roof against high winds. Slates now come in standard sizes with prepunched nail holes; tiles are manufactured in classic patterns that fit together like building blocks.

Although they all do the same job of keeping off the wind and weather, the roofing materials in the chart below vary strikingly in appearance. "Cost" refers to the relative cost of materials alone; it does not include the cost of labor. In most cases, the cost of professional installation is higher for the traditional roofing materials—slate, tile and wood shingles and shakes—than for the newer materials, which are designed to be installed more quickly. The minimum slope is the slope at which a specific material begins to provide adequate protection against water. All the materials listed can be applied to surfaces steeper than the minimum, but as slopes increase, such considerations as appearance and durability become more important. Roll roofing, for example, provides adequate covering for steep as well as gentle slopes, but its plainness and poor durability make it an unlikely choice for any but the most gradual slopes.

"Durability" is a rough measure of how long a roof will last with proper maintenance; the figures given apply to temperate climates. The columns listing advantages and limitations concentrate on installation, maintenance and repair.

Type	Cost	Durability (years)	Minimum slope	Advantages	Limitations
asphalt shingles	inexpensive	12-25	2 in 12	easy installation; available in a variety of weights and colors; requires little maintenance; easy to repair	poor fire resistance
roll roofing	inexpensive	5-10	1 in 12	easy installation and maintenance	poor fire resistance; drab appearance
built-up roofing	moderate	10-20	0 in 12	most waterproof of all roofing	poor fire resistance; must be installed professionally; leaks difficult to locate
wood shingles and shakes	moderate to expensive	15-30 (shingles) 25-75 (shakes)	3 in 12 (steeper in humid climates)	easy installation; attractive rustic appearance; natural insulator	highly flammable unless specially treated; shingles must be laid over open planks
slate	expensive	50-100	4 in 12	attractive traditional appearance; fire resistant	heavy, brittle; requires sturdy roof support; long and delicate installation may require special tools; needs regular replacement of damaged pieces; difficult to repair
ceramic tiles	expensive	50-100	4 in 12	attractive traditional appearance; fire resistant	heavy, brittle; requires sturdy roof support; time-consuming installation requires special tools; availability of replacement pieces unreliable; difficult to repair
metal panels	moderate	25-50	2 in 12	easy installation and patching; can be painted any color; fire resistant	subject to damage from wind, trees, any contact

Professional Tools for Reaching High Places

Professionals have a catalogue full of devices that make climbing to, working at and lifting materials to heights of 20 and 30 feet safe and easy. Most of these tools are available at rental agencies.

The basic tool, of course, is the extension ladder. For the jobs in this book use a Type 1 ladder, the strongest commercial ladder. New ladders are marked conspicuously with this classification. If you have doubts about the strength of a ladder you own, it is wise to rent a ladder that you can count on to support you and a bundle of shingles or siding.

Though a ladder is often used as a work platform for small siding repairs, larger jobs are more efficiently completed with a scaffold that extends at least 8 feet horizontally along the wall. It saves the time spent moving ladders. You can make a scaffold from a pair of extension ladders and special brackets called ladder jacks *(below).* A more versatile scaffold *(below, right),* designed to be moved up and down by foot power, is a better choice because it enables you to readjust the platform position easily to a comfortable working height. Both these devices support working platforms of 12-foot 2-by-10 fir planks of a type sold as scaffold grade. Use them in pairs supported every 9 feet; such a platform holds two workers plus about 75 pounds of materials. Elaborate scaffolds can be rented when extensive work on the side of the house needs to be done.

In addition to a ladder and possibly scaffolding, the equipment needed for roofing includes hooks to hold a ladder to the ridge or brackets to support a foot rest *(page 391).* If your roof slopes less than 4 inches in 12, you can probably work on it with no more assistance than rubber-soled shoes. For both roofing and siding work, you need support and access for materials as well as yourself. To lift the materials, says one contractor, the hardest way is often the easiest: lug the material, a batch at a time, up a ladder. However, you can ease some of this effort. Check to see if your roofing material supplier offers rooftop delivery, via a truck-mounted crane or conveyor. If not, use a ladder as a ramp, rent a crank-operated elevator *(page 392)*—or enlist a helper.

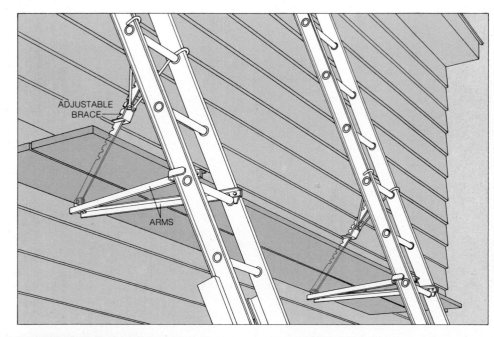

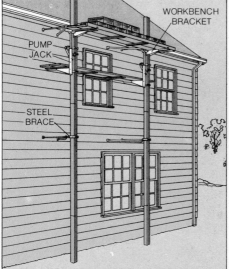

A scaffold hung from ladders. Ladder jacks, special plank supports designed to be hung from the rails and rungs of extension ladders, can support a work platform of 2-by-10s up to 9 feet long; they are useful for heights up to 20 feet above the ground. Suspend the jacks from two extension ladders leaned against the house so that the rungs are about 2½ feet from the wall at the height you wish to stand. Level the bracket arms with the adjustable brace on each ladder jack. Then enlist a helper to lay the planks so that they extend 1 foot beyond the arms.

An adjustable scaffold. Steel brackets called pump jacks travel up and down wood uprights to position a platform of planks—accessible by ladder—at working heights up to 30 feet. The uprights are usually set into shallow holes 9 feet apart anchored to the wall with steel braces *(page 390)* or to the roof deck edge under shingle tabs. The uprights also support brackets for a guardrail or a workbench for materials *(above).*

Pump Jacks and Scaffold: A Portable Freight Elevator

1 Constructing the uprights. Fasten 2-by-4s side by side with tenpenny nails to make two 4-by-4 poles. Drive the nails into both sides of the pole, spacing them a foot apart. To make a long upright—up to 30 feet—splice boards together, staggering joints at least 4 feet.

2 Bracing the upright. Braces clamped near the tops of the uprights and nailed to the wall or under roof shingle tabs hold the uprights vertical. Clamp the braces before erecting the uprights so that the bolts cross the pole seams, squeezing the halves together; then nail the braces to the uprights. If the uprights are to stand on a hard surface, install additional braces to secure the bottom of each upright; in soft ground, dig holes for the bottoms 4 inches deep and 32 inches from the wall.

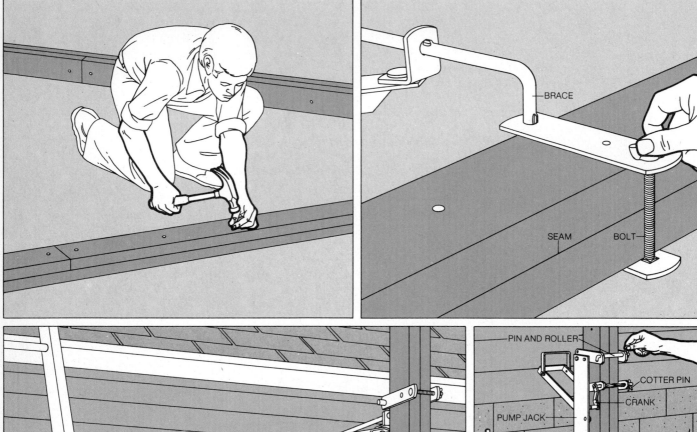

BRACE

SEAM BOLT

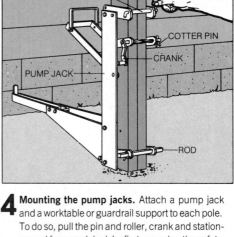

PIN AND ROLLER

COTTER PIN

CRANK

PUMP JACK

ROD

3 Anchoring a brace to the wall. Tilt each upright into position, and while a helper holds it, use 16-penny nails to fasten the arms of each bracket through the wall or under roof shingle tabs into studs or rafters. (If your home is brick or block construction, be sure to use 1½-inch masonry nails into mortar joints.) Anchor the longer arm of the brace between the poles *(above)*, then install additional braces as necessary to support the uprights every 7 to 10 feet of their height. For easy removal, use double-headed nails or 3-inch wallboard screws.

4 Mounting the pump jacks. Attach a pump jack and a worktable or guardrail support to each pole. To do so, pull the pin and roller, crank and stationary rod from each jack by first removing the safety cotter pins that prevent these components from working loose *(above)*. Rest the pump jack on the ground and, holding it against the pole, replace the pin and roller (use a new cotter pin each time), crank and stationary rod; secure them with the cotter pins. Worktable and guardrail supports are fastened to the poles above the pump jacks in a similar fashion but with fewer pins. Lay scaffold grade 2-by-10 planks across the jacks and worktable supports. Use a 2-by-4 as a guardrail.

FOOT LEVER

CRANK

ROD

5 **Operating the scaffold.** Raising or lowering the scaffold is best accomplished by two people working in unison, but you can do it alone. To lift the platform, raise and lower the foot lever on one pump jack until one end of the platform rises about a foot above the other, then repeat at the other end. When you have pumped the scaffold to the height you wish, leave the foot levers in the up position. To lower the scaffold, depress the stationary rod with your foot and turn the crank (inset). To jack past a brace, temporarily detach the brace from the upright and let it hang against the wall. Then raise or lower the scaffold past the brace and reattach it.

Secure Toeholds on a Sloping Roof

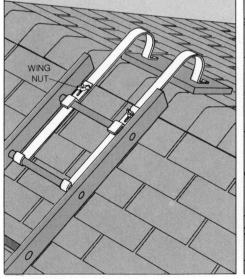

WING NUT

STRAP

MOUNTING SLOT

SHELF

UPRIGHT

LOCK

ADJUSTMENT SLOT

Using rungs as toeholds. Fitted with a pair of ladder hooks, a section of an ordinary extension ladder becomes a toehold for working on roofs. Simply clamp the hooks to the top two rungs of the ladder by tightening a wing nut, then suspend the ladder from the ridge as shown above. A wood block under the hooks spreads weight to prevent damage to shingles.

A roof-top scaffold. A pair of triangular metal platforms called roof brackets provides level storage or working area on asphalt shingles (and uncovered roof sheathing). Each bracket consists of a steel strap with slots or holes in one end for fastening to the roof. Attached to the strap is a shelf, braced by an upright, which supports a 2-by-10 plank. Adjustable brackets like the

ones shown above can fit any roof pitch and have a lock to keep the upright from slipping. To attach a bracket, bend back a shingle tab, insert an eightpenny nail in a bracket slot (or hole) and drive it through the shingle below. Remove a bracket with a hammer by knocking it toward the ridge and slipping it off the nail, then lift the shingle tab and pound the nail flush.

Two Ways to Hoist Heavy Loads

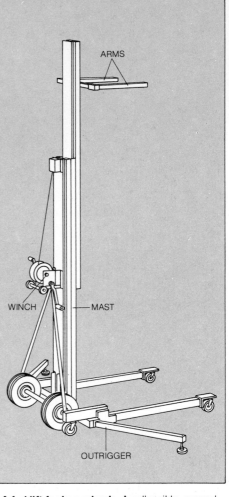

Hauling materials up a ladder. An extension ladder can serve as a ramp to steady a heavy or bulky object as you pull it up to a scaffold or a roof with a rope. Tie a length of half-inch rope around the load with a timber hitch (*inset*). Climb onto the scaffold or roof and pull the load up the ladder. For material as large as the 4-by-8-foot sheet of plywood sheathing (*above*), add a guide rope to be held by a helper on the ground.

A forklift for heavy loads. A collapsible, manual forklift from a tool rental agency can lift a 500-pound load of materials as high as 26 feet to a scaffold or an eave. The fork has adjustable arms to carry almost any size load and is cranked up the mast with a self-locking winch. (Small objects can be stacked on a plywood platform lashed to the arms.) The mast on this model automatically telescopes upward as the load is raised; on other types of forklift, the mast must be preassembled to the desired height. When using a forklift, be certain to set it on level ground and to extend the outriggers, if there are any, to prevent the forklift from tipping over. Also see that the casters are chocked to keep the forklift from rolling.

Roof Leaks: Hard to Find, Easy to Fix

The old joke that a roof leaks only during a rain, when you can't fix it, is at least half wrong—the trickiest part of repairing a leak is finding it, and that may be easier when the water is coming through. Even then, do not assume the damage is near the drip, for the multiple-layer construction of modern roofs *(below)* can lead water on a long and twisting course over several layers and through joints before it finally pours out into the house. Often it will travel down inside a second-story wall, across a first-floor ceiling and gush out around a lighting fixture.

Some leaks are caused by tears or punctures in the roofing surface, which you may be able to see from outside. Curled shingles, which admit wind-blown rain, are another visible cause. In winter, ice buildup on eaves can result in leaks. But equally common—and generally undetectable by inspection—are small openings in the metal flashing that should be installed at vents, chimneys, and corners or angles. The inevitable expansion and contraction of house parts loosens the sealant—called roofing cement—that covers the edges of flashing. The cement may also crumble with age, and it should be checked and renewed every few years.

Although a leak may be far from the drip, start your exploration there. Look for damage to the roof in the general area overhead. Or try to trace the leak from interior signs—even slight discoloration in a wall or ceiling suggests moisture. In an unfinished attic, you may be able to see gaps in the roofing from inside; look for pinpoints of daylight, and if you find a spot, mark it by poking a wire through. Remember that leaks may also arise in house siding, generally at cracks, breaks or vertical butt joints.

On the roof itself, always take on jobs of preventive maintenance as well as patching existing leaks. Check the flashings and reseal them if necessary *(pages 402-403)*—the same technique will work for leaks in a roof made entirely of metal—and replace missing or damaged shingles. The shingles that you are most likely to work with will be asphalt—low cost and light weight have made asphalt shingles *(page 394)* the most commonly used roofing material in the United States and Canada. Consisting of a felt base that is saturated with asphalt and coated with mineral granules, these shingles normally last anywhere from 15 to 25 years. And because they are relatively flexible, asphalt shingles are simpler for the amateur to repair or replace than are slate or wood shingles, which call for certain specialized techniques *(pages 396-398)*.

Asphalt shingles are usually packaged in bundles containing about 27 strips, 3 feet wide, and each composed of two or three shingle tabs separated by cutouts. Three bundles make a "square"—enough shingles to cover 100 square feet of roof surface. Although most shingles are sold by the square, many home-repair centers, building material suppliers and lumberyards will sell a smaller bundle or even individual shingles.

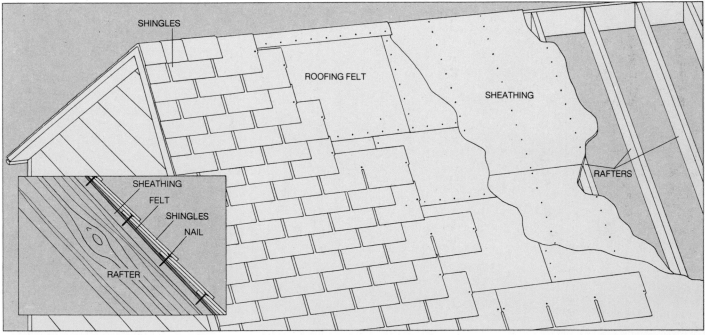

The anatomy of a roof. To provide a firm base for roofing materials, rafters are covered with sheathing—usually 1-by-6-inch boards or, on newer homes, 4-by-8-foot sheets of plywood. Overlapping layers of roofing felt or building paper are nailed or stapled to the sheathing, and the overlapping rows, or courses, of shingles are fastened with roofing nails that penetrate the underlying shingles as well as the felt and the sheathing *(inset)*. The tortuous path of water through these layers can make the source of a leak hard to find. When water leaks beneath a damaged shingle, it may soak directly through the underlying felt or flow downward until it reaches a loose seam or damaged area. At the sheathing, the water will generally run down to the joint between adjoining boards or plywood sheets, then along the joint to a loose butt joint over a rafter. Finally, the water may run along the rafter for a distance before dripping to the floor—far from the original hole in the shingle.

Repairing Asphalt Shingles

Reseating wind-blown shingles. If high winds lift or curl the tabs of asphalt shingles, wind-driven rain can penetrate the opened space beneath. To secure lifted tabs, use a caulking gun (page 18) to apply dabs of quick-setting shingle cement under the tab, then press it down into the cement. When replacing shingles, use the wind-resistant type, which has factory-applied adhesive on the upper surface an inch above the cutouts. After installation, the adhesive is softened by the heat of the sun, and holds the overlapping shingles in place.

Sealing small tears. If the damage does not extend under the overlapping shingles, coat the underside with roofing cement and press it flat. Nail both sides of the tear with 1-inch roofing nails and cover both the nailheads and the tear with additional cement. To replace a badly torn shingle, see the instructions on page 42.

Some Dos and Don'ts for Roofing Work

Working on a pitched roof is potentially dangerous: if you fear heights or if your roof is steeply pitched, the job is best left to a professional. But you can make repairs safely by taking these common-sense precautions:

☐ Never work in wet, windy or cold weather. Roofing materials can become dangerously slippery when wet, and asphalt shingles are brittle when cold, crumbling underfoot. In general, the less you walk around on a slate or wood shingle roof, the better.

☐ Wear sneakers or other shoes that have slip-resistant soles, and choose loose fitting clothes so that you can move about freely and comfortably.

☐ Use an access ladder that extends above the eave so that you need never step over the top of the ladder. Keep your hips between the ladder rails as you climb, and never lean over the side of the ladder to work on the roof.

☐ Enlist a helper to steady the ladder as you climb and to feed you tools and materials once you are up there.

☐ On a steep roof, use a roofing ladder with wood or metal brackets that hook over the roof ridge (page 391, bottom, left). These ladders not only provide secure hand- and footholds, but also distribute your weight over the roof's shingles. On brittle roofing materials such as slate, tile or asbestos, use a "chicken ladder" of the kind shown on page 396—a 1-by-12-inch board with 1-by-2-inch horizontal wood cleats nailed to it.

☐ If cutting asbestos wear a chemical cartridge respirator with a particulate filter approved for asbestos-containing dusts and mists to avoid inhaling carcinogenic asbestos fibers.

Replacing Asphalt Shingles

1 Removing the nails. To free a damaged shingle, you must pry out two rows of nails: a lower row on the damaged shingle, and an upper row that fastens both the shingle above and the upper edge of the damaged shingle. Each row usually consists of four nails, none of which are ordinarily visible. To get at the upper row, raise the shingle tabs two courses above the damaged shingle; insert the flat end of a pry bar under the nails thus exposed and remove them. Lifting the course above the damaged shingle will expose the second row of nails for removal with the pry bar.

2 Removing the damaged shingle. Carefully pull out the damaged shingle. If it resists, make sure you have removed all the nails holding it in place; then, with a putty knife, gently pry it away from the shingles above and below it. With the old shingle removed, apply roofing cement to all tears or holes in the shingle or roofing felt underneath.

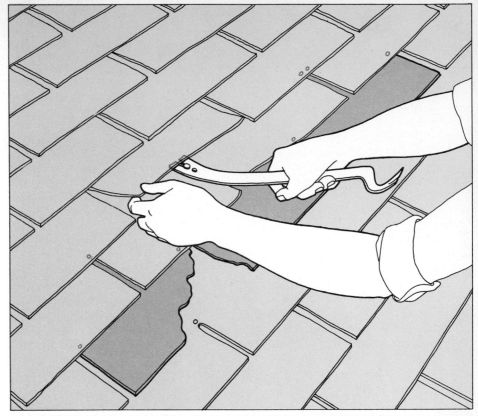

3 Installing the new shingle. Slide the shingle into place, aligning its bottom edge with the adjacent ones in its course. Then lift the second course above to expose the old nail holes in the first course above. Use these nail holes, nailing from one end of the shingle to the other to avoid buckling. To avoid curling the lifted tabs, do not try to lift the tabs high enough for hammering directly; instead, slide the flat end of a pry bar over the nailhead and hammer the bar just clear of the shingle's bottom edge *(above)*. For the lower nails, use the pry bar again to lift the first course above and to drive the nails. Locate two of them $\frac{5}{8}$ inch above the cutouts separating the tabs, and the other two an inch in from the edges.

Slate and Wood Shingle Roofs

Slate and wood shingles are not only two of the most attractive roofing materials, but when installed and maintained, they are exceptionally durable. And when repair is necessary, one or two pieces, rather than a whole strip, can be replaced. In general, keep walking and movement on a slate or wood shingle roof to a minimum. Follow the safety precautions on page 394 when working on either type of roof, and be especially careful on a slate roof: slate is brittle and it is extremely slippery when wet.

Lay wood shingles and shakes—thick hand-split shingles—with a ¼-inch spacing on either side to allow for expansion as they swell with moisture. You may find that the shingles were originally installed on spaced sheathing boards rather than solid sheathing; the open space beneath the shingles provides ventilation to dry out the wood. When cracks and splits do appear, act quickly. Work from a chicken ladder securely anchored at the ridge

with roof hooks, as shown below. Seal a small split or make a temporary repair on wood or slate *(below)*. If a shingle is badly split or rotted, replace it. The job will go faster if you use a roofing tool called a slate puller; if you cannot get one, use a hacksaw blade to cut the nails *(page 397)*.

Moss, which speeds decay, is a common problem on wood roofs, particularly in shady areas or damp climates. Scrape the moss off with a stiff brush and paint the affected area with a commercial wood preservative.

Loose slates are usually caused either by rusted nails or by cracks and breaks in the slate itself. Rusted nails can mean you need professional reroofing: the installer did not use corrosion-resistant nails. Cracks or breaks are most likely to occur in porous, moisture-absorbing slates; during freezes, water expands and cracks the slate. Fill hairline cracks with roofing compound; badly cracked or broken slates must be replaced.

Quick fix with a metal patch. To keep a split wood shingle from leaking—or to repair a badly damaged shingle or slate temporarily—make a patch from a sheet of copper or aluminum flashing. With a pair of metal shears, cut the patch to twice the width and about 3 inches longer than the exposed length of the damaged shingle. Apply roofing cement to the center of the patch, and slide the patch up and under the damaged shingle, cemented side down. Continue pushing the patch upward, using a wood block and hammer to tap it if necessary, until its top edge passes the butt of the shingles in the next course.

CHICKEN LADDER

BUTT

WOOD BLOCK

METAL PATCH

Replacing Wood Shingles

1 Removing the shingle. Using a mallet and a wood chisel, split the damaged shingle along the grain to break it into narrow strips and slivers. Then lift the end of each strip, work it from side to side to break it away from the hidden nails and pull it free.

2 Cutting the nails. The two nails that hold the damaged shingle in place are normally hidden, located about an inch from the edges of the shingle and about 2 inches up underneath the butt of the overlapping shingle. To remove them, use a slate puller *(page 398, top left),* if you have one. Or slip a long hacksaw blade under the overlapping shingle and cut through the nails flush with the shingle or sheathing beneath it. Protect your hand with a glove or by wrapping the blade end in heavy masking tape.

3 Installing the new shingle. To allow for expansion, use a replacement shingle ½ inch narrower than the space it will fill—trim the new shingle if necessary, using a hand plane or a small hatchet. Tap the shingle into place with a wood block and hammer; if any nails in the upper courses obstruct the new shingle, shorten it by cutting across its tapered end. Align the butt of the new shingle with the others in its course, then secure it with two galvanized roofing nails ¾ inch from each edge and just below the overlapping shingle. Coat the nailheads with roofing cement.

Replacing Broken Slates

1 **Removing the damaged slate.** Slide the end of a slate puller under the damaged slate and hook one of the two sharp puller notches around a nail holding the slate in place. With a hammer, strike sharply down against the puller handle to cut through the nail; repeat on the other nail and pull the damaged slate free. If you have no slate puller, use a hacksaw blade *(page 397, center).*

2 **Cutting a new slate to size.** Using the damaged slate as a guide, mark both sides of the replacement. Score along the lines on each side repeatedly with a cold chisel. Set a scored line at the edge of a flat surface and snap off the excess. Smooth the edges with emery cloth.

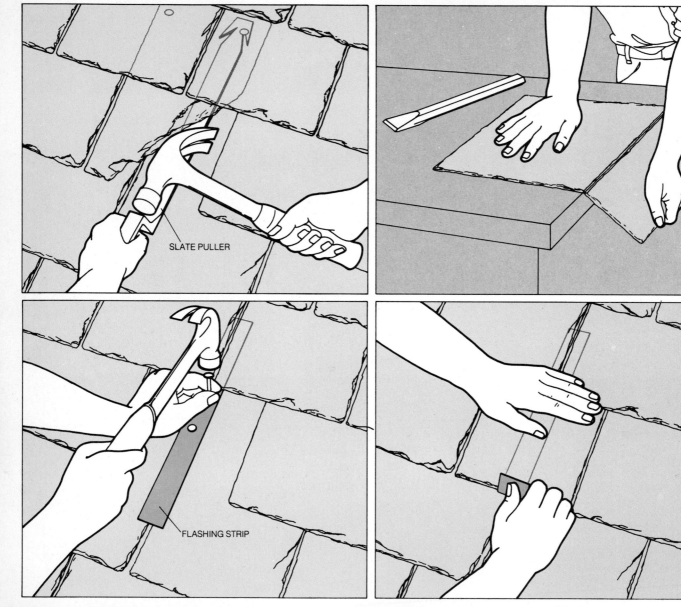

SLATE PULLER

FLASHING STRIP

3 **Installing a holding tab.** To hold the new slate in place, cut a strip of copper or aluminum flashing 2 inches wide and long enough to run for several inches under the slates above the damaged one and about 2 inches below the bottom edge of the replacement slate. Fasten the strip onto the joint between the underlying slates, using nails of the same metal as the flashing.

4 **Securing the new slate.** Coat the underside of the replacement slate with roofing cement and slide it into position over the holding tab and under the slates in the course above. Bend the holding tab up around the bottom edge of the slate, and secure it with a dab of cement.

Repairing Flat Roofs

Roofs that are flat or nearly flat usually are built up with as many as five alternating layers of roofing felt and hot tar or asphalt, fastened to the wood sheathing. This built-up roofing is often topped with a protective covering of gravel, pebbles or marble chips, or with a final layer of mineral-surfaced roll roofing; the light-colored stones or minerals help reflect the sun's rays from the dark, heat-absorbent surface.

A built-up roof should last from 10 to 20 years, before the sun's heat dries out the tar or asphalt and cracks develop over the entire surface. You can extend its life considerably by coating it with an asphalt-aluminum roof paint that slows the drying process and forms a stronger and more reflective surface.

When the roof does eventually fail, do not try to replace it yourself—that job calls for special equipment and the expertise of a professional roofer. But you can and should repair minor damages. Inspect the roof at least once a year for blisters, cracks, tears and storm damage. Blisters, which indicate that roofing felt has separated from the underlying layers or from the wood sheathing, should be treated immediately by the method shown at right, before they break open and admit rain water.

As you treat a blister, examine its interior. If it is dry, the blister is probably caused by poorly adhering or dried-out asphalt cement, and a simple patch can be an adequate repair. Interior moisture is a sign that water has leaked into the roofing and seeped along the sheathing to a point underneath the blister. Locate the point of leakage—possibly in loose flashings *(page 402)* at adjoining walls or around chimneys and vent pipes. If a substantial amount of water has penetrated the roofing, causing a large section to buckle or blister, cut out and patch the entire area *(page 400)*.

Treating a Blister

1 Cutting the blister open. Use a stiff brush to sweep dirt and loose gravel or mineral granules away from the blistered area. Then slice the blister open lengthwise with a hook-nosed linoleum knife *(right)* or a utility knife. If the felt layers beneath the surface are dry, proceed directly to Step 2. If they are damp, deepen the cut down to the wood sheathing and let the roofing dry out (you can use a portable electric heater-fan or hair dryer to speed the process) before proceeding to Step 2. To locate the source of the leak, feel for the spongy lines or patches leading from the blister to a faulty flashing or other damaged area. In that area make the more extensive repair that is shown opposite.

2 Sealing the cut. Use a putty knife to work asphalt roofing cement under both sides of the cut. Press the layers of roofing material flat against the sheathing and nail each side with 1½-inch flathead roofing nails, ¾ inch apart. If solid insulation board rather than sheathing lies immediately beneath the roofing, use nails long enough to reach into the wood.

3 Patching the cut. Cut a patch of 15-pound roofing felt large enough to overlap the blistered area about 2 inches in every direction. Cover an equivalent area over the cut with roofing cement and press the patch into place. Fasten the patch at its edges with 1½-inch roofing nails, and cover the nailheads and the edges of the patch with additional roofing cement.

Putting In a Patch

1 **Removing the damaged section.** Begin the repair of a large tear or a large blistered or buckled area by scraping off any gravel coating around the damaged area; then cut out a square or rectangle that includes the damage. Dip your knife in turpentine as you work to keep the blade free of tar and felt fibers, and pull out the layers of felt individually. If water has soaked the felt, remove all the roofing within the rectangle, down to the sheathing, and dry the area thoroughly as described in Step 1, page 399.

2 **Rebuilding the roofing.** Using one of the damaged layers as a guide, cut matching patches from new 15-pound roofing felt—one patch for each layer you have removed. Coat the bottom of the exposed roofing with asphalt cement, and work additional cement under the edges of the adjoining material. Lay a felt patch in the cement bed, press it into place, and coat its top with a bed of cement. Continue rebuilding the roofing layer by layer until it is level with the surrounding area. The top patch should overlap the cutout by 2 inches in every direction. Nail the top patch down with 1½-inch roofing nails spaced evenly around the edges.

3 **Adding a protective covering.** If the original roofing was covered with a layer of mineral-surfaced roll roofing, cut an oversized patch of the same material and press it into a bed of asphalt cement over the patched area. Nail down the edges of the patch and cover the nailheads and patch edges with cement. If the finish consists of gravel or marble chips, spread a thick layer of roofing cement over the top patch of roofing felt, sprinkle gravel or chips over the cement, and press the stones firmly into the cement with a flat board.

Replacing Vent-Pipe Flashing

1 Removing the old flashing. Scrape away gravel 2 feet around the vent pipe, cut into the roof just outside the edges of the flashing base plate with a utility knife and slip a pry bar into the cut and under the edge of the base plate. Pry the base plate up, using a scrap of wood as a fulcrum to prevent damage to the roof membrane. Make patches of roofing felt to fit the gap you have made, with a round hole in each patch to fit over the vent pipe, and fill the gap with alternating layers of roofing cement and felt.

2 Reflashing the vent pipe. Trowel cement around the area of the vent pipe and, wearing gloves, fasten a new flashing assembly over the vent pipe with roofing nails driven through the corners and into the roof; crimp the soft metal of the flashing barrel into the vent pipe. Cut two sheets of roofing felt or patching fabric, one 6 inches and the other 12 inches larger than the base plate. Cut holes at the centers of the sheets to make them fit snugly around the barrel of the flashing assembly. Spread cement around the base of the assembly, fit the smaller sheet over the pipe and embed it into the cement; repeat the process with the larger sheet. Coat the top sheet with roofing cement and on a gravel-coated roof spread gravel over the cement.

Repairs at a Parapet

Installing a flashing patch. Scrape off any gravel within 6 inches of the damaged area—work carefully to avoid tearing the roofing material, which is especially vulnerable at a parapet— and, using a pry bar and a scrap of wood as a fulcrum, lift the nails, if any, that fasten the metal cap flashing to the side of the parapet. When the nails are completely free pry the entire section of the cap up and away from the parapet.

Coat the damaged area with asphalt roofing cement and embed in it a sheet of patching fabric 3 inches larger in all directions than the area to be repaired. Apply a second coat of cement and lay a second piece of patching cloth, 6 inches larger all around. Coat this patch and the area under the cap flashing with roofing cement, then bend the flashing down over the parapet and replace the nails and gravel.

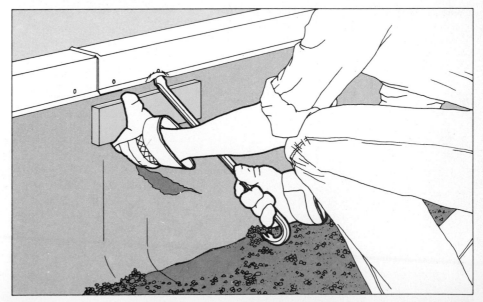

Flashing for the Weak Points

The weakest points in a roof, from a weatherproofing viewpoint, are the angles where slopes meet to form a valley and where chimneys and vent pipes project through the roofing. To protect these vulnerable areas, flashing is installed to make watertight seals between adjoining structures or surfaces. But without regular inspection and preventive maintenance, any flashing can become a funnel directing water into your home instead of into gutters and downspouts.

The best flashings are of rust-resistant metals such as copper, aluminum or zinc. Some older homes have galvanized-steel flashings. The life of more rust-prone flashings can be lengthened considerably if rust spots are removed promptly with a wire brush and the flashings are painted periodically with metal primer and aluminum paint. Metal flashings also are damaged by galvanic corrosion caused by an electrochemical reaction at spots where dissimilar metals meet; when repairing or replacing flashings, make sure the new metal and nails are the same materials as the old ones.

As a less expensive substitute for metal, some roofers use a double layer of mineral-surfaced roll roofing in valleys. Roof valleys take some of the hardest wear because they channel water from two roof slopes to the gutters. When inspecting valley flashings for leaks, remember that water can flow or seep uphill because of wind patterns or a heavier flow off one slope backing up the other side. The roofing cement sealing the shingle to the flashing also needs to be inspected and renewed regularly.

Chimney flashing is more complex and more vulnerable to leaks than other roof flashings. In the best installations a set of base flashings is secured to the roof sheathing and a set of overlapping cap flashings is embedded in the brickwork of the chimney. This construction allows slight movement and settlement without damage to the waterproofing seal. However, many chimney flashings consist of single metal pieces whose upper edge is set into the brick joints or simply cemented to the side of the chimney. The methods of repair are similar for both types.

The commonest problem with chimney flashings is deterioration of mortar or other seals; water then runs behind the top edge of the flashing and down the chimney into the house. Loose mortar should be replaced and all flashing joints resealed with asphalt cement *(opposite, top)*. Flashing that is loose or worn around a vent pipe is an equally serious problem that necessitates immediate attention. But new presized metal and plastic pipe flashings make replacements more practical than repairs. These flashings fit common pipes and include rubber or neoprene collars to form a completely watertight joint without caulking *(opposite, bottom)*.

Repairing valley flashing. If watermarks or other signs of damage are found inside the attic under the valley, inspect the flashing for holes. Repair holes in metal flashing by cleaning around the hole with a wire brush, coating the area with a thin layer of roofing cement and pressing a matching metal patch into the cement. The patch should overlap the hole several inches all around; seal the edges of the patch with additional cement and felt patches, following the instructions for repairing built-up roofs *(page 399-400)*.

If there is no visible damage to the flashing itself, the asphalt cement sealing it to the shingles probably has worked loose, allowing water to seep under. Starting at the eaves, pack roofing cement under the shingle edges with a putty knife *(above)* and press the shingles flat; do not nail shingles within 6 inches of the valley center.

Resealing a Chimney

1 **Cleaning the mortar joint.** Pry the loose cap flashings out of the mortar joint and lay them aside. Using a cold chisel and mallet, remove 1 to 1½ inches of mortar from the joint. Check that the top edge of the exposed base flashing is flush with the brickwork and seal the edge with roofing cement as necessary.

2 **Installing the flashing.** Dampen the open joint with a wet brush and insert the lip of the cap flashing in the joint. Using a tool called a joint filler (*below*), slide mortar off the edge of a board and tamp it into the joint, filling the space. When the mortar is firm but not hard, finish by shaping it to match the other joints.

3 **Sealing the joints.** Inspect the rest of the chimney for any crumbling mortar joints and repair them following Steps 1 and 2. Then seal all of the flashing joints and overlaps with a liberal coating of roofing cement, extending the cement 2 inches out on either side of the joints.

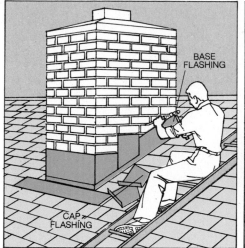

Resealing a Vent Pipe

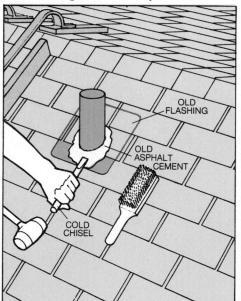

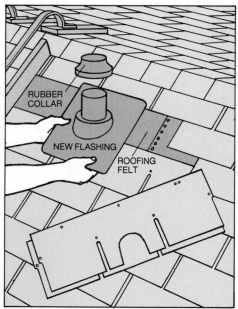

1 **Removing the old flashing.** Chip away the seal around the pipe. Expose the sides and upper portion of the flashing by removing the two shingle strips immediately above the pipe. Loosen the higher shingle first (*page 395, Step 1*) Remove any nails and loosen any cement holding the old flashing to the roof; if it is stuck to the roofing felt, cut away the felt and replace it by nailing a patch of 15-pound felt to the roof. Lift the flashing over the pipe and discard it.

2 **Installing the new flashing.** Seal all existing nail holes with roofing cement. Clean cement residue from the vent pipe with a wire brush and slide the new metal flashing down over the pipe until the flange is flush with the roofing. Then push the rubber collar down the pipe until it is flush with the metal flashing.

3 **Replacing the shingles.** Reinstall the shingle strips removed in Step 1, beginning with the lower shingle that overlaps the sides and back of the flashing. Follow the instructions for installing new shingles on page 395, but do not drive nails through the metal flange. Instead, seal the shingle edges to the metal with roofing cement.

How to Make Gutters Work

When gutters are clogged at blocked downspouts, rain water, left to find its own way, will pour off the eaves and settle into the ground below, and may then seep into the house. Gutters and downspouts need at least semiannual inspection, especially in regions that receive large snowfalls. The weight of snow and ice can force a gutter out of alignment or break it away from its supports. And, while many gutters today are made of weather-resistant aluminum and plastic, some are wood or steel, and these require inspection for rot or corrosion.

When you are inspecting a gutter, you may need a ladder stabilizer to keep the ladder's weight off the gutter. Debris in gutters, on screens or in downspouts not only slows the water flow, but speeds corrosion. Clear the downspout cage, gutters and gutter screens, if used.

To give momentum to the flowing water, gutters must be canted toward their downspouts. A telltale discoloration will mark any section where the gutter sags and retains a pool of water. Such sags can be mended by adjusting the gutter as shown (bottom right).

While up on the ladder, also inspect for peeling paint, rusted areas, loose hangers or joints, and split downspouts. Patch a small crack as shown opposite. Small patches of rust can be scraped clean with a wire brush, then coated with gutter cement or an asphalt-aluminum paint. Areas that have rusted badly or are badly cracked should be replaced with seamless aluminum runs (page 406). Check with local building suppliers for the length you need; runs of gutter longer than 10 feet may have to be custom made.

A downspout cage. To prevent downspouts from clogging with leaves and debris, install a wire or plastic cage or strainer (below). The strainer will trap leaves while permitting water to flow down the spout. Periodically inspect the gutter; unless collected debris is cleaned away from the cage it will mat and impede the water flow.

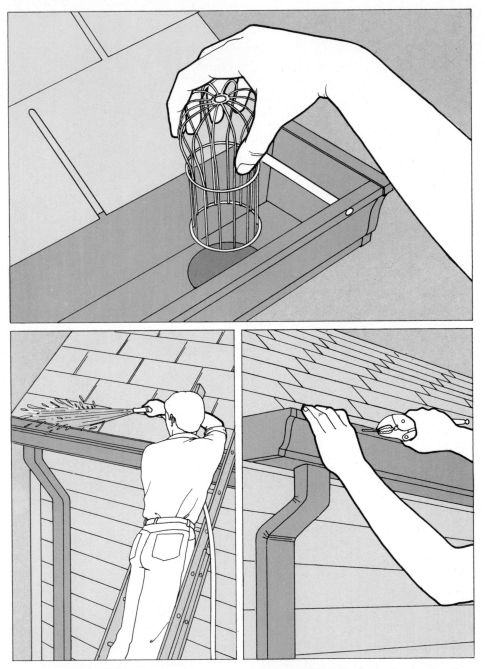

Detecting misalignment. To determine when a gutter is bent out of alignment, spray water on the roof with a garden hose (above). Then watch the flow of water along the gutter; it will pool in the low spots that need alignment.

Realigning gutters. If the gutter is supported by nails, use locking-grip pliers to twist them out (above); hammer claws would damage the rim of the gutter. Reposition the nails or gutter hangers to return the gutter to the proper alignment.

Patching a Crack or Small Hole

1 Cleaning the damaged area. Brush away leaves and dirt from around the crack. Roughen the trough of the gutter with a stiff wire brush or coarse sandpaper, removing any high spots or flaking paint. To ensure a good patch, wipe the area clean of dirt and moisture.

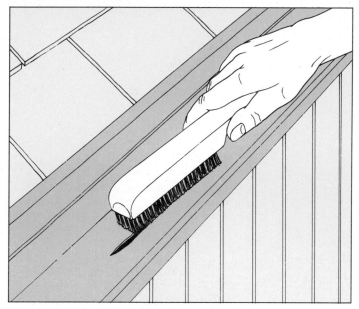

2 Applying roofing cement. To patch a crack or hole smaller than ¼ inch, apply a thin coat of roofing cement with a putty knife or stiff-bristled brush. The best repair is one that does not build up the bottom of the gutter too much; otherwise, water will not drain properly past this point. Cover an area 3 inches beyond the crack on both sides, wait an hour for the first coat to set to a leathery mat, then apply a second coat. Two thin coats are preferable to one thick coat, which may set unevenly.

3 Laying the patch. For longer cracks or holes between ¼—2 inches in size, apply a single, thin coat of roofing cement as in Step 2, then immediately lay in a thin metal patch cut at least 2 inches longer and wider than the damaged area. Push the patch into the cement with the putty knife so that the patch is securely embedded. Wait one hour for the cement to set, then apply a second coat, completely covering the patch.

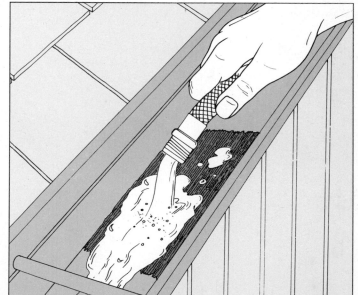

4 Testing the repair. When the cement has dried (about 24 hours), test the integrity of the patch by directing a steady stream of water through the gutter with a garden hose. Begin at the high end of each run, or in the middle if there are downspouts at both ends. This simple test can be used twice a year to check the condition of all the house's gutters and downspouts.

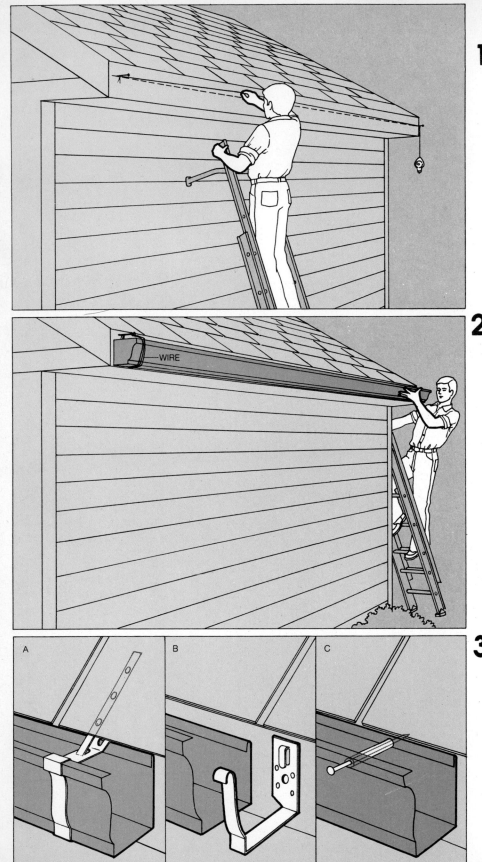

Replacing a Gutter

1 **Determining the pitch.** After removing the damaged gutter, string a line between two nails along the intended run of the gutter *(left)*. A carpenter's level may be used to check the line. Then determine the amount of incline needed for the run, using a ratio of 1 inch for every 16 feet, and lower the end of the chalk line near the downspout by that amount.

2 **Hanging the gutter.** Suspend one end of the gutter from a nail in the fascia board, using a circle of wire. Begin working at the other end of the run, nailing each hanger along the chalk line.

WIRE

3 **The fasteners.** Three types of fasteners are commonly used to suspend gutters: the strap hanger (A), nailed beneath the lowest strip of shingles on the roof; the fascia clip (B), which is screwed or nailed directly to the fascia board; and the spike and ferrule (C)—the easiest to install and realign. Drive the spike into a rafter.

A B C

Repairing a Rotted Cornice

1 Cutting away damaged wood. Starting just beyond an area of damaged wood in a fascia or soffit—the front and bottom parts of the overhanging cornice edging a roof—drill a pilot hole, then use a saber saw or keyhole saw to cut through the board. Avoid sawing into the rafter ends or the so-called lookouts—boards that anchor rafter ends to the house (*below*)—you can find both by looking for the nailheads in the fascia and soffit. Make a second saw cut on the other side of the damaged area. Use a chisel as necessary to complete the two cuts, then pry out the damaged section of board.

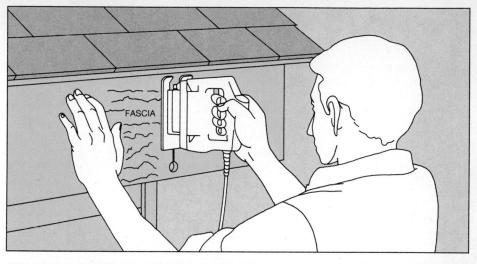

2 Doubling damaged rafter ends. If a rafter end has rotted, cut a piece of 2-inch-thick lumber to match the shape of the end of the rafter, long enough to reach back to sound wood. Soak it well with wood preservative or use pressure-treated lumber. Nail the new piece alongside the rotted end. If horizontal lookout boards are in the way, remove them before nailing on the new rafter ends. Replace rotted lookouts with new lumber cut to the same dimensions.

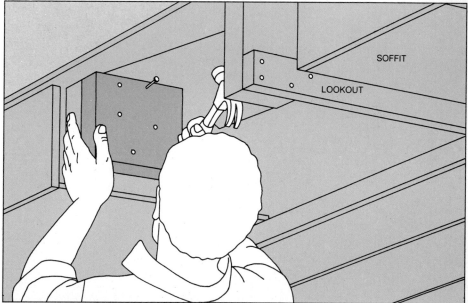

3 Attaching new fascia or soffit boards. Using galvanized screws, attach a 1-by-4 wood strip that will overlap the back of the new joint at each edge of the sound part of the fascia or soffit. Screw a replacement section to the strips and nail it to any rafter ends or lookouts that it crosses. Seal the joint at each end with exterior-grade wood putty before you paint.

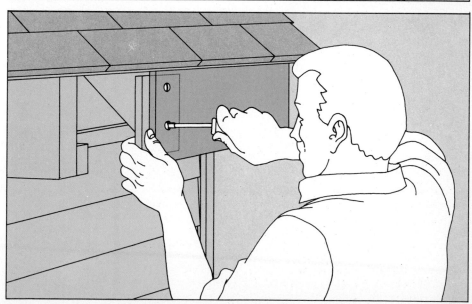

Repairing Siding

The greatest enemy of walls is water; the greatest protectors are shingles and siding. Water driven by wind or icing or capillary action defies gravity and flows upward, doing damage in hidden places. However, water cannot flow up the back of a shingle that overlaps the one beneath it. Lateral overlap, in staggered joints between shingles, prevents leakage from sideways flow. A soundly shingled surface tames water, causing it to meander in rivulets down the overlap of one shingle, dropping to the overlap of the next, until it reaches the bottom course and falls to the ground. The principle of overlap explains why you apply siding from bottom to top, and not the other way around.

Overlapping is also the key to clapboard, aluminum and vinyl siding. The materials are laid on in long, overlapped horizontal strips; they need only a few vertical joints, which can be staggered. In aluminum and vinyl siding, these vertical joints are also overlapped.

Repairs may require one shingle replacement or work with the deeper layers below the surface. Shingles and clapboard are supported from below by fiber or plywood sheathing, which is nailed to studs or rafters. In addition, many walls have a special barrier to dampness: asphalted building paper, nailed to the sheathing—and overlapped.

A Guide to Siding Materials

Siding type	Cost	Maintenance	Advantages	Limitations
wood panels	inexpensive (unfinished plywood) to moderate (finished hardboard)	regular painting or staining	quick installation; goes over most existing sidings; available in a wide variety of styles	poor fire resistance; installation always requires two workers, and can be especially difficult at the borders of windows, doors and rake
clapboard	moderate	regular painting or staining	goes over most existing sidings	poor fire resistance; installation requires two workers; some types are subject to rot
vinyl	inexpensive to moderate	none	easy installation; goes over most existing sidings	may melt near intense heat; brittle in very cold weather; narrow range of colors, subject to fading; cannot be painted
aluminum	inexpensive to moderate	none	easy installation; goes over most exiting sidings; fire resistant; available in wide variety of styles; can be repainted	scratches and dents easily; may clatter in wind and hail if not insulated; requires electrical grounding
wood shingles	expensive	regular replacement of missing or damaged pieces; regular painting or staining for some woods	goes over most existing sidings; single pieces easily replaced; can be left unfinished for rustic look	flammable; slow installation
wood shakes	expensive	regular replacement of missing or damaged pieces	goes over most existing sidings; single pieces exceptionally durable and easily replaced; can be left unfinished for rustic look	flammable; slow installation, often difficult around windows and doors
hardboard	inexpensive to moderate	pre-primed type must be repainted	easy installation; vinyl-clad in pre-finished colors; no knots or grain	limited color selection; flammable; requires low vapor barrier
stucco	moderate	none	fire resistant; surface can be molded or decorated	requires wire-mesh backing over wall or existing siding; long and difficult installation, requiring special skills and caustic materials, must be done in good weather; cracks or crumbles if incorrectly applied

Comparing siding materials. In the chart above, "Cost" refers to the relative cost of each material as compared with all the others; it does not include professional labor. In general, labor costs are considerably higher for the traditional materials—clapboard, wood shingles and shakes and stucco—than for the newer types of siding. With stucco, the materials alone are only moderately expensive, but if professionally installed, it is the most expensive of all sidings. For some materials a range of costs is given. Aluminum, for example, can be bought in two thicknesses, each with or without an insulation backing. Thin aluminum backing is inexpensive; thick aluminum with backing is moderately expensive. The column headed "Maintenance" indicates what must be done to keep a siding structurally sound and weatherproof. It does not take into account the gradual deterioration of materials like aluminum and vinyl. The last two colums summarize the general advantages and limitations of each material. Under these headings the most important considerations are ease of installation and the ability to cover existing siding.

Replacing Broken Shingles

Replace all broken or warped shingles before you finish them. Painting over bad shingles may disguise the damage, but it will permit water to seep behind the good shingles and cause further deterioration. The steps for replacing asbestos and wood shingles are basically similar, but asbestos shingles are more fragile and require extra care. When sawing or drilling asbestos shingles, avoid inhaling cancer-causing asbestos fibers: Wear a chemical cartridge respirator with particulate filter approved for asbestos-containing dusts and mists.

Before painting or staining shingles, be sure the surfaces are clean. Small patches of dirt can be washed off by hand with a rag, and bits of loose paint scraped off with a wire brush. If the whole house needs cleaning, rent a high-pressure spray cleaner.

Asbestos Shingles

1 Removing a shingle. Break up the damaged shingle with a hammer, taking care not to damage sound shingles around it—asbestos shingles are fragile. Slip a hacksaw blade under the course above the broken shingle, and saw off the nails that held it in place. Wear a glove to protect your hand. Remove all broken shingles.

2 Installing the new shingle. Slip the shingle under the upper course and hold it in place. Drill two new nail holes through the new shingle just below the bottom edge of the upper course, using a power drill with a carbide bit. The new shingle can then be nailed in place, using nonrusting galvanized or aluminum nails.

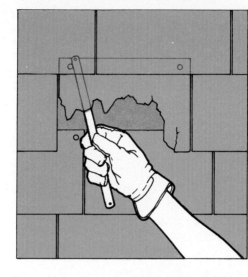

Wood Shingles

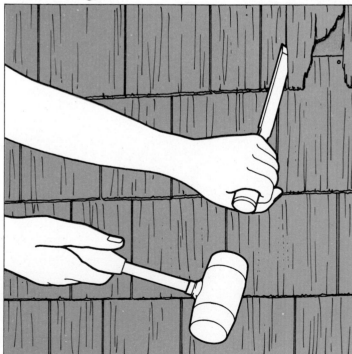

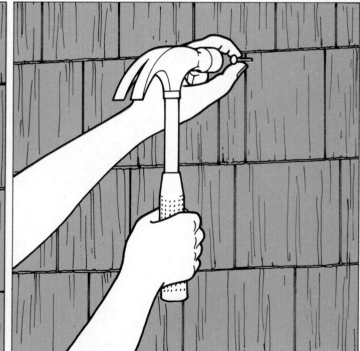

1 Removing a shingle. Split the shingle with a wood chisel along the grain, breaking it into narrow strips and slivers of wood. Cut the nails under the upper course with a hacksaw blade, following the method for asbestos shingles (above), and pull out all the pieces of old shingle.

2 Installing the new shingle. Slip the shingle under the upper course and hold it in place. Drive two or three galvanized or aluminum nails through the new shingle just below the bottom edge of the course above it. It is not necessary to drill nail holes through wood shingles first.

Metal and Plastic—Boards without Wood

Low cost and ease of installation make lightweight vinyl and aluminum siding the most popular materials for re-siding jobs, and increasingly for the outer covering of new walls. Both are available with insulation backing if desired.

Choosing between the two, which are remarkably similar in panel sizes and shapes, mounting techniques and durability, is mostly a matter of taste and availability. Vinyl is a bit easier to work, does not dent or show scratches and resists heat and cold better than aluminum. But it can crack when struck in cold weather and cannot be repainted.

Aluminum is usually less costly than vinyl, and comes in a brighter palette of factory-baked enamel finishes. But it is easily dented and scratched, and requires electrical grounding.

Whichever material you use, the key to professional-looking work is in the installation of the accesories—F channel, J channel, corner posts, starter strips and trim. When these are mounted level or plumb in their correct locations, the rest of the siding job is mostly routine sawing and hammering. Aluminum requires no special tools, but you will need a snaplock punch, available at hardware stores and siding dealers, to indent the edges of some vinyl panels. When replacing vinyl panels, you will also need a handy zipper tool *(above, right)*.

Both vinyl and aluminum siding expand and contract more than wood, and allowances must be made for this movement. Always provide a ¼- to ⅛-inch space at joints and panel ends. Never pull vinyl panels taut before nailing, since this may cause dimpling or rippling as they expand. With either material, drive nails straight into the wall through the centers of the oval nailing slots, leaving a gap of about ¹/₃₂ of an inch between the nailheads and the material—the thickness of a matchbook cover.

While it is possible to apply vinyl or aluminum siding without installing a new soffit—or vice versa—it is usually advisable to do both. If you already have a soffit, you may simply want to cover it

with new material. If you do not have one—or choose to rip out the old one—use at least one perforated panel every 10 feet for ventilation.

Like wood, vinyl and aluminum siding can be installed horizontally, vertically or—by special arrangements of mounting appliances—in both directions on the same wall. To make the lines of overlapping joints virtually invisible, begin siding at a point farthest from the usual viewing locations—front sidewalk, front entrance, driveway—and work toward those locations, lapping the previous panel. The finished wall will appear to be an unbroken expanse of siding when viewed from the "favored" side.

A Zipper and Cement for Replacements

Replacing a vinyl panel. Use a special tool called a zipper, available from siding dealers, to reach under the undamaged upper panel in order to hook into the locking strip inside the top of the damaged panel *(below)*. Pull down firmly while sliding the zipper the length of the damaged panel. This will unlock the upper panel, which can then be propped up high enough to remove the nails holding the damaged panel. Lock and nail the replacement panel, then use the zipper to relock the upper panel.

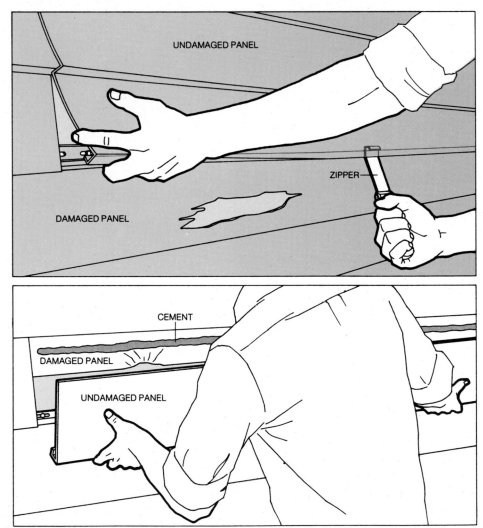

Replacing an aluminum panel. Use a utility knife to cut a slit along the center of the damaged panel, or just above the center groove on a panel that simulates a double row of siding. Unhook and discard the lower portion, leaving the upper portion intact. Cut off the nailing and locking strip of the replacement panel. Apply roofing cement the length of the damaged half-panel. Install the new panel by sliding its top edge under the locking hook of the panel above, while locking it into the lip of the panel below. Press down firmly to cement the panel.

Replacing Damaged Clapboard

A few rotting clapboards can turn an attractive house into an eyesore. In many cases, however, the offensive boards can be cut out and replaced. A good time to do this is just before you plan to paint the exterior, avoiding a mis-match of the spliced-in piece. But if you decide to apply an entirely new skin of wood siding, you have a wide choice of types.

Clapboards may be plain or beveled. Other styles of wood siding boards have interlocking edges, or join together to make a flat surface. Many types can be applied either horizontally or vertically, while some are suitable for one or the other. Siding ranges up to 1 inch in thickness, 12 inches in width and 20 feet in length. Though cedar is the most com-

mon siding wood, boards are available in redwood and in the man-made wood composition, hardboard. If your siding is plywood, use an exterior grade.

The only other major consideration before starting work is how to finish the corners. With horizontal siding, one option is to use corner boards. Alternatively, you can weave clapboards like cedar shakes or shingles. Or you can substitute metal corners for outside corner boards. These corners simulate the effect obtained by mitering the ends of siding boards, a procedure too demanding for all but a seasoned carpenter. Vertical siding is applied much like horizontal siding.

Siding must be fastened to a sound surface. Existing siding that is badly dam-

aged must be removed. Peeling paint may be a sign of moisture problems that must be corrected prior to new installation. Window frames, door frames and trim boards usually require building up to accomodate new siding. Downspouts and other fixtures must be removed. Furring strips are a necessity when re-siding over masonry or applying new horizontal siding over old clapboards. Horizontal siding on top of a flat wood surface, such as tongue-and-groove siding or vertically applied siding, requires no furring strips unless the surface of the wall is uneven. Nails should be stainless steel-siding nails with spiral or annular ring shanks; follow the nailing patterns used in securing the original siding.

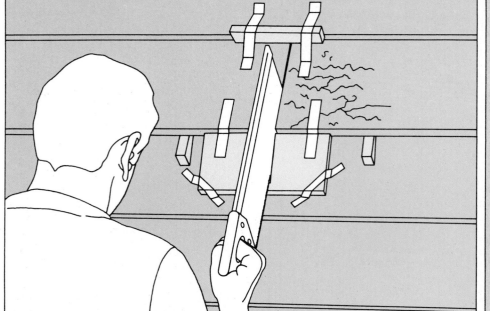

1 Cutting out damaged clapboard siding. Tap wedges under a damaged section of clapboard siding to separate it from the piece below, then use a backsaw to cut through it. Protect the boards above and below with wood blocks temporarily held in place with adhesive tape.

2 Finishing the cut. Move the wedges to the top of the damaged piece to raise the clapboard above, then finish the cuts, using a keyhole saw with the handle reversed. Use a hacksaw blade to cut through any nails under the damaged piece and remove the piece. Replace it with a new clapboard, driving nails through the lower part just above the top of the clapboard below.

If your siding is made of flush boards, cut out damaged wood with a hammer and chisel and replace it with new wood, using the techniques on pages 31-33 for repairing floorboards. If there is no sheathing beneath the siding, fasten new siding to old with the technique shown above for attaching a new fascia or soffit board.

Repairing Weatherworn Posts and Floors

Exposure to the outdoors eventually takes its toll on wood porches or decks. Both are particularly vulnerable to dampness and insect infestation.

Moisture, which fosters the growth of wood-rotting fungi and bacteria, becomes trapped in joints and between floorboards and is absorbed by the end grain of cut boards. Moisture may also collect around the bottom of porch and deck posts, and it can be absorbed directly from the earth wherever wood meets the ground. Wood-boring insects are even more destructive, gnawing through critical structural members and even reaching the roof of a porch.

To catch damage by these natural enemies of wood in its early stages and avoid the need for extensive repairs, inspect your porch or deck periodically. Spongy and discolored wood is an indication of rot; little piles of wood fibers or shed wings are signs of insect activity. If insects are present, exterminate them before beginning any repair work.

If rot or insect damage is widespread, it may be necessary to replace the entire porch or deck; but in most cases you can patch the structure by removing and replacing damaged supports or damaged sections of supports (below, page 414). Individual floorboards can also be replaced (page 415), and weakened joists reinforced (page 414). To retard future damage, always replace deck and porch parts with pressure-treated lumber, and use galvanized nails and anchors in order to prevent rust.

Before replacing a post or a column, first take the weight off it by bracing the structure that it supports with a screw-operated, telescoping jack. Or, to support low decks or porch floors, use a contractor's jack—a strong, bell-shaped screw jack about 1 foot tall. (You can increase a bell jack's working height by inserting a cut-to-fit length of 4-by-4 between it and the structure.) Both jacks are available at lumberyards and from tool-rental dealers. Do not use hydraulic jacks; they are not as reliable as the screw type.

In preparation for using a jack, grease its threads; then pad it at the bottom with a 2-foot length of 2-by-12 scrap lumber and at the top with a 1-foot length of 2-by-6, to distribute the load. If you are jacking a deck or a porch floor, place the bottom pad on the ground and level it before extending the jack. Always position the jack directly below the beam or header joist supported by the post you are removing, and as close as possible to the post. If you are jacking a porch roof, place the jack directly over a beam or joist on which the floor rests, to support the weight transferred to the jack.

In replacing a post that holds up a deck or porch floor, you will usually be dealing with a concrete footing. If the post is attached to the top of its footing with a metal post anchor, simply unbolt the damaged post and install a new one. But if the base of the post is embedded in the concrete, you will have to modify the footing before installing a new post.

The modifications will vary with the footing. If the top of the footing is at or near ground level, you can dig out the embedded wood, fill the cavity with concrete and install a post anchor (opposite, bottom). If the top of the footing is more than 8 inches below ground, remove as much of the wood as possible, then pour a new footing over the old one. Sometimes, if only a section of post is rotted, you can simply cut out the damaged area, splicing in a new section (page 414).

In replacing a traditional round porch column, you will first have to see if it is solid or hollow; to do this, drill into it in at least two places. A solid column is removed in the same way as a post. Inside a hollow column there usually is a post that supports the roof; if this inner support is sound, you need only replace the outer shell (opposite, top right).

After the repair is complete, several measures can prevent a recurrence of the trouble. If your porch or deck is painted, periodically scrape and repaint blistered and cracked sections that can trap moisture. If it is unpainted and is not made of pressure-treated lumber, treat it once a year with a wood preservative that is commonly used in your area. Keep the floor of a wood porch or deck swept clean of moisture-retaining leaves, and repair roof leaks promptly.

Removing Porch Posts and Columns

1 Jacking a porch roof. Set the jack on a 2-by-12 pad, lining it up between a floor joist and the roof header joist; lock the jack's telescoping tubes in the position that brings the top tube about 2 inches from the roof header joist, using the steel pins provided. While a helper holds the jack plumb and steadies a second pad between the jack and the roof header joist, raise the jack by turning the screw handle. When the jack is snug against the pads, give the handle another quarter turn, just enough for the jack to support the roof without lifting it.

2 **Disassembling the support.** To remove a porch post or a solid column *(below, left),* use a handsaw to make two crosscuts, about 1 foot apart, through the wood. Knock out the middle section with a mallet, and work the top and bottom sections loose. Making sure the anchor is firmly secured, install a new post in place of the old one.

To remove a hollow column *(below, right),* make two vertical cuts opposite each other down the length of the shaft, using a circular saw. Make a horizontal cut around the middle. Pull the two upper sections apart and remove them, staying clear of the capital if it falls—it may not be nailed to the header. Cut the capital in two

with a saber saw or a handsaw, and detach it from the support post. If the capital is attached to the header, free it with a pry bar. Remove the two lower shaft sections and the base. Check the inner support post to see if it is damaged, replace it if necessary. Cover the post with a new shaft, capital and base.

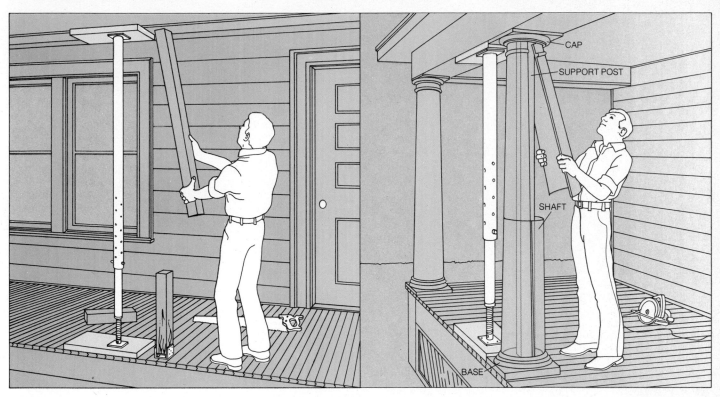

Salvaging the Usable Parts of a Deck Support

Reusing a ground-level footing. When the damaged post for a porch or deck floor rests on a concrete footing near ground level, sink a J-shaped anchor bolt in the footing to secure a post anchor as the base for a new post. To prepare the footing, jack up the floor, cut off the damaged post flush with the top of the footing and pry out the rotted wood with a wood chisel. Fill the footing cavity with new concrete, sink the anchor bolt in it and attach the post anchor *(inset),* establishing its position by hanging a plumb bob from the floor beam where the top of the post will be fastened. When the concrete has cured for 24 to 48 hours, cut a new post to fit between the floor beam and the post anchor. Nail it to the post anchor and fasten it to the beam, using the original hardware.

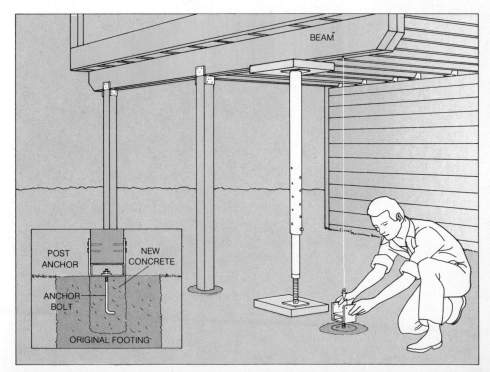

Building up a buried footing. When a damaged post for a deck or porch floor rests on a concrete footing that is well below ground level, build up the footing as a base for the new post. To prepare the new footing, jack up the floor, dig down to expose the entire top of the old footing and cut off the damaged post as close as possible to the top of the old footing. Fill in the hole with concrete, covering the remnants of the old post by at least 8 inches. Measure and cut a new post long enough to sink into the new footing about 1 inch, and lower it into the concrete. Hold the post plumb while a helper fastens it at the top with the same hardware used on the old post. Brace the bottom of the post with scrap lumber (*inset*), to hold the post plumb until the concrete has set.

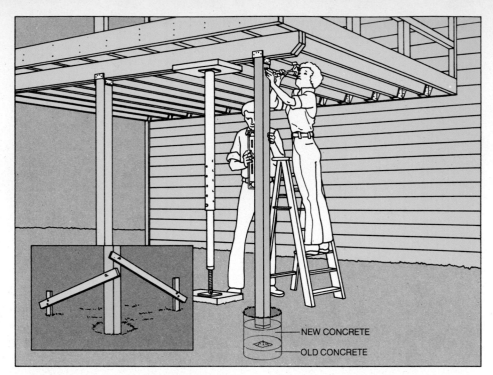

NEW CONCRETE
OLD CONCRETE

A Splice for a Weak Post

Replacing part of a post. When only the upper or lower part of a porch or deck post is rotten, you can splice in a new section instead of replacing the whole post. Jack up the floor or roof, and saw the post in two just beyond the damaged area. Measure and cut a replacement section, taking into account the change in length if a new footing is needed (*above*). Cut an L-shaped notch, half the thickness of the post and 6 inches long, in the end of the undamaged section, and a matching notch in one end of the replacement section. Clamp the notched sections together, and counterbore three ⅜-inch holes through the joint, staggering their positions. Secure the joint with ⅜-inch carriage bolts. Then attach the other end of the replacement section to the header joist or to the footing.

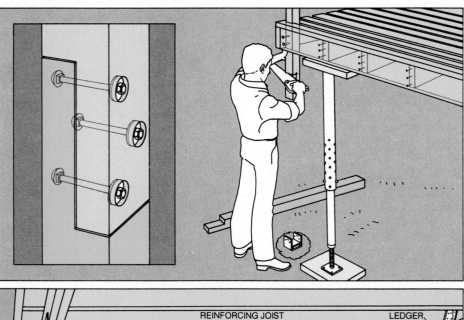

Reinforcing a damaged joist. To brace a weak joist, fasten a matching joist against it. Have a helper hold the new joist against the old, flush with the floorboards, while you secure its two ends to the ledger board and header with 7-inch galvanized angle plates or a double-width joist hanger held by fourpenny (1½-inch) nails. Then nail the two joists together with 12 penny (3-inch) nails, staggered top and bottom at 12-inch intervals. Then nail the floorboards to the top edge of the new joist.

If the old joist sags, jack it until its bottom edge is level with the new joist, and leave the jack in place until the two joists are nailed together.

REINFORCING JOIST   LEDGER

Patching a Tongue-and-Groove Floor

1 **Chiseling the damaged floorboards.** Use a 1-inch wood chisel to make cuts across both ends of each floorboard in the damaged section. To make each cut, first drive the chisel straight down, holding it so that the beveled edge faces the damaged part of the board. Then reverse the chisel, pointing it at an angle toward the cut that you have just made, and make a second cut, chipping out a deep groove. Center all of these cuts over the joists, and stagger them in such a way that no two adjoining floorboards are cut over the same joist.

2 **Removing the boards.** With a circular saw set to the thickness of the floor, make two parallel cuts down the middle of the longest damaged board, starting and stopping the saw just short of the chiseled ends. Complete the saw cuts with a wood chisel, then lift out the middle strip with a pry bar. Working first on the grooved side, then on the tongued side, pry out the rest of the board, using the pry bar to loosen the nails at the joists. Pry out the other damaged boards, using the opening left by the removal of an adjacent board as leverage space.

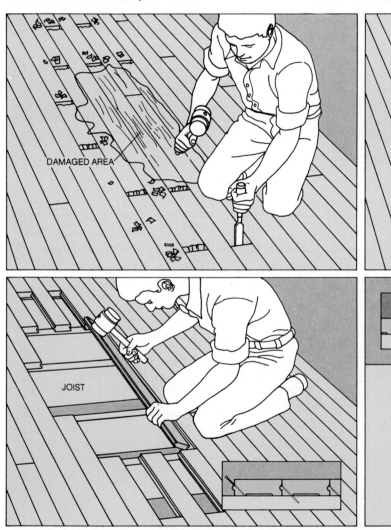

DAMAGED AREA

JOIST

3 **Inserting new boards.** Wedge a replacement board into position, fitting its grooved edge over the tongue of the undamaged adjacent board. Use a rubber mallet to force the new board into place. Then drive eightpenny (2½-inch) finishing nails through the corner of its tongue into the joists below (*inset*). Install as many boards as possible this way. For any pieces that cannot be wedged into place, use the alternate joining method described in Step 4.

4 **Installing the final boards.** When there is not enough maneuvering space to slide a replacement board into position, trim off the lower lip of its grooved edge with a chisel. Engage its tongued edge in the groove of the adjacent board, and drop its trimmed edge into place (*inset*), tapping it gently with a rubber mallet in order to seat it. Then face-nail the board at each joist with two eightpenny finishing nails, set at an angle, and fill the nail holes with wood putty.

Basic Techniques of Working with Mortar

Mortar is the basic bonding material that holds bricks, stones and blocks together. It also serves as a patching compound for concrete and, thinned down, becomes a grout for brickwork repairs. In all these jobs, a trowel is the essential tool. It is used to slice a batch of mortar into usable portions, to form the mortar into a foundation bed—or line—for bricks and blocks, to spread mortar on them and to shape the joints between them.

Once you master mixing and troweling mortar, you can fix walls or paving, or launch more ambitious projects such as installing a brick wall or laying a flagstone walk. The standard techniques are as useful for a five-minute repair job as for an elaborate masonry structure.

For most purposes, you can produce workable mortar by following either of the two recipes at right. They both contain portland cement as a bonding agent, sand to give strength and hydrated lime for pliability while the mixture is wet. The first recipe is frequently called a 1:1:6 mix. (The numbers refer to the ratio of the portland cement, lime and sand, and the ratio remains constant whatever the size of the mortar batch.)

The second recipe, a 1:3 mix, calls for a portland cement-lime mixture known as masonry cement to which you add the sand. You can also get the ingredients premixed—a dry mortar sold under several brand names—to which only water need be added. The ready-mixes are more expensive than ingredients purchased separately, but the cost may not matter when only small amounts are needed. Ready-mixed mortar comes in bags as small as 5 pounds, portland cement in 94-pound bags, masonry cement in 70- and 80-pound bags, and lime in 50-pound bags.

Sand for mortar can be any clean, dry, finely graded building sand. Generally it is sold in 50- and 60-pound bags. Never use beach sand; it contains salts that will weaken and discolor the mortar and prevent it from drying properly.

The exact amount of water required for the mortar depends on the humidity and temperature as well as the moisture in the sand and cannot be computed in advance. Add the water slowly in small amounts, stirring until it is all absorbed. But add as much water as possible without ruining the desired consistency. If the mortar is too wet, it will run out between joints; if it is too dry, it will not form a really tight bond.

While using the mortar, stir it often. If evaporation dries it out, add water from time to time—a process called retempering—to restore its workability. Mortar that starts to set before it can be used should be discarded. After the mortar has set —but before it hardens, usually within one or two hours—finish the joints by compacting and shaping the mortar between the bricks with a trowel or special finishing tool. Mortar only when the temperature is above 35°.

The recipes given here make 1 cubic foot—about what you need to lay 25 to 30 bricks and as much as you are likely to use before the mix hardens. The quantities are specified in gallons—easy to measure with a marked pail—although materials are sold by the pound. For ease in estimating your needs, weights are also listed. When mixing mortar, wear leather-palmed work gloves to protect your hands from irritants in the cement; keep them on when buttering and laying bricks as well. But such finishing jobs as shaping mortar joints are best done barehanded; you will get better control over the finishing tool, which will keep your hands safely away from mortar.

To make mortar decorative as well as structural, it can be colored—to accent joints between bricks or to help disguise and beautify repairs. Masonry cement comes in a variety of premixed colors, but pigments are available for creating shades in any mortar. Mix colors with the dry ingredients and, after adding water, stir until there are no streaks. Make a sample batch and let it set to see the final color; it lightens as the mortar dries. Colored mortar cannot be retempered without altering the shade.

Mixing and Testing Recipes

Ingredients to make 1 cubic foot of portland cement mortar:	Ingredients to make 1 cubic foot of masonry cement mortar:
1¼ U.S. gallons of portland cement (16 pounds)	2½ U.S. gallons of masonry cement (31 pounds)
1¼ U.S. gallons of hydrated lime (8⅓ pounds)	
7½ U.S. gallons of dry sand (100 pounds)	7½ U.S. gallons of dry sand (100 pounds)

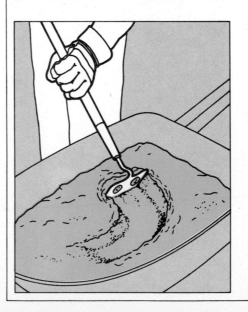

Making a batch of mortar. Measure cement. sand—and lime if required—into a wheelbarrow. Mix with a hoe, push the mixture to one end and pour 2½ to 3 gallons of water into the other end. Hoe the dry ingredients into the water. Working back and forth, add more water and repeat until the mortar has the consistency of soft mush and all lumps are eliminated.

Generally at least 4 to 5 gallons of water or so are required for a cubic foot. But be prepared to make adjustments as you test the consistency of the mix. To do this, make a curved furrow across the surface with a hoe. If the sides of the furrow stay in place and the clinging mortar shakes freely off the hoe, the mix is ready. If the sides of the furrow collapse, the mix is too wet—add small, proportional amounts of the dry materials. If the mortar does not shake freely off the hoe, it is too dry—add very small amounts of water, testing as before.

The Professional's Tricks for Simple Repairs

The monuments of the ancients prove that masonry can endure for millennia. But if its original attractiveness is to survive, cracks and crumbled sections must be repaired promptly—especially in northern climates. Even a crack $1/32$ inch wide will allow moisture to penetrate a wall or slab and, by freezing and thawing, spread destruction. Fixing masonry is a simple process with mortar or grout. The techniques shown here for repairing brick, block, concrete and stucco apply to paths and patios as well as walls—only the direction of the work changes. But the method employed depends on the defect. Three types are most common: crumbling mortar in joints; a broken section of a wall; and deteriorating concrete steps, sidewalks and driveways.

If you notice crumbling mortar joints in walls, repair them by employing the process masons call pointing: chisel out the old mortar and replace it with new. If the bricks themselves are cracked or have broken out of the wall, replace both bricks and mortar. On both of these jobs you can make the repairs almost invisible by finishing new joints to match existing ones.

If new brick walls suddenly show long cracks running from top to bottom, the normal shrinkage of hardening mortar is probably to blame; such cracks can be cleaned out and pointed with mortar or filled with grout. If the cracks open up again after a few weeks or months, call a mason. Such recurrent cracking may indicate that the wall foundation is settling, and the wall could be pulled apart. Similarly, you can easily repair small cracks or broken patches in stucco walls but you should call in a professional if the entire side of the house needs to be repaired.

Broken concrete sidewalks or cracked steps are too dangerous to leave unrepaired. The kind of material used to fix them varies with the dimensions as well as the type of defect. Small cracks, for example, can be filled with grout; large ones require mortar. When large pieces, still intact, break off steps, you can paste them on again with a sand-cement-epoxy mortar. But when sections of steps crumble away, you will have to build them up again with conventional mortar (pages 428-429).

In any job remember that mortar and grout must be kept damp for a three- to four-day period to cure properly and form a strong bond. Keep the repair covered if possible, and sprinkle mortar or grout with water as necessary—even four or five times a day in hot, dry weather.

Replacing Damaged Mortar

1 Cleaning out the joint. With a cold chisel and ball-peen hammer or maul, remove crumbling mortar from a joint to a depth of at least 1 inch. Then chop out enough additional old mortar to expose bare brick on one side of every joint. Brush out the joints, or clean them by blowing sharply into them. Caution: goggles are absolutely necessary to protect your eyes.

2 Laying the mortar. Dampen the joints slightly with a small, wet brush or garden hose set at a fine spray. Spread a ½-inch-thick layer of mortar (page 416) onto a hawk, a small mortarboard that has a handle so it can be easily held up to the work. With the bottom edge of a pointing trowel, which is smaller than a mason's ordinary trowel, slice off a thin piece of mortar: lift it from the hawk and press it into the joint. Because you push mortar away from you when pointing, always use the bottom side of the trowel. For extra-long horizontal joints—many bricks wide—you may want to use a narrow tool called a margin trowel.

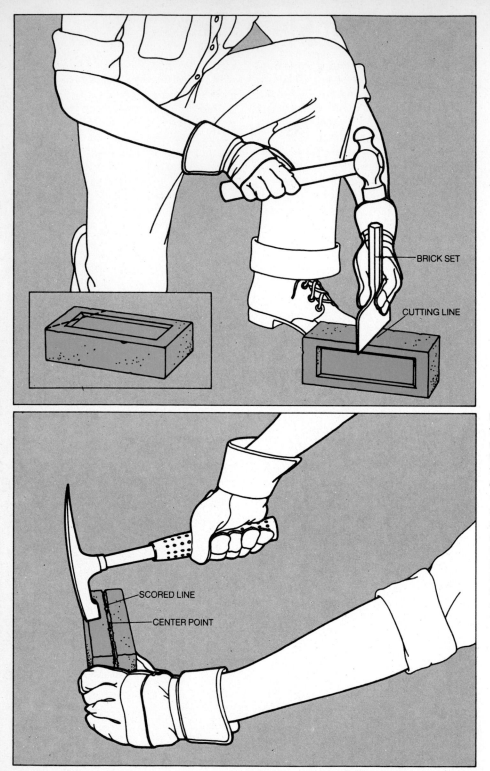

BRICK SET

CUTTING LINE

SCORED LINE

CENTER POINT

Splitting Brick

Crosswise cuts. Most brick jobs will probably require you to cut some bricks into smaller sections. It is easiest to cut them all at once. With a pencil and ruler, mark a cutting line across the long side edges of each brick. Mark on the diagonal (*inset*) if this shape is required. Put on goggles to protect your eyes from chips, and score along the cutting lines with a brickset, a broad-bladed chisel. Place the blade end of the brickset—beveled edge facing away from the part of the brick to be used—on the cutting line. Then tap the end of the handle with a ball-peen hammer.

Before cutting the brick, lay it on a bed of sand to cushion it. The long side edge should face up, and the part of the brick to be used should point toward you. Insert the brickset into the uppermost scored line, with the bevel again facing away from the part to be sued. Then strike the handle with a sharp blow of the hammer. The brick should separate into two pieces.

Lengthwise cuts. Find the center point of one of the long side edges of the brick. Measure and mark a continuous cutting line all around the brick. Wearing goggles, score the surface along the cutting line by tapping the line with the sharp edge of the square end of a bricklayers' hammer —or, for extra-hard bricks, with a brickset—as shown above. Grip the brick firmly in one hand, and strike the brick sharply with the flat side of the square end of the hammer, just beyond the center point of the scored line. (You may have to practice this technique several times before you will be able to halve the brick with a single blow.) Use the curved, chisel-like blade end of the hammer to clean off rough spots on the cut edges, removing small bits at a time.

Replacing a Broken Brick

1 **Removing a single damaged brick.** Wearing eye protection, tar with a mortar rake—a valuable tool if you can find one—or a chisel and ball-peen hammer. Because the mortar rake enables you to use both hands, it speeds up the job. Chisel out the damaged brick and brush the space clean.

2 **Replacing the brick.** Select a brick that fits the slot ot cut one to fit *(page 418).* Dampen the slot's surfaces and apply a thick coating of mortar. Hold the brick on a hawk about ½ inch above the course the brick will rest on. Ram the brick into the slot. Trowel in extra mortar if needed to fill the joints.

Filling In a Damaged Wall

Cutting out and replacing bricks. Remove all mortar surrounding damaged bricks and chop out all broken or cracked bricks with a board chisel (also called a brickset) and a ball peen hammer. When removing adjoining bricks, work from the top of mortar, brick and dust. Then, working from the bottom course upward, dampen all sur- faces of both old and replacement bricks, and lay mortar beds for the replacement bricks, trowel- ing and furrowing the bed just as you would for placing new bricks. Butter the bricks and lay them in place on the mortar beds. When the mortar is firm, finish the joints to match the rest of the wall.

Homemade Concrete in Convenient Batches

Concrete is man-made stone, and like stone it can last forever. Concrete steps or a post anchored in concrete will stand up to almost any kind of punishment. The great strength comes from the materials: gravel (called coarse aggregate), sand and cement. The coarse aggregate supplies bulk. The sand fills voids between the coarse pieces. And the cement, when it is moistened with water, binds the sand and aggregate into a durable monolithic solid.

For anchors on posts, clothesline supports and backyard gym poles, you can make concrete of plain portland cement. But for larger jobs such as building concrete patios or steps, you need air-entrained portland cement, which contains additives that produce and trap, or entrain, microscopic air bubbles in the concrete. When the concrete becomes wet, the bubbles act like tiny ball bearings to facilitate pouring and spreading. When the concrete dries, the bubbles form tiny spaces within the concrete so that it can expand and contract with a minimum of cracking. Because of this weather resistance, some local building codes require air-entrained cement for concrete that will be outdoors.

Cement comes in one-cubic-foot bags that weigh 94 pounds each (80-pound Canadian bags contain 7/8 cubic foot). Be sure the cement is dry before you use it. If a bag is hard around the edges, its contents have probably absorbed moisture but are acceptable—rolling the bag on the ground will generally break up the lumps. If the edges do not break this way, however, or if you find any lumps inside that do not break between your fingers, return the bag to your dealer.

Sand and coarse aggregate are also sold by the cubic foot. Sand for concrete, unlike the uniform sand needed for mortar, should contain particles of all sizes from dust to about 1/16 inch in diameter. Do not use beach sand; the salt in it will weaken concrete. Gravel aggregate should contain particles no larger than 1 inch in diameter for thin layers, such as you may need for a small fishpond; use 1½-inch aggregate where sections more than 4 inches thick are required, in such structures as steps, patios and sidewalks.

The amount of water required for a concrete recipe is critical; even a small amount of extra water can weaken the concrete. Most recipes are based on what is called wet sand, which forms a ball when squeezed in the hand but leaves no noticeable moisture on the palm. Since the sand you buy rarely matches this moisture level, you must adjust the amount of water added during mixing (page 422). The three recipes given below will produce variations of a basic 1:2:4 concrete mix—one part cement, two parts sand and four parts coarse aggregate—that is strong and workable yet viscous enough to be poured. To stiffen the mix for spreading rather than pouring —for making a bowl-like fishpond, for example—use about 2/3 the amount of water, added gradually only until the ingredients are thoroughly combined.

How you mix the materials depends on how much concrete you need. A small amount of plain (not the air-entrained type) concrete can be mixed by hand in a wheelbarrow, or on a driveway or other flat surface. But to mix enough air-entrained concrete to build steps or a footing for a wall, rent a gasoline- or electric-powered mixer and set it up close to your work area. Working with a power mixer, you probably will be able to pour and finish about 10 square feet of a six-inch thick slab before the concrete hardens too much to be finished. If you require larger quantities to be available, arrange for ready-mixed concrete delivered in a truck.

When mixing by hand, use a container marked in gallons to measure out and transfer the materials from bag to wheelbarrow or driveway work space (chart, below). For larger jobs requiring a power mixer, you may want to make a bottomless box, 12 inches square and 12 inches deep, to measure one cubic foot of dry ingredients. Set the box in a wheelbarrow, shovel the box full and lift the box out; then shovel the cubic foot of material into the mixer.

Three Basic Recipes

Ingredients to make one cubic foot of plain concrete:	Ingredients for one cubic foot of air-entrained concrete, using ¾-inch coarse aggregate:	Ingredients for one cubic foot of air-entrained concrete, using 1½-inch coarse aggregate:
1⅝ U.S. gallons plain portland cement (20 pounds or ⅕ cubic foot)	1⅝ U.S. gallons type 1A portland cement (20 pounds or ⅕ cubic foot)	1⅜ U.S. gallons type 1A portland cement (17 pounds or ⅙ cubic foot)
3¼ U.S. gallons sand (40 pounds or ⅖ cubic foot)	2⅞ U.S. gallons sand (35 pounds or ⅜ cubic foot)	2⅞ U.S. gallons sand (35 pounds or ⅜ cubic foot)
6 U.S. gallons ¾-inch gravel aggregate (80 pounds or ⅘ cubic foot)	6 U.S. gallons coarse aggregate (80 pounds or ⅘ cubic foot)	6⅜ U.S. gallons coarse aggregate (85 pounds or ⅞ cubic foot)
1¼ U.S. gallons water (10 pounds)	1¼ U.S. gallons water (10 pounds)	1¼ U.S. gallons water (10 pounds)

Caution: Portland cement is caustic when wet, and can cause serious burns to the eyes. Avoid bending over it when pouring dry ingredients and do not work on a windy day. When working with mixed concrete, protect your skin by wearing gloves.

Getting the Materials Ready to Use

Keeping the ingredients separate. Deposit cement, sand and coarse aggregate close to the work site. To prevent cement from absorbing moisture, stack bags against one another on a raised platform away from walls. On plastic sheeting, or a tarpaulin, pile sand and aggregate into several small adjoining mounds. Keep them apart with a board divider if necessary. If the materials must be stored longer than a few hours, place both open and unopened cement bags inside plastic bags, stack the bags on the platform and cover everything with a waterproof tarpaulin.

Cleaning Up After the Work is Done

Masonry cleanup usually consists of at least two different tasks: disposing of mortar or concrete that remains unused, and cleaning your tools.

Since most sanitation departments will not haul away leftover concrete or mortar, you may have to take it yourself to the nearest landfill for disposal. For easier handling, pour it into paper bags, or pile it in small heaps on sheets of paper and let it set into manageable lumps. Or mold concrete and save it for future use—for example, keep simple 2-by-4 wood forms ready for pouring excess concrete while it is still workable, and cast stepping stones.

Cleaning tools is an ongoing task that must be done every day. An easy way to eliminate much of the toil involved in cleaning tools individually is to put all of them in a wheelbarrow and hose them down together. Empty the dirty water into a street or road—do not let it run off into a drainage system or backyard, for even a small amount of hardened cement can clog drain traps and ruin lawns. (A town sewage system, which has large drainpipes and no traps, can carry the water off safely.) When the entire job is finished and you are ready to put tools away, wash them and coat them with petroleum jelly.

A power concrete mixer must be hosed out at the end of each workday. (Many rental companies charge an extra fee for a mixer that comes back dirty.) If you cannot clean the drum completely by using a hose, turn the mixer on and pour in a mixture of water and two shovelsful of aggregate to scour it out. Empty the mixer after three or four minutes, then hose it out again. If you have waited too long to clean the mixer, you may have to scrape bits of hardened concrete out with a wire brush or chip them off with a chisel. A dull-gray exterior film of dry cement should be sponged off with vinegar.

Mixing Concrete in a Wheelbarrow

1 Measuring the materials. Make no more than one wheelbarrow-sized batch of concrete—usually 2½ cubic feet—at a time. Measure out each of the ingredients *(recipes, page 420)* in a bucket (one marked in quarts is most convenient).

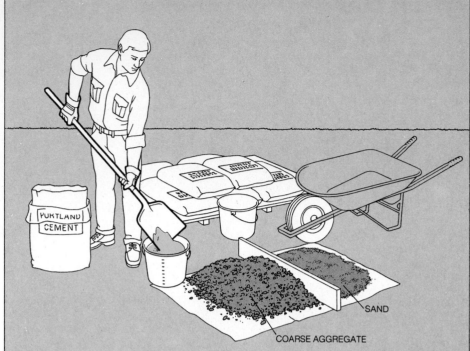

SAND

COARSE AGGREGATE

2 Combining the dry materials. Pour the sand into the wheelbarrow, and, using a hoe, shape the sand into a ring. Pour the cement into the center of the sand ring, then mix the ingredients. When the mixture is uniform in color—without streaks of brown or gray—shape another ring. Pour coarse aggregate into the center. Mix until the coarse aggregate is evenly distributed.

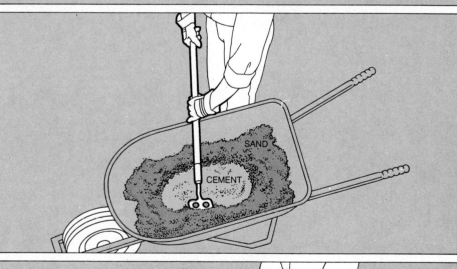

SAND

CEMENT

3 Adding the water. Push the sand-cement-coarse aggregate mixture to the sides of the wheelbarrow to form a bowl-like depression. Slowly pour about three quarters of the water into the depression. Pull the dry materials from the edges of the ring into the water, working all around the pile until the water is absorbed by the mixture. When no water remains standing on the surface, turn the concrete three or four times. Add the remaining water a little at a time until the mixture completely coats all the coarse aggregate. Leave any unused water in the measuring bucket until after you test the consistency of the concrete and make necessary corrections *(right)*. At the end of the day, clean up as explained on page 421.

CEMENT-SAND-COARSE AGGREGATE MIXTURE

A Power Mixer to Make the Job Go Faster

Before turning on the mixer, set the drum to the mixing position; then pour in half the water *(recipe, page 420)* and all the coarse aggregate. Turn on the mixer and add—in order—sand, cement and about half the remaining water. Wait three minutes, then add more water, little by little, until the mixture completely coats the coarse aggregate and the concrete is a uniform color. Test a few shovelfuls in a wheelbarrow *(below)*, and return the test batch to the mixer before making corrections. When the concrete is properly compounded, dump the mixerful into your wheelbarrow and hose out the drum. When you finish using the mixer, clean up as described on page 421.

Testing the Consistency

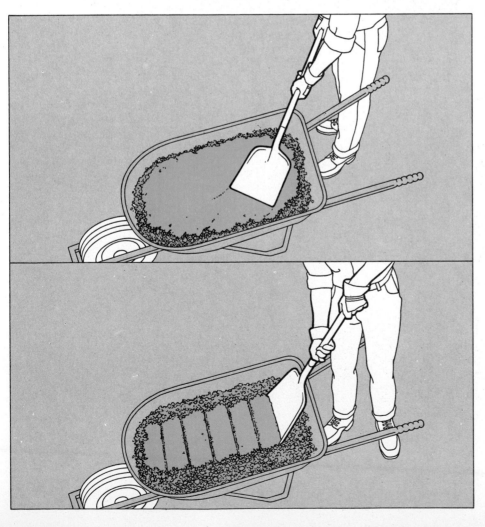

Judging and correcting the mix. Smooth the concrete in your wheelbarrow by sliding the bottom of a shovel or trowel across the concrete's surface. Then jab the edge of the shovel or trowel into the smooth surface to form grooves. If the surface is smooth and the grooves are distinct, concrete is ready to use *(left, bottom);* make sure you complete the job before it sets. If the surface roughens or the grooves are indistinct, add no more than a half-gallon of concrete-water mixture, using twice as much cement as water. If the surface is wet or the grooves collapse, add no more than a half-gallon of the cement-sand mixture combined in the original proportions. Retest the batch until the consistency is correct, then use it quickly, before it sets.

How to Restore Concrete

Paradoxically, concrete surfaces cannot be repaired with concrete—the coarse gravel aggregate in the new concrete would prevent a strong bond between the patch and the damaged area. Instead, the materials used are grout, mortar, sand-cement-epoxy compounds, or premixed cement or latex patching compounds that come in a box, can or cartridge.

Before using any of these materials, clear the repair area of damaged concrete, keep the area moist for several hours—preferably overnight—and remove all dirt, debris and standing water. Then apply a patch of the appropriate material. For cracks up to 1/8 inch wide, use either a grout made of portland cement and just enough water to make a paste that will hold its shape, or use a ready-mix patch *(page 438)*. Cement-based ready-mix in a cartridge can be applied directly with a caulking gun; force a canned mix or grout into the crack with a putty knife or a mason's trowel, and smooth it flush to the level of the surrounding concrete.

Mend larger cracks with mortar consisting of 1 part portland cement, 3 parts sand, and water; a latex-based ready-mix; or a sand-cement-epoxy mix. The epoxy compound produces an especially durable repair on surfaces from which concrete has flaked off in thin scales *(opposite, bottom)*. Wear gloves when repairing concrete, and goggles when breaking up the damaged surface.

Epoxy mixtures cure by themselves in 24 hours, but a grout or mortar patch must cure slowly in the presence of moisture. On a horizontal surface let the patch set for about two hours, then cover it with a sheet of plastic secured by bricks or rocks. For the next five to seven days, lift the cover daily and sprinkle some water on the patch. If a patch on a vertical surface cannot be covered conveniently, sprinkle it twice a day.

Treating Wide Cracks

1 Removing the damaged concrete. Chip away all cracked or crumbling concrete to about 1 inch below the surface, using a cold chisel and a ball-peen hammer. Wear goggles during this and the following step to protect your eyes from flying fragments.

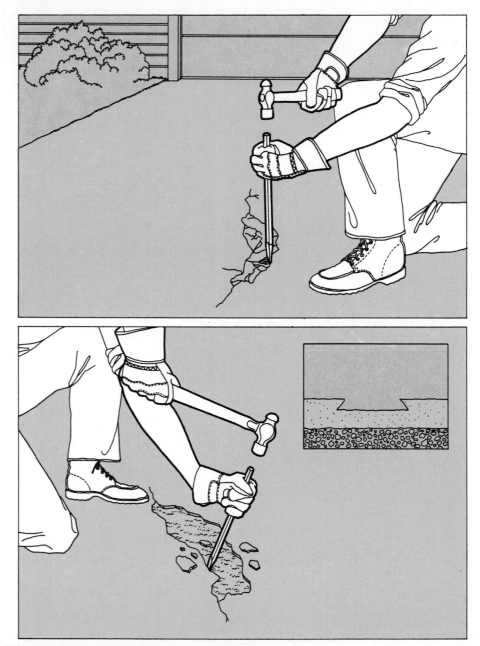

2 Undercutting the edges. To provide a better bond and keep the patch from heaving upward after the job is done, undercut the edges of the crack with the hammer and chisel until the hole you have made is wider at the bottom than at the top *(inset)*. Remove all rubble and dirt. Soak the crack with water for several hours; if possible, run a trickle from a garden hose through it overnight.

3 **Coating the edges with cement paint.** Thoroughly mix 1 part portland cement and 3 parts sand; add sufficient water to make a paste stiff enough to work with a trowel, and set it aside. Then mix a small batch of portland cement and water to the consistency of thick paint. Coat the edges of the crack with this cement paint and proceed immediately to Step 4. Caution: You must complete the repair before the paint dries.

4 **Filling the crack with mortar.** Pack the mortar firmly into the crack with a pointed mason's trowel, cutting deep into the mixture to remove air pockets. Level the mortar with a square trowel, let it stand for an hour, then spread it evenly back and forth across the crack, always with the leading edge of the trowel slightly raised (drawing). To cure the patch, follow the procedure described in the text on the opposite page.

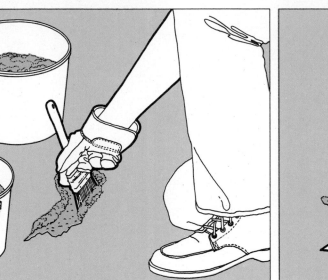

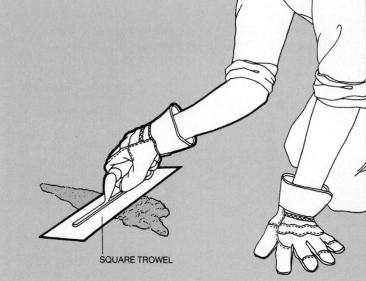

SQUARE TROWEL

Refinishing Scaling Surfaces

Using an epoxy mix. Wearing goggles to protect your eyes from flying fragments, break up large areas of scaling concrete with an 8-pound sledgehammer (let the hammer drop of its own weight, rather than swinging it hard against the surface); for small areas, use a ball-peen hammer and a cold chisel. Sweep up dust and debris, using a stiff wire brush, if necessary, to dislodge any small fragments. Wet down the damaged area and keep it moist several hours, preferably overnight. The area should still be damp but should contain no free water when you begin to apply the patch.

Prepare a sand-cement epoxy mixture according to the manufacturer's directions. Apply the mixture with a square trowel, bringing the new layer level with the surrounding concrete, and feathering it thinly at the edges. Let the patch stand for 24 hours before putting pressure on it.

Durable Patches
for a Concrete Floor

1 **Preparing the area.** Wearing gloves and goggles, break the damaged concrete into small, easily carried pieces with a sledge or an electric jackhammer and clear away the debris. Use a cold chisel and a hammer to angle the exposed edges of the slab toward the center of the hole you have made; roughen the edges of the slab with a wire brush and remove loose particles of concrete. Dig 4 inches below the bottom of the slab. Tamp the dirt inside the hole with the end of a 2-by-4 and fill the hole to the bottom of the slab with clean ¾-inch gravel.

2 **Cutting the reinforcing mesh.** Lay 6 x 6-10/10 gauge galvanized reinforcing wire over the hole and with metal shears cut a piece to fit the hole; the ends of the wires should rest against the exposed edges of the concrete slab. Reinforcing wire usually comes in rolls 5 feet wide; if you need a patch that is wider than 5 feet, join two strips of wire by twisting the free strands together. Set two bricks under the wire to keep it centered between the top and bottom of the hole when the new concrete is placed.

3 **Placing the patch.** Form a cone of ready-packaged concrete mix on a piece of plywood, hollow out the top and pour water into the center as specified by the manufacturer. Mix them together with a shovel until the concrete is firm but workable. Coat the edges of the hole with a concrete bonding agent. Before the coating dries, shovel the concrete into the hole, jabbing into it to force it against the sides of the hole; with the point of the shovel, push the concrete under the mesh to form a firm bed. Fill the holes to the level of the slab, then add a few extra shovels of concrete to allow for settling and shrinking. Be sure that none of the wire is exposed.

4 Finishing the patch. With a helper, sweep a straight 2-by-4 across the surface of the patch to level it, working the board back and forth as you sweep. If you find depressions in the surface, fill them with concrete and go over the patch again with the 2-by-4. A thin film of water will soon appear on the surface. When it evaporates and the surface sheen disappears, smooth the patch with a metal trowel for a smooth surface; if the surrounding surface is rough, use a broom to smooth the patch. If the patch is too large to trowel from its edges, kneel on boards laid across it and work backward from one side of the patch to the other, moving the boards as you go.

When the concrete hardens, sprinkle it with water and cover it with polyethylene to prevent moisture from escaping. Let the patch cure for three to seven days, checking it every day to be sure it is damp, and sprinkling it with water if needed.

Cosmetics for Concrete

A raw concrete floor has a certain rough beauty, but no one likes a stained floor and most people prefer one finished with a sealer or a paint. To remove stains or to paint, you must match materials and methods to your situation.

Most stains can be scrubbed away with a household detergent, but deep stains may require special treatment. Fold a piece of cheesecloth several times and lay it over the stained area. Then, pour one of the chemicals listed below over the cloth. The chemicals will dissolve the stain, and the cheese-cloth will absorb the chemicals. Use the following recipes for specific stains:

☐ Rust: use 1 part sodium citrate to 6 parts glycerin.

☐ Copper, bronze or ink: use 1 part ammonia to 9 parts water.

☐ Grease, oil or mildew: use a strong detergent.

☐ Iron: use 1 part oxalic acid to 9 parts water.

☐ Old paint: use a commercial paint remover.

Penetrating sealers are the least expensive and simplest finishes for concrete. They can be easily applied, dry in about eight hours and leave a thin film that protects against minor stains.

Until recently, concrete floors had to be specifically prepared for painting, because concrete contains alkalies that make most paints blister and peel. To neutralize the alkalies, the floors were treated with a strong solution of muriatic acid, difficult and somewhat dangerous to apply. The paints listed below can be used on an untreated concrete floor after a suitable waiting period. All can be spatter-dashed—a technique that obscures small stains in concrete and creates a decorative effect (left).

Epoxy-polyurethane coatings can be applied about a month after the concrete is poured. They are relatively expensive but more durable than other types. Most come ready to apply but a few manufacturers make "two-pot" coatings, for which resins and hardeners must be premixed. Epoxy-polyurethanes usually need two coats; a few types need a primer. Most dry in about six hours to a clear, tough, glossy finish.

Solvent-thinned, rubber-based paints, which are not as long lasting as epoxy-polyurethanes, are more water resistant; they can be applied to damp surfaces and are suited to humid areas. You will need three coats, the first applied two months after the concrete is poured. The paint dries in one half to four hours and the job can be done in one day. The paint solvents are noxious: If working indoors, open a window to make sure the room is well-ventilated.

Latex paints especially designed for concrete are cheaper than rubber-based or epoxy-polyurethane paints. Because they are water based, application and cleanup are easy, but they are far less durable than the others and can be damaged by freezing; do not use them on heavily trafficked areas or where sudden drops in temperature are common. Apply three coats, beginning two months after the concrete is poured.

Before spatter-dashing a floor, apply two coats of paint and mask walls with newspaper. Wearing goggles, gloves and a hat, load a brush with paint for the third contrasting coat (left) and strike it against the edge of a 1-by-2 board. Practice the technique over a sheet of paper.

Putting Back a Broken Step

1 Gluing the broken piece. Brush particles of dirt and cement from the broken piece and the damaged corner of the step. Mix a small batch of an outdoor-type epoxy glue, following the label directions, and coat the two surfaces that you are fitting together. Position the broken piece and hold it firmly for about 10 minutes, until the glue has hardened; if necessary, prop a board against the piece to hold it in place.

2 Completing the job. After the epoxy glue has set, use a scraper or putty knife to remove any excess that has oozed out between the piece and the step. You will probably find a small, irregular crack around the repair; patch it as you would any narrow crack, using the epoxy glue instead of grout. Avoid stepping on the repaired corner or bumping against it for at least 24 hours to allow the glue to harden completely.

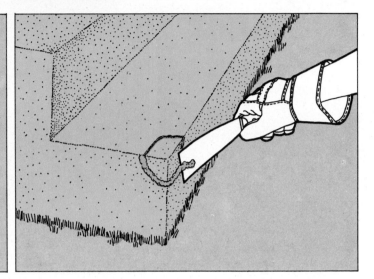

Rebuilding the Corner of a Step

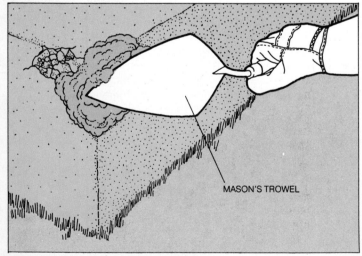

MASON'S TROWEL

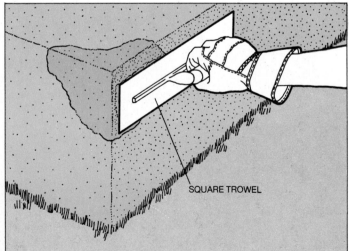

SQUARE TROWEL

1 Shaping a replacement piece. If the original corner of the step has crumbled away or been lost, clean and moisten the corner. Thoroughly mix a concrete patching agent and just enough water to make a paste that holds its shape. With a mason's trowel, apply the patch to the step in the rough shape of the original corner. Let the mortar harden until it retains a firmly impressed thumbprint (this may take up to five or six hours, depending on weather conditions).

2 Finishing the corner. Finish and smooth the corner flush to the adjoining parts of the step with a square trowel. Let the patch cure for a week, moistening it twice a day, and avoid stepping on the corner or bumping it for another three weeks; if a latex patch is used, curing is unnecessary.

Repairing the Chipped Edge of a Step

1 **Clearing the damage.** With a ball-peen hammer and a cold chisel held horizontally, chip off the damaged concrete all the way across the edge of the step. Be sure to wear goggles to protect your eyes from flying fragments.

2 **Undercutting a groove.** Still wearing the goggles, but holding the chisel at an angle, chip away enough of the step to make a V-shaped groove (*inset*). Clean off all debris and keep the edge damp for several hours, preferably overnight.

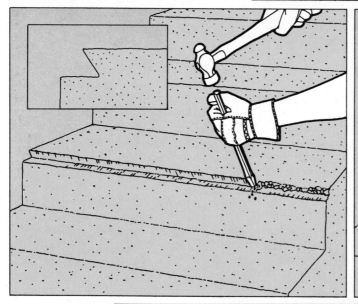

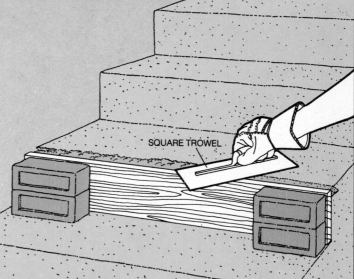

SQUARE TROWEL

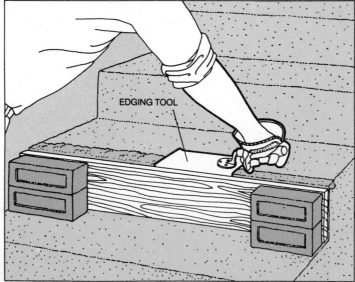

EDGING TOOL

3 **Rebuilding the edge.** Thoroughly mix a concrete patching agent with just enough water to make a paste that holds its shape; set aside. Make a form board as wide and high as the riser and set it against the step, holding it in place with heavy objects such as bricks or concrete blocks. Paint a concrete bonding agent onto the edge of the step, then immediately fill the V-shaped groove with patching compound, shaping and smoothing it flush to the adjoining surfaces with a square trowel.

4 **Completing the job.** Let the patch set for about an hour, finish the step to a rounded edge with an edging tool, then carefully remove the board. Unless a latex patcher is used, keep the area damp for at least a week to help the patch cure. Do not step on the new edge for two weeks.

Choosing the Right Remedy for a Wet Basement

The causes of a wet basement generally lie outside it, but even the best landscaping and gutter system may not solve the problem, and often cracks or holes in basement walls admit water that otherwise would stay outside. Much wetness can be eliminated by fixing interior walls, but work on the exterior may be necessary.

If the basement is damp but not wet—you see no patches of water but feel excess humidity or see its effects in mildew—the steps are fairly simple. Dampness may arise from water vapor generated by appliances in the house such as dish- and clothes washers—clothes dryers are the worst offenders and their exhausts should be vented outdoors.

Seepage through walls or floor may introduce water as well as humidity, and sometimes humid air generated inside the house may condense into liquid on masonry surfaces, suggesting that moisture is entering from outdoors. To determine whether the problem is inside or outside—and whether ventilation is a sufficient solution—perform the following test. Tape a 16-inch square of heavy plastic sheeting to the wall below ground level. Remove it after several days: dampness underneath means that water is seeping into the basement between grains of sand and cement in a wall that looks solid. If the plastic-covered area is

dry and the wall around it is damp, then water is condensing from moist air that is inside the basement.

If seepage is the problem, you may be able to block it with a coat of waterproof cement paint or, if necessary, layers of patching mortar over masonry interior walls and floor. A dirt floor is a common source of seepage; if you have one, cover it. Polyethylene plastic will do if you need not use the basement; if you must walk on the floor, lay sturdier covering —concrete or, at the least, roll roofing.

Cracks are more serious than seepage or condensation. They can be caused by settling, infiltrating tree roots, water pressure against walls or floor, or even by minor earthquake tremors.

You may first notice a crack on a rainy day as water streams into the basement. The flood can be stopped and the crack fixed by channeling water out through a short hose, then plugging the leak with hydraulic cement, which hardens on contact with water *(page 433)*.

Once the crisis has passed—or if you discover the crack before it floods the basement—check to determine whether it is a moving crack or a stationary one, since each type calls for a different remedy. Mark the wall or floor on each side of the crack and carefully measure the distance between the marks. Remeasure

the distance after two weeks. If it is unchanged, the crack is stationary. A change in the space between the marks indicates a moving crack. Try repairing stationary cracks from the inside of the basement first *(opposite)*. If such a patch proves ineffective by itself, the crack probably extends through the wall and you must seal the outside of the foundation too. A concrete patch will work for most cracks, but if the exterior wall of the foundation is badly damaged, you may have to excavate, patch and seal a large section of the wall.

Moving cracks almost invariably go through the wall. To seal hairline cracks effectively, you must make flexible interior patches out of fiberglass cloth and asphalt sealer. You can seal cracks up to an inch wide with mastic joint sealer, which is heated with a propane torch until soft and pushed with a putty knife into the crack. The mastic is then covered with a patching mortar.

Of all the cracks in a basement, the most troublesome are those that occur where the floor meets the wall. Try filling them with a joint sealer and epoxy resin, which are in turn covered by mortar. If this remedy fails to keep the basement dry, installing a sump pump *(page 435)* may be the only practical solution to expelling excess water.

Preventing seepage. Dampen the wall with a moist sponge and trowel on a ¼-inch layer of patching mortar mixed with a waterproofing additive such as silicone or latex. Work from the floor upward. After the cement dries but before it sets—about 20 minutes to one hour—use a stiff brush to apply a coat of waterproof cement paint, working the paint into the fresh cement.

PATCHING MORTAR

Patching stationary cracks. Wearing eye protection, open the crack with a cold chisel *(right)* until it is an inch wide, then remove loose concrete with a wire brush. Use a pointing trowel to wet the surfaces of the crack with patching mortar; then fill it with the mortar.

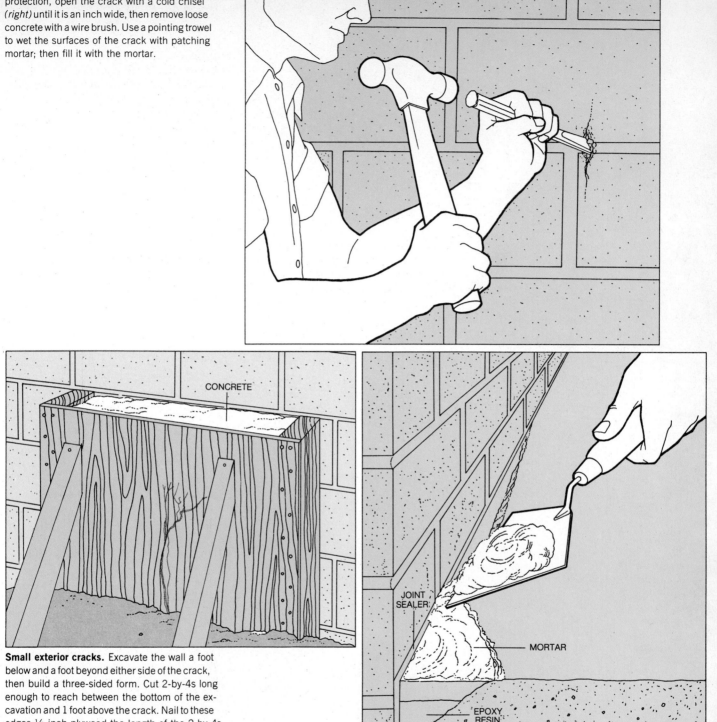

CONCRETE

JOINT SEALER

MORTAR

EPOXY RESIN

Small exterior cracks. Excavate the wall a foot below and a foot beyond either side of the crack, then build a three-sided form. Cut 2-by-4s long enough to reach between the bottom of the excavation and 1 foot above the crack. Nail to these edges ½-inch plywood the length of the 2-by-4s and 2 feet wider than the crack. Prop the form over the crack with 2-by-4 scraps and fill it with a standard concrete mix, tamped into place. Let the concrete set 24 hours before removing the form.

Filling wall-floor cracks. Widen the outside of the crack with a cold chisel, making a beveled slot. Dry the crack with a propane torch and line the slot next to the wall with a strip of mastic joint sealer ¼ inch thick to prevent bonding with the wall. Half fill the rest of the slot with epoxy resin to prevent the mastic from loosening, then mortar over the resin with a pointing trowel.

Repairing Small Moving Cracks

Repairing small moving cracks. Cut fiberglass cloth—the kind sold for patching walls—to cover the crack completely and extend at least 2 inches on all sides. Using detergent, clean the crack and the part of the wall to be covered by the patch. Brush on a coat of asphalt sealer, stick the patch to it, and cover it with more sealer.

FIBERGLASS

Repairing Large Moving Cracks

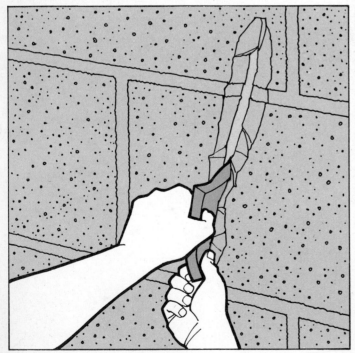

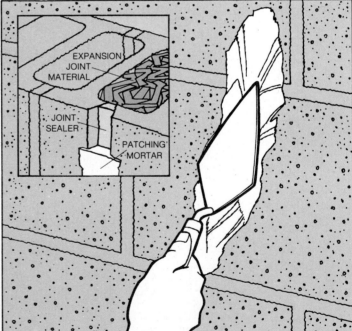

EXPANSION JOINT MATERIAL

JOINT SEALER

PATCHING MORTAR

1 Preparing the crack. Chip out the crack so that it is ¾ inch wide at the bottom and 1 inch wide at the surface of the wall. If the wall is concrete block, cut strips of expansion joint material, an asphalt-impregnated substance used between sections of sidewalk. Stuff the material through the crack—using a screwdriver, if necessary—to fill the hollow inside the block.

2 Sealing the crack. Use a propane torch with a wide tip to heat mastic joint sealer until it is soft, then press it into the crack with a putty knife. Fill the crack about halfway, then, with a pointing trowel, fill the crack to the top with patching mortar to complete the job.

Plugging Flowing Leaks

1 Inserting a bleeder hose. Chip loose concrete away from the hole. Divert the water into a bucket by inserting a piece of rubber hose—any size that fits—and fill around it with dry hydraulic cement, which sets within a minute or two after it comes into contact with water. It is available in hardware stores.

2 Inserting a plug. When the hole around the hose is filled, shape a conical plug of dry hydraulic cement, hold it in the palm of one hand, pull out the bleeder hose and jam the plug into the hole, holding it in place until the cement sets.

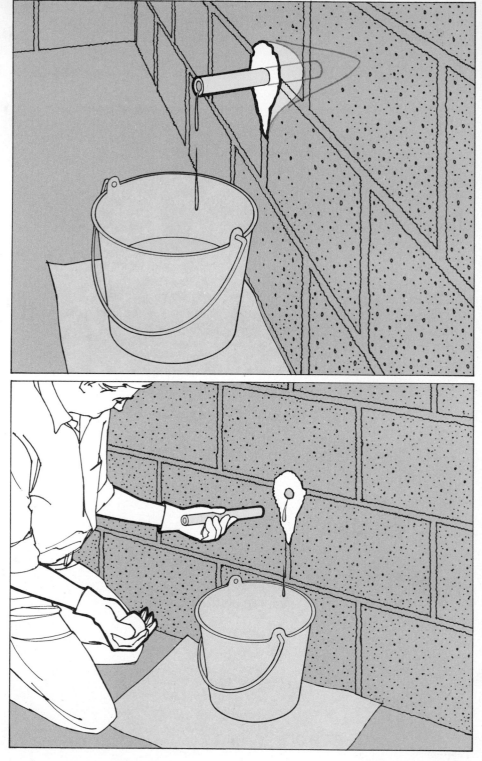

433

The Battle Against Moisture

Keeping the house dry is a twofold task. Inside the house, water vapor—moisture that is not in liquid form but is in the air as humidity—must be carefully controlled. Some water vapor enters the house from outside, but enormous amounts are generated inside by bathing, cooking and laundering. Problems caused by condensed moisture can be cured by improving the ventilation in your home. By installing strategically placed openings in the attic and basement, for example, you can ensure a constant movement of air that will push warm moisture outdoors, taking advantage of the natural tendency of hot air to rise. In problem areas—kitchens, bathrooms and laundries—ducting and electric fans may be needed to expel excess moisture. A dehumidifier can also help.

Outside the house, water must often be channeled off the house and away from the foundation. Leaks and seepage originating outdoors can often be corrected by taking such simple measures as redirecting the flow from downspouts and banking the earth around the foundation. If the dirt would cover part of a basement window, install a window well (below). Do not pile dirt any closer than 6 inches to wood siding; a pest problem may develop when insects use the embankment as a bridge into the house.

Areas directly below eaves must be protected from water coursing off the roof; raindrops can erode soil and expose the foundation. Gutters and downspouts are the common means by which this water is carried away; however, they have drawbacks. They need maintenance—painting, patching, repositioning—and replacement when they wear out (pages 404-406). They get clogged with leaves and debris. In northern climates they become blocked with snow and ice, causing buildups on the gutters and the roof itself.

Use gutters and downspouts where they are essential, but let rain fall freely off the roof if the ground below will bear it. A steep embankment often is protection enough. Thin strips of gravel, walks and patios are usually an even better solution for protecting against water runoff. And dense shrubbery planted under the eaves can impede erosion.

Wherever downspouts are used, the area around them must be given extra protection from the heavy concentration of water they spew forth. You may need to install a splash block or a downspout extension to stop erosion.

If the basement still leaks, try waterproofing the porous masonry from the inside with the appropriate paint, sealant or cement. More serious drainage problems, or a rising ground water level under the basement, will require digging a dry

Installing a window well. The cavity around a basement window that extends below ground level exposes the foundation to serious water damage unless proper drainage is provided. The solution is a window well. The liner of an inexpensive and easy-to-install well consists of a ready-made, oval-shaped sheet of galvanized steel, usually corrugated. Available at building-supply stores, the sheets come in a variety of sizes that will fit around almost any window.

Buy a liner 6 inches wider than the window. Dig a hole for the liner 1 foot deeper than the bottom of the window. Center the liner in the bottom of the hole (right). Spread 4 inches of gravel on the bottom of the well, both inside and outside the liner, then fill the rest of the hole behind the liner —away from the house—with earth. Plant sod or place a thin strip of gravel on top of the earth so that rain falling around the perimeter of the well will drain away naturally.

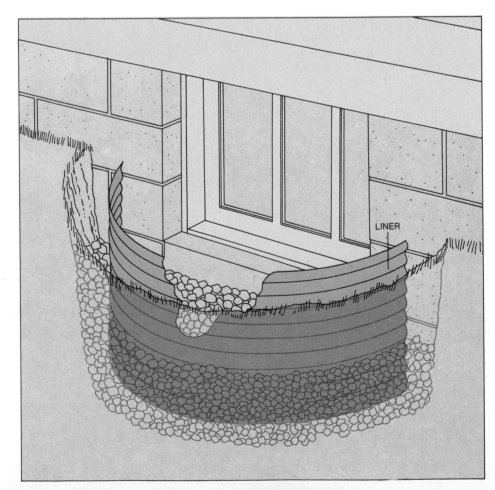

LINER

a dry well or excavating around the foundation—a heavy job you may want to have professionally done. You may also prefer hiring a professional if basement walls must be resurfaced with concrete. But the rest of the job is fairly simple to do yourself.

If the foundation is cracked, and the crack is shallow, you may be able to block it. Excavate the upper part of the basement wall to a depth of about 2 feet, then waterproof it with asphalt foundation coating and polyethylene plastic sheeting (right). If the leak is lower down, there is no alternative to excavating the entire basement wall down to the footing, then waterproofing the wall with concrete and laying drain tiles.

Even when these measures fail to keep water out of the basement, an electric sump pump (below) provides the last line of defense, discharging the water as fast as it enters.

If All Else Fails: A Sump Pump

Sometimes the best solution for a wet basement is a sump pump, especially in cases where a basement floods only when a severe storm occurs or the water table rises. Sump pumps are also good insurance against water damage from burst pipes and backed-up drains.

Sump pumps are available in portable models for use in emergency situations, or permanently installed models which usually operate on electricity; other types run on small gasoline engines or pressure from the water main.

The first step in installing a sump pump is to chop a hole—the sump—in the basement floor with an electric jackhammer, which can be rented. The sump should be big enough to accommodate a 15-inch diameter liner —a bottomless cylinder designed to prevent sump walls from caving in. Check your local plumbing code to see if you can run the discharge line into the sewer or storm drain. Sump pumps use 1¼- or 1½-inch discharge piping: Use plastic piping if possible.

Manufacturers recommend that power be drawn from a separate, unswitched outlet. Check local electrical codes to be sure that you use proper materials; call an electrician to make service panel connections.

ASPHALT

ROCKS

PLASTIC SHEETING

Waterproofing near the surface. Dig a trench 4 feet wide and 2 feet deep around the house, sloping it downward away from the house. With a trowel, apply a coating of asphalt to the wall from the bottom of the ditch to grade level. Smooth the coating with a stiff brush. Then press a sheet of polyethylene plastic against the asphalt and extend the sheeting to line the bottom of the entire ditch. Fill the trench with a 1½-foot layer of rocks and cover with topsoil.

Removing Grime from Brick, Concrete and Stone

Masonry is subject to two very different standards of cleanliness. Because of its strength and durability, it is often the material of choice for surfaces begrimed by the dirtiest dirt there is—the oil and grease of garage floors, the soot of fireplace interiors. No one expects these utilitarian surfaces to be spotless, but they do have to be cleaned occasionally—if only for safety's sake. At the opposite end of the cleaning spectrum are masonry surfaces whose decorative purpose entitles them to the same loving attention as fine wood-marble mantels, slate entry floors, patterned brick patios.

As it happens, the cleaning methods for both types of masonry are essentially the same: Decorative surfaces merely call for a little more patience. At the start of the cleaning process, a bit more elbow grease is substituted for strong chemicals, which are a last resort. In the final stages, more effort goes into erasing the last lingering shadows of a spot or stain.

Whatever the masonry surface, the cleaning power of a good natural-bristled scrub brush and a standard all-purpose household cleaner should not be underestimated. A surprising number of spots and stains will yield to such routine treatment. If this fails to dislodge the dirt, try a heavy-duty household cleaner or scouring powder. Be warned, however, that these stronger cleaners and powders may dull the stone's polished surface, which will later have to be restored.

Some stains and blemishes, of course, require more abrasion than a scrub brush can supply. When brick is speckled with paint or excess mortar, or discolored by the traceries left by ivy, you will have to resort to sanding—but not with sandpaper. Instead, use broken brick, whose gritty residue will be invisible.

Efflorescence, the white powdery deposit left by salts leached out from the interior of bricks when they are exposed to moisture (page 180), also requires special treatment. It must be removed with concrete etch (opposite), a mild acid. This is usually applied full strength follow the label directions. When the stain is gone, the etch in turn must be flushed with clear water.

When you work with an acid etch or with any other strong cleaning solution or solvent, be sure to wear protective clothing, and follow all the safety precautions given on the label.

Other cleaning regimens are less hazardous. A sprinkling of cat litter is helpful for soaking up oil and grease spills from a garage floor, and the remaining stain can be removed with a strong detergent. Lumps of spilled plastic that have hardened can be reduced to ash with a propane torch, then swept away; make sure it is safe to use an open flame in the area.

For large outdoor areas of masonry, such as a brick-walled house or a concrete driveway, you can rent a powerful machine called a pressure washer, which delivers a stream of water or detergent at pressures sufficient to blast out all but the most deeply ingrained dirt. The washer is powered by either a gasoline engine or an electric motor, but the gas-powered washer is much stronger and is preferable for large cleaning jobs.

For more stubborn stains that have worked into the pores of other masonry surfaces, a poultice may be preferable. Like the old-fashioned mustard plaster that was thought to draw poisons from the body, a cleaning poultice holds a strong chemical solvent in contact with the masonry long enough to penetrate and dissolve the stain. Meanwhile, the absorbent powder in the poultice soaks up the dissolving stain so that it can simply be brushed away. The powder in the poultice can be talc, whiting (also known as calcium carbonate) or hydrated lime—whichever is most readily available. The solvent, however, must be matched to the stain.

After the dirt or stain has been removed, you may also have to remove the effects of the cleaning process. Concrete and brick usually require nothing more than a thorough rinsing. Marble and slate may require buffing with a polish. One of the polishes recommended is tin oxide cream, widely used by jewelers to polish gemstones; the others are jeweler's rouge, a fine abrasive, and its slightly coarser relative, stone-polishing compound. All three are available at stores that carry supplies for lapidary work. Tin oxide cream is usually applied and rubbed by hand; jeweler's rouge and stone-polishing compound are applied and polished with a buffing attachment on an electric drill.

Finally, to protect newly cleaned masonry against soil, you may want to coat it with a silicone-base sealer, obtainable at most paint and hardware stores. Such sealers are best applied to smooth surfaces, such as marble, in several thin coats in succession. On rougher surfaces, such as brick and concrete, they are usually sprayed on with a pressurized sprayer in a single coat. The silicone sealer will impart a slightly unnatural gloss to the surface of the masonry, which is not to everyone's taste.

Asphalt-surfaced driveways and walkways also are often sealed after cleaning. Make sure that grease and oil spots on the driveway are completely removed; asphalt sealer will not adhere to the driveway surface if it is not cleaned properly. The sealant is an asphalt emulsion, which not only fills hairline cracks but restores the blacktop's sooty blackness. The emulsion, which is available at building-supply stores, is applied with a combination brush and squeegee made specifically for this job. The squeegee is used to spread the coating, the brush to smooth out irregularities on the driveway or walkway surface (page 440).

Dislodging Surface Deposits from Masonry

Sanding surface deposits from brick. Break a matching brick into fragments, and choose a fragment that will comfortably fit your hand. Working slowly and pressing lightly, rub the broken face of the fragment over the deposits in a back-and-forth motion. Avoid using the outside faces of the fragment; in firing, these faces become harder than the brick core, and they could scratch the brickwork.

Dissolving efflorescence. Before scrubbing the wall, protect the surface beneath the wall by covering it with a plastic dropcloth. Then protect yourself by donning safety goggles, a cap, heavy rubber gloves with cuffs, and old clothing—including a long-sleeved shirt. Then—from a plastic pail—use concrete etch full strength or as directed on the label.

After soaking the masonry with plain water, scrub the etch onto the wall with a natural-bristled scrub brush. When the acid stops bubbling, rinse the wall thoroughly with plain water.

When working indoors, open all the windows and wear a respirator in addition to the goggles and gloves. If your nose or eyes begin to sting, leave the room immediately and splash your face with cold water. Do not return to the task until the stinging subsides.

Simple Repairs for Walkways

Thawing, moisture and temperature changes can cause concrete walkways, patios and driveways to crack and buckle, resulting in small cracks and holes. Repairing this damage as soon as it appears can extend the surface's life. Three types of easy-to-use ready-mix concrete patching material can be found at hardware stores—cement made of latex, vinyl or epoxy. (For larger cracks and more serious concrete damage, use the methods described on pages 424-429.) Latex cement comes in two parts: cement and latex binder; mix together to form a thick paste. Vinyl cement is pre-mixed but requires water. Epoxy cement consists of dry cement, an emulsion and a hardener. Mix the emulsion and hardener together, then stir in the cement until you have the consistency you want. For any patching material, be sure to follow the drying time given in the instructions.

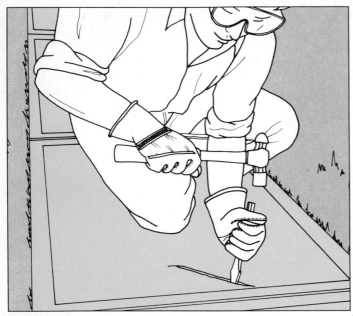

1 Preparing the crack. Wearing goggles and heavy work gloves, use a ball-peen hammer and cold chisel to undercut a crack *(above)*. Create an inverted triangle which will hold the patching material in place, then use a stiff brush to remove any debris in and around the crack.

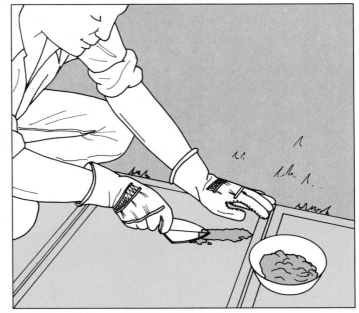

2 Filling the crack. Use a pointing trowel to spread the patching material evenly over the damage. Feather and smooth the material outward, while pushing the patching material into the crack. Allow the patch to dry according to the material's instructions.

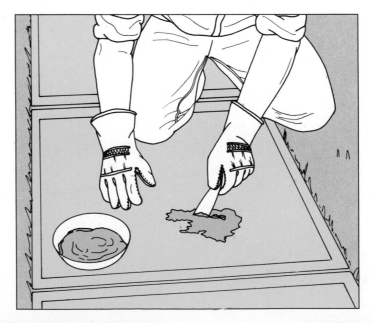

Patching small holes. Use a ball-peen hammer and cold chisel to undercut the perimeter of any holes, as in Step 1. Use a putty knife to fill the hole with the patching material and apply pressure to smooth the patch outward. Let the patch dry according to the material's instructions.

Patching Damaged Asphalt

The asphalt used to blacktop driveways and walks is actually a kind of concrete, a mixture of gravel with a binder. However, the binder is different—a crude-oil extract rather than cement holds the gravel together, giving asphalt its characteristic black color. Like any concrete, asphalt can develop cracks and holes from frost or ice-melting salts; it is vulnerable also to such substances as oil dripping from a car. To protect asphalt against most forms of deterioration, coat it once every four or five years with a waterproof and chemical-resistant sealer. Simply pour sealer straight from the can onto the driveway and spread it evenly, like thick paint, with a push broom or combination brush and squeegee *(page 440)*.

The coating process will also fill any cracks up to 1/8 inch wide that have appeared in the asphalt. For larger cracks —up to 1/2 inch wide—pour ready-to-use crack filler into the cavities one week before spreading the sealer. And for cracks up to an inch across, thicken sealer with sand to a putty-like consistency, push the mixture into the crack with a putty knife, then seal it over.

While sealer will fill most cracks, holes in a blacktop surface must be filled with "cold-mix" asphalt as illustrated at right. Cold-mix comes in two varieties: cutback asphalt and emulsion mix. Either type is satisfactory for dry holes, but damp holes require emulsion mix, which is made with water. Both types come ready-mixed in 66-pound bags, enough to patch about 1 1/3 square feet of asphalt to a depth of 4 inches.

If the temperature is below 40° F., asphalt should not be patched or sealed. If cool weather has hardened cold-mix into an unworkable lump, soften it by standing the bag in a heated room for a couple of hours before opening it.

How to Use Prepared Cold Mixes

1 **Preparing the hole for repair.** With a shovel, dig out the hole to a depth of 3 or 4 inches and remove any loose material. Cut back the edges of the hole to sound asphalt, making sure that the sides of the hole are vertical. Compact the bottom of the hole with a tamper made by fastening a pair of large door handles to opposite sides of a 4- or 5-foot-long 4-by-4.

2 **Adding the asphalt.** Fill the hole halfway with cold-mix asphalt. Slice through the asphalt with the shovel to open air pockets, then compact the asphalt with the 4-by-4 tamper *(bottom left)*. Add 1/2-inch layers of cold-mix, tamping each time, until the top of the patch is even with the surrounding blacktop. (If car wheels will run over the patch, make it 1/2 inch higher than the rest of the driveway; the weight of the car will flatten the hump.) Spread sand over the new asphalt until it dries (usually about two or three days) to keep it from sticking to your shoes.

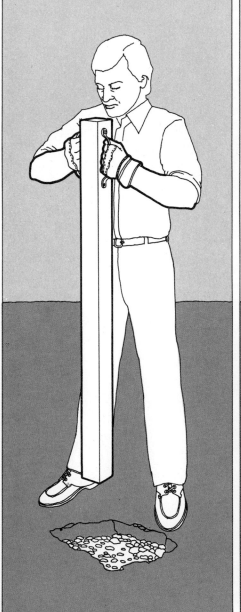
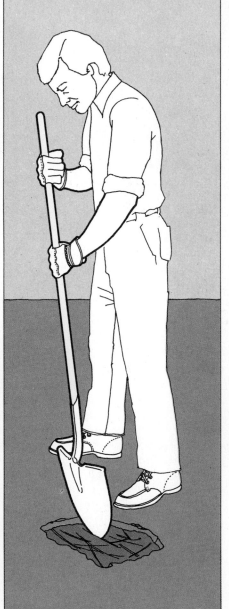

Resurfacing an Asphalt Driveway

When your asphalt driveway has whitish spots on its black surface and small cracks and fissures branching out across it, you know it is time to reseal it; otherwise, potholes will develop. Remedying this problem is a simple process, using asphalt sealer available in 5-gallon pails from hardware stores.

First remove patches of grease and oil from the surface using a cleaner meant for this purpose; otherwise these patches will prevent sealer from sticking to the surface. Clip any weeds that have pushed through the surface, and patch any holes and large cracks *(page 439)*. Next, use a broom to sweep away pebbles, rocks and debris. Before beginning the resealing, change into old clothes and put on shoes that can be discarded afterward: Sealer is sticky and hard to remove; don't let it end up on your floors.

Apply a convenient amount of sealer to the driveway surface with a push broom or combination squeegee-broom made especially for applying sealer to driveways. Pour some sealer from the pail onto the driveway and stand on one side. Extend the broom as far as possible and spread the sealer across the driveway with the bristle edge of the broom *(top);* repeat on the other side of the driveway. Using the squeegee edge, smooth the sealer over the asphalt surface *(middle),* then drag the broom toward the end of the driveway *(bottom).* Continue working in handy-sized sections, pouring more sealer on the driveway surface as needed. Let the new sealer set until dry to the touch—usually about 24 hours.

If the surface is not smooth and uniform, another coat of sealer may be needed. In that case, apply a second coat, then wait 36 hours for this coat to dry, or follow the drying directions given on the sealer label. Make sure the surface is completely dry before driving on it.

• Measurers and markers • Clamps and cutters • Hand and power saws • Router, chisels and screwdrivers • Electric drill and hammers • Wrenches and socket wrenches • Pliers and planes • Files and sanders • Safety equipment and other basic tools • Optional tools and fasteners

TOOLS FOR HOME REPAIR

The Right Tools

Most homeowners and apartment dwellers own tools, if only a hammer for hanging pictures or a drill and screwdriver for mounting a towel rack. But these few implements, however useful, hardly comprise a comprehensive tool kit for home repair. On the other hand, almost no project needs every tool found in a hardware store. Many of the items sold there are for rarely encountered contingencies; others may be gadgets of dubious value.

This section offers a guide of the items that make up a reasonably comprehensive, truly versatile tool kit for the home—one that will serve your needs for the majority of home repairs included in this book.

The tools are presented in categories—that is, devices for measuring, cutting, fastening, and so on, are listed together. The guide describes the features and the uses of each tool, and explains how to tell quality from inferior ones—for example, how to distinguish a hammer designed to drive nails straight and true from one that is likely to bend them. It also recommends which of the varieties of a particular tool you should own—how coarse a file, how many screwdrivers of what sizes, how long a saw—and gives maintenance pointers for tools that require them. The last pages are devoted to an assortment of tool-kit options, and to charts with which to identify screws, bolts and nails of various types and sizes. Potential craftsmen should be familiar with important considerations in assembling a set of tools and getting the most out of them: what tools are made of, how, when to acquire which tools, how to use them safely, and the ways to care for them to ensure long, faithful service.

The business ends of most tools are fashioned from one of three steels—carbon steel, low-alloy steel or high-speed steel. Carbon steel is a mixture of iron and carbon; low-alloy steel also contains small amounts of molybdenum or tungsten. Both metals are used in hand tools, such as hammers, chisels and socket wrenches, that generate little heat in use. High-speed steel, which contains relatively high percentages of molybdenum or tungsten, can withstand the heat of friction generated in a power tool by drilling, sawing or routing.

The cutting blades of the most expensive power tools are made of tungsten carbide—not a steel at all, but fine particles of a mixture of tungsten and carbon bonded at high temperature.

Methods for Making Tools

As important as the metal used in a tool is the method by which the tool is made. Most tools are formed by casting, forging or machining. In casting, molten steel is poured into a mold and allowed to cool. As the metal hardens, small bubbles form in the material, making it vulnerable to fracturing that can cause a wrench handle to break unexpectedly or a hammer to chip away. Therefore, casting is unsuitable for most tools; the exceptions are those that suffer little impact, such as vises and plane bodies.

The forging and machining processes start with an ingot of cast steel, heated until it is relatively soft, then squeezed between heavy rollers, which remove most of the bubbles in the casting. A small piece called a blank is cut from the rolled ingot. In machining, the blank is cut or ground into the shape of the tool. In forging, however, the blank is reheated, then stamped into a tool by a hammer weighing a ton or more. The blow of the hammer completes the elimination of bubbles, creating a tool that will withstand severe stresses. Tools formed in this way can often be identified by the words "drop-forged" stamped into the metal.

Three Steps for Hardening

Whether cast or forged, a tool is usually heat-treated to harden it. The process normally consists of three stages. First, the steel is fired to about 1,600° F. Then the metal is cooled (or, in technical language, "quenched") by plunging it into a bath of oil or water. The tool is now hard but brittle; it is tempered by reheating it to a lower temperature, between 400° and 1,000°. These steps produce a tool hard enough to hold a cutting edge, yet resilient enough to resist breaking.

When it comes to choosing tools, let the job pick them for you. In this way, you buy only the tools you need, when you need them. If you own only a few tools, or if they are of poor quality, the first project you tackle may require extensive purchases. But the second job, particularly if is it similar to the first, will mean the addition of only a few more tools, and eventually a complete set of good tools will all but assemble itself.

Buying tools to match the job also helps determine whether you will need hand tools, electrically powered models, or both. Hand tools are adequate for most small projects and have obvious advantages if you are working outdoors far from electrical outlets. However, a power tool is an asset where the amount of work to be done or the precision required justifies its price. The electric drill is so inexpensive and so facile at the basic carpentry skill of boring holes that a hand drill is all but superfluous. (Many recent models are battery-powered, so they can be used in places remote from a power source.) Also, anyone who has tried to carve long dadoes in cabinetry with a mallet and chisel will recognize a high-speed router as an irresistible work-saver and joy to use.

Such a buy-as-you-go philosophy is obviously inappropriate for some items. It makes more sense to take home a complete set of wrenches or bits for a drill, for example, than to buy them separately. They are always less expensive in sets, and purchasing them all at once avoids a trek to the hardware store each time you want to drill a hole of a different diameter or tighten a nut of another size.

Some projects, however, call for specialized tools that are not really part of a basic home tool kit. Included in this category are such items as long clamps for squeezing joints together while the glue is setting, industrial-sized sanders and polishers for finishing floors, and concrete mixers and smoothing tools for major patio repairs. Many of these tools, especially expensive ones that are used only once or twice, can be easily rented for a modest price from a tool rental agency. Bear in mind, however, that the rental fees can quickly add up to the purchase price of a tool if it is needed frequently or for a long period of time.

The Case for Quality

Do not be tempted by the price and proliferation of cheap tools. Shoddy screwdrivers and hammers will break, causing injury and damaging the work. A cold chisel stamped out of metal that is too soft cannot do the job it is designed for. Tools should help minimize errors, not create them; an unsquare square—or any other such inaccuracy in a tool—will make a home repair an exercise in futility and frustration even for the most skilled carpenter.

High-quality tools are sold at hardware stores, many lumberyards and department stores for reasonable prices—altogether, the tools in this section cost no more than, say, a top of the line sound system—and, because they last for years, they are the only true bargains in tools. On the other hand, it is rarely necessary to own the most expensive lines of tools; generally they offer only subtle improvements in balance and workmanship. For the average person these qualities may not justify the premium prices.

When selecting a tool, look for the name of a reputable manufacturer. Heft the tool to test its balance, making sure that it is neither too heavy to handle nor too light to do a good job. Try to test display models of power tools to observe them in operation. Examine each tool to confirm that it incorporates all the features recommended in this guide.

Before settling on any brand or model, read the terms of the manufacturer's guarantee. Many hand tools have unconditional, lifetime warranties that promise a replacement if the tool ever breaks in normal use. It is reasonable to expect power tools to be guaranteed for a full year, and parts should be easy to replace so the device will be inexpensive to repair.

Shop around for the best price available. Look for high-quality brand-name tools which are widely discounted and frequently on sale. Stick with double-insulated power tools; their shockproof, plastic housings will relieve you of any unnecessary concern about whether electrical outlets—and the tool itself—are properly grounded.

Use the right tool for the job. The wrong tool often makes it impossible to achieve professional-looking results. A good tool used incorrectly can be ruined, voiding its guarantee. Remember that tools should do most of the work for you; they become inefficient and difficult to control when too much force is applied during use. Swing a hammer so the weight of the head—not your muscle—drives the nail. Saw without excessive pressure; if the saw is as sharp as it should be, it will cut quickly enough and hold to a straight line with little force. Excessive force used with power tools can also overheat their motors and scatter dangerous fragments and bits. Other precautions—listed on pages 464-465—will go a long way toward preventing shop accidents.

Caring for Tools

Good tools function safely and reliably as long as they are properly looked after. Hang up tools instead of dumping them into a toolbox where they will be hard to find and subject to damage. Keep tools clean and free of rust. Wipe them after use and apply a coat of light oil to the metal to prevent oxidation. (But do not oil hammers, files or wrench handles: when slick, hammers can glance off nailheads, files will not cut and wrench handles can slip from your grip.) Metal that has rusted slightly from humidity or condensation can be restored by rubbing it with fine steel wool and kerosene. Turpentine is an excellent solvent for removing wood pitch from saw blades and other metal surfaces.

Keep tools sharp. You can renew the edges of plane cutters and chisels yourself. However, most saw blades, because of their compound bevels, and all drill and router bits require special sharpening tools and techniques that are available from professionals. To sharpen a chisel or plane, hold the blade so the bevel angle is flat against a whetstone coated with light oil. Rub the blade against the stone at the proper bevel angle until a thin curl of metal appears along the blade's edge. Turn the blade over again and, holding it at a slightly steeper angle than the bevel, give it a few strokes on the stone to hone the cutting edge.

Power tools, because of their electric motors, require special care. They must be regularly lubricated and cleared of sawdust; it can clog the vent in the motor housing and hinder the movement of a circular saw's safety guard.

Power cords must be protected from oil and solvent, and coiled loosely for storage to prevent damage to the inner wires. Never carry a tool by its cord; the cord can be pulled loose or damaged. Internal electrical contacts—called brushes and usually accessible through external screw caps—must be checked and replaced when worn.

All these details may sound like a lot of bother, but good tool habits, if cultivated from the outset, soon become second nature. Shown these considerations, the tool kit recommended here will give years of dependable service.

MEASURERS AND MARKERS

Center punch. Indents metal to provide a starting point for drill holes. Like an awl hole in wood, a center-punch dent keeps the drill on center as it bites into the metal. Center punches should be made of hardened steel, which will withstand hammering and dulling of the point. The squared end of the punch keeps it from rolling.

Awl. A steel scriber for marking lines on metal or wood and for starting drill holes in wood to keep the drill from wandering. The shank of the awl should extend through the handle and end in a steel cap, which will take the stress of mallet blows. Flat sides on the handle prevent the awl from rolling on work surfaces.

Combination square. A multipurpose tool for marking and checking not only square corners but 45° miters as well. It also serves as a depth gauge, a level for short spans and a precision 12-inch ruler. The ruler should be grooved so that the square's cast-iron head containing the level can be locked in position by a hand screw anywhere along the ruler. The heads of many squares include a scriber (small awl) for marking and are cast with a protective frame for the level.

Steel tape ruler. Flexible and retractable, it can measure curved and straight distances. The tape should be 12 feet long, ¾ inch wide (a ½-inch-wide tape is less bulky but cannot span as great a distance without buckling), and printed with inches, feet-and-inches and 16-inch stud marks. Most high-quality rulers have a replaceable tape with a protective plastic coating, a lock that controls retraction and a belt hook.

Carpenter's level. A device for determining whether a surface is level or plumb. A general-purpose level should be no less than 24 inches long and made of metal so it will not warp. It should contain indicators, or vials, for checking both horizontals and verticals. Plastic vials are superior to glass ones; they are almost unbreakable, and can be easily removed for replacement. An added convenience is a window located in an edge over the center vial. Handle a level carefully; dropping it can impair its accuracy.

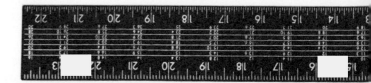

Folding extension ruler. Handy for determining vertical distances and measuring across wide spaces. A good wooden ruler has a brass extension for inside measurements. The ruler should be made of ⅛-inch hardwood for greatest rigidity, its segments joined with riveted hinges to prevent slipping, and its markings deeply etched and coated with plastic for long wear. Metal scuff plates on many rulers protect the markings when the ruler is opened or closed.

Steel square. Used for marking and checking square cuts, and for drawing parallel or vertical lines on large projects, and preferably made of rustproof metal darkened to reduce glare. The square's body (long arm) and tongue (short arm) are marked in $\frac{1}{12}$-inch increments for reading blueprints scaled 1 inch to the foot, and $\frac{1}{10}$-inch increments for calculators based on the decimal system. Some steel squares have markings for figuring board-footage, and for converting fractions to decimals and inches to centimeters.

T bevel. Records and transfers bevels and angles other than 90° and 45°. To duplicate angles called for in working plans or blueprints, a protractor *(below)* is used as a guide to set the blade of the T bevel. To match an existing bevel, the tool can simply be adjusted to fit the angle. The wing nut on the handle is tightened to secure the blade in the measured position.

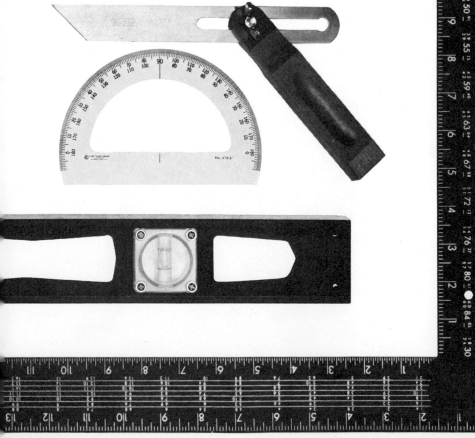

Chalk line. Marks long, straight lines. A 50- or 100-foot spool of string fits inside a case that is filled with chalk dust. Stretched tautly between two points, then lifted a few inches and snapped against a surface, the string leaves a straight, chalky mark. Suspended from a nail, the chalk line acts as a plumb bob for marking vertical lines. Worn strings can be replaced; chalk dust can be replenished after removing a cap at the bottom.

CLAMPS

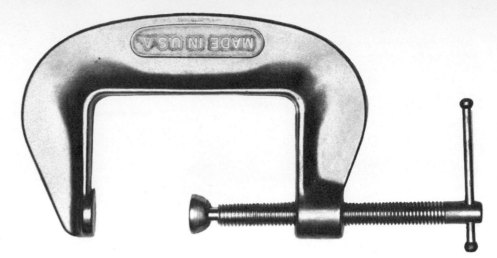

C clamp. Frequently used in pairs to hold pieces of work together for gluing, sawing or drilling. There are C clamps that open as wide as 12 inches; one pair of 6-inch clamps, made of either cast iron or aluminum, is adequate for most tool kits. The head atop the screw should swivel freely so the clamp will grip surfaces that are not quite parallel; the swivel feature also prevents the clamp from "walking" as it is tightened.

Spring clamp. A fast-action, clothespin-style clamp for holding freshly glued wood pieces together, and for other light-duty tasks such as mating pieces to be soldered or positioning a cutting guide. Spring clamps come in sizes up to 8 inches long with jaws that open 3 inches or more. A pair of the largest clamps, preferably with tips and handles sheathed in resilient plastic, are ideal for all but the most delicate applications.

Woodworking vise. Grips work for sawing, sanding, planing or drilling. The clamp-on model above has cast-iron jaws faced with wood or hardboard to keep them from marring the work. The vise is shaped to hold work vertically or horizontally, and should open at least 2½ inches. The faces should be removable so that they can be replaced when they become gouged or be set aside when the vise is used to grip metal. The virtue of the clamp-on feature is that the vise can be transferred from a workbench to any sturdy support, such as a table or a countertop.

CUTTERS

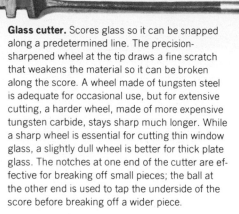

Glass cutter. Scores glass so it can be snapped along a predetermined line. The precision-sharpened wheel at the tip draws a fine scratch that weakens the material so it can be broken along the score. A wheel made of tungsten steel is adequate for occasional use, but for extensive cutting, a harder wheel, made of more expensive tungsten carbide, stays sharp much longer. While a sharp wheel is essential for cutting thin window glass, a slightly dull wheel is better for thick plate glass. The notches at one end of the cutter are effective for breaking off small pieces; the ball at the other end is used to tap the underside of the score before breaking off a wider piece.

Utility scissors. For trimming sandpaper, cutting cloth-backed tapes, making paper patterns and countless other workroom chores. This model has offset handles, which facilitates cutting material that is laid flat on a worktable. The carbon-steel blades are drop-forged and slightly curved toward each other to shear without jamming.

Tin snips. A device for cutting sheet metal and heavy cardboard. For easier handling, a compound lever action on the type shown is supplemented by spring-loaded handles covered with comfortable plastic grips. The jaws should be drop-forged for toughness and serrated to prevent slippage. A safety latch keeps jaws and handles closed when the snips are put away. For general use, select a pair of medium-duty, straight-cutting tin snips rather than snips designed specially for cuts to the right or left.

Retractable utility knife. A general-purpose cutting tool. The double-ended, reversible steel blade is slotted to mate with a sliding pin inside the metal handle. A knob on the handle slides the blade to adjust its extension, and retracts the blade completely when the knife is not in use. The hollow handle offers space for extra blades.

Wire stripper. Removes insulation from electrical wiring. This type has separate notches for the six wire sizes most commonly used in home electrical systems. Cutting edges inside the notches sever the insulation, but stop short of the wire, allowing the insulation to be pulled away. Made of tool steel, this stripper incorporates a wire cutter near the joint; the hole in each jaw is used to bend loops in the ends of heavy-gauge wires so that they can be attached to screw lugs on light switches and on outlets.

HAND SAWS

Coping saw. Cuts intricate patterns in wood or metal. Its narrow, ribbon-like blade is tensioned between two lugs by a screw handle and a stiff metal frame. The blade can be rotated through 360°, for negotiating tight corners, or reversed in the frame so that it cuts on the pull stroke for optimum accuracy. There is a variety of blades for diverse materials. The coping saw above is limited by its frame to cutting within 5 inches of an edge of a board, but deep-throated models, called scroll saws, extend the distance between the frame and the blade to 18 inches.

Compass or keyhole saw. Makes straight or curved cutouts for such purposes as mounting an electrical outlet in a wall or allowing the passage of pipes through a floor. The handle of the saw accommodates a variety of 12- to 14-inch crosscut-ground blades. Each blade is locked in place on the handle with a wing nut. The blades range from eight points for plywood to 24 points for cutting through plastics. When the handle is fitted with a shorter, narrower blade (*top*), the saw is capable of cutting sharper curves.

Crosscut saw. For cutting across the grain, the most frequent operation ih woodworking. The blade of a general-purpose crosscut saw should be 24 or 26 inches long, made of springy, tempered steel and attached to the replaceable handle with four or more fasteners. A blade with eight teeth to the inch is fine enough to leave a clean edge, yet coarse enough for fast cutting and ripping, or sawing along the grain. (When buying this type, specify ''an eight-point saw.'')

The blade of a high-quality saw is taper-ground to be thicker at the toothed edge than at the back. Its precision teeth are double-beveled and alternately bent, or set, to the sides of the blade to help clear the cut of sawdust and to reduce friction by making the cut slightly wider than the saw blade. A crosscut saw needs precision sharpening to maintain the proper set whenever the heavily used teeth in the middle of the blade feel duller to the touch than those at the ends; sharpening is best done at a saw-repair shop.

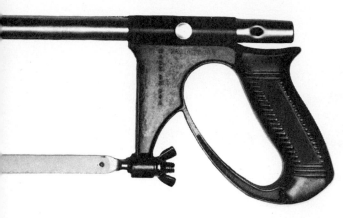

Hacksaw. For cutting metals. The saw's steel frame adjusts to accept 8- to 12-inch blades mounted between two lugs and tensioned by means of a wing nut. The frame must be rigid to keep the blade from flexing. A saw like the one at left can store extra blades inside the tubular frame above the handle: 24-point blades for general use, coarser ones for thick or soft metals, and finer ones for thin or hard materials. There are also round blades for sawing glass, ceramics and marble, and blades made of molybdenum steel, which, though more brittle, last four to six times as long as ordinary carbon-steel blades.

Backsaw and miter box. A specialized crosscut saw that makes extra-smooth cuts and tight-fitting joints, particularly 45° miters. A backsaw should have 13 teeth to the inch and a blade, usually 14 inches long, which is kept rigid for perfectly straight cuts by a spine along the back. The miter box holds the backsaw vertical and locks it at the chosen miter angle while the cut is made. A miter box should have adjusting devices for accurately setting a variety of miter angles, regulating the depth of the saw cut and accommodating saws of different thicknesses. Holes in the base make it easy to mount the box to a workbench with bolts or screws.

POWER SAWS

Saber saw. A versatile tool *(left)* capable of cross-cutting, ripping, sawing curves, beveling and starting a cut in the middle of a panel. Interchangeable blades *(below)*, so inexpensive that they are usually replaced rather than sharpened, enable the saber saw to cut a wide variety of materials, ranging from wood and metal to wallboard and ceramic tiles. For work around the home, a saber saw (sometimes called a jig saw) should have at least a $1/3$-horsepower, variable-speed motor capable of low speeds for cutting hard materials, and high speeds, up to 3,200 strokes per minute, for soft materials. Most saws have a $5/8$-inch blade stroke, sufficient to sever a 2-by-4 or $1/8$ inch of malleable steel. Choose a saber saw that cuts bevels and that blows sawdust from the cutting line. The saw should feel well balanced and should not vibrate excessively when cutting.

Types of blades. Wood-cutting blades, metal-cutting blades and special-purpose blades are available. Choose the shortest blade that will do the job; with the typical $5/8$-inch-stroke saber saw shown above, a job calling for a blade longer than 4 inches is apt to overtax the motor.

Blades for wood *(near right)*, made of high-carbon steel, have as few as six teeth per inch for fast, coarse cutting and as many as 14 teeth per inch for fine work. Most blades have teeth bent to alternate sides, but a taper-ground blade *(second from right)* has no set to its teeth and makes splinter-free cuts in plywood. A narrow blade, called a scroll bade, cuts sharp curves. Metal-cutting blades *(far left)*, which have between 12 and 32 teeth per inch, are made of high-speed steel for cutting both metal and plastic laminates. Special purpose blades *(center)* include a knife-edge *(blade at center)* for trimming materials such as linoleum or insulation, and a blade edged with abrasive chips of tungsten carbide, which cut hard metals and ceramics and saw hardwood so smoothly that it needs little or no sanding.

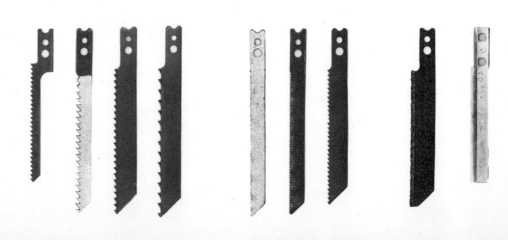

Circular saw. A heavy-duty tool *(left)* with interchangeable blades for sawing large numbers of long crosscuts, rips and bevels; also makes dadoes. The preferred model for a home tool kit should have a 7¼-inch blade—to permit cutting through 2-inch boards at a 45° angle—and a motor of at least 1¾ horsepower. A well-balanced saw with a wobble-free blade shaft, or arbor, makes the straightest cuts. Most saws have adjustments for the depth and angle of cut, and such safety features as a blade guard that springs into position when a cut is finished and an automatic clutch that helps to eliminate kickback if the blade should jam. There are some saws that are equipped with an electronic brake that stops the blade instantly when the saw is turned off. Other desirable features are sealed bearings that do not require any lubrication, an arbor lock to simplify changing the blades and a discharge chute to direct sawdust away from the work.

Types of blades. A combination blade, a crosscut blade and a plywood blade are an adequate complement for most home sawing. Made of tempered steel, these blades have teeth set to the sides like handsaws. Some blades are taper-ground to reduce friction and some have specially tempered teeth that stay sharp longer. A combination blade *(bottom)* is supplied with most circular saws. With its few coarse teeth (24, in this version), it is used both for ripping and for crosscutting where edge appearance is unimportant. The finer, crosscut blade *(near right),* with almost twice as many teeth, causes less splintering and is better for making miters. The plywood blade shown at top has 202 teeth, specially ground to minimize splintering the layers. These blades should be professionally sharpened.

451

ROUTER

High-speed router. Mills wood for tight-fitting joints, and cuts intricate patterns and contours. A router has a high-speed motor—18,000 to 35,000 rpm—mounted vertically on a two-handled base. A chuck on the motor shaft secures interchangeable bits *(below)*. Cut depth is altered by raising and lowering the motor with an adjustment ring on the housing. For home use, a router should have at least a ¾-horsepower motor. Some routers, like the model shown here, incorporate such safety features as a plastic chip deflector and a quick-stop switch in one handle. Convenience features on many good routers include permanently lubricated bearings, a depth scale on the housing, a built-in work light for better vision and a base faced with plastic to prevent marring surfaces of the wood.

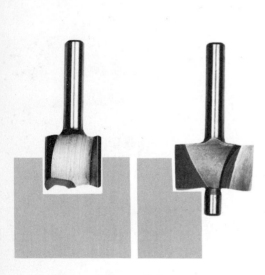

Jointing bits. A straight bit and a rabbet bit, both of which have vertical cutting edges—or flutes—are the only ones needed to make most joints. The straight bit *(far left)* makes dadoes, mortises and laps. For accurate routing it must be guided along boards clamped to the workpiece. The rabbet bit *(left)* has a polished shaft extension—a pilot tip—to ensure uniform width by guiding the bit along the edge of the board being notched.

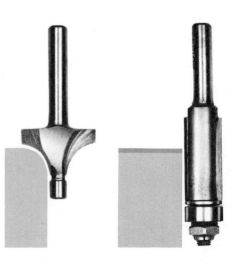

Finishing and decorating bits. The corner round *(right)* shapes edges of boards into professional-looking, rounded corners. The flush trimmer *(far right)* is used primarily to remove overhanging edges of wood and plastic counter-topping after it is glued to a plywood base. Both bits are pilot-tipped, but the flush trimmer rotates inside a ball bearing that will not mar finished surfaces. The flutes of the flush trimmer are tipped with tungsten carbide to withstand the abrasiveness of plastic laminates, and rarely need sharpening. The flutes of the corner round and the jointing bits described above, made of less expensive heat-tempered steel, dull more quickly. Both types are best sharpened by a professional.

CHISELS

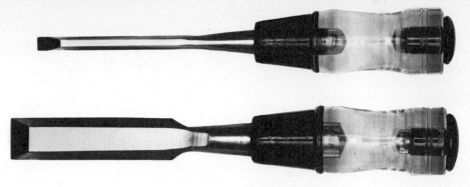

Wood chisels. Cutting tools for shaping, carving and trimming. They are particularly suited to removing small amounts of wood in tight spaces inaccessible to other tools. Two butt chisels— ¼ inch wide for fine detail and ¾ inch wide for bigger jobs—are a tool-kit minimum. To hold a sharp edge, chisel blades are made of hardened steel. Nevertheless, they require regular honing on a whetstone; sharpening must be carefully done to avoid altering the bevel of the cutting edge. If the handle is made of wood or plastic, it should have a metal cap so the chisel can be driven by a mallet or a hammer, as well as by hand.

Cold chisel. Cuts metal rods, bolts and rivets, severs light chain and chips away masonry. A cold chisel is a hexagonal rod of tool steel, beveled to a cutting edge—or bit—at one end and tempered for hardness. Designed to be struck with a ball-peen hammer, cold chisels come in several shapes; a ½-inch-wide flat-tipped chisel is best for most projects around the house. Cold chisels have few extra features, but vinyl grips on some models help absorb hand-stinging vibrations. If the head of the chisel should mushroom under constant hammering, it must be reground to restore it to its original shape; otherwise, dangerous metal splinters may break off.

SCREWDRIVERS

Flat-tipped screwdrivers. For screws with single slots. Four screwdrivers, with tip widths of ⅛, 3⁄16, ¼ and 5⁄16 inch, snugly fit most standard screwheads. The upper two screwdrivers shown here have cabinet tips—of uniform width—to reach deeply recessed screws. The lower two have standard tips—which widen for extra strength. They also have square shanks so that extra torque can be applied with a wrench. For comfort, select a screwdriver handle with wide rounded ribs or one fitted with a rubber grip. Cross-ground tips grip screws more securely than smooth tips. Though the best screwdrivers are forged of tough, resilient steel to resist twisting, bending and breakage, tips need occasional regrinding to keep them true. Screwdrivers are durable tools if used only for screws, but can be irreparably damaged if employed as a pry bar or chisel.

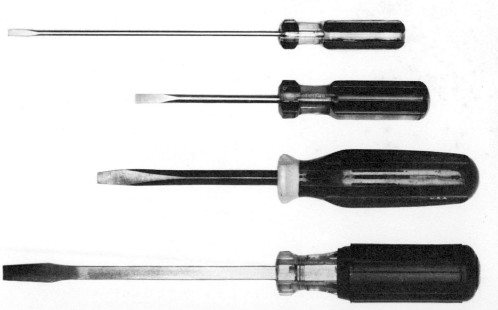

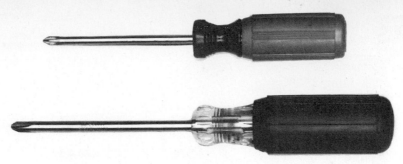

Phillips screwdrivers. For cross-slotted screws. Like the flat-tipped screwdrivers on the previous page, Phillips screwdrivers should have tough steel blades—long ones are preferable to short ones—and comfortable handles. Phillips screwdrivers come in five sizes, numbered 0 through 4. Two sizes—Nos. 1 and 2—will fit most Phillips-head screws used around the house.

Spiral ratchet screwdriver. For driving great numbers of screws quickly and efficiently. Interchangeable tips are snapped into a chuck. Pushing the spring-return handle causes the tip to make two and a half turns. A three-position control reverses the ratchet so the screwdriver can remove screws as well as drive them; in the center position, the ratchet control locks the tool for use as an extra-long conventional screwdriver. A multipurpose model like the one above comes with a ¼-inch standard tip and a No. 2 Phillips tip, but other tips, shown at far left, are available. To their right is an eight-bit drill set (¹⁄₁₆ inch to ¹¹⁄₆₄ inch) complete with the chuck adapter that is necessary to accommodate the smaller diameter of the drill shanks.

Offset ratchet screwdriver. For turning screws in hard-to-reach places where there is no space for a regular screwdriver. A ¼-inch flat tip and a No. 2 Phillips tip are positioned at opposite ends of a shaft mounted in the handle. Inside the handle, a ratchet controlled by an external lever makes it possible to drive or draw a screw without removing the tip from the screwhead.

ELECTRIC DRILL

Variable-speed drill. For boring holes, turning screws, buffing and grinding. The recommended model for a home workshop is a reversible, ⅜-inch drill (the chuck accepts bits with shanks up to ⅜ inch in diameter). It should have a trigger switch to control the speed and a button to lock the switch in the "on" position. A knurled knob on the switch of this model can be adjusted to set and maintain a chosen speed, and a lever directly above the trigger reverses the motor.

The chucks of all ⅜-inch drills are tightened with a geared "key." Many models also have an auxiliary handle to help hold the drill steady. Look for a drill with good balance and a light but positive switch. Check for undesirable play, or looseness, in the chuck and for destructive chattering from the internal gears during drilling.

Drill bits. To drill holes in wood, plastic, metal or masonry. High-speed twist bits like the top two bits are used to drill wood and plastic at high speeds or to drill metal at lower speeds. Twist bits are available in sets ranging from 1/64 inch in diameter to ½ inch, with the shanks of the larger bits usually machined to a diameter of ⅜ inch or ¼ inch.

Flat-bladed spade bits are used at medium speed to drill holes as large as 1½ inches in diameter in wood. Masonry bits have edges with hard carbide tips. They grind through such abrasive materials as cinder block, brick and concrete. To work efficiently, these bits should be used at low speeds.

Counterbore bit. Bores pilot and shank holes, and countersinks for wood screws all in one operation. Available for 6- through 12-gauge screws, the counterbore bit is a twist bit with an adjustable collar that slips over the bit and is secured by a setscrew. The collar is moved up and down so that the bit can make pilot holes of varying depths; the collar itself cuts the shank holes and countersink cavities for screwheads.

Screwdriver bits. Transform a variable-speed electric drill into a power screwdriver. Available in several sizes of standard and Phillips tips, screwdriver bits must be turned at low speeds. Standard-tipped bits must be kept perfectly aligned with the screw to keep the tip from twisting out of the slot and gouging the work. In a reversible drill like the one on the opposite page, the bits can also be used to remove screws.

Plug cutter. Carves round wood plugs used to conceal deeply countersunk screws and bolts. The plug cutter routs a circular groove into a board; the island of wood left behind is then chiseled loose. The device must be used with a drill stand (*overleaf*) to hold the drill securely, and the board supplying the plugs must be clamped securely to the drill-stand table.

Grinding wheel. An electric-drill attachment for abrading metals. Made of aluminum oxide, grinding wheels come in three grits: medium-coarse, for shaping metal quickly; medium-fine, for sharpening woodworking tools; fine, for sharpening knives and polishing. A grinding wheel fits on a shaft, or arbor, that is purchased separately. This grinder should be used only with a protective shield like the one on the drill stand at right.

Drill stand. Converts an electric drill into a compact drill press for precision jobs and cutting wood plugs. Choose a rigid stand built for your make and model, with preformed mounting holes. A well-designed stand has an adjustable stop that limits the depth of the holes, and a tilting table for boring holes at an angle. To make brushing or grinding jobs easier, the drill mount can be repositioned on the post to hold the drill horizontally. A semicircular shield—visible just to the right of the drill chuck in this picture—deflects debris from the wire brush or grinding wheel.

Polisher. For buffing wood or metal surfaces to a high luster. The polisher, preferably a ''bonnet'' made of lamb's wool, is tied around a flexible rubber backup pad; the pad has a spindle that fits into a drill's chuck. The polisher should be rotated at high speed to avoid swirl marks; however, apply only light pressure and keep moving the position of the bonnet to avoid burning the surface. The bonnet can also be used to polish wax on painted or stained surfaces or, coated with polishing and rubbing compounds, to brighten the surface on metal or wood finishes.

Wire brushes. For removing rust and paint, cleaning pitted surfaces, and brushing away burrs from metal surfaces. The cup-shaped brush is better when a drill is hand-held because it will deflect the debris downward. The wire wheel is used when a drill is mounted in a stand with a protective shield; both hands are then free to hold an object against the wheel. Made of either coarse or fine wire, the brushes usually come with a shaft attached; larger wheels require a separate arbor. You can lengthen the life of a wire wheel by occasionally installing it backward on the arbor; a wire cup lasts longer if the drill is operated alternately in forward and in reverse.

HAMMERS

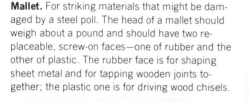

Nail set. Countersinks finishing nails. Made of hardened steel, the nail set has a knurled shank for a secure handgrip and a square head to keep it from rolling when set down. The concave tip has a sharp rim that will not slip from the nail-head. The device can also be used to back out protruding nails: simply place the tip against the point of the nail and strike the set with a hammer. A nail set is the only object, other than a nail, that should be struck with a curved-claw hammer. The best nail sets for home tool kits have tip diameters of $\frac{1}{32}$ inch and $\frac{2}{32}$ inch.

Mallet. For striking materials that might be damaged by a steel poll. The head of a mallet should weigh about a pound and should have two replaceable, screw-on faces—one of rubber and the other of plastic. The rubber face is for shaping sheet metal and for tapping wooden joints together; the plastic one is for driving wood chisels.

Curved-claw hammer. For driving or pulling out nails. Its head should weigh 16 ounces and be made of drop-forged steel. The poll, or striking part, is crowned to minimize surface denting, beveled to prevent chipping and angled slightly toward the handle so the hammer hits squarely. The inside edges of the claw should be sharp enough to grip smooth nail shanks. A hickory handle is satisfactory, but a rubber-sheathed handle made of fiberglass or steel, which is not affected by changes in temperature and humidity, will stay fixed in the head more securely.

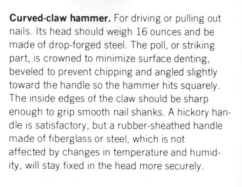

Ball-peen hammer. For hitting cold chisels and punches, as well as for bending or shaping heavy pieces of metal. The head, specially tempered to withstand impact on metals, should weigh about 20 ounces. Its poll, like that of the claw hammer, should be beveled to resist chipping. The hemispherical peen at the other end was originally designed to mushroom the heads of rivets so that they would hold securely.

Tack hammer. Handles light-duty hammering, such as driving carpet tacks and brads. The 5-ounce head has a magnetized poll at one end that holds a tack for the starting stroke. The other end is a claw for pulling tacks out.

WRENCHES

Adjustable wrench. A complete set of wrenches in a single tool. A knurled screw moves one of the jaws so that the wrench will fit nuts of all sizes. The recommended, 10-inch version opens to accept square or hexagonal nuts up to 1 inch across. Select a wrench with a precisely machined adjustment screw, which will keep the jaws at the chosen setting. The jaws should have tapered sides so that their ends can reach into tight places. When using an adjustable wrench, place the strain on the stronger, stationary jaw.

Open-end wrenches. For turning nuts and bolts. A typical set fits nuts from ¼ inch to 1 inch across. The ends are cocked 15° so that when the wrench is turned over, common hexagonal nuts can be tightened in cramped quarters that limit wrench swing to 30°. Many are chrome-plated to inhibit rust. All wrenches, open-end as well as the others shown here, should be made of drop-forged steel; softer metal is easily deformed.

Hex wrench. The hexagonal ends of the wrench fit into the socket of a setscrew typically used to secure handles, knobs and pulleys to shafts. A set usually has wrenches to fit setscrews measuring from ⁵⁄₆₄ inch to ¼ inch. Use the long end for extra reach, or for leverage against tight screws.

Pipe wrench. For gripping circular objects such as pipe. The loosely mounted upper jaw is adjusted by means of a knurled nut. When the wrench is tightened, the jaw tilts back to form a slight angle with the fixed lower jaw. Pulling on the wrench handle then jams the pipe between the jaws, and sharp teeth bite into the pipe to turn it. Two pipe wrenches—a 14-inch model, which opens to 3 inches, and a 10-inch model with a 1½-inch span—are recommended for the home tool kit. One wrench holds the pipe; the other turns the fitting. The tool can also be used to move nuts with damaged corners.

SOCKET WRENCHES

Reversible ratchet. Accepts a wide variety of sockets *(right)* and other attachments *(below)* for quickly tightening or loosening nuts, bolts and screws. High-quality ratchets are made of drop-forged steel, plated to resist rusting. Choose a ⅜-inch ratchet—that is, one with a ⅜-inch drive post. The internal mechanism should have closely spaced ratchet teeth so the wrench can turn fasteners in places where swing is limited to as little as 5°. A quick-release button on the back of the ratchet is a convenience that makes it easier to remove oily or tight-fitting sockets.

Types of sockets. There are two basic types: extra long, to reach recessed nuts and fit over the ends of long bolts, and regular length, for most other applications. Either type is available with six or 12 points (corners). Six-point sockets are slightly stronger, and better at gripping nuts with worn-down corners. Twelve-point sockets must be rotated only half as far as six-point models to slip onto a nut. Avoid eight-point sockets; they are for square nuts only. Sockets made for larger or smaller drive posts can be fitted to the handle with one of the adapters opposite. Recommended socket sizes for a ⅜-inch ratchet range from ⅜ inch to 1 inch; for use with a ¼-inch adapter, buy sockets ranging from 3/16 to ½ inch.

Universal joint. Allows a socket wrench to be used on fasteners that might otherwise be inaccessible. One end of this attachment snaps onto the ratchet, the other into a socket. Two hinges cause the joint to swivel when it is turned by the ratchet, allowing the drive post of the wrench to be angled to the socket.

Screwdriver tip. Turns the ratchet into a heavy-duty, offset screwdriver. Phillips tips like the one above, regular tips for slotted screws and hex-wrench tips are available in a wide range of sizes.

Extension bars. For otherwise inaccessible fasteners. As with the universal joint, one end of the extension fits over the drive post, the other into the socket. Though extension bars up to 24 inches long are available for ⅜-inch ratchets, the ones shown—3 inches, 6 inches and 10 inches—are usually adequate for a home tool kit.

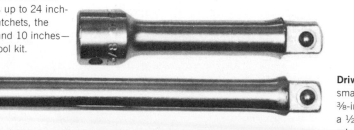

Drive adapters. Convert a ratchet to a larger or smaller drive. The adapter above right allows a ⅜-inch ratchet to be used with sockets having a ½-inch drive. The one above left reduces the ratchet to a ¼-inch drive; designed for the shorter handle of a ¼-inch ratchet, the small sockets that fit this adapter can break if full force is applied with the longer ⅜-inch handle.

PLIERS

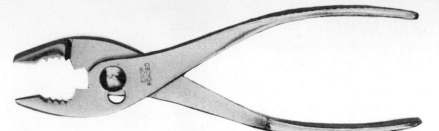

Slip-joint pliers. General-purpose gripping and bending tool. A pivot bolt in the handle slips from one of its positions to the other, allowing the jaws to accommodate either large or medium-sized objects. Choose an 8-inch pair of pliers whose drop-forged jaws have sharp serrations to hold work tightly, a wire cutter near the pivot and scored handles for a secure grip. Keep the jaw serrations sharp with a small, triangular file, and avoid using the pliers on finished surfaces; the jaws are capable of tripling the force exerted on the handles, enough to mar wood and many metals.

Locking-grip pliers. A clamping action keeps the tool from slipping and frees both hands. The jaws clamp onto an object and lock automatically as the handles are squeezed together. A knurled screw in one handle adjusts the gap between the locked jaws (shown here completely closed). A release lever on the other handle unlocks the jaws. Choose a 10-inch model with curved jaws for holding round objects almost 2 inches thick and with a wire cutter near the pivot; as the jaws lock, the cutter closes with as much as a ton of force, enough to sever a ¼-inch-thick steel rod.

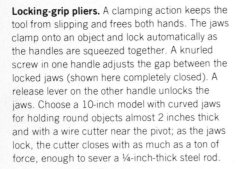

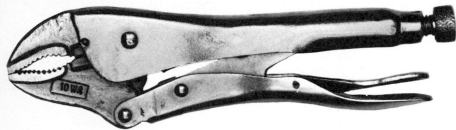

Long-nose pliers. Particularly suited to forming terminal loops in wires and to holding small screws and bolts. A wire cutter near the pivot is useful for snipping electrical wiring, and plastic grips make the pliers more comfortable to use, while protecting against electric shock. The recommended size for home use is 7 inches.

Channel-joint pliers. Especially useful for plumbing work. The jaw span is altered by mating a ridge on one side with one of seven grooves in the other. This arrangement keeps the jaws nearly parallel over a wide range of settings. Choose a 12-inch model whose long handles, often plastic coated for comfort, allow a tight grip on objects up to 2 inches thick.

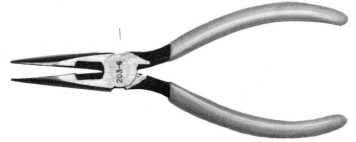

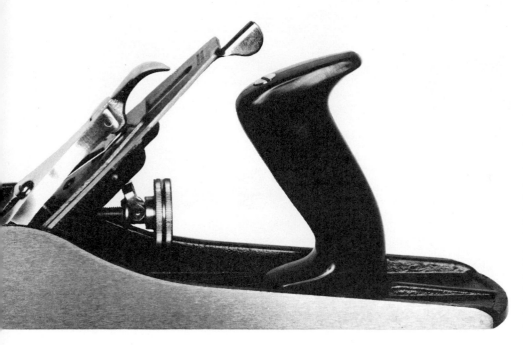

Jack plane. For use with two hands to size, trim, bevel and remove high spots from long boards. Choose a 14-inch plane; it spans and shaves down barely perceptible humps, which the shorter block plane would merely coast over. The jack plane has a knob near the toe for one hand and a handle near the heel for the other. Its compound blade—consisting of a cutter and a covering plate, or cap, under a locking mechanism—is adjusted much like the block plane's simple blade, except that the bottom edge of the cap must be set within ⅟₁₆ inch of the cutter's edge for smoothest planing. The mouth of the jack plane has a fixed opening. When the cutter of either a block or jack plane is honed to restore the knife-sharp edge, care must be taken to preserve its 30° to 35° bevel.

Block plane. For use with one or two hands to smooth and fit relatively small pieces of wood. Its tempered-steel cutter is angled between 12° and 21°. The low angle of the cutter keeps the plane from jamming when used to trim across the endgrain of a board, a job for which it is particularly suited. A typical block plane is about 6 inches long and has a cutter 1½ inches wide. On the model shown at right, an adjusting nut at the rear, or heel, of the plane moves a lever that runs the cutter in or out for thinner or thicker shavings; an adjustment lever above the nut aligns the cutter laterally. A third lever—secured by the knurled knob at the front, or toe—opens and closes the mouth in the bottom of the plane to accommodate shavings of various thicknesses.

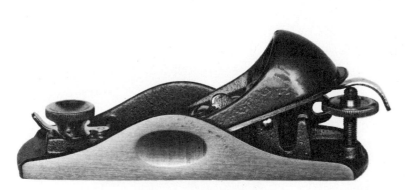

FILES

Half-round file. For shaping both hard and soft metals. Choose a "bastard" (medium-coarse) file, 10 inches long, shown below. The flat side should be "double-cut"—crisscrosses with ridges that form sharp cutting points—for fast shaping of flat and convex workpieces. The rounded side of the file is used on concave surfaces. Though made of tough, high-carbon steel, files are brittle and can snap in two if used as prying tools or dropped.

File handle. Fits over the pointed end, or tang, of a file to make it safer and more comfortable to use. The tang slips between two jaws in one end of the wooden handle; the recommended type has a screw knob at the opposite end that tightens the jaws for a secure grip.

POWER SANDER

Rasp. For shaping wood. The surface has large separated teeth for smoothing rough saw cuts, especially curves made with compass, keyhole or coping saws, and for improving the fit of wood joints. A 10-inch, half-round bastard rasp is suitable for general shopwork; it cuts quickly and shapes rounded as well as flat workpieces. Where a smoother finish is desired, rasped surfaces must be sanded to remove the deep tooth marks.

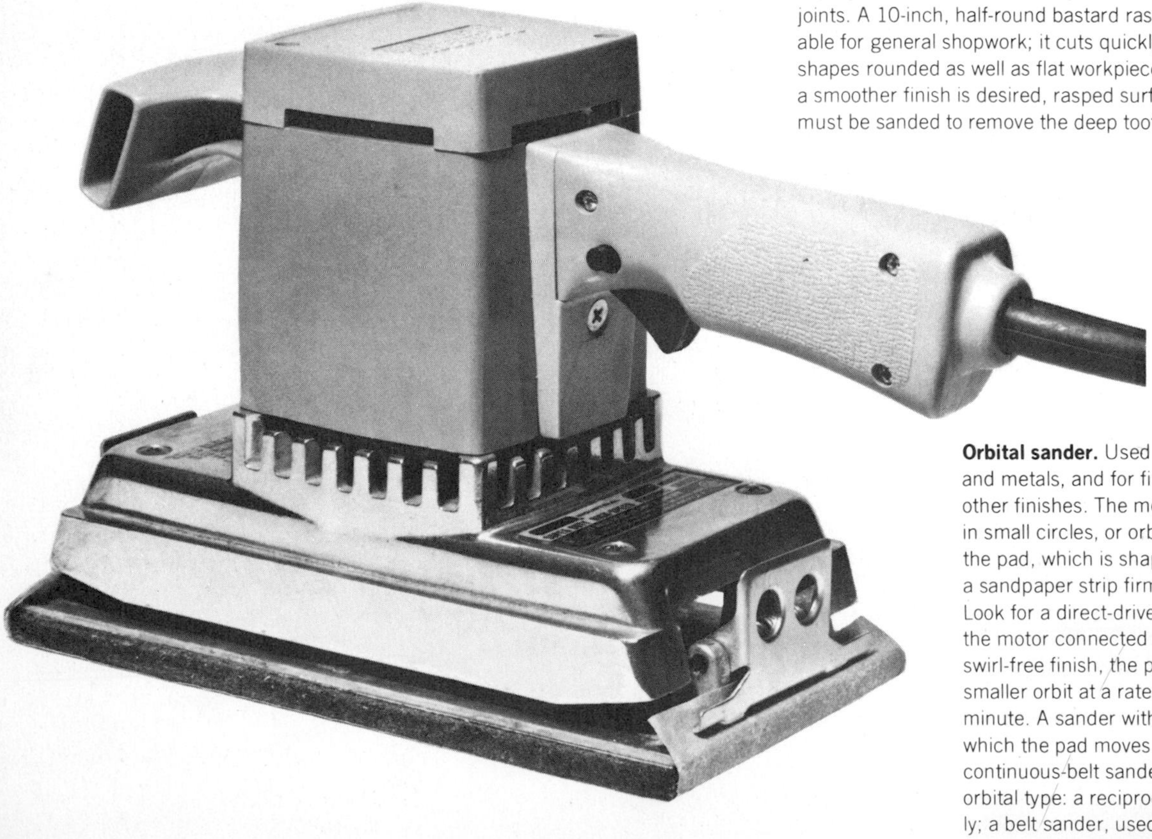

Orbital sander. Used for initial smoothing of wood and metals, and for final polishing of paint or other finishes. The motor turns a felt sanding pad in small circles, or orbits. Clamps on the ends of the pad, which is shaped to fit into corners, hold a sandpaper strip firmly against the rotating pad. Look for a direct-drive model—that is, one with the motor connected directly to the pad. For a swirl-free finish, the pad should make a ⅛-inch or smaller orbit at a rate of at least 9,000 orbits per minute. A sander with reciprocating action—in which the pad moves back and forth—or a continuous-belt sander is less desirable than the orbital type: a reciprocating model sands too slowly; a belt sander, used mainly on rough surfaces in industrial jobs, is difficult to control.

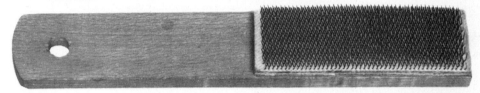

Round file. Shapes small concave surfaces and enlarges small holes in metal. Choose a 6-inch bastard type *(above)* that is slightly tapered. It often comes with a permanent handle.

Triangular file. For squaring the corners of holes in metal, removing burrs, sharpening the serrations of plier jaws and reshaping damaged threads of heavy bolts or screws. The 6-inch single-cut type recommended *(below)* has closely spaced teeth that leave a smooth surface. A triangular file, like all metal-working files, should be broken in on soft metal such as brass, and thereafter used with moderate pressure: too much or too little force dulls the file prematurely.

File card. A stiff wire brush for cleaning metal fragments from coarse files. The file card's soft-iron bristles are angled toward the handle so the brush can be pushed along the grooves of the file without snagging. Fine-toothed files like the triangular file can be cleaned with ordinary bristles, such as those on a toothbrush.

HAND SANDER

Rubber sanding block. Holds abrasive paper flat for smooth finishing; an improvement over a common wood block, it bends slightly for sanding curved surfaces. A piece of sandpaper is inserted into slots in the ends of the sanding block by lifting flexible rubber flaps; sharp pins inside the slots pierce the sandpaper, holding the paper securely. This type has finger grips molded into the sides and is shaped to fit the palm.

Abrasive Papers and Cloths

Flint paper. An inexpensive, relatively soft abrasive for sanding painted wood or metal, gummy woods and other materials that clog sandpaper grit quickly. The coating consists of quartz chips. Four grades of flint paper—identified by the words coarse, medium, fine or extra-fine printed on the reverse side—are commonly used. Like other abrasives, flint paper may be either closed-coat (completely covered with chips) or open-coat (50 per cent to 70 per cent covered). Closed-coat papers cut faster, but are more likely to clog than open-coat papers.

Garnet paper. An excellent abrasive for general wood sanding either by hand or with an orbital sander. The natural garnet chips last twice as long as the quartz chips used to coat flint paper.

Garnet papers are usually graded with a grit number that indicates the size of the abrasive particles: No. 36 for extra-coarse paper, a range of 40 to 60 for coarse, 80 to 120 for medium, 150 to 180 for fine and 220 to 320 for extra-fine. This abrasive is also available with a cloth backing; in this form, it is used for work requiring more durability and flexibility.

Aluminum oxide paper. For shaping, sanding and polishing hard metal like iron and steel, but also effective on wood. Aluminum oxide, a brown synthetic, cuts much faster and lasts much longer than garnet. It also comes with a durable cloth backing for flexibility and for heavy-duty applications such as rust removal and metal shaping. Waterproof cloth is available as a backing for use

with water or various lubricants. Aluminum oxide papers and cloths are graded by the same grit numbers as garnet abrasives.

Silicon-carbide paper. For sanding hardwoods and plywood, soft metals like brass and aluminum, and plastics; also used for smoothing glass edges and frosting glass surfaces. This fast-cutting synthetic is almost as hard as diamond but it is too brittle in the coarser grades for use on hard metals. Silicon carbide is backed with waterproof paper or cloth in grits as fine as No. 600. It can be used wet for fine hand sanding of paint or varnish between coats, or it can be coated with oil for smoothing and polishing metals. The oil and water help keep both the abrasive and the surface cool and float away grit-clogging wastes.

SAFETY EQUIPMENT

The equipment at right is recommended for a variety of repair jobs, and offers protection from potential hazards such as flying debris, the din and dust of power tools and caustic substances. In addition to using proper safety gear and handling tools with respect, the following precautions are suggested to prevent accidents while doing home repairs.

☐ Follow all the instructions that come with a power tool, and keep them for future reference.

☐ Unless a power tool housing is double-insulated, ground it through a three-hole outlet.

☐ Wear tight-fitting clothing, tie back long hair and remove all jewelry, including rings and watches, that might be caught in the tool as you work.

☐ Use clamps or a vise to lock workpieces firmly. On drill stands, small objects can be secured with blocks of wood bolted through the slots in the stand's base or table.

☐ Remember to disconnect power tools before changing blades or bits, and keep all adjustment nuts tight.

Work gloves. Protect hands from blisters as well as from cuts and splinters when handling hot, sharp or rough materials. This kind of glove shields the most vulnerable parts of the hand and the inside of the wrist with tough, supple leather. The back of the glove, made mostly of cloth for greater flexibility, has an elastic strap that helps hold the glove on the hand. A thick flannel lining softens the inside and absorbs moisture.

OTHER BASIC TOOLS

Pointing trowel. For small masonry jobs, including patching mortar between bricks (pointing) and filling small holes in concrete. Trowels must be cleaned and dried thoroughly after use, or the water in mortar and plaster will rust them.

Caulking gun. To fill cracks and crevices with a wide variety of sealing compounds. The sealers are available in interchangeable cartridges; when the trigger is pulled, a ratchet inside the handle advances the notched plunger, pushing caulking through a nozzle in the front of the cartridge. The tip of the sealed nozzle can be cut to any diameter up to $5/16$ inch. Turning the plunger so that the handle points down releases pressure on the cartridge, allowing it to be withdrawn.

Respirator. Filters out dust, mist and fibrous materials that can irritate the respiratory system and possibly cause lasting injury. A feltlike filter cemented across the front of this model stops small particles. The filter should be dusted with a clean paintbrush before it is put away, and the mask should be replaced after 24 hours of use or when breathing becomes difficult. Select a respirator with soft, rounded edges that form an airtight seal around the nose and mouth without causing discomfort. For protection against toxic substances, such as insecticides and some paints, use a respirator with an activated charcoal filter.

Noise muffler. Softens the din from power tools such as routers and circular saws. Distracting noise can lead to accidents; sustained loud noise can damage hearing permanently. The ear-muff device above, which cuts noise almost in half, has rigid plastic ear cups lined with foam rubber. The cups have air cushions that fit closely around the ear, sealing out sound without uncomfortable pressure. Simple ear plugs may also be used.

Goggles. Afford protection from flying chips of wood or metal during the use of hand tools as well as power tools. Held in place by an adjustable elastic band, the lightweight plastic goggles at right are large enough to fit over eyeglasses. The flexible frame, perforated with small air-circulation holes, provides a comfortable fit. The shatter-resistant eye piece on this model can be replaced when it becomes badly scratched.

Putty knife. For glazing windows, and smoothing, caulking and patching small imperfections in walls and woodwork prior to painting. A high-quality putty knife has a tempered steel blade that extends all the way through a wooden or shatterproof plastic handle. Select a knife with a flexible blade about 1¼ inches wide; it fits conveniently into small cans of patching materials.

Pry bar. For innumerable chores: prying, wedging, pulling, lifting, turning, etc. The tool should be drop-forged of high-carbon steel. Larger models, up to 6 feet long, are designed specifically for ripping out old construction, but a bar 18 inches long is adequate for home use. The claw in the sharply curved end, or gooseneck, has sufficient leverage to extract heavy nails.

Paintbrush. For small dusting jobs around the shop. Any inexpensive, 1½-inch paintbrush will do. Use it to brush wood chips out of corners, to clean the motor-cooling slots of power tools, and to clear sawdust from fine sandpaper.

Trouble light. Portable illumination for dark work spaces. A hook on the wire grate that protects the light bulb allows the lamp to be hung, freeing both hands. A reflector behind the bulb also keeps light out of a workman's eyes. Many such lamps have a convenience outlet in the handle. These outlets are not recommended for power tools, however, because the lamp's standard 25-foot cord is of insufficient electrical capacity.

Oil can. Two oil dispensers are needed around the home—one for medium (50-weight) oil, the other for light machine oil. A long spout is desirable for reaching recessed machinery and the cap should have a tight seal to prevent leaks.

Whetstone. Sharpens knives, chisels, planes and similar small tools. A 7-inch combination stone made of silicon carbide is recommended. One side is coarse-grained for rough sharpening, the other has a finer grit for final honing to a keen edge. A thin coating of light oil should be applied to the whetstone during use, both to keep it from losing its cutting ability and to float away steel particles ground from the tool.

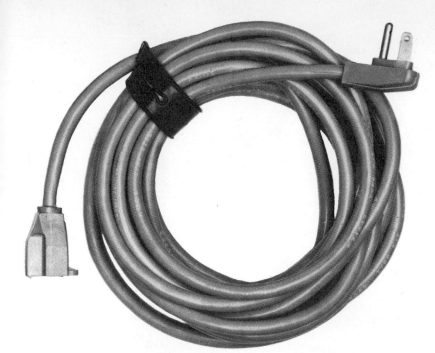

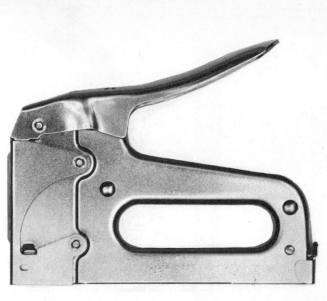

Heavy-duty extension cord. Permits use of power tools at remote locations. It should accept a three-prong grounding plug, and the wires inside should be 14 gauge. To minimize voltage drop and tangling, choose the shortest cord that will reach the normal work area easily. Light-colored sheathing is more visible, reducing the hazard of tripping over the cord. A plastic cinch keeps the cord neatly coiled when not in use.

Staple gun. A specialized fastening tool, it hammers home large staples with a single blow of a spring-driven plunger that is cocked and released when the trigger handle is squeezed against the grip. Choose a heavy-duty model that is capable of driving staples up to $9/16$ inch long into hard materials such as plywood and soft metals.

Slip-on attachments adapt the staple gun to special jobs. The curved fitting (*below, top*) is for attaching shades to rollers, the middle attachment tacks down electrical wires and the bottom adapter stretches screening across a frame.

Flashlight. A small, two-battery model provides enough light for most jobs where electricity is not available, or where it should not be used because there is danger of shock or explosion.

Wire brush. Strips away rust and flaking paint from rough or textured surfaces. Stiff, carbon-steel wires are folded double and stapled securely at the folds into holes in a hardwood handle. A curved handle protects against scraped knuckles. Keep wire brushes dry; water will rust the bristles and can warp or crack the handle.

Plumber's auger. Used to open clogged drains and traps. The recommended type resembles a tightly wound steel spring, 10 feet long, that bends and turns inside curved plumbing pipes. The auger is turned by its pipe handle, which can be locked in place with a thumbscrew anywhere along the shaft. A spiral hook at the top of the auger catches any obstruction and dislodges it.

Soldering iron. Bonds copper wire with rosin-core solder, an alloy of lead and tin. This 50-watt model *(above),* with its sharp, replaceable tip, is ideal for repairing small appliances. Always heat the metal, not the solder; melted by the hot metal, the solder will flow smoothly into the joint.

Voltage tester. Indicates whether electrical current is present in a wire or fixture. Its two probes are inserted into the slots of a receptacle, touched to the hot and neutral terminals of a light fixture, or, in the case of a switch, to the hot wire and a grounded object such as the switch box. If the circuit is live, the tester's neon bulb glows. When that occurs, electrical work should proceed only after a circuit breaker has been tripped or a fuse removed. The tester shown can be used for 120- and 220-volt service.

Plunger. Clears drains by means of water and air pressure. A rubber cup on the end of a wooden handle presses against the bottom of the drain to form a seal. When the handle is moved up and down, air is removed from the pipe and water pressure loosens the obstruction. Coating the lip of the cup with petroleum jelly improves the plunger action by making a tighter seal.

OPTIONAL TOOLS

Brad starter. Pushes small nails partway into wooden workpieces for easy hammering. A brad is inserted headfirst into the steel tube extending from the plastic handle. Inside the tube, a magnetized plunger keeps the brad from falling out and, when the handle is pushed, forces the point of the brad into the wood. Use as little force as possible on a brad starter; otherwise, the end of the tube may leave an imprint on the work.

Stubby screwdriver. For use in tight spaces —where a larger tool cannot fit. Available in standard and Phillips tips, this tool has a large-diameter handle that supplies considerable turning power even when the screwdriver can be grasped only with the finger tips.

Jeweler's screwdrivers. Fit screws used in eyeglasses, clocks and other small appliances. This set has five blades that lock into an aluminum handle—three with regular tips up to ³⁄₃₂ inch wide, one with a No. 0 Phillips tip and one shaped like an awl. The flared index-finger rest at the end of the handle revolves independently of the rest of the screwdriver, so that the tip can be firmly held in the tiny screw slot as the screw is turned.

Stud locator. Indicates the position of vertical wall supports. The operator slides the locator along a baseboard until a magnetic needle points to the hidden nails that have been used to fasten a lath or wallboard to a stud. Use this tool with caution: it will detect two nails at the edges of a stud as readily as a single nail at the center. Watch for two deflections of the magnetic needle an inch or so apart; the center of the stud probably is midway between these points.

Outsize screwdriver. Fits 12- and 14-gauge screws, large sizes not often used around the home. The broad tip combined with its large-diameter handle make this the only screwdriver with enough turning power to loosen large screws that have been frozen with rust. In addition, its size and strength—used wisely—make it a useful tool for minor levering and prying.

Screw starter. Grasps single-slot screws of 4 to 12 gauge for the first few turns in hard-to-reach holes. After these initial twists have been made, the tip of the tool is pulled out of the screw's slot, and the screw is tightened with an ordinary screwdriver. The model shown here is equipped with a convenient pocket clip and is topped with a magnet that helps to retrieve dropped screws and other small metal objects.

Sawhorse bracket. Used in pairs to build supports for workpieces during such operations as cutting, gluing and finishing. Because they will accept legs and crosspieces of varying lengths, such brackets can be used to build custom-fitted sawhorses for specific work areas. Each hinged bracket holds two legs and one end of the sawhorse crosspiece. The three pieces, all 2-by-4s, can be nailed permanently in place through small holes in the brackets, but the crosspiece is generally left unfastened. When this piece has been removed, the legs can be folded together on the brackets' hinges for compact storage.

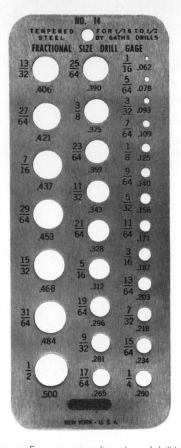

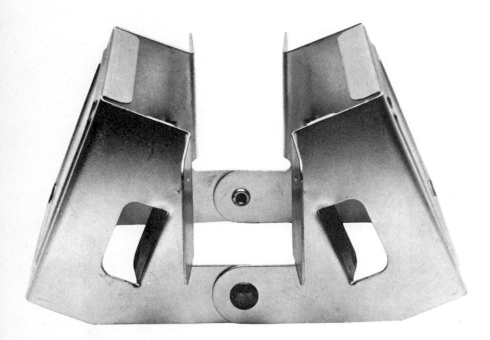

Drill gauge. For measuring diameters of drill bits with obliterated or unclear markings. This model indicates the size of a bit in fractions of inches. Made of heavy-gauge steel, the recommended version has 29 holes, ranging from 1/16 inch to 1/2 inch in steps of 1/64 inch. Under each hole is the fraction's decimal equivalent, a style of measurement used mainly by professionals.

Paint scraper. Removes old paint from wood. This model has a steel shaft with a nonslip vinyl grip. The angled head accepts a single, replaceable carbon-steel blade with four separate scraping edges: two opposing serrated edges for coarse work and two straight edges for fine work. Loosening the screw in the center of the head permits the blade to swing into position. Attaching the blade to the other side of the head changes the scraping angle for lighter applications.

Pickup claw. Bends around corners to retrieve fasteners, tools and other objects from otherwise inaccessible locations. The device consists of a flexible steel control cable with a movable wire core. One end of the core is fitted with a four-hook claw that opens when a plunger at the end of the handle is pushed in. Releasing the plunger retracts the claw, which closes on the object.

Fastening tool. Uses staple-like fasteners for such purposes as mending wire fences and securing upholstery springs to webbing. The sharp fasteners, designed to pierce leather, heavy cloth and similar materials, fit into grooves in the tool's jaws. Squeezing the handles bends the fastener into a triangular ring. File down the points of exposed fasteners to prevent cuts and scratches.

Paint mixer. Electric-drill attachment for distributing pigment evenly throughout a can of paint. The propellers have blades angled to force paint up from the bottom of the can and down from the surface to make a homogeneous mixture.

Window scraper. Removes paint, putty and labels from glass and other hard materials. A single-edged razor blade, slipped into a retractable holder, shaves the glass clean. After use, the thumb lock is depressed and the blade and its holders are withdrawn into the handle. To avoid cutting your fingers when you replace the blade, push it from the holder against a table edge.

Utility bar. All-purpose prying tool. Drop-forged and heat-treated for hardness, it comes in 15-inch and 5-inch lengths. The longer model is for heavy jobs, such as pulling nails and opening windows that have been painted shut. The shorter one is for lighter work, such as opening paint cans and pulling tacks or heavy staples. Both models have sharp edges to scrape paint, glue or caulking from narrow gaps and crevices.

FASTENERS

Types of screws. A screw is characterized by its slot, the shape of its head and whether it is designed for wood or sheet metal. Two basic slot designs, single slot and Phillips, and four common head shapes are shown at right. Flatheads can be concealed below the wood's surface; oval heads are partially countersunk; round and pan heads rest on the surface. Threading is designed specifically for either wood or metal: the first three drawings show wood threads, but sheet-metal screws are available with these heads. The pan head is found only on sheet-metal screws.

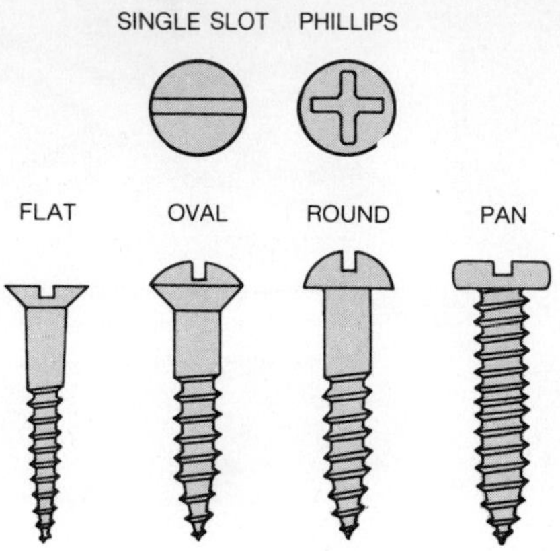

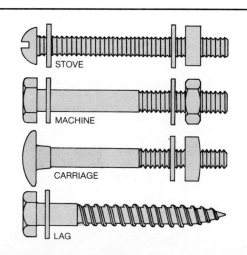

GAUGE	NO. 4	NO. 5	NO. 6	NO. 7	NO. 8	NO. 9	NO. 10	NO. 12	NO. 14
LENGTHS	¼"-1¼"	⅜"-1¼"	⅜"-1½"	½"-1½"	½"-2½"	¾"-2½"	¾"-3½"	¾"-3½"	1"-4"
STANDARD TIP	⅛"	⅛"	3⁄16"	3⁄16"	3⁄16"	3⁄16"	¼"	5⁄16"	5⁄16"
PHILLIPS TIP	NO. 1	NO. 2	NO. 2	NO. 2	NO. 2	NO. 2	NO. 3	NO. 3	NO. 3
PILOT-HOLE BIT	1⁄16"	5⁄64"	5⁄64"	3⁄32"	3⁄32"	7⁄64"	7⁄64"	⅛"	9⁄64"
SHANK-HOLE BIT	⅛"	⅛"	9⁄64"	5⁄32"	11⁄64"	3⁄16"	13⁄64"	15⁄64"	¼"

Screw chart. Screw sizes commonly found around the home are represented in this table. Because the screwheads and shanks are drawn life size, you can use the illustrations to identify and sort a jumble of screws by diameter, or gauge number. Use the columns below the drawings to find information about screw lengths, screwdriver tips and screw-hole diameters; the data are applicable to each screw, regardless of its slot, head shape or thread design. For example, a No. 8 screw comes in lengths ranging between ½ inch and 2½ inches. It should be driven by a screwdriver tip 3⁄16 inch wide or, if it is a Phillips screw, a No. 2 tip. Drilling a pilot hole for a No. 8 screw calls for a 3⁄32-inch drill bit; the wider opening for the shank, an 11⁄64-inch bit.

Bolts. Fasteners used for extra strength, for ease of disassembly or in place of screws larger than No. 14. The illustrations show four common bolts, along with the washers necessary to make removal easier and also to protect wood or metal parts against scratching. Light-duty stove bolts, tightened with a screwdriver and a wrench, and heavy-duty machine bolts, tightened with two wrenches, secure both wood pieces and metal pieces. Carriage bolts fasten wood pieces to either wood or metal bases; the rounded head of the bolt, which always rests against the wood piece, has a square shoulder that jams firmly into the pre-drilled bolthole, so that the nut can be tightened with a single wrench. Lag bolts are essentially heavy-duty wood screws, turned with a wrench rather than a screwdriver for extra leverage.

Common nails. For general construction and carpentry. These fasteners are made with broad heads that will not pull through a board, and with grooves at the top of the shank to keep the nail from working loose. You can avoid splitting boards by blunting the point of each nail with a tap of the hammer. Ideally, the length of a nail should be three times the thickness of the piece being fastened in place. Lengths of common nails are generally expressed in "penny" ratings, written as a numeral followed by the letter "d" (the symbol for "penny" in the old British monetary system), and the nails themselves are often sold by weight. Beneath each of the six common nails shown in full scale are its penny rating, its length in inches and the number in a pound.

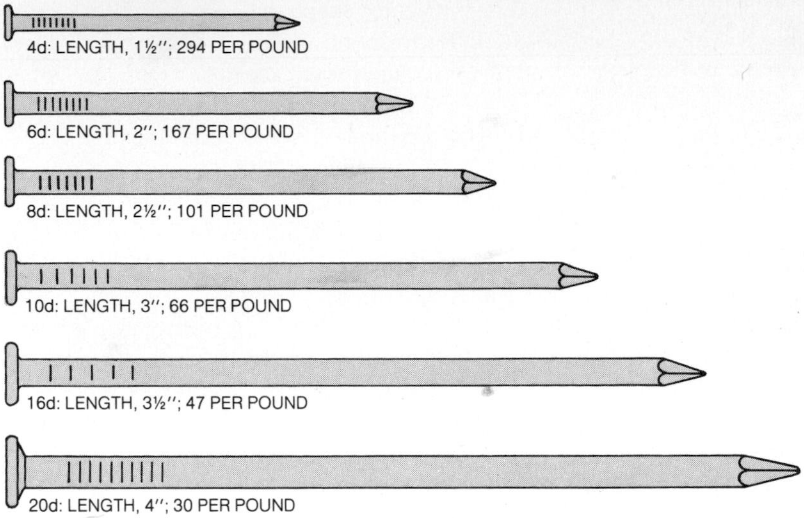

4d: LENGTH, 1½"; 294 PER POUND

6d: LENGTH, 2"; 167 PER POUND

8d: LENGTH, 2½"; 101 PER POUND

10d: LENGTH, 3"; 66 PER POUND

16d: LENGTH, 3½"; 47 PER POUND

20d: LENGTH, 4"; 30 PER POUND

A nail for every purpose. The various fasteners in this chart are tailored to jobs for which common nails are unsuited. All are available in a range of lengths. Finishing, box, scaffolding and cut nails are measured in penny ratings, as shown above, the other types simply in inches. Other characteristics vary by manufacturer; for example, some nails have coatings of zinc to resist rust, or rosin to increase holding power. Combine the information presented here with advice from your hardware dealer to select the most suitable nail for the task at hand.

Finishing nail. For invisible fastening. It has a small head that can be countersunk and completely concealed by a covering of wood filler.

Wire brad. Fine finishing nail identified not only by its length in inches, but also by the gauge, or diameter, of the wire from which it is made.

Box nail. Made with a narrower shank than a common nail to prevent a thin piece of wood from splitting when nailed near the edge.

Scaffolding nail. For temporary construction. A second head makes the nail easy to remove by keeping it from going all the way into the wood.

Cut nail. A flooring nail that is often used where a rustic look is desired. It has a blunt tip that helps prevent splitting of floor boards.

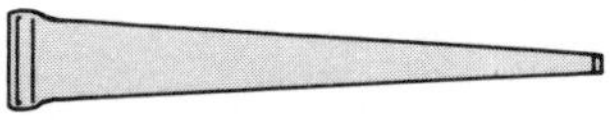

Spiral nail. Twists into the wood as it is driven. These comparatively costly nails offer a more permanent, screwlike grip than plain nails.

Fluted masonry nail. For fastening wood to concrete or cinder block. These nails require pilot holes to keep the masonry from crumbling.

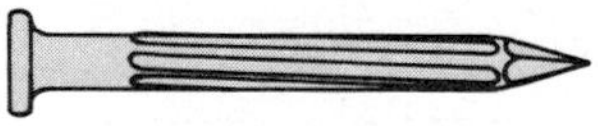

Annular ring nail. For driving into plasterboard. The sharp ridges circling the shank become embedded in the chalky material for a tight grip.

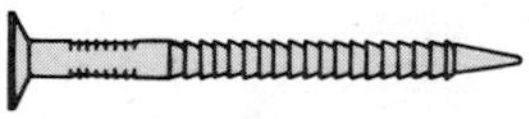

Roofing nail. The broad head of this galvanized nail keeps asphalt shingles from tearing loose. Roofing cement seals the shingles against leaks.

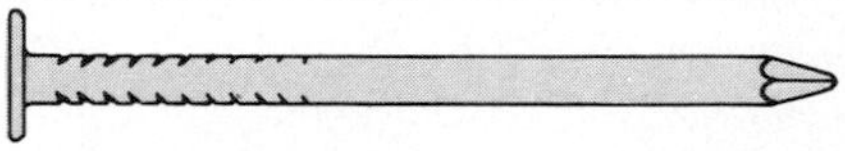

Self-sealing roofing nail. For metal roofing. This relatively expensive aluminum nail has a plastic washer to seal the nail hole against moisture.

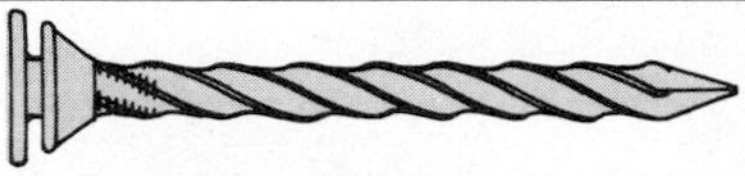

Corrugated fastener. For reinforcing a weak wood joint or holding the pieces of a new one in position while it is secured with nails.

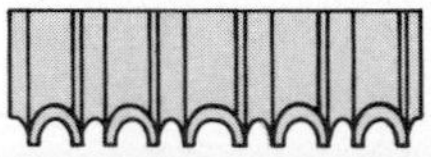

Index

Page references in italics indicate an illustration of the subject mentioned.

Acknowledgments

The editors wish to thank the following:

Paul Berens, Chief Chemist, Touraine Paints, Everett, Mass.;
Bert Bickerstaffe, Clog Busters Inc., Dedham, Mass.; John Cook,
Metropolitan Roofing and Sheet Metal, Alexandria, Va.;
Isabella Dealhoy, Montreal, Que.; D. Atwill Morin & Son Inc.,
General Contractors, St. Bruno, Que.; Leo Frenette, H.R. Cassidy
Ltd., Laval, Que.; Melanie Gagnon, Montreal, Que.; Kenneth
Larsen, C. Howard Simpkin Ltd., Montreal, Que.; Daniel
O'Brien, Heritage Restoration Inc., South Weymouth, Mass.;
Clifford O'Brien, Director, Architectural Promotion, Foster
Masonry Products, Westwood, Mass.; Richard L. Sweeney,
Stoneham Wallpaper and Paint, Stoneham, Mass.; Robert Payne,
Roofing Foreman, John G. Webster Co., Washington, D.C.;
Rob Smithwood, H.W. Foote & Co., Brighton, Mass.;
Joseph A. Tedesco, National Electrical Code Consultant,
President, J.A. Tedesco Associates, Inc., Weymouth, Mass.;
Waldo Bros. Concrete and Masonry, Boston, Mass.

The following persons also assisted in the preparation of this book:

Diane Denoncourt; Fiona Gilsenan; Solange Pelland;
Odette Sévigny; Natalie Watanabe